CRITICAL SURVEY
OF
DRAMA

CRITICAL SURVEY
OF
DRAMA

REVISED EDITION
Chu-Fra

2

Edited by
FRANK N. MAGILL

SALEM PRESS
Pasadena, California   Englewood Cliffs, New Jersey

∞ The paper used in these volumes conforms to
the American National Standard for Permanence of
Paper for Printed Library Materials, Z39.48-1984.

**Library of Congress Cataloging-in-Publication
Data**
Critical survey of drama. English language series/
edited by Frank N. Magill.—Rev. ed.
p. cm.
Includes bibliographical references and index.
1. English drama—Dictionaries. 2. American
drama—Dictionaries. 3. English drama—Bio-
bibliography. 4. American drama—Bio-bibliography.
5. Commonwealth drama (English)—Dictionaries.
6. Dramatists, English—Biography—Dictionaries.
7. Dramatists, American—Biography—Dictionaries. 8. Commonwealth drama (English)—Bio-
bibliography.
I. Magill, Frank Northen, 1907-
PR623.C75   1994
822.009'03—dc20   93-41618
ISBN 0-89356-851-1 (set)   CIP
ISBN 0-89356-853-8 (volume 2)

PRINTED IN THE UNITED STATES OF AMERICA

LIST OF AUTHORS IN VOLUME 2

CRITICAL SURVEY
OF
DRAMA

CARYL CHURCHILL

Born: London, England; September 3, 1938

Principal drama

Owners, pr. 1972, pb. 1973; *Moving Clocks Go Slow*, pr. 1975; *Objections to Sex and Violence*, pr. 1975, pb. 1985; *Light Shining in Buckinghamshire*, pr. 1976, pb. 1978; *Vinegar Tom*, pr. 1976, pb. 1978; *Traps*, pr. 1977, pb. 1978; *Cloud Nine*, pr., pb. 1979; *Three More Sleepless Nights*, pr. 1980, pb. 1990; *Top Girls*, pr., pb. 1982; *Fen*, pr., pb. 1983; *Softcops*, pr., pb. 1984; *Plays: One*, pb. 1985; *A Mouthful of Birds*, pr., pb. 1986 (with David Lan); *Serious Money*, pr., pb. 1987; *Ice Cream*, pr., pb. 1989; *Hot Fudge*, pr. 1989, pb. 1990; *Mad Forest: A Play from Romania*, pr., pb. 1990; *Churchill Shorts: Short Plays*, pb. 1990; *Plays: Two*, pb. 1990.

Other literary forms

Although Caryl Churchill is known primarily as a playwright, her writing career actually began with radio plays in the early 1960's, when *The Ants* was broadcast in 1962. *The Ants* was followed by other radio plays, including *Lovesick* (1967), *Identical Twins* (1968), *Abortive* (1971), *Not, Not, Not, Not, Not Enough Oxygen* (1971), *Schreber's Nervous Illness* (1972), *Henry's Past* (1972), and *Perfect Happiness* (1973). Churchill has also written several teleplays: *The Judge's Wife* (1972), *Turkish Delight* (1974), *The Legion Hall Bombing* (1978), *The After Dinner Joke* (1978), and *Crimes* (1981).

Achievements

Churchill is claimed by several political and artistic constituencies: She is hailed as a major voice for English socialists; is cited frequently by feminists; is the darling of proponents of workshops, or group construction, of plays; and is clearly a postmodern voice. Certainly, Churchill is each of these things, but, above all, she is a writer of the human presence and a champion of the individual choice. Her particular achievement is not to experiment but to experiment with a difference. Her unusual use of theatrical structure always aims to reveal the value of the eccentric individual over the concentricities of an exploitive social order. She is an established playwright whose work, though highly unusual in structure, is widely and well received in the English-speaking world, having been successfully produced both in London and in New York.

Biography

Caryl Churchill was born in London, England, on September 3, 1938.

She lived in Montreal, Canada, from 1948 to 1955, and there attended the Trafalgar School. From 1957 to 1960, she studied English literature at the University of Oxford and took her B.A. degree from that institution in 1960. Her first dramatic works were produced at the University of Oxford, but many of her early plays remain unpublished. In 1961, she married David Harter; she is the mother of three sons. As his wife's career developed, Harter gave up his lucrative private law practice so that his wife could spend more time writing. A prolific playwright, Churchill received her first professional stage production in 1972 when *Owners* was performed at the Royal Court Theatre. From that point on, she became closely associated with that theater. She has been a member of the Joint Stock Theatre Group, an organization dedicated to collective creation of theatrical work, and has worked with the Monstrous Regiment, a feminist theater union. Churchill has contributed frequently to the British Broadcasting Corporation's radio and television broadcasts. In an incident now notorious, she and her director, David Lan, insisted that their names be left off the credits of the BBC's 1978 television production of *The Legion Hall Bombing* because the producers had censored the work. As her reputation spread, Churchill's works were brought to the United States and were staged by Joseph Papp in New York. She is a playwright of considerable international importance.

Analysis

Caryl Churchill has become well known for her willingness to experiment with dramatic structure. Her innovations in this regard are sometimes so startling and compelling that reviewers tend to focus on the novelty of her works to the exclusion of her ideas. Churchill, however, is a playwright of ideas, ideas that are often difficult and, despite her bold theatricality, surprisingly subtle and elusive. Her principal concern is with the issues attendant on the individual's struggle to emerge from the ensnarements of culture, class, economic systems, and the imperatives of the past. Each of these impediments to the development and happiness of the individual is explored in her works. Not surprisingly for a contemporary female writer, many times she makes use of female characters to explore such themes.

In four of her best-known works—*Cloud Nine*, *Top Girls*, *A Mouthful of Birds*, and *Vinegar Tom*—Churchill presents woman as a cultural concept and displays the power of that concept to submerge and smother the individual female. In *Cloud Nine*, a parallel is suggested between Western colonial oppression and Western sexual oppression. This oppression is seen first in the family organization and then in the power of the past to demand obligations from the present. Although her characters use geographical distance and literally run away from the past, no one in *Cloud Nine* can exorcise the ghosts of established practices and traditions.

Top Girls is a depiction of the exploitation of women by women, a technique well learned through generations of women being exploited by men. The play portrays a group of friends, all successful women in the fields of literature and the arts, who gather for a dinner to celebrate Marlene's promotion to an executive position in the Top Girls employment agency. Viewers are introduced to scenes of Marlene's workplace and to her working-class sister and niece, Angie. In a painful end to *Top Girls*, Churchill reveals how one woman character is willing to sacrifice her very motherhood in order to maintain her position in the world of business, a world that the play shows to be created by and for men. Following a bitter argument between Marlene and her lower-class sister, it is also revealed that Marlene's "niece" is actually her illegitimate daughter.

The issues in *Top Girls* and *Cloud Nine*, however startlingly presented, are ones commonly addressed in modern culture, even if usually addressed with an attitude different from that of Churchill. *A Mouthful of Birds*, however, is altogether different, for it addresses the most sensitive and most taboo of all matters concerning women: sex and violence. Furthermore, in *A Mouthful of Birds*, Churchill turns the tables and considers sex and violence as perpetrated not by men on women but by women on men, thereby taking one more step into the forbidden matters of gender.

The theme of society's oppressed females is perhaps most powerfully presented in one of Churchill's earlier works, *Vinegar Tom*, a piece created especially for the Monstrous Regiment. *Vinegar Tom* is a play about witches, but there are no witches in it, only four women accused of being witches. Set in seventeenth century England, the play depicts four women accused by society of the vaguest of crimes: sorcery. Their only crime, however, has been to follow an individual impulse. Joan Nokes is simply poor and old, two conditions that are not supposed to happen simultaneously to Western women. Her daughter, Alice, understands sex as an individual matter and is inclined to enjoy a man if he suits her fancy. When Alice asserts her right to have an illegitimate child, she is labeled a "whore," since she is neither a virgin nor a wife. Betty, the play's third woman, is called a witch for refusing to marry the man picked out for her, and Susan, the fourth, is seen as a witch for choosing life over death: When put to the water test (witches float, the innocent sink), Susan elects to swim, thus saving herself but forcing society to find a way to kill her. All four women are emerging, strong-willed individuals whose only crime is to be themselves in an oppressive and conservative society. Since they will not carry out their assigned female roles, they are cast as witches and hanged as a logical consequence of their chosen life-styles.

It is virtually impossible to discuss thematic issues in Churchill's work without simultaneously considering her special treatment of dramatic structure. Each of her pieces is a unique construction, innovatively assembled and using unconventional and highly theatrical devices. Furthermore, Churchill's plays remain compelling, mysterious, and, at the same time, refreshingly accessible.

Cloud Nine presents, in part 1, an English family living in colonial Africa. The father, Clive, though far from home, "serves the Queen." He is father not only to his children but to the natives as well. Churchill has a special device for underscoring this male-dominated world. She calls for Billy, Clive's wife and the mother of the children, to be played by a male. To reinforce her statement, Churchill asks that the black servant, Joshua, be played by a white performer. Thus both characters, despite the race and gender of the performers, become whatever the white father wishes them to be. When a lesbian nanny, Ellen, appears, homosexual orientation is suspected in the children and the "perfect" family is created.

Part 2 has additional surprises. The colonial family returns to England without the father. In England, the grown-up children seek to realize their separate identities, but freedom to be fully choosing individuals still eludes them. They fret over not having the father to tell them what to do, and the traditions of the past weigh heavily on them, keeping them in their assigned roles. One of the daughters, Lin, a diminutive for Ellen, the lesbian nanny of part 1, had married to fulfill social expectations. Now divorced and having custody of her child, she openly lives with a female lover. Even that important change in sexual orientation, however, is not sufficiently liberating, for as Lin remarks, she can change whom she sleeps with but she cannot change everything. In a wistful scene, she attempts to conjure up a goddess, one she knows will never materialize, begging the deity to give her the history she never had, make her the woman she cannot be. In *Cloud Nine*, Churchill reverses the traditional immigration pattern. Often parents settle in a new land but bring the past and its old ways with them; in *Cloud Nine*, however, the children flee their past by returning to the old land, but they are still smothered by ancient habits, expectations, and icons. This preoccupation with the ghosts and hauntings of the past, indeed with the very nature of time itself, is further explored by Churchill in the unusual pieces *Traps* and *Moving Clocks Go Slow*.

A recurring device in Churchill's dramaturgy is to have one actor play several roles. Most of her better-known works—*Serious Money*, *Top Girls*, *Light Shining in Buckinghamshire*, and *Cloud Nine*—make use of multiple role playing. Although the device may be considered merely idiomatic with her, Churchill usually has a point to make in employing multiple role playing. In *Serious Money*, for example, the actors are assigned a series of roles that may be summed up in a single universal type, so that one actor, for example, plays a stockbroker or a financier while another plays various women who pander their bodies or their souls to men of high finance.

Even more idiosyncratic in structure is the powerful *A Mouthful of*

Birds, in which the stories of seven contemporary persons are interwoven with the ancient ritualistic events of Euripides' *The Bacchae* (c. 405 B.C.). Dionysus, the Greek God of wine, appears throughout the piece dancing in a modern woman's petticoat. Amid ancient scenes of ecstasy and emotional and physical violence, the modern characters appear in their normal daily activities. They each present a monologue in which they attempt to explain why they have failed to meet their obligations. Secret and mysterious problems of possession emerge. The atmosphere of the play is charged with the sensuality of accepted violence, violence intermingled with the irresistibility of sex. One woman character, for example, who is stereotypically squeamish about skinning a dead rabbit for supper, calmly tells her husband to go to the bathroom, where he will find their baby drowned. Churchill juxtaposes this modern violence against the culminating terror of *The Bacchae*, the gruesome moment when Agave, in a Dionysian ecstasy, tears apart the body of her son Pentheus.

An important factor in Churchill's proclivity for structural experimentation is her long and close association with workshop groups, whose aim is the collective creation of theater pieces through the interaction of actors, writers, directors, choreographers, and other artists. Two such groups have been especially influential on Churchill's artistic development: The first is the Monstrous Regiment, a feminist theater union that helped Churchill create *Vinegar Tom*; the other is the Joint Stock Theatre Group, with whose help she fashioned several important works, including *Cloud Nine*, *Fen*, and *A Mouthful of Birds.*

The Joint Stock Theatre Group, with directors such as Max Stafford-Clark, Les Waters, and David Lan, and choreographer Ian Fink, operates with suggestions that come from any group member. For example, *Light Shining in Buckinghamshire*, Churchill's first venture with the group, began with a member's suggestion concerning the motives for the mass immigration of villagers in seventeenth century England. After the initial proposal of the idea, the group set out to research the topic, following it with a theatrical workshop in which the group improvised scenes based on that research. These workshop scenes were interrupted by a "writing gap" during which Churchill wrote the script. Rehearsals came next, with more group interaction and improvisation on the script. *Fen* followed virtually the same process and was based on a suggestion to explore what it must have been like, in a rural English village, to have the social and agricultural habits of centuries suddenly overturned by the intrusion of modern capitalism, brought in the person of a Japanese businessman who buys all the village's farmland. In another example, the group's director, Lan, was interested in the politics of possession, while Churchill was interested in the theme of women becoming violent and rebellious rather than submitting to their traditionally assigned, passive role. The Joint Stock Theatre

Group went to work with these ideas, and *A Mouthful of Birds* was born. This creative method, which gives a privilege to experimentation and outright and frank theatricalism, seems to serve Churchill well.

Churchill also has a special relationship with London's Royal Court Theatre, where she was resident dramatist in 1974-1975 and where she has had many of her plays performed in the main playhouse and the experimental Upstairs Theatre. Churchill's radio and television works are often broadcast by the BBC, and her plays are frequently staged outside Great Britain, especially in the United States, where she was first introduced by Joseph Papp at the Public Theatre of New York City.

Churchill has openly proclaimed herself a feminist and a socialist. She is also emphatic in her position that the two are not one and the same. Indeed, her plays do not attempt to confound the two issues, although *Top Girls* does investigate the influence that capitalism can have on women and their willingness to forsake their humanity for economic gain. Churchill has examined with great sympathy, in works such as *Fen* and *Light Shining in Buckinghamshire*, the plight of the male, or of both genders, caught up in the destructiveness of inhuman economic forces. Churchill herself has argued that both issues are so important to her—the plight of women and the need for a socialist world—that she could not choose between them and would not have one problem alleviated without a concurrent solution to the other. In another sense, Churchill is interested in the greater issues of gender and the games of power played with gender at stake. Just so, she is equally committed to considering the individual and the power drained from that individual by the forces of modern economic and social systems.

Whatever her politics and philosophy, Churchill brings a fire and an energy, a special eye and ear, to the postmodern English drama. She is an inspiration to the feminist movement and to women intellectuals around the world. She remains a force crying out for the release of the individual of whatever gender from the oppressive imperatives of past practices and present expectations. To her art, she contributes an inventive mind and a willingness to invest great energies in wedding the play to the performance.

Other major works

TELEPLAYS: *The Judge's Wife*, 1972; *Turkish Delight*, 1974; *The After Dinner Joke*, 1978; *The Legion Hall Bombing*, 1978; *Crimes*, 1981.

RADIO PLAYS: *The Ants*, 1962; *Lovesick*, 1967; *Identical Twins*, 1968; *Abortive*, 1971; *Not, Not, Not, Not, Not Enough Oxygen*, 1971; *Schreber's Nervous Illness*, 1972; *Henry's Past*, 1972; *Perfect Happiness*, 1973.

Bibliography

Betsko, Kathleen, and Rachel Koenig, comps. *Interviews with Contemporary Playwrights.* New York: Beech Tree Books, 1987. In this provocative interview, the playwright discusses her concept of feminism and compares the London and New York productions of *Cloud Nine.*

Bigsby, C. W. E., ed. *Contemporary English Drama.* London: Edward Arnold, 1981. This collection of essays about the British theater provides a key to locating Churchill among her contemporaries. The essay by Christian W. Thomsen, "Three Socialist Playwrights: John McGrath, Caryl Churchill, Trevor Griffiths," is informative about contemporary socialist thought in England and about that thought as it is revealed in the plays of Churchill and her peers.

Cousin, Geraldine. *Churchill, the Playwright.* London: Methuen Drama, 1989. An excellent general study of Churchill's drama. All the issues present in Churchill's work are examined as they are found in the plays themselves.

Fitzsimmons, Linda, comp. *File on Churchill.* London: Methuen Drama, 1989. This brief volume is a compilation of "file material" on Churchill, including lists of sources to consult, quotations from articles about the playwright, biographical data, production information, and reviews of productions. An excellent and dependable source book.

Kaysser, Helen, ed. *Feminism and the Theatre.* Basingstoke, England: Macmillan, 1988. As the title suggests, this volume is a collection of essays on feminists in the theater, and includes an excellent essay on Churchill by a leading feminist critic in the United States, Sue Ellen Case. The volume is useful not only for the Case essay but also for aiding those interested in placing Churchill in the context of contemporary feminist thinking. It is also instructive in the uses of feminist thinking in Churchill's work.

Randall, Phyllis, ed. *Caryl Churchill: A Casebook.* New York: Garland, 1989. A collection of essays pertaining to Churchill as a working dramatist.

August W. Staub

COLLEY CIBBER

Born: London, England; November 6, 1671
Died: London, England; December 11, 1757

Principal drama

Love's Last Shift: Or, The Fool in Fashion, pr., pb. 1696; *Woman's Wit: Or, The Lady in Fashion*, pb. 1697, pr. 1699; *The Tragical History of King Richard III*, pr. 1699, pb. 1700 (adaptation of William Shakespeare's play *Richard III*); *Xerxes*, pr., pb. 1699; *Love Makes a Man: Or, The Fop's Fortune*, pr. 1700, pb. 1701; *The School Boy: Or, The Comical Rivals*, pr. 1702, pb. 1707; *She Wou'd and She Wou'd Not: Or, The Kind Imposter*, pr. 1702, pb. 1703; *The Careless Husband*, pr. 1704, pb. 1705; *Perolla and Izadora*, pr. 1705, pb. 1706; *The Comical Lovers*, pr., pb. 1707; *The Double Gallant: Or, The Sick Lady's Cure*, pr., pb. 1707; *The Lady's Last Stake: Or, The Wife's Resentment*, pr. 1707, pb. 1708; *The Rival Fools*, pr., pb. 1709; *The Rival Queens*, pr. 1710, pb. 1729 (burlesque); *Ximena: Or, The Heroic Daughter*, pr. 1712, pb. 1719; *Myrtillo*, pr., pb. 1715 (masque); *Venus and Adonis*, pr., pb. 1715 (masque); *The Non-Juror*, pr. 1717, pb. 1718; *The Refusal: Or, The Ladies' Philosophy*, pr., pb. 1721; *The Plays of Colley Cibber*, pb. 1721 (2 volumes), pb. 1980 (reprint); *Caesar in Aegypt*, pr. 1724, pb. 1725; *The Provok'd Husband: Or, A Journey to London*, pr., pb. 1728 (completion of Sir John Vanbrugh's play); *Damon and Phillida*, pr., pb. 1729 (ballad opera); *Love in a Riddle*, pr., pb. 1729 (ballad opera); *Papal Tyranny in the Reign of King John*, pr., pb. 1745; *The Lady's Lecture*, pb. 1748; *The Dramatic Works of Colley Cibber*, pb. 1777 (5 volumes).

Other literary forms

Colley Cibber wrote a number of nonfiction works in his later years: *An Apology for the Life of Colley Cibber* (1740), *A Letter from Mr. Cibber to Mr. Pope* (1742), *The Egoist: Or, Colley upon Cibber* (1743), *A Second Letter from Mr. Cibber to Mr. Pope* (1743), *Another Occasional Letter from Mr. Cibber to Mr. Pope* (1744), *The Character and Conduct of Cicero* (1747), and *A Rhapsody upon the Marvellous* (1751). In addition, having been made poet laureate in 1730, he wrote a series of annual New Year's and birthday odes celebrating the virtues of George II.

Achievements

Cibber's reputation rests on his career as an actor, manager, and playwright. As an actor, he was one of the principal comedians of his time, winning fame for his portrayals of a particular character-type, the foppish fool. As one of several actor-managers, he was the reader for Drury Lane and determined which new plays were performed and which were rejected. As a playwright, he wrote a series of successful dramas, including the first

sentimental comedy, *Love's Last Shift*. Today, his plays have chiefly historical interest, but a good half dozen became staples of the theatrical repertory during the eighteenth century. In his autobiography, *An Apology for
the Life of Colley Cibber*, Cibber likened his plays to his children: "I think
we had about a dozen of each sort [that is, children and plays] between us;
of both which Kinds, some dy'd in their Infancy, and near an equal number
of each were alive, when I quitted the Theatre." Cibber's autobiography
provides not only a record of his life but also a theatrical history of London
during the Restoration and early eighteenth century. Today, it is Cibber's
most widely read work.

Biography

Colley Cibber was the son of Jane Colley and Caius Gabriel Cibber, a
master sculptor from Flensburg, Schleswig. Cibber's father had intended
his son for the Church, but Cibber became stagestruck at an early age and
in 1689 joined the Theatre Royal as an unsalaried apprentice. Even though
his early years were not marked by financial success, in 1693, Cibber married Katherine Shore, the daughter of Matthias Shore, who held the post
of Sergeant Trumpet at court.

Discouraged by the poor roles he was assigned, Cibber wrote a play
(*Love's Last Shift*) with a role for himself. Sir Novelty Fashion was not the
main character in the play, but the part gave Cibber a chance to demonstrate his comic abilities. Shortly after the play's premiere in 1696, Sir John
Vanbrugh wrote *The Relapse: Or, Virtue in Danger* as a sequel to *Love's
Last Shift*. Cibber's performance as Lord Foppington (the new title for Sir
Novelty) in Vanbrugh's play confirmed his success in *Love's Last Shift* and
established him as one of the leading comedians of his day. As a playwright
and an actor, Cibber did not limit himself to comedy, but it was in this
genre that he enjoyed his greatest successes. In addition to writing and acting, Cibber became increasingly involved in the administration of Drury
Lane, eventually becoming one of the triumvirate of actor-managers who
ran the company.

The 1720's were marked for Cibber by well-publicized quarrels with
Alexander Pope, Henry Fielding, John Dennis, and Nathaniel Mist.
Cibber's popularity also declined during this decade; there appeared to be
a permanent claque in the audience that disapproved of everything Cibber
did. As reader for Drury Lane, Cibber was the most influential of the
three actor-managers. Many of his problems stemmed from his cavalier
treatment of new works that were submitted to the company for possible
performance.

In 1730, Cibber was named poet laureate. This new post proved a source
of both pleasure and aggravation for Cibber. It gave him an entry into the
highest levels of society but also made him the target of new volleys of ridi-

cule, since he was not a skilled poet.

In 1733, Cibber retired from the stage, but he continued to make guest appearances until 1745, when his play *Papal Tyranny in the Reign of King John* was presented, with the author playing Cardinal Pandulph. Neither the play nor Cibber's performance was well received; it marked his last appearance on the stage.

In 1740, his autobiography appeared and became an immediate success, quickly going through several editions. In 1743, Pope immortalized Cibber as the King of the Dunces in *The Dunciad* (1728-1743), thus bringing to a head their long-standing feud. Despite the attacks by Pope and other men of letters, Cibber enjoyed his final years, for he had achieved the status of a celebrity and was accorded preferential treatment by the finest families of England.

Analysis

As the reader for Drury Lane, Colley Cibber was widely hated for his many rejections of plays on the basis of their lack of theatricality. According to Richard Hindry Barker in *Mr. Cibber of Drury Lane* (1939), for Cibber, theatricality meant "effective situations, plenty of opportunities for stage business, good acting parts suitable for [Robert] Wilks, [Barton] Booth, Mrs. [Anne] Oldfield, and himself." These criteria are surely the outstanding characteristics of his own dramas. He knew what worked on the stage, and he fashioned his plays accordingly.

Today, Cibber is remembered as the creator of the first eighteenth century sentimental comedy; this accomplishment can best be understood in terms of the theatricality of his plays. Cibber did not set out to write a new kind of comedy. Rather, he set out to write a play that would show off the skills of his actors and that would leave his audience pleased and satisfied at the end of the evening. In his first play, he discovered a number of formulas that worked well on the stage. In a Cibber comedy, there are two plots involving a series of deceptions that lead up to discovery scenes in acts 4 and 5, in which the complications of the evening are resolved in a moral, decorous way. Usually, a leading character in the main plot comes to recognize that he has been living according to a false set of values. When he sees the errors of his ways, the problems of the evening are resolved. What makes Cibber a less than compelling dramatist is that this reversal usually does not grow out of characterization. Cibber's heroes and heroines perform what F. W. Bateson in *English Comic Drama, 1700-1750* (1929) calls a "psychological *volte-face*" in act 5, brought about by manipulations in the plot rather than by a process of self-discovery. The action in the secondary plot usually resembles the action in the main plot, but it does not depend on a character's sudden transformation for its resolution.

Cibber's plays are well crafted. No matter how complicated the plots become, they are always easy to follow, all conflicts being neatly resolved by the end of the performance. Cibber gave his audiences the satisfaction of seeing virtue rewarded and lovers correctly matched. His characters are, by and large, stock figures taken from the world of the Restoration comedy of manners. Many of the situations and plot complications also are part of the stock-in-trade of the Restoration stage. Nevertheless, his plays do represent a quite significant departure from the dramatic world of William Wycherley, Sir George Etherege, and William Congreve, in whose plays the endings are rarely so neat and uncomplicated.

Love's Last Shift was Cibber's first play and immediately established him as an important playwright. The main plot involves the reconciliation of a debauchee with the wife he had abandoned eight years before: Loveless "grew weary of his Wife in six Months; left her, and the Town, for Debts he did not care to pay; and having spent the last part of his Estate beyond Sea, returns to *England* in a very mean Condition." He thinks his wife Amanda is dead, but she in fact is alive, having remained faithful to him and come into an estate of her own with the death of a rich uncle. Amanda is not the witty heroine of Restoration comedy but a precursor of the noble heroine of eighteenth century drama, a model of fidelity and moral strength as she sets herself an all but impossible task:

> Oh! to reclaim the Man I'm bound by Heaven to Love, to expose the Folly of a roving Mind, in pleasing him with what he seem'd to loath, were such a sweet Revenge for slighted Love, so vast a Triumph of rewarded Constancy, as might persuade the looser part of Womankind ev'n to forsake themselves, and fall in Love with Virtue.

Loveless is a more familiar figure from the world of Restoration comedy, a rake who has lived according to a delusion of his sex and class about marriage: "an affectation of being fashionably Vicious, than any reasonable Dislike he cou'd either find in" his wife's "Mind or Person." Amanda, who has been altered (but not for the worse) by smallpox since Loveless last saw her, is persuaded by Young Worthy to trick her husband into her bed. This plot involves two transformation scenes. In act 4, the audience has the titillating experience of seeing the apparently virtuous Amanda abandon herself to the pleasures of "a lawless Love: I own my self a Libertine, a mortal Foe to that dull Thing call'd Virtue, that mere Disease of sickly Nature." In act 5, when Loveless discovers the mistake he has made, he admits the errors of his ways and returns to his faithful wife, a scene which reportedly brought tears to the eyes of the first-night audience.

These characters are one-dimensional figures committed to particular moral points of view, but the clash between these opposing views gives their scenes dramatic tension. Cibber also managed to leaven their scenes with laughter by introducing a subplot involving Loveless' servant Snap and Amanda's maid. Snap is placed under a table throughout Loveless' assignation with Amanda. After Loveless and Amanda retire, Snap sneaks up on Amanda's maid, who is listening at her mistress' door, and begins to take advantage of her. When she gets a chance, the maid tricks him into falling into the cellar, but Snap pulls her down with him and they spend the night together. Their brief scenes form an appropriate low-comedy contrast to the more serious affairs of their master and mistress.

The secondary plot ostensibly involves the correct mating of the Worthy brothers. Young Worthy loves Narcissa, who is betrothed to Elder Worthy, who loves Hillaria, Narcissa's cousin. At the end of the play, the couples are correctly matched, but Cibber's working out of this plot was perfunctory, since his real interest in this part of the play was Sir Novelty Fashion, the role which helped to establish him as an actor. One might expect Sir Novelty, a stock figure from Restoration drama modeled after Sir Fopling Flutter in Etherege's *The Man of Mode* (pr. 1676), to function as a possible rival for the hands of Narcissa and Hillaria, but he is so obviously a fool that no one, save himself, takes him seriously. Rather than using Sir Novelty to add complications to the secondary plot, Cibber used the plot as an occasion to display Sir Novelty. As a prank, the four young lovers lure Sir Novelty to St. James' Park with the promise of a rendezvous with Narcissa, whom he assumes must be enamored of his charms. Instead, he meets Mrs. Flareit, a used mistress he wants to get rid of. The scene, like so many of Cibber's big comic scenes, is filled with physical action. At its climax, the emotional Mrs. Flareit attempts to run Sir Novelty through with a sword. Occurring at the beginning of act 4, this scene with its broad humor balances the almost melodramatic meeting between Loveless and Amanda at the end of the act. In addition, the scenes thematically resemble each other, since both involve tricks played on male characters who are overly concerned with following the false dictates of fashion. Unlike Loveless, Sir Novelty experiences no moral reformation. He is simply exposed as the fool he is, to the general amusement of all.

In *The Careless Husband*, written eight years later, Cibber used more artfully many of the elements that had worked so well in *Love's Last Shift*. Sir Novelty reappears as Sir Foppington, but now he furthers the plot. He is still a fantastic fool, but not so ludicrous that he cannot make a devoted lover jealous when he ogles the lover's mistress. The double plot once again involves a similar situation played out with two couples, but here the characters in both plots are from the same genteel level of society and interact with one another. In the main plot, Sir Charles Easy is married to a faithful woman who sincerely loves him. Only at the end of the play does he learn to value her devotion and cast off the conventional role of jaded husband who must look outside his home for pleasure. In the secondary plot, Lady Betty Modish is pursued by a faithful suitor, Lord Morelove, who sincerely loves her. Only at the end of the play is she able to come to grips with her true feelings for him and to cast off her conventional role of the desirable beauty who delights in exercising her power over men and in keeping them on a string.

These characters neatly complement one another. Lady Easy is a model of virtue. Even when she discovers her husband sleeping with her maid, she suppresses her anger and thinks instead of his needs by placing a scarf "gently over his head" so he will not catch cold. Her only concern is that he should not wake and be irritated: "And if he should wake offended at my too-busy care, let my heart-breaking patience, duty, and my fond affection plead my pardon." Lady Betty Modish is a flirt. She cannot resist engaging in battle with the opposite sex and is satisfied with nothing less than victory: "Let me but live to see him once more within my power, and I'll forgive the rest of fortune." Sir Charles Easy is a man of the world, careless in his affairs, weary of the complicated games lovers play: "I am of late grown so very lazy in my pleasures that I had rather lose a woman than go through the plague and trouble of having or keeping her." Lord Morelove is so timid that he would never even attempt such an affair: "The shame or scandal of a repulse always made me afraid of attempting a woman of condition."

The reconciliations in act 5 are better prepared for here than in *Love's Last Shift*. Sir Charles Easy and Lady Betty Modish may not be in touch with their true feelings, but the audience is well aware of them. In this context Lady Easy is extremely useful. To a modern reader, she may appear impossibly prim and virtuous, but she is aware of the true feelings of Sir Charles and Lady Betty, and she helps expose what the characters themselves do not know. Here, for example, Lady Easy probes the feelings of Lady Betty:

> LADY BETTY MODISH: But still, to marry before one's heartily in love—
> LADY EASY: Is not half so formidable a calamity. But if I have any eyes, my dear, you'll run no great hazard of that in venturing upon my Lord Morelove. You don't know, perhaps, that within this half hour the tone of your voice is strangely softened to him, ha! ha! ha! ha!

At the end, the reader does not feel that the reconciliations have been imposed by the law of happy endings; they are rather the natural consequence of character in action.

Cibber's last successful play, *The Provok'd Husband*, was presented twenty-four years after *The Careless Husband*. Like so many of Cibber's works, it is not a completely original play. In this instance, Cibber revised an unfinished play which came into his hands after the death of its author, Sir John Vanbrugh. The changes Cibber made give a good indication of his theatrical interests. Vanbrugh's play consisted of two plots and was entitled *A Journey to London*. The main plot involved a well-to-do family from the country, the Headpieces, who come to London only to fall easy victims to the lures of the big city. The secondary plot involved the battling Loverules, who fight over Lady Loverule's extravagances. Peter Dixon suggests in his edition of the play that if Vanbrugh had finished the work, the Loverule plot would have issued "in an angry separation, without hope of reconciliation, but also without the possibility of divorce." Cibber, who had a reputation as the dramatist of genteel society, reversed the importance of the two plots. The disputes between the Townlys (the new name for the Loverules) became the primary plot, while the misadventures of the Wrongheads (the new name for the Headpieces) became the secondary plot. In act 5, Cibber provided a moral conclusion with the reconciliation of the Townlys.

The theme of a wife's financial excesses dominates the Townly plot. Lady Townly is addicted to gambling. Her fault is not simply a matter of extravagant expenditures, for she virtually abandons her husband for the pleasures of the hazard table, associating with the least reputable people in polite society and sleeping until five in the afternoon.

In act 5, however, Lady Townly reforms when she is threatened with the possibility of being cut off from her husband's wealth and her position as his wife. Her reformation is as unprepared for as Loveless' in *Love's Last Shift*. Both characters renounce their wicked ways after having spent a whole play demonstrating how committed they are to their profligate habits. In her recantation, Lady Townly sounds suspiciously like another Cibber character, Lady Betty Modish in *The Careless Husband*. Both ladies are great beauties who use their allure to gain power over men. Not surprisingly, both of these parts were written for Cibber's favorite actress, Anne Oldfield.

The secondary plot is also dominated by a conflict between spouses. Lady Wronghead quickly learns the main vice of the married lady in town—to spend money. She starts with knickknacks and fripperies, since "the greatest distinction of a fine lady in this town is in the variety of pretty things that she has no occasion for," but soon moves on to the pleasures of the hazard table, to which she is introduced by Lady Townly. At the end of the play, there is no recantation scene for Lady Wronghead. Rather, she is whisked back to the country, where she belongs and where she will do herself and others no harm. The Wrongheads, like Sir Novelty Fashion, exist to amuse the audience; moral reform is not possible for them.

In this late comedy, Cibber once more manipulated the character-types and situations with which he had worked for thirty years. Cibber's career as a dramatist does not reveal growth; rather, it reveals an early mastery of the requirements of the stage which sustained him for the rest of his career and made him the most important writer of comedies in the early eighteenth century.

Other major works

NONFICTION: *An Apology for the Life of Colley Cibber*, 1740; *A Letter from Mr. Cibber to Mr. Pope*, 1742; *The Egoist: Or, Colley upon Cibber*, 1743; *A Second Letter from Mr. Cibber to Mr. Pope*, 1743; *Another Occasional Letter from Mr. Cibber to Mr. Pope*, 1744; *The Character and Conduct of Cicero*, 1747; *A Rhapsody upon the Marvellous*, 1751.

Bibliography

Ashley, Leonard R. N. *Colley Cibber.* Rev. ed. Boston: Twayne, 1989. Ashley devotes one chapter to Cibber's youth and then gives an account of him as an actor, listing the various roles he played and counting his performances at 2,936. One chapter judges Cibber's work as a dramatist, and three chapters deal with his life in the theater. His quarrel with Alexander Pope is also summarized. A good bibliography completes this study.

Barker, Richard Hindry. *Mr. Cibber of Drury Lane.* New York: Columbia University Press, 1939. Reprint. New York: AMS Press, 1966. A well-written and comprehensive biography, especially good for the discussions of the rise of the actors-managers and their last years. The chapter entitled "The Struggle with Lincoln's Inn Fields" is an informative account of the theater at that location.

Cibber, Colley. *An Apology for the Life of Colley Cibber, with an Historical View of the Stage During His Own Time.* Edited by B. R. S. Fone. Ann Arbor: University of Michigan, 1968. First published in 1740, Cibber's autobiography, though usually faulted for being poorly written, is valuable for its intimate view of stage life during Cibber's time.

_____. *Colley Cibber: Three Sentimental Comedies.* Edited by Maureen Sullivan. New Haven, Conn.: Yale University Press, 1973. Sullivan has edited *Love's Last Shift: Or, The Fool in Fashion*, *The Careless Husband*, and *The Lady's Last Stake: Or, The Wife's Resentment.* She provides a forty-page introduction, an appendix with the first scene of *Love's Last Shift* as printed in the early quartos, and ample detailed notes.

Koon, Helene. *Colley Cibber: A Biography.* Lexington: University Press of Kentucky, 1986. Besides offering an authoritative biography, Koon includes invaluable appendices entitled "The Genealogy of the Cibber Family," "Cibber's Second Letter to Alexander Pope," "Colley Cibber's Will," and "Chronological List of Cibber's Roles." The notes and bibliography are excellent sources for further information.

Roper, Alan. "Language and Action in *The Way of the World*, *Love's Last Shift*, and *The Relapse.*" *Journal of English Literary History* 40 (1973): 44-69. Roper analyzes Cibber's *Love's Last Shift*, along with William Congreve's *The Way of the World* (pr., pb. 1700) and Sir John Vanbrugh's

The Relapse (pr., pb. 1696) and finds in the Cibber play a clash between the language of wit and that of morality.

Edward V. Geist
(Updated by *Frank Day*)

JOHN PEPPER CLARK-BEKEDEREMO

Born: Kiagbodo, Nigeria; April 6, 1935

Principal drama
Song of a Goat, pr., pb. 1961; *The Masquerade*, pb. 1964, pr. 1965; *The Raft*, pb. 1964, pr. 1966 (radio play), pr. 1978 (revised); *Three Plays*, pb. 1964; *Ozidi*, pb. 1966; *The Boat*, pr. 1981.

Other literary forms
John Pepper Clark-Bekederemo is recognized as a major poet for his collections *Poems* (1962), *A Reed in the Tide: A Selection of Poems* (1965), *Casualties: Poems, 1966-1968* (1970), and *A Decade of Tongues* (1981). He has also published literary criticism with *The Example of Shakespeare: Critical Essays on African Literature* (1970) and a travel diary, *America, Their America* (1964).

Achievements
Clark-Bekederemo was a member of an extraordinary group of creative young Nigerian writers and artists who began their careers in the early 1960's with publication in the legendary magazine *Black Orpheus.* Contributors besides Clark-Bekederemo included Chinua Achebe, the Nobel Prize winner Wole Soyinka, and Christopher Okigbo. The nature of this publication defined Clark-Bekederemo's subsequent work. He wished to establish and confirm the importance and dignity of his Ijaw inheritance in the river delta of Nigeria and yet communicate these roots through publication in English. Both in his poetry and in his drama, he presented with affectionate sensibility his ancestry. Yet because he had become an academic within the formal university system which the British had exported to West Africa, he was committed to linking this antecedence with the wider concept of international, universal human issues. His major works draw from the specific environment of his birth. He uses English to make profound statements about the conditions of humanity in the contemporary world, but an English skillfully adapted to express its African context.

Biography
John Pepper Clark-Bekederemo was born in the Western Rivers area of Nigeria in Kiagbodo, Warri Province, on April 6, 1935. His father, Clark Fuludu Bekederemo, was a chief. He attended several local schools, the most important being Government College in Ughelli. In 1954, he spent a year as a clerk in a government office before earning entrance to a college in Ibadan which would subsequently become the distinguished University

of Ibadan. At the university he rapidly entered the literary milieu and became editor first of *Beacon* and later of *Horn*, student magazines that offered early opportunities for publication to several writers who would become the first generation of Nigerian authors. In 1960, he was graduated with a B.A. in English, worked briefly as information officer with the Ministry of Information at Ibadan, and then was appointed an editorial writer for the *Express*, a Lagos newspaper. It was this position that permitted his appointment as Parvin Fellow at Princeton during the 1962-1963 academic year. For various reasons, this opportunity occasioned mutual dissatisfaction, and for Clark-Bekederemo, it provided the basis for a rather bad-tempered diary of that year, *America, Their America.* On his return to Nigeria, he spent a year as Research Fellow at Ibadan and began the field research that produced the *Ozidi* saga. In 1964, he married a Yoruba woman, Ebun Odutola, a talented actress. They had three children: two daughters, Ebiere and Imoyadue, and a son Ambekederemo. That same year, he joined the faculty of the University of Lagos and in 1972 was appointed professor of English. The years 1975 and 1976 saw him as Distinguished Fellow at Wesleyan University in Connecticut. In 1979, however, he chose to give up an academic career in order to concentrate on writing. Indicatively, he returned to his birthplace at Kiagbodo. He became influential in Nigerian theater, and in 1982 he formed the PEC Repertory in Lagos. After his return to Kiagbodo, he preferred to add his father's name, Bekederemo, to his own in formal matters, as demonstrated in his collection of plays and poems published in 1991.

Analysis

John Pepper Clark-Bekederemo's first play was *Song of a Goat.* Its title indicates the multiple cultural elements he integrates into his drama. There is obvious reference to classic Greek in that the very term "tragedy" translates as "goat song" (*tragos* meaning "goat," and *oide* meaning "song"). There is also a parallel tradition from Africa. By Ijaw custom, a goat is the appropriate sacrifice—in the manner of the Hebraic concept of scapegoat. Similarities with the Irish playwright John Millington Synge are also apparent. Clark-Bekederemo accepts Synge's view of the tragic dignity of humble people.

The plot of *Song of a Goat* presents a conflict between traditional and modern beliefs, though this does not seem to be the central element. The tragedy itself derives from urgent human responses. Zifa's wife, Ebiere, consults a "masseur," who is both doctor and priest, concerning her infertility. From her diffident explanations it becomes clear that the husband has become impotent: "I keep my house/ Open by night and day/ But my lord will not come in." The doctor argues that "some one has to go in, or they will take rust." He advises the tribal custom that someone within the family, such as Tonye, his younger brother, substitute for the husband. "That'll be a retying of knots" and there will be continuity of issue. Clark-Bekederemo presents a curious psychological ambivalence in response to this advice. Even though presumably the practice is legalized by long-term custom ("What I suggested our fathers did not forbid"), Ebiere is as horrified as any Western wife would be. "I'll not stay here longer to hear this kind of talk," she says. With ominous perception, she answers, "That will be an act of death." Her husband Zifa is also violently shocked by the suggestion. He prefers to wait: "The thing may come back any day." He is shamed that he will receive public scorn for his impotence. "Everybody will be saying, there/ Goes the cock. . . . " There are continuing hints that his problem is imposed by the gods as punishment for some very vaguely defined and unpurged offense committed by his father.

After some months of barrenness, Ebiere, bitter against her husband and lusting with thwarted passion, teases Tonye into seducing her. He resists at first, for the deed is wicked, but he embraces her with such ardor that there is no possible pretense that he is simply obeying the decrees of custom. This is naked adultery passionately performed. Zifa finds his incestuous brother in his bed and berates him: "I can't believe it. . . . My own brother who I have looked after." Zifa decides that he will kill the adulterer, but before he can do this, in shame Tonye goes and hangs himself. It seems there is nobility in this decision, for he takes upon himself the crime of suicide and frees Zifa from the penalty for committing the most heinous crime conceivable in Ijaw life: a deed that offends the gods. Zifa recognizes this sacrifice. "I thought to kill/ You but in that office you have again performed my part." Only now does his guilty self-condemnation confirm the possible justice of the act. "He went to my wife. . . . Was that not a brotherly act?" Ebiere is said to have miscarried in giving birth to his brother's son. Despairing at the disaster his own anguish and jealousy have wrought, Zifa commits suicide by drowning himself in the sea, yielding to the power of the gods whom in his life he has opposed. The masseur concludes by attempting words of comfort and reconciliation, rather than blame, in the face of tragedy that reduces men to misery and defeat. "It is enough/ You know now that each day we live/ Hints at why we cried at birth." Here is the moral essence of the tragic condition. The urgency in this play does not rest with the external cultural conflict, though this is often mentioned. The conflict between human passion and moral duty provides the trigger for the inescapable disaster constantly prophesied by an old woman who leads the neighbors in the role of Chorus. Cassandra-like, she issues warnings that are perceived but not heeded. This makes for absorbing drama in the classic tradition.

The richness of the language more than sustains the tension of the events. Clark-Bekederemo enjoys the long, extended poetic metaphor. Ebiere's unpregnant womb is compared to a "piece of fertile land—run fallow with elephant grass," an analogy he carries through to extreme development. This technique connects with the Ijaw preference for the riddle when matters are too intimate to be spoken of directly. There is the almost Shakespearean invective: "You lame thing, you crawling piece/ Of withered flesh." Clark-Bekederemo also employs the profoundest declamatory poetry. "You may well cry. But this is nothing/ To beat your breast. It was how/ We all began and will end." Here is something rare on the contemporary stage—a modern tragedy, a form that Western playwrights have only rarely achieved in the twentieth century.

The Masquerade closely links with the earlier play. It is essentially similar in mood and structure. One of the chief characters derives from *Song of a Goat.* It is now determined that Ebiere died giving birth to Tonye's son, Tufa. The earlier play spoke of her surviving a miscarriage. That minor point indicates that the two plays were not conceived originally as part of a single cycle. Tufa grows up and travels from his home, hoping like Oedipus to escape from the curse of his illegitimate origin. The play begins with a sense of foreboding. Without knowing the reason ("as far as I know no feasts have been left out," says one), the villagers see ominous signs: "The tilt [of the moon] is prominent,/ It is never so but there is disaster."

Into this situation comes Tufa. Titi is the local belle. A neighbor's description of her almost parodies the famous report of Cleopatra by Enobarbus: "Her head high in that silver tiara so/ Brilliant it was blindness trying to tell/ Its characters." Tufa immediately falls for her, and at first the affair seems blessed. The couple make love in lyric poetry: "Your flesh under flush/ Of cam flashes many times lovelier than gold/ Or pearls." Soon, however, gossip informs of the tragic but polluting events of Tufa's past: "His father/ Usurped the bed of his elder brother, yes,/ Brazenly in his lifetime, and for shame/ Of it hanged himself." Titi's father, Diribi, immediately condemns Tufa and forbids the marriage: "Consider the taint." He fears that the curse Tufa bears will spread among the entire family. If they associate with him, the gods will threaten them, too. The mother is equally dismissive, saying, "the man is no more your husband now happily/ His past and back are in full view." Tufa is told "leave my daughter alone, . . . and go your curse-laden way." To her father's horror, Titi defies him and argues that she will marry Tufa in spite of "this prospect of pollution." Her father curses Titi, calling her "this witch and bitch/ Who has quite infected her breed." Tufa, however, is touched by the generosity of her love and recognizes her devotion. Titi "called herself my wife, my bride ready to go with me/ In spite of my shame." Her father, in spite of his great affection, is more concerned with his consequent family shame and determines to kill her. Though "she tried tears, tried prayers," he shoots her with the very gun Tufa had given him as a present. He turns the gun upon Tufa and wounds him mortally. Tufa staggers out to join Titi, after confessing, "I am that unmentionable beast/ Born of woman to brother."

Borrowing from Greek, Clark-Bekederemo has the priests observe, "Who/ The gods love they visit with calamity." No action need be taken against the father. In this situation, no human punishment can add to the misfortune imposed. He has destroyed himself. He "who was so tall and strong/ Before. . . . Now at one stroke/ See him splintered to the ground." The tragedy that began with *Song of a Goat* has now worked itself out, purging the crime from which it originated in the manner of the great Greek tragedies.

Again, one should observe the controlled poetry that Clark-Bekederemo employs. Like that of Shakespeare, it can range without any apparent contradiction between colloquial conversation and great poetic feeling. Beautiful are the lines: "It is the time/ Of night. There is a catch in the air/ Will not hold. Not a rustle of leaves,/ Not a cry of a bird, nor the sudden charge/ Of sheep or goats. . . . "

The Raft explores a new topic, a circumstance reminiscent of Stephen Crane's famous short story "The Open Boat." It describes four workers: Olotu, the educated townsman; Kengide, the cynic; Ogro, the traditionalist, and Ibobo, the priest figure. They are camping on a huge raft of hard wood logs, sailing it downriver to the port. Owing to mischance or carelessness, the ropes tying it during the night come away and they drift helplessly down the river, unable to control direction or, since a heavy fog comes down, to determine where they are. This danger frightens them, and one by one these men are brought to the breaking point and die. The raft itself would seem to be a general symbol of individuals' inability to be masters of their environment, indicating their weakness when pitted against the superior power of circumstance. Some critics have argued that, since this was written when Nigerian political events seemed to be equally drifting before the resolution of an army coup, direct reference must be intended. The times may conceivably have been in Clark-Bekederemo's mind when he invented this plot, but the play is certainly far more universal in its concept than any political tract would be. The characters in the play do not represent public persons, even obliquely, nor are they conceived as representing generalized attitudes of the time. They are individuals battling fierce problems in a highly realistic setting. The play succeeds on the stage because the potential allegory is never allowed to intrude into the actual events.

The raft begins to drift when by some inexplicable means its mooring ropes break. "What I can't understand is how all/ The seven gave way. . . . Some madman/ Came aboard and cut us loose?/ Some ghost or evil god." The speculations indicate the cosmic nature of their plight. They find that they are being carried out to sea on the ebb tide. Desperately they apply all of their skill. As they contemplate the prospect of death, they agonize and discuss their chances, reminisce about their pasts, their families, their jobs, their hopes. Yet disaster cannot be avoided. First, Olotu is taken away when a part of the raft breaks off and he is unable to swim back. "He's adrift and lost!" is the cry. The greater truth comes in the responsive observation, "We are all adrift and lost!" Then they hear a ship coming. Ogro decides his best chance is to swim to it and be hauled aboard. The sailors see him and beat him away until he becomes entwined in the stern wheel and is killed. None will assist in escape. Now only Ibobo and Kengide remain. Ibobo thinks that he recognizes a small town they are passing and decides to jump overboard. Kengide holds him back, warning him of sharks, but Ibobo asks, "are/ You afraid to be alone?" With a more generalized recognition that typically links actual event to universality, Kengide says, "Aren't you afraid to be left alone/ In this world, aren't you?" They decide to shout in the hope of attracting attention. The last lines of the play are their forlorn and feeble voices crying "Ee-ee-eee!" which, in a stage direction, Clark-Bekederemo reminds his readers is "the long squeal as used when women go wood-gathering and by nightfall have still not found their way home." In a sense, the tragedy here is less personal, more cosmic. The suffering is not imposed upon the characters because there is some taint in their past, some evil to be assuaged. Here is the more pessimistic conclusion that all persons are doomed to suffer in a universe which is implacably indifferent to their fate. This view does not allow the note of hope that occurs in the final resolution of many tragedies when even death can be seen as a kind of liberation from the pains of enduring the arrows of life. Here, death is an end without purpose and without meaning imposed by powers beyond human beings' control and indifferent to their fate.

Ozidi brings a major change in the direction of Clark-Bekederemo's work. The original *Ozidi* is a traditional poetic saga of the Ijaw people. The playwright affirms its epic status, calling it "an old story, truly heroic in proportion, arising out of a people's sense of their past." In its original form, its performance lasts seven days and is embellished with dance, music, ritual masks, and costumes. In drawing upon the historical event, Clark-Bekederemo has departed from the universalist ideas of his earlier plays and immersed himself deeply in his African inheritance. This involvement makes it difficult for him to extract a sequence of action that will be appropriate for a formal theatrical presentation, inevitably restricted both in time span and area.

Clark-Bekederemo's concern for *Ozidi* has an extended history. He first heard the tale when Afoluwa of Ofonibenga recited it to an eager school audience. It had such an impact that he worked for ten years as a researcher to record permanently this oral, public event. The results were a film, a record of the music, and, in 1977, an Ijaw/English side-by-side transcription of nearly four hundred pages. While continuing this long-term study, in 1966 he attempted to distill the extensive epic into an English-language dramatized version. The result presents barriers to the non-African reader. The fullest comprehension may seem to require anthropological knowledge. Nevertheless, the play has moments of dramatic intensity and the basic plot is clear enough, even though compression requires external explication.

The story spans two generations. A new king must be selected, this time from the house of Ozidi. He refuses the honor and is amazed when his younger brother, Temugedege, a discreditable and feeble figure "dribbling with drink," demands his rights to the throne. He greedily imagines his power, intending to become "terror of all our/ Territories." The populace consider his pretensions ridiculous. Ozidi agrees with their judgments but insists that, as his brother has been made king, all the normal honors are due him, including lavish gifts: "A god is/ A god once you make him so," he says. His subjects have no intention of gratifying so feeble a monarch, for "nobody is going to serve Temugedege; he is an idiot." When Ozidi insists that the traditional generosities are required no matter how inadequate the recipient, there are murmurs of revolt. Rather than tax themselves for safety from the ruthless Ozidi, they prefer to plan his death. Since one of the expectations of a new king is a symbolic skull, they attack Ozidi, cunningly destroy his magic security, and send his head to his brother. "There is our tribute to you, King." He is too weak to do other than flee. Ozidi's grandmother Oreame escapes with his pregnant wife, Orea, who delivers a child also called Ozidi.

The second section deals with young Ozidi's upbringing largely at the hands of his grandmother, who uses her skills in magic to develop his courage so that he will be the means of revenge for his father's murder. She intends that he "must go forth and scatter death among/ His father's enemies." He returns to his father's home and reinstates himself: "Let's raise again the compound of my fathers." Urged by his grandmother and protected by her magic, he seeks out his enemies and throws down a challenge by shamefully and publicly stripping their wives. He singles out his opponents and fights them one by one. Though they confront him boldly, "Ozidi, I am going to eat you up today," he is always victorious. Others seeking to avenge their friends are equally eliminated, their magic brought to nothing against Oreame's spells. The sequence of deaths affects Ozidi, until a woman can ask, "is there nothing else you can do except kill?" Finally blinded by herbs, he kills both enemy and grandmother, for she has not thought to protect herself from her own grandson. He is attacked by fever and nursed by his mother. He wins that bodily battle and thus defeats King Smallpox, the ultimate enemy of the people, who will not "set foot again on this shore." The end is somewhat surprising, but it is clear that some general victory other than satisfied revenge is required to achieve Ozidi's full heroic status.

The events in this play are repetitive and sometimes confusing. The language, seeming sometimes close to Ijaw, makes for difficult interpretaion. At other times, it has the familiar Clark-Bekederemo lyrical conviction. "What need have/ We to stand up when silk cotton trees lie prostrate/ We are reeds only, mere reeds in the storm, and must/ Stretch our broken backs on the ground." *Ozidi* is less immediately accessible to a non-Nigerian reader, but it has the same tragic power and evocative language found in the earlier plays and exhibits Clark-Bekederemo's determination to draw ever more deeply from his African experience and culture.

For many years after his writing of *Ozidi*, Clark-Bekederemo seems to have preferred to concentrate on poetry, and perhaps his reputation in this genre is higher than his reputation as a dramatist; yet in the 1980's, his contribution to the theater continued with production of *The Boat*. He would not separate poetry from drama, and his ability to bring poetry and an African context and sensibility to the modern stage establishes his importance in contemporary world literature.

Other major works

POETRY: *Poems*, 1962; *A Reed in the Tide: A Selection of Poems*, 1965; *Casualties: Poems, 1966-1968*, 1970; *A Decade of Tongues*, 1981; *Mandela, and Other Poems*, 1988.

NONFICTION: *America, Their America*, 1964; *The Example of Shakespeare: Critical Essays on African Literature*, 1970; *The Philosophical Anarchism of William Godwin*, 1977; *State of the Union*, 1985.

EDITED TEXT: *The Ozidi Saga*, 1977.

MISCELLANEOUS: *Collected Plays and Poems, 1958-1988*, 1991.

Bibliography

Cartey, Wilfred. *Whispers from a Continent: The Literature of Contemporary Black Africa.* New York: Vintage Books, 1969. Clark-Bekederemo's *Song of a Goat*, *The Masquerade*, and *The Raft* are analyzed in considerable detail, toward Cartey's thesis that in Clark-Bekederemo's plays "man is indeed adrift and his actions to escape the drift are futile."

Egudu, Romanus. *Four Modern West African Poets.* New York: NOK Publishers, 1977. Only indirectly dealing with his drama, the chapter on Clark-Bekederemo nevertheless makes the point that, like his poetry, his drama takes on "the theme of calamity, of the tragic 'reality' of existence." Characters are victims of punishment, often undeserved, from society and the gods.

Esslin, Martin. "Two Nigerian Playwrights." In *Introduction to African Literature: An Anthology of Critical Writing from "Black Orpheus,"* edited by Ulli Beier. Evanston, Ill.: Northwestern University Press, 1967. Clark-Bekederemo is compared with Wole Soyinka, but with more theatrical authority than African expertise; this article first appeared in Clark-Bekederemo's own magazine. Particularly informative on the question of English-language theater for African writers.

Fearn, Marianne. *Modern Drama of Africa, Form and Content: A Study of*

Four Playwrights. Ann Arbor, Mich.: University Microfilms International, 1978. A section of chapter 3 deals with the verse theater of Clark-Bekederemo and his use of traditional music, dance, and folk characters. Strong bibliography on African drama.

Graham-White, Anthony. *The Drama of Black Africa.* New York: Samuel French, 1974. Chapter 5 gives a brief biography, then discusses the plays, from *Song of a Goat* to *Ozidi* (based on Ijaw traditional drama), in terms of Greek tragedy, cursed houses, and fallen heroes. Contrasts Clark's pessimism with Wole Soyinka's more positive views. Index and valuable chronology.

Irele, Abiola. Introduction to *Collected Plays and Poems, 1958-1988.* Washington, D.C.: Howard University Press, 1991. A substantial introduction to Clark-Bekederemo's dramatic and poetic work, discussing his debt to European theatrical tradition, especially the Theatre of the Absurd. *Ozidi* is cited as his "most fully realized play."

Povey, John. "Two Hands a Man Has." In *African Literature Today: A Journal of Explanatory Criticism*, edited by Eldred D. Jones. Vol. 1. London: Heinemann, 1972. An analysis of Clark-Bekederemo's poetry, which he himself refused to separate from his drama; T. S. Eliot's influence is noted. The title refers to Clark's recurring theme of the fundamental contradiction in individuals as a result of their dual parentage.

John Povey
(Updated by *Thomas J. Taylor*)

AUSTIN CLARKE

Born: Dublin, Ireland; May 9, 1896
Died: Dublin, Ireland; March 19, 1974

Principal drama

The Son of Learning, pr., pb. 1927 (as *The Hunger Demon*, pr. 1930); *The Flame*, pb. 1930, pr. 1932; *Sister Eucharia*, pr., pb. 1939; *Black Fast*, pb. 1941, pr. 1942; *As the Crow Flies*, pr. 1942 (radio play), pb. 1943, pr. 1948 (staged); *The Kiss*, pr. 1942, pb. 1944; *The Plot Is Ready*, pr. 1943, pb. 1944; *The Viscount of Blarney*, pr., pb. 1944; *The Second Kiss*, pr., pb. 1946; *The Plot Succeeds*, pr., pb. 1950; *The Moment Next to Nothing*, pr., pb. 1953; *Collected Plays*, pb. 1963; *The Student from Salamanca*, pr. 1966, pb. 1968; *Two Interludes Adapted from Cervantes: "The Student from Salamanca" and "The Silent Lover,"* pb. 1968; *The Impuritans: A Play in One Act Freely Adapted from the Short Story "Young Goodman Brown" by Nathaniel Hawthorne*, pb. 1972; *The Visitation*, pb. 1974; *The Third Kiss*, pb. 1976; *Liberty Lane*, pb. 1978.

Other literary forms

Austin Clarke was most prolific as a poet; all of his dramatic writings are also in verse form. Between 1917, when his first major poem, the narrative epic *The Vengeance of Fionn*, was issued by Maunsel in Dublin and London, and 1974, when his *Collected Poems* appeared just before his death, Clarke published numerous books of nondramatic verse as well as many individual poems. *Selected Poems*, edited and introduced by Thomas Kinsella, was published posthumously in 1976.

In addition to his dramatic verse, Clarke wrote in a variety of poetic genres—narrative epic poems, satires and epigrams, religious poems, confessional and meditative works, and erotic and love poetry. He also translated poems from the Gaelic. The subjects of his poetry—though diverse in some ways—are all related to aspects of Irish life and Irish culture, past and present.

Clarke wrote three novels, *The Bright Temptation* (1932), *The Singing Men at Cashel* (1936), and *The Sun Dances at Easter* (1952). Although these works are in the form of prose romance, full of adventure and fantasy, they also express Clarke's preoccupation with the problems of the development of the individual within the limits imposed by society, specifically Irish society. All three novels were banned at publication by the Irish Free State government. *The Bright Temptation* was reissued in 1973, but copies of Clarke's other two novels have virtually disappeared.

Besides poetry and novels, Clarke produced three book-length memoirs: *First Visit to England and Other Memories* (1945), *Twice Round the Black*

Church: Early Memories of Ireland and England (1962), and *A Penny in the Clouds: More Memories of Ireland and England* (1968). These books offer important insight into Clarke's development as a major writer in twentieth century Ireland.

Finally, Clarke was a prolific journalist, a frequent contributor of essays, reviews, and criticism to several major publications: *The Daily News and Leader* (London), which later became *The News Chronicle*; *The Spectator*; and *The Irish Times*. Between 1940 and 1973, he contributed more than a thousand articles on both narrowly literary as well as wide-ranging non-literary topics to *The Irish Times*. Clarke also wrote longer prose pieces for *The Dublin Magazine* and *The Bell*.

Achievements

In the judgment of many critics of Irish literature, Austin Clarke was the most important of the poets of the generation of Irish writers after William Butler Yeats. As a poet, Clarke's achievements are impressive. He wrote almost exclusively of Irish themes, myth, tradition, and history, and his own experience of Irish life and culture. Indeed, he has been called the "arch poet of Dublin," and his commitment to Gaelic poetic forms and pros-ody—assonantal patterns, vowel rhymes, tonic words—helped revise and preserve that poetic tradition.

Clarke was also a significant force in the revival of verse drama in Ire-land. In 1941, partly as a vehicle for performance of his own dramatic writings, Clarke, with Robert Farren, founded the Dublin Verse-Speaking Society, which performed on Radio Éireann and at the Abbey Theatre. In 1944, he and Farren founded the Lyric Theatre Company, which presented plays in verse form at the Abbey until the disastrous fire there in 1951.

Austin Clarke was a prolific man of letters, publishing a large amount of nonfiction and criticism for more than four decades in such respected out-lets as *The Bell, The Dublin Magazine*, and *The Irish Times*. Clarke's founding of a private small press, the Bridge Press, inspired other Irish writers to found small presses of their own that were later influential in the resurgence of Irish writing in the 1960's and 1970's. For thirteen years, Clarke presented a weekly broadcast on Radio Éireann on Irish poetry. He was president of the Irish branch of the International Association of Poets, Playwrights, Editors, Essayists, and Novelists (PEN) for six years, and in 1952, he became president of the Irish Academy of Letters.

Clarke received many awards and prizes in recognition of his achieve-ments as a writer. For his early lyric poetry, he was honored with the National Award for Poetry at the Tailteann Games in 1928. Later in life, Clarke was recognized and honored by the Arts Council of Ireland, Irish PEN, the Irish Academy of Letters, and the American Irish Federation. He was nominated by the Irish PEN for the Nobel Prize.

In 1966, on the occasion of his seventieth birthday, Clarke was presented with a festschrift containing poems and tributes by major Irish literary figures. A special issue of the *Irish University Review* was devoted to Clarke shortly before his death in 1974.

Austin Clarke's commitment to a literature that spoke most directly to the Irish themselves, within Irish literary and social traditions, about Irish themes, issues, and conflicts, has exerted unfortunate limitations on his general appeal, despite the fact that much of his work ultimately transcends its Irish context to deal with universals in human experience. The increasing critical focus on Clarke's works may help extend his reputation beyond the confines of Ireland.

Biography

Augustine Joseph Clarke was born in Dublin, Ireland, on May 9, 1896. His parents, Augustine Clarke and Ellen Patten Browne Clarke, produced twelve children; three daughters and one son, Austin, survived. The young Clarke was educated at Belvedere College (1903-1912) and then at University College of the National University of Ireland on a three-year scholarship of forty pounds a year.

At University College, Clarke studied with such prominent figures in Irish literary life as Douglas Hyde and Thomas MacDonagh, and he read Yeats, George Russell (Æ), George Moore, and other English and Anglo-Irish writers. Clarke began to immerse himself in Irish culture and the Celtic Twilight and to explore the literary movements of the time.

Clarke received his bachelor of arts degree with first class honors in English language and literature in 1916, the year of the Easter Rising, and the next year, his master of arts degree, again with first class honors in English. He was then appointed assistant lecturer in English at University College, to replace his teacher, MacDonagh, who had been executed by the British after the Easter Rising.

Clarke published his first significant poem, *The Vengeance of Fionn*, an epic in the Irish mythic tradition, in 1917. The poem was much praised and Clarke was hailed as a "new Yeats." For the next several years, Clarke devoted himself to the study of Gaelic prosody and Irish myth and folklore. In 1920, Clarke married for the first time, but the marriage was to last only ten days. He married again in 1930. In 1921, he was appointed assistant examiner in matriculation, National University of Ireland, a post he held until 1970.

By the mid-1920's, Clarke had shifted his attention away from early Irish themes and had turned instead to the Celtic-Romanesque medieval period as a source of poetic inspiration. The poems in Clarke's *Pilgrimage and Other Poems* (1929) deal with themes from this period and illustrate his commitment to Gaelic prosody.

In 1927, Clarke completed his first verse drama, *The Son of Learning*, and saw it produced at the Cambridge Festival Theatre in October of that year. Between 1922 and 1937, Clarke lived in England. During this period of "exile," he wrote several more verse plays. In 1932, Clarke's first novel, *The Bright Temptation*, was banned by the Irish Free State government; that same year, Clarke was made a member of the Irish Academy of Letters at the invitation of Yeats and George Bernard Shaw.

Between 1933 and 1937, Clarke served as a judge for the annual Oxford Festival of Spoken Poetry. In 1936, when he turned forty, his *The Collected Poems of Austin Clarke* was published with an introduction by Padraic Colum, and his second novel, *The Singing Men at Cashel*, was banned in Ireland.

In 1937, Clarke returned to take up permanent residence in Ireland and to become engaged in all aspects of Irish literary life. Clarke's next book of verse, *Night and Morning* (1938), marked another turn in his poetic career, from medieval Irish traditions to more complex themes dealing with the struggle between the individual conscience and constituted authority, between personal faith and belief and the Catholic Church in Ireland.

Though he would produce no more poetry for many years, Clarke engaged in a variety of literary activities during the time of his poetic silence. He began to offer literary broadcasts on Radio Éireann; he made regular contributions to newspapers and literary magazines; he set up his own private press, the Bridge Press; he held regular literary evenings at home on Sundays; he established the Dublin Verse-Speaking Society and the Lyric Theatre Company in cooperation with Robert Farren; and he worked with dramatic productions by these groups. During this period, Clarke also continued to write verse plays, and he completed his third novel, *The Sun Dances at Easter*, in 1952.

In 1955, Clarke published *Ancient Lights: Poems and Satires*, his first book of verse in nearly two decades. After a period of ill health, Clarke published his *Collected Later Poems* (1961), a volume that helped establish his reputation as a modern Irish poet. This was followed in 1963 by the publication of his *Collected Plays*, which contained all the plays he had written up to that time.

In 1964, for *Flight to Africa and Other Poems* (1963), Clarke won the Denis Devlin Memorial Award for Poetry from the Arts Council of Ireland. Like the best of his later poetry, the poems in *Flight to Africa and Other Poems* depart from the themes in his earlier works, dealing with issues of universal significance and exhibiting a more mature style.

The next year, Clarke was awarded a prize by the Arts Council of Britain. In 1966, an honorary degree was conferred on him by Trinity College. During the 1960's, Clarke published two memoirs, *Twice Round the Black Church* and *A Penny in the Clouds*.

In the closing years of his impressive career, Clarke was awarded the Irish Academy of Letters' highest award for literature, the Gregory Medal. He also received the American Irish Foundation's Literary Award. In 1972, Irish PEN nominated him for the Nobel Prize.

Clarke died in 1974, only a few months after the publication of his *Collected Poems*. Several of his plays were published posthumously, and a volume of his verse, *Selected Poems*, edited by Thomas Kinsella, appeared in 1976.

Analysis

Austin Clarke began his literary career as a poet. His first published works were several simple poems that appeared in 1916 and 1917 in a Dublin weekly, *New Ireland*. His first significant published poem was *The Vengeance of Fionn*. This epic poem and the other poems Clarke wrote early in his career drew heavily on Irish myth and the legends of pre-Christian Ireland. During the 1920's, Clarke turned from these themes to medieval Ireland and the monastic tradition as a source of poetic inspiration. In the 1930's, he abandoned these influences to write what could be called confessional poetry, particularly on subjects concerning the conflict between human intellect and the limits imposed by religious dogma. His own Catholic upbringing and subsequent difficulties with the Irish Catholic Church served as an important source of inspiration during this period.

After a self-imposed exile in England that began in 1922, Clarke returned to Ireland in 1937. Between 1937 and 1955, there was a long silence in Clarke's poetic output. Instead, he turned to the writing of verse drama and worked actively for the support of the production of his own verse plays and those of other Irish verse playwrights, including Yeats. Clarke's first two verse plays had been written in England: *The Son of Learning* and *The Flame*. All of his subsequent dramas were written in Ireland between 1939 and 1974. Two plays, *The Third Kiss* and *Liberty Lane*, were published posthumously.

None of the major writers of drama in post-Revival Ireland—Sean O'Casey, Lennox Robinson, George Shiels, Paul Vincent Carroll, the collaborators Frank O'Connor and Hugh Hunt—wrote verse plays. Clarke was essentially alone in his continued commitment to this dramatic form. At the Abbey Theatre, the only verse plays to have been presented in the first third of the twentieth century were those of Yeats.

Clarke's first play, *The Son of Learning*, was written in 1927 while he was in England. Although Yeats rejected it on behalf of the Abbey, it was performed at the Cambridge Festival Theatre in October, 1927. The performance was repeated by the Lyric Theater Company at the Abbey in 1945.

Clarke's poetic drama drew, like the poetry of his early and middle career, on Irish myth, the folklore and legends of pre-Christian Ireland,

and medieval Ireland and its monastic traditions. Although Clarke followed Yeats as a writer of verse drama, and although his own verse drama company performed Yeats's plays, the tenor of Clarke's own verse plays differs significantly from the austerity, formality, and symbolic structures Yeats favored. Like his own later poetry, Clarke's verse dramas focus on human conflicts and dilemmas, on the problems of individual freedom in the face of religious dogmatism. They blend, in an essentially satisfying way, comedy and tragedy. A comic view of life and a well-developed sense of the absurdity of the human condition motivate many of the major and minor characters in Clarke's dramas.

The plays in Clarke's dramatic canon are clearly uneven in quality. Although critics have varied in the rigor with which they have addressed and judged Clarke's drama, there is general agreement that a good part of the dramatic writing will today sustain the interest of only the most serious student of modern Irish literature.

Some of the less successful plays, such as *Black Fast*, *Sister Eucharia*, and *The Plot Is Ready*, are of interest mainly because of the intellectual questions and conflicts of conscience they present and the ambiguity in which the "resolution" in each play leaves the reader/viewer. *The Moment Next to Nothing* was simply an unsuccessful attempt to translate into dramatic form Clarke's last novel, *The Sun Dances at Easter*, which had been banned in Ireland.

Seven short, minor plays on various themes are of little dramatic consequence, except that they often display Clarke's fine sense of language and his ability to work within such earlier dramatic traditions as masque and farce. *The Kiss* and *The Second Kiss*, both written in couplets, are light, short pieces that deal amusingly with the amorous adventures of Pierrot and his love, Columbine. Two short plays drawn from Miguel de Cervantes, *The Student from Salamanca* and *The Silent Lover*, are bawdy little farces written in the form of the interlude, the brief diversions typically presented between medieval morality plays. Clarke's other minor plays are *The Impuritans*, *The Third Kiss*, and *Liberty Lane*. *The Visitation* appeared in a special issue of *Irish University Review* (1974) devoted to Clarke.

At least one critic has observed that several of the later minor plays, especially *The Impuritans* and the interludes from Cervantes, might most properly be considered along with the poems of Clarke's old age, which focus happily on erotic themes and celebrate human sexuality.

Clarke's remaining five plays, which will be considered briefly here, offer a sense of the kind of dramatic achievement in verse of which Clarke was clearly capable and also indicate the wide range of types and styles of verse drama he undertook.

The Son of Learning, as Clarke himself recalled, found its inspiration in a translation by Kuno Meyer of an Irish legend about King Cathal of Munster, who falls in love with Ligach, a noblewoman whose brother disapproves of the match. The brother causes Cathal to be cursed with a hunger demon. The unfortunate king is taken to the monastery in Cork to be rid of the demon. The play's central character, a wandering scholar, also arrives at the monastery, enrages the monks because of his audacious lack of piety, and is condemned to death. By virtue of his skill with words, however, it is the scholar, not the monks, who lures the demon out of Cathal and packs him off to Hell.

Within this simple framework, particularly in the conversations between the scholar and the monks, the scholar and the demon, Clarke explores the effects of religious dogmatism, the traditional discord between scholar and monk, intellect and faith. The overall tone is comic, based on exaggerated character, action, and speech.

In the end, which is characteristically ambiguous, the king is cured—but by what agency, exactly, Clarke is cunningly silent. Audience members are left to decide for themselves.

This first play shows how Clarke's verse dramas differ from the verse dramas of Yeats. They are less solemn, more comic; the speeches of the characters, while expressed in verse, are more human and idiomatic. In all, Clarke's plays are peopled not only by distant, legendary heroes but also by real people who have real foibles and who are faced with truly human dilemmas and choices.

Clarke's next play, *The Flame*, takes place in a convent and explores the conflict between the individual and the religious community. In *The Flame*, a young medieval nun secretly violates her order's rules by permitting her once luxuriant hair to grow again. Her preoccupation with herself causes her to neglect her duty—to tend the flame of Saint Brigid, which has burned at the convent for centuries. She is brought before the abbess for punishment. At the end of the play, the young nun is vindicated by an event one might call "miraculous." About its actual dimensions, the author is once again ambiguous.

As the Crow Flies is Clarke's most fully mature dramatic work in verse, written especially for presentation on radio. In it, he confronts all the challenges posed by an art form that must rely for effect almost entirely on voices, and he is particularly successful.

The play has a seemingly simple plot. Three monks, waiting out a terrible storm, take refuge in a cliffside cave that may have once been the dwelling of an ancient holy hermit. Over the din of the storm, they hear the voices of animals from Irish myth.

In an eagle's nest on the top of the cliff, the Crow of Achill, who has wrought evil for centuries, tells tales to the eaglet nestlings. When the eaglets wonder whether the storm that crashes about them is the worst storm there ever was, the Crow prompts the mother eagle to ask first the Stag of Leiterlone and then the Blackbird of Derrycairn. When they cannot answer her, the Crow urges the mother eagle to fly off to question Fintan, the Salmon of Assaroe, the wisest of all creatures. Fintan tells the eagle that he can recall the Deluge, surely the worst storm in history. He also tells her that through his endless existence, he has found no explanation for the violence, war, greed, and slaughter that seem to be the "unchanging misery of mankind." The eagle's joy in her newly found knowledge is dreadfully quenched: She returns to her nest to find that the evil Crow of Achill has devoured her babies.

All through the night, the three monks have listened to the conversations of the animals and, except for Aengus, seem to have comprehended their meaning only partially.

After the storm subsides, the monks, who have returned to their boat, watch the eagle hurl herself against the cliff where her babies perished. As he watches, Aengus shivers. He tells the others, "I know/ The ancient thought that men endure at night/ What wall or cave can hide us from that knowledge?"

As the Crow Flies is very probably Clarke's most fully realized verse drama. The dialogue is rich, vital, and evocative. The verse forms are intricate and challenging. The sound effects implied in the text suggest that a well-mounted production would be particularly haunting and memorable. Clarke effectively uses the voices of the blackbird and the other animals— creatures he has taken from Irish myth—to present and explore the theme of the duality of nature that is at the heart of this play. The responses of the three monks to the conversations they overhear convincingly represent three different ways of dealing with reality.

Overall, *As the Crow Flies* is a satisfying, if unsettling, presentation of Clarke's own inner conflicts, themes he had explored in earlier works and continued to probe until his death: the problems of good and evil in the world, of the clash between faith and reason, of the continuing tension between the rational and the irrational in human existence.

The Viscount of Blarney was written for performance on either stage or radio; it illustrates particularly well Clarke's depth and versatility in the creation of meaning-laden dialogue in verse. This play, the only one of Clarke's major works to be set more or less in the present, concerns the personal development of Cauth Morrissey, who has been reared in an orphanage and who is naïve in her interpretation of the world she encounters as a young adult. Some critics have suggested that the play is about the situation of youth in modern Ireland, caught between the oppressive teachings of the Catholic Church and their own natural desires, interests, and inclinations. Cauth is confronted by a variety of phantoms and demons, a pooka, and various primordial fears. She is finally rescued from her terrors and ignorance by a schoolmaster who coolly and methodically helps her get at the irrational roots of her fear.

Finally, there is *The Plot Succeeds*, not to be confused with the earlier, lesser work, *The Plot Is Ready*, mentioned above. The former is a poetic pantomime, a frankly easygoing work in which the comedic elements eclipse the weightier themes typical of most of Clarke's other verse plays. The play is a pleasant mélange of mistaken identities, magic spells, and clowning; the basic action turns on the attempt of the main character, Mongan, to "win back" his wife, Dulaca, whom he has lost in a card game. *The Plot Succeeds* demonstrates that Clarke had a genuine gift for comedy, had he chosen to develop it.

The best writing in Clarke's verse plays emphasizes his range and versatility as both poet and dramatist. Even in the least successful of his plays, Clarke's effects are neither entirely unsatisfactory nor entirely frivolous. Nearly every one of his plays is, at heart, a study of the conflict between the individual and the community—more specifically, between the Irish Church and Irish society, and the natural instincts of the common Irishman and Irishwoman. Clarke recast this basic conflict in settings as wide-ranging as those of his nondramatic poetry.

Other major works

NOVELS: *The Bright Temptation*, 1932, 1973; *The Singing Men at Cashel*, 1936; *The Sun Dances at Easter*, 1952.

POETRY: *The Vengeance of Fionn*, 1917 (based on the Irish Saga "Pursuit of Diarmid and Grainne"); *The Fires of Baal*, 1921; *The Sword of the West*, 1921; *The Cattledrive in Connaught and Other Poems*, 1925 (based on the prologue to *Tain bo Cuailnge*); *Pilgrimage and Other Poems*, 1929; *The Collected Poems of Austin Clarke*, 1936; *Night and Morning*, 1938; *Ancient Lights: Poems and Satires*, 1955; *Too Great a Vine: Poems and Satires*, 1957; *The Horse-Eaters: Poems and Satires*, 1960; *Collected Later Poems*, 1961; *Forget-Me-Not*, 1962; *Flight to Africa and Other Poems*, 1963; *Mnemosyne Lay in Dust*, 1966; *Old-Fashioned Pilgrimage and Other Poems*, 1967; *The Echo at Coole and Other Poems*, 1968; *Orphide and Other Poems*, 1970; *Tiresias: A Poem*, 1971; *The Wooing of Becfolay*, 1973; *Collected Poems*, 1974; *Selected Poems*, 1976.

NONFICTION: *First Visit to England and Other Memories*, 1945; *Poetry in Modern Ireland*, 1951; *Twice Round the Black Church: Early Memories of Ireland and England*, 1962; *A Penny in the Clouds: More Memories of Ireland and England*, 1968; *The Celtic Twilight and the Nineties*, 1969.

Bibliography

Farren, Robert. *The Course of Irish Verse in English.* New York: Sheed & Ward, 1947. This history of Anglo-Irish poetry since the eighteenth century provides important insights into the origins and development of Clarke's prosody. The insights are particularly valuable when used to connect Clarke's poetry with his verse plays. The author was closely associated with Clarke in the production of the latter's dramatic works.

Halpern, Susan. *Austin Clarke: His Life and Work.* Dublin: Dolmen Press, 1974. While this survey of Clarke's prolific output in prose and verse concentrates on the verse, Halpern does devote a chapter to Clarke's theory and practice of drama. She discusses all Clarke's plays and places them in the context of Clarke's work as a whole. Substantial bibliography.

Harmon, Maurice. *Austin Clarke: A Critical Introduction.* Dublin: Wolfhound Press, 1989. A comprehensive introduction to the life and work of Clarke. Drawing on a wide variety of sources, this study provides much background information and focuses on Clarke's verse. Devotes a substantial chapter to Clarke's drama. Exhaustive bibliography.

Irish University Review 4 (Spring, 1974). This special issue on Clarke contains a detailed account of his involvement with, and artistic contributions to, the Dublin Verse-Speaking Society and the Lyric Theatre Company, and it provides a complete list of the two organizations' productions. The issue also includes an overview that appraises the distinctive contribution made to the diversification and development of Irish theater by Clarke's dramatic works. The general conclusion is that Clarke's work for the theater is by no means a negligible part of his contribution to Irish literature.

Patricia A. Farrant
(Updated by *George O'Brien*)

MARTHA CLARKE

Born: Baltimore, Maryland; June 3, 1944

Principal drama

A Metamorphosis in Miniature, pr. 1982; *The Garden of Earthly Delights*, pr. 1984 (music by Richard Peaslee); *Vienna: Lusthaus*, pr. 1986 (text by Charles Mee, Jr., music by Peaslee); *The Hunger Artist*, pr. 1987 (text by Richard Greenberg, music by Peaslee, set by Robert Israel; adaptation of Franz Kafka's story and diaries); *Miracolo d'Amore*, pr. 1988; *Endangered Species*, pr. 1990.

Other literary forms

Martha Clarke is known for her extensive work as a choreographer and performer for the dance companies of Pilobolus and Crowsnest. Her dramatic works do not fall easily into any one genre: They incorporate elements of dance, music, and visual arts, as well as use of text, and involve collaborations with other artists.

Achievements

Clarke was already a highly acclaimed dramatic modern dancer performing in a world-renowned dance company, Pilobolus Dance Theater, when she crossed over into creating theatrical works. Her contributions as a choreographer include, with Pilobolus, *Ciona*, *Monkshood's Farewell*, and *Untitled*. These dances remain in the repertory of Pilobolus and are also presented by other major dance companies. Clarke has been compared to other experimental theater directors such as Robert Wilson, Ping Chong, and Meredith Monk for her ability to create multimedia theater pieces. Clarke's are noted for their visual beauty and a characteristic use of movement and timing. Clarke's innovative approach to her work encourages dancers, actors, designers, composers, and writers to work in a highly collaborative way toward a complex and richly textured performance-art object. Her first major theatrical production, *The Garden of Earthly Delights*, won a Village Voice Obie Award for Richard Peaslee's lush musical score. In 1988, she received a Guggenheim Fellowship intended for travel in Europe following the run of *Miracolo d'Amore*. Two years later, while rehearsing *Endangered Species*, Clarke was awarded a prestigious MacArthur Foundation Fellowship of $285,000 over the next five years. She is regarded as one of the most original directors in theater and one of the foremost innovators in American performance art.

Biography

Martha Clarke was born in Baltimore, Maryland, on June 3, 1944. As the second child and only daugnter in a financially secure and artistically inclined family, she was encouraged to pursue her creative interests at an early age. Her father was a lawyer who had been a jazz musician and songwriter. Her mother played the piano, and her mother's father, a businessman, presented string quartets at his home on Tuesday nights and collected antique musical instruments. Shirley Clarke, the avant-garde filmmaker, was Martha's aunt, on whose suggestion her niece was named after dancer/choreographer Martha Graham.

Clarke's childhood was spent in Pikesville, Maryland. She attended a small private school in Baltimore, at which her father was on the board of trustees. At age six, she began studying dance at the Peabody Conservatory of Music and taking drawing lessons on Tuesday afternoons at the Baltimore Museum. Horseback riding was another favorite activity and one she pursued in the summers at the Perry-Mansfield Camp in Colorado. There, in 1957, she met Helen Tamiris, who cast her, at age thirteen, as a child in *Ode to Walt Whitman*. Clarke says that she was hooked on dancing from the first time she worked with Tamiris.

When Clarke was fifteen, Tamiris and Daniel Nagrin asked her to attend their first summer workshop in Maine. Nagrin hoped to make Clarke an apprentice in the new company they were forming. Instead, Clarke chose to attend the American Dance Festival in Connecticut, where she first met Louis Horst, Merce Cunningham, Martha Graham, José Limón, Charles Weidman, and Alvin Ailey, and where she first saw the work of Anna Sokolow, whose dramatic dances greatly impressed her.

The next year, when she applied to the Juilliard School, Horst was on her jury, and he encouraged her to begin classes immediately and skip her senior year in high school. At Juilliard, she studied dance composition with Horst, who inspired and intimidated her. Horst's class in modern forms, in which dance studies are composed based on medieval and primitive art and Impressionist painting, was instrumental in developing her theatrical style.

Although Clarke was a Graham major and Horst was Graham's associate, it was the work of Sokolow and Anthony Tudor to which the young student was attracted. For two years, she studied with Tudor and as a sophomore danced a large part in a small ballet which he choreographed. She admired Tudor's work and its musicality. Also at Juilliard, she danced in the companies of Ethel Winter and Lucas Hoving, performing *Suite for a Summer Day* by the latter in 1962. She was in the first Dance Theater Workshop production with Jeff Duncan, after which she joined Sokolow's company. During her three years with the company she appeared in *Session for Six*, (at Juilliard), *Lyric Suite*, *Time + 7*, and *Dreams*. Clarke left the company because she found the work bleak and believed that she was becoming artistically limited.

Shortly after she was graduated from Juilliard, she married sculptor Philip

Grausman, a Prix de Rome winner. For the first five years of their fifteen-year marriage (they were divorced in 1980), Clarke stopped dancing. The couple lived in Italy for part of this time, immersing themselves in the art world. Shortly after their return to the United States, their son David was born. Grausman was named artist-in-residence at Dartmouth College, but Clarke saw herself as a twenty-seven-year-old mother and retired Anna Sokolow dancer. She and her husband moved into a large farmhouse, which resembled her childhood home, and built a dance studio for Clarke.

By this time, the four men who started Pilobolus were already touring. Clarke met Alison Chase, the Pilobolus men's dance teacher at Dartmouth, and the two became close friends. One of the members of Pilobolus, Robert Morgan Barnett, was an art major at Dartmouth and an assistant to Grausman. Barnett and Clarke began improvising dances in her studio after Barnett was forced to return early from a tour because of an injury. Clarke and Chase soon joined the previously all-male company. What drew her to Pilobolus was the company's irreverence and its rediscovery of the body. She believed that the inclusion of women in the company would allow the possibility of romance, gentleness, and delicacy to the male-oriented humor and gymnastics which were the company's trademarks. As a member of Pilobolus, she developed and performed *Ciona, Monkshood's Farewell*, and *Untitled*. In the seven years she was with Pilobolus, from 1972 through 1979, she created six solos, *Pagliaccio, Fallen Angel, Vagabond, Grey Room, Nachturn*, and *Wakefield*.

Her years with Pilobolus identified her as a clown and as a serious dramatic performer, but she wearied of the company's hectic touring schedule. Encouraged by Charles Reinhart, director of the American Dance Festival, and Lyn Austin, producer/director of the Music-Theater Group, Clarke left Pilobolus to start her own company, Crowsnest. Clarke joined with Felix Blaska, the French dancer and choreographer, whom she had met in Paris during her touring years with Pilobolus, and Pilobolus dancer Barnett. The trio worked collaboratively, and their work was described as a form of imagist movement-art when they first appeared at the American Dance Festival. Clarke and Blaska created *La Marquese de Solana*, and, with Barnett, *Haiku, The Garden of Villandry*, and *Fromage dangeureux*.

Clarke's first step into theater from dance was as choreographer for the Long Wharf Theater's production of Igor Stravinsky's *L'Histoire du soldat* in New Haven. For Lyn Austin, who first suggested that she direct, Martha Clarke and Linda Hunt created a two-woman dance-drama collage for the company's season in Stockbridge, Massachusetts. This work was followed by a production of *Elizabeth Dead*, a play by the humorist for *The New Yorker* George W. S. Trow. Clarke's debut as a New York theater director came with the production of *A Metamorphosis in Miniature*. The late David Rounds and Linda Hunt performed Clarke's dramatization of the Kafka story with a ten-page script and much physicalization.

In 1984, under the auspices of Music-Theater Group/Lenox Arts Center, Clark created *The Garden of Earthly Delights*. The hour-long work, based on the painting of Hieronymus Bosch, was a collaboration with Crowsnest and other dancers, with composer Richard Peaslee and musicians, and with lighting designer Paul Gallo. After a successful engagement at St. Clement's in New York, *The Garden of Earthly Delights* toured the United States and Europe.

By this time, Clarke was working on *Vienna: Lusthaus*. Like the Bosch piece, *Vienna: Lusthaus* began with visual images, initially inspired by an exhibition about *fin de siècle* Vienna which Clarke had seen in Venice. Once again, the project was a collaboration with dancers, musicians, composer Peaslee, set and costume designer Robert Israel, lighting designer Gallo, and with a text written by historian and playwright Charles Mee, Jr. Music-Theater Group/Lenox Arts Center again produced the work, which opened at St. Clement's for a two-week run before moving to The Public Theater on June 4, 1986.

Like the works before it, Clarke's next project was a collaborative creation. Clarke returned to the literary inspiration of Franz Kafka's writings to begin *The Hunger Artist*. This time, she used not only the story, "A Hunger Artist," but also the writer's own life in letters and diaries for inspiration. The company of dancers, actors, and musicians, along with Clarke, designer Israel, composer Peaslee, and playwright Richard Greenberg, focused on the themes of starvation and death, physical, emotional, and artistic. *The Hunger Artist* was also produced by the Music-Theater Group and opened at St. Clement's Theater on February 26, 1987.

The 1988 New York Shakespeare Festival in association with the Spoleto Festival produced Clarke's next work, *Miracolo d'Amore*. Clarke continued collaborating with the eminent team of Peaslee, Gallo, and Israel to produce a work closer to opera but with no plot and no actual text. *Miracolo d'Amore* opened at the Spoleto Festival in Charleston, South Carolina, amid an uproar over the nudity in the piece, though Clarke thought the real controversy was over the violence, especially toward women, depicted in this work. Nevertheless, when *Miracolo d'Amore* moved to New York, audiences and critics praised the visual beauty of the stage images, the evocative operatic score, and Clarke's idiosyncratic movement vocabulary used to expose the so-called miracle of love. Not all the criticism, however, was favorable. Some critics noted that though meticulously crafted and expertly produced, *Miracolo d'Amore* failed to provide any fresh perspectives on Clarke's favorite themes of men and women in love and conflict.

Clarke explained that the negative criticism of *Miracolo d'Amore* probably had something to do with her choice of subjects for her subsequent project, *Endangered Species*, produced in 1990 after nearly two years of preparation. The cast consisted of eleven actors and seven animals, among them an elephant from the Circus Flora who befriended Clarke when both were performing at the 1988 Spoleto Festival and whose trainer, one of the co-owners of the circus, talked at length with Clarke about the problems of animal poaching. Then, as Clarke describes it, ideas about animal rights, human slavery and racism, the American Civil War, and the Holocaust seemed to come together for her, with ideas for the text drawn from Walt Whitman's *Leaves of Grass* (1855). Clarke again gathered her collaborative team of stage designers (Gallo, Israel, and composer Peaslee) and brought in Robert Coe to adapt the text, but *Endangered Species* opened the Next Wave Festival at the Brooklyn Academy of Music to cool notices and closed after playing only fourteen of its scheduled thirty-five performances. Nevertheless, critics have not wavered in their belief that Clarke is an uncompromisingly precise theater director with a unique creative sensibility and artistic vision.

Analysis

Martha Clarke's works are in a performance genre which, as yet, has no name. It is a blending and fusion of dance, drama, music, gesture, light, scenic design, and text into performance pieces which mirror her unique artistic vision. Clarke is in a group of experimental performance artists as various as Robert Wilson, Ping Chong, Meredith Monk, and Peter Brook. Clarke's work as a conceptual director is distinguished from that of her peers by its painstaking use of movement and its density in a typically brief (usually one-hour) performance. Clarke achieves this synthesis of mediums by a collaborative, collagelike approach to composition.

Collaboration begins when rehearsals begin. Each performer, musician, composer, or designer is free to offer suggestions for the assemblage of fragments which will grow into a finished object of art. A long trial-and-error period ensues, during which the director develops movement phrases out of gestures and begins to keep a notebook of the ideas that work in rehearsal. She begins to distill the images and to dovetail the events while she looks for the contradictory images which will give the work texture and solidity. Clarke looks for a through-line that will unify her ideas, and she arranges and rearranges the scenes until they are compressed into their final form. She searches in works of art and writings for ideas that can be interpolated into the work. The final product is the result of the creativity of many people, but Clarke is responsible for the ultimate examination, selection, adaptation, and direction of all the elements.

Traces of Clarke's earlier work with Pilobolus Dance Theater can be seen in her theatrical direction and in her use of movement within the new works. In one of Pilobolus' best-known dances, *Monkshood's Farewell*, the members of the company, for the first time, began to organize the material with a dramatic logic instead of simply from an abstract point of view. The piece is reportedly based on the work of James Thurber, Hieronymus Bosch (for whose painting Clarke's work is named), Breughel the Elder, Geoffrey Chaucer's *The Canterbury Tales* (1387-1400), Sir Thomas Malory's *Le Morte d'Arthur* (1485), and a Craig Claiborne soup recipe, among other things. The four male members of the company joust, using the women as lancers, but later all six appear as the cretinous characters from the Bosch and Breughel paintings.

In *The Garden of Earthly Delights*, Clarke uses the Bosch painting as a point of departure for her own exploration and animation of the depicted world. She was attracted to the extremes of human emotion and behavior evident in the painting. The work is conceived as a left-to-right reading of the triptych, beginning in the Garden of Eden. The Garden of Earthly Delights and Hell are interrupted by an interpolation of the Seven Deadly Sins, the subject of another Bosch painting.

The director attempts to extract the qualities of the painting and condense its crowded, bustling panorama by giving Bosch's figures kinetic life. Though Clarke consulted science-fiction writer Peter Beagle, who wrote a book on the painting in 1982, for an interpretation of the qualities in the painting, her approach to the creation of *The Garden of Earthly Delights* is primarily choreographic. Each vignette in the work has some characteristic movement idea repeated rhythmically until it dissolves to make way for the next image.

In Clarke's hour-long enactment, seven dancers and three musicians are incorporated into a series of *tableaux vivants*. The vignettes include scenes of Eve wrapping her long hair around Adam, a serpent who produces the apple from between her thighs, performers who appear as musical instruments and trees, bawdy peasants, putti flying overhead, and angels falling through the heavens, transformed into demons, crashing in midair, and plummeting into Hell. Clarke summons the entire Bosch landscape, from the dreamlike Garden of Eden to medieval poverty to a nightmarish eternity.

The grotesque, acrobatic, and allegorical use of the human body always interested Clarke and the other members of Pilobolus. Clarke's exploration of metaphorical dance imagery developed differently, however, in the solo works she choreographed for Pilobolus and Crowsnest. Her work is characterized by its use of movement repetition, its languid, deliberate pacing, and the eroticism of the movement images. She believes that the slow pace allows the audience members time to respond to the complete scope of visual and textual associations with their own, more personal set of references.

The pleasure-garden idea returns in Clarke's *Vienna: Lusthaus*, but this time the director has chosen an entire city and culture, turn-of-the-century Vienna, as her point of departure. Clarke had worked at least twice before on a similar theme. One of the first dances by Alison Chase and Clarke, *Cameo*, was a study of the relationship between two Victorian women. In

Pilobolus' *Untitled*, two nine-foot women dance about the stage in flowing Victorian dresses until two nude men appear from beneath their skirts. *Vienna: Lusthaus* conjures an entire world, a dreamlike world of images that gradually shifts from a sensuous dream to an intensely disturbing nightmare, similar to the progression in *The Garden of Earthly Delights*.

Clarke's *Vienna: Lusthaus* was inspired by the art of the period, particularly that of Gustav Klimt and Egon Schiele, and by the political and social atmosphere at the traumatic beginning of the twentieth century in Vienna. The suicide of Prince Rudolf at Mayerling and the assassination of Archduke Ferdinand in 1914 provide the margins between which Clarke's surrealistic series of vignettes is set. Clarke was interested in a closer study of the veneer of graciousness, civility, and manners in Vienna that concealed the dark beginnings of twentieth century pyschosis and warfare.

On this work, Clarke enlisted a playwright, Charles Mee, Jr., to help develop a performance text. Mee used material from Sigmund Freud's *The Interpretation of Dreams* (1900), historical sources, and his own dreams to produce a text consisting of reminiscences spoken as monologue. These spoken memories, whose themes are primarily love and death, have an unashamed directness that makes them sound like dreams. Clarke and the performers worked to distill the text into vignettes, which are connected thematically rather than dramatically. Clarke thinks of this as an instinctual process rather than an intellectual one, and one that evokes the internal world of actors and audience.

The walls of the set are slanted, and a scrim is placed between the stage and the audience to distort the view. While some of the images are quite beautiful, others are ominous. A young couple caress and embrace each other on the floor in an erotic scene until the young woman is replaced by an old woman, whom the young man continues to kiss. Most of the men are dressed as soldiers, and the women are dressed in Victorian petticoats and long slips. Beautiful nudes pose as artists' models. Actors read fragments of Freud's letters. Skaters in plumed hats and waltzing soldiers and girls glide through the moonlight to fragments of the music of Richard Strauss. A booted man with a riding crop flicks it menacingly across a girl's face and then over her body.

A woman recalls her mother carrying an armful of flowers through the house on a summer day but then says that when her mother's mind began to wander, she walked through an open window and fell to her death. A half-dressed soldier appears with a girl in a petticoat, who sits in his lap and acts like a puppet. A clarinetist and accordion player begin tuneless renditions of carnival music. The waltzing young soldiers begin marching to a resounding martial drumbeat. At the end, snow begins to fall. A woman embraces the body of a dying soldier. She raises his dead body and bangs it against the floor. Eventually, she stops. The snow keeps falling as the dead man speaks.

He asks, "What colors does the body pass through in death?" Another man answers dispassionately, "First pink, then red, light blue, dark blue, and finally purple-red." Until this ending, these images are not presented linearly, but with amplifications, double meanings, contradictions, and a definite dramatic progression from the frivolous to the sinister.

Throughout, there is a sensuality and a surreal lack of logic. More than half the scenes are wordless but incorporate movements based on the same themes as those in the text. Clarke, once again, uses her characteristic technique of condensing, slowing down, and sharp-focusing the movement. Clarke finds that in working with actors and texts there is a natural sense of timing that corresponds to music. The speed and variation of certain phrases has a musical sense. She is interested in the slow development of a scene onstage which can mesmerize and stimulate the viewer's imagination. One of the actors turns into a horse, demonstrating the movements of the horse's arched legs and completing the transformation in one gesture. His foot becomes a hoof, and the man becomes an animal. Throughout *Vienna: Lusthaus*, the performers conjure scenes of the elegance and the decadence of this city of contradictions.

Following this work, Clarke began the process of researching, discussing, probing, and distilling new material once again. *The Hunger Artist* is not a revival of her earlier *A Metamorphosis in Miniature*, but a complete reworking of the Kafka material. Letters and diaries, as well as Kafka's body of fictional work, were consulted. Playwright Richard Greenberg worked with the actors to bring the letters to life. Scenic designer Robert Israel created a set which outlines a triangular house with striped walls, and placed a large box filled with earth onstage. Bentwood chairs are planted in the earth bed along with Dresden china and silverware, a nineteenth century rocking horse and cabbages. Peaslee's musical score contains phrases of Czech folk songs.

Clarke found a through-line in the theme of starvation and dying. In Kafka's famous story "A Hunger Artist," the main character earns his living by fasting and eventually starves himself to death. In Kafka's personal life, Clarke found evidence of emotional starvation in his relationships with his father and his fiancée Felice, and in his hunger for a normal life. One performer in *The Hunger Artist* resembles a Kafka insect when seen behind a World War II gas mask. Another performer poses in a small doorway, holding a hatchet, while one of the women performs a lyrical dance movement with a cabbage on her head.

Unlike her three previous theater works, Clarke's inspiration for *Miracolo d'Amore* was eclectic rather than drawn from one particular artistic, historical, or biographical source. Italo Calvino's *Fiabe italiane* (1956; *Italian Folktales*, 1975), Charles Darwin's *The Expression of the Emotions in Man and Animals* (1872), Giovanni Battista Tiepolo's paintings of *commedia dell'arte* characters (especially the Pulcinellas), French artist Grandville's nineteenth century illustrations of women as flowers from *The Court of Love*, as well as poetry by Dante and Petrarch, provided the wide range of sources from which Clarke began her process of sifting, extracting, and then creating the images that finally composed the fifty-five-minute piece with a cast of eight men and seven women.

In the opening moments of *Miracolo d'Amore*, an essentially indistinguishable hunched character, whose face and body are covered by ill-fitting sackcloth, slowly drags a stick across the stage. The set—composed of tilted walls, skewed doors, and angled windows and columns—is dimly lit but resembles a Venetian piazza in russet and ocher colors. Four nude women appear bathed in the golden light of a doorway, holding hands and tiptoeing into the first of several round dances with precise articulation but cool detachment. The group joins together, revolves in the space, then separates, and the figures dissolve one by one into the shadows of the set. The individual segments that compose *Miracolo d'Amore* are enacted between these slow and quiet round dances and seem to be complete and self-contained though they arrive at no particular narrative conclusion.

The vocal score for *Miracolo d'Amore* combines Peaslee's operatic songs of Italian love poetry sung by mostly soprano and countertenor voices with sounds of nature, the ocean and the wind, bird calls and cries, laughter and screams, and an inarticulate gibberish-Italian pseudolanguage that Clarke often uses in juxtaposition with an accompanying image of beauty or cruelty. The men, sometimes dressed as Pulcinellas, other times naked, masked, or otherwise disguised, approach the women with various intentions. At times they can be tender admirers, drawn to the beauty of the women dressed as flowers. Alternately, they portray predators whose fear or repulsion of the women turns to violence and commonly sends them back to the safety of the other men.

In one scene, a man slowly lifts a woman's skirt as she lies on the floor and puts his head between her legs; when his face reemerges, he lets out a great roar. Another man portrays a Christlike figure on a cross who is fed spaghetti from a bowl and who then transforms himself into an awkward bird looking for food and then a club-footed peasant limping offstage. A woman reaches between the legs of another woman and brings forth a seashell. A naked man, lying downstage, transforms himself into a fish. In the most climactic segment, if one could be described as such, the clownish men seem to woo the flowerlike women, engaging in tender caresses and embraces that gradually shift from lovemaking to gang rape and beating. The final moments of the piece set the gun-carrying men against one another in a shoot-out, yet the women reprise their silent, aloof hand-held dance off the stage.

Miracolo d'Amore may have been less successful than previous Clarke works in its attempt to illuminate the provocative subject of love, desire, and violence between women and men, but there seemed to be no question that Clarke succeeded once again in integrating theater, movement, art, and music with the haunting images of her imagination.

Clarke's next work, *Endangered Species* is, like *Miracolo d'Amore* and its predecessors, essentially a non-narrative series of vignettes for actors, singers, and dancers but with the addition of four horses, a monkey, a goat named Bert, and an elephant named Flora. Clarke described the roles of these animals as equal to those of the human company members in the creation and performance of this sixty-five-minute examination of animal and human oppression. The stage is covered with a plot of dirt and wood chips, an iron bed on the left, and a chair set in an otherwise empty space. Upstage, two oversized white doors are lit to reveal the shadows of the deftly moving actors or occasionally open for a glimpse of an elephant strolling back and forth. The score combines often loud recorded sound effects of bombings, a Nazi rally, and children screaming with a capella musical fragments, and the spoken snippets of Walt Whitman's *Leaves of Grass* text.

Endangered Species has a nightmarish quality in its scenes of violence and cruelty, yet the entire piece is, like Clarke's previous works, visually sensuous and deceptively beautiful. In one sequence, a woman writhes suggestively on the back of a horse that stands perfectly still. Sometimes the horses circle the stage, at times with riders standing on their backs. In one scene, a white woman sits in a black man's lap while he caresses her, yet another woman is sexually abused by one of the men. A white man beats one of the black men. A horse ambles through, then a naked man runs past and is shot. His limp body hangs overhead until the end of the piece, when the others are all shot to the sounds of a massacre and bombing. In the closing moments, a man walks through reciting Whitman's words "I think I could turn and live with animals."

Ultimately, criticism of *Endangered Species* centered on what Frank Rich of *The New York Times* considered Clarke's inability to contribute to the audiences' knowledge or sense of urgency about the horrors of violence and oppression. Clarke herself considered this a very personal and risky project in both her choice of material and her choice of casts, but *Endangered Species* may have proven to be too thematically varied for the kind of treatment Clarke envisioned.

Bibliography

Clarke, Martha. Interview by Arthur Bartow. In *The Director's Voice.* New York: Theatre Communications Group, 1988. An interview with Clarke made during the development of *Miracolo d'Amore.* Bartow says that audiences respond to Clarke's "images in the same manner as they are created—viscerally." The interview is concerned with the intricacies of

Clarke's creative process from the moment she conceives a work through its collaborative creation. Clarke discusses her transition to the theater from dance and each of the projects she has produced since beginning work with the Music-Theater Group.

Gussow, Mel. "Clarke Work." *The New York Times Magazine*, January 18, 1987, 30-34. Gussow provides extensive biographical information and discusses Clarke's major theatrical works, collaborations, and artistic vision. He says that "Clarke's work is distinctive in its passion, its use of movement, its brevity and its concern with art and culture." Includes quotations from an interview in which Clarke discusses her creative process while rehearsing *The Hunger Artist*. Also contains photographs from productions of *The Garden of Earthly Delights* and *Vienna: Lusthaus.*

Nadotti, Maria. "What Becomes of the Brokenhearted?" *Artforum* 27 (September, 1988): 117-121. A thorough critical analysis of *Miracolo d'Amore* that examines the various literary and artistic sources for the work and provides clear descriptions of the visual effects and stage designs. Nadotti also offers a brief overview of Clarke's previous theater projects in order to place this piece in context. Illustrated with photographs from the Public Theatre production of *Miracolo d'Amore* and reproductions of the Tiepolo paintings upon which the work is based.

Osterle, Hilary. "Alas, No Giraffe." *Dance Magazine* 64 (October, 1990): 46-49. Osterle provides background information on the creation of *Endangered Species*, speaks with Clarke and the performers about this unusual theatrical adventure, and discusses the various ideas and concerns that shaped this piece over its two-year formation. Color photographs of Clarke rehearsing the animals before moving the work to the Brooklyn Academy of Music.

Rothstein, Mervyn. "Martha Clarke's Thorny Garden." *The New York Times*, July 12, 1988, pp. 1, 26. A feature article on Clarke following the opening of *Miracolo d'Amore* at the Spoleto Festival. Rothstein provides insightful glimpses at this work in particular, as well as a substantial interview with Clarke. He describes *Miracolo d'Amore* as "quintessential Clarke as Charleston is quintessential South—a Clarke whose previous, intensely personal visions of Boschian brushwork, Freudian Vienna and Kafkaesque neurosis have made her a law unto herself in the world of performance art."

Diane Quinn

PADRAIC COLUM

Born: Longford, Ireland; December 8, 1881
Died: Enfield, Connecticut; January 11, 1972

Principal drama

The Children of Lir, pb. 1901 (one act); *Broken Soil*, pr. 1903; *The Land*, pr., pb. 1905; *The Fiddler's House*, pr., pb. 1907 (revision of *Broken Soil*); *The Miracle of the Corn*, pr. 1908; *The Destruction of the Hostel*, pr. 1910; *Thomas Muskerry*, pr., pb. 1910; *The Desert*, pb. 1912; *The Betrayal*, pr. 1914; *Three Plays*, pb. 1916, 1925 (revised), 1963 (revised; includes *The Land*, *The Fiddler's House*, *Thomas Muskerry*); *Mogu the Wanderer: Or, The Desert*, pb. 1917, pr. 1932 (revision of *The Desert*); *The Grasshopper*, pr. 1917 (adaptation of Eduard Keyserling's play *Ein Frühlingsofer*); *Balloon*, pb. 1929, pr. 1946; *Moytura: A Play for Dancers*, pr., pb. 1963; *The Challengers*, pr. 1966 (3 one acts; includes *Monasterboice*, *Glendalough*, *Cloughoughter*); *Carricknabauna*, pr. 1967 (also as *The Road Round Ireland*); *Selected Plays of Padraic Colum*, pb. 1986 (includes *The Land*, *The Betrayal*, *Glendalough*, *Monasterboice*; Sanford Sternlicht, editor).

Other literary forms

Padraic Colum's career as a writer spanned nearly three-quarters of a century. His first one-act play was published in 1901, and he continued to write poetry until his death in 1972. For most of his life, his living was made largely from his children's books, many of which have become classics. Like all truly good books of their kind, they are readable and engaging for adults as well as for children. Such works as *A Boy in Eirinn* (1913), *The King of Ireland's Son* (1916), *The Adventures of Odysseus* (1918), *The Children of Odin* (1920), *The Golden Fleece and the Heroes Who Lived Before Achilles* (1921), and *Legends of Hawaii* (1937) won for him respect both as a children's writer and as an expert on folklore and mythology. "The storyteller," he wrote, "must have respect for the child's mind and the child's conception of the world, knowing it for a complete mind and a complete conception. If a storyteller has that respect, he need not be childish in his language. . . . If children are to will out of the imagination and create out of the will, we must see to it that their imaginations are not clipped or made trivial."

Colum's literary output also included two novels, *Castle Conquer* (1923) and *The Flying Swans* (1957), several travel books, a literary recollection of James Joyce (written with Mary Colum), and a biography of Arthur Griffith, one of his earliest friends and the first president of the Irish Free State. A bibliography of Colum's separately published books would run to more than seventy titles. If miscellaneous works were added to this—books he edited, prefaces, introductions, and periodical publications of poems, stories, and essays—the number would be in the thousands.

In all Colum's prose works, his style is direct, lucid, and graceful, but his literary reputation rests most securely on his poetry, which has been widely anthologized and warmly praised by writers and critics since his poems first began to appear in the opening years of the twentieth century. The poet George Russell (Æ), one of Colum's earliest and most enthusiastic admirers, wrote in 1902 that he had "discovered a new Irish genius: . . . only just twenty, born an agricultural labourer's son, laboured himself, came to Dublin two years ago and educated himself, writes astonishingly well, poems and dramas with a real originality. . . . I prophesy about him." By 1904, Colum's poems had begun to appear in anthologies in Ireland and the United States, and since then every major collection of Irish poetry has included his work. Critics have consistently placed his name high on lists of the best Irish poets, but his poems have inspired few detailed scholarly studies. His poetry, in fact, resists such treatment: It is not easily identified with any particular school or movement, and it contains no esoteric philosophy to be glossed or obscure passages and patterns of symbolism to be unraveled. Indeed, its most distinguishing characteristics are simplicity and clarity. Often the poems are dramatic lyrics spoken by Irish peasants. Many are acutely accurate observations of commonplaces, as are those in his *Creatures* (1927) and *The Vegetable Kingdom* (1954).

Achievements

Although few scholars have written about Colum's poetry, scholars and poets have been generous in honoring him. He was elected president of the Poetry Society of America in 1938 and won its medal in 1940. He also received honorary doctorates from the University of Ireland and Columbia University and awards from the Academy of Irish Letters and the American Academy of Poets. Critic Edmund Wilson, after reading a collection of Colum's poems, wrote to him that "I wept while reading . . . some of them—not for sentiment, which doesn't often make me weep, but for the beauty of the lines. If everybody in Ireland hadn't been so overshadowed by Yeats, you would certainly have stood out as one of the best poets in English of your time."

Colum's reputation as a poet was well deserved, but it was one that did not altogether please him. He did not disown the title of poet, but he frequently objected to the exclusiveness of the label when it overshadowed his accomplishments in the theater. On one occasion, while discussing with a friend how future generations would remember him, he insisted that the popular notion that he was primarily a poet was a misconception. "I am primarily a man of the theatre," he argued, "and always have been." Colum repeated this judgment several times toward the end of his life. A few weeks before his death at the age of ninety, he told a reporter from *The*

New York Times that he was often prouder of his plays than of anything else he had written. Whenever he was in a position to influence the shaping of his public identity, he was careful to point out the close connection between his poetry and his plays. One such opportunity came when he was being interviewed by a writer who was preparing an introductory study of his works. "In the early part," Colum directed, "put my poems and plays together. The sort of plays I was writing for the theatre and the sort of poems I was writing are about the same sort of people and treat them in the same sort of way." Referring to such early poems as "The Plougher" and "An Old Woman of the Roads," he suggested that "you would put it best by saying that they were dramatizations. They're really characters in a play that hadn't been written." He was given another opportunity when Irish Radio invited him to sketch a prose portrait of himself. "Anything I have written, whether verse or narrative," he said during the broadcast, "goes back to my first literary discipline, the discipline of the theatre."

Biography

Padraic Colum wrote his first play when he was nineteen and his last when he was eighty-five. In all, he wrote about two dozen plays of varying lengths, many in several different versions. His plays have been produced at the Abbey and Gate theaters in Dublin, on Broadway by David Belasco and Iden Payne, Off-Broadway, at the Dublin Theatre Festival, on Irish television, in the little theaters that flourished in Dublin in the 1960's, and by amateur groups in Ireland, England, the United States, the Middle East, and Australia.

There was little in Colum's family background to suggest a career as a playwright. Unlike William Butler Yeats, John Millington Synge, Lady Augusta Gregory, and most of the other playwrights of the Irish Literary Renaissance with whom he became associated, his background was rural, Catholic, and working-class. His mother was the daughter of a gardener, and his father the son of a tenant farmer. Colum's father seems to have been temperamentally unsuited to handle the responsibilities of a growing family and, according to Colum, "was always unlucky looking for jobs." He worked first as a teacher in a national school and later taught the children of paupers at Longford Workhouse in the Irish midlands; he eventually became master of the workhouse but had to resign the position because of his drinking and mishandling of funds. He left Ireland for a few years to work at various jobs in the United States but returned when Colum was nine and moved the family to Sandycove outside Dublin, where he had found a job as a clerk in the railway station. Padraic entered the local national school, though his attendance became irregular when he was old enough to take a part-time job. He and his brother Fred worked as delivery boys for the railroad and took turns attending school, one going one day, the other the next. When he was seventeen, Colum left school after passing his examinations and began work as a clerk at the Railway Clearing House on Kildare Street in Dublin.

Colum soon became interested in drama, though all he knew about plays and playwriting was what he had learned from the national school curriculum, from books he found in the local library, and from rare visits to the theater in Dublin, where the fare tended to be a mixture of music-hall variety shows and popular English comedies. He recalled later that when he began writing his first play, he "knew nothing whatever about the theatre. I had seen [Dion Boucicault's] *The Colleen Bawn*, *The Shaughraun*, and some shows put on by amateurs, and I had gone to the Gaiety Theatre, and spent a whole shilling for a seat in the pit... to see Mr. and Mrs. Kendall in a play called *The Elder Miss Blossom*." This was in 1899, and there was as yet no such thing as a native Irish drama, apart from the melodramas of Boucicault. The Abbey Theatre, which would provide models for the next generation of playwrights, was still six years from being founded, and the Irish Literary Theatre, which Yeats, Lady Gregory, and Edward Martyn had established with the aim of creating a native drama, was only in its first year of production. Colum saw none of the Irish Literary Theatre's plays that year and, in fact, saw none of its subsequent productions except the final one on October 21, 1901. This was a double bill featuring *Diarmuid and Grania* by Yeats and George Moore and *Casad-an-Sugan (The Twisting of the Rope)*, Douglas Hyde's play in Irish.

Colum's first effort at playwriting was, instead, a result of his attendance at the *tableaux vivants* that the patriotic Daughters of Ireland were staging to promote nationalistic sentiment. "They were statuesque groups introduced by some familiar piece of music, and holding their pose for some minutes—an elementary show in which costume, music and striking appearance were ingredients," Colum later wrote. "I was in an audience that witnessed 'Silent, O Moyle, Be the Roar of Thy Waters.' I felt there should be words to give life to the pathos of children transformed by an enchantress stepmother; my mind was already on plays. I began a one act play in verse, *The Children of Lir*, and sent it to [the Daughters of Ireland]." Although they did not produce the play, Colum succeeded in getting it published in *The Irish Independent* on September 14, 1901. It was his first published work. During the next three years—what Colum called his apprentice period—he published several more one-act plays, including plays based on Irish history and mythology, Ibsen-like problem plays, a dramatic monologue, and a melodramatic propaganda play, written to discourage enlistments in the British Army. As might be expected, these early plays are, for the most part, awkward and immature, and Colum made no later effort to revise or republish them. They do, however, show a precocious grasp of dramatic techniques and a rapidly developing skill.

Colum's full-length play *Broken Soil* was produced by the Irish National Theatre Society in 1903, the same year it produced the first plays of Synge and Lady Gregory. Almost immediately he was recognized as a playwright of great promise and sound dramatic judgment. When he was only twenty-three, he was selected by the National Theatre Society to be a member of its first reading committee, a role he shared with Yeats and Æ. Yeats was particularly impressed by Colum's work, describing him in 1904 as "a man of genius in the first dark gropings of his thought" and noting that "some here think he will become our strongest dramatic talent." Colum's plays and poems also won for him the patronage of Thomas Hughes Kelly, an American millionaire living near Dublin, who awarded him a five-year grant—beginning at seventy pounds and increasing by ten pounds per year—to support his literary work. With this subsidy, Colum was able to quit his job as a railway clerk in 1904 and devote his full time to writing. He quickly developed into an accomplished playwright, and the popularity of his next play, *The Land*, helped to confirm Yeats's prediction. Produced in 1905 after the Irish National Theatre Society was reorganized as the Abbey Theatre, it gave the Abbey what it much needed when many were criticizing it for being something less than the national theater it purported to be—a play that was both a critical and a popular success. Irish and English critics hailed it as "the best play yet given us by the dramatic movement" and "one of the most important plays which have appeared in English for a long time." Although this praise was perhaps extravagant, the play did add a new dimension to the dramatic movement. As one reviewer explained: "What we have been waiting for is a play that should be at once good and popular. Mr. Yeats has proved a little too abstruse, and Mr. Synge a little too bizarre to get fully down to the hearts of the people."

The Land was the first of a series of three plays dealing with life in the Irish midlands that firmly established Colum's reputation as a major playwright and a pioneering figure in the realistic movement. The second in the series was a thorough reworking of *Broken Soil*, which he retitled *The Fiddler's House*. It was performed in 1907 by the Theatre of Ireland, a splinter group formed after Colum and others had left the Abbey in a dispute over theater policy a year earlier. By all accounts, the Theatre of Ireland production was inept. As a result, the play did not receive the public exposure it deserved, even though most critics thought it a much better play than *The Land*. Andrew E. Malone, for example, described it as "in every respect Colum's best play" and considered it "equal to the greatest in the Irish theatre." After Colum left the Abbey Theatre, he never fully reestablished his association with it. He did, however, give it *Thomas Muskerry*, the third of his realistic Irish plays, for production in 1910. The public reception of this play was mixed, with opinions turning on the harshness of its characterization of small-town merchants: While some reviewers found the play brilliant, others damned it as libeling the Irish national character. The issues raised by *Thomas Muskerry* were debated for several weeks in the columns of Dublin's newspapers. Like Synge's *The Playboy of the Western World* (pr. 1907) and Sean O'Casey's *The Plough and the Stars* (pr. 1926), however, the play survived the controversy it aroused and is now generally considered to be Colum's masterpiece.

In 1912, Colum married Mary Catherine Gunning Maguire, whom he had met while she was a student at University College, Dublin. By then, his five-year grant had expired, and his income was now dependent on his free-lance writing. He and Mary supplemented this by teaching in a private school but soon decided that if Colum was to earn a living as a writer, he would have to find a wider market than Dublin offered. When his aunt in Pittsburgh offered to pay their fare to the United States, they accepted, hoping to make careers for themselves there as writers. They left for the United States in 1914, and both subsequently succeeded in their goals, Colum by his voluminous output of books, essays, and literary journalism, and Mary by becoming a highly respected literary critic, writing reviews for *The New York Times* and several other major newspapers and literary journals and serving as literary editor of *Forum*.

In the ten years between the end of his apprenticeship in 1904 and his emigration to the United States, Colum wrote a number of other plays. None was in the manner of his three major realistic plays, and none was given a successful production until several years after he left Ireland. *The Miracle of the Corn*, written for the Irish National Theatre Society, was accepted and put into rehearsal in 1904 but for some reason was not performed. The Theatre of Ireland staged it in 1908 in a production that seems to have been less competent than that of *The Fiddler's House*. One critic in the opening-night audience commented that the actors spoke their lines so softly that they could not be heard in the first row. Colum wrote an adaptation of the medieval miracle play *The Second Shepherds' Play* at Yeats's suggestion in 1911, but the Abbey did not produce it. Of the other plays, only *The Destruction of the Hostel* was staged while Colum still lived in Ireland, and this was in an amateur production by the boys' acting class of St. Enda's School. After leaving the Abbey, Colum hoped to make a name for himself in the London theater and wrote three plays for production there. He was unable, however, to find a producer for *The Desert* or "Theodora of Byzantium," and a London production of *The Betrayal* was canceled after Lady Gregory refused to grant permission for a group of actors under contract with the Abbey to act in it.

Colum's interest in the theater continued after his arrival in the United States. His first job there was at the Carnegie Institute in Pittsburgh, where he was hired to assist in the production of a series of Irish plays. His *The Betrayal* was given its first production as part of the series. In 1915,

Colum moved to New York, where he lectured on Irish drama and announced his intention of joining John P. Campbell, a former artistic director of the Ulster Literary Theatre, in establishing the Irish Theatre of America, to be modeled after the Abbey Theatre. Colum and Campbell held an organizational meeting, issued a statement of plans to the press, and produced their first play in February, 1915, but the group failed to gather momentum and disbanded soon afterward. Over the next forty-five years, Colum's contacts with the theater became less frequent. *The Grasshopper*, his adaptation of Eduard Keyserling's *Ein Frühlingsofer*, was produced on Broadway in 1917 and at the Abbey in 1922. *The Fiddler's House* received its first Abbey Theatre production in 1919 and was revived in New York in 1941. *Mogu the Wanderer*, a revised version of *The Desert*, was produced at Dublin's Gate Theatre in 1932 with a young Orson Welles in a leading role. Michael Myerberg, who had successfully produced Thornton Wilder's *The Skin of Our Teeth* (pr. 1942), bought the option on *Balloon*, an experimental play modeled partly on the Italian *commedia dell'arte* and partly on American comic strips, published by Colum in 1929, and tried it out for two weeks in 1946 in Ogunquit, Maine, but did not take it into New York. Myerberg also commissioned Colum to write the screenplay for a 1954 adaptation of Engelbert Humperdinck's opera *Hansel and Gretel* (pr. 1893), in which the actors were animated dolls. Also in 1954, Colum assisted Marjorie Borkenstein in adapting James Joyce to the stage in *Ulysses in Nighttown*.

Such activities kept Colum sporadically in touch with the theater but were not enough to keep alive the reputation as a playwright he had established decades earlier in Dublin. Although his notebooks for these years show that the theater was rarely far from his mind, most of his writing efforts for the stage went into adaptations of other people's work and seemingly endless revisions of plays he had written years before. He produced only one wholly new play between 1912 and 1961. This was *Balloon*, and an anecdote about it reveals how difficult it was for Colum to keep alive his reputation as a man of the theater. His friend Charles Burgess tells of an encounter with him in New York during the 1950's. "You are talking to a dead man," Colum said, and Burgess recalls:

> That afternoon he had called on a producer to whom he had recently sent a play. . . . As they had discussed the possibility of a production, the producer had said to him, off-handedly, that of course they'd have to use a different name.
>
> Colum, rising to his work's defense, had replied, "Well, I don't know. . . . Most of the people who know the play tell me that *Balloon* is a very good name for it."
>
> "Oh, I don't mean the title of the play," the producer had countered, "it's the name Padraic Colum I'm referring to. There was another playwright by that name at the turn of the century and I think we'd be criticized if we used his name."

In the last ten years of his life, Colum stepped up his efforts in the drama and succeeded to some degree in bringing his name again before the playgoing public. In 1960, he began work on a cycle of Yeatsian Nō plays, the first of which, *Moytura*, was published in 1963. Also in 1963, he published a significantly revised edition of his realistic *Three Plays*. The revisions demonstrated a good sense of dramatic structure and revealed that Colum's mastery of dialogue was better than it had ever been. *Moytura* was performed at the Pike Theatre in Dublin in 1963, and productions of it and of other Nō plays followed on Irish radio and television. Three of the plays, *Monasterboice*, *Glendalough*, and *Cloughoughter*, were gathered together under the title *The Challengers* and staged in 1966 at Dublin's Lantern Theatre. The following year, *Carricknabauna*, a dramatic adaptation of some of Colum's poems, was performed Off-Broadway and, as *The Road Round Ireland*, at the Lantern.

Despite Colum's final flurry of activity, his dramatic efforts, spaced over a period of more than sixty years, do not add up to a distinguished career in the theater and hardly seem to justify his insistence that "if I am not a playwright, I am nothing." There is clearly an element of exaggeration in such a statement, but if there is, Colum's need to exaggerate is at least partially understandable as a protest against premature burial by literary historians who persisted in reporting that he had abandoned the stage for good in 1910 and Broadway producers who thought him long dead. There is also a temptation to dismiss Colum's repeated assertions that he was primarily a playwright as the wishful thinking of an old man who had never quite got over his first flush of success on the stage. Such an attitude does not do Colum justice, for his plays have never been fully evaluated, and the importance of their position in his identity as an artist has never been acknowledged.

Analysis

Padraic Colum was a major figure in Ireland's Literary Renaissance both because he was the first to deal realistically with the Irish peasant farmer and because of the influence his plays had on the playwrights who followed him. Something of the pervasiveness and power of his influence comes through in the open letter that Yeats wrote to Lady Gregory in 1919, in which he announced that he was giving up public theater for a more private theater of the drawing room. Yeats wrote that while he had sought to create a poetic drama, the Abbey playwrights, following Colum's lead, had instead succeeded in "the making articulate of all the dumb classes each with its own knowledge of the world, its own dignity, but all objective with the objectivity of the office and the workshop, of the newspaper and the street, of mechanism and of politics." It was, nevertheless, the realistic drama of peasant life that won for the Abbey Theatre its international recognition.

Colum himself did not claim to have been the inventor of the peasant play; he said that he shared the distinction with Synge. "My *Broken Soil* and Synge's *In the Shadow of the Glen* were produced within a month of each other," he wrote. "These two plays inaugurated the drama of peasant life. W. B. Yeats' *Cathleen ni Houlihan*, in which the characters are peasants, was produced first, but *Cathleen ni Houlihan* is symbolic and not a play of actual peasant life." "A play of actual peasant life" aptly describes what Colum sought to write, and it was with this type of play, in his view, that Ireland began to have a truly native drama—plays he described as being "authentic in idiom and character" and expressing "the sum of instincts, traditions, sympathies that made the Irish mind distinctive." Probably the most important concept in Colum's view of drama was that plays should *express* Irish life. Synge and others poeticized the life of the peasant; Colum saw a poetry within that life and expressed it realistically. In doing so, he saw his work as being distinctly "democratic, not only because it deals with the folk of the country and the town, but because it is written out of recognition of the fact that in every life there are moments of intensity and beauty." Other Irish playwrights wrote about peasants, but none accepted them on their own terms. They saw them as outsiders would see them: Yeats's peasants are romantic idealizations, Lady Gregory's are caricatures—only slightly less broad than the nineteenth century "stage Irishmen"—and Synge's, for all the richness and beauty of their language, are exaggerations of the Irish peasant. Of all the early Abbey Theatre playwrights, only Colum, who grew up among peasant farmers and small-town merchants, accurately reflected their character, their language, and their concerns.

Because of their realistic portrayal of Irish life, Colum considered *The Land*, *The Fiddler's House*, and *Thomas Muskerry* to be his most important and most influential plays. Most literary historians agree with this judgment. What gives each of the plays its dramatic vigor and depth of characterization is the tension inherent in Colum's view of Ireland. Each presents a pair of characters whose energy or imagination is too strong to be held back by the dreary inertia of Irish country life. Matt Cosgar and Ellen Douras in *The Land*, Maire Hourican and her father, Conn, in *The Fiddler's House*, and Muskerry and Myles Gorman in *Thomas Muskerry* all experience a conflict between their feelings of responsibility to something in this spiritually cramped existence and a deeper need to rise above it. The attention which Colum gives to realistic detail in the plays is a means of emphasizing the part in the conflict played by everyday life in Ireland. Permeating the three plays as a motivating force and linking them thematically is the struggle for freedom that is resolved in *Thomas Muskerry*'s final triumphant symbol, Myles Gorman, whom Colum described as "a man of energy set free on the roads."

Because he considered these plays so central to his reputation as a playwright, Colum revised them frequently throughout his life. He first gathered them together as *Three Plays* in 1916 and later published revised editions of the collection in 1925 and 1963. With the exception of *The Land*, which received only light revision, the plays in the 1963 edition differ significantly from the versions that were staged nearly a half a century earlier. *The Land* was inspired, Colum said, by the Land Act of 1903, which enabled Irish tenant farmers to purchase their land. The play's central conflict is between two generations: the farmers, who have fought to win their land, and their children, who are tempted by the call of the larger world outside. The younger generation prevails in the end, with Matt Cosgar and Ellen Douras departing for the United States and leaving their claims to their fathers' farms to Ellen's less imaginative brother Cornelius and Matt's slow-witted sister Sally.

Although Colum referred to it in 1910 as only "a sketch for a play" and wrote in 1963 that "if staged these days *The Land* would have to be played as an historical piece and for character parts," the play is notable for its strong characterization of Sally and the two fathers, Murtagh Cosgar and Martin Douras. It also has a strongly unified plot and a clean story line. By unfolding his plot against the larger historical backdrop of the farmers' progress from tenants to landowners, Colum managed to reinforce the irony of the exodus of Ireland's most gifted young people at the very time when the country had something to offer them.

The Land plays well on the stage—when the Dublin International Theatre Festival was inaugurated in 1957, it was the only early full-length Abbey Theatre play selected—but it is inferior to Colum's other two realistic dramas. The plot is perhaps too neatly constructed and the characters too conveniently paired off; the son and daughter of Murtagh Cosgar wed the son and daughter of Martin Douras, and six young emigrants to America in act 2 are balanced against six farmers who commit themselves to the land in act 1. Matt and Ellen, moreover, are too thinly characterized for the parts they play, and Cornelius' curtain speech is too obviously propagandistic. Nevertheless, because of both the popular support it won for the Abbey and its value as a commentary on social and political changes, the play has undeniable historical importance. *The Land*, in fact, is the only one of the three plays about which it can be said with any justice that historical value outweighs literary worth.

The Fiddler's House is similar to *The Land* in both theme and plot: An aging fiddler, Conn Hourican, leaves the farm that his daughter Maire has inherited to follow the roads, playing at festivals and in public houses. Maire, whose increasing sense of affinity with her father is matched by a growing aversion to Brian McConnell, the man whom she had intended to marry, decides to follow her father on the roads and deeds the farm to her younger sister, Anne. *The Fiddler's House* was probably Colum's most frequently revised play, and through several revisions the focus switched back and forth between the two main characters. In a letter to his patron, Kelly, in 1910, Colum revealed his fascination with the characters of Conn and Maire and suggested that Maire dominated the unpublished *Broken Soil.* "Now that I read the plays," he wrote, "Conn Hourican and [Maire] Hourican in *The Fiddler's House* are more vivid to me than any of the people in *The Land.* I know that you prefer *Broken Soil* to *The Fiddler's House*, the play that has taken its place. . . . But I thought Conn Hourican worth a play, and I tried to make a new one for him." Conn dominated both the 1907 and 1925 versions of the play. Later, however, Maire began to grow in Colum's imagination. In the preface of the 1963 edition of *Three Plays*, he says:

> The motive in its early version was simply "the call of the road." It became *The Fiddler's House* when a real conflict was seen as developing in it, the conflict between father and daughter in which reconciliation came when Maire Hourican becomes aware that she, too, has the vagrant in her. Later, when produced in New York by Augustin Duncan, something else in her character was made explicit. Her recoil from her lover is due to her fear of masculine possessiveness—a recoil not extraordinary in a girl brought up in the Irish countryside.

In the 1963 revision of the play, Maire regained the ground that she had lost in the versions of 1907 and 1925, and the characters settled into a state of equilibrium, each interesting for different reasons. While the divided focus of the play kept it from greatness, it also gave the Irish stage two memorable characters. The complexly motivated Maire is particularly well drawn. When Brian tries to dominate her and threatens to carry her off by force to marry him, she begins to realize that, more than marriage, she wants freedom. When she leaves to follow her father at the play's close, the possibility of reconciliation with Brian is more remote than it had been in the earlier plays. Through the various revisions, Colum gradually transformed her from a girl who wants only a home and a husband to a woman who wants to shape her own life.

Thomas Muskerry went through a similar evolutionary process of revision, and by the time he completed the process, Colum had transformed his weakest play into his strongest. Andrew E. Malone, writing about the early Abbey Theatre version of the play, termed it "in every respect inferior to *The Land* and *The Fiddler's House*; Robert Hogan, writing in 1967 about the final revision, called it Colum's "masterpiece." Most critics concur with Hogan's judgment. In writing the play, Colum drew on his earliest childhood experiences at the Longford Workhouse. As the play begins, Muskerry, master of a workhouse in the Irish midlands, is at the end of a successful career and looking forward to a pleasant retirement in the cottage he plans to buy with his life savings. By the play's end, he lies dead in a pauper's bed at the workhouse. In the intervening scenes, it is discovered that he had accidentally mismanaged the workhouse's funds, and the Crilly family, into which his daughter had married, persuades him to resign as master to save the family's reputation in the village. They also persuade him to give up his plan of buying a cottage and to live with them behind their shop. Once he abdicates his power to the Crillys, however, they become increasingly neglectiul of him, even as he uses his savings to keep their shop from foundering. At the end of the play, he is penniless and spiritually broken by the ingratitude of his daughter and her in-laws and by the humiliating taunts of Felix Tournour, the workhouse porter. The only person who shows him any sympathy is Christy Clarke, an orphan whom he had befriended.

The 1910 version of *Thomas Muskerry* was little more than the bare bones of a play and had succeeded only on the merits of an unusually moving final act; it had little else to recommend it. The first act did scarcely more than lay an Ibsen-like foundation of complex exposition and introduce a large cast of sparsely drawn characters—each arriving and departing at too obviously opportune moments. The succession of events necessary for the play's later developments was more mechanical than dramatic and too rapid to be credible. The second act moved along at the same quick pace, carrying Muskerry mechanically through the events that led finally to his death. Muskerry in the closing scenes achieved—in his mixture of pathos and tragedy, failure and triumph—a grandeur reminiscent of Lear. The play, in fact, resembled William Shakespeare's tragedy in many ways and gained strength from the underlying but unspoken allusion to *King Lear* that reverberated through the unfolding pattern of filial ingratitude.

The later version of *Thomas Muskerry* more than compensates for the artistic deficiencies of the early version. Structurally, Colum's innovations slow the pace and allow the play to build more powerfully to its climax. What was merely a mechanical succession of events in the first version takes on an aura of inevitability in the revision. In rewriting the play, Colum divided the first act into two scenes by reshuffling the exposition and spreading the action over two evenings instead of one. He also suggests early in the first scene that Felix Tournour has information that may later damage Muskerry's reputation and jeopardize his pension. In the earlier version, Tournour's knowledge had come as a surprise late in the play and had no real effect on the action. With this small change, Colum was able to foreshadow the most important turning point in Muskerry's fortunes and to orchestrate Tournour into a nemesis who lurks through four acts before he finally strikes.

Between the original first and second acts, Colum inserted a new act that accomplishes several things. It begins with the senile bantering of two elderly inmates who reflect on the change in masters and, in the process, reveal to the audience the old master's record of humane kindliness. Their reverential comments continue in choric counterpoint behind the main action, in which Muskerry is quietly shunted aside to make room for his successor. Like the early slights of Goneril and Regan in *King Lear*, the early shifts in the way his daughter and her in-laws treat the retired Muskerry provide the first glancing blows at his dignity and prefigure the larger insults that follow. Into the new second act Colum also introduced a traveling photographer whose uncertainty about whether Muskerry is still master of the workhouse helps to bring into focus the other characters' attitudes toward the protagonist.

The third act of the 1963 play is the original second act; in the revision, Colum polished and augmented the dialogue to improve characterization and made the act a third again as long by the introduction of another character, Peter Macnabo, who, like Muskerry, is a former workhouse master fallen into disgrace. The addition of Macnabo alone would have been enough to improve the overall quality of the play. His indomitability, industrious self-sufficiency, and rising fortunes as he begins a new life for himself provide a strong contrast to Muskerry's decline. The positioning of his visit between the petty quarrels of the Crilly family and examples of Tournour's growing arrogance gives the new version's third act a dramatic intensity almost equal to that of act 4, and the combination of naïveté and shrewdness that prompts Macnabo at the age of sixty to attempt a new career manufacturing traditional Irish clay pipes makes him one of the play's most finely drawn characters.

The fourth act differs little from the strong concluding act of the original. Colum's major change was to expand the part of Muskerry's young ward, Christy Clarke, so that in the closing scenes he functions as something of an adopted Cordelia in ironic contrast to the Goneril and Regan of Muskerry's daughter and the Crilly family. Colum's changes in the play involved more than simply improving its structure and adding new characterization and dialogue. While the 1910 version presented an array of broadly sketched characters, the revision contains a gallery of fully delineated personalities. Muskerry, already a powerfully conceived protagonist in the original, is a truly memorable one in the final version. The revised play also features three unusually strong supporting characters in Christy Clarke, Peter Macnabo, and Felix Tournour. The remaining characters in the revised version all have the fullness and clearly defined identities that they lacked in the original. The dialogue, moreover, shows the sure hand of an artist with more than fifty years of experience as both a poet and a playwright.

Despite the high quality of his art and the glowing predictions of fellow writers such as Yeats and Æ, Colum never became truly famous. His emigration to the United States probably had much to do with this. His best plays were the early Abbey Theatre works about rural Irish life; when he left Ireland, he lost the stimulus of a convenient stage and an appreciative audience. Though he had been famous as a poet and playwright in Dublin, he was virtually unknown in New York and had to begin again to make a name for himself while expending much of his creative energy on the children's books and literary journalism that provided his income. Perhaps he was partially a victim of his own personality and of his ability to do many things well. If he had been flamboyant, irascible, or conspicuously tormented, he might have become a literary personality, as have many writers of less talent. Instead, he was a quiet, good-natured, and apparently happy man. If anything, he was conspicuously unflappable. "Every serious Irish writer has a pain in his belly," Æ once chided Frank O'Connor, who was complaining of indigestion. "Yeats has a pain in his belly; Joyce has a terrible pain in his belly; now you have a pain in your belly. Padraic Colum is the only Irish writer who never had a pain at all."

Other major works

NOVELS: *Castle Conquer*, 1923; *The Flying Swans*, 1957.

SHORT FICTION: *Selected Short Stories of Padraic Colum*, 1985 (Sanford Sternlicht, editor).

POETRY: *Wild Earth and Other Poems*, 1907; *Dramatic Legends, and Other Poems*, 1922; *Creatures*, 1927; *Way of the Cross*, 1927; *Old Pastures*, 1930; *Poems*, 1932; *Flower Pieces: New Poems*, 1938; *The Collected Poems of Padraic Colum*, 1953; *The Vegetable Kingdom*, 1954; *Ten Poems*, 1957; *The Poet's Circuits: Collected Poems of Ireland*, 1960; *Images of Departure*, 1969; *Irish Elegies*, 1976; *Selected Poems of Padraic Colum*, 1989 (Sanford Sternlicht, editor).

NONFICTION: *My Irish Year*, 1912; *The Road Round Ireland*, 1926; *Cross Roads in Ireland*, 1930; *A Half-Day's Ride: Or, Estates in Corsica*, 1932; *Our Friend James Joyce*, 1958 (with Mary Colum); *Ourselves Alone: The Story of Arthur Griffith and the Origin of the Irish Free State*, 1959.

SCREENPLAY: *Hansel and Gretel*, 1954 (adaptation of Engelbert Humperdinck's opera).

CHILDREN'S LITERATURE: *A Boy in Eirinn*, 1913; *The King of Ireland's Son*, 1916; *The Adventures of Odysseus*, 1918; *The Boy Who Knew What the Birds Said*, 1918; *The Girl Who Sat by the Ashes*, 1919; *The Boy Apprenticed to an Enchanter*, 1920; *The Children of Odin*, 1920; *The Golden Fleece and the Heroes Who Lived Before Achilles*, 1921; *The Children Who Followed the Piper*, 1922; *At the Gateways of the Day*, 1924; *The Island of the Mighty: Being the Hero Stories of Celtic Britain Retold from the Mabinogion*, 1924; *Six Who Were Left in a Shoe*, 1924; *The Bright Islands*, 1925; *The Forge in the Forest*, 1925; *The Voyagers: Being Legends and Romances of Atlantic Discovery*, 1925; *The Fountain of Youth: Stories to Be Told*, 1927; *Orpheus: Myths of the World*, 1930; *The Big Tree of Bunlahy: Stories of My Own Countryside*, 1933; *The White Sparrow*, 1933; *The Legend of Saint Columba*, 1935; *Legends of Hawaii*, 1937; *Where the Winds Never Blew and the Cocks Never Crew*, 1940; *The Frenzied Prince: Being Heroic Stories of Ancient Ireland*, 1943; *A Treasury of Irish Folklore*, 1954; *Story Telling, New and Old*, 1961; *The Stone of Victory, and Other Tales of Padraic Colum*, 1966.

Bibliography
Bowen, Zack. *Padraic Colum: A Biographical-Critical Introduction.* Carbondale: Southern Illinois University Press, 1970. A comprehensive critical review of Colum's prolific output in various genres. Beginning with a biographical introduction and a consideration of the historical context of Colum's work, the study goes on to deal in turn with Colum's poetry, drama, fictional and nonfictional prose, and children's literature. Extensive bibliography.

Colum, Mary. *Life and the Dream.* Garden City, N.Y.: Doubleday, 1947. A first-hand account by the playwright's wife of the impact of the Irish Literary Revival. The events and personalities of that creative period are regarded nostalgically and rather uncritically. Gives some immediate access to the atmosphere in which Colum's plays were produced and received.

Hogan, Robert, Richard Burnham, and Daniel P. Poteet. *The Rise of the Realists.* Atlantic Highlands, N.J.: Humanities Press, 1979. This volume of an ongoing history of theater in modern Ireland concentrates on the years of Colum's involvement with the Abbey Theatre and the national theater movement. The authors' documentary approach ensures the inclusion of much first-hand, specialist material pertaining to the production and reception of Colum's most important plays.

Journal of Irish Literature 2 (January, 1973). This special issue on Colum contains a miscellany of Colum material, including tributes from a number of Irish scholars, a substantial interview, and articles surveying Colum's achievements. Also included is a portfolio of work by Colum, including two plays, poems for children and other verse, and various prose pieces, one of which is a self-portrait.

Sternlicht, Sanford. *Padraic Colum.* Boston: Twayne, 1985. An introductory study of Colum's long life and various literary achievements. Much attention is given to Colum's poems. Also contains a detailed chapter on the prose and another on Colum's works of mythology, which are associated with his children's writing. Includes a chronology and a bibliography.

Gordon Henderson
(Updated by *George O'Brien*)

WILLIAM CONGREVE

Born: Bardsey, Yorkshire, England; January 24, 1670
Died: London, England; January 19, 1729

Principal drama

The Old Bachelor, pr., pb. 1693; *The Double Dealer*, pr. 1693, pb. 1694; *Love for Love*, pr., pb. 1695; *The Mourning Bride*, pr., pb. 1697; *The Way of the World*, pr., pb. 1700; *The Judgement of Paris*, pr., pb. 1701 (masque); *Squire Trelooby*, pr., pb. 1704 (with Sir John Vanbrugh and William Walsh; adaptation of Molière's *Monsieur de Pourceaugnac*); *Semele*, pb. 1710 (libretto), pr. 1744 (modified version); *The Complete Plays of William Congreve*, pb. 1967 (Herbert Davis, editor).

Other literary forms

Although William Congreve is remembered today as a dramatist, his first publication was a novella, *Incognita: Or, Love and Duty Reconcil'd*, which appeared in 1692. He also published a translation of Juvenal's eleventh satire and commendatory verses "To Mr. Dryden on His Translation of Persius" in John Dryden's edition of *The Satires of Juvenal and Persius* (1693), as well as two songs and three odes in Charles Gildon's *Miscellany of Original Poems* (1692). Later, Congreve reprinted these odes, together with translations from Homer's *Iliad*, in *Examen Poeticum* (1693). His other translations from the classics include Ovid's *Art of Love, Book III* (1709) and two stories from Ovid in the 1717 edition of *Ovid's Metamorphoses*. His original poetry was first collected with his other writings in *The Works of Mr. William Congreve* (1710) and frequently reprinted throughout the eighteenth century. After 1700, Congreve abandoned serious drama in favor of social and political interests, although he did write a masque and an opera after that date and collaborated with Sir John Vanbrugh and William Walsh on a farce. In response to Jeremy Collier's attacks on Restoration playwrights, Congreve wrote a short volume of dramatic criticism, *Amendments of Mr. Collier's False and Imperfect Citations* (1698). Congreve's letters have been edited by John C. Hodges and are available in *William Congreve: Letters and Documents* (1964).

Achievements

Congreve's first play, *The Old Bachelor*, was an instant success; its initial run of fourteen days made it the most popular play since Thomas Otway's *Venice Preserved* (pr., pb. 1682). *The Double Dealer* was not as instantly successful, but *Love for Love* was so popular that Congreve was made a manager of the theater. *The Mourning Bride* was still more successful; in 1699, Gildon said of the work that "this play had the greatest Success, not only of all Mr. Congreve's, but indeed of all the Plays that ever I can remember on the English Stage." Congreve's last comedy, *The Way of the World*, though now universally regarded as his best and arguably the best Restoration comedy as well, met with little support at the time, and its cool reception drove Congreve from serious drama.

Throughout the eighteenth century, Congreve's reputation remained high, both for his poetry and his plays. Edward Howard, in his *Essay upon Pastoral* (1695), said that Congreve possessed the talent of ten Vergils. Dryden, who equated Congreve to William Shakespeare on the stage, declared that in his translations from the *Iliad* Congreve surpassed Homer in pathos. Alexander Pope's translation of the *Iliad* (1715-1720) was dedicated to Congreve, as were Sir Richard Steele's *Poetical Miscellanies* (1714) and his 1722 edition of Joseph Addison's *The Drummer: Or, The Haunted House*. In the nineteenth century, Congreve's reputation declined, along with the public's regard for Restoration comedy in general, because of the sexual licentiousness depicted in the plays. With the twentieth century, however, came a reevaluation; when *The Way of the World* was revived at Cherry Lane Theatre in New York in 1924, it ran for 120 performances. That work and *Love for Love* remain among the most frequently acted of Restoration plays, and Congreve's other two comedies are also occasionally staged. Although Congreve's one tragedy has not worn as well, he may be today the most popular and most highly regarded English dramatist between Shakespeare and George Bernard Shaw.

Biography

William Congreve was born on January 24, 1670, at Bardsey, Yorkshire, England. In 1674, his father, also named William, received a lieutenant's commission to serve in Ireland, and the family moved to the garrison of Youghal. In 1678, the elder William was transferred to Carrickfergus, another Irish port, and again, the family accompanied him. Congreve's knowledge of port life may have contributed to his depiction of the sailor, Ben, in *Love for Love*; Ben's use of nautical terms demonstrates the playwright's familiarity with this jargon. When the elder Congreve joined the regiment of the Duke of Ormond at Kilkenny in 1681, his son was able to enroll in Kilkenny College, which was free to all families who served the duke. Here, Congreve received his first formal education and his first exposure to the high society that gathered around the wealthy Duke of Ormond. After spending four and a half years at Kilkenny, Congreve entered Trinity College, Dublin (April 5, 1686), where he had the same tutor as Jonathan Swift, St. George Ashe. The theater in Smock Alley, Dublin, was at this period being run by Joseph Ashbury, who, like Congreve's father, served under the Duke of Ormond. Congreve may already have known Ashbury before coming to Trinity College, and Congreve's frequent absences from college on Saturday afternoons suggest that he was spending his time at the theater. Here, he would have seen a fine sampling of contemporary drama and could have begun to learn those dramatic conventions that he perfected in his own works.

In 1688, James II fled to Ireland. Perhaps fearing a massacre of Protestants in retaliation for their support of William of Orange against the Catholic Stuart king, the Congreves left Ireland for their family home in England. Congreve went first to Staffordshire to visit his grandfather at Stretton Manor; there, he wrote a draft of *The Old Bachelor* before coming to London to enroll in the Middle Temple to study law. Congreve was not, however, an ideal law student. Like Steele's literary Templar in *The Spectator*, he frequented the Theatre Royal in nearby Drury Lane and Will's Coffee House rather than the Inns of Court.

At Will's, Dryden held literary court; by 1692, Congreve had become sufficiently friendly with the former laureate that he was asked to contribute a translation of Juvenal's eleventh satire to Dryden's forthcoming edition of the satires of Juvenal and Persius. Together with Arthur Manwayring and Thomas Southerne, Dryden was helpful to Congreve in revising *The Old Bachelor*. (In 1717, Congreve partially returned the favor, editing and writing an introduction to a posthumous edition of Dryden's *Dramatick Works*.) The play opened at the Theatre Royal in Drury Lane on March 9, 1693, with a brilliant cast, including Anne Bracegirdle as Araminta. Congreve was soon in love with Bracegirdle, who would play the heroine in each of his succeeding works and who may have been his mistress. In December, 1693, Congreve's second comedy, *The Double Dealer*, was performed. Though Dryden praised it profusely, the play was not initially well received. After Queen Mary requested a special performance, however, its popularity increased.

Love for Love needed no royal sponsorship for its success. The first play to be performed in the restored Lincoln's Inn Fields Theatre (April 30, 1695), it ran for thirteen nights. Congreve was made one of the managers of the theater in return for a promise of a play a year, if his health permitted. Congreve needed two years to complete *The Mourning Bride*, which opened on February 27, 1697. The tragedy was worth the wait, for it was eminently successful. Three more years elapsed before Congreve's next play. Meanwhile, in 1698, Jeremy Collier attacked the Restoration stage in general, and Congreve in particular, for immorality. Congreve replied with his *Amendments of Mr. Collier's False and Imperfect Citations*. Between ill-health and the controversy with Collier, Congreve was unable to stage *The Way of the World* until March, 1700. Dryden recognized its genius, writing to Mrs. Steward on March 12, "Congreve's new play has had but moderate success, though it deserves much better." Coupled with Collier's attacks, the poor reception of *The Way of the World* convinced Congreve to abandon serious drama, but he continued to write and remain interested in the theater.

On March 21, 1701, *The Judgement of Paris*, an elaborate masque, opened at Dorset Garden with Anne Bracegirdle as Venus. With Vanbrugh and Walsh, Congreve adapted Molière's *Monsieur de Pourceaugnac* as *Squire Trelooby*, which was performed in March, 1704. He also wrote the libretto to an opera, *Semele*, which was not performed in his lifetime. For a brief time, too, Congreve, Vanbrugh, and Walsh managed a theater in the Haymarket.

Although Congreve held a variety of government posts throughout his life—the type of minor posts with which men of letters were often rewarded in that era—he did not have a lucrative position until 1705, when he was made a commissioner of wines, with an annual salary of two hundred pounds. Congreve was an ardent Whig, but he had so agreeable a personality that when the Tories came to power, Jonathan Swift and Lord Halifax (to whom Congreve had dedicated *The Double Dealer*) intervened to help him retain this income. Dryden was not merely flattering when he wrote, "So much the sweetness of your manners move,/ We cannot envy you, because we love." Not until almost a decade later, when the Hanoverians came to power, did Congreve enjoy a substantial income, receiving the post of Secretary of the Island of Jamaica. He discharged his duties by a deputy, continuing to lead a placid, retired life in London during the winter and in various country houses during the summer. As he wrote to Joseph Keally, "Ease and quiet is what I hunt after. If I have not ambition, I have other passions more easily gratified."

One passion was for Henrietta, Duchess of Marlborough, whom he met in 1703. In 1722, Congreve went to Bath for his health, and Henrietta accompanied him, even though she was married to the son of Lord Treasurer Godolphin. The following year, when she gave birth to her second daughter, Mary, it was assumed that Congreve was the child's father. Henrietta was by his side when he died on January 19, 1729, and when she died four years later, she was buried near him in Westminster Abbey.

Analysis

William Congreve began writing some thirty years after the Restoration, yet his plays retain many of the concerns of those written in the 1660's and 1670's. Foremost among these concerns is what constitutes a gentleman; that is, how one should act in society. The seventeenth century, particularly after 1660, was very interested in this matter; some five hundred conduct books were published during the century, the majority of them after the Restoration.

The response that Congreve gives, which is identical to that of Sir George Etherege, William Wycherley, and other Restoration dramatists, may be summed up in a single word: wit. This wit encompasses far more than mere verbal facility. By the time Sir Richard Blackmore attacked wit as suitable "only to please with Jests at Dinner" ("A Satyr Against Wit," 1700), the term had lost much of its significance. For Congreve, Dryden's definition is more relevant than Blackmore's: "a propriety of thoughts and words"—and, he might have added, of conduct. As Rose Snider wrote in *Satire in the Comedies of Congreve, Sheridan, Wilde, and Coward* (1937), "Decorum (true wit) might be defined simply as a natural elegance of thought and conduct, based on respect for sound judgment, fidelity to nature, and a due regard for beauty."

What constitutes propriety and fidelity to nature is subject to varying interpretation. To the nineteenth century, Restoration comedy was at best "the Utopia of gallantry, where pleasure is duty, and the manners perfect freedom" (Charles Lamb, "On the Artificial Comedy of the Last Century"), at worst the height of immorality. Chastity was not a requirement for the late seventeenth century gentleman, though it was for the lady. Charles de Saint-Denis de Saint-Évremond expressed well the age's sexual ethics: "As for the Hatred of villainous Actions, it ought to continue so long as the World does, but give leave to Gentlemen of refin'd Palates to call that Pleasure, which gross and ill-bred People call Vice, and don't place your Virtue in old musty Notions which the primitive Mortals derived from their natural Savageness."

In keeping with this genial libertinism is a rejection of prudence, financial as well as sexual. Money is not to be saved but spent, and spent on pleasure. Business is rejected as an improper pursuit. In the first scene of *The Old Bachelor*, Congreve presents in the dialogue between Bellmour and Vainlove a catalog of unworthy occupations for the genteel and indicates that the proper pursuits are witty conversation and love.

To a certain extent, this hedonism was a reaction to the restraints imposed by the Puritan Protectorate. After the Restoration, playwrights, who had lost their occupation under Cromwell, continued to portray the final victory of Cavalier over Roundhead. The Puritan cleric is a standard butt of Restoration satire. So, too, is the "cit," the merchant—not only because he was likely to be a Dissenter rather than an Anglican but also because mercantile London supported Cromwell while in general the country squires remained loyal to the Crown. Those who suffered the most under the Protectorate, the Court party, took their revenge in their plays when they returned to power.

Restoration comedy does not, however, restrict itself to negatives, nor to rejecting conventional morality and ridiculing its followers. The Truewit is indeed a libertine and often a spendthrift and freethinker, but he espouses positive values that offset these signs of youthful exuberance. Bravery, for example, is highly prized. The wit will not tolerate an insult; a sign of wit is a willingness to defend one's honor. A character such as Captain Bluffe (in *The Old Bachelor*), who draws his sword only when all danger is past, or Fainall (in *The Way of the World*), who draws his sword on a woman, shows himself to be no true wit.

Urbanity is another attribute of the Truewit. He must be able to engage in brilliant repartee; his conversation must never be dull, vulgar, overly serious, or abstruse. A wit must never lose his temper, for reason should always control emotion. He must be aware of the latest fashions and observe them. Excesses in dress, manner, or speech are scorned, as are rusticity and bad taste. Because the wit must fit into polite society, the rustic is a butt of humor on the stage even though his political views probably harmonized with those of the playwrights who were mocking him.

Yet another virtue is intelligence, of which one outward sign is again brilliant conversation. A further indication is the ability to outsmart those who would thwart the wit's desires—generally comic villains who try to prevent his attaining a suitable wife and estate. Although these villains make a pretense of being clever and urbane, their speeches and action expose their flawed nature, which leads to their punishment at the end of the play.

Selflessness is also a Restoration ideal. Prodigality is not a vice but rather a manifestation of generosity. Fondlewife (*The Old Bachelor*) leaves his wife to secure five hundred pounds and is almost cuckolded during his absence. By contrast, Valentine (*Love for Love*) is willing to give money to a discarded mistress (though not to a creditor). When wits scheme, they are trying to secure what should rightfully be theirs; when fools and Witwouds plot, they are trying to secure what should belong to another. The latter are greedy and so are frustrated.

Restoration comedy is thus moral in its intent, punishing those who deviate from societal values and rewarding those who are faithful to those norms. These values are not Victorian, nor are they the values of religious fanatics, Puritans, or nonjurors such as Jeremy Collier—hence the repeated charges of immorality brought against Congreve and his contemporaries. In emphasizing intelligence, generosity, urbanity, and bravery, though, these dramatists were drawing on a tradition that went back to Aristotle's *Nicomachean Ethics* (fourth century B.C.), and their view of comedy is Aristotle's as well. Defending himself against Collier, Congreve conceded that he portrayed vice on the stage, but he did so because comedy, according to Aristotle, depicts "the worst sort of people." It portrayed such people, Congreve continued, because "men are to be laugh'd out of their Vices in Comedy; the Business of Comedy is to delight, as well as to instruct: And as vicious People are made asham'd of their Follies or Faults, by seeing them expos'd in a ridiculous manner, so are good People at once both warn'd and diverted at their Expense." Collier and his successors did not find this response persuasive; they saw little to choose between Bellmour and Heartwell (*The Old Bachelor*) or between Mirabell and Fainall (*The Way of the World*). On the other hand, Congreve's appreciative audiences have always understood the important distinction.

At the same time that Congreve's plays are the artistic consummation of the traditions of Restoration comedy, they also reveal a breaking away from those traditions. Though these plays accept societal norms, and though the hero and heroine must be able to conform to societal expectations, they recognize the flaws of society also. Instead of trying simply to blend into society, the true wits seek to establish a private world beyond it. They recognize that beneath the glittering costumes and language lurk hypocrisy and brutality. Marriages are more often made in countinghouses than in heaven; a wedding is often the beginning of a domestic tragedy rather than the end of a social comedy. Life does not always proceed smoothly, and even when it does, it leads to a loss of youth, beauty, attractiveness. Congreve reaffirms the *carpe diem* spirit—eat, drink, and be merry—but he does not blink from the rest of the refrain—for tomorrow we die.

The sadness beneath the surface of Congreve's plays also derives from his refusal to dehumanize the targets of ridicule. Restoration comedy is social rather than psychological, and Congreve's plays are primarily concerned with how one should act in society. For the first time in the period, though, those who do not conform are not simply dismissed as fools. In fact, Pope wondered whether Congreve actually portrayed any fools, and in his dedication of *The Way of the World*, Congreve noted that audiences had difficulty distinguishing "betwixt the character of a Witwoud and a Truewit" in that work. Congreve probes beneath action to motivation to reveal what Heartwell, Fondlewife, Lord Plyant, and Lady Wishfort are thinking. These characters recognize their weaknesses; they are not merely two-dimensional types but three-dimensional people capable of suffering. By granting humanity to would-be wits and fools, Congreve was unconsciously moving away from the purely satiric toward sentimental comedy.

His one tragedy, which is actually a tragicomedy, similarly uses many of the conventions of the period while showing significant variations. The diction is inflated, as is typical of heroic tragedy. The action is remote in time and place, the characters of noble birth and larger than life, the conflict Hobbesian as rivals ruthlessly contend. Unlike earlier heroic tragedy, however, the resolution to the conflict comes not through a Leviathan, not through some divinely ordained ruler, but rather through a Glorious Revolution that overthrows unjust, though otherwise legitimate, authority in favor of a benign, popularly proclaimed monarch as exponents of power yield to advocates of love. The influence of John Locke and the deposition of James II echo in the play, especially when contrasted with Dryden's tragedies, which espouse the divine right of kings.

Congreve may have begun *The Old Bachelor* as early as 1689, at the age of nineteen. Although Dryden proclaimed it the best first comedy he had ever seen, it shows in many ways evidence of being an apprentice piece. It is the only one of Congreve's comedies that lacks dramatic tension. There is no reason why Bellmour and Belinda could not marry in the first scene, since there are no blocking characters to prevent the match. Another flaw is Congreve's ambiguous attitude toward Belinda. In the *dramatis personae*, he describes her as "an affected Lady," and in his *Amendments of Mr. Collier's False and Imperfect Citations*, he indicates that she is not intended to be admirable. Anne Bracegirdle, who always played the heroine in Congreve's works, took the role of Araminta; Belinda was played by Susanah Mountfort, who performed as the obviously foolish Lady Froth in *The Double Dealer*. Since role and performer blended with each other in Restoration drama, audiences would expect that Belinda/Mountfort was intended as a butt of ridicule for her affectation and that Araminta would be the ideal to be admired. Yet at the end of the piece, Belinda is rewarded with marriage, while Araminta remains single.

The Old Bachelor also suggests its author's youth in its close adherence to the conventions of Restoration drama. It is, for example, the only one of Congreve's comedies that has for its hero a practicing, rather than a reformed, rake. It introduces, somewhat gratuitously, standard butts of Restoration satire: a rustic boor (Sir Joseph Wittol), a pretender to valor who is in fact a coward (Captain Bluffe), a Puritan merchant (Fondlewife), and an old man who, according to the *dramatis personae*, while "pretending to slight Women, [is] secretly in love."

Aside from the treatment of Belinda, the play does show a sure hand in exposing these various pretenders and in providing suitable punishment for them. Sir Joseph Wittol is tricked out of one hundred pounds and married to Vainlove's discarded mistress. Captain Bluffe is shown to be aptly named; he is valorous only in the absence of danger. He is beaten and kicked by Sharper and married off to Silvia's maid, Lucy, who had been Setter's mistress. Heartwell, who pretends to misogyny and candor, is punished by being made to believe that he has married Silvia and then being informed that she is not as chaste as he had assumed. Though he is again unmarried, he is tormented and mocked for his folly. Fondlewife has married a woman too young and sprightly for his years; additionally, he devotes himself to business, which Bellmour calls "the rub of life [that] perverts our aim, casts off the bias, and leaves us wide and short of the intended mark." Fondlewife narrowly escapes cuckolding, and one senses that the escape is only temporary. As Vainlove notes, "If the spirit of cuckoldom be once raised up in a woman, the devil can't lay it, 'till she has done 't."

Congreve shows great skill in handling the dialogue. Bellmour and

Belinda exemplify the witty couple of Restoration comedy; as is typical of duels between the witty man and woman, Belinda has the better of their exchanges. Vainlove and Araminta, too, engage in witty debate, and again the woman proves the wittier; in one dialogue, Araminta reduces Vainlove to a defeated "O madam!," at which point she dismisses the conversation—and her suitor—with a call for music. The men and women also engage in repartee among themselves, deftly leaping from one topic to another, devising fresh and apt similes, coining paradoxes, brilliantly sketching a character in a line. The play abounds in the sheer joy of words, as when Barnaby tells Fondlewife, "Comfort will send Tribulation hither." Restoration audiences attended comedies less for their plots than for their wit, and the success of *The Old Bachelor* shows that Congreve did not disappoint them in this regard.

While Congreve was offering largely conventional fare in his first comedy, even here one finds hints of sadness beneath the comic surface. John King McComb argues (in his essay "Congreve's *The Old Bachelor:* A Satiric Anatomy") that Bellmour, Vainlove, Heartwell, Fondlewife, and Spintext are stages in the rise and fall of the lover—from rake, to fop, to gull, and finally, to cuckold. The "cormorant in love," as Bellmour describes himself in the first scene, admits that "I must take up or I shall never hold out; flesh and blood cannot bear it always." Vainlove has been a cormorant in love, too, but now contents himself with arousing desire and leaving to others the task of satisfying it. Heartwell, too, was a rake in his youth, but his passion has ebbed; unlike Vainlove, he no longer can excite women at those rare instances when he wishes to and so must attempt to purchase love. At the last stage are Fondlewife and Spintext; the latter never appears in the play but is mentioned as being a cuckold, while the audience sees Fondlewife first almost suffering the same fate and then refusing to believe the ocular proof. Bellmour, too, will age, Congreve seems to suggest; he will lose his looks and gaiety and perhaps be reduced to the state of a Heartwell or Fondlewife. The last speech of the play, which Congreve gives to Heartwell, projects such a fate for the youth.

Restoration satire is also muted in the play through the humanization of Heartwell and Fondlewife, both of whom show more sense than the typical comic butt. Heartwell's pretended aversion to "the drudgery of loving" must be exposed, since love is the chief concern of the Truewit and thus not to be slighted. Neither can pretense go unpunished. Yet Heartwell himself understands his dilemma as he is caught between reason and desire. Standing before Silvia's house he declares, "I will recover my reason, and begone." He is, however, fixed to the spot; his feet will not move: "I'm caught! There stands my north, and thither my needle points.—Now could I curse myself, yet cannot repent." After Heartwell is caught and exposed, Congreve does not mask his real anguish. In a speech reminiscent of Shylock's "Hath not a Jew eyes," Heartwell turns upon his mockers: "How have I deserved this of you? any of ye?" Vainlove urges Bellmour to stop ridiculing Heartwell—"You vex him too much; 'tis all serious to him"— and Belinda agrees: "I begin to pity him myself."

Similarly, Fondlewife, Puritan, banker, old man that he is—and any one of these characteristics would suffice in itself to render him ridiculous in a Restoration comedy—has moments of self-knowledge that grant him a touch of humanity. When he discovers Bellmour with his wife, he, too, speaks with dignity. Though Bellmour kisses Laetitia's hand at the very moment she is being reconciled to her husband, Fondlewife's tears and professions of kindness take some of the edge off the satire. If one must choose between the world of Bellmour and that of Fondlewife, one will certainly prefer the former; even so, Congreve understands that with all its admirable qualities, its wit, grace, youth, and intelligence, that World, too, is not devoid of faults.

Congreve's second play, *The Double Dealer*, demonstrates much greater control over his material; it also contains a more fully developed negative portrayal of society. In *A Short View of the Profaneness and Immorality of the English Stage* (1698), Jeremy Collier noted, "There are but Four Ladys in this Play, and Three of the biggest of them are Whores. A Great Compliment to Quality to tell them there is not above a quarter of them Honest!" Despite Congreve's efforts to dismiss Collier's observation, Congreve does indeed indict the fashionable world, and his epigram from Horace— "Sometimes even comedy raises her voice"—suggests that he intended to go beyond the conventional butts of Restoration satire. Small wonder that fashionable society returned the favor with a cool reception of the piece.

Artistically, *The Double Dealer* is much more coherent than *The Old Bachelor*. As Congreve wrote in the dedication, "I made the plot as strong as I could, because it was single; and I made it single, because I would avoid confusion." This single plot revolves around the love between Cynthia and Mellefont, who wish to marry, and the efforts of Maskwell and Lady Touchwood to prevent the match. The intrigues of these blocking figures, though conventional in comedies of the period, provide dramatic tension lacking in Congreve's earlier piece.

Congreve's handling of this central conflict, however, is less conventional. Typically, the Truewit defeats the Witwoud through his greater intelligence and so proves himself worthy of the witty heroine. When Mellefont proposes that he and Cynthia elope and thereby end the plotting and counterplotting, she rejects so simple a solution, demanding "a very evident demonstration of" her lover's wit. Until Maskwell overreaches and betrays himself, though, Mellefont is powerless to direct the action of the play; instead, he acts as Maskwell directs.

The conversation is not as sprightly as in Congreve's other plays or in

Restoration comedy generally. Mellefont and Cynthia are too good-natured to take verbal advantage of the follies of those around them. While their benevolence makes them likable, it also tends to make them dull. They seem to anticipate the comedies of Steele rather than looking back to those of Etherege and Wycherley. Like Maskwell, the Witwouds are left to expose themselves: Lady Froth attempts a heroic poem on "Syllabub," for which Brisk provides inane commentary; Lord Froth claims that the height of wit is refraining from laughing at a joke, yet he laughs incessantly; Lady Plyant thinks herself a mistress of language but contrives such convoluted sentences that her lover, Careless, is driven to exclaim, "O Heavens, madam, you confound me!"

These Witwouds are as vain as they are foolish. In a telling piece of by-play, Lord Froth takes out a mirror to look at himself; Brisk takes it from him to admire himself. This sign of vanity is repeated when Lady Froth hands her husband a mirror, asking him to pretend it is her picture. Lord Froth becomes so enamored of the image he sees that his wife declares, "Nay, my lord, you shan't kiss it so much, I shall grow jealous, I vow now." Like false wit, vanity is left to mock itself.

Even sex, treated so cavalierly in other comedies of the period, is here largely a disruptive rather than a regenerative force. Each of the married women in the play is false to her husband. Lord Froth and Sir Paul Plyant are old and foolish and so "deserve" to be cuckolded, but the same cannot be said of Lord Touchwood. Lady Touchwood's passion for her nephew Mellefont threatens to upset Cynthia's marriage as well as her own and to subvert, through incest, proper familial relationships. Her passion for Maskwell, meanwhile, threatens to allow a member of the servant class to become a lord, as she contrives to have Maskwell supplant Mellefont as her husband's heir. The seriousness of this sexual promiscuity is manifest at the end of the play; Lady Touchwood is to be divorced and so lose her position in society.

Surrounded by vanity, infidelity, folly, and knavery, Cynthia has good reason to wonder whether she and Mellefont should continue to participate in the social charade. "'Tis an odd game we are going to play at; what think you of drawing stakes, and giving over in time?" she asks Mellefont. She understands that marriage is not a great improver: "I'm thinking, though marriage makes man and wife one flesh, it leaves them still two fools." The song that concludes this conversation with Mellefont warns of yet another threat: "Prithee, Cynthia, look behind you,/ Age and wrinkles will o'ertake you;/ Then, too late, desire will find you,/ When the power must forsake you." To become like her stepmother, Lady Plyant, or Mellefont's aunt, Lady Touchwood, may be the fate reserved for Cynthia. The melancholy implicit in *The Old Bachelor* here rises to the surface. Mellefont remains cheerful, but his optimism seems misplaced. He has grossly misjudged

Maskwell; he may be misjudging all of reality. Though the true lovers marry, and though Maskwell and Lady Touchwood are banished at the end of the play, Congreve had not yet found, as he did in his last play, a way to reconcile the private world of virtue with the public world of folly, sham, and pretense. Cynthia and Mellefont remain apart from society; they do not control their actions, nor do they appear much in the play. The implication is that one can preserve one's innocence only by avoiding the fashionable world. The play thus foreshadows the gloom of the Tory satirists as well as the sentimental comedy of the next age.

Congreve was stung by the cool reception of his bitingly satiric *The Double Dealer*. Although he believed that satire is the aim of comedy, in his next play, *Love for Love*, he disguised his attacks on fashionable society offering a more traditional Restoration comedy. As he notes in the prologue: "We hope there's something that may please each taste. . . ." Much of the satire of *Love for Love* is confined to Valentine's mad scenes in the fourth act. By putting these comments into the mouth of a seeming madman, Congreve can be harsh without offending; it is as if he were stepping outside the world of the play to deliver these observations. Valentine in his madness is utterly Juvenalian, railing against all aspects of the fashionable world. There is more truth than wit in such observations as, "Dost thou know what will happen to-morrow?—answer me not—for I will tell thee. Tomorrow, knaves will thrive through craft, and fools through fortune, and honesty will go as it did, frost-nipped in a summer suit." Scandal, Valentine's friend, is also harsh in his analysis of society: "I can shew you pride, folly, affection, wantonness, inconstancy, covetousness, dissimulation, malice, and ignorance, all in one piece. Then I can shew you lying, foppery, vanity, cowardice, bragging, lechery, impotence and ugliness in another piece; and yet one of these is a celebrated beauty, and t'other a professed beau." Beneath the surface, the way of the world is vicious and foul.

By the end of the play, though, Valentine abandons his feigned madness, and Scandal is willing to take a kinder view of the world than that expressed in the song: "He alone won't betray in whom none will confide;/ And the nymph may be chaste that has never been tried." Although society in *Love for Love* has its faults, these spring more from folly than from vice; the world here is closer to that of *The Old Bachelor* than to that of *The Double Dealer*. There are no villains such as Maskwell or Lady Touchwood, no divorce, no banishment from society.

As in *The Old Bachelor*, there *is* considerable pretense that must be exposed and, to an extent, punished. Tattle pretends to be a great rake, a keeper of secrets, and a wit. Foresight pretends to be wise, to be able to foretell the future, and to be a suitable husband for a "young and sanguine" wife. Sir Sampson Legend pretends to be a good father and a fit husband for Angelica. Each of these pretenders is exposed and punished. Tattle is married off in secret to Mrs. Frail, a woman of the town. Fondle-wife is cuckolded. Sir Sampson's plan to cheat his son of his inheritance and his fiancée is frustrated. These characters are Witwouds because they fail to adhere to the ideals of Restoration society. Sir Sampson is greedy; Foresight has failed to acquire wisdom with age; Tattle seeks a fortune rather than pleasure. They all want to be Truewits, but they are unable or unwilling to conform to the demands of wit.

Below them are Ben and Miss Prue, respectively a "sea-beast" and a "land monster." Neither has had the opportunity to learn good manners, Ben because he has spent his life at sea and Prue because she has been reared in the country rather than the town. They are no match for even the pretended wits. Tattle quickly seduces Prue; Mrs. Frail seduces Ben. Society has no place for these characters, who return to their element at the end of the play.

Above the fools and would-be wits are Valentine and Angelica. She is the typical Restoration witty lady, able to manipulate Foresight and Sir Sampson and control Valentine to attain her goal, which is a suitable marriage. Valentine has many of the characteristics of the wit—he is generous, he prefers pleasure to prudence, he is a clever conversationalist—but Angelica will not marry him until she is certain that he really is a proper husband.

At the beginning of the play, there is some question as to his suitability, not because he has been a rake, not because he has spent money reck-lessly—these are actually commendable activities—but because he has been trying to buy Angelica's love. Valentine's lavish entertaining has been to impress her; he seems to regard her as mercenary and must learn her true character. Having failed to purchase her with his wealth, Valentine next tries to shame her with his poverty; here, again, he fails. Then he tries to trick her into expressing her love by feigning to be mad. As a Truewit, Angelica is able to penetrate this disguise also. Only when Valentine abandons all of his tricks and agrees that Angelica should have free choice of a husband does she accept him. Marriage for her is a serious business; she must be certain she is not submitting to tyranny or being pursued solely for her large fortune.

The blocking figure in *Love for Love* is, then, Valentine himself, and the plot of the play concerns his learning how to interact in society. Ben and Miss Prue do not learn how to do so, in part because of their previous experiences, in part because their teachers are would-be instead of true wits, in part because they lack intelligence and so are easily deceived. Foresight, Tattle, and Sir Sampson fail to learn because their characters are flawed. Foresight thinks he will learn from astrology, while Sir Sampson and Tattle think so highly of themselves that they are not even aware that they need to be taught anything.

Congreve indicates in *Love for Love* that one must live within a society that is less than perfect but that one can do so pleasantly enough if one adheres to the ideals of Restoration comedy. The despair in *The Double Dealer* yields here to a happier vision. Valentine and Angelica, unlike Mellefont and Cynthia, understand their society and have shown their ability to survive in it.

Because Congreve recognizes the limitations of the fashionable world, he is sympathetic to characters who do not quite fit in. Ben is not simply a butt of ridicule because he is an outsider. Whereas Tattle is punished with Mrs. Frail, Ben escapes that fate. Because he does not share society's viewpoint, Ben is also able to make some telling comments. He speaks his mind, shuns pretense, is generous, and understands that he will be happier at sea than in London. Prue, too, is honest; though she is Tattle's willing pupil, she does escape marrying him. The innocent fools suffer less than do the Witwouds.

With *Love for Love*, Congreve has found his true voice—a combination of satire, compassion, and wit. His hero and heroine understand both the attractions and faults of society and therefore are able to skate deftly on the surface of their world without succumbing to its folly, as Bellmour and Belinda may, or being overwhelmed by its viciousness, as Mellefont and Cynthia may be. It is a shorter step from *Love for Love* to *The Way of the World* than from *The Old Bachelor* to this comedy.

Before making that step, however, Congreve turned to tragedy, though *The Mourning Bride* resembles Congreve's other plays, for, like the comedies, it explores the questions of how the individual should act in society and what constitutes a proper marriage. On the one hand are Zara and Manuel, who rely on royal birth and power. They believe that power can command even love; Manuel wants to compel his daughter to marry Garcia, the son of the king's favorite, and Zara seeks to force Osmyn to marry her. Manuel is therefore another version of Sir Sampson Legend, who would have his child act as he himself wishes, regardless of the child's desires. Zara is a tragic rendition of Lady Touchwood, who would rather murder the man she loves than see a rival marry him. Significantly, Elizabeth Barry played both Lady Touchwood and Zara. Zara and Manuel serve as blocking figures, much like Maskwell and Lady Touchwood, but with more power to do evil.

Contrasted to these two are Osmyn and Almeria. They, too, are of royal birth, but instead of using power to create love, they use love to get power. They are generous, brave, intelligent, like their comic counterparts. Like them, too, they are young, confronting a harsh world controlled by their elders. As in the comedies, the values of the young triumph, but in the process the villains are not simply exposed but, as befits a tragedy, killed.

Critical Survey of Drama

The true lovers wed; Zara and Manuel also "marry"—at the end of the play, Zara drinks to her love from a poisoned bowl, embraces him, and dies by his side exclaiming, "This to our mutual bliss when joined above." Like Tattle and Mrs. Frail, the unworthy characters are joined. The analogy is strengthened by the masked wedding each undergoes. Just as Tattle and Mrs. Frail do not recognize their partners until it is too late, so Zara believes she is dying beside Osmyn rather than Manuel.

The deposition of the old by the young marks a triumph of love over power. It also addresses the question of what constitutes legitimate power. The older generation believes that birth and rank alone are sufficient; Manuel and Zara sense no obligation to anyone but themselves. Theirs is the belief in the divine right of kings to govern wrongly. Osmyn and Almeria have a different view. Though of royal birth, Osmyn is elevated to the throne by the people, who rebel against Manuel's tyranny. Congreve, staunch Whig, is portraying the Glorious Revolution, in which the hereditary monarch, because he has abused his power, loses his crown to a more worthy, because more benevolent, successor.

In the first scene of the fourth act of *The Way of the World*, Congreve directly addresses the issue of how two people can live harmoniously with each other while retaining personal autonomy and dignity on the one hand and remaining part of the social world on the other. This famous "Proviso" scene has a long theatrical history. A scene that first gained prominence in Honoré d'Urfé's *Astrea* (1607-1628), versions appear in four of Dryden's comedies—*The Wild Gallant* (pr. 1663), *Secret Love: Or, The Maiden Queen* (pr. 1667), *Marriage à la Mode* (pr. 1672, pb. 1673) and *Amphitryon: Or, The Two Socia's* (pr., pb. 1690)—in James Howard's *All Mistaken: Or, The Mad Couple* (pr. 1667), and Edward Ravenscroft's *The Careless Lovers* (pr.1673) and *The Canterbury Guests* (pr. 1694). As he did so often, Congreve used a well-established convention but invested it with new significance and luster. The proviso in *The Way of the World* is not only the wittiest of such scenes but also the most brilliantly integrated into the theme of the play. Indeed, the scene illuminates the plight of every witty heroine who had appeared on the Restoration stage and summarized the hopes and fears of all fashionable couples to that time.

Millamant does not want to "dwindle into a wife"; Mirabell does not want to "be beyond measure enlarged into a husband." She wishes to be "made sure of my will and pleasure"; he wants to be certain that his wife's liberty will not degenerate into license. In the Hobbesian world of self-love, rivalry, and conflicting passions, these two therefore devise a Lockean compact, creating a peaceful and reasonable accommodation between their individual and mutual needs. They will not act like other fashionable couples, "proud of one another the first week, and ashamed of one another ever after." They will act more like strangers in public, that they may act more like lovers in private. Millamant will remain autonomous in her sphere of the tea table, but she will not "encroach upon the men's prerogative." She will not sacrifice her health or natural beauty to fashion or whim; otherwise, she may dress as she likes. Together the lovers create a private world divorced from the follies and vices of the society around them while retaining the freedom to interact with that society when they must.

In contrast to this witty couple are Fainall and Marwood. As the names suggest, Fainall is a pretender to wit, and his consort, Marwood, seeks to mar the match between Mirabell and Millamant because of her love—and then hate—for Mirabell. She, too, is a pretender, a seeming prude who in fact is having an affair with Fainall. Whereas the witty couple seek to preserve their private world inviolate, Fainall and Marwood attempt to exploit private relationships. Fainall has married for money, not love, and once he has secured his wife's fortune, he intends to divorce her, marry Marwood, and flee society. Later, he and Marwood conspire to secure half of Millamant's and all of Lady Wishfort's estate by threatening to expose Mrs. Fainall's earlier affair with Mirabell, hoping that Lady Wishfort will pay to keep secret her daughter's indiscretion and prevent a public divorce.

On yet another level are Lady Wishfort, Petulant, and Witwoud, who have no private life at all. Lady Wishfort cannot smile because she will ruin her carefully applied makeup; the face she presents to society must not be disturbed by any unexpected emotion. All of her efforts are directed to appearing fashionable—hence her fear of Mrs. Fainall's exposure. Hence, too, her inflated rhetoric when she tries to impress the supposed Sir Rowland. Petulant wishes to appear the true Restoration wit and so hires women to ask for him at public places. He will even disguise himself and then "call for himself, wait for himself; nay, and what's more, not finding himself, sometimes [leave] a letter for himself." Witwoud, as his name indicates, seeks to pass himself off as a wit but must rely on his memory rather than his invention to maintain a conversation. His cowardice or stupidity prevents his understanding an insult, and he mistakes "impudence and malice" for wit. He will not acknowledge his own brother because he believes it unfashionable to know one's own relations, thus surrendering private ties to public show. Sir Willful, Witwoud's half brother, is the typical rustic. Like Ben and Prue in *Love for Love*, he has no place in society. He withdraws from social interaction first by getting drunk and then by returning to his element, leaving the urban world entirely.

Congreve thus offers four ways of coping with the demands of society. One may flee completely, as Sir Willful does and as Marwood, Fainall, and Lady Wishfort talk of doing. Mirabell and Millamant could adopt this solution, too. If they elope, Millamant will retain half of her fortune, enough to allow the couple a comfortable life together, but they would lose the pleasures of the tea table, of the theater, of social intercourse—of all the benefits, in short, that society can offer. One can also submit one's personality completely to society and abandon any privacy (Petulant and Witwoud). One can use private life only to serve one's social ends (Fainall and Marwood), or one can find a suitable balance between them. Presented with these choices, Mirabell and Millamant wisely choose the last.

The question posed here is not only one of surfaces, of how best to enjoy life, although that element is important. Additionally, Congreve here explores differing ethical stances. The opening conversation between Mirabell and Fainall establishes the moral distinction between them. Fainall states, "I'd no more play with a man that slighted his ill fortune than I'd make love to a woman who undervalued the loss of her reputation." Mirabell replies, "You have a taste extremely delicate, and are for refining on your pleasures." Fainall's may be the wittier comment, but it is also the more malicious. True wit in *The Way of the World* embraces morality as well as intelligence. Mirabell does prove more intelligent than Fainall, outwitting him "by anticipation" just as he has cuckolded Fainall by anticipation. Even so, in their conversations the difference in cleverness is not as apparent as it is between Witwoud or Mirabell or Lady Wishfort and Millamant. Congreve once more is moving toward sentimental comedy by creating an intelligent hero who is also sententious. He is foreshadowing Addison's attempt in the *Spectator* "to enliven Morality with Wit, and to temper Wit with Morality."

The tone is bittersweet—another anticipation of the next age. Like Belinda in Pope's *The Rape of the Lock* (1712, 1714) Millamant must grow up. Just as she cannot be a coquette forever, so Mirabell must put aside his rakish past. One has a sense of time's passing. Even amid the witty repartee of the proviso scene, Mirabell looks ahead to Millamant's pregnancy, and to the time beyond that when she will be tempted, as Lady Wishfort is now, to hide her wrinkles. Her maid will one day say to her what Foible tells her lady: "I warrant you, madam, a little art once made your picture like you; and now a little of the same art must make you like your picture."

With this new sense of the future coexists a new sense of the past, a sense that one's earlier actions have consequences. Valentine is able to dismiss a former mistress with a gift of money and to redeem his earlier extravagances through an inheritance and a good marriage. Mirabell is not so fortunate. His previous affair with Mrs. Fainall is not immoral—no one condemns Mirabell for it—but neither is it a trifle to be quickly forgotten. Because of that affair, Mrs. Fainall has had to marry a man she dislikes and who hates her; she is not merely asking for information when she inquires of Mirabell, "Why did you make me marry this man?" Nor has Mirabell escaped all consequences, for this affair gives Fainall the opportunity to seize half of Millamant's—and thus half of Mirabell's—estate.

The artificial world and golden dreams of *The Old Bachelor* have essentially vanished in *The Way of the World*. The form remains—the witty couple contending successfully against the Witwouds and the fools; the young struggling against the old; the flawed but brilliant urbane society opposing vulgarity and rusticity. Congreve has elevated this form to its highest point; there is no more lovable coquette than Millamant, no Restoration wit more in control of his milieu than Mirabell. Yet the substance, the sense of passing time, of the sadness of real life, is undermining the comedy of wit. Alexander Pope called Congreve *ultimus Romanorum* (the ultimate Roman). He is truly the greatest of the Restoration dramatists, but he is *ultimus* in its other sense as well—the last.

Other major works

NOVELLA: *Incognita: Or, Love and Duty Reconcil'd*, 1692.

POETRY: "To Mr. Dryden on His Translation of Persius," 1693; *Poems upon Several Occasions*, 1710.

NONFICTION: *Amendments of Mr. Collier's False and Imperfect Citations*, 1698; *William Congreve: Letters and Documents*, 1964 (John C. Hodges, editor).

TRANSLATIONS: *Ovid's Art of Love, Book III*, 1709; *Ovid's Metamorphoses*, 1717 (with John Dryden and Joseph Addison).

MISCELLANEOUS: *Examen Poeticum*, 1693; *The Works of Mr. William Congreve*, 1710; *The Complete Works of William Congreve*, 1923 (4 volumes).

Bibliography

Avery, Emmett L. *Congreve's Plays on the Eighteenth-Century Stage*. New York: Modern Language Association of America, 1951. An account of the reception of Congreve's plays in the eighteenth century that attempts to clarify the degree to which the plays were appreciated by the changing tastes of three or four generations. Because he was then regarded as representative of the most brilliant comic drama of the late seventeenth century, the reception of his plays illuminates the status of Restoration comedy as a whole, especially the work of such comparable authors as William Wycherley, Sir George Etherege, and Sir John Vanbrugh. Bibliography.

Lindsay, Alexander, and Howard Erskine-Hill, eds. *William Congreve: The Critical Heritage*. New York: Routledge, 1989. The excellent series of essays in this volume trace Congreve's critical reception from the immediate acclaim that greeted his first comedy to the emergence of modern academic criticism in the twentieth century. The editors include a generous selection of dramatic reviews, particularly from the eighteenth century, when all five of his plays were a standard part of the repertory.

Love, Harold. *Congreve*. Totowa, N.J.: Rowman & Littlefield, 1975. This well-written discussion of Congreve's plays places the works within the historical-theatrical context in which they were written. Love stresses the necessity of active aural and spatial imagination in understanding Congreve. Encourages readers to see Congreve's scenes as he himself would have viewed them and gives information about the great performers for whom he wrote. Brief bibliography, chronology.

Markley, Robert. *Two Edg'd Weapons: Style and Dialogue in the Comedies of Etherege, Wycherley, and Congreve.* New York: Oxford University Press, 1988. Theoretical discussions about the nature of style and historical questions about stylistic theory and practice in the late seventeenth century form the broad outline of this study. Markley argues that studying John Dryden's plays and the critical comments, as well as the plays of Sir George Etherege, William Wycherley, and Congreve, can offer valuable insights into seventeenth century stylistic theory, dramatic artistry, ideology, and conceptions of dramatic style. Focuses on both the definition and interaction of style and ideology in these dramatists' works. Bibliography.

Novak, Maximillian E. *William Congreve.* New York: Twayne, 1971. In this study, Novak attempts to treat Congreve and his plays specifically in terms of English art and society after the Glorious Revolution of 1688. For the most part, this book is concerned with explication and close examination of Congreve's writings while keeping in mind the specific context of that last decade of the seventeenth century in which a brilliant style of comedy flourished. The author argues that Congreve always adapted his plays to his decade. Excellent bibliography, chronology.

Williams, Aubrey L. *An Approach to Congreve.* New Haven, Conn.: Yale University Press, 1979. Against the views that Congreve's plays reflect a post-Christian universe, a secularized or despiritualized world, this well-argued study attempts to provide the evidence and context for an approach that takes into account the essential compatibility of Congreve's one novella and five plays with a commonly shared and fundamentally Christian seventeenth century worldview. Bibliography.

Joseph Rosenblum
(Updated by *Genevieve Slomski*)

MARC CONNELLY

Born: McKeesport, Pennsylvania; December 13, 1890
Died: New York, New York; December 21, 1980

Principal drama

Dulcy, pr., pb. 1921 (with George S. Kaufman); *To the Ladies*, pr. 1922, pb. 1923 (with Kaufman); *Merton of the Movies*, pr. 1922, pb. 1925 (with Kaufman; adaptation of Harry Leon Wilson's story); *The Deep Tangled Wildwood*, pr. 1923 (with Kaufman; originally as *West of Pittsburg*, pr. 1922); *Helen of Troy, N.Y.*, pr. 1923 (with Kaufman; music and lyrics by Bert Kalmer and Harry Ruby); *Beggar on Horseback*, pr. 1924, pb. 1925 (with Kaufman; based on Paul Apel's play *Hans Sonnenstössers Höllenfahrt*); *Be Yourself*, pr. 1924 (with Kaufman; music by Kalmer, lyrics by Ruby); *The Wisdom Tooth*, pr., pb. 1926; *The Wild Man of Borneo*, pr. 1927 (with Herman J. Mankiewicz); *The Green Pastures: A Fable*, pb. 1929, pr. 1930 (adaptation of Roark Bradford's sketches in *Ol' Man Adam an' His Chillun*); *The Farmer Takes a Wife*, pr., pb. 1934 (with Frank B. Elser; adaptation of Walter D. Edmond's novel *Rome Haul*); *Everywhere I Roam*, pr. 1938 (with Arnold Sundgaard); *The Flowers of Virtue*, pr. 1942; *A Story for Strangers*, pr. 1948; *Hunter's Moon*, pr. 1958; *The Portable Yenberry*, pr. 1962.

Other literary forms

Marc Connelly is known primarily for his plays, but he also wrote many short humorous stories for *The New Yorker* and other magazines, a number of essays, a novel (*A Souvenir from Qam*, 1965), and an autobiography (*Voices Offstage*, 1968).

Achievements

Connelly is known mainly as a writer of polite farce of a conventional stamp. He enjoyed the partnership of a first-rate collaborator (George S. Kaufman) in his early years, the services of the stars of Broadway to speak his words, and one enduring artistic and commercial success, *The Green Pastures*, which won the 1930 Pulitzer Prize for Drama and made him a millionaire. He broke new ground in wedding his romantic views to Expressionistic techniques in a way that was suitable for the popular audience of the day. While his early successes were generally predictable comedies of manners, he was never content to restrict his plays to a single type, freely using features of the progressive theater of the time. His greatest work, *The Green Pastures*, which may seem condescending and simplistic to readers in the 1980's, represented a breakthrough for the theater of 1930: an all-black cast in a recasting of the Bible, set in the rural South. Connelly's dreams of an earthly paradise where the common man can find fulfillment despite his self-doubt and his burden of anxiety about the world are realized most completely in this play, set far from New York with characters different from the often fatuous urban types he had drawn so successfully. When audiences of the mid-1920's wanted someone to celebrate their heady exuberance and make them laugh, Connelly provided the gags and the situations to which they could respond; when the audiences of the Depression era wanted to find some hope in the future, Connelly responded again with a worldview pure in its simplicity, self-assured in its happy resolutions of misfortune, and delightful in its crackling wit.

Four of Connelly's collaborations with Kaufman in the years prior to *The Green Pastures* were successful: *Dulcy* and *To the Ladies* arose from a character already popular in a New York newspaper column; *Merton of the Movies*, one of the earliest satires on Hollywood, adapted cinematic techniques to the stage; and *Beggar on Horseback* introduced Expressionism to Broadway. Later, *The Wisdom Tooth*, written by Connelly alone and chosen by Burns Mantle for *Best Plays of 1925-1926*, once more employed two realistic scenes flanking a fantasy.

Connelly's good taste, solidly American values, and ready wit made him a successful writer in other areas as well, from his radio play, *The Mole on Lincoln's Cheek* (1941), to his fiction, both long and short. In the same year that *The Green Pastures* won the Pulitzer Prize, Connelly also won the O. Henry Award for the 1930 short story "Coroner's Inquest." He was given honorary degrees by Bowdoin College (1952) and Baldwin-Wallace College (1962).

Connelly's plays have been rarely revived in recent years, and except for *The Green Pastures* his works are read only by historians of the stage. Nevertheless, his lasting achievement, *The Green Pastures*, is a monument of the American theater, distinguished by the purity of its sentiment, the richness of its language, and the charm of its imagination and humor.

Biography

Marcus Cook Connelly was born December 13, 1890. The year before, his parents, Patrick Joseph and Mabel Louise Fowler (Cook) Connelly, two touring actors, had settled in McKeesport, Pennsylvania, blaming the death of their first child on the hardships of the touring life. His father managed the White Hotel, a favorite stop for traveling circus troupes and theatrical companies, who imbued young Marc with what he later described as "the early feeling that going to the theatre is like going to an unusual church, where the spirit is nourished in mysterious ways, and pure magic may occur at any moment."

Connelly's father died of pneumonia when his son was twelve, and following the failure of the White Hotel in 1908, Connelly's hopes for college were dashed. When he and his mother moved to Pittsburgh, Connelly began a career with local newspapers, finally becoming second-string drama critic and author of a humorous weekly column, "Jots and Tittles," for the Pittsburgh *Gazette Times*. He also spent his evenings writing, directing, and stage-managing skits for the Pittsburgh Athletic Association. In 1913, Connelly wrote the lyrics for Alfred Ward Birdsall's *The Lady of Luzon*, which so impressed local steel magnate Joseph Riter that Connelly was commissioned to write the lyrics and libretto for a play that Riter was producing on Broadway, *The Amber Princess*. The play, which after two years of rewriting finally contained only Connelly's title and the lyrics to one song, failed, and the hopeful young playwright was forced to return to newspaper work, this time far from home.

While covering the theater district for the New York *Morning Telegraph* in 1917, Connelly met George S. Kaufman, who was then second-string drama critic for *The New York Times*. At the suggestion of the producer George C. Tyler, Connelly and Kaufman collaborated on a vehicle for Lynn Fontanne entitled *Dulcy*, which opened August 13, 1921, and was so popular (running for 246 performances) that they immediately created a sequel as a vehicle for another young star, Helen Hayes, entitled *To the Ladies* (which ran for 128 performances). The team again collaborated on a misguided effort, *The Deep Tangled Wildwood*, which was shelved following a disastrous out-of-town tryout in May, 1922, and later reworked and produced on Broadway on November 5, 1923, running for only sixteen performances. Their greatest success as a team came with *Merton of the Movies*, the story of an innocent shop clerk who seeks stardom in Hollywood. It opened in November 13, 1922, and played for 398 performances.

At this same time, Connelly was firmly entrenched as a member of that group of literary and theatrical wits who lunched together at the Algonquin Hotel. In addition to the charter members, Franklin P. Adams, Jane Grant, Harold Ross, and Alexander Woollcott, the group included Robert Benchley, Dorothy Parker, Ring Lardner, Heywood Broun, Robert E. Sherwood, and others. In 1925, Grant, Ross, Woollcott, Kaufman, Connelly, and others founded *The New Yorker*, to which Connelly contributed numerous essays and pieces of short fiction between 1927 and 1930.

Kaufman and Connelly collaborated on three more plays, two of them musicals: *Helen of Troy, N.Y.*, with songs by Bert Kalmer and Harry Ruby, and *Be Yourself*, which starred Queenie Smith; the third was the fantasy *Beggar on Horseback*. When *Be Yourself* closed, the partnership was effectively over, although the two remained friends and were said to have been working on a musical about a union boss at the time of Kaufman's death.

Connelly went to Hollywood in 1925 to write the screenplay of a Beatrice Lillie vehicle, *Exit Smiling* (1926), returning to Broadway for his directorial debut in his play *The Wisdom Tooth*, a showcase for the actor Thomas

Mitchell, which ran for 160 performances. Connelly next collaborated with Herman J. Mankiewicz on a failed production, *The Wild Man of Borneo*, which closed after fifteen nights. For the next two years, Connelly avoided the theater and concentrated his efforts on *The New Yorker*.

In the fall of 1928, Connelly's cartoonist friend Rollin Kirby recommended that he read a book by a New Orleans newspaperman, Roark Bradford, entitled *Ol' Man Adam an' His Chillun*, a series of stories from the Old Testament told in the language of a black Southern preacher. Connelly immediately took to the book and visited Bradford in Louisiana, where he refined his knowledge of the dialect and found the spirituals a chorus would sing between the scenes. Once the play was written, Connelly spent the better part of a year seeking financial backing, as most producers feared offending both blacks and whites, the religious and the nonreligious. Finally, a broker, Rowland Stebbins, put up the necessary money, and on February 26, 1930, *The Green Pastures* had the first of its more than sixteen hundred performances. This play, for which he derived not only great financial rewards but also the deepest sense of fulfillment, formed the summary moment of his long career in the theater, a moment he never approached later in his life.

In 1930, Connelly married the actress Madeline Hurlock; they were divorced in 1935. It was during this period that Connelly wrote his last hit, *The Farmer Takes a Wife*, written with Frank B. Elser from his play *Rome Haul* (based on Walter D. Edmond's novel) and starring Henry Fonda. None of Connelly's remaining plays—*Everywhere I Roam* (written with Arnold Sundgaard), *The Flowers of Virtue*, *A Story for Strangers*, *Hunter's Moon*, and *The Portable Yenberry*—played more than fifteen performances. During this time, Connelly became involved in projects outside the theater. He directed his own adaptation of *The Green Pastures* for film (1936) and wrote several other screenplays as well, including *Captains Courageous* (1937). He also wrote a successful radio play, *The Mole on Lincoln's Cheek*, and, much later, a humorous novel, *A Souvenir from Qam*, as well as his autobiography, *Voices Offstage*, all the while contributing numerous pieces, mostly on his travels, to popular magazines. He occasionally acted, playing the Stage Manager in a 1944 production of Thornton Wilder's *Our Town*, and Professor Charles Osnan in Russel Crouse and Howard Lindsay's *The Tall Story*, both on Broadway (1959) and in the film (1960); also he served as the Narrator for the Off-Broadway revue *The Beast in Me* (1963), drawn from the writings of James Thurber. A founder of the Dramatists Guild, past president of the Authors' League of America, he was president of the National Institute of Arts and Letters from 1953 to 1956. From 1946 to 1950, he taught playwriting at Yale and frequently conducted seminars in the years following. Connelly's quiet humor remained keen to the end. On his ninetieth birthday, after receiving a certificate of appreciation from Mayor Ed Koch of New York, he said, "Some days I feel like an old man of 137, and other days like a mere boy of 136."

Analysis

Marc Connelly's early plays were highly successful largely because they adequately fulfilled audience expectations. He chose his collaborators well, as he did the books and plays that he adapted. While not a man of surpassing originality, he nevertheless brought a distinctive tone of gentility and sweet romanticism to his humor, tempering the brusque manner of Kaufman or the cynicism of Paul Apel. Throughout his work runs an implicit faith in people's ability to act for the good of themselves and of humankind. For Connelly, humor brings forth all the elements of an earthly paradise: happiness, laughter, freedom from care, and harmony with others.

After a brief friendship, Connelly and Kaufman began their collaboration with *Dulcy*. A popular character in Franklin P. Adams' New York *World* column "The Conning Tower," Dulcinea was a chic suburban wife given to wearing fashionable clothes and uttering fashionable platitudes. A kind of satiric weather vane of the rising New York social set, she was ripe for appropriation for the stage, and she was taken by Connelly and Kaufman with Adams' full support. Characteristically, they did not make her an object of satiric attack; rather, they made her language and that of her friends a vehicle for laughter. The play centers on Dulcy Smith, who in her Westchester home hosts a weekend party for her husband Gordon's new business partner, C. Roger Forbes. Forbes wants to acquire Gordon's jewelry business for only a fraction of its real value. Dulcy sets out to get more money from Forbes, a fairer price, and upon her efforts the action of the play turns.

The other houseguests provide the heroine with a sufficient variety of difficulties to resolve before the final curtain. Dulcy's brother, William Parker, falls in love with Forbes's daughter Angela, who is already loved by another guest, screenwriter Vincent Leach. Schuyler Van Dyck is an otherwise attractive man who continually talks about the fortune he does not have, while Henry is a reformed forger whom Dulcy has converted into a butler.

Leach is supposed to encourage Mrs. Forbes's desire to write for the movies, but Forbes is antagonized by Dulcy's ploy, for he does not want his wife to become involved in the movie business. Dulcy further angers Forbes by helping his daughter Angela, who plans to elope with Leach; indeed, Forbes becomes so angry that he threatens to leave at once, canceling his offer to buy Gordon's business.

Dulcy is "a clever woman," however, and in the third act, all the complications are resolved. Forbes agrees to pay twenty-five percent for Gordon's business, rather than the sixteen and two-thirds percent initially offered. Instead of eloping with Leach, Angela is married off to Dulcy's stockbroker brother, William, pleasing her father no end. Schuyler Van Dyck is taken by Forbes for what he pretends to be, and Henry is exonerated of the charge of having stolen a pearl necklace.

If the action is uninspired, the *au courant* dialogue charmed contemporary audiences. Dulcy's trite expressions are played off against those of the clever characters, the most clever of whom is her brother, who is rewarded with the girl of his dreams. The jargon of various professions is exquisitely mocked: Leach speaks the language of Hollywood (particularly in his account of his movie *Sin*, the play's finest satiric set piece); Forbes speaks the language of Wall Street; and an incidental character, Tom Sterrett, an "advertising engineer," speaks the lingo of Madison Avenue. Broadway found itself laughing at this congenial burlesque of jargon, for the authors never make their satire sting but rather invite one to pardon these amiably foolish types.

Adams provided the impetus for another Connelly-Kaufman collaboration when he recommended in his column of February 3, 1922, *Merton of the Movies*, a novel by Harry Leon Wilson. The producer George C. Tyler then suggested it to the team, and the play opened November 13, 1922. Wilson's novel is a biting attack on the hypocrisy and meretriciousness of Hollywood and its reflection of the pervasive lack of culture in the United States; Connelly and Kaufman viewed Hollywood with an air of such superior amusement that they could not feel themselves threatened enough to knot the lash of their satire any more than they had with *Dulcy*. Instead, they made the play a story of one man realizing his dream to be a Hollywood star, ultimately becoming as vapid and cynical as those he had so long worshiped on the screen. The play was a critical and popular success, running for 398 performances.

Merton Gill is a clerk in a general store in Simsbury, Illinois, who gains stardom in Hollywood. His knowledge and interest in the "art" of the movies is limited to the fan magazines and public relations interviews he devours, and so at the beginning of the play he is as easy a butt for jokes as is the movie industry itself. The summation of all of his dreams is Beulah Baxter, the lead in the popular *Hazards of Hortense* serials to which Merton became addicted back in Simsbury. When he finally meets her, he finds not the sweet and simple ingenue she portrays but an oft-married, selfish starlet whose concerns about her art are as limited as her vocabulary. Tricked into appearing in a parody of his cinematic idol, Harold Parmalee, Merton becomes an overnight star. His gimmick is playing amusing roles seriously, which leads everyone (including the audience) to imagine that poor Merton is being used. In his final speech, however, which endeared him (and the play) to the Broadway audiences, Morton claims that he was not unwittingly used but that he had known what he was doing all along: He was creating satire so clever that most of his fans did not understand it.

Merton of the Movies was not the first parody of Hollywood, but it was one of the first stage productions to attempt the rapid scene shifts common to the medium it was satirizing. There are four acts and six scenes in this play, where *Dulcy* had three acts and one set only. Moreover, the action of the play unfolds before the audience as if they were watching a film in the process of being shot.

This play also presents the typical Connelly-Kaufman character: the innocent but honest man whose dreams are often compromised or negated by his own unwillingness or inability to act properly. Despite Connelly's dreamily romantic views of life, his leads tend to gain only ironic successes, as here, when Merton's very lack of talent makes him a star; the meaning of what he has learned about Hollywood (that is, that lack of talent does not make bad entertainment in the eyes of the moguls, but is perceived as "satire") is lost on him. Still, Connelly and Kaufman could not be accused of writing satire in *Merton of the Movies*, for the message of the play is too light and the attacks too gentle.

Beggar on Horseback declared itself more forcefully on the subject of the worthwhile in art and also represented a further advance in the team's stagecraft. Suggested by the German Expressionist Paul Apel's play *Hans Sonnenstössers Höllenfahrt* (pr. 1911), the play nevertheless is essentially Connelly and Kaufman's own, as Alexander Woollcott pointed out in his introduction to the printed version.

Beggar on Horseback develops the old chestnut, "Put a beggar on horseback and he'll outride the devil," by depicting, in Connelly's words, "a fantasy in which a young musician would go through a maze of kaleidoscopic experiences, the basic theme of which would be the ancient conflict of art and materialism." Neil McRae is a good composer but an improvident man who compromises his talent by writing cheap orchestrations of the sort that periodically drift in his window from the street. His wealthy neighbors are the Cady family: Mr. Cady is a businessman from Neil's hometown; Mrs. Cady is a society volunteer for worthy causes; their daughter, Gladys, is a ray of sunshine who brings Neil candy for his tea, while Homer, the son, is perpetually morose. Neil's friend, Dr. Albert Rice, suggests to Gladys that she marry Neil to give him the emotional and financial support he needs to get on with his writing. To calm his nerves, Neil takes a sleeping pill, and as he drifts off to sleep, Cynthia, to whom Neil has proposed, turns him down because she cannot support him as well as Gladys can.

The dream sequence that follows was remarkable for the Broadway stage of 1924: As Neil's future life is played out, he watches himself marry Gladys, whose bouquet is made of dollar bills, in a ceremony accompanied by the kind of sporty music he had heard in his apartment. The hectic pace of their social life prevents Neil from composing, and when he takes a job in Cady's widget business he begins to amass a fortune by day which he and Gladys will spend at jazz clubs by night. He finally sells his symphony, but Gladys destroys the manuscript, and Neil in a rage kills all four Cadys.

Neil comes to trial with Mr. Cady as the judge; the chief witness is Mrs. Cady, the prosecutor is Homer, and the members of the jury are all dance instructors. Neil loses his case after presenting as evidence on his behalf a ballet composed by himself and Cynthia, and he is sentenced by the jury to write popular songs for the rest of his life. Bent on suicide, he takes another pill, and Cynthia promises to stand by him forever.

The dream sequence ends with Cynthia knocking on the real door of Neil's apartment. Gladys breaks the engagement when she realizes that Neil's true love is Cynthia, and the lovers remain together.

Here, for the first time, Connelly and Kaufman do more than merely ridicule: They state clearly what is valuable for the artist both objectively (in the realistic sequences) and subjectively (in the dream sequence). The realistic sections are portrayals (in the manner of *Dulcy* and *Merton of the Movies*) of the lovable innocents and the mendicant fools of 1920's society. When in the dream one butler becomes two and those two become four, and so on, until the stage is literally filled with hustling butlers, the audience sees a dramatic representation of wealth overrunning the individual who possesses it. The play is also remarkable for the integral role that music plays in it. The authors were not afraid to follow their own artistic prescriptions, involving the music of Connelly's friend (and for a time, roommate), the composer and critic Deems Taylor, as an essential part of rather than accompaniment to the dramatic movement of the play, both in the realistic and in the dream sequences. While many more revolutionary developments were taking place in the 1920's in American experimental theaters—as well as in Europe—*Beggar on Horseback* introduced Expressionism to Broadway, and for this alone the play deserves a place in American theatrical history.

The Green Pastures marked a significant advance in Connelly's ambitions as a dramatist. In his previous plays, he had focused on a limited area of modern life: society life, Hollywood, business. In *The Green Pastures*, he attempted a unified retelling of the principal document of our culture within the context and language of rural Southern blacks. He was interested not in theological exactitude but rather in the humanistic message that even "De Lawd" comes to accept through His suffering: Man's essential imperfection must be accepted, for man's nature is to sin without regard to De Lawd's praise or damnation; this is the cross both man and God, as symbolized by Jesus on the Cross at the end of the play, must bear. Suffering ennobles the sufferer, be he man or God, and the anguish of the realization of man's nature is, in the closing words of the play, "a terrible burden for one man to carry."

The first part of the play covers events from Creation to the Flood. These ten episodes begin with a Sunday school lesson presided over by Mr. Deshee, who tells his children about Heaven, Creation, Adam and Eve, Cain and Abel, and Noah, showing how man fell from grace and how, with the Flood, he must begin again. Here is where *Dulcy, Merton of the Movies*, and *Beggar on Horseback* would have ended, full of promise, but Connelly was no longer satisfied to end on such a note. The end of part 1 finds De Lawd merely hopeful of the success of His new start and Gabriel downright uncertain.

Part 2 begins with two Heavenly Cleaners in De Lawd's office complaining that a little speck on De Lawd's horizon, Earth, is taking up too much of His time; Gabriel reports that the supply of thunderbolts is depleting without sufficient benefit for their use. De Lawd resolves to try once again with mankind, and He shows Moses how to trick Pharoah into letting His people out of Egypt. Joshua finally gets them to the Promised Land, but soon, in the words of Mr. Deshee, "dey went to de dogs again." The scene changes to a Harlem-style nightclub with golden idols and money-changing priests that bring De Lawd to renounce His creation and declare that He will not save man again.

In scene 6 of part 2, the fall of Jerusalem is played out. De Lawd is so moved by the statement of faith in the God of Hosea given by Hezdrel—a character created without biblical authority and in certain respects morally superior to even De Lawd—that He turns to a dialogue with Gabriel on the nature of man, who can be so evil, yet so noble and courageous in the face of suffering. De Lawd realizes that He, too, must suffer for each new thing He learns about mankind, and the joint suffering of God and man is made manifest in the Crucifixion, seen in shadow on De Lawd's wall. With this scene witnessed, the severe, noble black Lawd, now given hope in His creation for the first time, smiles broadly as the chorus sings "Hallelujah, King Jesus."

The play was received with overwhelming critical and popular praise, even from blacks, who, if they were offended by the stereotypical poverty and near-illiteracy of Mr. Deshee and his charges, were nevertheless elated at the acceptance Broadway audiences gave this all-black cast, behaving, with the exception of the Harlem-speakeasy Babylon scene, in a good and proper way. To what extent the simplistic figures of De Lawd and His minions and the hot-tempered, immoral, and occasionally violent characters such as Cain, Zeba, the Children of Noah, and the Children of Israel represented caricatures with which the New York audience could feel comfortable, and to what extent they represented behavioral archetypes that transcend race, is an open question. Connelly himself left no doubt about how he viewed them:

I never saw my play—and I certainly don't now—as part of any civil rights movement, as for or against *any* movement. It was no more simply about a race of people than [Gerhart Hauptmann's] *The Weavers* say, or [Maxim Gorky's] *The Lower Depths* was simply about one particular class of people. My play had little to do with Negroes—or, rather, it had as much to do with yellow and white and red as it did with black. *Green Pastures* was, at heart, about humanity, but maybe that's a little hard to explain today.

This play of simple faith in mankind came at the right time, as the United States was sinking into the Depression; with confusion and despair all around, Connelly brought hope and laughter to a darkening country.

Other major works

NOVEL: *A Souvenir from Qam*, 1965.

SHORT FICTION: "Luncheon at Sea," 1927; "Gentlemen Returning from a Party," 1927; "Barmecide's Feast," 1927; "The Committee: A Study of Contemporary New York Life," 1928; "The Guest," 1929; "Coroner's Inquest," 1930.

NONFICTION: *Voices Offstage: A Book of Memoirs*, 1968.

SCREENPLAYS: *Whispers*, 1920; *Exit Smiling*, 1926; *The Suitor*, 1928 (short); *The Bridegroom*, 1929 (short); *The Uncle*, 1929 (short); *The Green Pastures*, 1936; *I Married a Witch*, 1936; *Captains Courageous*, 1937 (with others); *Crowded Paradise*, 1956.

RADIO PLAY: *The Mole on Lincoln's Cheek*, 1941.

Bibliography

Brown, John Mason. *Dramatis Personae: A Retrospective Show.* New York: Viking Press, 1963. This comprehensive history of the American theater in the twentieth century also covers the long career of Marc Connelly in theater, radio, and Hollywood.

Connelly, Marc. *Voices Offstage: A Book of Memoirs.* Chicago: Holt, Rinehart and Winston, 1968. A short and witty autobiography by one of the United States' most prolific playwrights.

Daniel, Walter C. *"De Lawd": Richard B. Harrison and "The Green Pastures."* New York: Greenwood Press, 1986. In this volume, Daniel reviews African-American contributions to the American theater and the role of Connelly in stage history.

Nolan, Paul T. *Marc Connelly.* New York: Twayne, 1969. Nolan provides a concise but useful study of the colorful author and supplements his book with a useful bibliography.

Quinn, Arthur Hobson. *A History of the American Drama from the Civil War to the Present Day.* New York: Appleton-Century-Crofts, 1964. This standard account includes some material on Connelly and his era.

Ward W. Briggs

(Updated by *Peter C. Holloran*)

NOËL COWARD

Born: Teddington, England; December 16, 1899
Died: Port Royal, Jamaica; March 26, 1973

Principal drama

I'll Leave It to You, pr. 1919, pb. 1920; *Sirocco*, wr. 1921, pr., pb. 1927; *The Better Half*, pr. 1922 (one act); *The Young Idea*, pr. 1922, pb. 1924; *London Calling*, pr. 1923 (music and lyrics by Noël Coward and Ronald Jeans); *Weatherwise*, wr. 1923, pb. 1931, pr. 1932; *Fallen Angels*, pb. 1924, pr. 1925; *The Rat Trap*, pb. 1924, pr. 1926 (wr. 1918); *The Vortex*, pr. 1924, pb. 1925; *Easy Virtue*, pr. 1925, pb. 1926; *Hay Fever*, pr., pb. 1925; *On with the Dance*, pr. 1925; *The Queen Was in the Parlour*, pr., pb. 1926; *This Was a Man*, pr., pb. 1926; *Home Chat*, pr., pb. 1927; *The Marquise*, pr., pb. 1927; *This Year of Grace!*, pr. 1928, pb. 1929 (musical); *Bitter Sweet*, pr., pb. 1929 (operetta); *Private Lives*, pr., pb. 1930; *Some Other Private Lives*, pr. 1930, pb. 1931 (one act); *Cavalcade*, pr. 1931, pb. 1932; *Words and Music*, pr. 1932, pb. 1939 (musical); *Design for Living*, pr., pb. 1933; *Conversation Piece*, pr., pb. 1934; *Point Valaine*, pr., pb. 1936; *Tonight at 8:30*, pb. 1936 (3 volumes; a collective title for the following nine plays, which were designed to be presented in various combinations of three bills of three plays: *We Were Dancing*, pr. 1935; *The Astonished Heart*, pr. 1935; *Red Peppers*, pr. 1935; *Hands Across the Sea*, pr. 1935; *Fumed Oak*, pr. 1935; *Shadow Play*, pr. 1935; *Family Album*, pr. 1935; *Ways and Means*, pr. 1936; *Still Life*, pr. 1936); *Operette*, pr., pb. 1938; *Set to Music*, pr. 1939, pb. 1940 (musical); *Blithe Spirit*, pr., pb. 1941; *Present Laughter*, pr. 1942, pb. 1943; *This Happy Breed*, pr. 1942, pb. 1943; *Sigh No More*, pr. 1945 (musical); *Pacific 1860*, pr. 1946, pb. 1958 (musical); *Peace in Our Time*, pr., pb. 1947; *Ace of Clubs*, pr. 1950, pb. 1962; *Island Fling*, pr. 1951, pb. 1956; *Relative Values*, pr. 1951, pb. 1952; *Quadrille*, pr., pb. 1952; *After the Ball*, pr. 1954 (musical; based on Oscar Wilde's play *Lady Windermere's Fan*); *Nude with Violin*, pr. 1956, pb. 1957; *South Sea Bubble*, pr., pb. 1956; *Look After Lulu*, pr., pb. 1959; *Waiting in the Wings*, pr., pb. 1960; *High Spirits*, pr. 1961 (musical; based on his play *Blithe Spirit*); *Sail Away*, pr. 1961 (musical); *The Girl Who Came to Supper*, pr. 1963 (musical; based on Terence Rattigan's play *The Sleeping Prince*); *Suite in Three Keys: Come into the Garden Maude; Shadows of the Evening; A Song at Twilight*, pr., pb. 1966; *Cowardy Custard*, pr. 1972, pb. 1973 (also as *Cowardy Custard: The World of Noël Coward*); *Oh! Coward*, pr. 1972, pb. 1974 (also as *Oh Coward! A Musical Comedy Revue*); *Plays, One*, pb. 1979; *Plays, Two*, pb. 1979; *Plays, Three*, pb. 1979; *Plays, Four*, pb. 1979; *Plays, Five*, pb. 1983.

Other literary forms

Noël Coward was an extraordinarily prolific playwright, lyricist, and composer, writing more than fifty plays and musicals during his lifetime. He did not limit his literary endeavors solely to the drama, but ventured into other genres as well. These diversions into the realm of fiction, nonfiction, and poetry proved equally successful for him. In addition to his plays, Coward wrote three novels (two unpublished), several collections of short stories, satires, a book of verse, and several autobiographical works, *Present Indicative* (1937), *Middle East Diary* (1944), and *Future Indefinite* (1954).

Coward's versatility is also apparent in his original scripts for five films, his screenplays and adaptations of his hit plays, and his several essays on the modern theater which appeared in popular journals and in *The Times* of London and *The New York Times*. Like his plays, Coward's other works reveal his distinctive satiric style, sharp wit, and clever wordplay.

Achievements

In 1970, Coward was knighted by Queen Elizabeth II for "services rendered to the arts." The succinct phrasing of this commendation is as understated as some of Coward's best dialogue, considering his long and brilliant career in the theater. Coward wrote plays specifically designed to entertain the popular audience and to provide an amusing evening in the theater. Few of his plays champion a cause or promote a social issue. His most noteworthy achievement came in the writing of scores of fashionable comedies, revues, and "operettes" which were resounding successes on the English, American, and Continental stages and which continue to enjoy success today. For this insistence on writing light comedy, he received substantial criticism, and several of his works were brusquely dismissed as "fluff" by critics. These same plays, however, never wanted for an audience, even during the most turbulent, politically restless years.

Coward came to be associated with the 1920's in England in much the same way that F. Scott Fitzgerald was identified with the Jazz Age in America. Whereas Fitzgerald seriously examined the moral failings of his prosperous characters, however, Coward treated them lightly. His plays chronicle the foibles, fashions, and affairs of the English upper class and provide satirical vignettes of the social elite. Coward's life and work reflect the same urbane persona; indeed, he wrote his best parts for himself. Coward's world was that of the idle rich, of cocktails, repartee, and a tinge of modern decadence; this image was one he enjoyed and actively promoted until his death.

For all their popularity, most of Coward's plays are not memorable, save for *Private Lives*, *Blithe Spirit*, *Design for Living*, and possibly one or two others, yet his song lyrics have become part of the English cultural heritage. "Mad Dogs and Englishmen," from *Words and Music*, achieved immortality when its famous line "Mad dogs and Englishmen go out in the mid-day sun" was included in *The Oxford Dictionary of Quotations*.

Coward's reputation rests less on the literary merits of his works and more on the man, who as an accomplished actor, entertainer, and raconteur displayed enormous resilience during his five decades in the public eye. One of the obvious difficulties in producing a Coward play is finding actors who are able to handle the dialogue with the aplomb of "the master." What made Coward's plays successful was not so much a strong text, but virtuoso performances by Gertrude Lawrence, Jane Cowl, Alfred Lunt and Lynn Fontanne, and Coward himself. The public continues to be amused by his works in revivals, especially when performed by actors, such as Maggie Smith, who can transmit Coward's urbane humor to today's audiences.

Biography

Noël Pierce Coward was born December 16, 1899. He was the child of Arthur Sabin Coward and Violet Agnes Veitch, who married late in life after meeting in a church choir. Coward's family on his father's side was very talented musically. They helped nurture the natural virtuosity of the child, instilling in him a lifelong love of music.

Since his birthday was so close to Christmas, Coward always received one present to satisfy both occasions, but on December 16, his mother would take him to the theater as a special treat. He first attended a matinee at the age of four, never realizing he would spend the next seventy years of his life in service to the dramatic muse. As he grew older, he found these junkets to the theater more and more fascinating, and upon returning home would rush to the piano and play by ear the songs from the production he had just seen.

Coward made his first public appearance, singing and accompanying himself on the piano, at a concert held at Miss Willington's School. Though obviously a very talented child, Coward's precocity did not carry over to his formal education. At best, his schooling was sporadic. For a time, he attended the Chapel Royal School at Clapham in hopes of becoming a member of the prestigious Chapel Royal Choir. Failing his audition as a choir member, he was taken from school and did not attend any educational institution for six months, at which time he was sent to school in London. He was ten years old.

Coward was an incorrigible, strong-willed child, given to tantrums when he did not get his way. These traits, inherited from both sides of his argumentative family, are evident in his characters, and each of his plays contains a rousing altercation scene. He was indulged by his mother, who became the stereotypical stage mother during his early years, and it was at his mother's insistence that he began attending Miss Janet Thomas' Dancing Academy in addition to his regular school in London. Soon, Miss Thomas' school usurped the position of importance held by traditional academic fare, and Coward became a child performer.

Coward's first professional engagement, and that which launched his long career, was on January 28, 1911, in a children's play, *The Goldfish*. After this appearance, he was sought after for children's roles by other professional theaters. He was featured in several productions with Sir Charles Hawtrey, a light comedian, whom Coward idolized and to whom he virtually apprenticed himself until he was twenty. It was from Hawtrey that Coward learned comic acting techniques and playwriting. He worked in everything from ballets to music halls and made it a point to study the more experienced performers to learn to "catch" the audience quickly. This skill was one he actively drew upon in the writing of his plays.

At the tender age of twelve, Coward met one of the actresses who would help contribute to his overwhelming success, Gertrude Lawrence; she was then fifteen and a child performer as well. The occasional acting team of Coward and Lawrence would become synonymous with polished, sophisticated comedy during the 1920's, 1930's, and 1940's.

When he was fifteen, Coward was invited to stay at the country estate of Mrs. Astley Cooper. This stay, and subsequent visits, influenced his life markedly in two ways: He grew to know intimately the manners and mores of the upper class, and, through Mrs. Cooper, he came to meet Gladys Calthrop, who was to become his lifelong friend and the designer for his productions.

Coward began his writing career when he was sixteen by writing songs and selling them for distribution. He turned his hand to playwriting when he was seventeen and found that he was very good at writing dialogue. Success came quite early to Coward. He was already accepted as an accomplished actor on the London stage when he began writing. By 1919, his play *I'll Leave It to You* was produced in the West End with Coward in the leading role. One of the idiosyncrasies of Coward's writing is that often he wrote "whacking good parts" for himself or for people he knew. Some of his best plays are essentially vehicles for his own talents or those of Gertrude Lawrence and later of the Lunts.

I'll Leave It to You met with moderate success, and Coward received great praise from critics for his playwriting abilities, although Sir Neville Cardus, writing in the *Manchester Guardian*, faulted the play for its narrow focus on the world of the idle rich. This criticism dogged Coward throughout his career.

Coward went to New York for the first time in 1921 and arrived virtually penniless. He sold three satires to *Vanity Fair* in order to support himself. Though he may have begun the 1920's in penury, Coward's position as the most popular playwright in the English theater became secure during this decade. In 1924, *The Vortex* was produced in London. Coward's most important serious play, *The Vortex* broke with English theatrical tradition in its choice of subject matter: drug addiction. This Ibsenesque approach to a problem created quite a sensation. It was hailed by many critics as an important play but also found dissenters who labeled it "filth" and "dustbin drama."

In late 1927, Coward purchased 139 acres in Kent called Goldenhurst Farm. This was the first residence he used as a retreat to escape the glitter of the stage. Eventually, he would own others in Jamaica, Paris, Geneva, and London. The years from 1928 to 1934 are regarded by many as Coward's "golden years." His string of successes during this period include some of his best and most famous plays and revues: *This Year of Grace!*, *Bitter Sweet*, *Private Lives*, *Cavalcade*, *Words and Music*, *Design for Living*, and *Conversation Piece*. According to Coward, in a letter written to his mother, *Bitter Sweet* was the only show that played to capacity houses in New York during the stock market crash of 1929. By the 1930's, the opening of a Coward play in London was regularly attended by royalty and other prominent socialites.

Coward took his success and the responsibility of fame seriously. When asked to aid the Actors' Orphanage, he did so willingly and subsequently became president of the organization, a position he retained from 1934 to 1956.

After World War II, Coward fell from grace with many critics, who regarded him as being past his literary prime. The year 1949-1950 proved the lowest point in his career as he received poor reviews for his plays and scathing reviews for his film, *The Astonished Heart*. The drama was changing during these restless years that would produce playwrights such as John Osborne, and Coward was momentarily out of step with the times. He turned to the writing of fiction and produced several short stories and his autobiographical work *Future Indefinite*.

By the late 1950's, audiences were once again in love with Coward. His plays, revues, and nightclub appearances were extremely successful. The critics, however, remained vitriolic, but their rancor failed to dim the enthusiasm of the general theatergoing public, who clamored for more Coward plays. In 1969, there was a seventieth birthday tribute to Coward in London which lasted a full week. On January 1, 1970, Coward's name appeared on the Queen's New Year's list as a Knight Bachelor, for services rendered to the arts. For the remaining years of his life, he was Sir Noël Coward. In the same year, he was awarded a special Tony Award by the American theater for Distinguished Achievement in the Theatre. In 1972, he received an honorary Doctor of Letters from the University of Sussex.

Coward died of a heart attack in Jamaica on March 26, 1973, bringing to an end a career of more than sixty years in the theater. The most lasting tribute awarded to Coward is the continued success which meets revivals of his plays and musicals. Coward created a mystique about himself during his lifetime, and this intangible quality of wit and sophistication has become part of the Coward legend, which has become a part of the colorful heritage of the theater.

Analysis

Betty Comden and Adolph Green observe of Noël Coward in Roddy McDowall's book *Double Exposure* (1966), "To us he represented class . . . and we don't mean that in a superficial sense. We mean the highest of wit, of style, of discipline, and craftsmanship." As a playwright, composer, lyricist, producer, director, author, and actor, Coward spent his life entertaining the public. This he did with a flair, sophistication, and polish that are not readily found in twentieth century drama. He wrote farce, high comedy, domestic and patriotic melodramas, musical comedies, and revues. His plays were popular fare in England and America for years because Coward recognized that the "great public" for which he wrote his plays wanted, above all, to be entertained.

All of Coward's plays fall into easily recognizable stylized patterns. Essentially, Coward wrote modern comedies of manners which are as reflective of twentieth century mores and sentiments as their Restoration forebears were of those in the seventeenth century. For the most part, his plays are set in drawing rooms and usually have a couple involved in a love relationship as the central characters. He draws heavily on his theatrical background and populates his plays with theatrical and artistic characters. These temperamental personages allow Coward to involve them easily in the constant bickering and verbal fencing that came to be the trademarks of a Coward play. Each of his characters vies to get the upper hand over the others. Arguments are central to his work, and much of his humor relies on sophisticated insults. Coward's dialogue bitingly exposes hypocrites and the petty games played by the upper class; his plays parody Mayfair society mercilessly. Unfortunately, his plays involve little else. There is little motivation of character, less development of theme, and what thin remnant of plot remains is swept along in the incessant bantering of the characters. Robert Greacen, referring to *Fumed Oak*, remarked that "an observant foreigner might sit through the entire play . . . and simply hear people talking and believe that no action was taking place at all." Such statements apply to most of Coward's plays.

This criticism reveals both the strongest and the weakest aspects of Coward's theater. He was capable of writing brilliant, naturalistic dialogue with an astonishing economy. In spite of this enormous talent for writing dialogue, however, little happens in his plays to advance the plot. Most of his plays remain structurally flawed, relying heavily on the use of *deus ex machina* and coincidence for plot resolutions.

Thematically, Coward's comedies examine true love, adulterous affairs, and domestic upheavals. His more serious plays focus on a variety of topics, including drug addiction, infidelity, and patriotism. The few patriotic plays he attempted strongly support solid middle-class values and promote a stereotyped image of the stoical Englishman.

Though his works appear to have identifiable themes, they lack a thesis. Coward's plays realistically depict modern characters in absorbing situations, but the characters are not as fully developed as the situations in which they find themselves. Their motivations remain obscured. Even in the serious plays, his position on his subject is never clearly revealed. Most of his serious dramas fail because he never brings the moment to a crisis, and so his plays end anticlimactically. According to Milton Levin, Coward's plays "raise no questions, they provide few critical footholds, they simply ask to be praised for what they are, sparkling caprices."

Generally, the success of Coward's plays depended on the ability of the actors to carry his rapier-sharp dialogue. He freely admitted tailoring choice roles to his talents and those of his friends. Coward and Gertrude Lawrence in *Private Lives*, Coward and the Lunts in *Design for Living*, Coward with Beatrice Lillie in *Blithe Spirit* mark legendary moments in theatrical history that cannot be replicated. When criticizing drama, one must consider the text in production. It is this consideration that elevates the relatively weak scripts of Coward's plays to modern classics.

One finds embodied in Coward a theatrical trinity of actor, playwright, and producer. The inability to separate completely one from the other in studying his works contributes to the mystique which surrounds the man. Rarely are his works found in academic anthologies of the genre, but the imprint of his productions is still discernible in the theater today.

Design for Living was the end result of a plan by Coward, Alfred Lunt, and Lynn Fontanne to act in a play together, written specifically for them. They originally conceived of this idea in the early 1920's, and the gestation period required for Coward actually to write and produce the play lasted eleven years. *Design for Living* scrutinizes a free-spirited and occasionally painful *ménage à trois* comprising Gilda, an interior decorator, Otto, a painter, and Leo, a playwright. The most striking quality of the play is its completely amoral stance on marriage, fidelity, friendship, and sexual relations. Pangs of conscience are fleeting in these characters as their relationships as friends and lovers become apparent to one another and to the audience.

It is the amorality of the characters, rather than a perceived immorality, that has provoked criticism of this play. Coward forms no conclusions and passes no judgment: The play ends with the three characters embracing and laughing wildly on a sofa, and the audience is provided no clue as to how they should judge these amorous individuals. They are asked to watch and accept without being given a resolution to the plot. Most of the criticism directed at the production resulted from a misunderstanding of the title on the part of the critics. Coward intended his title to be ironic. It was taken to be an admonition that the Bohemian life-style depicted onstage was not merely acceptable but was actually preferable to conventional ways as a "design for living."

Design for Living was a vehicle for the formidable talents of Coward and the Lunts. The dialogue is quick and sharp as the three characters alternately pair off, argue, and reunite. The theme stressed most strongly in this play, and the one which offers its most redemptive qualities, is that of friendship. Gilda, Otto, and Leo value their mutual companionship, but their active libidos complicate their relationships. *Design for Living* was judged to be "unpleasant" by the critics, but it enjoyed a phenomenal success with audiences in England and America.

Private Lives, considered one of Coward's best plays, "leaves a lot to be desired," by the author's own admission. The protagonists, Amanda and Elyot, are divorced and meet again while both are honeymooning with their new spouses. Their former affection for each other is rekindled, and they abandon their unsuspecting spouses and escape to Paris. Here, they are reminded of what it was in their personalities that prompted them to seek a divorce. The scene is complicated by the arrival of the jilted spouses, who come seeking reconciliation, but who eventually are spurned as Amanda and Elyot, after arguing violently, leave together, presumably to lead a life of adversarial bliss.

Amanda and Elyot are interesting, fairly well-drawn characters; these roles were written with Gertrude Lawrence and Coward in mind. The secondary characters, the spouses, Victor and Sibyl, are two-dimensional and only provide a surface off which to bounce the stinging repartee of the reunited couple. Coward himself has described *Private Lives* as a "reasonably well-constructed duologue for two performers with a couple of extra puppets thrown in to assist the plot and to provide contrast."

Coward was a highly developed product of the 1920's and the 1930's and of the social milieu he frequented, and, to a not inconsiderable extent, the current popularity of his work originates in the nostalgic hunger of contemporary audiences for an age more verbally sophisticated and carefree than their own. Nevertheless, at their best, Coward's plays continue to sparkle with their author's lively sense of wit, talent for dramatic dialogue and construction, and genius for the neat twist in dramatic action. These significant talents make Coward's theater instructive as well as delightful.

Other major works

NOVEL: *Pomp and Circumstance*, 1960.

SHORT FICTION: *Terribly Intimate Portraits*, 1922; *Chelsea Buns*, 1925; *Spangled Unicorn*, 1932; *To Step Aside*, 1939; *Star Quality: Six Stories*, 1951; *The Collected Short Stories*, 1962; *Pretty Polly Barlow and Other Sto-*

ries, 1964; *Bon Voyage and Other Stories*, 1967; *The Complete Stories of Noël Coward*, 1985.

POETRY: *Not Yet the Dodo*, 1967; *Noël Coward: Collected Verse*, 1984.

NONFICTION: *Present Indicative*, 1937; *Australia Visited*, 1941; *Middle East Diary*, 1944; *Future Indefinite*, 1954; *The Noël Coward Diaries*, 1982; *Autobiography*, 1986.

SCREENPLAYS: *Bitter Sweet*, 1933; *In Which We Serve*, 1942; *This Happy Breed*, 1944; *Blithe Spirit*, 1946; *Brief Encounter*, 1946; *The Astonished Heart*, 1949.

TELEPLAY: *Post Mortem*, 1931.

MISCELLANEOUS: *The Lyrics of Noel Coward*, 1965; *The Noël Coward Song Book*, 1980; *Out in the Midday Sun: The Paintings of Noël Coward*, 1988.

Bibliography

Briers, Richard. *Coward and Company.* London: Robson Books, 1987. A short, well-illustrated biography of the English actor, playwright, composer, director, producer, and bon vivant.

Lahr, John. *Coward the Playwright.* London: Methuen, 1982. A concise but thoughtful evaluation of Coward as a writer.

Lesley, Cole. *Remembered Laughter: The Life of Noël Coward.* New York: Alfred A. Knopf, 1976. This volume provides a thorough study of Coward's colorful life in the London theater. It was published in London under the title *The Life of Noël Coward*, also in 1976.

Levin, Milton. *Noël Coward.* Boston: Twayne, 1989. This short but updated biography of the playwright contains a useful bibliography.

Morley, Sheridan. *A Talent to Amuse: A Biography of Noël Coward.* London: Heinemann, 1969. The best and most thoughtful biography, written before Coward's death in 1973.

Susan Duffy
(Updated by *Peter C. Holloran*)

MART CROWLEY

Born: Vicksburg, Mississippi; August 21, 1935

Principal drama
The Boys in the Band, pr., pb. 1968; *Remote Asylum*, pr. 1970; *A Breeze from the Gulf*, pr. 1973, pb. 1974.

Other literary forms
Mart Crowley is known primarily for his plays. He wrote the screenplay for a 1970 film adaptation of *The Boys in the Band*.

Achievements
Crowley brought the subject of male homosexuality into the open in the American theater with his 1968 comedy-drama *The Boys in the Band*. His plays are characterized by a clashing mix of personality types and a keen comic sense for one-liners. The significance of Crowley's work rests entirely on his first play and its introduction of a once-taboo subject. The play and the subsequent film adaptation of it are important milestones in the history of gay activism in the United States. Unlike Tennessee Williams, William Inge, and Edward Albee, who kept the topic of homosexual passions on the periphery of their work, Crowley made the initial leap which openly established gay drama and unapologetically linked his own life with his writing. The playwright's outrageously comical dialogue and his daring display of his own emotional failures are the most impressive and perhaps the most enduring of his contributions to the stage.

Biography
Martino Crowley was born in Vicksburg, Mississippi, on August 21, 1935. Crowley's parents were conservative and religious, and they scrupulously brought up Mart, their only child, in the teachings of the Roman Catholic Church, enrolling him in a parochial high school in Vicksburg. His father, an Irishman from the Midwest, owned a pool hall called Crowley's Smokehouse, which bore the motto "Where all good fellows meet." As a child, Crowley was asthmatic and sickly, a condition which changed, he claims, immediately after his departure from Vicksburg. An avid filmgoer and starstruck reader of Hollywood gossip magazines since early childhood, he left home in the early 1950's, moving to Los Angeles, where he took a number of low-paying jobs in order to be near the motion-picture studios. His father, who had cherished the hope that his only son should attend Notre Dame, finally compromised and convinced Mart to attend Catholic University of America in Washington, D.C. After two years there, Crowley, unhappy with the conser-

vative social atmosphere in Washington, returned to Hollywood and began working on a degree in art at the University of California, Los Angeles, hoping to become a scenic designer in films. Crowley returned to Catholic University not long afterward and worked in the university theater. At one point, he collaborated with fellow collegian James Rado, later one of the writers of the rock musical *Hair* (which ran concurrently in New York with Crowley's hit *The Boys in the Band* in 1968), and the two of them produced a revue sketch. Crowley also worked in summer-stock theater in Vermont.

After his graduation from Catholic University in 1957, Crowley briefly considered joining the Foreign Service but moved back to Southern California instead, where he wrote a number of unproduced scripts for motion pictures and television. He took jobs with various film production companies, working on such films as *Butterfield 8* (1960) and *Splendor in the Grass* (1961). He also worked as a scriptwriter in the early 1960's for several television production companies. The popular film star Natalie Wood, whom Crowley met while both were working on *Splendor in the Grass*, hired him as a private secretary in 1964, a position he held until 1966. During this time, he wrote a screen adaptation of Dorothy Baker's novel *Cassandra at the Wedding* (1962) expressly for Wood and French director Serge Bourguignon. The film was never produced. Ridden with anxiety and depression, Crowley moved to Rome for a winter, staying with film star Robert Wagner and his wife, Marion.

In 1967, Paramount Studios completed a film from an original screenplay by Crowley entitled *Fade In*. The project was a hectic and disappointing experience for the young writer, and after all of his effort, the studio did not release the film. After six months of rest and psychoanalysis to cope with this ego-flattening experience, Crowley got the idea to write a play about homosexual friends at a birthday party. (His notes on the theme of homosexuality, including fragments of dialogue and character sketches, were begun as early as 1959.) Crowley finished the play, *The Boys in the Band*, in five weeks during the summer of 1967 while he was house-sitting in the Beverly Hills home of performer Diana Lynn. The agent he subsequently contacted about the script replied that although the play was very good, she did not believe the American stage was ready for a drama almost exclusively about homosexual men. She nevertheless sent a copy of the play to producer Richard Barr, who liked it and decided to produce it at his Playwrights Unit workshop. Robert Moore, an actor who had known Crowley at Catholic University and in summer stock, expressed interest in making his debut as a stage director with the play. More difficult, however, was the task of finding performers willing to be cast in the play. A number of actors read the play and liked it but refused to risk their professional images by performing homosexual characters onstage. The play was finally cast with an ensemble of largely unknown performers.

The Boys in the Band first appeared at the Vandam Theatre in January of

1968. Three months later, the play made its debut on the New York stage at Theatre Four. It was a success both at the box office and with most of the theater reviewers. Apart from viciously homophobic reviews from critics such as Martin Duberman and John Simon, the reviewers judged the play for its composition and production, rather than for its subject matter. Surprisingly, the play became controversial not so much in the heterosexual as in the homosexual community. The source of the contention may be inferred from the emphasis and wording of some of the favorable mainstream reviews, which commented on the play's portrayal of the "tragic" or even "freakish" aspects of the "homosexual life-style." Such generalizations were not, however, necessarily invited by the play. The production ran for more than one thousand performances in New York and was produced with great success in London, in regional theaters across the United States well into the 1970's, and as a 1970 film featuring the original Off-Broadway cast directed by William Friedkin. The play's director, Robert Moore, won a Drama Desk Award, and Cliff Gorman, who played the role of Emory, received an Obie Award (for performances in Off-Broadway theaters). The play was also included in several lists and anthologies of "best plays" of the 1960's. Many persons accounted for the play's success by observing that it offered the homosexual community a chance to see and hear itself represented onstage and the heterosexual community a chance to eavesdrop upon the former. By the time the play had been made into a motion picture, however, a considerable portion of the gay public objected to the play on the grounds that it made homosexuality seem like a form of neurosis characterized by religious guilt, loneliness, and self-loathing.

The year the film adaptation of *The Boys in the Band* was released, an earlier play by Crowley, *Remote Asylum*, was produced in California to universally unfavorable reviews. Opening at the end of 1970 at the Ahmanson Theatre in Los Angeles, *Remote Asylum* was not subsequently produced in New York. A third play, *A Breeze from the Gulf*, opened at the Eastside Playhouse in New York in October of 1973 to a somewhat better response. The writer's most intimate play, *A Breeze from the Gulf*, though praised for its competent writing and acting, lacked the audience appeal and the ability to stir up controversy which had made his first play a success. Its run was scarcely longer than *Remote Asylum*'s, but it took second place for a New York Drama Critics Circle Award. Crowley thereafter retired from playwriting and returned to television.

In 1986, he began writing and adapting novels, such as James Kirkwood's *There Must Be a Pony* (1986), for television. According to interviews, he has also explored some areas for new theatrical productions.

The success of Crowley's work signaled a social change that allowed artistic discussion of the gay personality in the hands of more competent playwrights, as with Michael Cristofer's *Shadow Box* (pr. 1975, pb. 1978),

Lanford Wilson's *Fifth of July* (pr., pb. 1978), and Martin Sherman's *Bent* (pr., pb. 1979). Contemporary plays dealing more directly with the gay experience, such as Harvey Fierstein's *Torch Song Trilogy* (pr. 1979, pr. 1981) and Larry Kramer's *The Normal Heart* (pr., pb. 1985), about the acquired immune deficiency syndrome (AIDS), owe much to Crowley's groundbreaking achievement.

Analysis

Mart Crowley's plays are not entirely autobiographical, but, as the playwright points out in an interview with Mel Gussow, "Any fool knows you have to live through something to write about it." As a device for giving his plays immediacy, however, each play contains a character named Michael, whom the audience is invited to let stand for the playwright himself. Crowley's persona is spared little in the psychological flayings which are characteristic of the writer's work. Contrary to what one might expect of an autobiographical protagonist, Michael/Mart does not embody positive, ideal, or necessarily healthy outlooks on life. In all of Crowley's plays, but especially in *The Boys in the Band*, Michael is characterized as self-pitying, debt-ridden, guilt-stricken, and vindictive; a failure as a friend, son, lover, and artist; a victim of excessive, intense self-scrutiny. The other characters stand in contrast to this negative image, or, to be more accurate perhaps, their personalities are in tension with his, caught in a web which alternately feeds and falls prey to Michael's repression, egotism, and anger.

Each play divulges a different part of the author's life, and consequently each play presents a separate but related galaxy of affection and social belonging. As they were produced, the plays run in reverse chronological order. *The Boys in the Band* presents a thirtyish Michael in the company of his homosexual friends and former lovers in his rented lower-Manhattan apartment. The setting for *Remote Asylum* is a run-down mansion in Acapulco, and its *dramatis personae* include a bizarre assortment of misfits and outcasts surrounding an aging female film star. The characters abuse one another in a sort of shark frenzy of emotions, and the result is a more vicious, more bleak version of Lanford Wilson's multicharactered comedies, with Crowley's emphasis falling more definitely upon decadence. *A Breeze from the Gulf* presents Michael from age fifteen to age twenty-five. It is the most intimate of the three plays. Its only characters are Michael, his mother, Loraine, and his father, Teddy. Most of the dramatic action occurs in their family home in Mississippi, though the stage setting is only suggestive, avoiding naturalism or a sense of definite place. The play is not a simple exercise in nostalgia. The Connelly family is pathogenic; each of the three members is both victim and abuser of the other two. The play does not idealize bygone times. Its focus, which becomes gradually evident in the first act, is the painful psychological interdependency of son, father, and mother. The second act portrays a scene out of the playwright's life to which Crowley's previous two plays had only referred: the father's dying confession in the arms of his son on the floor of a hospital ward. The impact of this scene in the context of all the others is to assert that family relationships can be, and often are, morbidly corruptive to the individual human spirit.

Of the three plays Crowley produced within half a decade, only one, *The Boys in the Band*, earned a reputation for its writer. Twenty years after its New York opening, the play was still regarded as a landmark (historical, if not ideological) of gay drama. Its chronological proximity to the Stonewall Riots of June, 1969, lends added significance to its first production. Critic James W. Carlsen made the play the dividing point in the dramatic representation of gay men on the stage, his subtitles demarcating "Pre–*The Boys in the Band* perceptions" and "Post–*The Boys in the Band* Portraits." The changing attitudes toward homosexuality that the play helped to inspire turned eventually against the neurotic and self-demeaning "boys" in the drama. Without making an undue claim to "literary greatness" for the play, it is possible to defend it against its detractors, whose objections are primarily ideological, by asserting its social importance as a vehicle for making gay men more visible, and thus more vocal and politically viable, in American society. While the play does reinforce certain stereotypes of male homosexuality in the characters of Michael and Emory, *The Boys in the Band* also includes a number of other "types" which were hitherto unrepresented on the stage: The gay man as athletic, virile, capable of both fidelity and promiscuity, self-knowing, "ordinary," or "masculine" appeared in this play for the first time. The play also debunked a number of flattering truisms about homosexuals, such as that all gay men are more sensitive, tasteful, or witty than heterosexual men.

The focus of most of the criticism the play has received is its central character, Michael, who experiences more than his share of bitterness and self-loathing because of his homosexuality. As his friend Harold points out to him at the end of the play, Michael's problem is not his homosexual nature but his failure to accept himself as he is. Psychologists call this type of homosexuality "ego-dystonic," and the condition is considered a treatable psychological problem. It is thus possible to interpret Michael's personality as indicative of a real psychological disorder and not as symbolic of an inherent or typical maladjustment of the homosexual mind. That it is not the latter is evident in that other characters, such as Harold, Hank, and Larry, do not appear to suffer from the same self-hatred, and in that Michael's identity problem is explicitly compared to Bernard's, who struggles with feelings of inferiority because he is black. The charge that the play reinforces the prejudice that all gay men are really unhappy and that homosexual relationships are spurious is largely accurate, but it fails to take into account the tremendous step that was taken by the playwright in presenting even a somewhat compromising portrait of gay culture.

The Boys in the Band falls into a category of mid-twentieth century American drama sometimes labeled "comedy of exacerbation": An assortment of characters reveal themselves to themselves and to one another through some sort of excruciating ordeal, often, ironically, a party game. Whatever device is used, the veneer of each participant is stripped in order to bare the fact that the basis for much of his existence is rationalization, repression, or fantasy. The characters' relationships with one another flicker between love and loathing, and the repartee is savagely witty and unnervingly accurate. The epitome of this style of drama is Edward Albee's comedy-drama *Who's Afraid of Virginia Woolf?* (pr. 1962), to which *The Boys in the Band* is often compared. Albee's "Get-the-Guests" scene is structurally similar to Crowley's second act. In both, the device of a game is used in order to trick one of the participants into making a painful admission. Yet Michael's obsessive attempt to make his college friend Alan admit that he had a homosexual affair with a mutual friend fails and, like George and Martha's "game," backfires on him, revealing his own vulnerability and sadness.

The least that can be said for Crowley's contribution to the American theater is, sadly, also the most that can be said for it: His play *The Boys in the Band* opened up the subject of homosexuality to dramatic treatment. Though less positive than its successors, the play is no less forthright, and dramas such as Harvey Fierstein's *Torch Song Trilogy* and Jane Chambers' *Last Summer at Bluefish Cove* (pr. 1981, pb. 1982) would perhaps have never been were it not for Crowley's timely and trailblazing effort.

Other major works

SCREENPLAY: *The Boys in the Band*, 1970.

TELEPLAYS: *There Must Be a Pony*, 1986 (from the novel by James Kirkwood); *Bluegrass*, 1988; *People Like Us*, 1990.

Bibliography

Carlsen, James W. "Images of the Gay Male in Contemporary Drama." In *Gayspeak: Gay Male and Lesbian Communication*, edited by James W. Chesebro. New York: Pilgrim Press, 1981. A serious examination of the effects of Crowley's play on social perceptions of homosexuals in the early 1970's, and of subsequent changes in the dramatic interpretations of gay characters, such as in Lanford Wilson's *Fifth of July* (pr. 1978) and Martin Sherman's *Bent* (pr., pb. 1979).

DeGaetani, John L. *A Search for a Postmodern Theater: Interviews with Contemporary Playwrights.* New York: Greenwood Press, 1991. Discusses *The Boys in the Band*, especially Michael's Catholicism; Crowley notes that the "Catholic Church still [1991] teaches that homosexual practices are a sin." Good update on Crowley's views on gay rights, homophobia, Cardinal John Joseph O'Connor, and AIDS.

Duberman, Martin. Review of *The Boys in the Band. Partisan Review* 35 (Summer, 1968): 418. Surprisingly nonsupportive, maybe a little jealous, Duberman attacks Crowley's craftsmanship, calling him "essentially a gag writer, a man with a brilliant flair for one-liners." Sees his treatment of the gay theme as "a retrogressive more than a forward step for the theater."

Gussow, Mel. "The New Playwrights." *Newsweek*, May 20, 1968, 115. Looks at Israel Horovitz and Ed Bullins as well as Crowley, letting the playwright speak for himself: "One has so little time. There's no point wasting it on lying." Of *The Boys in the Band*, Crowley says, "It's a play about self-destruction, about being one's own worst enemy."

Simon, John. Review of *The Boys in the Band. Commonweal* 88 (May 31, 1968): 335-336. Lists the stereotypes without acknowledging the three-dimensionality, then admits "a certain pioneering sensationalism, some genuine merit, and enough surface polish to achieve a success it almost deserves." Distancing himself by overintellectualizing the real theater experience, Simon hurries his judgment here.

Joseph Marohl
(Updated by *Thomas J. Taylor*)

JOHN CROWNE

Born: Shropshire, England; c. 1640
Died: London, England; April, 1712

Principal drama

Juliana: Or, The Princess of Poland, pr., pb. 1671; *The History of Charles the Eighth of France: Or, The Invasion of Naples by the French*, pr. 1671, pb. 1672; *Calisto: Or, The Chaste Nymph*, pr., pb. 1675 (music by Nicholas Staggins); *The Country Wit*, pb. 1675, pr. 1676; *The Destruction of Jerusalem by Titus Vespasian, Parts I and II*, pr., pb. 1677; *The Ambitious Statesman: Or, The Loyal Favorite*, pr., pb. 1679; *Thyestes*, pr., pb. 1681; *City Politiques*, pr., pb. 1683; *Sir Courtly Nice: Or, It Cannot Be*, pr., pb. 1685 (adaptation of Agustín Moreto y Cabaña's comedy *No puede ser: O, No puede ser guardar una mujer*); *Darius, King of Persia*, pr., pb. 1688; *The English Friar: Or, The Town Sparks*, pr., pb. 1690; *Regulus*, pr. 1692, pb. 1694; *The Married Beau: Or, The Curious Impertinent*, pr., pb. 1694; *Caligula*, pr., pb. 1698; *The Dramatic Works of John Crowne*, pb. 1872-1874 (4 volumes; James Maidment and W. H. Logan, editors); *The Comedies of John Crowne*, pb. 1984 (B. J. McMullin, editor).

Other literary forms

John Crowne is remembered primarily for his plays, although he also wrote some verse and a novel, *Pandion and Amphigenia: Or, The History of the Coy Lady of Thessalis* (1665).

Achievements

Crowne was one of many playwrights who flourished in the small but intense theatrical world of Restoration London. In some ways, he is the archetypal dramatist of the time. He wrote to gain royal favor and to advance socially; he wrote in several genres to satisfy the taste of his aristocratic audience: court masques, historical tragedy, heroic tragedy, comedy of wit, and tragicomedy. Crowne's plays commented, directly and indirectly, on contemporary political and social issues. Despite the attention to relevance, Crowne patterned his plays on the best models: Seneca, William Shakespeare, and Jean Racine in tragedy; Lope de Vega and Molière in comedy. That Crowne's career spanned a quarter of a century suggests that he was popular and skillful, and an important playwright.

From the dramatic variety of the time, two genres emerge as characteristically Restoration. The first is heroic tragedy. John Dryden was the preeminent practitioner of the form in plays such as *All for Love* and *The Conquest of Granada by the Spaniards*. Crowne is somewhat beneath Dryden's level of achievement. Lacking Dryden's skill in poetry and subtlety in psychological conflict, Crowne successfully created larger-than-life heroes and placed them amid spectacular action.

The second genre is the comedy of wit. Here again, Crowne ranks immediately below the best writers, such as Sir George Etherege and William Wycherley. Though somewhat weak in plotting, Crowne excelled in creating ingenious situations, introducing farcical stage business, and portraying eccentric *dramatis personae*—the sort good character actors very much like to play.

Though his tragedies are badly outdated by their idealism about monarchy and their relevance to Restoration politics, his comedies are less so. Several were revived occassionally in the 1700's. The gem among them is *Sir Courtly Nice*, which remained a staple of the eighteenth century theater and is refreshingly amusing still.

Biography

John Crowne was the son of William Crowne, who fought on the Parliamentary side in the English Civil War. In 1657, he accompanied his father to America, and while the elder Crowne established a proprietorship in Nova Scotia province, young Crowne enrolled in Harvard College. William Crowne's claim to Nova Scotia was made doubtful by a partner's perfidy and by the Restoration of Charles II; thus, in 1660 John Crowne accompanied his father to London, where they sought royal protection for the proprietorship. In the meantime, Crowne earned a living by becoming a gentleman-usher to an elderly lady and by writing a prose romance in the style of Sir Philip Sidney's *Arcadia* (1590). The family's hopes for reclaiming the proprietorship ended in 1667 when Charles II ceded Nova Scotia to the French.

Most scholars agree that Crowne wrote plays in order to provide an income and to secure Charles II's royal favor that might compensate the family for its lost lands. Crowne succeeded in the first goal but not in the second. For fourteen years (1671-1685), Crowne strove mightily to please Charles and his court. He wrote plays virtually on command, often following the king's advice for themes, characters, or Continental models to imitate. Crowne's dramas in these years are clearly Royalist in sentiment: They articulate aristocratic values, and they defend Charles against his enemies. Unfortunately for Crowne, Charles had more people who sought favors than he had resources with which to favor them.

After Charles's death in 1685, Crowne continued to support himself by his pen. He wrote, saw produced, and had published six plays in the next thirteen years. By the late 1690's, however, his health was failing; he was plagued by what he described as "a distemper, which seated itself in my head, and threatened me with an epilepsy." Crowne secured an annual pension from Queen Anne which lasted until 1706. After that, it is unclear how he was able to live; presumably, he resided in poverty and went unremarked by a new generation. In 1712, he died.

Analysis

John Crowne wrote seven tragedies and five comedies, frequently repeating character-types, plot devices, and thematic concerns from play to play. His method and his achievement can be best understood by a close analysis of three plays. *The Destruction of Jerusalem by Titus Vespasian* was his most popular tragedy and remains a good example of the peculiar type of Restoration tragedy called "heroic drama." In *Sir Courtly Nice*, Crowne's most successful comedy of wit, clever men and women of fashion compete with one another in wordplay and intriguing. *City Politiques* is unlike Crowne's other comedies; it relies on farce and on the ridicule of specific contemporary personalities for its impact, but even the modern reader who does not understand the political allusions can appreciate Crowne's ability to keep the stage filled with interesting characters and action.

Like Restoration tragedies in general, *The Destruction of Jerusalem by Titus Vespasian* interweaves complex love plots and complicated political plots. The complexities of love Crowne borrowed from the same source that all of his fellow dramatists used: French romances and tragedies of the early and middle 1600's. The political complications Crowne took from the world around him. The restoration of the monarchy in 1660 had neither ended the competition for power between the king and Parliament nor stilled the loud debate over whether the English throne should be occupied by a Protestant or a Catholic monarch.

Crowne's *The Destruction of Jerusalem by Titus Vespasian* was patterned after John Dryden's *The Conquest of Granada by the Spaniards*, which had been a great success in the early 1670's. Like Dryden, Crowne wrote his play in rhyming couplets (imitating the French tragedies that Charles II loved) and doubled the normal length to ten acts. In both plays, the action centers on several monarchs who are caught in a maze of political and romantic obligations. Finally, Crowne followed Dryden in using special stage effects to heighten the tension. If Crowne had lived three centuries later, he could have easily written scripts for cinema epics.

The action of *The Destruction of Jerusalem by Titus Vespasian, Part I* commences on the eve of Passover, A.D. 72. The city of Jerusalem awaits the arrival of a Roman army under Titus Vespasian. The city's high priest and governor, Matthias, works to prepare the defenses, but he faces insubordination from John, leader of the Pharisee party, who believes that Matthias is secretly in the Romans' pay. Matthias governs in the place of the Jewish king, recently killed under mysterious circumstances. The dead monarch's sister Berenice, appointed by the Romans to rule, has returned to the city in the hope of preventing resistance to the imperial army.

Berenice's heart, however, is not in her mission, because she is in love with Titus, the son of the Emperor Vespasian.

Also present in the city are two exiled monarchs, Phraartes and Monobazus, who have fallen in love with Jewish noblewomen. Phraartes, who believes that religion is a myth supporting the divine right of kings, loves Matthias' daughter Clarona, a vestal virgin of the temple. Clarona is attracted to Phraartes but refuses to violate her vow of eternal virginity. Monobazus loves Berenice, but his ability to woo is inhibited by his secret knowledge that he is her brother's murderer. Berenice, smitten by Titus, hardly notices Monobazus.

Though neither king makes progress in courting his beloved, both use their swords effectively. First they fight off the Edomites, a neighboring tribe invited by John to invade the city on the pretext of forestalling the Romans. Next they rescue Matthias when John leads the Pharisees in open rebellion and captures the Temple. Phraartes demands from Matthias Clarona's hand in marriage as his reward. The high priest is willing if a loophole can be found in the law which would release Clarona from her vows. As they deliberate his daughter's fate, a messenger announces that the Roman army has made camp on nearby hills. On this ominous note, *Part I* ends.

Part II opens with Titus pacing in his tent, torn between his love for Berenice and his duty to the empire. Titus' second-in-command convinces him that duty is superior to love, and two allied kings convince Titus to conquer before the Jews can rally under a new leader. Berenice arrives at the Roman camp soon afterward, but after a long and passionate interview, Titus pushes her away.

Inside Jerusalem conditions worsen as food supplies dwindle. John continues his efforts to kill or capture Matthias. Phraartes is wounded in a second skirmish against the Pharisees; as Clarona binds his wound, she admits her love and hints that if the two of them can save the city, she might renounce her vow. In the meantime, the Jews lose an ally: Monobazus follows Berenice to the Roman camp.

Phraartes departs in search of food supplies. Returning with some provisions, he finds Matthias again in the hands of the Pharisees and once more rescues him. Phraartes now promises Clarona that he will bring in his own Parthian troops to save the city. Titus acts to counter Phraartes' plans even though Berenice attempts to distract the Roman general by threatening to kill herself if her love is not requited. With a heavy heart, Titus chooses duty over love. Berenice fails to carry out her threat.

Monobazus, now ashamed of his beloved and his love, returns to join Phraartes in the city's defense. The two kings find the Temple desecrated by John's forces and discover Matthias and Clarona mortally wounded. After his beloved dies in his arms, Phraartes decides to give up his life fighting the invaders. Monobazus decides to do the same after passing up the chance to flee the doomed city. They die like brothers, side by side in combat.

Titus enters the city in triumph and spares the survivors. Berenice visits him one last time, and when he again refuses to return her love, she goes into permanent and secret exile. As the play ends, Titus stands alone onstage, still agonizing whether duty can be worth such a sacrifice.

It is easy to discern political themes in the play in which the Restoration audience could see their own concerns reflected. The Jews face aggression from the greatest power in the world, Rome, just as England feared domination by neighboring France, which, under Louis XIV, was Europe's most potent nation. The Jewish resistance against the invader is hampered by internal dissension, just as Charles's policies were hampered by opposition from anti-Royalist groups.

The most important political theme centers on the rulers in the play: Phraartes, Monobazus, Matthias, and Titus. The hero is not any of these but rather the institution of kingship itself. The four represent facets of Charles II, his life, his obligations, and his privileges. Phraartes and Monobazus are kings in exile, echoes of the Charles who was in exile in the 1650's. Although they have no kingdoms that obey them, Phraartes and Monobazus speak and act with a natural and convincing authority; clearly, they believe that the authority of kingship flows from divine approbation rather than from popular will. Matthias represents the besieged ruler who struggles bravely against the odds when domestic rebels join foreign enemies in threatening the State. Titus shows the personal sacrifice that kingship demands: For the good of the State, he must deny the longings of his own soul and reject the woman he loves. There is not a consistent political allegory in the play; rather, Crowne presents several vantage points from which to survey the character of a king.

All of the rulers speak eloquently about political obligation: Their diction is elegant and their imagery rich in metaphor. Phraartes and Titus speak with the same poetic force about love. Phraartes with Clarona and Titus with Berenice engage in lengthy debates that reveal the depth of their commitment. What makes the lovers' anguish such good stage business is that each pair is caught in an inescapable dilemma: Clarona has made eternal vows to a religion Phraartes despises; Berenice and Titus must be traitors in order to be lovers. As Crowne devises the situations, lifelong doubt, exile, or death are the only solutions.

Spectacular staging heightens the emotional impact of the play's political themes and romantic dilemmas. An angel appears against the ceiling of the temple to prophesy the doom of the city, and the ghost of Herod walks abroad to do the same. The laments of enslaved citizens and dying warriors are heard offstage, and there is an abundance of swordplay, chases, and stabbings onstage. In the tenth act, the temple catches fire, and Phraartes and Monobazus (seen in silhouette) fall from a prominent battlement as they are fighting Romans. The stage itself is an ambitious multilevel setting whence Matthias can look down at rebel Pharisees, the exiled kings can glare down at invaders, and the nightdress-clad Clarona can gaze down at her lover. No wonder *The Destruction of Jerusalem by Titus Vespasian* was Crowne's greatest success in the 1670's.

Among his comedies, *Sir Courtly Nice* was Crowne's most popular play, and it has retained its reputation as his best. Like other Restoration comedies of wit, it combines a love plot with social commentary. Its themes are love, marriage, and independence: *Sir Courtly Nice*'s dual heroines struggle to achieve the third without sacrificing the first two.

Violante, in love with Lord Bellguard, hesitates to marry him because of his treatment of his unmarried sister Leonora. Bellguard has set a maiden aunt and two eccentric kinsmen (the religious fanatic Testimony and the antireligious zealot Hothead) to watch over the girl. These three sentinels hinder Leonora's romance with Farewel, the son of a rival noble family. Bellguard is cautious because he thinks that all women are promiscuous by nature. Violante and Leonora decide to teach Bellguard a lesson.

Violante asks Farewel to help, and he suggests that they employ Crack, a poor but ingenious scholar expelled from the university for studying magic. Their first victim is Surly, a cynical and unpleasant man in love with Violante. She promises to respond to Surly's awkward advances if he chases away Bellguard's choice of suitor for Leonora, Sir Courtly Nice. Meanwhile, Crack, disguised as a traitor, gains access to Leonora and gives her a locket containing Farewel's picture.

Surly visits Sir Courtly, a man of elegant, even fastidious, manners. Arriving drunk, Surly annoys Sir Courtly by announcing his intention to woo Leonora. Surly annoys him to an even greater extent when he exhales his foul-smelling breath.

Bellguard meanwhile finds Farewel's picture in Leonora's possession and accuses her of being a wanton. With the sentinels in an uproar over the accusation, Crack enters in a new guise and manages to right the situation. Pretending to be Bellguard's crazy but rich cousin, Sir Thomas Calico, he provides Leonora with an absurd alibi. Bellguard, deferring to the wisdom of the wealthy, accepts the lame excuse. Crack tells Leonora that Farewel will visit her that night.

Sir Courtly comes courting. Leonora's aunt wishes to remain behind to supervise the lovers, but Bellguard escorts her out of the room. Leonora listens to Courtly's smug and silly avowals of love and responds mockingly. Surly interrupts to woo Leonora himself and to taunt Courtly. Against his will, Courtly timorously challenges Surly to a duel in order to save face.

Meanwhile, Crack sneaks Farewel into Leonora's room. Her aunt discovers his presence, and an alarmed Bellguard hunts for the intruder throughout the house. Crack comes to the rescue again by declaring that it was he who let Farewel, whom he identifies as his future brother-in-law, into the house. Bellguard is willing to forgo suspicion if Leonora promises to listen once more to Courtly's proposal. She tries, but she indignantly leaves the room as Courtly professes love and offers marriage as he stands gazing fondly on himself in a mirror. The aunt, entering the room and seeing no other woman, takes Courtly's words as applying to herself. When she loudly accepts, Courtly is too preoccupied to notice her misinterpretation.

Leonora takes her fate into her own hands, leaving Bellguard's house to marry Farewel. Violante praises her friend's love and brave spirit, contrasting it with the aunt's betrayal of trust at the first opportunity. Bellguard is finally convinced that not all women need close supervision. As a final test, Violante teases Bellguard by flirting with Surly. When Bellguard responds with passionate declarations rather than jealous accusations, Violante knows she has a man on her terms. No longer afraid that Bellguard will try to control her as he did Leonora, Violante agrees to become his wife.

Crowne wrote *Sir Courtly Nice* as an adaptation of a Spanish comedy, *No puede ser: O, No puede ser guardar una mujer* (1661), by Agustín Moreto y Cabaña. Charles II himself suggested the adaptation to Crowne, who revised the original to suit an English audience and his own dramatic skills. The Spanish play had used the framing device of a debate about the nature of women which leads to a wager. Crowne abandoned that device and began his comedy *in medias res*. One of Crowne's favorite techniques was to multiply character-types; thus, in *Sir Courtly Nice*, he uses not one eccentric kinsman but two and has Crack appear in a variety of disguises. The effect is a more lively play; more characters enter and leave the stage than in most comedies.

Crowne's strength was not in the creation of memorable leading characters but in forming a cast with several strong roles. Indeed, the enduring popularity of *Sir Courtly Nice* can in part be attributed to its appeal to acting companies. There are numerous good parts, and even the smaller roles add distinctively to the whole. It is a play that depends for success not on one or two stars but on the successful interaction of the company. Crowne worked closely with actors and actresses, often tutoring them about the way he imagined his characters being played. *Sir Courtly Nice* is an actor's play as much as it is the author's play.

All of Crowne's characters are strong. Violante and Leonora are atypical Restoration heroines who possess more initiative and spirit than women—real or fictitious—were allowed in the seventeenth century. Testimony and Hothead are bold caricatures of mentalities that were powerful and respected in the age. Sir Courtly is a magnificent fop whose folly is not exposed by others so much as it is revealed by his own actions; his every mannerism betrays the narcissism that leads to his comeuppance in the mirror scene. Surly is a delightful foil to Courtly—one of the crudest of numerous ill-mannered Restoration rakes. These characters interact in a comedy that is always funny, though not always kind. Their story is one that does not pale, the perennially interesting tale of young lovers who must use ingenuity to circumvent the objections of the older generation—or of their peers who prematurely think like the older generation.

Crowne's other important play, *City Politiques*, does not fit into any established genre of comedy. It is too politically oriented to be a romantic comedy; it has too many scenes of farce to be a comedy of wit or a comedy of manners. It is a play of its time, when a playwright employed his dramatic skills on behalf of his patron or of his party. The years from 1678 to 1682 were a time of serious political crisis in England, and when King Charles emerged victorious from that crisis, Crowne celebrated the triumph with a satiric production that ridiculed the Whigs, the enemies of royal rule. *City Politiques* laughs at the issues and personalities of the Popish Plot from the safe vantage of hindsight.

The Popish Plot crisis began in 1678 when an ex-clergyman, Titus Oates, claimed that he had uncovered a plan by which English Catholics, the pope, and the French king intended to assassinate the Protestant Charles II and replace him with his Catholic brother, James. On the sworn testimony of Oates and several others, thousands of Catholics were implicated and arrested; two dozen were put to death. Charles's opponents united to campaign for the Exclusion Bill, which would remove the incentive for a plot by barring James from the succession. Charles opposed the measure, but for the next two years, both Parliament and the city of London were dominated by the bill's supporters. With many of his nobility and the country's major city hostilely disposed, Charles's reign became difficult. In 1681, after much of Oates's testimony had been discredited, the king dissolved the Whig-dominated Parliament. By 1682, the Whig control of London had collapsed, and many leaders of the party fled the country. Except for the emotional scars, the crisis was over.

City Politiques, a series of connected sketches more than a coherent play, ridicules the assumptions and practices of the Whigs during the Popish Plot. It shows ambitious statesmen relying on false oaths to gain selfish ends, citizens defying authority under the cover of respectability but actually motivated by mere whimsy, and lawyers using the laws against the source of all law, the king. Contemporaries delighted in drawing connections between the characters Crowne put on the stage and the actual persons who had important roles in the plot. Modern readers do not enjoy such identifications long after the fact, but they can enjoy Crowne's clever dramatization of mankind's less respectable motives for action.

The action of *City Politiques* occurs in Naples, where the rakish nobleman Florio plans to seduce Rosaura, the young second wife of the newly elected Podesta (mayor of the city). To attain his goal Florio pretends to be a supporter of the Podesta; he also pretends to be incapacitated by venereal disease. In the course of his scheme, Florio befriends the Podesta's son, Craffy, who confides one day that he is in love with his stepmother. When Florio threatens to tell the Podesta, Craffy replies that he will get a dozen paid informants to swear that Florio is the woman's lover.

The Podesta and his followers, openly called Whigs, celebrate his election by acting rudely to the royal governor. When the governor refuses their request to have the Podesta knighted, the mayor vows to gain revenge by fomenting rebellion. One of his supporters is the lawyer Bartoline, who has recently married a much younger woman, Lucinda. Her beauty immediately attracts the eye of another rake, Artall, who disguises himself as Florio. Thinking "Florio" a dying man, Bartoline leaves Lucinda with him while he goes about the Podesta's business. Artall uses the opportunity to teach her the difference between a virile nobleman and an impotent lawyer.

The Podesta continues to harass the governor. He calls the citizens to arms by spreading rumors that a foreign army is poised to invade, and he hires Bartoline to prepare a false indictment against the governor. Bartoline, however, is playing a double game: at the same time he helps the Podesta indict the governor, he is helping the governor press charges against the Podesta and his followers. Florio meanwhile harasses the Whigs by publishing a mock proclamation against them.

Florio goes to Rosaura's apartment. A drunken Craffy interrupts their assignation, attempting to seduce Rosaura while Florio pretends to be the Podesta asleep on the couch. When the real Podesta enters the house, Rosaura tricks Craffy into attacking his father while Florio escapes. Father and son wrestle each other to the ground before realizing their mistake.

Later, Artall again tricks Bartoline. Hoping that the dying Florio (Artall in disguise) will include Lucinda in his will, Bartoline allows his wife to visit Florio's bedroom. At the same time, Craffy discovers the real Florio making love to Rosaura in a nearby room. Craffy calls the Podesta, but the mayor is assured by Bartoline that Florio is with Lucinda and must not be disturbed. Thus, the two rakes complete the double cuckolding while Craffy is deemed mad. Afterward, "Florio" brazenly carries Lucinda from her husband's house while Bartoline watches helplessly.

Florio plays one more trick on the Podesta. His servant Pietro pretends to be a Spanish nobleman with influence upon the governor. Pietro promises to help the Podesta become lord treasurer if he will betray his followers, and the Podesta enthusiastically agrees. When the governor arrives at the mayor's house, however, it is with a warrant, not a knighthood, in hand. The Podesta is under arrest for causing false alarms among the citizens. Bartoline, too, is under arrest: To gain revenge upon "Florio," he paid several informants to accuse him of treason. When he identifies Artall as Florio, Bartoline is arrested for harassing an innocent bystander. The governor concludes the play by warning everyone to leave politics to those properly in authority.

City Politiques shows that once a citizen has broken faith with his legitimate ruler, he can expect no one to keep faith with him. After the Podesta begins to plot against the governor, his son attempts to steal his wife, his best friend succeeds in seducing her, and his lawyer tries to frame him. Likewise, if a man has betrayed his ruler, he will betray anyone, as the Podesta plans to betray his followers. Political rebellion leads to the loss of fidelity at all levels of society.

Phrased this way, the theme of *City Politiques* is indeed serious, but its onstage execution is humorous. Florio and Artall are witty seducers, as anxious to puncture the husband's pomposity as to enjoy the wife. Craffy is a zany and incompetent would-be rake, so infatuated with Rosaura that he talks to himself about his passion even in his father's presence. Bartoline lisps peculiarly and gratingly, making numerous inadvertent puns. The stage business is as inventive as the characters' speaking habits. Craffy's wrestling match with his father wrecks the entire room; the dual cuckolding unfolds daringly and rapidly.

Proof that Crowne's satire struck home was his fate after the play opened: Outraged Whigs assaulted him on the street. Whatever pains Crowne suffered on that occasion must have been eased by his knowledge that the play was a success. London audiences relished his satiric depiction of those who, only months before, had been powerful and feared enemies.

Other major works

NOVEL: *Pandion and Amphigenia: Or, The History of the Coy Lady of Thessalìs*, 1665.

POETRY: "A Poem on the Death of King Charles," 1685; "The History of a Love Between a Parisian Lady and a Young Singing Man," 1692.

Bibliography

Canfield, J. Douglas. *"Regulus* and *Cleomenes* and 1688: From Royalism to Self-Reliance." *Eighteenth Century Life* 12 (November, 1988): 67-75. Crowne's tragedy *Regulus*, like John Dryden and Thomas Southerne's *Cleomenes, the Spartan Hero* (pr., pb. 1682), shows a Royalist perspective upon the Revolution of 1688. The play draws a parallel between Great Britain and ancient Carthage, suggesting that by banishing warriors loyal to the righful rulers, rebel leaders invite divine vengeance upon the kingdom. Crowne argues dramatically that faithfulness is the most important virtue in a nation's political life.

Cordner, Michael. "Marriage Comedy After the 1688 Revolution: Southerne to VanBrugh." *Modern Language Review* 85 (April, 1990): 273-289. Crowne's *The Married Beau* is one of many comedies in that decade whose plot concerns the marital disharmony following a wife's discovery of her husband's real or supposed adultery. Unlike Restoration wives who repaid infidelity with infidelity, postrevolutionary wives remained determinedly virtuous. In a new age, dramatists unhesitatingly changed the convention of Restoration comedy.

Hume, Robert D. *The Development of English Drama in the Later Seventeenth Century.* Oxford, England: Clarendon Press, 1976. Crowne is one of many minor dramatists of the period who illustrates Humes's provocative thesis: Criticism of Restoration drama has overemphasized the major playwrights (William Wycherley, William Congreve, John Dryden) and obscured the fact that the theater was a popular medium where the political, philosophical, and social ideas of the age were presented and debated in entertaining genres. The "minor" dramatists gave the theater its vigor by competing through sensational plots and timely themes for both audience and reputation.

Kaufman, Anthony. "Civil Politics—Sexual Politics in John Crowne's *City Politiques.*" *Restoration: Studies in English Literary Culture, 1660-1700* 6 (Fall, 1982): 72-80. The games of seduction and sexual competitiveness that form the plot of Crowne's most famous comedy are a metaphor for the political struggle between Whigs and Tories during the Popish Plot and Exclusion crisis of 1678-1682. Crowne portrays Whigs as self-seeking individuals engaged in a quest for political power that threatens government, society, and literature itself.

Murrie, Eleanor Boswell. *The Restoration Court Stage, 1660-1702, with a Particular Account of the Production of "Calisto."* New York: Benjamin Blom, 1960. Part 3 of this study of plays performed at Charles II's court focuses on the production of Crowne's masque *Calisto.* It reports in fascinating detail the information that has survived about the performance: the lists of ladies and gentlemen of the court who performed in minor roles and in the chorus, the cost of the elaborate sets, the ushers' instructions for seating the audience, and the costumes worn by the royal princesses who took the leading roles.

Robert M. Otten

RICHARD CUMBERLAND

Born: Cambridge, England; February 19, 1732
Died: Tunbridge Wells, England; May 7, 1811

Principal drama

The Banishment of Cicero, pb. 1761; *The Summer's Tale*, pr., pb. 1765; *The Clandestine Marriage*, pr. 1766; *The Brothers*, pr. 1769, pb. 1770; *The West Indian*, pr., pb. 1771; *The Fashionable Lover*, pr., pb. 1772; *The Choleric Man*, pr. 1774, pb. 1775; *The Walloons*, pr. 1782, pb. 1813; *The Mysterious Husband*, pr., pb. 1783; *The Carmelite*, pr., pb. 1784; *The Natural Son*, pr. 1784, pb. 1785; *The Box-Lobby Challenge*, pr., pb. 1794; *The Jew*, pr., pb. 1794; *The Wheel of Fortune*, pr., pb. 1795; *First Love*, pr., pb. 1795; *Don Pedro*, pr. 1797, pb. 1831; *False Impressions*, pr., pb. 1797; *The Unpublished Plays of Richard Cumberland*, pb. 1991 (edited by Richard J. Dircks).

Other literary forms

Richard Cumberland is remarkable for the volume and variety of his literary output, if for nothing else. Experimenting in several different genres, he earned a reputation in his day as a distinguished man of letters. Most of his works, however, have not survived.

Cumberland had early ambitions as a poet, his first publication being an imitation of Thomas Gray, *An Elegy Written on St. Mark's Eve* (1754). He was to publish *Odes* in 1776, and a volume entitled *Miscellaneous Poems* two years later. A religious epic, *Calvary: Or, The Death of Christ* (1792) sold well, which encouraged him to collaborate with Sir James Bland Burgess in *The Exodiad* (1807). Cumberland rendered some fifty psalms into English meter in *A Poetical Version of Certain Psalms of David* (1801) and reflected on his life in verse in *Retrospection* (1811).

Cumberland also won renown as an essayist for his multivolume work *The Observer*, which first appeared in 1785, with editions following in 1788 and in 1798. It featured a discussion of the early Greek drama with some original translations (notably of Aristophanes' *The Clouds*, 1798). Cumberland wrote pamphlets—defending his grandfather's reputation, among other causes—and a religious tract. He entered the realm of art history with his *Anecdotes of Eminent Painters in Spain During the Sixteenth and Seventeenth Centuries* (1782) and published the first catalog of the paintings housed in the royal palace at Madrid.

The pathetic scenes which mark Cumberland's drama are also found in his fiction: *Arundel* (1789), an epistolary novel of the form popularized by Samuel Richardson, and *Henry* (1795), a conscious imitation of Henry Fielding. Cumberland's active involvement in the theater resulted in numerous prologues and epilogues as well as an edition of *The British Drama* with biographical and critical comments, published posthumously in 1817. In 1809, Cumberland also founded *The London Review*, which invited signed articles from contributors; it appeared only twice. His *Memoirs of Richard Cumberland, Written by Himself* (1806-1807), perhaps the most lasting of his nondramatic productions, preserved for posterity the record of his long and productive career.

Achievements

Cumberland is remarkable for his long and varied contribution to the theater. During his career, which spanned forty years, he wrote some fifty dramatic pieces, including musical comedies and operas, a masque, classical historical and domestic tragedies, translations and adaptations, farces, and occasional pieces. The genre in which he excelled was sentimental comedy, and for years he was the most successful writer in the field. His sentimental comedies held the stage against the masterpieces of Oliver Goldsmith and Richard Brinsley Sheridan. His very preeminence, however, made him vulnerable to attack, and unfortunately he has been handed down to posterity, through the eyes of his opponents, as "the Terence of England, the mender of hearts," according to Goldsmith in *Retaliation* (1774).

Indeed, Cumberland is remembered primarily for his place in the debate between sentimental and laughing comedy. The issues were hotly contested: What is the primary purpose of the stage? Should comedy be realistic or idealistic? Should it ridicule vices and follies or present models worthy of imitation? Should playwrights appeal to the intellect or to the emotions? Should they aim to provoke superior laughter or sympathetic tears? Stated in these terms, the answers seem obvious, with the common verdict in favor of "true," or laughing, comedy. One should not forget, however, the response of Cumberland's contemporaries. In his day, he was enormously popular as well as influential. Many imitators followed Cumberland's lead, ensuring the dominance of the sentimental school to the end of the century.

Cumberland was convinced of the moral utility of the drama and took his role seriously as reformer of the age. He created characters specifically to combat national prejudices, and he attacked fashionable vices. This was done both by means of admonitory examples (the ruined gambler in *The Wheel of Fortune*) and by direct statement. Aphorisms are to be found throughout Cumberland's plays, and a useful lesson is often expounded at the end.

Cumberland was unusual as a "gentleman" playwright and was considered a credit to the profession. He was well educated in classical as well as English stage tradition and drew on his knowledge for his works. His writing was admired for its elegance and accurate portrayal of high life. The refined sensibility of his heroines and the tearful pathos they inspired were highly commended.

Cumberland was superior to other writers in this genre in that he was able to blend humor with sentiment. In almost all of his plays, one finds "low" characters, included for comic relief, as well as sprightly ladies, amorous spinsters, and henpecked husbands. Strongly patriotic, he liked home-grown English characters and created some memorable types, such as the Irishman Major O'Flaherty. He could also employ local color to advantage, as he did in the seaside scenes in *The Brothers.*

Through his long acquaintance with the theater, Cumberland developed a good sense of what would work onstage; it was often remarked that his plays performed better than they read. He was able to utilize all the resources at his disposal (scenery, costumes, and so on) to enhance his plays. He also knew the abilities of the performers and could write parts which would exploit their talents. Some of these roles—Penruddock or Belcour, for example—were favorite acting parts.

Famous in his own time, Cumberland was the last and the best of the sentimental dramatists. Of his many plays, *The West Indian* survives as a classic.

Biography

Richard Cumberland was born on February 19, 1732, in the Master's Lodge at Trinity College, Cambridge, into a family of clergymen and scholars of whom he was justly proud. His father, Denison Cumberland, later Bishop of Clonfert and Kilmore, was descended from the Bishop of Peterborough, who wrote an influential treatise in refutation of Thomas Hobbes, *De Legibus Naturae, Disquisito Philosophica* (1672). Cumberland's mother, Joanna, was the daughter of the famous classics scholar Richard Bentley. Cumberland cherished fond memories of this learned man and upheld Bentley's reputation all of his life.

At the age of six, Cumberland was sent to school at Bury St. Edmunds, where, encouraged by headmaster Arthur Kinsman, he stood first in his class. In 1744, he entered Westminster School contemporaneously with Warren Hastings, George Colman, and William Cowper. In Cumberland's school days, an interest in the drama was awakened by his mother's reading of William Shakespeare; on an early trip to the theater, he was much impressed by the innovative acting of the young David Garrick.

In 1747, Cumberland was admitted to Trinity College, Cambridge, where he enjoyed the quiet life of study and intellectual exertion. He took his bachelor of arts degree in 1751 with high honors and was elected to a fellowship two years later. He felt drawn to an academic or clerical career and relinquished his calling with some regret when more worldly prospects presented themselves.

The great Whig Sir George Montagu Dunk, second Earl of Halifax, out of gratitude to Cumberland's father, offered to take Cumberland as his private secretary. Cumberland moved to London to take up the post, which gave him the opportunity to move in political circles. In 1759, he married Elizabeth Ridge, with whom he was to have four sons and three daughters. Fortunately for his growing family, he was appointed the Crown Agent for Nova Scotia and Provost Marshal of South Carolina, which added to his income.

Cumberland accompanied Lord Halifax to Ireland in 1761 as Ulster Secretary. This experience was later to bear fruit in Cumberland's drama, when he brought original Irish characters to the stage. The relationship with his patron cooled upon Cumberland's refusal of a baronetcy, and when Halifax became Secretary of State in 1762, he appointed a rival as Under Secretary. Cumberland was forced to accept a minor position as Clerk of Reports on the Board of Trade.

With little to do and in need of money, Cumberland began in earnest his career as a dramatist. His first play, *The Banishment of Cicero*, was refused, but in 1765, *The Summer's Tale* was produced, a musical comedy imitative of Isaac Bickerstaffe. This provoked a charge from which Cumberland was often to suffer, that of plagiarism, and he turned his efforts to a genre more conducive to his talents, that of sentimental comedy. In 1769, *The Brothers* played at Covent Garden to great applause.

An unexpected compliment to Garrick in the epilogue won Garrick's friendship and led to a very productive association between the two. As actor-manager of Drury Lane Theatre until 1776, Garrick produced several of Cumberland's plays, which benefited from Garrick's expert knowledge of stagecraft. Their first effort was also the most successful: *The West Indian*, which appeared in 1771, enjoyed an extraordinary first run of twenty-eight nights, was frequently revived and held the stage to the end of the century. When his third comedy, *The Fashionable Lover*, also won favor, in 1772, Cumberland was established as the leading dramatist of the sentimental school.

Cumberland's preeminence in the theater won for him his entrée into the leading social and literary circles of the time. At the British Coffee House, he met Samuel Johnson, Sir Joshua Reynolds, Edmund Burke, and Samuel Foote. He patronized the painter George Romney. He dined at Elizabeth Montagu's ("Queen of the Blues"); he knew Hester Thrale and irritated Horace Walpole. As to the latter, although Cumberland moved in society with ease, proud of his dignified position as "gentleman playwright," he had a temperament that provoked as much enmity as friendship.

Most unsatisfactory were his relationships with fellow dramatists, for Cumberland was reputed to be envious of all merit but his own. His discomfiture at the success of Sheridan's *The School for Scandal* (pr. 1777) was widely reported. As the most popular exponent of sentimental comedy, Cumberland was vulnerable to attack by those who preferred laughing comedy, and when Goldsmith's famous essay on the subject, "An Essay on the Theatre," appeared in 1773, Cumberland took it as a personal affront. He replied in a vitriolic preface to his (appropriately entitled) play *The Choleric Man*. Proud of his accomplishments though professing humility, and sensitive to criticism though pretending to lofty indifference, he exasperated even Garrick, who called him a "man without a skin." Cumberland was identified by contemporaries as the original of Sheridan's caricature in *The Critic* (pr. 1779) and was known as Sir Fretful Plagiary.

Cumberland's literary career was interrupted in 1780 by involvement in political affairs. He had been appointed Secretary to the Board of Trade in 1775 through the interest of his patron and friend Lord George Germain. For this nobleman, then Colonial Secretary, Cumberland undertook a secret mission to Spain to arrange a separate peace treaty. When negotiations failed in 1781, Cumberland was recalled and was treated ungratefully by the government, which refused to reimburse him for his expenses. Moreover, he lost his post when the Board of Trade was abolished in 1782. Disappointed and in need of money, Cumberland retired to Tunbridge Wells, where he tried through unceasing literary activity to recoup his fortunes.

The first work produced after Cumberland's return, *The Walloons*, a play with a strong Spanish flavor, failed to please, but he had more success with a domestic tragedy, *The Mysterious Husband*, in 1783. *The Carmelite*, staged in 1784 with an impressive Gothic setting, displayed the extraordinary talents of actress Sarah Siddons as the heroine. Cumberland won little approval for his next few ventures, and it was not until 1794 that he again found his audience.

The Box-Lobby Challenge, produced early that year, was amusing fare, and a few months later *The Jew* was widely acclaimed. For the title role of the latter, Cumberland created a sympathetic character whose apparent avarice cloaked benevolent actions. Another powerful figure animated *The Wheel of Fortune* in 1795, giving actor John Philip Kemble one of his favorite roles. *First Love*, in the old vein of sentimental comedy, also won favor. These plays briefly restored Cumberland to his former popularity, but in the years to come, he was unable to match their success. He continued to write prolifically up to his death but for the most part failed to suit the taste of the audience and complained of the degeneracy of the stage.

Perhaps for this reason, Cumberland turned to other channels, and the years of his retirement saw a tremendous outpouring of fiction, poetry, and prose. This unremitting literary activity was at least partly a result of financial pressure. Toward the end of his life, his unfortunate situation attracted notice, as one unworthy of a venerable man of letters.

By 1800, Cumberland had outlived his own generation and was viewed by his younger contemporaries as a figure from another era. He enjoyed his position as elder statesman and was accorded respect for his age and accomplishments. He liked to encourage young writers of talent, entertaining them with anecdotes of his own younger days. Always staunchly patriotic, he raised a corps of volunteers to meet the threat of a Napoleonic invasion; two of his sons died serving their country. At his death, at the age of seventy-nine, Cumberland left a modest estate to his youngest daughter. He lies buried in the Poets' Corner of Westminster Abbey.

Analysis

Richard Cumberland took seriously his role as moralist and reformer and set himself a novel didactic task:

> I thereupon looked into society for the purpose of discovering such as were the victims of its national, professional or religious prejudices; . . . and out of these I meditated to select and form heroes for my future dramas, . . .

In his popular play *The West Indian*, he defends the character of a Creole. The basic plot is a familiar testing device, set up in the opening scene. Stockwell awaits the arrival from Jamaica of his unacknowledged son; he decides to defer acknowledgment of their relationship until he has had an opportunity to evaluate the young man's behavior. Should his son, Belcour, satisfy this scrutiny, Stockwell will reward him with legitimacy, a fortune, and a place in English society.

Interest in Belcour is awakened before his entrance and increased by the parade of black porters. Nor is he likely to disappoint expectations; he enters breezily, complaining of the rapacious mob at the waterside. As a stranger to English society, he is able to view it objectively and provide satiric commentary. Moreover, as a "child of nature," his viewpoint should be a healthy corrective. Generous and honorable himself, he does not suspect duplicity in others; while this makes him an easy dupe of the scheming Fulmers, it redounds to his credit as a proof of his innocence.

Belcour's lack of guile is an endearing trait: The candor with which he acknowledges his faults to Stockwell disarms reproof, and his ingenuous confession to Charlotte of the loss of her jewels wins an easy forgiveness. This West Indian shows the human heart in its natural state—impulsive, mercurial, and uncontrolled. He himself bemoans the violence of his passions, blaming them on his tropical constitution. He is driven by his powerful urges; inflamed by the beauty of Louisa Dudley, he sacrifices every other tie to possess her. Plunging headlong into error, he is chastened by the mischief that ensues. Like so many other libertines, Belcour is reclaimed by a virtuous woman. Kneeling at her feet, he pledges his love, grounded now on principle. In their union, the ideal of a feeling heart tempered with reason will be achieved.

Belcour is valued above all for his benevolence. A creature of instinct, his first impulse on hearing of distress is to relieve it. His follies and virtues proceed from the same source—a warm heart. He reflects the fundamental belief of sentimental drama in the natural goodness of people and contradicts the orthodox Christian view of human beings' sinfulness. Sympathy with one's fellow creatures is the moral touchstone for all the characters in the play—a quality conspicuously lacking in Lady Rusport, who represents the Puritan position: She was taught never to laugh; she abhors the playhouses; and she upholds the letter of the law over the spirit of charity. She is rightfully excluded from the happy ending.

Cumberland's fallible but generous hero, who would not be out of place in a laughing comedy, resembles Fielding's Tom Jones and Sheridan's Charles Surface. The play abounds with high spirits; besides the amusing peccadilloes of Belcour, there is a subplot involving the lively Charlotte Rusport. She is unexpectedly forthright, avowing her love for Charles although uncertain of its return. This reversal of roles, where a lady takes the active part in the wooing, is frequently seen in Cumberland's plays. Charlotte's witty repartee, directed even at the sentimental heroine, prevents Louisa's distresses from appearing too pathetic.

A similar defusing of sentiment is accomplished by Major O'Flaherty. He is a stage Irishman with a difference; while retaining some national traits, he has many admirable qualities, showing courage, loyalty, and generosity. It is he, after all, who discovers and delivers the will which brings about the happy reversal of fortune. His joyful exuberance animates this otherwise tearful scene. He punctures the Dudleys' formal rhetoric with irreverent comments, undercuts Lady Rusport's tirade, and interrupts the highly emotional father-son reunion.

In *The West Indian*, Cumberland skilfully blends comic and sentimental elements. It is unique in this regard; more often, his plays are thoroughly imbued with sentiment. *The Fashionable Lover*, for example, shows more clearly what is meant by the "tearful Muse."

The opening of *The Fashionable Lover* is reminiscent of a comedy of humors, in which each character appears onstage to exhibit his or her particular foible. A Scotsman complains of extravagance to a foppish French valet; a railing misanthrope irritates a dissolute aristocrat; and a musty Welsh antiquary squares off with a vulgar merchant. The tone is one of satire until the introduction of the sentimental plot. This involves a poor orphan, surprised by the rakish lord into a compromising situation. Wherever Miss Augusta Aubrey turns in her hapless state, tears are sure to follow.

Cumberland aims to inspire pity through the picture of virtue in distress. He presents characters in a middle walk of life, with whose problems the audience can identify. The appeal to the heart is beneficial and instructive; it enlarges one's sympathies and strengthens one's affections. To evoke this response, Augusta is cast upon the world bemoaning her hard lot. Nor is she likely to minimize her sorrows: "I have no house, no home, no father, friend, or refuge, in this world." The smallest problems are magnified in her eyes; the awesome prospect of independence overwhelms her. Preoccupied as she is with her troubles, it is difficult to rouse her from self-pity. Even when informed of her good fortune, Augusta weeps, reflecting how unaccustomed she is to happiness.

As Augusta is unlikely to show stoic fortitude, so she is incapable of acting spiritedly on her own behalf. Her most likely resource at this critical pass would be her fiancé, but rather than appeal for his aid, she advises him to forget her. When he demands an explanation, she replies ambiguously that she accepts her fate. It is not surprising that Mr. Tyrrel concludes that she is guilty, for she makes no effort to deny it.

The heroine's extraordinary passivity is the result of her extreme sensibility; she is tremblingly alive to every sensation and fearful of aggression. Ushered into the presence of a man who eyes her keenly, Augusta complains, "his eyes oppress me." She is delicate of body as well as of spirit, and the least exertion exhausts her. Reunited with her long-lost father, she weeps, faints, and has to be carried away. Her feminine frailty endears her to the hero, since she so evidently depends on his protection.

Such a pathetic heroine requires a rescuer. A conventional figure is an elderly gentleman somewhat removed from the action who wanders through the play doing good. He appears at propitious moments to solve difficulties, remove obstacles, and shower benefits on the needy. In *The Fashionable Lover*, there are at least three rescuers. Colin MacLeod is the most colorful of these and the linchpin of the plot. He is on hand at every critical juncture: He meets Augusta in the street and later saves her from rape; he intercepts her father on his return and masterminds the final discovery. An attractive character with his homely, forceful dialect and blunt humor, he was intended by Cumberland to combat prejudice against the Scots. It is clear that Colin is economical on principle and not parsimonious; he disapproves of wasteful expenditure and lives frugally that he may be the more generous to others. He is the mouthpiece for several moral maxims which serve the playwright's didactic purpose.

Colin's confederate is a stock type, not quite so original. Like Tobias Smollett's Matthew Bramble, Mortimer cloaks his charitable deeds under an affected cynicism. Extremely susceptible to human suffering, he hides his soft heart within a crusty shell. He succors the afflicted, expecting no reward but his own gratification. He proves that one acts benevolently for purely selfish reasons and calls himself a voluptuary in virtue. Besides protecting Augusta, he is determined to extricate Lord Abberville from the snares of evil. The return of the prodigal is a familiar motif in Cumberland. He frequently attacks fashionable vice in his plays: Dueling is discussed in *The West Indian* and condemned as ignoble murder. Gambling is another favorite topic and is treated as a serious crime; typically, it leads to other follies. Lord Abberville, for example, comes to realize that "gaming has made a monster of me"; grateful for his reprieve on the brink of ruin, he promises to reform.

The ending is conventional: The dishonest are chastised, the wicked repent, and the chaste lovers, blissfully united, are lavishly endowed with fortune. This is the "tin money" of which Goldsmith complained; the conclusion demonstrates the sentimentalist's rather simplistic view of poetic justice. Virtue need not wait for the hereafter; Cumberland himself takes on the role of Providence, distributing appropriate rewards and punishments before the curtain falls.

Romantic love is often at the center of Cumberland's plots, which typically revolve around a young couple who encounter difficulties in bringing their attachment to fruition. The obstacles they face recur: parental opposition, difference of class or fortune, misleading appearances, or the waywardness of one of the parties. A conventional pair of star-crossed lovers appears in *The Wheel of Fortune*. What is surprising is that their affair is secondary, significant only for its effect on the protagonist.

Roderick Penruddock is an unusual hero for a Cumberland play in that he is well past the age of courtship. In his youth, he was cruelly betrayed by his friend and robbed of his beloved. Bitter and disillusioned, he has withdrawn into gloomy seclusion. The play opens on his inheritance of a vast estate, to which the property of his enemy has been mortgaged. His accession to wealth gives him the power to destroy his foe and rouses in him long-suppressed emotion. The conflict of the play is internal, as he is tempted by, contends with, and eventually vanquishes the spirit of revenge.

In this brooding figure, the play shows signs of the taste for melodrama that was to dominate the English stage in the nineteenth century. There are also certain Romantic tendencies that link it to a later era. Immediately striking is the setting; the first scene takes place in a wild and remote landscape, extremely picturesque. The character of the misanthrope is well adapted to his environment: Penruddock is not only an isolated but also an alienated man. Deeply passionate, he has never forgiven his injuries. Inexorable in anger, he is equally tenacious in love. Though rejected and forgotten by his betrothed, he retains her image fresh in his mind and is haunted by her voice. The anguish of his loss has driven him close to madness.

The turbulence of Penruddock's mind is shown by the intemperance of his language. He rails at the beguiling world which entices only to destroy: "Away with all such snares! There's whore upon the face of them." At home in a stormy wasteland, he is out of place in London. In a gaily festooned ballroom, he looks "like a gloomy nightpiece in a gilded frame." In the streets, the beggars shrink away from his grim visage, which bears the "mark of Cain." He is almost Byronic in his role as a man set apart by a fateful destiny.

Penruddock also shows the Romantic need to escape the corrupting influence of society. He is more content in a simple cottage than in the splendid mansions of the city. He is loath to leave his humble abode and anxious to return. When he has won his battle of conscience, he looks forward to the solace of a self-approving conscience in his rural retreat.

This is a familiar notion in a sentimental play, that good deeds are also pleasurable. One finds an increasingly greater emphasis as the century progresses on sensual gratification, on luxuriating in emotions for their own sake. Penruddock shows signs of this preoccupation; he is completely engrossed by his own subjective experience. Wandering the streets of London, he considers the tumult outside as a reflection of his own state of mind. At every stage of the action, he feels his own mental pulse. Moreover, he deliberately seeks out potentially stimulating situations. He rereads Mrs. Woodville's letter for the tender melancholy it produces, which he indulges to the full. His self-consciousness is characteristically Romantic.

Despite these innovative features, Penruddock is contained within the structure of a sentimental play, and in the end he is reclaimed. The change begins in the third act, when he abandons his aloof and ironic pose to defend his actions. He sympathizes strongly with Henry and is finally able to forgive his debtor. Consonant with Cumberland's philosophy, the spirit of vengeance has been a brief aberration in an otherwise benevolent soul. Apparently, Penruddock's former state of alienation has also been a distortion of his true nature, to which he is now restored. By the end of the play, he has grown remarkably sociable. He compares his heart, overflowing with sympathy, to a river flooding its banks. The bonds have been reestablished, and Penruddock has been accepted back into society.

In *The Wheel of Fortune*, enormously popular in its day, Cumberland demonstrated his ability to adapt to the latest literary trends, yet he was later to fall back on his old recipes for success, despite the fact that these outmoded forms failed to please. In his last years, he complained of the deterioration of standards, to which he would not accommodate himself, and pleaded for tolerance. Cumberland's influence on the theater effectively ended in 1795.

Other major works

NOVELS: *Arundel*, 1789; *Henry*, 1795.

POETRY: *An Elegy Written on St. Mark's Eve*, 1754; *Odes*, 1776; *Miscellaneous Poems*, 1778; *Calvary: Or, The Death of Christ*, 1792; *A Poetical Version of Certain Psalms of David*, 1801; *The Exodiad*, 1807 (with Sir James Bland Burgess); *Retrospection*, 1811.

NONFICTION: *Anecdotes of Eminent Painters in Spain During the Six-*

teenth and Seventeenth Centuries, 1782; *The Observer*, 1785; *Memoirs of Richard Cumberland, Written by Himself*, 1806-1807; *The Letters of Richard Cumberland*, 1988 (edited by Richard J. Dircks).

TRANSLATION: *The Clouds*, 1798 (of Aristophanes' play).

MISCELLANEOUS: *The London Review*, 1809 (editor); *The British Drama*, 1817.

Bibliography

Bevis, Richard. *The Laughing Tradition*. Athens: University of Georgia Press, 1980. Focusing on the varieties of comic theater in the age of actor David Garrick, Bevis investigates the traditional critical dichotomy between an entrenched, uninspired sentimental mode and an upstart, imaginative laughing mode. He discusses Cumberland's major comedies as a response to audience demands for "clean fun" and morally uplifting themes. Bevis describes Cumberland's plays as the ancestors of melodrama. The book has an excellent appendix on trends in criticism of the Georgian theater and provides thorough, illuminating notes.

Campbell, Thomas J. "Richard Cumberland's *The Wheel of Fortune*: An Unpublished Scene." *Nineteenth Century Theatre Research* 11 (1983): 1-11. This article demonstrates what can happen to a play as it passes from text to performance. The omitted scene was probably cut by John Kemble, who played the comic lead of Penruddock in the first performance. Apparently, Kemble thought that the scene's suggestive lines and bantering tones were out of harmony with the sentimental mode of comedy, which audiences preferred.

Detish, Robert. "The Synthesis of Laughing and Sentimental Comedy." *Educational Theatre Journal* 20 (1970): 291-300. Detish argues that a proper reading of Cumberland's most important play, *The West Indian*, requires a recognition of the tension between laughing comedy aggressively espoused by Oliver Goldsmith in the 1770's and sentimental comedy dominant since the days of Richard Steele. *The West Indian* is a bridge between the rival schools of comedy.

Dircks, Richard J. *Richard Cumberland*. Boston: Twayne, 1976. The only modern, full-length critical study of Cumberland's life and works. It evaluates Cumberland's little remembered novels and poems, as well as the more important plays, to present a complete picture of a writer who produced literature popular with contemporary audiences but uninspiring to, and not influential on, the next generation of authors.

Traugott, John. "Heart and Mask and Genre in Sentimental Comedy." *Eighteenth Century Life* 10 (1986): 122-144. The author considers Cumberland's *The Jew* among the worst sentimental comedies of the eighteenth century for its "genteel vulgarity." In contrast to the plays of Oliver Goldsmith and Richard Brinsley Sheridan, Cumberland's work coyly courts a sense of worldliness that it affects to scorn. Traugott offers on thematic grounds an explanation for the lack of reputation of Cumberland's later plays.

Williams, Stanley T. *Richard Cumberland: His Life and Dramatic Works.* New Haven, Conn.: Yale University Press, 1917. The author is mostly concerned with Cumberland's thirty-year career on the Board of Trade and his most noted stage successes. Williams judges Cumberland's plays unsympathetically, showing little appreciation for the artistry of even the best work, *The West Indian.* Williams' approach typifies the old scholarship that Richard Bevis' book (above) challenges.

Lorna Clarke
(Updated by *Robert M. Otten*)

SIR WILLIAM DAVENANT

Born: Oxford, England; February, 1606
Died: London, England; April 7, 1668

Principal drama

The Cruell Brother, pr. 1627, pb. 1630; *The Tragedy of Albovine, King of the Lombards*, pb. 1629; *The Just Italian*, pr. 1629, pb. 1630; *The Siege: Or, The Collonell*, pr. 1629, pb. 1673; *Love and Honour*, pr. 1634, pb. 1649; *The Witts*, pr. 1634, pb. 1636; *News from Plimouth*, pr. 1635, pb. 1673; *The Temple of Love*, pr., pb. 1635 (masque); *The Platonick Lovers*, pr. 1635, pb. 1636; *The Triumphs of the Prince d'Amour*, pr., pb. 1636 (masque); *Britannia Triumphans*, pr., pb. 1638 (masque); *The Fair Favorite*, pr. 1638, pb. 1673; *Luminalia: Or, The Festival of Light*, pr., pb. 1638; *The Unfortunate Lovers*, pr. 1638, pb. 1643; *The Distresses*, pr. 1639, pb. 1673 (also as *The Spanish Lovers*); *Salmacida Spolia*, pr., pb. 1640 (masque); *The First Days Entertainment at Rutland House*, pr. 1656, pb. 1657 (music by Henry Lawes); *The Siege of Rhodes, Part I*, pr., pb. 1656, *Part II*, pr. 1659, pb. 1663; *The Cruelty of the Spaniards in Peru*, pr., pb. 1658; *The History of Sir Francis Drake*, pr., pb. 1659; *Hamlet*, pr. 1661, pb. 1676 (adaptation of William Shakespeare's play); *Twelfth Night*, pr. 1661 (adaptation of Shakespeare's play); *The Law Against Lovers*, pr. 1662, pb. 1673; *Romeo and Juliet*, pr. 1662 (adaptation of Shakespeare's play); *Henry VIII*, pr. 1663 (adaptation of Shakespeare's play); *Macbeth*, pr. 1663, pb. 1674 (adaptation of Shakespeare's play); *The Playhouse to Be Lett*, pr. 1663, pb. 1673; *The Rivals*, pr. 1664, pb. 1668; *The Tempest: Or, The Enchanted Island*, pr. 1667, pb. 1670 (with John Dryden; adaptation of Shakespeare's play); *The Man's the Master*, pr. 1668, pb. 1669.

Other literary forms

Apart from his plays, Sir William Davenant is best known for his unfinished heroic poem, *Gondibert* (1651).

Achievements

Sir William Davenant began his career as a playwright in the age of Ben Jonson and ended it in the age of John Dryden. Already a well-established playwright and poet laureate before the closing of the playhouses at the beginning of the English Civil War in 1642, Davenant managed a limited revival of theatrical entertainments toward the end of the interregnum. Despite the Puritan prohibition against staging plays, Davenant succeeded in obtaining government consent to present "entertainments" at Rutland House in London in 1656. These "entertainments" were musical rather than strictly dramatic, with set declamations instead of plots and entries instead of acts and scenes, but their popularity kept the theater from vanishing entirely during the protectorate of Oliver Cromwell and kept it poised for a revival after the restoration of Charles II in 1660.

Davenant may be credited with having introduced the first actress on the English stage, when Mrs. Edward Coleman sang the role of the heroine Ianthe during the production of his "opera" *The Siege of Rhodes* at Rutland House in the fall of 1656. This production also made use of the changeable scenery hitherto restricted to private theaters and court masques. After the Restoration, Davenant retained and expanded his use of changeable scenery, designing his new theater in Lincoln's Inn Fields to take advantage of its possibilities and spurring imitation by his competitors. Thus, the staging of almost every kind of drama was radically altered.

Davenant operated his theater under a patent that was granted to him by Charles II. In need of plays to produce, he revived some of Ben Jonson's and adapted several of William Shakespeare's. Indeed, Davenant's adaptation of *Macbeth* held the stage well into the eighteenth century, and his adaptation of *The Tempest* well into the nineteenth. As an innovator and an impresario, Davenant changed the course of English theatrical history and extended his influence well beyond his own age.

Biography

Sir William Davenant (or D'Avenant), son of John Davenant, a vintner, was born at Oxford, England, near the end of February, in 1606. As a young man, he wrote his first plays while living in the household of Sir Fulke Greville, and by 1638, he was sufficiently established as a poet and playwright to succeed Ben Jonson as poet laureate. When civil war broke out in 1642, Davenant, a staunch Royalist, risked his life for the Stuart cause. He fled to the Continent for a time, and in 1650 he was on his way to America to become lieutenant governor of Maryland when his ship was intercepted and he was captured and imprisoned in the Tower of London. It was there that he wrote most of his unfinished heroic poem *Gondibert*. Influential friends finally secured his release from the Tower, after which Davenant managed to live on good terms with the Puritan government. He eventually secured official permission to stage operatic entertainments at Rutland House in London, beginning in May of 1656.

Four years later, when the monarchy was restored, Davenant expected court preferment on the basis of his past service to the Stuarts. Although Charles II did grant him a patent to operate a theater, Davenant never regained the favor he had enjoyed under Charles I. Therefore, instead of relying on the patronage of the court, he busied himself with writing and staging plays for the Duke's Company, which he managed at Lincoln's Inn Fields in the public playhouse that he himself built to accommodate the changeable scenery that had been the prerogative of the earlier private theaters. His post-Restoration career lasted only seven years, but during that time, he managed to establish actresses on the English stage, to change play production radically, and to create a new appreciation of Shakespeare's plays, even if in a greatly altered version.

Davenant was married three times. In 1632, he wed a still unidentified woman to whom he was reputed to have been unfaithful. After her death (the date of which is unknown), Davenant married Dame Anne Cademan in 1652. She died in 1655; in that same year, he married Henrietta-Maria du Tremblay, who had four sons by previous marriages. They subsequently had nine sons. He had only one daughter, with one of his first wives. After Davenant's death in 1668, Henrietta-Maria helped prepare an edition of his works. Davenant was buried in Westminster Abbey. His epitaph epitomizes his achievements: "O rare Sir Will. Davenant."

Analysis

Thematically and technically, Sir William Davenant's plays link the theater of Charles I with that of Charles II. For example, the seeds of Restoration comedy are embedded in *The Witts*, in which Davenant explores the subject of wit, using heroes and heroines who prefigure those of Sir George Etherege, William Wycherley, and William Congreve. His early tragedies and tragicomedies, such as *Love and Honour*, explore the love and honor conflicts that later dominate Restoration heroic drama, beginning with Davenant's own *The Siege of Rhodes*. His court masques for Charles I and his queen, Henrietta Maria, used the movable scenery that he would popularize in the public theater after the Restoration. His revivals of the plays of Ben Jonson and his adaptations of Shakespeare's plays preserved and advanced the reputations of those writers during the reign of Charles II.

The Witts is perhaps the best of Davenant's early comedies. During the seventeenth century, the term "wit" came to have multiple meanings. It could mean simply verbal cleverness expressed in appropriate and sustained repartee; it could mean the synthetic faculty of the mind that could see similarities in apparently dissimilar things; it could mean the ornamentation of discourse; it could mean gamesmanship, implying a superior understanding of "the way of the world."

Gamesmanship comes closest to the meaning that concerns Davenant in *The Witts*. Most of the characters in this work are concerned with outmaneuvering their opponents in games of love and legacy. The contest is between the Truewits—those who truly have wit—and the Witwouds—those who think they have wit but do not. Davenant represents the first in the characters of Young Pallatine and Lady Ample; the second, in the characters of the Elder Pallatine and his companion, Sir Morglay Thwack, a country squire.

These last two characters come to London to live by their wits, which to them means seducing rich women who will afterward support them lavishly. Young Pallatine, already in London, has been successful at this game, having gone so far as to persuade his mistress Lucy to sell her belongings to pay for his indulgences. When the brothers Pallatine meet in London, the elder rejects his younger brother's plea for money, and Young Pallatine plots how he may reap both revenge and reward at his brother's expense.

Young Pallatine enlists Lucy in his plot. When Lucy's aunt finally turns her out of her house, she seeks aid from a friend, the wealthy Lady Ample, who, of all the play's characters, turns out to be the wittiest because she can best understand and control her own and others' actions. Lady Ample eventually uses that wit to foil her guardian, Sir Tirant Thrifty, who has picked out an inappropriate husband for her.

In one of the play's key scenes, Lady Ample discusses her wit with Lucy, whom she first takes to task for being so dull-witted and traitorous to her sex as to support a man. Lady Ample, who says she draws her wit from nature, argues instead for tempting "the Fowl" until it can be "caught" and "plume[d]." She then proceeds to demonstrate the application of this principle by acquiring complete mastery over the Elder Pallatine.

After a series of twists, turns, and deceits, engineered by Young Pallatine, Lucy, and Lady Ample herself, the Witwouds are totally humiliated. Sir Morglay Thwack resolves to return to the country while the Elder Pallatine is forced to recant his pretensions to wit. Surprisingly, however, Lady Ample, eager to escape the match arranged by her miserly guardian, agrees to marry the Elder Pallatine because she likes being able to dominate one who has so much money and so little wit.

Lady Ample further demonstrates her mastery over him by forcing him to sign certain bonds without him knowing what it is he is signing. It turns out to be a deed to part of his estate that he has unwittingly signed over to his younger brother. This generous settlement allows Young Pallatine and Lucy to marry. That done, Lady Ample confirms her intention to marry the Elder Pallatine, whom she "has the wit to govern." This scene, in which an independent woman sets the terms upon which she will be married, is a forerunner of the famous "proviso" scenes of Restoration comedy in which like-minded heroines set forth the terms upon which they will consent to marry. Thus, Lady Ample clearly proves to be the best gamester, and therefore the greatest wit, among all the characters. With the addition of more polished repartee and a worthier adversary, Congreve at the end of the seventeenth century would refine a charming Lady Ample into the brilliant Millamant of his *The Way of the World* (pr. 1700).

The English Civil War temporarily halted Davenant's playwriting career, but toward the end of the interregnum, Davenant succeeded in convincing the Puritan government that theatrical entertainments could be useful in teaching morality. Davenant was granted permission to set up a semiprivate stage at Rutland House, his London residence, and to present *The First Days Entertainment at Rutland House* on May 23, 1656. Carefully avoiding even the semblance of drama, Davenant's entertainment was little more than two debates, interspersed with musical interludes. The first debate concerned the usefulness and morality of public entertainments. Indeed, *The First Days Entertainment at Rutland House* was itself designed to demonstrate that public entertainments need not threaten either public morals or the Puritan government. The second debate concerned the relative merits of Paris and London, with, of course, English nationalism triumphant.

Encouraged by the success of this initial enterprise, Davenant again used Rutland House to present his "opera" *The Siege of Rhodes* in the fall of 1656. This time Davenant was more daring, moving his entertainment a step closer to drama by giving it a thin plot and characters developed beyond those of the debaters in *The First Days Entertainment at Rutland House*. In fact, Edward J. Dent in his *Foundations of English Opera* (1928) argues persuasively that *The Siege of Rhodes* was originally written as a play but altered to include instrumental and vocal music to circumvent the Puritan prohibition against the staging of plays. Nevertheless, Davenant was careful to call his work neither drama nor opera, but *The Siege of Rhodes: Made a Representation by the Art of Prospective in Scenes, and the Story Sung in Recitative Musick*. He even avoided the designation "act" by borrowing the term "entry" from the court masques, which he had composed during the reign of Charles I. Thus, *The Siege of Rhodes* has five "entries" instead of five "acts."

From the court masque, Davenant also borrowed the idea of using changeable scenery in his entertainments at Rutland House. Scenes were changed in full view of the audience and indeed were themselves sometimes the most important part of the entertainment. In his preface to *The Siege of Rhodes*, Davenant complains that the narrowness and shallowness of the stage at Rutland House greatly limited his use of spectacle. To create his effects, Davenant used a proscenium arch to frame movable backflats and wings. No attempt at realism was made; instead, the various scenes merely suggested an appropriate atmosphere (though not without inevitable incongruities). Generally, the actors played on the stage apron in front of the proscenium rather than close to the scenery behind it.

Women had long taken part in the court masques. Usually the queen and some of her ladies-in-waiting would appear as goddesses, often accompanied by spectacular scenic effects. On the English public stage, however, men customarily acted women's roles. The closing of the theaters in 1642 meant that by 1656 Davenant had no readily available young actors specifically trained to interpret female roles. Furthermore, Davenant's exile in France had accustomed him to seeing actresses rather than actors in women's roles. Thus, his first production of *The Siege of Rhodes* also marked the first appearance of an actress on the English public stage, when Mrs. Edward Coleman sang the role of the heroine, Ianthe.

After the Restoration, Davenant converted this work into a heroic play. The essence of this genre was the conflict between love and honor. Its heroes and heroines either were exemplary in virtue or were Herculean figures not subject to customary moral niceties. Its verse form was the heroic couplet—the rhymed iambic pentameter closed couplet—deemed most suitable for the expression of heroic ideals. Finally, it emphasized spectacle, sometimes at the expense of sense, as George Villiers, Duke of Buckingham, was to point out in *The Rehearsal* (pr. 1671), which burlesqued the conventions of the genre.

The Siege of Rhodes is a quasi-historical drama. In 1522, the Ottoman Turks besieged Rhodes, garrisoned by the Knights of St. John, under the command of Villiers de L'Isle-Adam. The knights fought valiantly and, though defeated, won the respect of the Turks and safe conduct from the island. Into this story Davenant inserts his hero, Alphonso, and his heroine, Ianthe. Alphonso is one of the defenders of Rhodes; Ianthe, his bride, having sold her jewels in Sicily to procure arms for the garrison, sets sail for Rhodes but is intercepted by the Turkish Fleet and taken prisoner by its commander, the sultan Solyman. Ianthe conquers the sultan by her virtue, and he grants her safe passage to Rhodes. Alphonso is less than happy to see her, since he assumes her safe conduct has been granted because Solyman has enjoyed her favors. Overcareful of his honor, Alphonso fails to recognize honor in others. His resultant jealousy momentarily overwhelms his love, but when the siege resumes and both he and Ianthe are wounded, he at last realizes his folly, and the pair are reconciled, though the outcome of the siege is left in doubt.

To balance Alphonso's jealousy, Davenant introduces Roxolana, Solyman's wife, who is jealous of her husband's appreciation of and attention to Ianthe. Their marital discord is less definitely and happily reconciled, since their marital peace is achieved not by love or trust but by the watchfulness of Roxolana's waiting-women, who have been charged to report any infidelity of Solyman.

Indeed, the notion of reconciliation is crucial to an understanding of *The Siege of Rhodes*, since much of the play's structure seeks a creative rather than a destructive tension between opposites, especially between love and honor. Thus, antitheses abound. For example, West and East are represented by the Rhodians and the Turks respectively, Christian and Muslim by Alphonso and Ianthe and by Solyman and Roxolana; the play's diction is liberally sprinkled with references to order and chaos, public and private worlds, harmony and discord, passion and reason, and light and darkness.

Viewed from this perspective, the marital discords of Alphonso and

Ianthe and of Solyman and Roxolana take on new meaning. The former resolve their discord through the creative power of love and thereby reach a new harmony; the latter achieve only the appearance of a resolution, since the destructive power of jealousy still mars their relationship. These private reconciliations, however, are played out against the backdrop of a larger and much more public discord—the siege itself, which is left unresolved.

This larger conflict was not resolved until Davenant wrote part 2 of *The Siege of Rhodes*. Always the impresario, he staged parts 1 and 2 on alternate days at Lincoln's Inn Fields Theatre. Part 2 continues Davenant's theme of love and honor. This time, the defenders of Rhodes, threatened by famine and by the inevitability of a direct Turkish assault, must choose either an honorable death or an ignoble surrender. Ianthe is sent to negotiate with Solyman, who once again treats her honorably. Alphonso's jealousy is reawakened but eventually subordinated to his fear for Ianthe's safety. Roxolana's jealousy, also rekindled, is somewhat assuaged by her awe of Ianthe's virtue, which lies not so much in Ianthe's reputation as in a sense of personal integrity that allows her to risk her reputation by returning to Solyman's camp. Similarly impressed, Solyman allows Ianthe to set honorable conditions for the surrender of Rhodes. Thus, Ianthe's virtue reconciles both private and public tensions—a happy ending indeed for an England still struggling with the destructiveness of its civil war and the uncertainties of its restored monarchy.

A different sort of reconciliation must be effected in Davenant's *The Playhouse to Be Lett*. The prologue likens this work to a new-fashioned "monster" whose disproportionate limbs "are disjoyn'd and yet united too." Davenant, the successful theater manager, takes his audience behind the scenes to observe the workings of a Restoration playhouse, empty for the summer but about to be rented for various entertainments. The housekeeper and a player must choose among such prospective tenants as a dancing master, a musician, a gentleman, and a poet.

Four entertainments are selected, three of which are by Davenant himself. The French farce presented in act 2 is Davenant's own translation of Molière's *Sganarelle: Ou, Le Cocu imaginaire*. Acts 3 and 4 revive two of Davenant's Rutland House entertainments: *The History of Sir Francis Drake* and *The Cruelty of the Spaniards in Peru*. Act 5 is a travesty of Katherine Philips' tragedy *Pompey* (1663).

Interesting as each of these entertainments may be, it is the action of the frame story that is of most importance, for *The Playhouse to Be Lett* is really a play about the problems of managing a playhouse. Together with plays about the problems of producing a play, it belongs to the sizable group of Restoration plays concerned with theatrical self-consciousness. Many of these plays use a frame story in which a playwright and one or more critics attend the rehearsal of a play, whose action is often interrupted by their comments or by those of the actors themselves, who step out of character momentarily. The epitome of this genre was *The Rehearsal*, which satirized John Dryden and poked fun at the absurdities of heroic drama.

Davenant, whose work preceded *The Rehearsal*, uses a rehearsal framework only in the loosest sense of that word. There is a rehearsal of what will be presented for the summer season, but there is no attempt to interrupt or to correct the individual presentations. In fact, the player and the housekeeper are not even the final judges of what is to be presented. Near the end of the first act, a crowd is gathering outside the theater in order to "see strange things for nothing." The player sends a dozen laundry maids with "tough hands" to keep them out. Nevertheless, at the end of *The Playhouse to Be Lett*, this imaginary audience is revealed to be, in reality, the actual theater audience that has been watching Davenant's entertainment. The player observes that somehow their neighbors have been let in; if they elect to stay, they are likely to hear "An Epilogue, since they have seen a Play." Thus, Davenant's audience is suddenly brought into the action of *The Playhouse to Be Lett*, and the frame characters' awareness of the audience is responsible for the abrupt ending of Davenant's entertainment with no judgments among the prospective renters having been made by the player and the housekeeper. Instead, those judgments will be made by the spectators themselves—a process Dryden was later to term the law of "pit, box, and gallery." The audience alone will determine the profitability of an entertainment. Indeed, throughout act 1, the housekeeper and the player discuss possible audience responses to the kinds of entertainments proposed by the prospective renters and even discuss packing the audience with favorable critics, including a one-handed man who claps by striking his hand against his cheek. Therefore, in giving the audience a look behind the curtain of the playhouse, Davenant also gives the audience a look at itself. His parading before them of the popular entertainments of the town, generated by his audience's insatiable appetite for novelty, would later be enlarged upon by Henry Fielding in the third act of *The Author's Farce* (pr., pb. 1730), in which emblematic representations of the "pleasures of the town" vie for a chaplet to be awarded by the Goddess of Nonsense to her favorite devotee—an honor which eventually goes to Signior Opera.

Davenant's jest at the expense of his playhouse audience illustrates his capacity to play with the paradoxes of the imagination. One of the primary meanings of "imagination" in Davenant's day was the capacity to form images. As the player and the housekeeper in the first act of *The Playhouse to Be Lett* discuss the anticipated responses of their projected audience, they create the image of an early Restoration audience eager for novel entertainments. At the end of act 5, this image fuses with its underlying reality when this imaginary audience is identified with the audience present at Davenant's play. In turn, *The Playhouse to Be Lett*, termed a dramatic "monster" in its prologue, becomes an image of the audience, since it reflects their tastes.

In this sense, Davenant's plays as a whole reveal the "imagination" of two ages—that of Charles I and that of Charles II. The heroes and heroines of Restoration tragedy and comedy are nascent in Davenant's early plays and reach their maturity in his later plays, reflecting the heroic ideals and pragmatic cynicism of the age of Charles II. Indeed, the unpleasantness of the English Civil War and the uncertainties of the restored monarchy seem both to have enhanced expectations for a new heroic age and to have tempered those expectations with the wisdom of the recent past.

However well Davenant may have reflected his world, he also dared to try to shape it, both politically and theatrically. He was no mere spectator during the English Civil War but risked his life in the service of the Crown. In the theater, he risked Puritan opposition to present his entertainments at Rutland House, and he risked introducing actresses and innovative staging in the public playhouse. Like Young Pallatine in *The Witts*, Davenant had wit; like Alphonso in *The Siege of Rhodes*, he had heroic ideals; but above all, like the player and the housekeeper, he had a "playhouse to be lett." To his credit, he filled its stage with exceptional entertainments.

Other major works

POETRY: *Madagascar: With Other Poems*, 1638; *Gondibert*, 1651 (unfinished); *The Seventh and Last Canto of the Third Book of Gondibert*, 1685; *The Shorter Poems and Songs from the Plays and Masques*, 1972 (A. M. Gibbs, editor).

NONFICTION: *The Preface to Gondibert with an Answer by Mr. Hobbes*, 1650 (with Thomas Hobbes).

MISCELLANEOUS: *Works*, 1673, 1968 (reprint).

Bibliography
Blaydes, Sophia B., and Philip Bordinat. *Sir William Davenant*. Boston: G. K. Hall, 1981. This volume in the Twayne series begins with a chapter on Davenant's life and times and then surveys the early plays, the masques, and the Restoration plays. The bibliography is excellent, including even dissertations and theses as well as the usual primary and secondary sources. A good place to begin studying Davenant.

_____. *Sir William Davenant: An Annotated Bibliography, 1629-1985*. New York: Garland, 1986. This bibliography casts a wide net in 365 pages. The primary bibliography is divided into "Collected Works," "Separate Works," and "Miscellaneous Works." The secondary bibliography is broken down into four sections, treating Davenant century by century, and the last section is subdivided into decades. An exceptionally useful tool for Davenant scholars.

Collins, Howard S. *The Comedy of Sir William Davenant.* The Hague: Mouton, 1967. After a chapter on Davenant's career, Collins surveys the general topic of seventeenth century comedy before discussing *The Witts*, *News from Plimouth*, and *The Playhouse to Be Lett.* He then discusses the comedy in ten tragedies and tragicomedies and in six translations and adaptations by Davenant. Select bibliography.

Edmond, Mary. *Rare Sir William Davenant.* New York: St. Martin's Press, 1987. A scholarly study, with rich notes, that treats the whole career. Davenant as man of the theater is considered in chapters treating the early plays and masques, *Gondibert*, the opera, the formation of the "Davenant/Killigrew stage monopoly," and Davenant as theater manager and stage director. Helpful bibliography.

Harbage, Alfred. *Sir William Davenant: Poet Venturer, 1606-1668.* Philadelphia: University of Pennsylvania Press, 1935. Reprint. New York: Octagon Books, 1971. A very good introduction to Davenant. Besides being well written, it sketches Davenant fully enough to give a good picture of the intellectual life of the times. The scholarly bibliography is still helpful. The analysis of Davenant's works is supplemented by a chapter entitled "Adaptations of Shakespeare."

Nethercot, Arthur H. *Sir William Davenant: Poet Laureate and Playwright-Manager.* Chicago: University of Chicago Press, 1938. Reprint. New York: Russell & Russell, 1967. The longest and most detailed study of Davenant. Besides focusing on Davenant as a man of the theater world, Nethercot includes scholarly appendices on the questions of Davenant's wife as William Shakespeare's "Dark Lady," the Chancery Suit against Urswick, Mary Davenant's will, and Thomas Warren's death.

Summers, Montague. *The Playhouse of Pepys.* London: Kegan Paul, Trench, Trubner, 1935. Summers' first chapter, "Sir William Davenant: His Earlier Work and the Opera," is an admiring study of his subject. The ten pages of notes should not be overlooked, and the other chapters—especially the one entitled "Thomas Killigrew and the History of the Theatres Until the Union of 1682"—contain helpful background material for students of Davenant.

Valerie C. Rudolph
(Updated by *Frank Day*)

ROBERTSON DAVIES

Born: Thamesville, Ontario, Canada; August 28, 1913

Principal drama

Overlaid, pr. 1947, pb. 1949 (one act); *Eros at Breakfast*, pr. 1948, pb. 1949; *Hope Deferred*, pr. 1948, pb. 1949; *The Voice of the People*, pr. 1948, pb. 1949; *At the Gates of the Righteous*, pr. 1948, pb. 1949; *Eros at Breakfast and Other Plays*, pb. 1949 (includes *Hope Deferred*, *Overlaid*, *At the Gates of the Righteous*, *The Voice of the People*); *At My Heart's Core*, pr., pb. 1950; *King Phoenix*, pr. 1950, pb. 1972; *A Jig for the Gypsy*, pr. 1954 (broadcast and staged), pb. 1954; *Hunting Stuart*, pr. 1955, pb. 1972; *Love and Libel: Or, The Ogre of the Provincial World*, pr., pb. 1960 (adaptation of his novel *Leaven of Malice*); *Hunting Stuart and Other Plays*, pb. 1972 (includes *King Phoenix* and *General Confession*); *Question Time*, pr., pb. 1975.

Other literary forms

Robertson Davies is known primarily as a novelist. His most highly acclaimed novels form the Deptford Trilogy: *Fifth Business* (1970), *The Manticore* (1972), and *World of Wonders* (1975). These three novels were preceded by another trilogy, set in the fictional community of Salterton: *Tempest-Tost* (1951), *Leaven of Malice* (1954), and *A Mixture of Frailties* (1958). Another trilogy consists of *The Rebel Angels* (1981), *What's Bred in the Bone* (1985), and *The Lyre of Orpheus* (1988). His novel *Murther and Walking Spirits* (1991) continues his interest in reconstructing the main character's past by means of supernatural devices. His earliest success was the publication of three books based on a newspaper column, "The Diary of Samuel Marchbanks," in which he offered witty observations on the social pretensions of a small Ontario town: *The Diary of Samuel Marchbanks* (1947), *The Table Talk of Samuel Marchbanks* (1949), and *Marchbanks' Almanack* (1967).

Davies also has written a teleplay, *Fortune, My Foe* (1948), and he enjoys a considerable reputation as a critic. His articles, essays, and observations have been collected in several books, including *A Voice from the Attic* (1960), *One Half of Robertson Davies* (1977), *The Enthusiasms of Robertson Davies* (1979), and *The Well-Tempered Critic* (1981). Subjects to which he has turned his sharp pen include contemporary Canadian theater, the manners and mores of small-town residents, the humor of Stephen Leacock, the history of the Stratford Shakespearean Festival, and the Canadian national identity. His scholarly writing has centered on theater history and dramatic literature, particularly of the nineteenth century.

In all of his nondramatic writing, Davies demonstrates a keen sense of the absurdity of social pretension, an awareness of the dark world of the unconscious, and a love of magic. In many of his fictional works, the theater plays an important part, whether it be the amateur production of William Shakespeare's *The Tempest*, which sets the stage for *Tempest-Tost*, or the flamboyant actor-manager of the melodramatic school who holds center stage in *World of Wonders.* Regardless of genre, Davies' perspective is that of the ironic, detached, urbane, yet sensitive observer, a reporter of the quirks of fortune which act upon human existence and which serve to reveal the inner workings of the heart.

Achievements

Davies is recognized as one of Canada's leading writers, and, although his influence is predominately in fiction, his impact on the emergence of drama and theater uniquely Canadian is widely appreciated. The source of this influence is divided between his position as a respected critic and scholar and his original and striking dramatic writing. As Master of Massey College, a position he held from 1962 to 1981, and as founder and senior scholar of the Graduate Centre for the Study of Drama, Davies influenced two generations of students at the University of Toronto.

The period immediately following World War II was of great significance to the development of indigenous Canadian drama. A spirit of nationalism, arising in large part from the important contribution of Canadian regiments to the victory in Europe, fueled a renewed interest in plays about the Canadian experience. At the same time, there was a sharp increase in the number of plays being performed in theatrical centers such as Toronto. The new professional theater companies were looking for new plays which would appeal to local audiences and with which they could make their reputations. One such company was the Crest Theatre, and several of Davies' plays were written for this group. Other influential plays by Davies were written for amateur companies and became staples of the amateur repertoire in Canada. As a result, between 1945 and 1965 Davies was the dominant English-Canadian playwright.

Davies was awarded the Leacock medal for humor in 1955, the Lorne Pierce medal for contribution to Canadian literature in 1961, and, in 1973, the Governor-General's Award for Fiction. He is a fellow of the Royal Society of Canada, the recipient of honorary degrees from more than ten universities, an honorary member of the American Academy (the first Canadian to be so honored), and a Companion of the Order of Canada.

Biography

William Robertson Davies was born on August 28, 1913, in Thamesville, Ontario, to William Rupert Davies, editor of the *Thamesville Herald*, and

Florence Sheppard McKay Davies. In 1926, the Davies family moved to Kingston, where William Rupert Davies became owner and editor of the Kingston *Whig* and later, when the two local papers merged, of the Kingston *Whig Standard*. The fictional town of Salterton, which provides the environment for three of Davies' novels, bears a remarkable resemblance to the town of Kingston.

Davies was greatly influenced by the literary and dramatic activities of his parents, both of whom had a lively interest in music and theater. At that time, there was little professional theater in the small towns of Ontario, but the family traveled regularly to Toronto, Ottawa, and Detroit to see productions touring out of New York or London. The influence of the great masters of the art of acting is felt in much of Davies' work, but most notably in *World of Wonders*, which is a fictional treatment of the Canadian tour of John Martin-Harvey, one of the last proponents of the nineteenth century school of Romantic acting.

Davies' love of theater was evident throughout his academic career. As a schoolboy, he dramatized classic novels for his fellow students to perform. He acted in local amateur theater productions in the community and at school. At Balliol College, Oxford, he was active in the Oxford University Dramatic Society as an actor, stage manager, and director. He also did his bachelor of literature thesis on Shakespeare's boy actors, publishing it in 1939.

The young Davies determined to make his career in theater, and, as there was virtually no professional theater in Canada at the time, he remained in England and found employment at the Old Vic Repertory Company. He performed only minor roles and proved more valuable in teaching theater history in the company school and doing literary work for the director, Tyrone Guthrie, an old school friend from Oxford. It was there that he met Brenda Mathews, a young Australian actress and stage manager, whom he married in 1940.

The theaters in London closed with the outbreak of World War II, and the Davies returned to Canada, where Davies became literary editor of *Saturday Night*, a monthly cultural magazine. In 1942, they moved to Peterborough, and Davies became the editor and publisher of the *Peterborough Examiner*, a position he held until 1962. In 1943, he began the syndicated column "The Diary of Samuel Marchbanks," featuring satiric observations and anecdotes about fictional characters, situations, and attitudes in a small Ontario town, as seen through the eyes of a thinly disguised Robertson Davies. Selections from this column were collected in three books: *The Diary of Samuel Marchbanks*, *The Table Talk of Samuel Marchbanks*, and *Marchbanks' Almanack*.

It was also at this time that Davies and his wife became active in local amateur theatricals. He began to write full-length and short plays, submitting one of them, *Overlaid*, to a play competition in Ottawa in 1947. As the winning play, it was produced by the Ottawa Drama League. The same group produced his next short comedy, *Eros at Breakfast*, the following year, and entered their production in the national amateur dramatic competition, the Dominion Drama Festival. The production won a trophy for best production of a Canadian play and Davies won the prize for author of the best Canadian play. Moreover, the production was selected to represent Canada at the Edinburgh Festival in Glasgow in 1949.

With this encouraging beginning, Davies went on to write, in quick succession, *Fortune, My Foe* (which carried off the same prizes as *Eros at Breakfast*), *At My Heart's Core*, and *King Phoenix*. By 1948, Davies had become the most produced English-Canadian playwright, with amateur groups across Canada performing his plays.

Nevertheless, at this time, Davies' energies were being directed more and more toward the writing of full-length fiction. *Tempest-Tost*, *Leaven of Malice*, and *A Mixture of Frailties* were published in the 1950's, and in 1953, Davies discontinued the Marchbanks column. He did not, however, entirely turn his back on the theater; on the contrary, his writing benefited from two exciting new developments in Canadian drama. In 1953, the Stratford Shakespearean Festival was founded, and Davies became a member of the board of directors, a position he held until 1971. From 1953 to 1955, he published an annual record of the history of the festival, which was then under the leadership of his friend Tyrone Guthrie. These volumes were published as *Renown at Stratford* (1953), *Twice Have the Trumpets Sounded* (1954), and *Thrice the Brinded Cat Hath Mew'd* (1955). The second development was the emergence of a fully professional theater company in Toronto, the Crest Theatre, for which Davies wrote several plays. The company produced his *A Jig for the Gypsy* in 1954 and *Hunting Stuart* in 1955. *General Confession* was written in 1956 for the same group but was never performed.

Davies' considerable energies were further diverted when, in 1962, he was appointed by Vincent Massey to be the first Master of Massey College, a college for graduate students at the University of Toronto. In 1960, Davies had been appointed a professor of English and began his teaching career. He remained a member of the academic community for twenty years but was always skeptical about his adopted world, as is evident in the pointed satire in his novel *The Rebel Angels* (1981).

In 1960, Davies attempted a dramatization of his novel *Leaven of Malice*, entitled *Love and Libel*, which Tyrone Guthrie directed for the New York Theatre Guild. Reviews were mixed; the production closed after four days, and Davies himself was dissatisfied with his adaptation. He consented to rework the script for an amateur production at Hart House Theatre at the University of Toronto in 1973 under the same title as the novel, and it was this version which was produced at the Shaw Festival in 1975. In 1975, Davies wrote *Question Time* for Toronto Arts Productions, a leading Toronto professional company. Again, the results were not entirely positive. The reviews were mixed, and audiences were puzzled by the play's nonrealistic style. Davies was more comfortable writing for amateur groups, including the theater group at his old school Upper Canada College, which produced *A Masque of Aesop* in 1952 and *A Masque of Mr. Punch* in 1962. In 1967, the year of the centennial celebrations in Canada, he contributed one segment to *The Centennial Play*, which was written expressly for amateur audiences. It was given its first full-scale production by a group with which Davies had been associated at the beginning of his writing career, the Ottawa Little Theatre.

In 1981, Davies retired from his duties as Master of Massey College to dedicate himself full-time to his writing. Thereafter, he continued to contribute to scholarly and popular periodicals on a regular basis but concentrated on his novel writing. He contributes regularly to *The New York Times Book Review*, *Maclean's*, *Harper's*, and other literary periodicals. A television documentary on Davies, "The Magic Season of Robertson Davies," was aired in 1990.

Analysis

The dramatic writing of Robertson Davies stands far removed from the mainstream of mid-twentieth century drama. The majority of modern drama is realistic in language and characterization, if not in form. Davies rejects this trend for older and blatantly theatrical models such as medieval masques and morality plays and nineteenth century Romantic comedies and melodramas. In his commentary on his own plays, Davies confirms his commitment to alternatives to realism. He rejects the naturalistic school of drama, which seeks to reproduce daily life on the stage, for, as Davies notes, it is the paradox of the theater that plays are sometimes most like life when they are least like a photograph of reality.

Davies' love for some of the older forms of drama springs from his conviction that these forms were closer in spirit to the original, primal function of all art. He seeks theater that will fill audiences with a sense of wonder. The theater, in Davies view, should be a place of spiritual refreshment, and this is particularly the case, he suggests, in melodrama and in the earliest forms of drama. Theater began, he reminds his audience, as a temple, a place where people expected to experience the full range of human emotion—the glorification of the godlike in man as well as his invigorating wickedness.

Davies readily admits to being an old-fashioned playwright longing for a theater which has perhaps entirely disappeared. He writes plays which call for acting in the classic Romantic style he remembers so fondly from visits to the theater during his youth. His plays necessitate this larger-than-life manner because they deal with fundamental conflicts between archetypal forces.

Davies is equally unfashionable in the strongly didactic tone of his plays. He defines himself as a moralist, one who perceives several insidious diseases of the spirit and seeks to cure them with the powerful antidote of laughter. So strong are Davies' opinions that he eschews subtlety in favor of direct statement, as well as a decidedly oracular tone thinly disguised with a sugary coating of wit.

Davies recognizes that his attitudes run against the *Zeitgeist*, but he remains true to his original commitment to the magical rather than the ordinary. As a result, his dramatic writing is remarkably unified in style.

The predominant identifying feature of Davies' plays is their language. Modern fashion leans toward dramatic dialogue that is colloquial, filled with slang and expletives, and minimal. Davies has chosen the opposite extreme, and his plays are linguistic feasts of wit, flights of fancy, and lucidity. Davies defends his style by pointing out that, for those with intelligence, style, sensitivity, and the wit to give form to random human discourse, conversation is an art. Davies' attitude toward conversation is expressed in *Fortune, My Foe* by Professor Rowlands, who describes himself as having a gift for something which is undervalued: good talk. Rowlands claims to be an artist, a master of poetry that is verbal and extempore but that is still poetry. Indeed, in general, the characters in the plays of Robertson Davies speak in a manner remarkably reminiscent of that of the playwright himself.

Davies' carefully constructed sentences are the perfect vehicle for another dominant attribute of his writing, his satire and parody of Canadian institutions and attitudes. There is nothing oblique about this element of Davies' dramas: The incorporation of the satiric element is very much a part of the moral thrust of the plays. Virtually every character in every play is given at least one well-constructed aphorism, and characters have a decided tendency to address one another in short moral lectures. At times these digressions threaten to slow the dramatic movement of the plot to a standstill, but the sheer pleasure of Davies' language retains the goodwill of the audience.

The witty repartee characteristic of a Davies play is generally given plausible motivation, given the setting and the intellectual attributes of the speakers. Chilly Jim and Idris Rowlands, who exchange quips and aphorisms in *Fortune, My Foe*, are two such plausible moral wits. Rowlands, as noted above, is a university professor who describes himself as a professional talker, a poet of conversation, while Chilly confesses that language is his hobby. Their conversations, which are filled with the most carefully crafted language, are entirely believable. Modern audiences are used to fast-paced and tightly edited forms of entertainment, but Davies crafts his plays for a premodern, slow-moving dramatic form and for audiences who prefer to savor *bons mots*.

In dramatic structure, Davies' plays are also strongly influenced by archaic forms. Several of his plays, most notably *Question Time*, take the form of a morality play, with a central character representing mankind interacting with personifications of the human psyche on a journey toward self-discovery. In *Question Time*, Peter MacAdam is a representative of humanity (his name means "son of Adam") and of all Canadians (as Prime Minister of Canada) who is launched upon a journey into his unconscious mind after a plane crash in the Arctic. While he lies in a coma, his mind is freed to explore his inner landscape in search of his true identity. He encounters personifications of his own attributes—totem animals—and finally convenes the Parliament of the Irrational, wherein two versions of himself lead the debate as to whether he should live or die.

Debate is another traditional element of the morality play, and Davies' characters frequently engage in such contests. Many of his plays focus on two essential forces in conflict, with the balance clearly weighted toward one of the two parties. This is the case in *Overlaid*, where Pop represents life-affirming forces (Eros), and Ethel, life-denying forces (Thanatos).

In drawing on an archaic form such as the morality play, Davies does not stifle audiences with dusty scholarship. Rather, he adapts the model to realize the potential of the modern stage to become a forum for an exploration of those deep concerns humanity shares. Davies replaces the absolute Christian moral doctrines espoused by the medieval morality plays with a standard of judgment that is not external but internal. Davies is concerned with individuals' judgment of themselves, their perception of their soul in its entirety, and their recognition of the unlived lives that, if unattended, are sure to have their revenge.

In characterization, Davies also rejects the expected naturalistic layering of details or the question-filled outlines of the contemporary theater. Instead, he relies on character-types as symbolic vehicles for his morality lessons. He generally structures a play around a single protagonist whom he presents in the most exciting and positive manner. He surrounds this character with a variety of less fully developed creations, all of whom exist to fulfill a thematic function, to embody a force against which the hero reacts. Minor characters are given single and striking identifying characteristics and then allowed to interact within situations that are crafted to bring essential conflicts to the surface.

Davies' heroes share the attributes of the artist, and those characters who stand in opposition embody those forces which seek to destroy or limit the artistic function. Davies' sharp juxtapositions of these forces indicate his condemnation of certain attitudes. Ranged against the positive force of art, which is linked with spiritual enrichment, intuition, sensitivity, perception, and wonder, are narrow materialism, ignorant respectability, cultural philistinism, dogmatic religion, science, modern impatience, insufficient education, and the absence of laughter. Those characters who lack a sense of humor are perhaps the most barren, pretentious, and emotionally undernourished (as well as the least appealing to the audience). Their grim devotion to principle—whether it be religious, social, or scientific—is the most effective force against the joyful spirit of the healthy soul.

In his most successful novels and plays, Davies explores the relationship between human consciousness, trapped as it is in the perceptions of daily reality and blinded by the limitations of sensibility, and the unconscious, that vast, uncharted, terrifying world whence springs all art, all vitality, and all meaning. From Davies' perspective, the conflicts of the unconscious mind are more real than the trivial, day-to-day concerns of observable reality.

Davies' fascination with the internal workings of an individual dates, he reports, from the health dialogues in which he acted as a child. These little skits were set in such locales as the stomach and featured naughty foods as well as the angelic Miss Milk and Mr. Apple. In one of his earliest plays, *Eros at Breakfast*, Davies returns to this idea and shows us a young man's soul when he first experiences love. With this fantasy, Davies is able to teach a few lessons about the inner workings of the mind: Love comes, we learn, not from the mind, but is initiated by sentiment, enhanced by the liver, and finally affects the soul. In his later plays, Davies takes on increasingly complex aspects of human experience, until he comes to grips with the nature of identity and strives to define more clearly the soul itself. En route, Davies' expert knowledge of and defiant admiration for melodrama is transferred to the interior landscape, so that striking character-types merge with psychological allegory. In this method, he is greatly influenced by the theories of Carl Jung, in particular the definition of the three attributes of the personality: the persona, the anima, and the shadow. In his scholarly writing, Davies has explored the relationship between Jungian archetypes and melodramatic character-types, and scholars have traced a similar correspondence in Davies' fiction. In melodrama, they appear as the hero, the heroine, and the villain; in Davies' plays, they emerge in a variety of forms as he experiments with the dramatic presentation of this theory.

An early, unproduced experiment is *General Confession*, which Davies has singled out as his favorite play. An elderly Casanova entertains two young lovers with three conjured figures: the philosopher Voltaire, the evil magician Cagliostro, and an unnamed beautiful woman. The figures act out scenes from Casanova's past, and in the last act, Casanova is put on trial for his sins, with the philosopher as adviser, the woman as defender, and

the magician as accuser. Finally, Davies gives these last three figures allegorical titles: they are, respectively, Casanova's Wisdom, his Ideal of
Womanhood, and his Contrary Destiny. Casanova and his two young
friends learn an important lesson in identity: Everyone has within him a
wise adviser; an ideal, to provide direction; and an enemy, against which to
test himself.

This dramatization of Jung's theory of the personality has injected Davies' writing with an atmosphere of the mystical, which underlies the surface narrative he presents. In *Question Time*, he jettisons the external reality within which he tried to work in *General Confession*, using the patterns
of dreams for his dramatic form and the images of Jungian theory for characters and setting. The *terra incognita* into which Peter MacAdam journeys
in *Question Time* is the world of the unconscious, here made remarkably
theatrical by Davies' image of the Arctic as the last unchartered realm of
our world and so the perfect metaphor for the unchartered territory of the
mind. His description of the stage presentation indicates the mystical atmosphere he wished to evoke; he asks for music that is not the conventional movie sound track, but something truly mysterious, embracing, alive.
The set, he suggests, should create the effect of a landscape that, although
unfriendly, is of transporting beauty.

Along with his old-fashioned dramatic form, Davies often alienates audiences by expressing attitudes which it is unfashionable to state publicly,
though they may be widely held. In two areas, in particular, he has in-
curred the wrath of sectors of the public. Davies has strong feelings about
class divisions, as is evident in the characterization in his plays. In *Question
Time*, the representatives of the working classes are Madge and Tim, and
the portrait is not at all flattering. Crude language, cruder vision, and the
most narrow-minded selfishness characterize these figures. Tim is much
given to simplistic, clichéd pronouncements against the rich, and he makes
several references to his union. He is particularly irritating in the second
half of the play, where he disrupts the formal rituals with obnoxious and
ignorant objections. Davies seems to be implying that the common people
are easily led, uneducated, brutish, and totally lacking in any sensitivity to
the world of the spirit. Regardless of the veracity of this portrait, it is in
sharp contrast to the egalitarian ideals mouthed by most contemporary
playwrights.

Davies is openly elitist about the world of art and espouses an aristocracy
of the soul: Some people are open to its magic, and some are closed. This
capacity is not always tied to class and education, for some of Davies' most
obtuse and closed characters suffer from an excess of money and schooling.
More often than not, however, the most appealing, witty, sensitive, and
attractive of Davies' characters are members of the social elite. Davies
describes repeatedly the natural grace and acquired good taste of the ladies

in *At My Heart's Core*, qualities which are very much part of their breeding as gentlewomen. Contrast is provided by Sally and Honour, the first an Indian servant whom Davies describes as giggling at the most inopportune moments or brandishing a skillet, and the second an uneducated Irish settler who has just borne a child to her foster father. In a telling scene, Mrs. Frances Stewart, whom Davies portrays as the most beautiful and gracious of the ladies, suggests that, if Honour does not wish to stay in bed to recover from the birth of her child, she might just as well go out into the kitchen and help Sally. Frances means no insult here, nor does Davies. Honour is more comfortable serving Frances, and both women accept the responsibilities and privileges of their different positions. There is no hint of these two having been born equal.

Another issue on which Davies has expressed decided and unpopular ideas is gender. In direct statement as well as by implication, Davies communicates his belief that women and men are different and that the world runs most smoothly when both sexes know their strengths and limitations and do not attempt to shatter the natural order. For Davies, women are the more sensitive, the givers, the supporters. This does not mean that they are incapable of intelligence, of spirit, or of strength, but theirs is a distinctly feminine intelligence, spirit, and strength. Frances Stewart is a woman witty enough to match swords with the devilish tempter Edmund Cantwell, intelligent enough to admit his success and attempt to deal with the dissatisfaction with which he attempts to poison her life, and strong enough to deliver a baby, outface a drunken settler, and remain alone in the forest eight miles from her closest neighbor. When her husband returns, however, she bows to his masculine wit, intelligence, and strength and allows him to solve the social entanglement in which she finds herself. It is Thomas Stewart who hands out justice to the erring settler, who gets to the bottom of the plotting of Edmund Cantwell and who embodies the most vital and theatrical love of life, exemplified by his mimicry of the music-hall clown Grimaldi.

The explanation for Davies' attitude toward his female characters rests partially in his personal Victorian sensibilities but also in his use of the female gender to embody the values of the spirit. The most striking example of this occurs in *Question Time*, in the figure of La Sorcière des Montagnes de Glace. In the final moments of the play, Davies explicates her symbolic function: She is the ultimate authority in the world of the soul, the final reality, the life force, a power so old that she "makes all monarchies seem like passing shadows on her face, and all forms of power like games children tire of." Women cannot complain that Davies dislikes their sex, but they are perhaps correct when they say that he does not portray them realistically on the stage.

Given Davies' concern with the interior of the human mind, it is no surprise to discover two perennial themes in his dramatic writing: the quest for personal identity and the magic of art. These are not new themes, and Davies' treatment of the importance of self-knowledge and the unique properties of art and artists is not new. What is striking is the way in which he unites these two themes with a third concern which figures largely in his dramatic writing: the relationship between art, personal identity, and the national identity of Canadians. When asked to describe the theme of *Question Time*, Davies' reply was brief and to the point; he stated that the play was about the relationship of the Canadian people to their soil and about the relationship of a man to his soul, both of which we neglect at our peril.

These relationships, and the parallels between the two, form the thematic content of many of Davies' plays. Canada, he suggests, suffers from a lack of emotional stimulation, from a denigration of the arts which might have been appropriate in a pioneer society but which is sadly out of place in the twentieth century. By evoking the magic and power of art, Davies hopes to awaken his audiences to the need for the life-giving spirit of art in their lives.

Nowhere is the pure magic of the performing arts more powerfully evoked than in *Fortune, My Foe*. Here the art form is puppetry, and the artist is Franz Szabo, a refugee who has brought to Canada a European artistic discipline and awareness. Franz gives voice to Davies' view of artistic creation when he describes his profession. It takes sixteen years to acquire the skill of a marionette master, but once acquired, it allows the puppet master to infuse his creation with a part of his own soul, so that the figure is more real, more truly alive, than the puppet master himself. Although his new Canadian friends warn him that Canada is a cold country, inhospitable to artists, Franz is determined to remain and find an audience for his puppets. In the course of the play, he is partially successful in this quest.

The individual most deeply affected by his encounter with the artist Szabo is Nicholas, a young university professor on the brink of leaving Canada for a more lucrative career in the United States. Nicholas has despaired of ever achieving a decent income in Canada, a country where the questions he asks meet only with blank incomprehension and where the yearnings he feels find no understanding. He realizes the importance of art to the health of the soul: Art fills a need in the heart; it provides brilliant color, the warmth and gaiety that people crave. Others who come in contact with Franz Szabo respond less favorably. Vanessa Medway is enchanted and eager to become involved, but her impatience bars her from partaking of an artistic experience which requires a minimum of two years' training. Vanessa exemplifies a worldview that Davies labels as distinctively modern: detached, unemotional, fast-moving, quickly tiring of things and people, yet capable of perception and honesty. Ursula Simonds wants to alter Szabo's art to pure didacticism; she claims that art without a message is worthless, while Szabo argues that art is not to be trusted unless it is in the hands of artists, not educators or revolutionaries.

The least appealing response comes from Mrs. E.C. Philpott and Ovrille Tapscott, representatives from the local recreation board, whom Davies uses to satirize certain educational theories that emphasize the scientific approach. Tapscott and Mrs. Philpott regard puppets as ideal for instruction in oral hygiene and for developing manual dexterity in young girls. Their belief in their power to do good is so powerful that it blinds them to the simple, pure message of Szabo's little theater. They are, Davies suggests, the half-educated, who are the least likely to appreciate art. They find Szabo's dramatization of the story of Don Quixote immoral, offensive, and antisocial. Terrified of any art which ventures into the area of deep personal concerns, they are blind to their own need for art to save them from emotional starvation.

Szabo has the strength to survive the condemnation of the emotionally barren and the impatience of the modern. He reminds his friends that a real artist is tough; as long as he keeps the image of his work clear in his heart, he will not fail. Canada is his country now, and though he foresees struggle, he will continue his search for an audience. His optimism tips the balance for Nicholas, and the play ends with the young man's announcement that he, too, will stay in Canada.

It is the cynical Chilly Jim, however, who voices Davies' most powerful evocation of the potential of the theater. Chilly has seen three murders, but nothing has moved him like Szabo's puppets. The theater makes him feel something he has not experienced since he was a boy, a kind of religious wonder:

> You've always suspected that something existed, and you've wished and prayed that it did exist, and in your dreams you've seen little bits of it, but to save your life you couldn't describe it or put a name to it. Then, all of a sudden, there it is, and you feel grateful, and humble, and wonder how you ever doubted it. That little stage makes me feel like that—quiet and excited at the same time.

This is the power of the theater that Robertson Davies celebrates in his writing.

Other major works

NOVELS: *Tempest-Tost*, 1951; *Leaven of Malice*, 1954; *A Mixture of Frailties*, 1958; *Fifth Business*, 1970; *The Manticore*, 1972; *World of Wonders*, 1975; *The Rebel Angels*, 1981; *What's Bred in the Bone*, 1985; *The Lyre of Orpheus*, 1988; *Murther and Walking Spirits*, 1991.

NONFICTION: *Shakespeare's Boy Actors*, 1939; *Shakespeare for Younger Players: A Junior Course*, 1942; *The Diary of Samuel Marchbanks*, 1947; *The Table Talk of Samuel Marchbanks*, 1949; *Renown at Stratford: A Rec-*

ord of the Shakespeare Festival in Canada, 1953, 1953 (with Tyrone
Guthrie); Twice Have the Trumpets Sounded: LA Record of the Stratford
Shakespearean Festival in Canada, 1954, 1954 (with Guthrie); Thrice the
Brinded Cat Hath Mew'd: A Record of the Stratford Shakespearean Festival
in Canada, 1955, 1955 (with Guthrie); A Voice from the Attic, 1960; The
Personal Art: Reading to Good Purpose, 1961; Marchbanks' Almanack,
1967; Stephen Leacock: Feast of Stephen, 1970; One Half of Robertson
Davies, 1977; The Enthusiasms of Robertson Davies, 1979; The Well-
Tempered Critic, 1981; Reading and Writing, 1993.
TELEPLAY: Fortune, My Foe, 1948.

Bibliography

Davies, Robertson. "Robertson Davies: An Interview." Interview by Michael Hulse. Journal of Commonwealth Literature 22, no. 1 (1987):
119-135. A warmhearted chat by the fireside, mainly on Davies' novel
characters, but touching at several points on his writing methods. Briefly
mentions Question Time and Davies' process for revising drafts.
_____. The Well-Tempered Critic: One Man's View of Theatre and
Letters in Canada. Toronto: McClelland and Stewart, 1981. The first half
of this volume is a collection of essays on the theater, spiced with
Davies' own acerbic wit but revealing his benevolent attitude toward traditional, even medieval, dramatic forms. Contains many reviews of the
festival seasons at Stratford, Ontario.
MacLulich, T. D. Between Europe and America: The Canadian Tradition in
Fiction. Toronto: ECW Press, 1988. Despite its title, this study deals with
Davies' earliest plays, Hope Deferred and Overlaid, before a brief synopsis of Fortune, My Foe and At My Heart's Core. Much on Davies'
prose work as well. Helpful index.
Peterman, Michael. Robertson Davies. Boston: Twayne, 1986. A general
study of Davies' novels and essays, as well as two chapters on his plays,
early and late. Contains a chronology, a bibliography, and an interesting
discussion of his first, unpublished play, The King Who Coult Not
Dream. Index.
Steinberg, M. W. "Don Quixote and the Puppets: Theme and Structure in
Robertson Davies' Drama." In Dramatists in Canada: Selected Essays,
edited by William H. New. Vancouver: University of British Columbia
Press, 1972. Originally published in Canadian Literature: A Quarterly of
Criticism and Review in 1961, this essay is a structural analysis of Da-
vies' early plays, notably Fortune, My Foe, At My Heart's Core, and A
Jig for the Gypsy. "Eminently stageworthy and . . . a valuable contribu-
tion to a genre that Canadian talent has unfortunately neglected," Stein-
berg notes.
Woodcock, George. "A Cycle Completed: The Nine Novels of Robertson

Davies." *Canadian Literature: A Quarterly of Criticism and Review* 126 (Autumn, 1990): 33-48. A good overview of Davies' major literary contribution, as a backdrop for his dramatic output. Woodcock sees Davies' "traditional" forms as "calming and comforting" in an otherwise "permissive" literary world.

Leslie O'Dell
(Updated by *Thomas J. Taylor*)

OWEN DAVIS

Born: Portland, Maine; January 29, 1874
Died: New York, New York; October 14, 1956

Principal drama

For the White Rose, pr. 1898; *Through the Breakers*, pr. 1899; *The Confessions of a Wife*, pr., pb. 1905; *The Family Cupboard*, pr. 1913, pb. 1914; *The Detour*, pr. 1921, pb. 1922; *Icebound*, pr., pb. 1923; *The Nervous Wreck*, pr. 1923, pb. 1926; *The Haunted House*, pr. 1924, pb. 1926; *The Good Earth*, pr., pb. 1932 (with Donald Davis; adaptation of Pearl Buck's novel); *Jezebel*, pr., pb. 1933; *Ethan Frome*, pr., pb. 1936 (with Donald Davis; adaptation of Edith Wharton's novel); *Mr. and Mrs. North*, pr., pb. 1941 (adaptation of Frances and Richard Lockridge's novel).

Other literary forms

In addition to more than three hundred plays, Owen Davis wrote a radio series entitled *The Gibson Family* (1934), which lasted for thirty-nine weeks. He was also a screenwriter in Hollywood, where his work included *Icebound* (1924), *How Baxter Butted In* (1925), *Frozen Justice* (1929), and *Hearts in Exile* (1929).

In 1930, dissatisfied with Hollywood and its exploitation of the writer, Davis returned to writing for the stage. In 1931, he published a volume of autobiography, *I'd Like to Do It Again*; he updated his life story in 1950 with *My First Fifty Years in the Theatre.*

Achievements

Owen Davis' career spanned almost sixty years, and during that period he wrote more than three hundred plays, most of which were performed professionally. Inasmuch as his work was produced in New York for thirty-seven consecutive seasons, and twenty of his plays were produced in Hollywood as movies, he was, from 1900 to 1950, America's most prolific playwright. Indeed, drama critic George Jean Nathan called Davis "the Lope de Vega of the American Theatre."

Davis began his career as a writer of "'Ten-Twent'-Thirt'" melodramas, and by 1910 he achieved recognition as the dominant writer in this dramatic form. Motivated to be a serious writer, Davis wrote *The Family Cupboard*, which enabled him to move from the visually dominated melodramas to comedy. Always seeking to grow as an artist, Davis shifted from situation comedy to psychological melodrama; perhaps his finest work in this form was the 1923 play *Icebound*, for which he received the Pulitzer Prize and for which he was inducted into the National Institute of Arts and Letters. Later, he would serve on the Pulitzer Prize selection committee.

In addition to his work as a dramatist, Davis sought to free the writer from managerial abuse and plagiarism. Thus, he became actively involved in founding the Dramatists' Guild, serving as its president in 1922. As president, he addressed himself to such issues as film rights, actors' homes, loans, and other issues germane to the theater profession. Davis had a gift for organization and administration and was drafted continually into leadership positions.

Biography

Writing plays like "a freshman writes home for money—as frequently and with as little effort," Owen Davis became America's most prolific dramatist. Born in 1874, Davis was one of eight children of Abbie Gould Davis and Owen Warren Davis. His father, a graduate of Bowdoin College and a Civil War veteran, was primarily in the iron business, owning the Kathodin Iron Works and serving one term as president of the Society of American Iron Manufacturers. Later, he operated a photography studio on New York's Forty-second Street. He died in 1920 of a heart attack.

Davis went to school in Bangor, Maine, and at the age of nine wrote his first play, "Diamond Cut Diamond: Or, The Rival Detectives." At the age of fourteen, he enrolled as a subfreshman at the University of Tennessee. To satisfy his father, Davis left after one year and attended Harvard. Because Harvard did not have a theater and drama department, Davis first majored in business and then transferred, in 1893, to the sciences to become a mining engineer. While at Harvard, Davis participated in football and track and organized the Society of Arts, under the auspices of which he produced his verse dramas. In 1893, he left Harvard without a degree and followed his family to Southern Kentucky, where he was hired by the Cumberland Valley Kentucky Railroad as a mining engineer. Dissatisfied, Davis decided that he wanted to become a playwright or an actor. In 1895, with twelve dollars in his pocket, he quit his job and went to New York City. Meeting with continual discouragement, Davis was finally aided by theater manger A. M. Palmer, whose influence helped Davis get work as a utility actor, stage manager, press agent, advance man, company manager, and in some instances assistant director for the Fanny Janauschek Troupe. Davis left the company in 1896, committed to becoming a writer.

Giving full attention to writing, Davis tried to sell his first play, *For the White Rose*. Meeting with rejection after rejection, he became determined to figure out a formula for the then-running successful plays. After studying the melodramas and the audiences, Davis discovered that he needed to write for the "eye rather than the ear"—that is, he needed to emphasize scenic elements. Davis also concluded that the successful melodramas depended on such common features as a strong love interest, the triumph of good over evil, and stock comic characters. Although *For the White*

Rose was finally produced in 1898, *Through the Breakers* was to be Davis' first successful play.

In January, 1901, Davis met Elizabeth Drury "Iza" Breyer, whom he married on April 23, 1902. They remained married for fifty-five years and had two sons. In 1902, Davis and Al "Sweetheart" Woods signed an agreement that led in 1905 to the well-known "Owen Davis-Al Woods Melodrama Factory," from which fifty-nine plays were produced, the first being *The Confessions of a Wife* in 1905. While pouring out "Davidrama" after "Davidrama," as his particular brand of melodrama was labeled, at a rate of eight or more per year, Davis began using such pseudonyms as Arthur Lamb, Martin Hurly, Walter Lawrence, George Walker, and John Oliver.

Not satisfied with his success as a popular playwright, Davis struggled to write serious drama. In 1918, he moved from the melodrama of the "Ten-Twent'-Thirt'" theaters to try his luck on Broadway. Success on Broadway was not easy to achieve, and Davis again studied the work of other successful writers (such as Clyde Fitch) to ascertain the necessary formula. Besides writing plays, he also published articles on the theater in *The New York Times* and other periodicals.

Disturbed and sobered by World War I, Davis read works by Henrik Ibsen, Maxim Gorky, Gerhart Hauptmann, and other serious dramatists whose naturalistic emphasis on the influence of heredity and environment is apparent in such Davis plays of the early 1920's as *The Detour* and *Icebound*. Another departure in Davis' work occurred with his farce *The Nervous Wreck*, which Davis called "the terrible play which made us all rich." Whereas his Pulitzer Prize drama, *Icebound*, made one thousand dollars weekly, *The Nervous Wreck* brought in twenty-one thousand dollars a week. Made into the musical *Whoopee* (1928), remade as *Up in Arms* (1944), and later adapted for the screen (Davis was not involved in these projects), *The Nervous Wreck* was Davis' most popular and most lucrative work. During the years from 1924 to 1941, Davis worked on movies, on radio, and on drama at the Lakewood Theatre in Skowhegan, Maine (known as "Broadway in Maine"), as well as on Broadway. His play *Jezebel* failed in New York, but as a 1938 movie it earned for Bette Davis an Academy Award. Davis' last major achievement was his adaptation of Edith Wharton's *Ethan Frome* (1911). Failing eyesight and bad health slowed his output, and his last substantial work was *Mr. and Mrs. North*. Davis died in New York City on October 14, 1956.

Analysis

Under the influence of naturalistic drama, Owen Davis wrote one of his finest plays, *The Detour*. Still using the melodramatic form, Davis varied his approach with a realistic style. The characters are thus depicted as products of heredity and environment, placed in circumstances in which they struggle physically and psychologically against these forces. Despite their efforts to circumvent their fate, the destiny that shapes their ends prevails. The central character, Helen Hardy, exemplifies this determination in the face of hardship.

For ten years, Helen has scrimped and sacrificed for the sake of her daughter, Kate, who aspires to be a painter. Helen's dream for Kate is in reality her own unfulfilled dream "to get away and go to New York, or somewheres where bein' born and bein' dead wasn't the only things that ever happened." Her efforts to escape her environment, however, fail when fate intercedes in the guise of Stephen Hardy. Helen admits that, in her loneliness, "somehow I got to loving him before I knew it." Married and feeling trapped, Helen doggedly tells Kate, "Your life isn't going to be like this:" Helen's struggle against destiny becomes the central conflict of the play.

The struggle focuses on Kate's suitor, Tom Lane, and takes on larger proportions when Tom, echoing a widely held viewpoint, affirms that "women ought to just cook, and clean, and sew, and maybe chop a little wood, and have the babies. . . . And if a woman sometimes gets to thinkin it ain't quite fair" and decides to alter the situation, "she's flyin' in the face of Providence." In order to expedite Kate's departure to New York, Helen sells her bedroom wardrobe and with the additional money plans for Kate to leave immediately. Again, Stephen Hardy intercedes. Obsessed with owning land, and needing money to buy what he considers a prime section, Stephen takes the money intended for Kate. This makes the men happy: Stephen will get his land, and Tom will get Kate. Stephen's act is a villainous one, and inasmuch as Tom supports Stephen, he must share that guilt. Thus, the men in *The Detour* symbolize society and its failure to guarantee equal rights for women. The play ends with the forces of tradition victorious: An art critic seriously questions Kate's talent, and Kate decides to remain with her family and Tom. Despite this defeat, Helen is undaunted; "she stands, her face glorified, looking out into the future, her heart swelling with eternal hope."

The influence of naturalism is also apparent in Davis' prizewinning play *Icebound*. In this work, despite his intention to move away from melodrama, Davis retained many of the basic elements of that form. Unlike tragedy, which contains highly serious action that probes the nature of good and evil, melodrama generally lacks moral complexity; in melodrama, good and evil are clearly defined. While the plot of *Icebound* is essentially melodramatic, the play also features an element of psychological complexity that distinguishes it from straight melodrama.

Jane Crosby is an adopted second cousin to the Jordan family. Taken in by the family's matriarch, Jane is considered an outcast by the rest of the family, especially as the mother is dying and the Jordan wealth is to be inherited. Responding to her enemies, Jane asserts her "hate" for the Jordans and her plans "to get away from them." As for the dying mother, "she was the only one of you worth loving, and she didn't want it." When the mother dies, fate intervenes in the guise of the dead woman's will: Jane is left the Jordan home and money. When the will's contents are revealed, the Jordan family's sentiments are summed up: "We'll go to the law, that's what we'll do." Thus, Jane is pitted against the greedy and vengeful Jordan clan. The conflict is clearly defined, and the audience is sympathetic to Jane.

Had Davis kept the focus solely on the conflict between Jane and the Jordans, the play would be a simple melodrama; instead, he chose to emphasize the role of Mrs. Jordan's son Ben, the black sheep of the family. Ben is a "wild, selfish, arrogant fellow, handsome but sulky and defiant"; indicted by the grand jury for his "drunken devilment," he has run away to avoid state prison. While he is still a fugitive, Ben, risking capture, returns to see his dying mother, and after her death, he is arrested. Alone and without money, Ben is befriended by Jane, in whose custody the court places him. Four months later, Ben comes to grips with his past. Ashamed and feeling remorse about his past behavior, Ben struggles to express his repressed emotions. Admitting love for his mother and for Jane, Ben beseeches Jane to "help me to be fit." With Ben's reformation, society's positive values emerge triumphant over the baneful influence of the Jordan family. No longer emotionally icebound, Ben marries Jane, who gives him his rightful inheritance.

Davis was active as a playwright for many years after the appearance of *Icebound*, but the only significant work of this later period was his adaptation of *Ethan Frome*, Edith Wharton's short novel set in a harsh New England landscape. Ethan "lives in a depth of moral isolation too remote for casual access." He is married to Zenobia, whom Davis characterizes as cruel, harsh, impersonal, and drab, like the play's New England winter setting. In that she represents those forces which seek to enslave Ethan's body and soul, and in that she drives the action to catastrophe, Zenobia (or Zeena) is the villain.

Despite her sickly appearance, Zeena is a forceful personality, and on issues of importance to her, her strength surfaces. For example, she demands that her cousin Mattie Silver be allowed to come and live with them as a hired girl. Citing a complete lack of money, Ethan protests against this demand, but Zeena settles the issue by curtly asserting, "Well—she's comin' just the same, Ethan!" The consequences, however, are not what Zeena intended: Mattie's presence "thaws" Ethan, and eventually, the two fall in love. Jealousy rages within Zeena, who conspires to get rid of Mattie. For years, Ethan has felt trapped by the farm that he inherited, and with Mattie leaving, Ethan's "desire for change and freedom" are resurrected. Ethan tells Zeena that he plans to go West for a fresh start and that Zeena may have the farm. Zeena, however, wishes to keep Ethan enslaved, and, playing on his strong sense of duty, she makes Ethan realize that he is a "poor man, the husband of a sickly woman, whom his desertion would leave alone and destitute." Ethan and Mattie decide to kill themselves by sledding at high speed "into that big elm . . . so't we'd never have to leave each other any more." Their decision gives the play an element of high seriousness; it is a tragic action rather than a melodramatic one. The act of crashing into the elm is also symbolic in that it dramatizes the perennial conflict between human beings and nature. Typical of characters in tragedy whose decisions cause their undoing, Ethan and Mattie survive. Not only does their survival create a reversal in the action, but also it suggests nature's superior force. Although crippled, Ethan can walk, but Mattie is partially paralyzed and is confined to a wheelchair. Ethan and Zeena are tied down to a daily existence of caring for the farm and for Mattie. Nature has demonstrated its mastery over human destiny.

Other major works

NONFICTION: *I'd Like to Do It Again*, 1931; *My First Fifty Years in the Theatre*, 1950.

SCREENPLAYS: *Icebound*, 1924; *How Baxter Butted In*, 1925; *Frozen Justice*, 1929; *Hearts in Exile*, 1929.

RADIO PLAY: *The Gibson Family*, 1934 (series).

Bibliography

Davis, Owen. *I'd Like to Do It Again.* New York: Farrar & Rinehart, 1931. Davis' initial autobiographical sketch covers his theater apprenticeship and his prolific work in the "'Ten-Twent'-Thirt'" melodramas.

_____. *My First Fifty Years in the Theatre.* Boston: W. H. Baker, 1950. One of two Davis autobiographies, this book covers the actors, managers, and playwrights with whom he worked from 1897 to 1947. Its chatty and informal style suggests the ease with which Davis wrote, but it is sometimes inexact with regard to specific dates and places.

Goff, Lewin. "The Owen Davis-Al Woods Melodrama Factory." *Educational Theatre Journal* 11 (October, 1959): 200-207. One of the first major scholarly articles on Davis. Goff examines the unique, exclusive contract between Davis and controversial theatrical producer Al Woods, whereby the writer turned out fifty-eight plays over a five-year period.

Moses, Montrose J. *The American Dramatist.* Boston: Little, Brown, 1925. Moses describes the development of Davis in the context of the many forms of American melodrama. He includes many quotations from an interview with the author.

Rahill, Frank. "When Heaven Protected the Working Girl." *Theatre Arts*

38 (October, 1954): 78-92. This piece reviews Davis' work in the "Ten-Twent'-Thirt'" drama, with specific examples of how popularly priced plays were created. It focuses on some of the social and political events that became the subjects of many of the melodramas.

Witham, Barry B. "Owen Davis: America's Forgotten Playwright." *Players* 46 (October/November, 1970): 30-35. Witham's article is a complete synopsis of Davis' dramaturgy from the melodramas to the award-winning later plays. It also reviews Davis' accomplishments outside the theater, such as his pioneering work on behalf of the Dramatist's Guild and the Authors' League of America.

Loren Ruff
(Updated by *Barry B. Witham* and *Michael L. Quinn*)

THOMAS DEKKER

Born: London, England; c. 1572
Died: London, England; August, 1632

Principal drama

The Whole History of Fortunatus, pr. 1599, pb. 1600 (commonly known as *Old Fortunatus*); *The Shoemaker's Holiday: Or, The Gentle Craft*, pr., pb. 1600 (based on Thomas Deloney's narrative *The Gentle Craft*); *Patient Grissell*, pr. 1600, pb. 1603 (with Henry Chettle and William Haughton); *Satiromastix: Or, The Untrussing of the Humourous Poet*, pr. 1601, pb. 1602; *Sir Thomas Wyatt*, pr. 1602 (as *Lady Jane*), pb. 1607; *The Honest Whore, Part I*, pr., pb. 1604 (with Thomas Middleton); *Westward Ho!*, pr. 1604, pb. 1607 (with John Webster); *Northward Ho!*, pr. 1605, pb. 1607 (with Webster); *The Honest Whore, Part II*, pr. c. 1605, pb. 1630; *The Whore of Babylon*, pr. c. 1606-1607, pb. 1607; *The Roaring Girl: Or, Moll Cutpurse*, pr. c. 1610, pb. 1611 (with Middleton); *If This Be Not a Good Play, the Devil Is in It*, pr. c. 1610-1612, pb. 1612 (as *If It Be Not Good, the Devil Is in It*); *Match Me in London*, pr. c. 1611-1612, pb. 1631; *The Virgin Martyr*, pr. c. 1620, pb. 1622 (with Philip Massinger); *The Witch of Edmonton*, pr. 1621, pb. 1658 (with William Rowley and John Ford); *The Noble Soldier: Or, A Contract Broken, Justly Revenged*, pr. c. 1622-1631, pb. 1634 (with John Day; thought to be the same as *The Spanish Fig*, 1602); *The Wonder of a Kingdom*, pr. c. 1623, pb. 1636; *The Sun's Darling*, pr. 1624, pb. 1656 (with Ford); *The Welsh Embassador: Or, A Comedy in Disguises*, pr. c. 1624 (revision of *The Noble Soldier*); *The Dramatic Works of Thomas Dekker*, pb. 1953-1961 (4 volumes; Fredson Bowers, editor).

Other literary forms

Thomas Dekker was also known in his time as a prolific pamphleteer. His pamphlets are characterized not by a failure of moral judgment, as some critics have charged, but by a deliberate strategy of refraining from gratuitous finger-pointing. *The Wonderful Year* (1603), for example, presents two long poems that are supposed to be the prologue to a play and a summary of its action and, in a prose section, that action—stories of English reaction to the death of Elizabeth I; Dekker leaves the reader to decide whether there is a thematic relationship in the tripartite structure of the work which links the death of Elizabeth and the devastating plague of 1603, whether these disasters are to be regarded as retribution for England's sins, and whether the accession of James represents God's gift of unmerited grace. Such implications are there, but the author draws no final conclusions. In this and other pamphlets, Dekker typically adopts the role of observer-reporter, who, like the Bellman of London, carries his lantern into the darkest corners of his dystopian world to reveal the deepest degradations of the human spirit. In this regard, like modern social critics, he is content to "tell it like it is"; the selection of specific detail furnishes the didactic underpinning of his vision. In works such as *The Bellman of London* (1608) and the different versions of *Lanthorn and Candlelight* (1608, 1609; revised as *O per se O*, 1612; *Villanies Discovered*, 1616, 1620; and *English Villanies*, 1632, 1638, 1648), the reader discovers an alarming truth: The social and political organization of the underworld is a grotesque parody of polite society and the Jacobean Establishment. Thus, rogues and thieves have their own laws, codes of ethics, and standards of "scholarship" which hold a wide currency in both town and country. As demonstrated in *The Gull's Hornbook* (1609), they have even developed their own professional language. In this world, God is not an immediate presence, although He may work out His providential purposes in the hearts and minds of human beings; Dekker, however, is chiefly interested in sociological rather than theological sins, as seen in *The Seven Deadly Sins of London* (1606), in which he carefully adapts the traditional medieval framework to fit his own experience of life in the city of London. Even in his numerous descriptions of Hell, Dekker presents an essentially secular view of the afterlife, designed to show that the community of rogues is an integral part of the Jacobean commonwealth.

Another significant feature of the pamphlets—significant for an understanding of the plays—is the evidence they give of Dekker's familiarity with and manipulation of a wide range of literary forms and conventions. *The Wonderful Year* combines elements of narrative journalism, the frame-tale, the morality play, and the jestbook. *The Seven Deadly Sins of London* involves some knowledge not only of the medieval tradition of the sins but also of morality drama, estates satire, and pageants. *The Bellman of London* parodies the Utopian travelogue, while *The Gull's Hornbook* should be read in the tradition of education books such as Baldassare Castiglione's *The Courtier* (1528). Such a review only scratches the surface of Dekker's diverse reading and interests; it is only in works such as *Four Birds of Noah's Ark* (1609), modeled upon contemporary prayer books, that the author maintains a relatively simple structure. An awareness of Dekker's breadth is of the first importance for a reading of his plays, which also draw on a multiplicity of forms. To some extent, the plays also represent a necessary thematic balance to the moral vision of the pamphlets, for in his drama, Dekker provides the role models usually missing in his prose works—protagonists such as Moll in *The Roaring Girl*, the saintly Dorothea in *The Virgin Martyr*, and the Subprior in *If This Be Not a Good Play, the Devil Is in It*, who rise above worldly temptations. Such characters suggest that, while it is often impossible to make clear moral distinctions in a world where knaves and politicians are easily confused, one can successfully rely upon one's own moral intelligence. The key to this steadfast vision might well be summarized by a brief passage from *The Seven Deadly Sins of London*: "Wee are moste like to God that made us, when wee shew love to another, and doe most looke like the Divell that would destroy us, when wee are one anothers tormentors."

Achievements

Although he had a hand in some aspect of the creation of at least seventy plays, it is unfair to dismiss Dekker as a mere refurbisher of old plays, for there is no question that his frequent collaboration with lesser dramatists was a necessity forced upon him in his constant struggle against bankruptcy. His equally frequent collaborations with such outstanding dramatists as Thomas Middleton, John Webster, and John Ford indicate that he was held in high esteem as a playwright. In fact, a fair estimate of his achievement may never be possible, since at least forty-five of his plays have not survived, and much of the work attributed to him remains a matter of critical conjecture. On the other hand, extant plays, such as *Old Fortunatus* and *Satiromastix*, that are attributed solely to Dekker reveal little sense of moral, thematic, or structural unity. The playwright's handful of genuine masterpieces, including *The Shoemaker's Holiday*, the two parts of *The Honest Whore*, and *If This Be Not a Good Play, the Devil Is in It*, conclusively prove, however, that he was capable of transcending the difficulties which mar his lesser works.

At his best, Dekker was an excellent lyric poet, as illustrated in the pastoral scenes of *The Sun's Darling* and the poignant love songs and laments which appear throughout his works. He was also the master of lively and racy dialogue, particularly in the characterization of clowns, rogues, citizens' wives, and old men. Owing to his creation of such memorable characters as the voluble Eyre and his uppity wife Margery (*The Shoemaker's Holiday*), Orlando Friscobaldo and the scoundrel Matheo (*The Honest Whore*), Scumbroth and the devils (*If This Be Not a Good Play, the Devil Is in It*), and Elizabeth Sawyer (*The Witch of Edmonton*), Dekker has gained a reputation as a "realist"; while it is true that he is at his best among the shops and stalls of London, it is more accurate to recognize Dekker as a dramatist who breathed new life into essentially old forms and conventions, for the roots of his invention lie in the chronicle play, folklore, the mystery plays, and moral interludes of the previous age. His dramatic preferences are clearly revealed in his typical choice of subject, such as legendary biography (in *The Shoemaker's Holiday*), Prudential psychomachia (in *Old Fortunatus*), medieval hagiography (in *Patient Grissell* and *The Virgin Martyr*), anti-Catholic polemic (in *The Whore of Babylon*), and the use of diabolical temptation similar to that found in such old plays as Christopher Marlowe's *Doctor Faustus* (in *If This Be Not a Good Play, the Devil*

Is in It). Dekker's drama, more fully than that of any of his contemporaries, demonstrates the continuing vitality of medieval themes and conventions in Renaissance theater. His greatest achievement was to re-create these traditions upon the Jacobean stage with moral force and perspicuity.

Biography

The phrase "my three-score years" in the dedicatory epistle to the 1632 edition of *English Villanies* suggests that Thomas Dekker was born in 1572, probably in the City of London. His broad knowledge of Latin literature suggests that he received a grammar school education, although all such speculation about his early years is mere conjecture. Since he was ranked by Francis Meres, in 1598, among the best English writers of tragedy, he must have begun writing plays as early as 1595; his name first appears in Philip Henslowe's diary in 1598 as the author of the lost play *Phaeton*, and he may also have collaborated with Anthony Munday, Henry Chettle, Thomas Heywood, and William Shakespeare in *The Booke of Sir Thomas More* (c. 1595-1596). Numerous other references in Henslowe's papers and on the title pages of published plays show that Dekker remained extremely busy from 1598 to 1613, writing for the Lord Admiral's Men and occasionally for the Children of Paul's. He was also constantly in debt during this period and was forced to supplement his income by the publication of pamphlets. In 1613, he was imprisoned for debt for the third time and remained in the King's Bench prison until his eventual release in 1619. During his last years, Dekker wrote several plays for the Palsgrave's Men and published several more pamphlets. He apparently refused to attend church from 1626 to 1629 in order to avoid being arrested for debt and was consequently indicted for recusancy. It is believed that he was buried in the parish of St. James, Clerkenwell, on August 25, 1632. The fact that his widow, Elizabeth, refused administration of his will suggests that Dekker had no estate to administer and that death came as his final release from the specter of debtors' prison.

Analysis

Critical condemnation of Thomas Dekker as "a moral sloven" or as a hack with a marginal understanding of dramatic structure is chiefly based upon unsympathetic readings of such early plays as *Old Fortunatus*, *Patient Grissell*, and *Satiromastix*. To some extent, the adverse assessments are justified, for these plays are quite severely lacking in structural coherence. Part of the problem, however, may lie in the sheer intransigence of Dekker's sources. The fact that Dekker did possess a keen sense of dramatic structure and moral integrity can easily be demonstrated by an analysis of two of his finest works, *The Shoemaker's Holiday* and *The Honest Whore, Part II*.

Based upon Thomas Deloney's prose narrative *The Gentle Craft* (1597–c. 1598), *The Shoemaker's Holiday* reveals its structural strategy in the opening scene, in which a discussion between Sir Roger Otley, Lord Mayor of London, and Sir Hugh Lacy, the powerful Earl of Lincoln, is animated by the latent hostility which divides the landed nobility and the wealthy, self-made citizenry of London. Both men fear an elopement between the earl's nephew, Rowland Lacy, and Rose, the Mayor's daughter. Rather than expose his treasury to the frivolous exploitation of a courtly son-in-law, Sir Roger has ordered his daughter into rustic banishment. The earl, to avoid besmirching the family dignity and turn his nephew's attention elsewhere, has arranged to have his nephew lead one of the regiments about to invade France. Lacy, however, leaves his command in charge of his cousin Askew, but before he can escape, he is temporarily interrupted by a shoemaker, Simon Eyre, and his men, who try, unsuccessfully, to intercede for the newly married journeyman Rafe, who has been pressed for service in France. Realizing the futility of his plea, Eyre then encourages Rafe to fight for the honor of the gentle craft of shoemakers. The poignant departure scene is highlighted by the generous monetary gifts showered upon Rafe and by Rafe's gift of a pair of monogrammed shoes he has made for Jane, his bride. Rafe's obedience provides a stark contrast to the irresponsibility of Lacy, who, though he insists upon Rafe's loyalty, has no intention of fulfilling his own patriotic duty. Meanwhile, Jane's distress is reflected in a parallel scene in which Rose learns of Lacy's orders to leave for France. Lacy, however, has decided to use his knowledge of the shoemaker's trade learned on an earlier trip to Germany, to find work with Eyre, who will be shorthanded without Rafe's services. In the following scene, the audience is entertained by the lively bustle of Eyre's shop as he drives his men into honest industry and heaps torrents of loving abuse upon his wife, Margery, when she tries to exert a little domestic authority over his employees. Lacy, now posing as Hans Meulter, a Dutchman who speaks only broken English, appears to apply for a job but is hired only because of the strong support of Hodge and Firke, Simon's other workmen. This scene reinforces the central theme of class conflict, because it demonstrates both that true love knows no social barriers and that a resourceful courtier can humble himself to the level of mere apprentice.

By stark contrast, in act 2, Dekker introduces the character of Hammon, an upstart citizen who, in the hope of impressing the exiled Rose, dresses in the height of fashion and ludicrously affects the language of courtly love. Even though his suit is favored by Sir Roger, Hammon is sternly rebuffed when he proposes marriage to Rose. Ironically, Sir Roger is far more impressed by the citizen who apes courtly manners and speech than by the true nobility of Lacy, who is willing to sacrifice all, including social status, for the sake of love. In the third scene, Lacy repays his employer's kindness by introducing him to a Dutch captain who sells Eyre a cargo of valuable merchandise at a great bargain. In order to impress the captain and effect the deal, Simon disguises himself as an alderman, a post he later achieves.

The first scene of act 3 renews Sir Roger's entertainment of Hammon as a suitable husband for Rose, but once again Rose firmly rejects the proposal, much to her father's disgust, and when he learns of Lacy's desertion, Sir Roger's suspicions are highly aroused. In the second scene, Simon's men play upon Margery's vanity by suggesting how she should respond to the news that Simon has been elected High Sheriff of London. The festivities are dampened by the unexpected return of Rafe, who has suffered the amputation of a leg. His grief is doubled when he discovers that Jane has secretly left the Eyre household. His distress, however, is swept aside by the triumphal entrance of Eyre, wearing the sheriff's chain of office. The third scene, in which Sir Roger honors Eyre at a banquet, is pivotal to the main plot, for it provides an opportunity, when Simon's men perform a morris dance, for Lacy to reveal his identity to Rose. This scene also reinforces the striking contrast between the pretentious gravity of Sir Roger and the bluff good nature of Simon Eyre. Margery's amusing efforts at courtly decorum also provide an ironic commentary upon citizen snobbery. Having been unsuccessful in his pursuit of Rose, Hammon subsequently proposes to Jane, now working as a seamstress, and when she rejects him on the grounds that she is still married, Hammon concocts a false report of Rafe's death in battle. In spite of her evident grief, Hammon relentlessly presses his case until Jane agrees to marry him.

Act 4 begins with excited speculation that Simon will become the next Lord Mayor, but the shoptalk is interrupted by Rose's maid, Sybil, who has been sent to arrange a secret meeting between Rose and Lacy. In the following scene, Rafe learns that Jane is going to marry Hammon when Hammon's servant is dispatched to Eyre's shop to have a pair of shoes made after the exact model of those which Rafe had given Jane. The wily Firke promises to devise a scheme to prevent the marriage. In scene 3, Lacy is surprised during his secret assignation with Rose by Sir Roger, yet he eludes detection by pretending, in the character of Hans, to measure Rose for shoes. When, shortly after, Sir Hugh is announced, Hans and Rose manage to slip away undetected. When Sybil eventually reveals their elopement, Sir Hugh, fully aware of his nephew's experience as a shoemaker in Wittenberg, realizes how he has been duped. At this point, Firke enters with the shoes which Rose had actually ordered and, seeing the danger to Hans, manufactures a story that misdirects the two enraged elders to St. Faith's, where a marriage, but that of Hammon and Jane, is scheduled. It is important to note that Dekker uses pairs of shoes throughout act 4, in both the main plot and the subplot, to effect the union or reunion of souls.

In the opening scene of act 5, Simon Eyre, who has been elevated to the office of Lord Mayor, agrees to intercede on behalf of Rose and Lacy to the king himself, who has accepted an invitation to dine with him that same day. Simon undertakes this potentially dangerous mission because he will not "forget his fine Dutch journeyman." In the scene following, Rafe, Firke, and Hodge intercept Hammon and his men who are escorting Jane to St. Faith's. Realizing that her husband still lives, Jane immediately rejects Hammon, while the shoemakers give his men a sound thrashing. Sir Hugh and Sir Roger appear at this moment, only to discover that Firke has deceived them, for Rose and Lacy have already been married at the Savoy. Finally, Eyre and his men entertain the king at a great banquet, dedicating the day to their gentle craft and their patron Saint Hugh. This saint's association with the city of London suggests good fortune not only for shoemakers but also for Lacy, who as the Earl of Lincoln's heir and as a shoemaker himself, embodies the best of both worlds. In spite of the earl's vigorous objections, the king, responding graciously to Eyre's humble petition, pardons Lacy's desertion. The shoemaker-mayor, "one of the merriest madcaps" in the land, carries the day, and the king reconciles Sir Roger and Sir Hugh to the marriage of Lacy and Rose.

In adapting Deloney's novel for the stage, Dekker drastically revised the character of Simon Eyre, who in Deloney's work seems much more like Dekker's Sir Roger Otley, a ceremoniously grave and ambitious man who plots his rise to power. Thus, Dekker suppresses the darker side of the bargaining for the Dutch merchandise and creates in Simon an irrepressible force for good. Furthermore, although Deloney's Eyre believes in thrift and hard work, Dekker's Eyre is less motivated by purely economic considerations than he is by an exhilarating sense of the value of work *as* work. It is also important to note that *The Shoemaker's Holiday* is not a dynamic play, for Dekker's treatment of his main characters permits no internal conflict, no self-discovery, and no essential growth. Simon, Lacy, Rose, and the shoemakers remain, throughout, perfectly secure in the holiness of their hearts' affections, and their knowledge is instinctive rather than based upon systems of moral philosophy or codes of social behavior. In the very integrity of their words and actions, their lives exemplify the theme of the comedy: that love and nobility transcend such considerations as wealth, class consciousness, or political status. Although Simon Eyre achieves all the social distinctions which mean most to men such as Sir Roger and Sir Hugh, he remains completely oblivious to them. His love of life, his concern for his men, and his innate patriotism are never corrupted. From beginning to end, he remains "the merriest madcap" in the land, whose triumphs are based upon goodwill and honest industry. It is also significant that his victory over class prejudice is realized through the royal intervention of the legendary King Henry V, who recognizes in Eyre's raucous good humor a strain of genuine nobility which escapes the pettier understanding of such men as Sir Hugh and Sir Roger. In fact, it is tempting to see in Eyre and his men a group of individuals who represent the exact social obverse of Shakespeare's Falstaff and his predatory followers.

Throughout the play, Dekker skillfully interweaves the various strands of plot to achieve both a structural and thematic unity, not only in the resolution of the romantic intrigues but also in the establishment of a new social order that sweeps aside the trivial differences which divide courtiers and citizens. Beginning with the class conflict developed in the initial debate between Sir Roger and Sir Hugh, each consecutive scene either opposes or reinforces the class harmony which must eventually prevail in the final scene. Lacy's decision to work as a tradesman and the friendship and loyalty he finds in the assistance of Hodge and Firke counterpoise the noble pride of the Earl of Lincoln. The truth of Lacy's love for Rose, for which he risks all, is neatly balanced against the unscrupulous conduct of Hammon, whose romantic affectations and courtly love language are offset by Lacy's true nobility and Rafe's simple devotion to Jane. Rose and Jane suffer the anguish of forced separation from their lovers, and both are reunited in scenes which involve the manufacture and delivery of shoes from Eyre's premises. Sir Roger's preference for Hammon provides a ludicrous commentary upon the blindness of class snobbery, as do Margery's feeble attempts at gentility and decorum. The one flaw in Lacy's behavior, his desertion from patriotic duty, is structurally necessary to justify his employment in Eyre's shop and thematically essential to provide the reason for the king's intervention against the feuding parents. The act of royal clemency, in turn, affirms the primacy of love and resolves the theme of class conflicts, and the royal pardon itself is based upon the king's affirmation of Simon Eyre as the exemplar of social and political harmony.

Dekker's greatest work, however, is *The Honest Whore, Part II*, a tragicomedy utilizing most of the characters from the first part (written in collaboration with Thomas Middleton), in which is dramatized the moral conversion of the whore Bellafronte by Hippolito, the son-in-law of the Duke of Milan. In the resolution of *The Honest Whore, Part I*, the scoundrel Matheo has been forced to marry Bellafronte because he had been initially responsible for leading her into a life of sin. The subplot of the first part features the tempting of Candido, a patient man who triumphs over the constant humiliations heaped upon him by his shrewish wife Viola.

The second part of *The Honest Whore* begins with Bellafronte and an unnamed scholar waiting to make petitions to Hippolito. His summary dismissal of the scholar is ominous, for the clear implication is that the scholar is willing to sell his genius for money. The suggestion that the scholar is an intellectual prostitute, however, may be more a reflection upon the prince's mind than upon the scholar's integrity. On the other hand, Hippolito does listen to Bellafronte's request that he intercede on behalf of the profligate Matheo, who has been condemned for killing a man in a duel. At the same time, finding himself strangely attracted to the fallen woman whom he had once redeemed, he also promises to reconcile her, if he can, to her estranged father Orlando Friscobaldo, who had abandoned his support when she resorted to prostitution. Hippolito makes good his promise in the following scene when he intercepts Orlando and urges him to forgive his daughter, who has turned away from sin. The old man appears totally intransigent in his repugnance for Bellafronte and rebukes Hippolito for disturbing his peace, although secretly he resolves to keep an alert watch over Bellafronte and her disreputable husband. In the third scene, a number of gallants visit the linen-draper Candido, who has remarried after Viola's unexpected death. Urging him to subdue the pettish whims of his new bride, lest she too turn into an untamable shrew, they together devise a scheme in which Ludovico Sforza, in the role of an apprentice, will test her mettle.

Act 2 begins with Matheo's return from prison, although it is immediately apparent that he has not changed his ways, a fact which sorely distresses Bellafronte, who has now been reduced to virtual destitution. Their quarreling is interrupted by Orlando, who has disguised himself as his own servingman, Pacheco. When he and Matheo exchange disparaging remarks about her father's honesty, Bellafronte will not tolerate their insults, even though the old man has abandoned her to humiliation and direst poverty. Reassured by this successful testing of his daughter's virtue, Orlando offers his services to Matheo and gives him money for safekeeping. When Hippolito visits Bellafronte, Orlando quickly discerns the drift of the prince's interest in his daughter and watches anxiously to see how she will react to even greater temptations. Later, however, she dispatches Pacheco with a letter and a diamond she wishes to return to Hippolito. She also gives the old man a cryptic message which rejects the prince's lecherous designs. In the following scene, Candido reduces his new wife to submission after challenging her to a duel with yardsticks. This scene highlights the virtue of a wife's loyalty and obedience to her husband in a test which clearly parallels Bellafronte's support for a far less worthy husband.

Act 3 opens with Orlando's delivery of Bellafronte's letter not to Hippolito but to Infelice, who subsequently confronts her husband with positive proof of his treachery. Hippolito feigns contrition but nevertheless resolves to give full rein to his lust. With "armed Devils staring in [his] face," like Angelo in William Shakespeare's *Measure for Measure*, the young prince is less captivated by Bellafronte's beauty than by her persevering virtue. In the meantime, Orlando returns to find that Matheo has squandered all the money he had entrusted to him and has even robbed his wife of her gown, which he intends to sell to satisfy his desire for a cloak and rapier. Matheo even urges her to return to her profession in order to keep him supplied with ready cash. After the husband's angry departure, Orlando consoles his daughter and plots an appropriate revenge. Bellafronte's trial is further reflected in the following scene, in which Candido's wife is tested by the gallants who lure the husband into a protracted discussion of his wares while Lieutenant Bots, a denizen of the local stews, tries unsuccessfully to lure her into prostitution.

Orlando appears in his own person, in the first scene of act 4, to accuse Matheo and Bellafronte of maintaining a bawdy house, but his daughter disclaims her past and pleads with the old man not to leave her destitute, since poverty may drive her back into a life of sin. After engaging in a shouting match with Matheo, Orlando storms out of the house, only to return moments later in the guise of Pacheco, who commiserates with Matheo and promises to help him burglarize his father-in-law's house. After the husband's departure, Hippolito appears and argues with Bellafronte in the hope of making her turn "whore/ By force of strong perswasion." His argument, however, is unconvincing, because he merely reverses the claims he had presented in his earlier conversion speech in *Part I*; Bellafronte triumphs because her arguments are firmly based upon the real shame and degradation she has actually experienced as a whore. Though soundly defeated in this exchange, the prince swears to press his case "even to Hell's brazen doores." In scene 2, Orlando enlists the duke's aid in having Matheo arrested for theft committed against two peddlers who are actually Orlando's own men in disguise. Aware of Hippolito's infidelity to Infelice, the duke also orders the arrest of all harlots and bawds, including Bellafronte. In the third scene, the gallants, including Matheo, entertain Bots and Mistress Horseleach and lure the unsuspecting Candido into drinking their health while Orlando delivers the stolen goods for their appraisal. When the trap is set, the constables arrive, first to arrest the bawdy-house keepers and Candido, and second to apprehend Matheo for theft and possession of stolen goods.

The final act begins with Ludovico informing Hippolito of Bellafronte's arrest, the news of which drives the prince into a frenzy of rage. He races off to storm the Bridewell, where the duke and Infelice lie in wait for him. All the interwoven threads of intrigue are carefully drawn together in the long final scene as Orlando and the duke confront Matheo and Hippolito with the enormity of their behavior. Still disguised as Pacheco, Orlando orchestrates the arraignment of Matheo, who first tries to pin the blame upon Bellafronte and then upon Pacheco himself. He even accuses Hippolito and Bellafronte of whoring, claiming to have caught them together in bed. When Infelice demands justice against the bewildered Bellafronte, Hippolito confesses his miserable failure in trying to tempt Bellafronte; at this moment, Orlando casts off his disguise to exonerate his daughter of Matheo's malicious accusation, while at the same time certifying the veracity of the prince's confession. Matheo is saved from the charge of theft, since the men he had robbed are Orlando's own servants. Matheo is not pardoned for his merits, or even in the hope that he will reform, but as a reward for Bellafronte's patient loyalty to him. Similarly, Candido, who remains the soul of patience, is elevated to the rank of "king's counselor." Hippolito is ignored but is doubtless restored to Infelice's good graces.

It was a stroke of realistic genius on Dekker's part to leave Matheo only grudgingly repentant at the end of the play, for his insolent prodigality and his cruelty toward Bellafronte make it impossible for his crimes merely to be whitewashed. The main point of the resolution is to demonstrate how completely the "whore" has overcome the obstacles which have constantly threatened her progress. In *Part I*, Bellafronte's conversion becomes the continuing butt of scurrilous jests and innuendos, which partly suggest that she will be unable to sustain her penitence and purity of moral purpose. Her final victory in *Part II* is earned against almost insuperable odds, in spite of the seemingly mitigating fact that her father has been watching over her, for there is no question that Orlando undertakes his role with a view to testing fully her reformed character. The implication is clearly that he will once again abandon Bellafronte if she suffers a relapse. In fact, her conversion to chastity in *Part I* would ultimately have proven unconvincing had not Dekker submitted her to the protracted trials and grief of *Part II*, for which Matheo's thorough, unrelenting evil is thematically essential.

It seems likely that Dekker was attracted to a reexamination of the temptation theme after his less than successful effort at reworking the legend of patient Griselda. Unlike the saintly Grissell, who has never experienced the pleasures of forbidden life and who is never seriously threatened by Gwalter's cruelty, Bellafronte undergoes a series of much more realistic temptations. Her chastity is severely tested not because her resolution is weak but because she faces the constant fear of degrading poverty and starvation. In this light, Hippolito's importunate lust represents no serious threat, since her resistance is firmly based upon the clear recollection of the disgust and shame she has actually experienced as a prostitute. On the other hand, Matheo's repulsive suggestion that she return to her "profession" poses a genuine threat because it represents a terrifying dilemma; she must choose between a return to prostitution or continued resistance to her husband's will. The stripping away of her self-respect reaches its nadir with Matheo's theft of her gown, which is sold to feed his uncontrollable greed. It is at this point that Orlando knows he must intervene to uncloak Matheo's villainy, but he only makes this decision when he is thoroughly convinced that her steadfast resistance to temptation is genuine.

Structurally, the subplot provides consistently strong reinforcement of the trial theme in the main plot, particularly since it involves not only the enduring patience of Candido, whose unassailable virtue reminds one of Grissell's, but also the successful resistance of Candido's new wife to the schemes of Bots, Horseleach, and Ludovico. The duke's Milan, plagued as it seems by all the seven deadly sins, is Dekker's re-creation of the Jacobean London so vividly depicted in the rogue pamphlets. In such a world, Hippolito, Matheo, the bawds, prostitutes, and gallants "doe most looke like the Divell that would destroy us, when wee are one anothers tormentors," and they are frequently described in terms of diabolic imagery. Furthermore, true to Dekker's basically Arian moral thought, Bellafronte demonstrates that love, obedience, and perseverance are the constant virtues of a distinctly possible reformation. In this play and in *The Shoemaker's Holiday*, Dekker left at least two works which demonstrate architectonic unity and a keen sense of moral values. For this achievement, he deserves to be ranked among the excellent second-rank dramatists of the Elizabethan-Jacobean stage.

Other major works

NONFICTION: *The Plague Pamphlets of Thomas Dekker*, 1925 (F. P. Wilson, editor).

MISCELLANEOUS: *The Magnificent Entertainment Given to King James*, 1603 (with Ben Jonson and Thomas Middleton); *The Wonderful Year*, 1603 (prose and poetry); *The Double PP*, 1606 (prose and poetry); *The Seven Deadly Sins of London*, 1606; *News from Hell*, 1606; *The Bellman of London*, 1608; *Lanthorn and Candlelight*, 1608, 1609 (revised as *O per se O*, 1612; *Villanies Discovered*, 1616, 1620; *English Villanies*, 1632, 1638, 1648); *The Gull's Hornbook*, 1609; *Four Birds of Noah's Ark*, 1609; *A Work for Armourers*, 1609; *Dekker, His Dream*, 1620 (prose and poetry); *Penny-Wise and Proud-Foolish*, 1630; *The Non-Dramatic Works of Thomas Dekker*, 1884-1886 (4 volumes; Alexander B. Grosart, editor); *Thomas Dekker: Selected Prose Writings*, 1968 (E. D. Pendry, editor).

Bibliography

Berlin, Normand. "Thomas Dekker: A Partial Appraisal." *Studies in English Literature* 6 (Spring, 1966): 263-277. Berlin discusses the following plays in an attempt to boost Dekker's reputation: *The Shoemaker's Holiday*, *The Honest Whore*, *Westward Ho!*, *Northward Ho!*, and *The Roaring Girl*. He questions Muriel Bradbrook's characterization of Dekker as a "moral sloven" for it "too strongly undermines a basically severe moralist."

Conover, James H. *Thomas Dekker: An Analysis of Dramatic Structure.* The Hague: Mouton, 1969. Conover devotes a chapter each to six plays: *The Shoemaker's Holiday*; *Old Fortunatus*, *The Honest Whore, Part II*, *The Whore of Babylon*, *If This Be Not a Good Play, the Devil Is in It*, and *Match Me in London.* A useful feature is the appendix with scene-by-scene summaries of each of the six plays discussed. The "List of Works Cited" is convenient.

Hunt, Mary Leland. *Thomas Dekker: A Study.* New York: Russell & Russell, 1964. Hunt's chapters on the young Dekker are followed by accounts of the earliest plays, the quarrel with Ben Jonson, and the association with Philip Henslowe. Separate chapters analyze the influence of Thomas Middleton, sum up the prose, survey the work of the 1610-1619 period and the imprisonment, and comment on the plays of Dekker's last years.

Kaplan, Joel H. "Virtue's Holiday: Thomas Dekker and Simon Eyre." *Renaissance Drama,* n.s. 2 (1969): 103-122. Kaplan stresses the "moral ambiguities" in Simon Eyre's rise to Lord Mayor of London in *The Shoemaker's Holiday.* The analysis reveals a pattern of rhetoric that creates "the impression not of a disreputable shoemaker, but of a disreputable society that seems to melt away in his presence." Simon's vitality transforms "virtue into festival."

Manheim, Michael. "The Thematic Structure of Dekker's 2 *Honest Whore.*" *Studies in English Literature* 5 (Spring, 1965): 363-381. *The Honest Whore, Part I* and *Part II,* studies "the problem of corruption in seemingly virtuous individuals." The play is structured around the testing of Matheo, Bellafronte, and Hippolito by the standards of Orlando's speech on the happy man in *Part I.* The play thus treats a standard Elizabethan theme: "the revelation of real and seeming virtue."

Price, George R. *Thomas Dekker.* Boston: G. K. Hall, 1969. Price provides all the standard virtues of the Twayne volumes: a succinct chronology, a chapter on the life, and three chapters of analysis followed by a summarizing conclusion. The detailed notes and annotated bibliography make this study an excellent starting place for students of Dekker.

Waage, Frederick O. *Thomas Dekker's Pamphlets, 1603-1609, and Jacobean Popular Literature.* 2 vols. Salzburg: Universität für Englische Sprache und Literatur, 1977. Although these two scholarly volumes do not deal directly with Dekker's plays, they are full of commentary on Dekker's ideas and his life. The first chapter on Dekker's career, 1603-1609, is informative, and the seventeen-page bibliography offers researchers a good beginning point.

E. F. J. Tucker
(Updated by *Frank Day*)

SHELAGH DELANEY

Born: Salford, England; November 25, 1939

Principal drama

A Taste of Honey, pr. 1958, pb. 1959; *The Lion in Love*, pr. 1960, pb. 1961; *The House That Jack Built*, televised and pb. 1977, revised for stage 1979.

Other literary forms

Three of Shelagh Delaney's screenplays have become successful films: *A Taste of Honey* (1961, with Tony Richardson), based on her stage play of the same title; *Charlie Bubbles* (1968), based on one of her short stories; and *Dance with a Stranger* (1985), based on a celebrated murder case and trial in the mid-1950's. Two other screenplays were not as successful: *The White Bus* (1966), from a Delaney short story, filmed but never released, and *The Raging Moon* (1970). Delaney has done several teleplays, including *St. Martin's Summer* (1974), *Did Your Nanny Come from Bergen?* (1970), and *Find Me First* (1979). She has one television series to her credit, *The House That Jack Built* (1977), adapted for stage performance in New York in 1979. She has also written two radio plays, *So Does the Nightingale* (1980) and *Don't Worry About Matilda* (1983), which was very favorably reviewed. In 1963, a collection of semiautobiographical short stories appeared: *Sweetly Sings the Donkey*. A number of her essays appeared in the 1960's in *The New York Times Magazine* and *Cosmopolitan.*

Achievements

Delaney is highly regarded for her ability to create working-class characters and to express the difficulties of their lives in industrial northern England. She is a playwright of a particular region and social class. Both *A Taste of Honey* (which won the New York Drama Critics citation as best foreign play of 1961) and *The Lion in Love* employ such settings and characters. Her focus on the domestic tensions in the lives of working-class families is especially sympathetic to women, though never sentimental. Delaney's early work for the stage and her later television, film, and radio plays seem to revolve around the dreams and frustrations of women in contemporary society. While she was at first mistaken as an "Angry Young Woman," her focus has generally not been on large social issues but on individuals confronting their economic and social limitations and dealing with their illusions. *A Taste of Honey*, *The Lion in Love*, and several of her works in other media study characters who belong to families yet who are isolated even from those closest to them. That her characters face their difficulties with humor and wit sets her apart from many of her contemporaries, such as John Osborne.

Biography

Shelagh Delaney was born on November 25, 1939, in Salford, Lancashire, England. She remembers her father, Joseph, a bus inspector, as a great story-teller and reader. Delaney's education was erratic, marked by attendance at three primary schools and her failure of the eleven-plus qualifying examinations for grammar school. She was admitted to the Broughton Secondary School, and after a fair record of achievement, she was transferred to the more academic local grammar school. At fifteen, she took her General Certificate of Education, passing in five subjects, and at age seventeen she left school. She held a number of jobs in succession, as a shop assistant, as a milk depot clerk, as an usher, and finally as an assistant researcher in the photography department of a large industrial firm.

The encouragement Delaney received at Broughton School led her to continue her writing later. She had already begun a novel when she saw a performance of Terence Rattigan's *Variation on a Theme* (1958), which she disliked and which she thought she could better. This experience served as a catalyst for reshaping her novel into the play which became *A Taste of Honey*. She sent the revision to Joan Littlewood, leader of a radical London group called Theatre Workshop, who began rehearsals immediately. Its initial run began May 27, 1958, at the Theatre Royal, Stratford East, and lasted a month. Restaged six months later at the Theatre Royal, it eventually opened in London, on February 10, 1959. When it opened in New York, in October, 1960, it was very well received and ran for 391 performances.

Delaney's second play, *The Lion in Love*, was heavily criticized on its opening in Coventry in September, 1960. Attacked as verbose, without unity and focus, its London run was brief. After *The Lion in Love*, Delaney turned her efforts to television and film, and even some of this material has been adapted from her short stories. In 1961, she worked with director Tony Richardson to produce a successful film version of *A Taste of Honey*, one which differed markedly from the stage version in its realism. The production won for her a British Film Academy award. Her 1963 collection of short stories, *Sweetly Sings the Donkey*, also contains a version of "The White Bus," later filmed but never released. Her successful screenplay for *Charlie Bubbles*, reportedly based on a short story, won for her a Writers' Guild Award. Throughout the 1970's, most of her work was in television, including a series, *The House That Jack Built*, which she adapted for an Off-Off-Broadway production in 1979. Her 1985 screenplay *Dance with a Stranger*, her first work based on historical, rather than imagined, characters and situations, was a notable success; in the same year, she was made a Fellow of the Royal Society of Literature.

Analysis

Shelagh Delaney's stage plays *A Taste of Honey* and *The Lion in Love*, though very different in style, share several themes and emphases. Despite early critics' comments that the plays have "no ideas" and nearly no plot, both communicate effectively the loneliness of their working-class characters and their dreams and frustrations as they deal with the realities of love. In both plays, families are portrayed who, except by accident of birth and location, are strangers. Cut off from security and stability by education, social class, and economics, these characters are further isolated by a peculiar stubbornness and pride, in part a defense against the vulnerability love brings.

A Taste of Honey is briefly told in two acts. As the play opens, Helen, a "semi-whore," and her sixteen-year-old daughter Josephine, or Jo, are moving into a desolate two-room flat in Manchester. Helen soon decides to marry Peter, a raffish one-eyed car salesman, and the two abandon Jo. Jo, too, has a love interest, in a black sailor, who proposes to her and consoles her as Helen and Peter leave. The second act, set six months later, introduces Geof, a homosexual art student, who moves in with Jo, now pregnant from her Christmas affair. He fixes up the apartment, attempts to help Jo accept the child, and eventually offers to marry her. In Jo's last month of pregnancy, Helen returns, her marriage having broken down. She bullies Geof into leaving and takes over as Jo goes into labor. When she discovers that the baby may be black, she leaves, ostensibly for a drink, promising to return. Jo's last lines are from a nursery rhyme of Geof's, holding out the promise of a benefactor who will care for her.

A Taste of Honey succeeded in part because of its daring plot, but primarily because of the strength of its characterizations, especially of Jo. Delaney's realistic dialogue creates a sense of authenticity of character which masks considerable implausibility. Particularly in the opening scenes with Helen and Jo, the rhythm of attack and defense, the revelation of past failures, the barely concealed insults, the self-deprecation, the sharpness and sustained talk tantalize the audience. Out of fragments of conversation, partial revelations, and even asides to the audience, Delaney creates individuals with deep and universal human needs. Out of this battle of words, partially revealing Jo's hope for love and her need for affirmation from her mother, come the forces which propel her into her love affair.

Delaney's male characters are significantly weaker than her women. Peter is more a caricature, some of his mannerisms suggesting a middle-class dropout now slumming with Helen. His villainy is stereotypical: Complete with eyepatch for a war wound, he carries a walletful of pictures of other girlfriends, though courting Helen. Geof is equally vague, in part because of his homosexuality. He is clearly the more sympathetic, in that he makes no demands on Jo, but is an easy and deferential target for Helen when she returns.

Although it may be said that little happens in the play, its physical and verbal compression makes the interaction of the characters overwhelming. Jo and Helen's two-room flat reflects a world lacking intellectual and physical privacy, in which the characters literally lack room to grow and develop. Similarly, the play's allusiveness contributes to a sense of the mythic nature of the action: References to other works of literature ranging from nursery rhymes to Sophocles' *Oedipus Tyrannus* (c. 429 B.C.) are embedded in the dialogue. That they are suggested, rather than developed fully, may reflect Delaney's youthfulness.

The play's style, a result of the production techniques of the Theatre Workshop, makes it a mixture of gritty realism and dreams. Both the dialogue and the situation seem realistic: The language has the distinct flavor of a region and a class, and the characters' reactions to their situation seem authentic. Yet the text also seems stylized and Brechtian in its rapid pacing, asides in the third person to the audience, and a music-hall style of humor, including insults and songs. A small jazz band plays between scenes and provides music to which the characters enter and exit, many times dancing as they do. Significantly, the play never becomes abstract or allegorical, as do Bertolt Brecht's *Der kaukasische Kreidekreis* (1944-1945; *The Caucasian Chalk Circle*, 1948) and *Der gute Mensch von Sezuan* (1938-1940; *The Good Woman of Setzuan*, 1948), dealing with similar situations.

The collaboration of the Theatre Workshop is important, for *A Taste of Honey* was significantly reshaped from the original text. John Russell Taylor studied the original text of the play as it went to the Theatre Workshop and the final printed version. Aside from minor cutting to tighten dialogue, two major changes in the performance version are evident. First, the character of Peter is much weakened in performance, and he becomes a much more sinister figure. His marriage to Helen, successful in the original draft, now fails. The original draft employs his marriage to Helen as the basis for a more radical plot change from performance: He offers to take in both Jo and the baby. As the play ends, Jo seems destined to return to her mother. Geof is left alone onstage, holding the doll which he had given Jo, all that he will have of the relationship. This seems to suggest much greater optimism in the original text than in performance and also a significant focus on and greater sympathy for Geof.

A Taste of Honey, by structure and characterization, indicates both the intense needs of its characters for love and affirmation and the likelihood of their failure to meet those needs. Most of the characters voice a longing for affection and love, but nearly all are defensive and uneasy in relationships with others. While Jo is the most fully realized character, Geof is, though shadowy, more sympathetic, for his willingness to become what Jo needs. Yet his love for her leads to his willingness to leave when Helen pushes him out. Despite Helen and Jo's reunion at the play's end, the inability of the characters to adapt their personal needs to those of others leaves only guarded optimism about the future.

The Lion in Love, a three-act play set in the north of England, is both more compressed than *A Taste of Honey* and simultaneously more diverse. Delaney has extended her range of characters with an entire family, the Freskos: grandfather Jesse, his daughter Kit and her husband Frank, and their children, Banner and Peg. She further includes minor characters: Nora, who is having an affair with Frank; Loll, Peg's boyfriend and fiancé; and Andy and Nell, the former character an injured acrobat and pimp for the latter.

Instead of nine months' action, as in her previous play, Delaney dramatizes three days several weeks apart. Yet this does not tighten the structure of the play. Although characters confront opportunities for fulfillment, through hesitation or fear most of them lose their chance. The action consequently seems either directionless or circular, with little external change. Frank, who sells toys from a suitcase stand in the marketplace, spends most of his time with Kit arguing and being insulted. Either a permanent booth or Nora's offer to set up a shop with him would mean personal and economic security. In the end, Frank gains neither, and he remains trapped in his complex and antagonistic relationship with Kit. Peg and Loll, though able to see what has happened to the older generation, seem no wiser or better able to govern their emotions, and Peg apparently elopes with Loll. Only Banner, in his departure for Australia, is able to escape the limitations of marriage, but at the cost of abandoning his family and any support it may offer. Even Nell and Andy and their dreams of a new act for performance are blighted: He is not as good a dancer as she thought.

The title of the play is from an Aesopian fable in which a lion permits a forester to remove his claws and teeth as preconditions for marrying the forester's daughter. Once he submits, the forester kills him. The moral, "Nothing can be more fatal to peace than the ill-assorted marriages into which rash love may lead," applies to both the parents and children of the Fresko family. Both Kit and Frank seem to have lost by their marriage, and Loll and Peg may do the same. The banter of the partners back and forth, the attempt at friendship and intimacy, the defensiveness and caution are the same in both the younger and older lovers.

Once again, Delaney focuses more on the women of the play than the men. Although Kit does not enter immediately, she dominates the action and provides the center of interest. In a sense, the other members of her family exist only in their reaction to her. Her love of life and excitement, her determination not to behave as an adult and accept adult limitations, her chosen independence from children, husband, and father, make her a dynamic figure in an otherwise unchanging situation. She seems always to transcend the limitations of situation, class, and economic factors. Yet her "liveliness" is in fact destructive, provoking her husband's affairs and her daughter's disillusionment and eventual elopement. Although Peg is much less developed than

Kit, her history will likely be the same. She has the wit, insight, and longings of her mother.

Delaney's men are, once again, shadowy or insufficient figures. While each has plans and dreams, none seems able to realize them or even develop commitment to them. They wander aimlessly, which may communicate a psychological truth but which confuses audiences. Jesse, the grandfather, the garrulous commentator on life, the link with the past, seems despite his history to have little to offer. Frank is much more fully realized, but his motives are still confused, and he is unable to confront his motives for returning to Kit. Banner and Loll are undeveloped, each with a dream which necessitates leaving and which has only vague longings to support it.

The Lion in Love has a quite different production style from that of *A Taste of Honey*. Gone are the Brechtian elements, the asides, the jazz band in the wings, the dancing entrances and exits. Although the stage directions indicate that the set is "suggested rather than real," with a backdrop which is "a fantastic panorama" of the city and "the local bombed-site" at the back, the play is much more conventionally realistic. While the stage action is at points quite lively, as at the opening of act 2, set on market day, the pacing throughout is measured. The biting humor of *A Taste of Honey* remains, but not the mixture of fantasy and reality.

Delaney has been applauded for her realism, especially in her language and her treatment of relationships. She deserves, however, equal praise for her creation of a mythic world, filled with powerful symbols of brokenness. When the plays appeared, critics recognized her regionalism, humor, and vivid women characters. Yet Delaney's early critics frequently assumed that the plays should be closed, climactic, showing issues resolved and measurable growth. Neither *The Lion in Love* nor *A Taste of Honey* fulfills such expectations. Instead, Delaney's world is one in which change is slight and in which circularity is common: Sons behave like fathers, and daughters follow their mothers. This world is, despite Delaney's humor, a difficult one. Her characters fear and hurt too much to become vulnerable, and they are ultimately detached from one another save for brief moments of consolation followed by antagonism.

Other major works

SHORT FICTION: *Sweetly Sings the Donkey*, 1963.

SCREENPLAYS: *A Taste of Honey*, 1961 (with Tony Richardson); *The White Bus*, 1966; *Charlie Bubbles*, 1968; *The Raging Moon*, 1970; *Dance with a Stranger*, 1985.

TELEPLAYS: *Did Your Nanny Come from Bergen?*, 1970; *St. Martin's Summer*, 1974; *The House That Jack Built*, 1977 (series); *Find Me First*, 1979.

RADIO PLAYS: *So Does the Nightingale*, 1980; *Don't Worry About Matilda*, 1983.

Bibliography

Anderson, Lindsay. "A Taste of Honey." Review of *A Taste of Honey. Encore* 5 (July/August, 1958): 42-43. An early review of the play, before its London opening, which compares Delaney's writing to J. D. Salinger's novel *The Catcher in the Rye* (1951). The character of Jo is praised for her spontaneity, sophisticated innocence, and candor. Anderson separates her from the "angry young men" of the current theater for her toughness, resilience, and lack of bitterness.

Delaney, Shelagh. "How Imagination Retraced a Murder." *The New York Times*, August 4, 1985, p. B15. Delaney discusses how she came to write the screenplay for the first nonfiction drama she had written, *Dance with a Stranger*. Relates briefly the facts of the life of the protagonist, Ruth Ellis, then argues for the validity of Delaney's imaginative reconstruction of the character, criticized by people who knew Ellis. Delaney uses the wildly differing opinions of others to argue that her reconstruction is adequate, because "we are all figments of each other's imaginations" and cannot really know or understand one another.

Gillett, Eric. "Regional Realism: Shelagh Delaney, Alun Owen, Keith Waterhouse, and Willis Hall." In *Experimental Drama*, edited by W. A. Armstrong. London: G. Bell & Sons, 1963. Compares Delaney and three other "regional" playwrights, discussing their authentic handling of characterization and dialogue. Notes the weakness in plotting, but general improvement in characterization, in Delaney's second play.

Kitchin, Laurence. *Mid-Century Drama*. London: Faber & Faber, 1960. A brief interview with Delaney, suggesting elements that went into her style in *A Taste of Honey:* a storytelling tradition from her father, a welfare state upbringing that left her disenchanted with socialism, and popular cinema.

MacInnes, Colin. "A Taste of Reality." Review of *A Taste of Honey. Encounter* 12 (Spring, 1959): 70-71. This early review focuses on Delaney's inclusion of believable character types foreign to the popular English stage in the 1950's. Suggests that her popularity was aided by shocking the audience and by suggesting an authentic, though never staged, picture of England.

Oberg, Arthur K. "*A Taste of Honey* and the Popular Play." *Wisconsin Studies in Contemporary Literature* 7 (Summer, 1966): 160-167. Studies Delaney's first play as a product of collaboration between the playwright and the radical Theatre Workshop. Delaney's stylistic borrowings from music-hall theater and Victorian melodrama create much of the vitality of the play, but Oberg believes that they ultimately inhibit the play's aspiration to rise to serious drama. He argues that an audience cannot take the characters and situation seriously because of the associations that these elements raise.

Taylor, John Russell. *The Angry Theatre: New British Drama.* New York: Hill & Wang, 1969. Presents the first careful analysis of the original script of *A Taste of Honey* and its adaptation by the Theatre Workshop and further contrasts several major features of the play with the film version, done in a realistic mode, in 1961. Major changes in production included tightening of dialogue, revision of the roles of two of the male characters, and a significant change in the play's ending. Taylor continues with an examination of *The Lion in Love*, the short-story collection *Sweetly Sings the Donkey*, and the screenplay for *Charlie Bubbles.*

Wellarth, G. E. *The Theatre of Protest and Paradox.* Rev. ed. New York: New York University Press, 1971. Links Delaney's first play, in its examination of the problems of loneliness and failed communication, to Samuel Beckett, Eugène Ionesco, Jean Genet, and Arthur Adamov. Points out that the asides to the audience in *A Taste of Honey* conceal the characters' ability to communicate to the audience, but not with one another.

Richard J. Sherry

MERRILL DENISON

Born: Detroit, Michigan; June 23, 1893
Died: Bon Echo, Ontario; June 13, 1975

Principal drama

Brothers in Arms, pr. 1921, pb. 1923 (one act); *From Their Own Place*, pr. 1922, pb. 1923 (one act); *Balm*, pr. 1923, pb. 1926; *Marsh Hay*, pb. 1923, pr. 1974; *The Weather Breeder*, pb. 1923, pr. 1924 (one act); *The Unheroic North*, pb. 1923 (includes *Brothers in Arms*, *From Their Own Place*, *Marsh Hay*, *The Weather Breeder*); *The Prizewinner*, pr., pb. 1928; *Contract*, pr. 1929; *Haven of the Spirit*, pb. 1929 (one act); *The U.S. vs Susan B. Anthony*, pb. 1941 (one act).

Other literary forms

Merrill Denison not only contributed to the emergence of indigenous Canadian drama for the stage but also was involved in the establishment of radio as a medium for drama. On the invitation of the radio department of the Canadian National Railways, Denison wrote a series of radio dramas based on incidents from Canadian history, which were broadcast as the *Romance of Canada* series in the winter of 1930-1931. He produced a similar series for American radio, entitled *Great Moments in History*, broadcast during 1932 and 1933. He continued to write original radio dramas and adaptations until 1944. Denison's historical writing also took the form of company biographies, histories of large corporations which were more than mere self-serving eulogies or lists of directors. The first of these was *Harvest Triumphant* (1948), about Massey-Harris Company, the farm equipment manufacturers. He also wrote about Canada's largest brewery in *The Barley and the Stream: The Molson Story* (1955) and about the Royal Bank, in *Canada's First Bank: A History of the Bank of Montreal* (1966-1967). Denison's major prose works are *Boobs in the Woods* (1927), a series of comic anecdotes about tourists and residents of the backwoods of Ontario, and *Klondike Mike* (1943), a biography of the Yukon Gold Rush prospector Michael Ambrose Mahoney. Both books have been praised as essentially accurate accounts freed from the restrictions of factual documentation. Denison also regularly contributed both fiction and nonfiction to newspapers and magazines. His collected papers are housed at Queen's University in Kingston, Ontario.

Achievements

Denison was the first and most successful of a group of writers in the 1920's who sought a truly indigenous Canadian dramatic literature. He has been called Canada's first nationalist dramatist and the founder of modern

Canadian drama. This reputation is based on but four short comedies and one full-length drama. When these plays were first presented to the public, critics agreed that Denison showed great promise. Edith Isaacs, editor of *Theatre Arts Monthly*, in reviewing the publication of *The Unheroic North*, a collection of Denison's plays, called him a Canadian Eugene O'Neill. Ironically, this praise appeared at the same time Denison was turning his back on the theater and beginning his exploration of radio as a forum for his writing. It was not until 1971, on the fiftieth anniversary of the production of *Brothers in Arms*, that the Canadian literary community attested unequivocally Denison's contribution to the evolutionary growth of Canadian literature, and it was not until 1974, one year before his death, that his best play, *Marsh Hay*, received a public performance. Given the small quantity of his contributions to theater and the admittedly flawed nature of his dramatic writing, how can it be that Denison holds such a significant position in the history of Canadian drama?

The answer to that question lies only partly in the barren nature of Canadian dramatic literature before the 1960's. W. S. Milne, in reviewing *The Unheroic North* for *Canadian Forum* in 1932, commented with bitter sarcasm, "Some half dozen plays, mostly of one act; four of them dealing with the same restricted milieu; not a bit of imagination in one of them, unless by accident. A small thing almost perfectly done. That is the dramatic achievement of Merrill Denison, and he is Canada's greatest dramatist." At that time, Denison was one of the very few playwrights exploring issues of interest to Canadians and presenting a realistic picture of life in Canada. As a leading member of the first wave, his position in history books is assured, but the achievement of his dramatic writing is not limited to its historical significance. A close examination of the plays allows for a rebuttal to Milne's condemnation of "not a bit of imagination in one of them" and supports the praise given by those dramatists who followed Denison's leadership and innovation. In his attitude toward contemporary social issues, Denison provided a model for the social realism that became the mainstay of several of Canada's leading playwrights and theater companies. The same is true of Denison's commitment to historical subjects. His influence was apparent in the lively theater scene in Toronto in the 1960's, which was dominated by plays that bore a remarkable resemblance, in form, content, and impact, to Denison's work. In particular, the docudramas of this period, based on incidents from history or observation of real-life situations and people, followed Denison's commitment to dramatizing only those situations which he himself had observed.

In retrospect, Denison is worthy of the title Father of Canadian Drama not only because he was the first but also because his plays demonstrate all the potential of a great dramatist as well as all of the flaws of a young writer. The tragedy is that Denison, for whatever reasons, turned his back on playwriting before the promise of his first works could be fulfilled. He needed an ongoing relationship with professional actors and directors and a sympathetic public in order to grow as a writer, and in Canada at that time he was cut off from these. One can only speculate that he might indeed have become the Canadian O'Neill—if only he had had a Canadian Provincetown Players.

Biography

Merrill Denison was born in Detroit, Michigan, on June 23, 1893. That he was born an American rather than a Canadian resulted from the fact that his mother wanted her child not to be a subject of the British Crown. Shortly prior to the birth, she had traveled from her home in Toronto to Detroit in order to accomplish this. A well-known feminist, Flora MacDonald Denison was a descendant of Nathaniel Merrill, who had left Connecticut in 1774 to settle in Kingston as part of the second exodus of United Empire Loyalists. Flora continued the family tradition of outspoken individualism. In 1905, after five years as a manager of the women's wear department of a large department store, Flora refused to punch in on the newly installed time clock, on the grounds that the newfangled system fostered class distinctions.

Merrill Denison was an only child, and the influence of his mother on his private and public life was strong. He supported her stand on women's issues; he was president of the University Men's League for Women's Suffrage in Canada. By contrast, Denison's father, Howard, had little influence. A commercial traveler, he was at home only irregularly, although his son remembers him as a friend. Flora was responsible for Merrill's literary bent as well as his social awareness. She contributed a regular column on women's suffrage to the *Sunday World* of Toronto and took every opportunity to speak and write about religious, social, and political controversies. Another enduring love that passed from mother to son was of the Bon Echo resort on Lake Mazinaw in northern Ontario. This backwoods area not only became Denison's holiday and retirement home but also provided the setting and characters for his most significant dramatic writing. Flora first took the eight-year-old Denison to Bon Echo in 1901; in 1910, she bought the twelve-hundred-acre resort; Denison managed a summer hotel there from 1921 to 1929; and in 1959 he turned the property over to the Ontario government for use as a provincial park.

As a young man, Denison studied at the University of Toronto for one semester and then departed "by mutual consent." After a series of odd jobs, including work as a journalist, drama critic, advertising agent, and timekeeper in a steelworks plant, he returned to the University of Toronto to study architecture. In 1916, he departed to serve two years with the American Ambulance Field Service in France. In 1919 and 1920, he worked as an architectural draftsman in Boston and New York, but architecture was not to be his career. In fact, he wrote a critique of his architectural education, which appeared in 1922 in *The American Architect*. The magazine's publishers reportedly offered him the editorship, which he refused. After he returned to the family home in Toronto, he was approached by Roy Mitchell, the dynamic and forward-looking director of Hart House Theatre at the University of Toronto, to become the theater's art director. His first stage designs were for a production of Euripides' *Alcestis* in February of 1921. He also tried his hand at acting and became a playwright by the end of the season.

Denison tells an amusing story of how this came about. Mitchell had planned an evening of three Canadian plays for April, but only two, both tragedies, had been found. Five weeks before the opening, Denison and Mitchell were joking about where to find a true Canadian. Denison claimed that the only untainted Canadians he had known were the backwoodsmen near Bon Echo, the subject of so many of the amusing stories with which he had regaled his friends. The result: He was locked in the director's room and told to turn out a play based on his famous story of the Upper Canada College principal trying to acquire the use of a boat from a backwoodsman. As Denison reports, "Well, with no inhibitions and a deadline, I was able to accomplish the feat in about four and a quarter hours."

Brothers in Arms, as this play was called, enjoyed remarkable popularity, appearing in ten editions from 1923 to 1975, and was performed an estimated fifteen hundred times from 1921 to 1971. The initial response, however, was not undivided. Hart House was governed by a theater committee which had to give approval to all scripts. This group, shocked by the ungrammatical language of backwoodsmen and by the satire of patriotism that fuels the comedy, rejected Denison's script. After Mitchell threatened to resign, however, the play was added to the program, and theater history was made.

Denison continued with Mitchell at Hart House Theatre and saw productions of *The Weather Breeder* on April 21, 1924, and *The Prizewinner* on February 27, 1928. The one-act format was necessitated by Mitchell's commitment to an evening of short plays by three different writers, but in 1929, Denison was given a chance to provide an entire evening's entertainment. He wrote *Contract*, described by the Toronto *Star* as "good-natured satire . . . charged with local allusions . . . convincing and clever." Other reviews were equally positive, but this was to be Denison's last major stage production. The first twentieth century English-Canadian playwright to attempt to make a living from his writing in Canada was forced to abandon the stage in order to earn enough money to survive.

In 1929, Denison was approached by Austin Weir, who was then in charge of radio programs for the Canadian National Railways, with the idea of presenting episodes from Canadian history over the air. At first, Denison was dubious about the potential of such a venture, having an ambivalent regard for the medium and questioning, as he later admitted, anyone's ability to discover in Canadian history the material out of which half a dozen, let alone twenty-five, romantic dramas could be written. He soon warmed to the task, however, and became fascinated with the potential of radio for dramatic presentation. The result was the radio series known as *Romance of Canada* directed by Tyrone Guthrie and broadcast in the winter of 1930-1931 over a transcontinental chain by Canadian National Railways' Radio Department. Six of the scripts were published in 1931 under the title *Henry Hudson and Other Plays*. So successful was this series with both audiences and critics that Denison was commissioned by the J. Walter Thompson Company to write a similar series dealing with American history. Denison produced a forty-week series of half-hour programs, broadcast during 1932 and 1933, entitled *Great Moments in History*, and he continued to earn his living writing for American radio networks through World War II. He was best known for his ability to dramatize historical events in a manner both educational and entertaining. During the war, he wrote for American, British, and Canadian radio, including the British Broadcasting Corporation's *Home Hour*, for which he produced dramatized commentaries explaining the American war effort to United Kingdom listeners.

Denison's storytelling skills led him to several prose treatments in both short and full-length form. *Klondike Mike*, a biography of Michael Ambrose Mahoney, a survivor of the Klondike Gold Rush, was a best-seller within weeks of its publication and was a Book-of-the-Month Club selection. It was reprinted in 1965 and received the accolades of another generation of Canadians. Nevertheless, playwriting and storytelling were insufficient sources of income, and Denison's attempt at resort management was also not a financial success. His alternative career was in journalism; as a regular contributor to leading daily newspapers and monthly magazines, Denison spoke out on cultural and social issues that concerned him deeply. These included the state of drama in Canada, the potential of radio as a social and cultural force, the hardships endured by those trying to survive in the less developed regions of Canada, and the need for a strong conservationist policy to protect the natural beauty of the unspoiled north.

In 1922 and 1923, Denison was a contributing editor of *The Bookman*, from which position he analyzed the causes of the slow emergence of indigenous Canadian literature. His theory, that Canadians suffer from an inferiority complex—or "an intellectual timidity born of a false feeling of inadequacy or inability"—has profoundly influenced subsequent theories and later practitioners. Being an American by birth and citizenship and a

Canadian by choice of residence, Denison was also able to comment insightfully on relations between these neighbors. Though against nationalism as a divisive international force, Denison remained throughout his life an ardent advocate of Canadian nationalism because of his sense of the feelings of inferiority suffered by Canadians, despite prodigious accomplishments in many areas. "You will have to find out about yourselves and know and appreciate yourselves before you can expect other people to know and understand you," he advised in 1949. In 1967, the year of the Canadian Centennial, his message had altered as little as the problem he addressed: the ignorance of Canadians about their own past achievements.

An interest in history, biography, and journalism made Denison a logical choice for the Massey-Harris Company when it celebrated its one hundredth birthday in 1947 with a booklet outlining its history. Denison admitted that "farm implements had never been numbered my irrepressible enthusiasms," but he soon became fascinated with the technological advancements pioneered by the firm, as well as the position of the company in the social, economic, and international history of Canada. He received permission to prepare a full-length biography which was published in 1948 as *Harvest Triumphant*. Company biographies usually are of little interest save to those members of past and present management who receive the praise which seems to be the sole motive for their production, but in this case, Denison's book not only was an overwhelming commercial success but also set a creative precedent for the company biographies that followed.

Denison was much in demand, following the success of *Harvest Triumphant*, to record the achievements of other companies. The most respected of these biographies were *The Barley and the Stream*, a history of the powerful Molson brewery empire; *The People's Power: The History of Ontario Hydro* (1960); and *Canada's First Bank*. In each of these company biographies, which involved several years of historical research and for which Denison demanded freedom from interference by company management, Denison remained true to his commitment to the importance of the country's history for an understanding of what it meant to be a Canadian. He did not limit his definition of history to political events. History, he said,

is to be found in the nature of the land itself, dominated by the Laurentian Shield. It is to be found in the struggles of a tiny population to subdue that and other regions, in the long wait for the tools with which to master the Prairies and the Far North, the Shield and its inaccessible forests and once-useless water power. It is linked to canals, railroads, hydro-electric power, diamond drills, airplanes and caterpillar tractors, far more than it is to fluctuating fortunes of political parties or the decisions of the Privy Council. The story is to be found in the mineshafts and the lumber camps and the holds of the Great Lakes Freighters; in the tellers' cages of banks from Canso to the Yukon; in the custom brokers' records of a hundred ports around the world.

Merrill Denison, master storyteller, dedicated his life to transmitting, in a variety of forms, incidents from real life, contemporary and historical, that would hold a mirror up to the Canadian people, in which they might more clearly see themselves. He tried to battle the inferiority complex that he saw around him in order to give the citizens of his adopted country the same love for the land and its people that he so fervently felt.

Analysis

Merrill Denison was one of the group of Canadian writers who, in the 1920's, first attempted to dramatize the uniquely Canadian aspects of their national experience. If this were his only achievement, he would be a provincial writer of interest only to his immediate contemporaries and to theater historians. It is his unique attitude to the Canadian experience that marks his contribution to dramatic literature and gives it enduring value.

Three aspects of Denison's dramatic writings distinguish his work. His plays are first and foremost realistic, based entirely on personal experience and observation and written with careful attention to believable dialogue, setting, action, and characterization. Second, he is both antiheroic and antiromantic, dedicated to debunking the false image of Canada as the home of Mounties and noble, simple hunters—natural heroes of the virgin wilderness. Finally, he brings to his writing a sense of comedy tempered with commitment to justice—a commitment that leads him to explore so- cial problems objectively and in defiance of contemporary morality. The result is a group of plays that have not become dated with the passage of time.

In his short comedies, Denison uses character-types, two-dimensional creations that function within a limited plot line. The plays turn on a single narrative device, usually a reversal. In *From Their Own Place*, city dweller Larry Stedman turns the tables on the backwoodsmen who have attempted to sell him the furs from illegally trapped animals for an inflated price (while arguing over who is the rightful owner of the furs) by calling in the game warden to witness all three men deny ownership. The tricksters are tricked into parting with the furs, and the naïve city dweller pays only for the cost of the trapping license.

Even within the limitations of the one-act structure, Denison creates evocative and well-crafted explorations of life in the northern areas of On- tario. His attention to language demonstrates the fine ear of a raconteur adept at mimicry. The ungrammatical utterances of the locals might offend university committees, but this language provides authenticity and a rich comic texture. Denison does not use foul language, but he still manages to capture the flavor of backwoods speech. When Alec, one of the tricksters, swears that half of the furs are his, he vows, "If they aint will the Lord strike me down right here where I'm stanin and send me to burnin hell for ten thousand years wiv a cup of cold water just beyond my lips and me not able to reach it."

Denison does not incorporate these vivid colloquialisms for mere comic effect; language is always tied to the characters and to their social environment. Sandy, caretaker for the Stedmans, and Cline, who habitually sells them worthless objects, debate the relative morality of their positions: Sandy attacks first, saying, "You've sold him enough trash now to satisfy anybody but a MacUnch." Cline indignantly defends his family name with "That's a fine thing for you to say, and you married to a MacUnch yourself and had three children by her. And the hull of you half starved till you got a job from the old lad. It aint everyone can get a job caretakin and not have nothin to do." Sandy retorts, "No, there aint but one can get it and that's me and it wouldn't matter if Emmy had twelve children and all of them twins, I wouldn't be like yous MacUnches trying to sponge off'n the only friend the backwoods has." Buried in this amusing exchange is the presentation of a serious socioeconomic situation. The duplicity of Sandy and Cline evolves into a hilarious farce of entrance and exit, lie and counterlie, as they conspire to cheat Stedman and then betray each other, but their convoluted relationship also points to a condition of inbreeding that Denison had observed and on which he had commented in his letters and articles, and their actions are motivated by a poverty that is tragic. "It's a hopeless country to try and make a living in. Even if it is the most beautiful spot in the world," comments Harriet Stedman, in an effort to excuse the stealing and lying of Sandy, Cline, and Alec.

Brothers in Arms, like *From Their Own Place*, features two-dimensional characters, simple plot devices, comic exchanges, and serious social commentary. J. Altrus Browne, a businessman, and his wife, Dorothea, have ventured to a hunting camp in the backwoods. Dorothea exhibits all of the romanticism of an outsiders' view of Canada; she wants to meet a *coureur de bois* (a French or half-breed trapper), one of the romantic figures of whom she had read in books or seen in movies about Canada. Her husband is presented even less sympathetically, as an impatient, insensitive, and pompous fool. Having received word of a business deal worth twenty-five thousand dollars, he is determined to catch the next train to Toronto but must wait for Charlie to drive them out in the only car. Dorothea views her environment through a glaze of romanticism: "I think your camp is adorable. It's so simple, and direct. So natural." Browne judges by a different standard: "I should never have come up into this God-forsaken hole at all." Syd, an authentic *coureur de bois*, unrecognized by Dorothea, and a fellow veteran (a brother-in-arms), unrecognized by Browne, sees his surroundings with the clear vision of a man who is resigned to the reality of survival in a "wild, virgin country," where there are a few deer left, although most have been scared off by the neighbor's hounds. Although

Syd lives far from civilization, that "keeps folks outa here in the summer. City folks is a kinda bother. . . . They's always tryin to get a feller to work. One way and another they figger they's doin a feller a favour to let him work for em." Dorothea tries to fit Syd into her preconceived notions, suggesting to him that he wants to be left alone to lead his own simple life, but Syd defies romanticism. His relaxed manner and unconventional attitudes might entice audience sympathy, but Denison undercuts this by also presenting his laziness and destructive shortsightedness. The hunters tear up the floorboards rather than split firewood, so the abandoned farmhouse they use for their camp is slowly being destroyed.

Denison has some pointed comments to make about the army. Syd and Browne were both soldiers, but their experiences in the war were quite different. Syd's view of "their war" is "they wasn't no sense to it to my way of thinkin." Syd's version of sentry duty—"They wasn't a German this side of the ocean and they wasn't no sense hangin around in the cold. So I went in and went to bed"—horrifies Browne but arouses in Dorothea continued romanticism: "Don't you love his sturdy independence? It's so Canadian." Denison tempers this satire with a bitter image when Syd voices his most pointed criticism of officers and businessmen: "Perhaps you ain't used to listenin much in your business. We got a feller up here that got his eyes blew out in France can hear most a mile away." Finally, Denison, having created a vehicle for his satiric portrait of romanticism and the army, ends the piece with the comic reversal. Charlie arrives at last, only to inform the Brownes that Syd, with whom they have been talking all along, could just as well have driven them to the train, being half owner of the car. Browne explodes with the question, "Why didn't you say you could drive us?" to which Syd replies, "You never ast me."

In *The Weather Breeder*, Denison explores a theme which plays a part in all of his dramatic writing: the relationship between character and natural environment. Old John, a backwoods farmer, is gloomy when the weather is glorious because he is certain that a storm is blowing. When the storm arrives, he is overjoyed because his sour predictions have come true; when the storm passes by and causes minimal damage to the vulnerable crops, he becomes gloomy again. Old John's attitude toward the weather becomes a metaphor for his pessimistic outlook: "It aint natural to have three weeks without a storm and the longer she waits the worse she'll be. We'll have to pay for it." As Jim, John's young helper, notes, John makes life miserable for everybody with his sour prophesying of inevitable doom. Even the most perfect of days becomes merely an excuse to prophesy that an entire summer's worth of bad weather is building up, waiting to descend on them all at once.

Denison based *The Weather Breeder*, like all of his plays, on attitudes that he had observed in the communities around Bon Echo. For the bare subsistence farming such an environment provides, weather can destroy the hopes of a lifetime. Old John expects a certain amount of hardship every year, and, when it holds off for a time, he expects his share of disaster to occur in one huge cataclysm. This bleak outlook, ingrained in Old John's personality, is largely played for comic effect, and the serious implications of his pessimism are further undermined by a rather mundane motivation for his sour spirits: Old John has been laid up with a serious injury; his foot was caught in a thresher.

Thus, in his short plays, Denison did not give full expression to his harsh vision of Canadian life. In his full-length drama *Marsh Hay*, however, he directly addressed the devastated state of the northern backwoods, where, as a result of unrestricted lumbering from 1850 to 1890 and ravaging forest fires, the land had been transformed. As Barnood, a struggling farmer in *Marsh Hay*, recalls, "I can remember when a man could drive a team through a stand of white pine for days... but the lumber companies and the fire gouged her clean. Turned it into so much bare rock and scrub popple." The farms of the area were abandoned by those with the resources and vision to escape. Those who remained were forced into a cruel, grasping search for survival. Outsiders such as Thompson, the city lawyer (a less satiric portrait than Browne), might call them lazy and shiftless, but Barnood defends his fellow survivors: "I don't know as you call a man that works fourteen or sixteen hours a day, lazy. They don't make much of a livin, Mr. Thompson. Pick up a few dollars from the city people that summers on the lakes back here... do a little trappin... kill a deer or two... raise a few potatoes between the rocks and cut marsh hay."

Marsh Hay tells the story of the Serang family. John, the father, like the John in *The Weather Breeder*, is a sour, bitter man, so broken by the desperation of his effort to scratch a living in this desolate region that he is incapable of any positive feeling. He summarizes his life thus: "Twenty years of a man's life gone into workin fifty acres of grey stone... cuttin marsh hay to keep a couple of sows and a half dead horse alive. Cuttin marsh hay because the land won't raise enough fodder to winter a rat. A dozen scrawny chickens... twelve children. Five dead, thank God. Twenty years of a man's life." There is an alternative, to travel west to the fertile land of the prairies, but for John Serang, this is the bitterest twist of fate he must endure: When he was young enough to go, he could not break free, and now he is too worn out to summon the energy and too poor to finance the trip. As he ironically notes, "If we'd lived in England they'd a paid our fare."

John sees no hope for change in his situation and expects no help from a change in government. As he says to his neighbor Barnood, "Andy, the only thing a change in government ever changes, Andy, is the government." A government cannot make the weather good or make the hay stand shoulder high in the marshes, nor is the government even likely to build railroads all through the back country, a more realistic hope at which John also sneers.

John's wife, Lena, shares this desolation, so reflective of the barren environment. Their marriage is one of continued accusation and bitterness. John calls her a damned sow, and she replies, "It's a wonder I aint killed you before this John. Callin me... look at me! Look at me! Worn out before my time... bearin your children. And you call me that. It's a wonder I aint killed you." Denison's stage direction notes, "Lena comes slowly to John, vehemence and heat forgotten and nothing but cold, bitter rage left her." John replies, indifferently, "I wish you had."

In this sort of home, it is not surprising to find that the children are dispirited, cruel, and desperate for any means of escape. John's bitterness has been passed on like a disease to his surviving offspring. Sarilin, fifteen years old, says, "Paw don't like us to do nothin. It don't make no difference to him but he won't let nobody have no fun. He never has done hisself and he don't know what it is." Her solution is to follow in the path of her sister Tessie, who runs off with a boy at the beginning of the play. The result is that Sarilin finds herself pregnant. Walt, who is the father of the child, tries to escape an enforced marriage which, as even old John admits, would be a cruel trap. This has been John's own experience, but Denison does not wholly doom the next generation to this horrible cycle. Pete, John's youngest, is determined to continue to attend school despite the eight-mile walk each way. "I want to get some learnin so's I can get out a this back country and go out front. I aint goin to spend my life workin this farm."

The most profound hope for the family comes from an unlikely source. Sarilin's pregnancy, which is viewed by the community as a shameful and tragic event and by the minister as a heinous sin, is for Lena an inspiration for dignity and renewed caring. This comes about through a chance meeting with a city woman (based on Denison's mother), who shares with Lena the unconventional philosophy that no child is illegitimate. As Lena reports it, "She said it was natural ... she told me people is ruled by laws ... just like a tree is ... and she says no one was to blame." Lena resolves to follow unflinchingly the woman's recommendation never to let Sarilin feel ashamed, and to give the baby the best chance they can. The strength of her conviction has a profound effect on the family. The two boys, Jo and Pete, share in her caring for Sarilin, and even John finds himself half believing her. The house itself reflects the transformation. In his stage direction, Denison says, "Where before was a feeling of extreme squalor, poverty, tragic futility, there is a feeling of regeneration. The place lacked self-respect before... all echo the evident attempt to make the place decent to live in."

The regeneration, however, is short-lived. Tessie infects her younger sister with a cynical realism that arises naturally out of being reared in hatred. Children are only another mouth to feed, another link on the chain of entrapment. She suggests a self-induced abortion, and Sarilin complies. The final act of the play brings us full circle, to a scene of abject misery. The despair is palpable, made all the more bitter by John's begrudging respect for Sarilin's decision: "I don't know but what she showed pretty good sense, too." The same recriminations are voiced by John and Lena, and even Lena's last residue of gentle feeling, "We must've been kinda fond of each other to stick together all these years, John?" is shattered by John's brutal and uncompromising reply, "Fond? Fond be damned. We stuck together because we couldn't get away from each other. That's why we stuck. We're chained here. That's what we are. Just like them stones outside the door, there. Fond? Bah!"

The dramatic writings of Merrill Denison exhibit many of the weaknesses of any young dramatist. He has been criticized for simplistic characterization, particularly of the women in his short plays, who have a tendency to utter the most inane superficialities. Even *Marsh Hay*, his most ambitious work, suffers from a lack of complexity in the delineation of the relationships and emotions of the central characters. In dramatic structure, his plays rely on twists of plot that are at times difficult to believe, and his language, though vigorous and amusing, is also repetitious, particularly in the longer drama, which is weighted with so many references to "fifty acres of grey stone" that it begins to read as though it were "fifty acres of grey prose."

These flaws, however, do not outweigh Denison's real achievement. It is his unflinching commitment to the recording of events, attitudes, and problems he observed in the area around his beloved Bon Echo that merits most praise. Unfortunately, his most exciting attribute as a dramatist may well have been a factor in Denison's unwillingness to write another play after *Marsh Hay*. The documentation of observed social phenomenon was fine when it was sugarcoated with comedy, but in a serious form it was unpalatable to audiences.

Denison was passionately committed to the social message he wished to convey, but the public was not ready to hear it. It is to be regretted that this gifted playwright did not find the environment within which to fulfill his early promise.

Other major works

SHORT FICTION: *Boobs in the Woods*, 1927.

NONFICTION: *Klondike Mike*, 1943, 1965; *Harvest Triumphant*, 1948; *The Barley and the Stream: The Molson Story*, 1955; *The People's Power: The History of Ontario Hydro*, 1960; *Canada's First Bank: A History of the*

Bank of Montreal, 1966-1967 (2 volumes).

RADIO PLAYS: *Henry Hudson and Other Plays*, 1931 (6 plays from the *Romance of Canada* series).

Bibliography

Fink, Howard. "Beyond Naturalism: Tyrone Guthrie's Radio Theatre and the Stage Production of Shakespeare." *Theatre History in Canada/Histoire du Théâtre au Canada* 2 (Spring, 1981): 19-32. Denison wrote scripts for Tyrone Guthrie when he came to Canada in 1931 to produce radio plays. Guthrie returned to Canada in 1952 to found the Stratford Shakespeare Festival. Fink traces the influence of Denison and radio on Guthrie's staging of Shakespeare's plays.

Guthrie, Tyrone. *A Life in the Theatre.* London: Hamilton, 1961. Guthrie's autobiographical reminiscences cover his time with Denison producing the radio series *Romance of Canada* in the early 1930's. Denison wrote all the scripts for that series, and Guthrie remembers that the playwright gradually grew exhausted and drained of new ideas.

Johnson, Chris. "Merrill Denison." In *Dictionary of Literary Biography*, Vol. 92, edited by W. H. New. Detroit: Gale Research, 1990. Johnson offers a later biographical sketch of Denison. He reviews Denison's place in literary history as a major pioneer of Canadian drama. He points out that Denison finally received recognition for his contributions in the 1970's.

Wagner, Anton. Introduction to *Canada's Lost Plays.* Vol. 3 in *The Developing Mosaic: English-Canadian Drama to Mid-Century*, edited by Anton Wagner. Toronto: Canadian Theatre Review Publications, 1980. Wagner describes the Canadian theatrical scene in the early twentieth century and Denison's place in it. He says that Denison could have been the Eugene O'Neill of Canada except that he was not connected to a theater troupe, so many of his plays were not produced. This volume contains Denison's play *The Weather Breeder.*

Weir, E. Austin. *The Struggle for National Broadcasting in Canada.* Toronto: McClelland & Stewart, 1965. Weir recaps the history of radio in Canada and Denison's role in establishing it. The Canadian radio networks were originally run by the Canadian National Railroad (CNR). In 1930, the CNR decided to diversify beyond its musical programming. That is when it hired Denison to write his historic radio series.

Leslie O'Dell
(Updated by *Pamela Canal*)

JOHN DRINKWATER

Born: Leytonstone, England; June 1, 1882
Died: London, England; March 25, 1937

Principal drama

Ser Taldo's Bride, pr. 1911 (one act; adaptation of Barry Jackson's play); *Cophetua*, pr., pb. 1911; *An English Medley*, pr., pb. 1911 (masque; music by Ruthland Boughton); *Puss in Boots*, pr., pb. 1911; *The Pied Piper: A Tale of Hamelin City*, pr., pb. 1912 (masque; music by S. W. Sylvester); *The Only Legend: A Masque of the Scarlet Pierrot*, pr., pb. 1913 (masque; music by J. Brier); *Rebellion*, pr., pb. 1914; *Robin Hood and the Pedlar*, pr., pb. 1914 (masque; music by Brier); *The Storm*, pr. 1914, pb. 1915 (one act); *The God of Quiet*, pr., pb. 1916 (one act); *The Wounded*, pr. 1917; *X = O: A Night of the Trojan War*, pr., pb. 1917 (one act); *Abraham Lincoln*, pr., pb. 1918; *Oliver Cromwell*, pb. 1921, pr. 1923; *Mary Stuart*, pr., pb. 1921; *Robert E. Lee*, pr., pb. 1923; *Robert Burns*, pb. 1924; *The Collected Plays of John Drinkwater*, 1925 (2 volumes); *The Mayor of Casterbridge*, pr., pb. 1926 (adaptation of Thomas Hardy's novel); *Bird in Hand*, pr., pb. 1927; *John Bull Calling: A Political Parable in One Act*, pr., pb. 1928; *A Man's House*, pr. 1931, pb. 1934; *Napoleon: The Hundred Days*, pr., pb. 1932 (adaptation of Giovacchino Forzano and Benito Mussolini's play *Campo di Maggio*); *Laying the Devil*, pr., pb. 1933; *Garibaldi: A Chronicle Play of Italian Freedom in Ten Scenes*, pb. 1936.

Other literary forms

Starting in 1903 with *Poems*, John Drinkwater published a number of volumes of poetry, the most significant of which are *Poems 1908-1914* (1917), *Poems 1908-1919* (1919), *Selected Poems* (1922), *New Poems* (1925), and *The Collected Poems of John Drinkwater* (in three volumes, two published in 1923 and one in 1937). His most important critical and biographical studies are *William Morris: A Critical Study* (1912), *Swinburne: An Estimate* (1913), *Lincoln, The World Emancipator* (1920), *The Pilgrim of Eternity: Byron—A Conflict* (1925), *Mr. Charles, King of England* (1926), *Cromwell: A Character Study* (1927), *Charles James Fox* (1928), *Pepys: His Life and Character* (1930), and *Shakespeare* (1933). His autobiographical volumes are *Inheritance* (1931) and *Discovery* (1932); they cover only the period to 1913.

Achievements

For three decades, from early in the twentieth century until he died in 1937, Drinkwater was a consummate man of the theater—a playwright, actor, producer, director, and critic. Foremost among his achievements was his role in the organization and development of the Birmingham Repertory Theatre, one of Great Britain's most innovative and influential companies. In addition, the popular success of his verse dramas encouraged other playwrights to work in the same genre, and his prose play *Abraham Lincoln* was the most notable historical-biographical play of its time. Both it and the earlier verse drama *X = O* were important expressions of antiwar sentiment, to which audiences responded enthusiastically, and *Abraham Lincoln* enjoyed long runs in London and New York. Active as he was in the theater, Drinkwater was also a prolific man of letters. He wrote critical studies of Algernon Charles Swinburne, William Morris, and William Shakespeare; biographies of such famous men as Abraham Lincoln, King Charles I, Oliver Cromwell, Samuel Pepys, and Lord Byron; a novel; essays; and film scripts. He also was a major poet in the Georgian movement; according to John Middleton Murry (in 1922), only John Masefield rivaled Drinkwater in popularity. (His popularity notwithstanding, critics did not regard his poetry favorably, labeling it derivative, unimaginative, and sentimental.)

Though public and critical interest in him had faded by the time of his death, and he and his work have been largely ignored in the decades that followed, Drinkwater merits at least a footnote in studies of modern English drama for his attempts to revitalize poetic drama in the twentieth century and to develop the chronicle play into a viable modern dramatic form. More than most playwrights, he brought to his craft (as Arnold Bennett put it) "a deep, practical knowledge of the stage."

Biography

John Drinkwater was born on June 1, 1882, in Leytonstone, Essex, England, to Albert Edwin and Annie Beck Brown Drinkwater. His father, headmaster of the Coburn Foundation School at Bow, in East London, had been active in amateur theatricals and, in 1886, embarked on a career in the theater as an actor, playwright, and manager (setting a pattern for his son to follow years later). Because his mother was terminally ill, young Drinkwater was sent to live with his maternal grandfather in Oxford when he was nine. An indifferent student, he left Oxford High School in 1897 for Nottingham, where he worked for the Northern Assurance Company and did some acting in amateur productions. His transfer in 1901 to the Birmingham branch of the firm was a fortuitous move, for there he met Barry Jackson, a well-to-do theater enthusiast (two years older than Drinkwater) who presented plays at his father's palatial home. When Jackson's group went public as the Pilgrim Players, Drinkwater joined them, and, in 1909, he gave up his career in insurance to work for the Players, becoming general manager in 1913 (by which time the Pilgrim Players had become the Birmingham Repertory Theatre and had a theater). By the time he left

Jackson's employ in 1918, Drinkwater had directed more than sixty productions, had appeared (under the name of John Darnley) in about forty roles, and had written a number of plays, including $X = O$ and *Abraham Lincoln*. His wife, Kathleen Walpole, whom he had married in 1906, also acted in the company (as Cathleen Orford).

The presentation of *Abraham Lincoln* at Sir Nigel Playfair's theater, the Lyric, in a London suburb, starting on February 19, 1919 (it had a run of four hundred performances), and its subsequent New York production made Drinkwater a celebrity on two continents. Birmingham gave him an M.A. in 1919, and he was in demand for lecture tours of the United States. On his return home, in 1921, from his second trip to the United States, Drinkwater met and fell in love with the violinist Daisy Kennedy. This shipboard romance led to an affair which culminated in the breakup of Drinkwater's marriage to Kathleen Walpole and of Kennedy's to Russian pianist Benno Moiseiwitsch. Drinkwater and Kennedy married in 1924 and during the next decade traveled widely on concert, lecture, and stage tours in the United States, on the Continent, and in Britain. They also became major figures on the London social circuit. Through this entire period, Drinkwater wrote for the stage; wrote articles, poems, and biographical and critical studies; did screenplays as well as lyrics for films; wrote two volumes of autobiography; and edited anthologies. He also continued to act, and shortly before he died—at his London home on March 25, 1937—appeared in the role of Prospero in a Regent's Park, London, production of Shakespeare's *The Tempest*.

Analysis

In the preface to his collected plays, John Drinkwater says that his "affections have never been divided between poetry and drama, " and he recalls that he hoped "to help as far as one could towards the restoration of the two upon the stage in union." Despite John Galsworthy's admonition to him that "the shadow of the man Shakespeare is across the path of all who should attempt verse drama in these days," Drinkwater was not deterred, and his first solo venture as a playwright (he previously had put a Barry Jackson sentimental comedy, *Ser Taldo's Bride*, into rhymed verse) was *Cophetua*, a one-act play in verse about a stubborn king who resists the demands of his mother and counselors that he wed but then decides to marry a beggar-maid, whose beauty and purity win over the aghast mother and counselors. Though the play has neither literary nor dramatic merit, it is of some interest, for the independent-minded Cophetua is a character-type that reemerges in later Drinkwater plays. Drinkwater wrote the play as a conscious experiment: "I used a variety of measures for the purpose of seeing whether a rapid and changing movement of rhyme might not to some extent produce the same effect on the stage as physical action." The effort failed, but Drinkwater concluded: "The experiment, I think, showed that there were exciting possibilities in the method, and if I had been born into a theatre that took kindly to verse as a medium I believe that interesting things might have been done in its development."

Drinkwater's only full-length poetic drama, *Rebellion*, also was a failure, in large part because of its overly rhetorical blank verse (which Drinkwater "stripped . . . of a little of its rhetoric" in the printed version). Nevertheless, it remains interesting because it recalls William Butler Yeats's *The King's Threshold* (pr. 1904), also about a struggle between a king and a poet, and foreshadows later Drinkwater plays that focus on war and the conflict between liberty and tyranny.

Little more than a curtain raiser, *The Storm* also has an Irish connection, for it is a contemporary rural tragedy that echoes John Millington Synge's *Riders to the Sea* (pb. 1903). The only one of Drinkwater's poetic dramas with a contemporary setting, *The Storm* is about women vainly awaiting the return of the man of the house, who is lost in a storm. The conflict centers on the boundless optimism of the young wife and the insistent pessimism of an old neighbor. Though blank verse is too stately a measure for the occasion, the play does possess tragic intensity, primarily because of the fully developed character of the wife, Alice, who is Drinkwater's most memorable creation.

The death in 1915 of poet Rupert Brooke, who was serving in the Royal Naval Division, heightened Drinkwater's antipathy toward war. He had met Brooke through Sir Edward Marsh, editor of *Georgian Poetry* (1912-1922), in which both were represented, and the two had become close friends. Drinkwater's last verse plays, *The God of Quiet* and $X = O$, are complementary works that reflect both sorrow over Brooke's death and disdain for war. The earlier of these one-act plays is the lesser of the two.

In *The God of Quiet*, war-weary people (young and old beggars, a citizen, and a soldier) meet at a life-size statue of their god, a Buddha-like figure, where they are joined by their king, who also has tired of the lengthy conflict and now preaches humility and love. The enemy king comes in prepared to resume the battle, denounces the God of Quiet for having "slacked the heat" and turned the people against war, and drives his dagger into the god's heart. The effigy comes to life, cries out "Not one of you in all the world to know me," and collapses. The first king is angered ("Why did you do it? He was a friendly god,/ Smiling upon our faults, a great forgiver . . . / He gave us quietness—"), curses his enemy, draws his sword, and vows "to requite the honour of this god." The din of war is heard as the curtain falls. Although the message is clear, the play lacks impact because the generalized characters are merely two-dimensional (not at all universal types), the dialogue is stilted, and the setting lacks precision.

On the other hand, $X = O$, the theme of which is the same, is a play of enduring sensitivity and impact. Briefer even than *The God of Quiet*, $X = O$ was a critical and popular success when first presented, and the passage of time has not dimmed its luster. Its structure is simple: Set during the ninth year of the Trojan War, the parallel scenes of the play show a pair of Greek soldiers and then two Trojan warriors lamenting what they consider a futile war, regretting the need to kill their adversaries, and yearning to return home. Each man is named and distinctively individualized, and all share an appreciation of the beauty and promise of life; as the mathematical equation in the title suggests, the erstwhile enemies are portrayed as sharing character traits and aspirations.

One of the youths in each camp must leave for his daily chore of killing an enemy soldier. The Greek who remains, a poet, is killed by the Trojan who is a would-be statesman with a dream of "Troy regenerate"; the Trojan who stays behind, a sculptor, is killed by the Greek who wants to become a politician. On each side, then, an artist is slain by an aspiring politician, a representative of the state, a detail that surely has its genesis in the deaths of Brooke and other young poets of Drinkwater's generation in World War I, which was at its height when Drinkwater wrote the play.

In writing his five verse plays, Drinkwater attempted "to find some other constructional idiom whereby verse might be accepted as a natural thing by a modern audience." By 1917, however, despite the popular success of $X = O$, Drinkwater had (as he reports in his autobiography) "a growing conviction that if I was to take any effective part in the practical theatre of my time, I should have to abandon verse for prose. Full of reforming ideas as we all were, I soon began to realise that in this fundamental matter of expression it would be futile, and indeed pointless, to try to alter the habit of an age." Somewhat defensive about his decision, he says in the preface to the collected plays:

> The transition from verse to prose, from $X = O$, that is, to *Abraham Lincoln*, was not a surrender, but a recognition that any chance of development in one's dramatic technique depends upon an acceptance of the fact that if one insists on staying in the theatre at all one may be anything one likes so long as one is not doctrinaire. The problem to be solved was how to keep in the sparest prose idiom something of the enthusiasm and poignancy of verse. In the days when verse was the natural speech of the theatre, its beauty, like the beauty of all fine style, reached the audience without any insistence upon itself. The guiding principle of the speech of these plays later than $X = O$ has been, so far as I could manage it, to make it beautiful without letting anybody know about it.

Abraham Lincoln was a transitional work for Drinkwater; although it was his first prose play, the dramatic tableaux that dominate this chronicle are linked by choral odes in verse. The play was closely tied to its immediate predecessors by its theme as well, for it is as obviously an antiwar drama as is $X = O$. It also set the pattern for Drinkwater's plays *Oliver*

Cromwell and *Robert E. Lee*; all three of these historical plays dramatize the problem of leadership, and each is developed in a series of episodes that chronologically traces the development of the hero and cumulatively delineates his personality. Indeed, Drinkwater said that he conceived of the three plays as a unit and according to "a more or less definite plan."

In a note included in the first edition of *Abraham Lincoln*, Drinkwater says that his "purpose is not that of the historian but of the dramatist . . . of the dramatist, not that of the political philosopher," and that his "concern is with the profoundly dramatic interest of [Lincoln's] character, and with the inspiring example of a man who handled war nobly and with imagination." Given his primary aim, he has "freely telescoped [historical] events, and imposed invention upon [their] movement, in such ways as I needed to shape the dramatic significance of my subject."

Abraham Lincoln begins in Springfield, Illinois, with townsmen talking of their neighbor's nomination for the presidency; it concludes with the assassination of the President at Ford's Theatre. Lincoln is portrayed as a peace-loving man who endures the agonies of war for the sake of lasting freedom. His last speech, given to the theater audience immediately before his assassination, epitomizes his character; he concludes: "With malice toward none, with charity for all, it is for us to resolve that this nation, under God, shall have a new birth of freedom; and that government of the people, by the people, for the people, shall not perish from the earth." Drinkwater's use of Lincoln's words in this context typifies the dramatic license that he exercises throughout the play.

When originally produced at the Birmingham Repertory Theatre on October 12, 1918, the play was a great hit. This provincial success did not assure a West End opening, however; in fact, managers either ignored or rejected it, and the London production was at Hammersmith, a suburb. Enlightened by its popularity there, West End managers tried unsuccessfully to convince Sir Nigel Playfair to bring it to the city. Finally, the city came to the play. The public loved it, for *Abraham Lincoln* was timely and obviously touched a responsive chord, a pervasive concern among people living with war and desiring peace, and brought admiration for a strong, principled leader who could guide his country through a dangerous period. Another determining factor in the popular success of the play was that the United States and Great Britain had jointly fought in a common cause, and the British, who had become increasingly interested in American history, saw in the play a reflection of their own sufferings and triumphs. In like manner, when *Abraham Lincoln* was produced in New York (for which production Drinkwater made his first trip to the United States, appearing in the play as a chronicler), Americans responded favorably to the patriotic theme and noted the intended parallels between Lincoln and Woodrow Wilson. In sum, it matters not that today, *Abraham Lincoln* seems closer to melodrama than it is to tragedy; it was the right play for its time.

Among Drinkwater's other plays (and masques, a form of which he was fond), *Bird in Hand* merits attention, in part because it is an atypical light comedy in the tradition of Oliver Goldsmith's *She Stoops to Conquer* (pr. 1773), but also because it shows Drinkwater's skill at orchestrating a varied group of well-developed characters in a realistic Midlands setting. His familiarity with the Cotswolds, where he rented a cottage for a time and about which he wrote in *Cotswold Characters* (1921), is apparent. The plot revolves about the reluctance of an innkeeper to permit his daughter to marry the son of a local baronet, since he believes that people should keep to their station in life. The efforts of his daughter, wife, and assorted guests fail to persuade him to renounce his prejudices, and he is moved to consent only through trickery. Although the plot is not very original, the play succeeds because Drinkwater gave his characters—stereotypical though they are—a measure of individuality, and he had them speak realistic dialogue. Further, the frivolity of the complications and the lightness of style and tone do not obscure the serious dimension of the play: an examination of the perennial problem of the generation gap. Coming almost ten years after the success of *Abraham Lincoln*, which prompted him to move to London, *Bird in Hand* marked Drinkwater's triumphant return to the Birmingham Repertory Theatre. The play was first produced there, with Drinkwater directing and including Peggy Ashcroft and Laurence Olivier as the young lovers. Its subsequent popularity in London and New York rivaled that of *Abraham Lincoln*, and reviewers on both sides of the Atlantic were generally more enthusiastic than they had been about any of Drinkwater's other plays.

In an early essay, "The Nature of Drama," Drinkwater says that a man chooses to write drama "quite definitely with the response of a theatre audience in his mind, and it is for this, and not because of any inherent virtue which he finds in this form and in no other, that his choice is made." The public reaction to at least three of his plays—*X = O*, *Abraham Lincoln*, and *Bird in Hand*—suggests that he chose well.

Other major works

POETRY: *Poems*, 1903; *Poems 1908-1914*, 1917; *Poems 1908-1919*, 1919; *Selected Poems*, 1922; *New Poems*, 1925; *The Collected Poems of John Drinkwater*, 1923-1937 (3 volumes).

NONFICTION: *William Morris: A Critical Study*, 1912; *Swinburne: An Estimate*, 1913; *Lincoln, The World Emancipator*, 1920; *Cotswold Characters*, 1921; *The Pilgrim of Eternity: Byron—A Conflict*, 1925; *Mr. Charles, King of England*, 1926; *Cromwell: A Character Study*, 1927; *Charles James Fox*, 1928; *Pepys: His Life and Character*, 1930; *Inheritance*, 1931; *Discovery*, 1932; *Shakespeare*, 1933.

Bibliography

Abercrombie, Lascelles. "The Drama of John Drinkwater." _Four Decades of Poetry, 1890-1930_ 1, no. 4 (1977): 271-281. Abercrombie was a fellow dramatist who also wrote one-act verse plays in the 1920's, though they were less successful than Drinkwater's plays. This article, an edited version of a previously unpublished 1934 lecture, opens with a discussion of verse drama and the possibilities for its acceptance by twentieth century audiences; Abercrombie then proceeds to analyze his friend's plays. Admiring critic though he is, the discussions are thorough, balanced, and insightful.

Anniah Gowda, H. H. _The Revival of English Poetic Drama in the Edwardian and Georgian Periods._ Bombay, India: Orient Longman, 1972. Chronicling the largely unsuccessful attempts of Drinkwater and others to revive verse drama on the English stage, this book contains a dozen pages on Drinkwater, devoted mainly to play summaries, but the author does provide a detailed analysis of $X=O$ as a "crowning achievement" and the only one of the works that effectively blends poetry and drama.

Berven, Peter. "John Drinkwater: An Annotated Bibliography of Writings About Him." _English Literature in Transition: 1880-1920_ 21 (1978): 9-66. Introduced by a two-page biographical-critical statement, this comprehensive work contains almost five hundred annotated entries, covering the full range of Drinkwater's career as playwright, poet, critic, biographer, and anthologist. Many of Berven's items (whose usefulness he rates on a one to five scale) are periodical and newspaper reviews, making the bibliography valuable as a source of contemporary reactions to Drinkwater's work.

Morgan, Arthur Eustace. _Tendencies of Modern English Drama._ Freeport, N.Y.: Books for Libraries Press, 1969. In the fourteen pages of his chapter on Drinkwater, Morgan acknowledges the playwright's considerable achievements in poetic drama, though he also faults all the early plays for weak characterization. He calls _Abraham Lincoln_ a "new and interesting experiment" in dramatic structure but believes that the conclusion "weakens the tragic effect." He is similarly critical of the denouement of _Oliver Cromwell_, which he regards as a static play, "a study of spiritual endurance rather than of conflict."

Nicoll, Allardyce. _English Drama, 1900-1930: The Beginnings of the Modern Period._ Cambridge, England: Cambridge University Press, 1973. Useful for its handlist of Drinkwater plays from 1905 to 1928, this encyclopedic survey of three decades of English drama devotes only several pages to a discussion of Drinkwater, but it effectively places him in the context of the post-Edwardian period. Nicoll believes that _The Storm, The God of Quiet,_ and $X=O$ are "among the most stageworthy verse plays of the period" and that _Abraham Lincoln_ is "at the head of a lengthy line of historical-biographical plays."

Sutton, Graham. *Some Contemporary Dramatists.* New York: Doran, 1925. Reprint. Port Washington, N.Y.: Kennikat Press, 1967. Starting his twenty-page chapter on Drinkwater by comparing passages from $X = O$ and *Abraham Lincoln* with lines from plays by the Greek Euripides, Sutton points to a heroic spirit in Drinkwater's early drama. The last of the verse plays, $X = O$, according to Sutton, is "an embryonic *Lincoln* or *Lee*," and he regards the first of the chronicles as the playwrights' major achievement because of its "exquisite austerity [and] vision of character." Of interest is Sutton's focus on what he calls "the matriarchal tendency" in *Abraham Lincoln* and *Oliver Cromwell*; ironically, *Mary Stuart* lacks this trait, he says, and is a less successful play overall.

Thouless, Priscilla. *Modern Poetic Drama.* Oxford, England: Basil Blackwell, 1934. Reprint. Freeport, N.Y.: Books for Libraries Press, 1968. Noting that Drinkwater's verse dramas are distinguished by his realistic subject matter, Thouless compares $X = O$ and *The God of Quiet* to morality plays in theme and form. She deems these two Drinkwater's most successful works, although she criticizes his inability to create visual imagery. While recognizing the contemporary relevance of *Abraham Lincoln*, she concludes that it and the other chronicle plays "are not of great value . . . for they are neither very strong historically nor very creative."

Gerald H. Strauss

JOHN DRYDEN

Born: Aldwinckle, England; August 19, 1631
Died: London, England; May 1, 1700

Principal drama

The Wild Gallant, pr. 1663, pb. 1669; *The Indian Queen*, pr. 1664, pb. 1665 (with Sir Robert Howard); *The Rival Ladies*, pr., pb. 1664; *The Indian Emperor: Or, The Conquest of Mexico by the Spaniards*, pr. 1665, pb. 1667; *Secret Love: Or, The Maiden Queen*, pr. 1667, pb. 1668; *Sir Martin Mar-All: Or, The Feign'd Innocence*, pr. 1667, pb. 1668 (adaptation of Molière's *L'Étourdi*; with William Cavendish, Duke of Newcastle); *The Tempest: Or, The Enchanted Island*, pr. 1667, pb. 1670 (adaptation of William Shakespeare's play; with Sir William Davenant); *An Evening's Love: Or, The Mock Astrologer*, pr. 1668, pb. 1671 (adaptation of Thomas Corneille's *Le Feint Astrologue*); *Tyrannic Love: Or, The Royal Martyr*, pr. 1669, pb. 1670; *The Conquest of Granada by the Spaniards, Part I*, pr. 1670, pb. 1672; *The Conquest of Granada by the Spaniards, Part II*, pr. 1671, pb. 1672; *Marriage à la Mode*, pr. 1672, pb. 1673; *The Assignation: Or, Love in a Nunnery*, pr. 1672, pb. 1673; *Amboyna: Or, The Cruelties of the Dutch to the English Merchants*, pr., pb. 1673; *Aureng-Zebe*, pr. 1675, pb. 1676; *The State of Innocence, and Fall of Man*, pb. 1677 (libretto; dramatic version of John Milton's *Paradise Lost*); *All for Love: Or, The World Well Lost*, pr. 1677, pb. 1678; *The Kind Keeper: Or, Mr. Limberham*, pr. 1678, pb. 1680; *Oedipus*, pr. 1678, pb. 1679 (with Nathaniel Lee); *Troilus and Cressida: Or, Truth Found Too Late*, pr., pb. 1679; *The Spanish Friar: Or, The Double Discovery*, pr. 1680, pb. 1681; *The Duke of Guise*, pr. 1682, pb. 1683 (with Lee); *Albion and Albanius*, pr., pb. 1685 (libretto; music by Louis Grabu); *Don Sebastian, King of Portugal*, pr. 1689, pb. 1690; *Amphitryon: Or, the Two Socia's*, pr., pb. 1690; *King Arthur: Or, The British Worthy*, pr., pb 1691 (libretto; music by Henry Purcell); *Cleomenes, the Spartan Hero*, pr., pb. 1692; *Love Triumphant: Or, Nature Will Prevail*, pr., pb. 1694; *The Secular Masque*, pr., pb. 1700 (masque); *Dramatick Works*, pb. 1717; *The Works of John Dryden*, pb. 1808 (18 volumes).

Other literary forms

If one follows the practice of literary historians and assigns John Milton to an earlier age, then John Dryden stands as the greatest literary artist in England between 1660 and 1700, a period sometimes designated "the Age of Dryden." In addition to his achievements in drama, he excelled in poetry, translation, and literary criticism. He wrote some two hundred original English poems over a period of more than forty years, including the best poetic satires of his age, memorable odes, and a variety of verse epistles, elegies, religious poems, panegyrics, and lyrics. His prologues and epilogues, attached to his dramas and those of his contemporaries, stand as the highest achievements in English in that minor poetic genre.

For every verse of original poetry Dryden wrote, he translated two from another poet. Moreover, he translated two long volumes of prose from French originals—in 1684, Louis Maimbourg's *Histoire de la Ligue* (1684) and, in 1688, Dominique Bouhours' *La Vie de Saint François Xavier* (1683)—and he had a hand in the five-volume translation of Plutarch's *Parallel Lives* published by Jacob Tonson in 1683. The translations were usually well received, especially the editions of Juvenal and Persius (1693) and Vergil (1697).

Dryden's literary criticism consists largely of prefaces and dedications published throughout his career and attached to other works, his only critical work published alone being *An Essay of Dramatic Poesy* (1668). As a critic, Dryden appears at his best when he evaluates an earlier poet or dramatist (Homer, Vergil, Ovid, Geoffrey Chaucer, William Shakespeare, Ben Jonson, John Fletcher), when he seeks to define a genre, or when he breaks new critical ground, as, for example, in providing definitions of "wit" or a theory of translation.

Achievements

In a period of just over thirty years (1663-1694), John Dryden wrote or coauthored twenty-eight plays, an output which made him the most prolific dramatist of his day. His amplitude remains even more remarkable when one considers the amount of poetry, criticism, and translation he produced during the same period. This prolific production is equaled by the variety of the plays: heroic plays, political plays, operas, heroic tragedies, comedies, and tragicomedies. In his prefaces and other prose works, Dryden commented at some length upon the various types of plays, seeking to define and to clarify the dramatic forms in which he wrote.

Yet Dryden himself recognized that his dramas were not likely to wear well, and his literary reputation today rests largely upon his poetry and criticism. The operas *King Arthur* and *The State of Innocence* (which was not produced during his lifetime) survive primarily in their lyrics; like other operas of the time, they were somewhat primitive, judged by modern standards, with relatively little music—something more akin to the masque or to modern musical comedy than to grand opera. The heroic plays are too artificial to appeal to any but the most devoted scholars of the period, and Dryden's comedies and tragicomedies suffer in comparison with those of his contemporaries, Sir George Etherege, William Wycherley, and William Congreve, not to mention his predecessors in English drama. As an index to the taste of the Restoration, however, the plays remain valuable and instructive, reflecting the levels of achievement and prevalent values of dramatic art of the time. Further, a study of Dryden reveals much about both aesthetic and intellectual influences on the drama of his period and the development of the dramatic genres of his age.

Biography

John Dryden was the eldest of fourteen children in a landed family of modest means whose sympathies were Puritan on both sides. Little is known of his youth in Northamptonshire, for Dryden, seldom hesitant about expressing his opinions, was reticent about details of his personal life. At about age fifteen, he was enrolled in Westminster School, then under the headmastership of Dr. Richard Busby, a school notable for its production of poets and bishops. Having attained at Westminster a thorough grounding in Latin, he proceeded to Cambridge, taking the B.A. in 1654. After the death of his father brought him a modest inheritance in the form of rents from family land, Dryden left the university and settled in London. Though little is known of his early years there, he served briefly in Oliver Cromwell's government in a minor position and may have worked for the publisher Henry Herringman. He produced an elegy on the death of Cromwell, yet when Charles II ascended the throne, Dryden greeted the new ruler with a congratulatory poem, *Astraea Redux* (1660). After the Restoration, he turned his main interest to the drama, producing an insignificant comedy, *The Wild Gallant*, and collaborating with Sir Robert Howard on a heroic play, *The Indian Queen*. He married Lady Elizabeth Howard, Sir Robert's sister, a marriage which brought him a generous dowry and, eventually, three sons in whom he took pride.

Throughout his career, Dryden was no stranger to controversy, whether literary, political, or religious; in fact, he seemed all too eager to seize an occasion for polemics. In literature, he challenged Sir Robert Howard's views on the drama, Thomas Rymer's on criticism, the Earl of Rochester's and Thomas Shadwell's on questions of literary merit and taste. After receiving encouragement from Charles II, Dryden entered the political controversy over succession to the throne with *Absalom and Achitophel* (part 1, 1681; part 2, with Nahum Tate, 1682). Later, he explained his religious views by attacking Deists, Catholics, and Dissenters in *Religio Laici* (1682); then, he shifted his ground and defended Catholicism in *The Hind and the Panther* (1687).

For a variety of reasons, Dryden was the most often assailed among major poets in his time, a fact attributable in some measure to envy. In an age when almost everyone prized his own wit, Dryden attained eminence without obviously possessing more of that quality than many others. Yet his willingness to plunge into controversy won him a host of enemies, and his changes of opinions and beliefs—literary, religious, political—made him vulnerable to criticism. Examining Dryden's changes of allegiance and point of view one by one, a biographer or critic can provide a logical explanation for each. This task is perhaps most difficult in literary criticism, where Dryden defended a position with enthusiasm only to abandon it later for another, which he advocated with an equal enthusiasm. To his contemporaries, some of his changes were to be explained by self-interest, and, rightly or wrongly, the charge of timeserving became a potent weapon in the hands of his critics.

In 1668, Dryden was appointed poet laureate, a position he held for twenty years, and he also signed a lucrative contract with the Theatre Royal to produce three new plays each year. Though he was unable to produce this stipulated number over the decade of the contract, he nevertheless received his share of theater revenues. During his term as laureate, he received a two-hundred-pound annual stipend, an amount that was later increased to three hundred pounds when he became historiographer royal, but irregularly paid. He was active as a dramatist throughout the 1670's, though he gradually turned his interest to poetic satire, beginning with *Mac Flecknoe* (1682).

With events surrounding the Popist Plot (1678) posing a threat to the government of Charles II, Dryden all but abandoned the theater, writing instead satires, translations, and then his religious poems. Initially, he carried the field for the king, but after the fall of James II and the loss of his political cause, he also lost the laureateship and its accompanying pension.

During the final period of his life, 1688-1700, Dryden made a brief return to the theater, producing an additional five dramas, but he devoted most of his considerable energy and talent to translations of poetry, achieving success with his patrons and public.

Analysis

Marriage à la Mode is usually considered John Dryden's best comedy. His others rely heavily upon farcical situations and double entendre and, at times, inept licentiousness that makes comedies such as *The Assignation* and *The Kind Keeper* seem unnecessarily coarse even by the standards of his time. *Marriage à la Mode* combines in its two distinct plot lines the conventions of the romantic tragicomedy and the Restoration comedy of manners, a genre not fully established when Dryden produced his play.

The tragicomic plot involves the theme of succession, perhaps Dryden's most frequent dramatic theme after love and honor. Polydamas, having usurped the throne of Sicily, discovers two young persons of gentle birth but unknown parentage who have been living among fisher folk under the care of Hermogenes, a former courtier. When Hermogenes tells the usurper that Leonidas is his son, born after his wife had fled from him, the king accepts this as correct, even though Leonidas is actually the son of the king he had deposed. When Polydamas insists that Leonidas marry the daughter of his friend, Leonidas refuses because of his love for Palmyra, the girl with whom he had been discovered. To frustrate this passion, Polydamas seeks to banish her, whereupon Hermogenes declares that Palmyra is the king's daughter and claims Leonidas as his own son, for he cannot risk revealing the truth about Leonidas, in reality the rightful successor. Polydamas than seeks to have Palmyra marry his favorite, Argaleon, and banishes Leonidas, later changing the sentence to death. Facing execution, Leonidas manages to proclaim his right to the throne, to bring his captors over to his side, and to oust Polydamas, whom he generously forgives as the father of his beloved Palmyra.

The tragicomic characteristics are all present—the unusual setting; the usurper; the long-lost noble youth; the faithful servant; the idealization of romantic love, struggling successfully against the odds and triumphing. To heighten the tone, Dryden uses blank verse rather than prose and, in the most serious passages, employs rhymed heroic couplets. The tragicomic plot, in the manner of John Fletcher, reveals a significant debt to Elizabethan and Jacobean tragicomedies.

Whereas in the main plot the attitude toward love is idealistic, the subplot represents a sharp contrast in the value placed upon both love and marriage. Dryden creates two witty couples—Rhodophil and Doralice, Palamede and Melantha—the first pair married and the second engaged by arrangement of their parents. Their attitudes toward marriage and love are as cynical and sophisticated as is standard in the comedy of manners. Palamede hopes before marriage to carry off an affair with his friend Rhodophil's wife, while Rhodophil hopes to make Melantha his mistress. They freely satirize Puritans and country folk, and the prevailing attitude of society toward marriage is indicated by Rhodophil when he speaks of his wife, "Yet I loved her a whole half year, double the natural term of any mistress; and I think, in my conscience, I could have held out another quarter, but then the world began to laugh at me, and a certain shame, of being out of fashion, seized me." Disguises, masked balls, and assignations keep the plot lively and suspenseful, though the couples' goals are never realized because all plans either are intercepted or go awry, and at the end, they part still friends. Throughout, the dialogue sparkles with repartee unequaled in any of Dryden's other plays. It includes Melantha's affected French expressions along with much double entendre and innuendo, yet it is never brutally licentious in tone, as is true of dialogue in comedies such as *The Kind Keeper.*

Though the two plots are loosely connected, Rhodophil does bring the newly found gentlefolk to the court, and both he and Palamede unite to support Leonidas in the final act. Further, the attitudes of parents who arrange marriages are condemned in both plot lines. For the most part, however, the plots occur in two separate worlds—the witty and sophisticated world of the comedy of manners and the idealistic and sentimental world of tragicomedy.

During the period from 1663 to 1680, Dryden wrote, entirely or in part, twenty-one plays. His initial success came with his heroic plays from *The Indian Queen* to *Aureng-Zebe*, by which time the genre had almost run its course. The heroic play was influenced by a variety of sources, including the English dramas of John Fletcher, the French tragedies of Pierre Corneille, and the French poetic romances of Madeleine de Scudéry and Gautier de Costes de La Calprenède. The most prominent feature which set the genre apart from the usual tragedy was the dialogue in heroic couplets, attributed to the playwrights' efforts to please Charles II, who, it was said, had come to enjoy the rhymed French drama he saw during his years in exile. Dryden defended the artificiality of rhymed dialogue on the grounds that the plays dealt with conflicts and characters above the commonplace; thus, the stylistic elevation provided by rhyme was appropriate. The characters, however, engage in lengthy rhymed speeches, usually with two characters confronting each other, and the result has seemed in a later time excessively artificial.

The plays frequently employ spectacle, enhanced by songs, dances, and elaborate costumes. The settings are usually exotic rather than English, thus heightening their romantic appeal. *The Indian Queen* and *The Indian Emperor*, for example, are set in Mexico, whereas both parts of Dryden's *The Conquest of Granada by the Spaniards* are set in Spain. Warfare, conquest, and striving dominate the plays.

The characters belong to a set of types that include as the protagonist the love-honor hero, who finds himself involved in intrigues and power-struggles which put those virtues to the test. Like the other characters, he does not change; the tests the characters encounter are intended to show the strength of their virtue or the depth of their depravity. The hero is surrounded by such Fletcherian types as the sentimental maiden, whom he loves; the evil woman, who shamelessly attempts to gain him for herself; the weak king, whom others are attempting to topple from the throne; the faithful friend; and an antagonist who is almost but not quite a Machiavellian villain motivated solely by ambition. The hero is sometimes fortunate and prevails over all of the obstacles he encounters; at other times, he dies without any success other than preserving his love and honor.

The romantic excesses of heroic plays were satirized by George Villiers, Duke of Buckingham, in his burlesque *The Rehearsal* (pr., pb. 1672), which has as its major character John Bayes, a brilliant satiric depiction of Dryden. Villiers parodies many of the absurd and inflated lines of Dryden and others who wrote in the form, yet *The Rehearsal* failed to drive the heroic drama from the stage. The genre remained viable for nearly two decades, until the late 1670's, when the playwrights began shifting their efforts to a less flamboyant form of tragedy.

Aureng-Zebe, the last of Dryden's heroic plays, was judged by him to be his best, though in the prologue he announced that he had grown weary of rhyme, an indication of his imminent shift to blank verse as the appropriate meter for serious drama. By comparison to Dryden's earlier heroic dramas, *Aureng-Zebe* makes less use of song and dance and includes less rant and bombast, yet it clearly preserves the major elements of the genre.

Set in India at the time of the Mogul Empire, it derives events and characters from history, though Dryden freely alters the sources. The aging emperor, a stereotypical weak king, finds his throne challenged by several of his sons, the loyal Aureng-Zebe being an exception. Aureng-Zebe is depicted by his friend Arimant, Governor of Agra, as "by no strong person swayed/ Except his love," a hero of unshakable loyalty who hopes that he will attain the hand of the captive queen Indamora for his support of the emperor.

While *Aureng-Zebe* is tame by earlier standards of the heroic play, echoes of the swashbuckling, superhuman hero remain. In armed conflict, the hero defeats two rebellious brothers, Darah being the first, "Darah from loyal Aureng-Zebe is fled,/ And forty thousand of his men lie dead." The threat represented by Morat, the ambitious villain of the play, is not so easily parried, for he has raised an immense force thus described by Abbas: "The neighb'ring plain with arms is coverd o'er;/ The vale an iron harvest seems to yield/ Of thick-sprung lances in a waving field." The hyperboles, typical of the genre, suggest the physical threat posed by Morat; his character also serves as a foil to that of Aureng-Zebe, for he does not properly control his passions. Primarily motivated by a desire for power, he also wishes to abandon his faithful wife, Melesinda, for Aureng-Zebe's beloved Indamora, who finds him repulsive. Further complications arise when the emperor falls passionately in love with Indamora, and the Empress Nourmahal, Aureng-Zebe's stepmother and the "evil woman" of the play, conceives a strong passion for her stepson. Confronted with news of his father's love for Indamora and his placing her under arrest, the hero accepts the challenge involving both his love and honor.

Aureng-Zebe finds himself threatened from many directions when he intercedes with the emperor and attempts to prevent the emperor's petulant imprisonment of Nourmahal. No sooner has the emperor seen Nourmahal taken away than he summons the rebellious Morat with the intent of making him his heir, all because of Aureng-Zebe's love for Indamora. Boldly entering unannounced, Aureng-Zebe attempts to end the alliance between the emperor and Morat by offering to disband his army if Morat will withdraw his forces from the city, leaving the emperor in control. Despite these peace-making efforts, the emperor orders Aureng-Zebe's arrest when he will not renounce his love for Indamora. When

Indamora pleads for Morat to spare the life of Aureng-Zebe, he demands her love in exchange, which she curtly refuses. The alliance between the emperor and Morat is broken when the emperor learns of Morat's passion for Indamora. After Aureng-Zebe has been released through the efforts of Indamora and Arimant, Indamora finds great difficulty in convincing the jealous hero that she has remained faithful and has not betrayed him with Morat. Meanwhile, having lost the favor of the emperor, Morat rebels against him.

The outcome is obscured when Arimant, in a disguise that results in his being mistaken for Aureng-Zebe, is killed and Morat has to break off a long seductive speech to Indamora to quell an uprising. In the final battle, Aureng-Zebe leads the emperor's forces to victory, and Morat, mortally wounded, manages to prevent his mother from murdering Indamora. Her violent passion frustrated, Nourmahal poisons herself, and the Emperor grants Aureng-Zebe both the state and Indamora.

In *Aureng-Zebe*, the characters who retain their honor reap the rewards of both love and honor, whereas those who do not control their passions and ambition encounter misfortune. The abruptness and violence of passions are appropriately accompanied by abrupt and violent actions in the plays. A major difference between good and evil characters becomes the measure of control over passions, not the violence of the passion itself. As D. W. Jefferson has pointed out, Dryden's characters, both the good and the bad, express themselves blatantly where sexual passions are concerned, a phenomenon not limited to the characters of the heroic plays.

Of *All for Love*, his tragedy based upon Shakespeare's earlier great work *Antony and Cleopatra*, Dryden himself commented that he had never written anything "for myself but *Antony and Cleopatra.*" The drama reflects Dryden's vision of tragedy, sometimes designated by critics as "heroic tragedy" to indicate certain similarities to the heroic play. The chief among Dryden's works in the type include *Oedipus, Troilus and Cressida, Don Sebastian, King of Portugal* and *Cleomenes, the Spartan Hero.* Unlike the heroic plays, these are written in blank verse and their sources are Shakespearean or classical. They demonstrate fewer of the epic dimensions of the heroic play, and the heroes are more nearly realistic characters. Although Dryden succeeds more fully in presenting human emotions in these dramas, in part because the medium of blank verse is more suited to emotional expression, he achieves the effects of pathos and sentiment rather than pity and fear.

In *All for Love*, Dryden follows the dramatic unities of time, place, and action, which he regarded as ornaments of tragedy, though not indispensable. The hero, Antony, is presented on the final day of his life, which happens to be his birthday. Facing imminent defeat at the hands of Octavius, he encounters temptations to abandon the great passion of his life, Cleopatra, in order to prolong the contest or to minimize the consequences of the loss. Restrictions inherent in the dramatic unities result in characters which are not nearly so complex as those of the source, Shakespeare's *Antony and Cleopatra*. Cleopatra neither wavers in her devotion to Antony nor reflects at length upon her role as queen, as she does in Shakespeare's tragedy. Dryden's Ventidius shares qualities drawn from Shakespeare's character of the same name but also from Shakespeare's Enobarbus, the devoted adviser who abandons Antony. Ventidius strives to deliver Antony from his passion for Cleopatra, while, at the same time, her servant Alexas is scheming with Cleopatra to keep Antony's devotion. Caught in the struggle between love and duty, Antony appears a weak hero. Ventidius first offers Antony, then under attack by Octavius, the support of twelve legions if he will abandon Cleopatra, pointing to this as a necessary condition since the legionnaires refuse to come to Egypt and insist that Antony join them to assume command. Seizing upon this chance for victory, Antony agrees, only to change his mind when he receives a parting gift, a bracelet, from Cleopatra, who unexpectedly arrives to put her gift on his arm.

Ventidius next arranges for Antony to make an honorable peace with Caesar, leaving him with limited power, if he will return to his wife Octavia. When Octavia appears with their two daughters, Antony is unable to withstand their pleas and agrees to return to her, dispatching Dolabella to deliver a farewell to Cleopatra. This episode reveals the flaws in Alexas' and Ventidius' calculations. Alexas reasons that Cleopatra may win Antony back by arousing his jealousy through Dolabella, whereas Ventidius assumes that jealousy will convince Antony that Cleopatra was worthless. Thus, both adversaries steer Antony in the same direction for different ends. The result is that Octavia becomes so distressed at Antony's obvious jealousy over their reports that she leaves him. In return for Antony's hostility and anger and after the loss of a battle at sea, Cleopatra sends word of her death, which Antony cannot bear. Following his self-inflicted mortal wound, he is taken to Cleopatra, whose death following his brings a sense of triumph.

While scenes such as that between Antony and Octavia involve a generous amount of sentimentality, Dryden achieves in *All for Love* an intensity that is lacking in most of his plays, one whose emotional effects are not dissipated through digressions or loosely related subplots. The play reveals a tightly unified plot line in which characters' motives and actions are influenced primarily by strong romantic love.

Dryden's tragedy *Don Sebastian, King of Portugal*, written after the Glorious Revolution, is his longest drama and, in the view of critics from Sir Walter Scott to Bruce King, his finest dramatic achievement. In the play's preface, Dryden acknowledges that the players cut more than twelve hundred lines from the acted version. Though the play's themes are universally appropriate for tragedy, it includes a closely related comic subplot, and it ends not with the death of the hero or heroine but with their retirement from the world of affairs. The play incorporates numerous qualities and dramatic techniques that Dryden employs elsewhere in his work and may be the most fruitful play to examine for clarifying his dramatic art.

The play is set in North Africa, where Don Sebastian, King of Portugal, and his allies have been defeated and captured after warring against the Moors. Sebastian's chief desire is to marry the woman he loves, Almeyda, Christian Queen of Barbary, also held captive. This he manages to do after the Emperor Muley-Moluch has given him a measure of freedom so that Sebastian can attempt to win Almeyda's hand for the emperor. Sebastian and Almeyda escape the emperor's retribution for their marriage, because he is slain in a rebellion, but they do not escape fate. In the final act, they learn from the old counselor Alvarez, who has just been freed from captivity, that they are half brother and sister, having had the same father. The incestuousness of their relationship, unknowing though it was, forces them to part, with each retiring to a separate religious house.

The Moors are portrayed throughout the play as riven by factions, the chief threat being the effort of the emperor's favorite, Benducar, to topple him from the throne, ostensibly in favor of the emperor's brother, Muley-Zeydan, but in reality for himself. In this attempt, he involves the populace, the religious leader Mufti Abdalla, and Dorax, a Christian who has turned against Sebastian and has joined the Moors. Dorax later joins Sebastian, after the fall of the emperor, to defeat the uprising and restore worthy leaders to their places. A comic subplot involves the efforts of the Christian captive Don Antonio to flee the household of the Mufti with his daughter Morayma and his treasure, in much the same way that Lorenzo and Jessica flee Shylock in Shakespeare's *The Merchant of Venice*.

The exotic setting, the theme of heroic love, the stock characters, and the broils and warfare represent familiar themes and situations of Dryden's dramas. Occasionally, one also finds in the dramas some exceptional improbabilities. In this play, for example, Dorax, having lost the confidence of the Moors, is poisoned by two of them, Benducar and the Mufti, but survives because each poison neutralizes the effect of the other. Yet *Don Sebastian, King of Portugal* illustrates other characteristics of Dryden's dramatic art that are less obvious but more influential and significant: the theme of incest, actual or suppressed; anticlericalism; political satire and allusions; and scenes of reconciliation. In *Don Sebastian, King of Portugal*, unwitting incest occurs between Sebastian and Almeyda after they are married, and such is their consternation when they discover they have violated the taboo that Sebastian believes suicide the only escape until Dorax dissuades him. The situation resembles somewhat that of Oedipus in the version of the old Greek drama that Dryden and Nathaniel Lee produced for the Restoration stage. It is as though love in Dryden is so exalted, wrought up to such a pitch, that introduction of the taboo acts to heighten it and make the plight of the lovers more poignant. In *Don Sebastian, King of Portugal*, the theme is counterbalanced by the story of Violante, who denied affection to the husband Sebastian had chosen for her and awaited for many years her beloved Dorax.

It is unclear why anticlericalism becomes such a prominent theme in the works of Dryden, though it seems plausible that his profound distrust and dislike of Puritan influence on political affairs may in part explain it. The Mufti represents the typical clergyman in Dryden, usually the object of satire in both the poems and the plays. He is ambitious, avaricious, sensual, officious, and usually hypocritical. The Mufti appears ridiculous in both political and personal affairs, becoming the object of humor and scorn. Dryden does not, of course, ridicule clergymen of the Church of England, but wherever he introduces a pagan, a Moslem, or a Catholic religious figure, the character becomes the object of satire.

In its political theme, the play concerns betrayal and misappropriation of power. The emperor, having usurped the throne, discovers that he can trust no one, least of all Benducar, his closest adviser. Benducar incites the mob to rebellion, and they manage to defeat and kill the emperor, barbarously showing his head on a pike as that of a tyrant. Like a true Machiavellian, Benducar muses on the thesis that might makes right: "And I can sin but once to seize the throne; all after-acts are sanctified by power." Such passages as this in Dryden's plays, poems, and translations following the Glorious Revolution usually serve as oblique satire of the new monarchs, and his distrust of the judgment of the common people where political affairs are concerned is a recurring theme throughout his work.

A final characteristic of Dryden's theater is evident in act 4, scene 3, often considered the most successful scene of the play. It depicts the intense quarrel of the two friends, Dorax and Sebastian, and their reconciliation. Dryden may have based this scene on the quarrel of Brutus and Cassius in Shakespeare's *Julius Caesar*; similar scenes occur in other works of Dryden, notably in *Troilus and Cressida* and *Cleomenes, the Spartan Hero*. Although Dorax has fought on the side of the Moors, he defends and spares the life of Sebastian—so that he can kill him to exact his own revenge. He holds a powerful grudge because Sebastian did not adequately reward him for his prior service and awarded the hand of Violante to another courtier, Henriquez. Facing an imminent fight to the death with Dorax, Sebastian explains that Henriquez had sought the hand of Violante first, that Henriquez had died defending Sebastian, and that Violante now waits for Dorax. Accepting Sebastian's explanation, Dorax submits, is restored to favor, and promises that he will serve Sebastian as faithfully as Henriquez had done. In the final act, Dorax helps Sebastian bear manfully his sense of guilt and loss. Scenes of intense confrontation permit the dramatist to display a range of emotions in a brief space, as well as a heightening and diminution of passions. Dryden's ability to capture such a range of tones compensates to a degree for his lack of a greater gift as a dramatist—the ability to show growth and development of his characters.

Other major works

POETRY: *Heroic Stanzas*, 1659; *Astraea Redux*, 1660; "To My Lord Chancellor," 1662; *Prologues and Epilogues*, 1664-1700; *Annus Mirabilis*, 1667; *Absalom and Achitophel*, 1681; *Absalom and Achitophel, Part II*, 1682 (with Nahum Tate); *Mac Flecknoe*, 1682; *Religio Laici*, 1682; *Threnodia Augustalis*, 1685; *The Hind and the Panther*, 1687; "A Song for St. Cecilia's Day," 1687; *Britannia Rediviva*, 1688; *Eleonora*, 1692; "To My Dear Friend Mr. Congreve," 1694; *Alexander's Feast: Or, The Power of Music*, 1697; "To My Honour'd Kinsman, John Driden," 1700.

NONFICTION: *An Essay of Dramatic Poesy*, 1668; "A Defense of *An Essay of Dramatic Poesy*," 1668; "Preface to *An Evening's Love*," 1671; "Of Heroic Plays: An Essay," 1672; "Preface to *All for Love*, 1678; "The Grounds of Criticism in Tragedy," 1679; "Preface to *Sylvae*," 1685; "Dedication of *Examen Poeticum*, 1693; *A Discourse Concerning the Original and Progress of Satire*, 1693; "Dedication of the *Aeneis*," 1697; "Preface to *The Fables*," 1700.

TRANSLATIONS: *Ovid's Epistles*, 1680; *The History of the League*, 1684 (of Louis Maimbourg's *Histoire de la Ligue*); *The Life of St. Francis Xavier*, 1688 (of Dominique Bouhours' *La Vie de Saint François Xavier*); *The Satires of Juvenal and Persius*, 1693; *The Works of Virgil*, 1697.

Bibliography

Barbeau, Anne T. *The Intellectual Design of John Dryden's Heroic Plays.* New Haven, Conn.: Yale University Press, 1970. In this scholarly study of Dryden's five heroic plays, Barbeau argues that Dryden did not attempt to compete with Elizabethan or French dramas but pursued a direction of his own. She elucidates this direction in her close reading of the plays and also in her discussion of Dryden's dramatic theory, political theory, and ethics. The early narrative poems are compared with the heroic plays in order to underscore their common sense of values.

Bywaters, David. *Dryden in Revolutionary England.* Berkeley: University of California Press, 1991. This book describes the rhetorical stages by which Dryden, in his published works between 1687 and 1700, sought to define contemporary politics and to stake out for himself a tenable place within them. The volume attempts to situate these works in political and literary contexts familiar to Dryden and his readers. The study reveals much about the relationship between Dryden's politics, polemics, and art. Contains an epilogue and extensive notes.

Hammond, Paul. *John Dryden: A Literary Life.* New York: St. Martin's Press, 1991. This study of Dryden's life examines the texts that he produced and the relationship of these texts to the society they reflect. The work consists of chapters on different aspects of Dryden's works. They are arranged approximately chronologically to suggest the shape of his career and to explore his own developing sense of his role as the premier writer of Restoration England, both dominating and detached from the world in which he moved. Select bibliography and extensive notes.

Schilling, Bernard N. *Dryden: A Collection of Critical Essays.* Englewood Cliffs, N.J.: Prentice-Hall, 1963. An excellent collection of critical essays on Dryden's poetry and drama. The author's thesis is that, of the major English poets, Dryden has stood most in need of balanced judgment and informal reappraisal. The book attempts to make the reader more fully aware of the meaning and value of Dryden's work and to assess his literary stature. Contains a chronology of important dates and a bibliography.

Winn, James Anderson. *John Dryden and His World.* New Haven, Conn.: Yale University Press, 1987. This lengthy work is a fresh attempt to transport its reader to Dryden's time. It examines the man, his work, and the world in which he lived. Considers the subtle relations linking this world's religious beliefs, its political alliances, and the literary styles it favored. Views Dryden's work as a product of his particular historical situation. Includes illustrations and appendices on Dryden's family history.

Stanley Archer
(Updated by *Genevieve Slomski*)

WILLIAM DUNLAP

Born: Perth Amboy, New Jersey; February 19, 1766
Died: New York, New York; September 28, 1839

Principal drama

The Father: Or, American Shandyism, pr., pb. 1789 (revised as *The Father of an Only Child*, pb. 1806); *Fountainville Abbey*, pr. 1795, pb. 1806; *The Archers: Or, Mountaineers of Switzerland*, pr., pb. 1796 (opera; music by Benjamin Carr); *The Man of Fortitude: Or, The Knight's Adventure*, pr. 1797, pb. 1807; *Tell Truth and Shame the Devil*, pr., pb. 1797 (adaptation of A. L. B. Robineau's play *Jérome Pointu*); *André*, pr., pb. 1798; *False Shame: Or, The American Orphan in Germany*, pr. 1798, pb. 1940 (adaptation of August von Kotzebue's play *Falsche Schaam*); *The Stranger*, pr., pb. 1798 (adaptation of Kotzebue's play *Menschenhass und Reue*); *Don Carlos*, pr. 1799 (adaptation of Friedrich Schiller's play *Don Carlos, Infant von Spanien*); *Lovers' Vows*, pr. 1799, pb. 1814 (adaptation of Kotzebue's play *Das Kind der Liebe*); *The Italian Father*, pr. 1799, pb. 1800; *The Virgin of the Sun*, pr., pb. 1800 (adaptation of Kotzebue's play *Die Sonnen Jungfrau*); *Pizzaro in Peru: Or, The Death of Rolla*, pr., pb. 1800 (adaptation of Kotzebue's play *Die Spanier in Peru: Oder, Rollas Tod*); *Fraternal Discord*, pr. 1800, pb. 1809 (adaptation of Kotzebue's play *Die Versöhnung*); *Abaellino, the Great Bandit*, pr. 1801, pb. 1802 (adaptation of J. H. D. Zschokke's play *Abällino der Grosse Bandit*); *The Glory of Columbia—Her Yeomanry!*, pr. 1803, pb. 1817 (adaptation of *André*); *Ribbemont: Or, The Feudal Baron*, pr. 1803 (originally as *The Mysterious Monk*, pr. 1796); *The Wife of Two Husbands*, pr., pb. 1804 (adaptation of Guilbert de Pixérécourt's play *La Femme à deux maris*); *Leicester*, pb. 1806 (originally as *The Fatal Deception: Or, The Progress of Guilt*, pr. 1794); *The Dramatic Works of William Dunlap*, pb. 1806, 1816 (3 volumes); *Thirty Years: Or, The Life of a Gamester*, pr. 1828, pb. 1940 (adaptation of Prosper Goubaux and Victor Ducange's play *Trente Ans*); *A Trip to Niagara: Or, Travellers in America*, pr. 1828, pb. 1830; *Four Plays, 1789-1812*, pb. 1976; *Adaptations of European Plays*, pb. 1988; *Five Plays*, pb. 1991.

Other literary forms

Many of William Dunlap's nondramatic works have earned for him solid status among students of literature and visual art. His biography of his contemporary Charles Brockden Brown, America's first major Gothic novelist, remains a standard reference tool. Dunlap's other biographical works—a shorter piece on Brown, sketches of Gilbert Stuart and Thomas Abthorpe Cooper, and a book on George Frederick Cooke—are valuable portraits by one who was on the scene for many of the events presented. Because of his career as a painter, Dunlap's *A History of the Rise and Progress of the*

Arts of Design in the United States (1834) also remains a work worth consulting for this aspect of America's early cultural history.

Still more important is *A History of American Theatre* (1832). Dunlap's account of the American theater from the 1790's through the first third of the nineteenth century is at times blurred by faulty memory. Nevertheless, before the work of George O. Seilhamer, George C. D. Odell, Arthur Hornblow, and Arthur Hobson Quinn, Dunlap offered a rich history of American drama. His firsthand account also furnishes an autobiography of its author, and altogether, it remains a classic in the annals of the American stage.

Dunlap also wrote verse, and several of his short stories, published in periodicals during the final decade of his life, merit critical attention. Many of his periodical pieces were unsigned, making definite attribution difficult. Dunlap intended to bring out a collected edition of his plays, in ten volumes. Only three volumes of *The Dramatic Works of William Dunlap* appeared, however, the first in 1806, the following two in 1816.

Achievements

Customarily designated the "Father of American Drama," Dunlap lived a long life through a period of extraordinary historical change in American culture. He was the first American playwright who turned to writing plays and managing theaters for a livelihood. His output of original plays and adaptations or translations from foreign dramas adds up to more than fifty titles. He gained considerable fame, as well as the love of many who were connected with early American theater, during his management of playhouses in Philadelphia and New York. Dunlap also deserves praise for his interest in and knowledge of German language and literature, as a result of which he was able to bring plays by August von Kotzebue, Friedrich Schiller, and J. H. D. Zschokke to the American stage at the turn of the nineteenth century. Such fare continued to be popular for many years. Dunlap also adapted from French theater, particularly from the then fairly new melodrama. His own pleasure in melodramatic and sensational scenes informs many of his original productions; he adapted many sentimental-sensational plays for his theaters because he well comprehended the desires of his audiences. His striving in his writing and in his theaters for high standards of morality, however, countered common tendencies to cater mainly to less admirable impulses of audiences eager for thrills and sexually suggestive titillation. At times, too, Dunlap's intense patriotism, centered on his admiration for George Washington, saved his own plays from running overmuch into sleazy melodramatics. On the other hand, that overt patriotism emphatically dates these plays and limits their appeal today, except as valuable literary history.

Dunlap as dramatist furnishes a curiosity in the accounts of anthologists and scholars of our national literature, in that most collections of eighteenth and early nineteenth century American plays have featured only *André*. Richard Moody, however, in his anthology *Dramas from the American Theatre, 1762-1909* (1966), provides other specimens from Dunlap's canon, *The Glory of Columbia—Her Yeomanry!* and *A Trip to Niagara*. The first is a reworking of *André*; the second demonstrates Dunlap's experimental combination of dramatic and visual-arts techniques. Dunlap's interests as playwright and painter make such a blending understandable. Possibly more than any other playwright of his age, Dunlap has come down through chronicles of American drama, such as those of Arthur Hobson Quinn, Montrose J. Moses, and Oral Sumner Coad, as the author of a single play, although Quinn's account in his history of early American drama does reveal other facets of Dunlap's work.

Dunlap's decided inclination toward the Gothic, obvious in *Leicester*, *Fountainville Abbey*, and other plays and clearly coursing through works in which other concerns are primary, has been sadly neglected, although this interest led to some of Dunlap's outstanding achievements. The early historians of American literature tended to follow too closely in the footsteps of Ralph Waldo Emerson, championing a distinctly national literary art. As a result, they generally regarded Gothicism as a product of European decadence, a genre not conducive to the production of a genuinely indigenous American literature. Dunlap himself recognized the excesses to which literary Gothicism was prone, as is evident in his short stories: There, as often as not, such exaggerations were subjected to hoax treatment. In the manner of Washington Irving and Edgar Allan Poe, Dunlap deftly mingled horror and humor.

Dunlap's partiality toward the Gothic has not been the only aspect of his work to be noted unfavorably by critics and historians. Dunlap's twin interests, the theater and painting, have often been used against him by those who believe that he achieved slightly less than greatness in either, simply because he was engaged in two careers. Partly as a result of such prejudices, Dunlap's work as a playwright has been undervalued. At a time when bombast clouded much of American literature, Dunlap experimented with vernacular speech on the stage. He managed to effect compelling characters by such means. His practical experience of theater management gave him a command of his medium that many of his contemporaries did not enjoy, as, for example, the career of James Nelson Barker reveals. All of his limitations notwithstanding, William Dunlap merits greater attention than he has received from students of American drama.

Biography

William Dunlap, the only child of Samuel and Margaret Sargeant Dunlap, spent his early years in Perth Amboy, New Jersey, where he was born. The wealth of his father, a merchant specializing in the china and looking-glass trade, enabled the boy to receive a fine education. He was particularly fortunate in studying classical literature with the elderly Thomas Bartow, whose store of learning in the classics enriched the mind of his young friend. In the spring of 1777, Samuel Dunlap, whose sympathies were Loyalist, moved his family to New York City, where William was first introduced to stage drama. This interest was to continue throughout his life, and although reverses in fortune later dogged Dunlap, he never lost his enthusiasm for any aspect of the stage. In 1783, after the close of the Revolutionary War, the Dunlaps returned to Perth Amboy. Shortly thereafter, during the convening of Congress at Princeton, Dunlap first saw George Washington, and during the winter of 1783-1784, the young man painted a portrait of his hero.

From 1784 to August, 1787, Dunlap spent time in London, studying painting with Benjamin West and increasing his acquaintance with playgoing and with theater personages. Richard Brinsley Sheridan's plays were among his favorites. Returning to the United States, Dunlap tried to establish himself as a portrait painter, but the theater soon came to be uppermost in his mind and work. The success of Royall Tyler's *The Contrast* (pr. 1787) inspired Dunlap to create his own first play, a comedy entitled "The Modest Soldier: Or, Love in New York," which was accepted by the American Company but never performed; the young playwright had failed to fashion parts suitable for the manager and his wife. Correcting that circumstance in his next work, *The Father*, written in 1788 and performed in 1789, Dunlap launched himself on a career as a dramatist that lasted for the next thirty years and made him famous. His experiments with numerous dramatic forms, his introduction of Kotzebue and other European playwrights to the American stage, and his career as a manager in Philadelphia and New York, as well as his ventures into painting (most notably portraits) and into other forms of writing, filled his life.

Dogged by financial misfortunes after he lost his fortune as a theater manager, Dunlap maintained a good temper, as well as the respect and love of a wide circle of friends. His marriage, in 1789, to Nabby Woolsey, of an old New York family, brought him into contact with many well-known figures of his day, including Timothy Dwight, his wife's brother-in-law, who was to become President of Yale University. Always a social being, Dunlap also maintained connections with several literary clubs. The Friendly Club numbered among its members, in addition to Dunlap, many who shaped the cultural history of the United States during its early national period. Dunlap died in New York on September 28, 1839, after suffering a stroke.

Analysis

The Father: Or, American Shandyism was William Dunlap's first play to be performed; it was also the second comedy by an American playwright to enjoy public notice. As such, it deserves examination as a follow-up to Tyler's *The Contrast. The Father* still can entertain readers; its comic misunderstandings and mishaps, its portraiture of the typical Yankee character, and its lively dialogue retain their power to amuse.

The marriage of the Rackets has entered the doldrums; Mr. Racket believes that solace will come in the arms of country-bred Susannah, a pert household maid, while Mrs. Racket hopes to intensify her husband's love by inciting him to jealousy of their friend, Ranter. Ranter, however, has designs on her sister, Caroline. At an inopportune moment, Colonel Duncan, guardian to the sisters, enters and discovers Mrs. Racket fainting into Ranter's arms—and suspects the worst. The colonel and his servant, Cartridge, function, as Cartridge observes, like Laurence Sterne's Mr. Toby Shandy and Corporal Trim from the novel *The Life and Opinions of Tristram Shandy, Gent.* (1759-1767), a tale abounding in comic high jinks such as Dunlap tries to approximate with American characters. Ultimately, a solid reunion of the Rackets is effected by means of the exposure of Ranter's rascalities, the relevation that Caroline's lover, the long-lost son of Colonel Duncan, is alive, and the proper disposition of Susannah to Dr. Quiescent, a comic figure who has provided relief to tempestuous or grave incidents.

Dunlap deftly revised this play into *The Father of an Only Child*, which was possibly never performed, although it certainly reads well and could be a lively performance piece. A more distinctly American tinge is emphasized by means of comic reference to the *American Monthly Magazine*, in the vernacular speech of some of the characters, principally the maid Susannah, and in diminishing the Latinate names (Dr. Quiescent becomes Dr. Tattle). The Rackets are still the bibulous Irishman who has an eye for the ladies, and the long-suffering, determined wife who wrongheadedly tries to use jealousy to regain her husband's affections. The Colonel, renamed Campbell (his aide is renamed Platoon), with his concern for the only son he left to others long ago, gives the new title to the play. The background (the recent adoption of the United States Constitution) provides plausibility for the drunken revelry at the opening of the play. The menial, Jacob, adds to the cast a comic "Dutch" character, soon to become a stereotype in American plays. The outcome of this play is similar to that of *The Father*, except that Susannah is destined for Platoon.

Susannah's speeches in particular are noteworthy for their colloquial flavor, as when she repulses Racket's advances: "I'm a poor Yankee girl, and you are a rich town gentleman, and I'm sartin sich are no more fit to go together than a *pumpkin* and a pine-apple. Now mister Platoon don't go for higher than a good ripe ear of Indian corn, and a pumpkin needn't be ashamed of coming upon the same table any day." She remarks at this same juncture that "a body ought to keep company with a body's likes. Some folk's place is the keeping-room, and some folk's place is the stirring-room." Along with Platoon's praise for Colonel Campbell freeing his slaves (Dunlap's own action upon his father's death), such speeches serve to add homey, American touches to *The Father of an Only Child*. The exposure of the villainous servant's machinations against his master—the long-lost lover of Mrs. Racket's sister—in both versions suggests that European villainy is more vicious than the rather tame misdoings of Americans (the Rackets are new Americans). Ranter-Marsh-Rushport has his disguise stripped from him, and the revelation that he is the ne'er-do-well son whose mis-deeds killed his clergyman father and whose ring is that of Caroline's be-trothed recalls the confusions of identity, duplicitous and otherwise, charac-teristic of the Gothic romance so much in vogue at that time.

Similar comedies wherein misapprehension of motives furnishes the dra-matic conflict are *False Shame*, adapted from Kotzebue, *Thirty Years*, adapted from Goubaux and Ducange, and Dunlap's original *A Trip to Niagara*. In this last play, Dunlap put together suitable dramatic action to enhance a diorama or revolving set of scenery that moves the audience from New York Harbor to Catskill Landing, during which action the merits of the United States, as Dunlap's audience knew it, were debated—to the final yielding to its excellences by the British antagonist. Too easily dis-missed by critics, *A Trip to Niagara* is not poor dramatic art. The dialogue is spirited, the situation—of Amelia Wentworth's lover having to win her brother to things American in order to marry her—is good comic material, and the portraiture of comic stage types (French, Irish, Yankee) is compel-ling. The dialects, especially the American colloquial (although John Bull, Amelia's lover, merely impersonates a familiar Yankee figure), are well handled. Dunlap also presented the first serious portraiture of a black character of the American stage in Job Jerryson, who is a far cry from the amusing black minstrel who became a popular stage type during the nine-teenth century. Despite Dunlap's apparent writing of this play upon com-mission, he managed to create a comedy of no mean order.

Dunlap's tragic muse also inspired him to write several plays of high quality; these tragedies often derive from Gothic tradition. *Leicester*, *Fountainville Abbey*, *Ribbemont* (originally staged as *The Mysterious Monk* in 1796), and *The Man of Fortitude* abound in eerie scenery; foreboding characters and settings in equally mysterious situations; intense, emotion-filled scenes; and death—with accompanying moral loftiness triumphing. Derivative as it is from William Shakespeare's *Macbeth*—itself an inspira-tion for Gothic fiction—*Leicester* conveys splendidly the tensions of char-acters motivated by ambition, thwarted or illicit passion, and murderous impulses. The shifts in scenes, physical and psychological, through numer-ous shadows and glooms or fears and hysteria artistically support the strained verbal interchanges among the *dramatis personae*.

Fountainville Abbey, even more literary than historical in inspiration, was founded on Ann Radcliffe's famous Gothic novel, *The Romance of the Forest* (1791), and a play that was based on it, by the British dramatist James Boaden, *Fountainville Forest* (pr. 1794). Dunlap's play, first performed in 1795, is another of his works that has been neglected in favor of historical-patriotic creation, although Elihu Hubbard Smith, thoroughly knowledgeable in cultural currents at the time, pronounced it the best tragedy he had seen in twenty years, adding that if Dunlap fulfilled his promise, he might well become the most respected dramatist of his time.

In Dunlap's hands, the British sources are transmuted into exceptional verse drama. Fleeing creditors, La Motte, his wife, and his servant, old Peter, along with Adeline, a girl mysteriously brought along by La Motte, find shelter in abandoned Fountainville Abbey. The darkness and obscurity of that locale blend well with a seeming ghost—who in the end turns out to be old Peter harmlessly going to and fro—to produce a rational supernaturalism, after the manner of Radcliffe and akin to what Dunlap's contemporary, the novelist Charles Brockden Brown, would soon purvey in his fiction. (Dunlap, however, should be credited with being the first American Gothicist.) The wicked Marquis de Montalt, whom La Motte had attempted to rob, soon appears on the scene, lusts after Adeline, and then tries to browbeat La Motte into murdering the girl when he discovers that she is his niece, daughter of the brother and rightful marquis, whom he had murdered. In the end, justice and virtue triumph, but that happy conclusion occurs only after moments of great trauma. Adeline is restored to her rightful status, and with her wealth she will bring good fortune to La Motte as well. The Marquis unsuccessfully tries to commit suicide—and thus departs from his origins in Radcliffe and Boaden, wherein he does kill himself. La Motte, a man dogged by guilt, finally, and symbolically, is brought from darkness, in setting and spirit, to light and salvation. The backdrops are functional in enhancing the psychic upsets (more significant than physical action) in *Fountainville Abbey*. Dunlap's poetic heights in this play are not matched in *Ribbemont*. Reminiscent of the *Romeo and Juliet* situation of poisoning, this play of apparently illicit love and murder is marred by too many overstrained speeches and too little action.

The Man of Fortitude, *The Stranger*, *The Italian Father*, *Don Carlos*, and *Abaellino, the Great Bandit*—adaptations from older English or from German plays—contain fine scenes. They are interesting in that they exemplify types of stage fare, such as the Gothic, the robber play, or the sentimental, much sought in the period of Dunlap's career. Overall, however, these works do not measure up to the high standards achieved in dramas such as *Leicester* or *Fountainville Abbey*.

André, Dunlap's best-known drama, though unsuccessful in its 1798 performance, reaches heights of psychological tension that are matched only in the Gothic plays written shortly before, in the 1790's. It has also appealed to those whose tastes in early American drama turn decidedly toward the patriotic. The plot is simple: Major John André, en route to Benedict Arnold, is captured and sentenced to hang as a spy against the American cause during the Revolution. He ultimately goes off to die after successive emotionally charged attempts to save him fail. The dramatic interest centers on delineating the psychological workings of those who argue for André's life. Even George Washington finds admirable traits in André's personality, although he realizes that to pardon him would be to encourage treason. The action of young Bland, André's great friend, in throwing down his cockade before Washington, was hissed by the American audience on the opening-night performance, but his subsequent repentance of his rashness toned down the suggestion of treason in his anger. Dunlap did not observe strict historical accuracy in creating his play—only one, but the best, of several on the popular André theme. Documents reveal that the love affair between André and Honora, who in Dunlap's play appears to plead for him, was romanticized by the playwright. He also invented the Blands, a mother and son who, in their pleadings, doubtless appealed to an American audience's love of sentimentality.

The André theme is reworked in *The Glory of Columbia—Her Yeomanry!*, nine of the fifteen scenes of which were taken from *André*, but to no great advantage. As the title change suggests, the center of interest shifts from André, who in both plays recalls the villain-hero of many tragedies, to the common people of America. Dunlap's handling of colloquial idiom is the single positive feature in this otherwise too fervently patriotic play, so blatantly calculated to wring the nationalistic hearts of American playgoers. Nevertheless, *The Glory of Columbia—Her Yeomanry!* was for some time revived each year to celebrate the Fourth of July.

Other major works

NONFICTION: *Memoirs of the Life of George Frederick Cooke*, 1813 (2 volumes), 1815 (revised as *The Life of Cooke*); *The Life of Charles Brockden Brown*, 1815 (2 volumes); *A History of American Theatre*, 1832; *A History of the Rise and Progress of the Arts of Design in the United States*, 1834 (2 volumes); *Thirty Years Ago: Or, The Memoirs of a Water Drinker*, 1836 (as *Memoirs of a Water Drinker*, 1837); *A History of New York for Schools*, 1837 (2 volumes); *Diary of William Dunlap*, 1931, 1969 (Dorothy C. Barck, editor).

Bibliography

Argetsinger, Gerald S. "Dunlap's *André*: The Beginning of American Tragedy." *Players* 49 (Spring, 1974): 62-64. Argetsinger demonstrates how

André established Dunlap as the first major American dramatist and how it stands alone as the representative eighteenth century American tragedy. This article is significant in that it provided the foundation for later treatments of Dunlap as a dramatist.

Canary, Robert H. *William Dunlap.* New York: Twayne, 1970. Canary emphasizes Dunlap's importance because of his place at the beginning of the United States' history as a nation. The biography charts Dunlap's emergence as representative of the artists who made a place for the arts in the new nation. The criticism directs the reader to what is still of interest and suggests directions for literary analysis. Dunlap's most important works are described together with the personal and critical principles that governed his work. Notes, references, and annotated bibliography.

Coad, Oral Sumner. *William Dunlap: A Study of His Life and Works and of His Place in Contemporary Culture.* 1917. Reprint. New York: Russell & Russell, 1962. The standard biography and introduction to the works of Dunlap. Coad places Dunlap and his dramatic writings into the context of early American history and culture. In separate chapters, he examines Dunlap's original plays, dramatic translations, and nondramatic writings. Contains five illustrations of Dunlap and his paintings, a complete listing of Dunlap's writings, and an index.

Meserve, Walter J. *An Emerging Entertainment: The Drama of the American People to 1928.* Bloomington: Indiana University Press, 1977. Meserve provides an excellent overview of Dunlap's career, detailing his various contributions and their impact on his audience, then summarizes the major critical evaluations of Dunlap's work. Several other references to Dunlap are found throughout the volume. Bibliography and index.

Quinn, Arthur Hobson. *A History of the American Drama from the Beginning to the Civil War.* 1923. Reprint. New York: Appleton-Century-Crofts, 1951. The chapter "William Dunlap, Playwright and Producer" provides a basic introduction to his life and writings. It places his work in historical and literary contexts and evaluates his achievements. Quinn emphasizes that Dunlap decried of the values of commercial theater and that he repeatedly called for a national, state-supported theater. Includes a complete list of American plays from 1665 to 1860 and an index.

Wilson, Garff B. *Three Hundred Years of American Drama and Theatre.* Englewood Cliffs, N.J.: Prentice-Hall, 1973. A survey of Dunlap's life and works in narrative form. Wilson labels Dunlap "the father of American drama" and draws attention to his character and how his optimistic patriotism, generosity, and honesty imbued all of his work. Illustrations, bibliography, and index.

Benjamin Fisher
(Updated by *Gerald S. Argetsinger*)

LORD DUNSANY
Edward John Moreton Drax Plunkett

Born: London, England; July 24, 1878
Died: Dublin, Ireland; October 25, 1957

Principal drama

The Glittering Gate, pr. 1909, pb. 1914; *King Argimenes and the Unknown Warrior*, pr. 1911, pb. 1914; *The Gods of the Mountain*, pr. 1911, pb. 1914; *The Golden Doom*, pr. 1912, pb. 1914; *The Lost Silk Hat*, pr. 1913, pb. 1914; *Five Plays*, pb. 1914; *The Tents of the Arabs*, pr. 1914, pb. 1917; *A Night at an Inn*, pr., pb. 1916 (one act); *The Queen's Enemies*, pr. 1916, pb. 1917; *The Laughter of the Gods*, pb. 1917, pr. 1919; *Plays of Gods and Men*, pb. 1917; *If*, pr., pb. 1921; *Cheezo*, pr. 1921, pb. 1922; *Plays of Near and Far*, pb. 1922; *Lord Adrian*, pr. 1923, pb. 1933; *Alexander*, pb. 1925, pr. 1938; *Mr. Faithful*, pr. 1927, pb. 1935; *Seven Modern Comedies*, pb. 1928; *The Old Folk of the Centuries*, pb. 1930; *Plays for Earth and Air*, pb. 1937.

Other literary forms

Lord Dunsany did not limit himself to a particular literary format; his prolific output comprised novels, short stories, poems, translations, extensive periodical publication, and a wide range of literary and social criticism presented as lectures. Although his drama is historically significant, he is best remembered for his short tales and stories, which are still available in various reprints and anthologies. In these works, his fertile imagination best combined with a natural style to produce an appropriate single effect. Dunsany made little attempt to develop character or to probe the nuances of an individual mind. Instead, he created self-contained mythological worlds which depend upon plot and highly stylized language to move the action to its inevitable conclusion. Dunsany's novels suffer from an excess of invention without a firm grounding in reality or psychological depth; as a remarkable curiosity of verbal ingenuity and fantasy, however, *The King of Elfland's Daughter* (1924) remains a classic. The critical reception of his poetry has been kind, but his work in this genre has never been considered anything but minor. Distinguished by an enviable range of interest in all aspects of art, Dunsany believed that the task of the artist is to create or reveal beauty; for him, the beauty evoked by the written word could be expressed in any form.

Achievements

Dunsany's first play, *The Glittering Gate*, was commissioned by William Butler Yeats for production at the Abbey Theatre, Dublin, in 1909. Having read Dunsany's earlier tales, Yeats thought him a genius and wished to include his work as part of the Irish Renaissance. Although public response to the play did not equal the furor provoked by John Millington Synge's *The Playboy of the Western World* (pr. 1907), Dunsany's delineation of the capriciousness of the gods and the emptiness of Heaven on the other side of the gate nevertheless raised a minor disturbance which seemed to ensure Dunsany a place in the group.

Yeats, however, was interested in developing a literature that was purely Irish in tone and subject matter, and his desire to include Dunsany as part of this movement seems to have been based upon a misperception of Dunsany's point of view. While Dunsany may have been technically Irish, his was not the mystical outlook of Yeats or James Stephens but rather the sensibility of a certain type of Englishman, in the same strain as Rudyard Kipling, John Buchan, or J. R. R. Tolkein, a direct inheritor of the Romantic tradition of Lord Byron and Samuel Taylor Coleridge. In his youth, Dunsany's imagination was fueled more by the Brothers Grimm, Hans Christian Andersen, Edgar Allan Poe, and the Greek writers of the Golden Age than by Irish legends. His closest affinity to Ireland came through his appreciation of the lush beauty of its landscape, evoked with power and mystery in the best of his works.

His early plays were well received, the English casts often featuring respected actors such as Claude Rains (in *The Gods of the Mountain* and *The Golden Doom*), Cathleen Nesbit (in *The Queen's Enemies*), and Gladys Cooper (in *If*). *The Laughter of Gods* was translated into Czech (as *Smich Boha*) and was also performed at the Moscow Art Theatre. Another of his early plays, *The Lost Silk Hat*, was produced in Russia, in 1915, and, even more unexpectedly, in China, at the end of World War I. Americans were his most admiring audiences, however, responding to the initial production of *A Night at an Inn*, according to *The New York Times*, "half-hysterical with excitement for the play is stirring beyond belief." His American biographer Edward Hale Bierstadt declared, "The three great contemporary dramatic poets of Ireland are Synge, Dunsany and Yeats."

Although Dunsany's literary influence has not been widespread, it has been important to the minor fictional area of fantasy. His successful Billiards Club series, for example—stories related by a retired adventurer to his cronies at the club—is echoed in Arthur C. Clarke's *Tales of the White Hart* (1957) and also in the Gavigan's Bar stories of Fletcher Pratt and L. Sprague de Camp. Both C. S. Lewis and H. P. Lovecraft were directly indebted to him, and today many of their followers, although not familiar with Dunsany's work at first hand, pursue the same tradition.

Dunsany was a fellow of the Royal Literary Society and of the Royal Geographical Society as well as president of the Authors' Society. He won the Harmsworth Award and was accorded an honorary doctor of letters degree, in 1939, from Dublin University.

Biography

Lord Dunsany was born Edward John Morton Drax Plunkett, becoming eighteenth Baron Dunsany upon the death of his father in 1899. He spent his early boyhood at Dunstall Priory in Kent, but in later years his principal residence was Dunsany Castle in Meath, Ireland. The influence of the Irish side of his heritage was muted greatly by political connections to England, his grandfather being seated in the House of Lords and his father and two uncles holding seats in the House of Commons. Dunsany himself stood as Conservative candidate for the Commons but lost in a local election.

Educated in England at Eton, Cambridge, and Sandhurst Military Academy, Dunsany accepted his role in the conventional upper-class life and adopted most of the attitudes and habits current among his peers. While writing was important to him, he gave every evidence of pursuing his literary career in a gentlemanly fashion, claiming that it engaged no more than three percent of his time.

In the spirit of the country gentleman, Dunsany led an active life as a sportsman, enjoying fishing, horseback riding, cricket, and hunting. He was a crack shot and became pistol-shooting champion of Ireland. A yearning for adventure led him to more serious pursuits in the military, and he first saw action at age twenty in the Coldstream Guards, fighting for the British in the Boer War. While in South Africa, he met Rudyard Kipling, a man similar in temperament and outlook, who was to remain his friend for life. Like Kipling, Dunsany was preoccupied with the conflict between the instinctive, primitive nature of human beings and the rational, respectable façade of civilization.

After leaving the army and experiencing the disappointments of political life, Dunsany married Lady Beatrice Villiers, the daughter of the Earl and Countess of Jersey, in 1904. Two years later, the Dunsanys' only child, Randall, was born. During this period, Dunsany wrote three volumes of stories, beginning with *The Gods of Pegāna* (1905). In these early tales, Dunsany set the tone for much of his later writing, evoking magical worlds of his own creation with great originality and humor. The language in which they are presented is poetic, biblical; they stress the beauty of the land, the power of fate, and the impotence of human intellect.

Dunsany's first play, commissioned by Yeats, was received with some acclaim by Abbey Theatre audiences, but when his second opened there, it was given little notice. He offered at least two other plays, *The Golden Doom* and *The Tents of the Arabs*, to Yeats and the Abbey Theatre and was rather hurt when they were rejected as "unsuitable." Because of this rejection, their differing views of the purpose of "Irish drama," and an awkward social situation created when Dunsany learned of some rather malicious remarks made about him, Dunsany's friendship with Yeats and

Lady Augusta Gregory cooled and he severed his relationship with their group.

Many of the great and near-great of his time did like Dunsany, however, including writers Padraic Colum, George Russell (Æ), George Moore, Oliver St. John Gogarty, and H. G. Wells, as well as members of the nobility. His position on political affairs, particularly the Irish question, was hard to categorize. As a landlord in Ireland, Dunsany thought the Sinn Fein rebels and traitors. On the other hand, the reviews of his novel *Up in the Hills* (1935), a good-natured satire on the Troubles, were as enthusiastic in Ireland as in England.

Dunsany's brief flirtation with the Irish National Theatre at least induced him to continue writing plays, and from 1909 to 1922 he produced drama of interest, including *King Argimenes and the Unknown Warrior*, *The Gods of the Mountain*, *A Night at an Inn*, *The Tents of the Arabs*, and *If*. These plays often reached the stage in Britain and the United States, but with the return of realism in the 1920's, they were judged to be dated and facile.

Dunsany was thirty-six when World War I began in 1914. He enlisted in the National Volunteers and, shortly after, joined the Royal Inniskilling Fusiliers. After seeing action in France, Dunsany was wounded in Dublin during the Easter Rebellion in 1916; while out on a weekend pass, he was shot in the face and spent a week in a rebel hospital before his release. Subsequently, Dunsany joined the War Office to write propaganda.

Between the two world wars, Dunsany wrote with extraordinary energy and, although unsuccessful as a playwright, enjoyed popular acclaim for such novels as *The King of Elfland's Daughter* and *The Blessing of Pan* (1927), for his collections of poetry, and for the tales of his most ambitiously rendered character, Mr. Joseph Jorkens. The demand for Jorkens, the boastful, Dickensian drunk of the fictional Billiards Club, became so extraordinary that Dunsany was forced to write four more volumes to satisfy his growing public. Ever restless in his creativity, Dunsany also took up painting as a hobby and perfected his chess game enough to reign as Irish champion. His victories led to friendship with the famed world chess master José Raul Capablanca, who became a regular visitor at Dunsany Castle. Dunsany's taste for a fight did not diminish, either; at the age of sixty-two, he joined the Local Defence Volunteers in preparation for a possible Nazi invasion. When this service proved uneventful, he accepted an invitation from the British Council to take the Byron Chair of English Literature at the university in Athens and set off for that city in 1940, an experience that culminated in *Guerilla* (1944), a novel about the war of resistance in Greece. One of his few semirealistic books, this novel demonstrated that he could control conventional fiction and also receive favorable response from tough-minded modern critics.

From 1945 to the end of his life, Dunsany's inventiveness never failed, but old age moderated his productivity. Eccentric, but no longer embittered by the brave new world's lack of appreciation for his work, Dunsany lived contentedly until his death after an appendix operation in 1957.

Analysis

Lord Dunsany's writing consists of many elements found in his early reading of the tales of the Brothers Grimm, of Hans Christian Andersen, and of Greek mythology. His religious temperament was formed intuitively by the beauty and terror of mysterious fictional worlds rather than by formal theology. Dreamlands of mystery and mythology, filled with marvels and the exotic, confrontations between gods and heroes—or mere mortals—these were the center of most of his works. He found such subjects attractive in part because without them, life was less fun, less exciting, less colorful. While he managed to retain a childlike wonder at the vastness of the universe and the power of external forces which people disregard at their own peril, Dunsany was also a well-educated, sophisticated man of the world, and this dichotomy shows through. Just when his work seems ready to lapse into sentimentality, irony, satire, or an unexpected twist is encountered. Instead of bemoaning the dimness of the Celtic Twilight, Dunsany celebrated the adventuresome spirit of humankind. He continually pointed out that the dawning of the Age of Reason may have been announced, that worship of industrialization and technology may have swept the earth, but whenever humans become too confident in themselves and think they have safely pigeonholed the universe, the universe will surprise them by upsetting their pet ideas.

In his essay on playwriting, "Carving the Ivory" (1928), Dunsany claims that, as a playwright, he follows no formal rules of dramatic composition. He merely carves the play, "the ivory block," as a sculptor carves his material. The result is a finished shape which assumes a natural form, refined to its fruition as if no authorial hand was implicated in its making. Dunsany wrote quickly, with little revision—*A Night at the Inn*, for example, was completed between his noon meal and teatime—but his preoccupation with the mysteries of aesthetic romanticism is quite deceptive. The poetic language of his plays, often delivered in perfect hexameters, and their effective rhetorical devices reveal a thoughtful and cunning artist at work, adept at rendering a limpid style.

The Glittering Gate, which Dunsany said he had written chiefly to please Yeats, is not characteristic of Dunsany's work. It opens in a lonely place of rock suspended in an abyss hung with stars. Close to the landscape littered with thousands of beer bottles is a golden gate hinged in a wall of granite. Jim, a thief hanged for crimes on earth, wearily and cynically uncorks the bottles, but none of them contains beer. He is joined by Bill, formerly his student of burglary, who has died from a gunshot wound while attempting to break into a house. At various points, there is faint and unpleasant laughter in the background. Bill is convinced that his jemmy, his "old nut-cracker" burglary tool, can open the heavenly gate; beyond it, he hopes to find angels, gold, apples, and his mother. Jim has a moment of astonishment as Bill succeeds in prying the door ajar. As they look out at the emptiness, cruel, violent laughter rises.

Dunsany's cynicism is apparent in this play, and although many critics downplay this quality in him, it is not uncharacteristic of his work. The case against the gods is one-sided in that the reader or viewer is not allowed to see what eventually happens to "good people"—unless, in ultimate cynicism, Dunsany wishes to indicate that even the best of mankind is, to the gods, no better than Jim or Bill. Each of the characters pays for his actions in the world and is abandoned to a form of punishment particularly suited to him: Jim will be perpetually thirsty, possibly more for hope than for beer, and Bill will never see his mother again. Even in the afterlife, each continues to be true to his criminal nature. Instead of feeling remorse, they seek a way out; they do not give in to the gods any more than the gods give in to them.

The play has parallels to the myth of Sisyphus. Like Sisyphus, forever rolling his stone up the mountainside only to have it roll back down again, Jim opens his beer bottles to find them empty. He knows he will not find beer, but he hopes that, if only once, the gods' trick might not work. His placid statement at the end, as he looks into nothingness, is that it is characteristic of the gods to have arranged such an anticlimax. In a similar way, Sisyphus understands his predicament but must nevertheless repeat the cycle of his condemnation. Jim's monologue on the meaninglessness of the years and the futility of confinement with Bill is also reminiscent of Jean-Paul Sartre's *No Exit* (pr. 1944).

Two closely related plays, *The Gods of the Mountain* and *A Night at an Inn*, clearly illustrate Dunsany's major theme of the arrogance of men provoking retribution at the hands of intransigent gods. In *The Gods of the Mountain*, set somewhere in the East, a group of beggars, led by Agmar, wish to enter the city to seek riches at a time when the gods seem to be asleep and the divine in men seems to be dead. The beggars suggest posing as lords or kings, but Agmar insists that they impersonate gods. Disguised as the seven green jade idols of Marma, they fool a skeptical populace through the will and intellect of Agmar. Dunsany's admiration of Friedrich Nietzsche's *Thus Spake Zarathustra* (1883-1885) is reflected in the characterization of Agmar. Agmar dismisses the idea of subservience to anyone, but when the real gods enter to seek vengeance on the usurpers, Agmar's genius fails, and all the beggars are turned to stone.

A Night at an Inn, a slighter play, demonstrates that human pride is as dangerous close to home as it is in the mysterious East. Three merchant sailors and their leader, A. E. Scott (the Toff), steal the ruby eye from a green idol, Klesh. The Toff remains aloof and calm upon hearing that the priests of Klesh are following them. He says that they will not come until he is ready to receive them. After all, he says, he is able to see into the future. When the three priests appear, the Toff formulates and carries out a clever plan to murder them. The blind idol, however, claims his ruby eye and leaves the inn; offstage, a seductive voice calls the names of the sailors, and, against their will, they exit into the darkness. On his way out, the Toff comments in despair that he did not foresee this conclusion.

These two works read better than they play. Unlike *The Glittering Gate*, both melodramas call for the physical presence of the gods, which lessens the mystery considerably in a staged version: The problem for Dunsany was to make the audience believe that an abstraction could operate on the material level; the attention commanded by the idols leaves the message out of focus and depersonalized. In reading, at least, each individual can create his own image of the idols.

It may always be difficult to evaluate Dunsany's work fairly, since it is an admixture of so many strains. Audiences conditioned by the work of filmmakers George Lucas and Steven Spielberg may not object to the speaking statues or the ominous laughter of the gods, and audiences accustomed to Samuel Beckett, Eugène Ionesco, and T. S. Eliot may enjoy the stylized soft-edge mysticism—unfortunately, the two types rarely overlap.

In his search for eternal values in imaginative expression, Dunsany produced a body of work of considerable diversity and quality. His private mythological universe may seem too arcane for today's taste, but it is one of surprising richness and beauty. Dunsany's provocative plays are models of sophistication and verbal precision and certainly deserve more recognition than they have been afforded.

Other major works

NOVELS: *The Chronicles of Rodriguez*, 1922; *The King of Elfland's Daughter*, 1924; *The Charwoman's Shadow*, 1926; *The Blessing of Pan*, 1927; *The Curse of the Wise Woman*, 1933; *Up in the Hills*, 1935; *My Talks with Dean Spanley*, 1936; *Rory and Bran*, 1936; *The Story of Mona Sheehy*, 1939; *Guerilla*, 1944; *The Strange Journeys of Colonel Polders*, 1950; *The Last Revolution*, 1951; *His Fellow Men*, 1952.

SHORT FICTION: *The Gods of Pegāna*, 1905; *Time and the Gods*, 1906; *The Sword of Welleran and Other Stories*, 1908; *A Dreamer's Tales*, 1910; *The Book of Wonder*, 1912; *Fifty-one Tales*, 1915; *Tales of Wonder*, 1916 (also as *The Last Book of Wonder*); *Tales of War*, 1918; *Tales of Three Hemispheres*, 1919; *Unhappy Far-off Things*, 1919; *The Travel Tales of Mr. Joseph Jorkens*, 1931; *Jorkens Remembers Africa*, 1934; *Jorkens Has a Large Whiskey*, 1940; *The Man Who Ate the Phoenix*, 1947; *The Fourth Book of*

Jorkens, 1948; *The Little Tales of Smethers*, 1952; *Jorkens Borrows Another Whiskey*, 1954; *The Food of Death: Fifty-one Tales*, 1974.

POETRY: *Fifty Poems*, 1929; *War Poems*, 1940; *To Awaken Pegasus and Other Poems*, 1949.

NONFICTION: *If I Were Dictator: The Pronouncements of the Grand Macaroni*, 1934; *My Ireland*, 1937; *Patches of Sunlight*, 1938; *While the Sirens Slept*, 1944; *The Sirens Wake*, 1945; *A Glimpse from a Watch Tower*, 1946.

TRANSLATION: *The Odes of Horace*, 1947.

Bibliography

Bierstadt, Edward Hale. *Dunsany the Dramatist.* Boston: Little, Brown, 1917. Analyzes the plays of Dunsany and relates them to the Irish Literary Theatre (Abbey Theatre Company). Includes photographs of scenes, some letters between Dunsany and Stuart Walker, a bibliography, and a list of play casts.

Boyd, Ernest A. *The Contemporary Drama of Ireland.* Boston: Little, Brown, 1917. Boyd says that the production of *The Glittering Gate* at the Abbey Theatre in 1909 revealed a "new force" in Irish drama. *King Argimenes and the Unknown Warrior* is a good play, but *The Gods of the Mountain* is Dunsany's best. Boyd's judgment—in 1917—is that Dunsany is "the only worthy successor of Yeats in the history of the Irish Theatre."

Hammond, Josephine. "Wonder and the Playwright, Lord Dunsany." *The Personalist* 3 (January, 1922): 5-30. Hammond admits the lack of "authentic character creation" in Dunsany's work but praises the psychological insights of his "excursions, primarily, into the fantastic and grotesque." An admiring appreciation of Dunsany's works.

Harris, Frank. *Contemporary Portraits.* 1919. Reprint. 2d ser. New York: Kraus Reprint, 1970. Harris praises *A Night at an Inn* as "excellent melodrama" and *The Tents of the Arabs* for its love story of the king and the gypsy. *The Gods of the Mountain* is Dunsany's "finest work," but it also reveals his weaknesses.

Littlefield, Hazel. *Lord Dunsany: King of Dreams.* New York: Exposition Press, 1959. Littlefield points to Dunsany's genius in dealing with human passions, particularly as seen in *Alexander*. She remarks that as a prophet, Dunsany was "gentle with dullness, but impatient of all that was shallow and insincere."

Malone, Andrew E. *The Irish Drama.* London: Constable, 1929. Malone calls Dunsany Ireland's "only practitioner in magic in the contemporary theater." He invented a theogony, or genealogy of the gods, useful for his stage magic, and he was more English than Irish. Judges his best plays to be *The Glittering Gate, The Gods of the Mountain*, and *A Night at an Inn.*

Yeats, W. B. Introduction to *Selections from the Writings of Lord Dunsany.* Churchtown, Ireland: Cuala Press, 1912. Yeats finds Dunsany's main theme to be the passing away of gods and people under the sway of time. He admires Dunsany's skill at transfiguring common things with beauty, and he marvels at Dunsany's power to delight him although he cannot identify the source of that power.

James C. MacDonald
(Updated by *Frank Day*)

CHRISTOPHER DURANG

Born: Montclair, New Jersey; January 2, 1949

Principal drama

The Greatest Musical Ever Sung, pr. 1971; *The Nature and Purpose of the Universe*, wr. 1971, pr. 1975 (radio play), pr. 1979 (staged), pb. 1979; *Better Dead than Sorry*, pr. 1972 (libretto, music by Jack Feldman); *I Don't Generally Like Poetry but Have You Read "Trees"?*, pr. 1972 (with Albert Innaurato); *The Life Story of Mitzi Gaynor: Or, Gyp*, pr. 1973 (with Innaurato); *The Marriage of Bette and Boo*, pr. 1973, pb. 1976, rev. pr. 1979, pb. 1985; *The Idiots Karamazov*, pr. 1974, pb. 1976 (with Innaurato, music by Feldman); *Titanic*, pr. 1974, pb. 1983; *Death Comes to Us All, Mary Agnes*, pr. 1975, pr. 1979; *When Dinah Shore Ruled the Earth*, pr. 1975 (with Wendy Wasserstein); *'dentity Crisis*, pr. 1975, pb. 1979; *Das Lusitania Songspiel*, pr. 1976 (with Sigourney Weaver, music by Mel Marvin and Jack Gaughan); *A History of the American Film*, pr. 1976, pb. 1978; *The Vietnamization of New Jersey (A American Tragedy)*, pr. 1976, pb. 1978; *Three Short Plays*, pb. 1979; *Sister Mary Ignatius Explains It All for You*, pr. 1979, pb. 1980; *The Actor's Nightmare*, pr., pb. 1981; *Beyond Therapy*, pr. 1981, pb. 1983; *Christopher Durang Explains It All for You*, pb. 1983; *Baby with the Bathwater*, pr., pb. 1983; *Sloth*, pr. 1985; *Laughing Wild*, pr. 1987, pb. 1988; *Chris Durang and Dawne*, pr. 1989; *Naomi in the Living Room*, pr. 1991; *Media Amok*, pr. 1992.

Other literary forms

Christopher Durang is known primarily for his plays. He has written a screenplay of *Beyond Therapy* (1987).

Achievements

Durang belongs to a tradition of black humorists and fabulists who first emerged in the 1950's with the novelists Joseph Heller, Kurt Vonnegut, Jr., and Thomas Berger. His plays are ridiculous comedies which agitate the audience without propagating a particular political viewpoint, attacking every "Great Idea" of Western literature and philosophy merely because it is assailable. His writing centers on the enduring questions of human suffering and authority. His most popular play, *Sister Mary Ignatius Explains It All for You*, was hotly debated by theologians and theater critics alike and won an Obie Award as the best new Off-Broadway play of 1980. His other honors include grants from the Rockefeller Foundation and the Lecomte du Nuoy Foundation, fellowships with Guggenheim and the Columbia Broadcasting System, and a Tony nomination for his musical *A History of the American*

Film. His work is characterized by energy and a sense of the ridiculous in life and art, sustained by anger and despair. The targets of his abusive wit are the sacred cows of contemporary American society: religion, family life, hero-worship, law and order, and success.

Biography

Christopher Durang was born in Montclair, New Jersey, on January 2, 1949. A very humorous autobiographical sketch is given in the introduction to his plays in *Christopher Durang Explains It All for You*, beginning with his conception and ending with the reviews of *Beyond Therapy*. His parents, Francis Ferdinand and Patricia Elizabeth Durang, were devout Catholics who fought constantly until they were divorced, when Durang was still in grade school. Durang's interest in theater and playwriting became evident early in life. He wrote his first play while in the second grade in a Catholic elementary school. He subsequently attended a Catholic preparatory high school run by Benedictine priests. He continued to write plays, and though a fairly conservative and conventional student, he often inserted hints of sex for their shock effect. In high school, Durang was overcome with religious zeal and the desire to enter a monastery upon graduation, but soon afterward he lost his faith and his interest in the Roman Catholic religion.

He attended Harvard University with the hope and expectation of discovering a more intellectual and less conservative dimension of Catholicism but was disappointed. In his second year at Harvard, he entered psychoanalysis with a priest. He became obsessed with motion pictures and neglected his academic studies. Although he had been a prodigious writer in high school, he wrote almost nothing in college until his senior year, when he wrote (as a form of therapy for his feeling of religious guilt) a musical-comedy version of the life of Christ called *The Greatest Musical Ever Sung*, which included such irreverent show-tune lampoons as "The Dove That Done Me Wrong" and "Everything's Coming up Moses." The play stirred up a local religious controversy but was well received by audiences, encouraging the young playwright to write more. His next effort, the ambitiously titled *The Nature and Purpose of the Universe*, was eventually produced in New York and, following Durang's graduation from Harvard in 1971, was submitted as part of his application to the Yale School of Drama.

At Yale, Durang met and worked with a number of actors and playwrights who were, along with him, to make their marks in the American theater. Among his classmates were Albert Innaurato (with whom Durang collaborated on several plays), Meryl Streep (who appeared in a Durang play in college), Wendy Wasserstein (with whom Durang wrote *When Dinah Shore Ruled the Earth*), and Sigourney Weaver (who appeared in several Durang plays in New York and with whom he wrote *Das Lusitania Songspiel*). His chief supporter at Yale and later in New York was Robert Brustein, who was dean of the drama school while Durang was enrolled there and artistic director of the Yale Repertory Theater. Durang received his M.F.A. in 1974 but remained in New Haven for an extra year, performing and writing at Yale, teaching drama at the Southern Connecticut College in New Haven, and working as a typist at the medical school.

Durang moved to New York in 1975. *Titanic*, which he wrote for a class at Yale, and *The Nature and Purpose of the Universe* were produced in Off-Broadway theaters. In 1976, his musical play *A History of the American Film* was produced in Waterford, Connecticut, as part of the Eugene O'Neill Playwrights Conference, and in 1977 it was produced simultaneously on both coasts at the Hartford Stage Company in Connecticut, the Mark Taper Forum in Los Angeles, California, and the Arena Stage in Washington, D.C. In 1978, the play opened on Broadway at the American National Theatre. The play's subsequent failure on Broadway precipitated a period of depression which climaxed with the death of Durang's mother in March of 1979. Watching his mother die of incurable bone cancer and reassessing his Catholic upbringing, Durang started writing the play upon which his reputation as a playwright would be secured, *Sister Mary Ignatius Explains It All for You*. The play was first produced in December of 1979 by Curt Dempster's Ensemble Studio Theatre in New York, along with other one-act plays by David Mamet, Marsha Norman, and Tennessee Williams. Two years later, Andre Bishop's Playwrights Horizons produced the play Off-Broadway with two members of the original cast of six, along with Durang's *The Actor's Nightmare*, which he wrote as a curtain raiser.

Sister Mary Ignatius Explains It All for You brought Durang to the public's attention, not only through the show's popularity but also through several battles against censorship when various Catholic organizations attempted to close down the play. The Phoenix Theatre commissioned Durang to write *Beyond Therapy*, which opened in 1981 and then, almost a year and a half later, was rewritten and produced on Broadway at the Brooks Atkinson Theater. Later, Durang revised and expanded two plays he originally wrote at Yale, *Baby with the Bathwater* and *The Marriage of Bette and Boo*, which also were produced in New York. A 1987 film version of *Beyond Therapy* directed by Robert Altman was a box-office failure, and Durang expressed his unhappiness with the experience. Nevertheless, he subsequently expressed his disenchantment with the New York theater scene and his intention to pursue work in film, which, he stated, offers more permanence and reaches a larger audience than live drama.

Analysis

The plays of Christopher Durang are remarkable for their absurdist approach to the important questions of modern philosophy, for their hilarious disregard for social conventions and traditional sexual roles, and for their uncompromisingly bleak assessment of human politics and society. As early as the satirical travesties he produced in college, Durang's abiding themes have been suffering and paternalism. The cutting edge of his humor is his insistence on the commonplaceness of suffering in the world. His plays are populated by archetypal sadists and victims, and the comedy is usually cruel (as the audience is made to laugh at the exaggerated and grotesque misery of the characters) and nearly always violent; death, suicide, disaster, and murder are never too far away in typical Durang slapstick. In a note accompanying the publication of *The Nature and Purpose of the Universe*, the writer explains that the violence of the play must appear simultaneously vicious and funny, demanding that performers make the audience sympathize with the victim and yet feel sufficiently "alienated" (in the sense of Bertolt Brecht's "alienation-effect") from the theatrical action to be able to laugh at it. Presiding over the sufferers is a figure of authority, always coldly detached and frequently insane, who "explains" the suffering with banal truisms taken from philosophy, religion, and pop psychology, while in fact he or she acts as the instrument of the oppression and mindless malice.

Fear and insecurity are the principal components of Durang's comedy of paranoia. While his plays are repeatedly criticized for not being positive and for not suggesting any remedy to the problem of human evil, they are in fact relentlessly moral, fueled by a profound sense of outrage at the crimes against human dignity. Like Eugène Ionesco, Joe Orton, and Lenny Bruce, Durang attempts to shock the audience out of its complacency through the use of vulgarity, blasphemy, violence, and other forms of extremism. If his endings seem less than perfectly conclusive, and if his characters seem to be no more than cartoons, still, underneath all the madcap and sophomoric nonsense is a serious and humane plea for tolerance, diversity, and individual liberty. The object of the writer's most satirical attacks is the incompetent guardian, a sometimes well-intentioned but always destructive figure of patriarchal authority who appears in many different guises: parent, husband, teacher, analyst, hero, nanny, doctor, author, and even deity. This figure embodies for Durang all the evil elements of human nature and social hierarchy.

Durang's drama of the mid-1970's, the plays which grew out of his college exercises at Yale, is chiefly parodic and yet contains kernels of the preoccupation with suffering characteristic of his later works. *The Idiots Karamazov*, which he wrote with Innaurato, is a musical-comedy travesty of the great Russian novelists of suffering, Fyodor Dostoevski and Leo Tolstoy. The principal character, Constance Garnett, is the translator, an older woman confined to a wheelchair and attended by a suicidal manservant, Ernest. In Durang and Innaurato's version of Dostoevski's *The Brothers Karamazov*, the holy innocent and idiot savant Alyosha becomes a pop music star, and the "Great Books," along with other academic pretensions to cultural importance, are thus trivialized as commodities in a money-and-glitter-oriented enterprise. Durang ridiculed Hollywood and the motion pictures in *A History of the American Film*, a 1976 musical which opened on Broadway in 1978. The five principal characters are caricatures based on familiar Hollywood types. Loretta (as in Loretta Young) is the long-suffering and lovingly innocent heroine. Jimmy (as in James Cagney) is the tough guy, part hoodlum and part romantic hero. Bette (as in Bette Davis) is the vamp, a vindictive but seductive figure who enjoys nothing more than making Loretta suffer. Hank (as in Henry Fonda) is the strong and silent all-American good guy, who eventually turns psychotic. Eve (as in Eve Arden) is the ever-present true friend, who covers up her own sexual frustration with dry witticisms and hard-boiled mottoes. True to its title, the play satirizes the gamut of Hollywood kitsch, including jabs at *Birth of a Nation* (1915), *The Grapes of Wrath* (1940), *The Best Years of Our Lives* (1946), *Psycho* (1960), *Who's Afraid of Virginia Woolf?* (1966), and *Earthquake* (1974). On a deeper level, the play exposes the American motion-picture industry as a manufacturer of glamorous façades for real-life misery and fear. In *The Vietnamization of New Jersey*, Durang takes on the legitimate theater itself. Using David Rabe's controversial Vietnam-era satire *Sticks and Bones* (1969) as a starting place, Durang makes the social and political pretensions of "serious theater" seem silly, while castigating the various "isms" of contemporary culture: liberalism, consumerism, racism, militarism, and sexism. The play treats the horrors of war, mental illness, inflation, unemployment, and suicide with chilling comedy.

In the late 1970's, when Durang wrote *'dentity Crisis*, *The Nature and Purpose of the Universe*, and the phenomenally successful *Sister Mary Ignatius Explains It All for You*, the playwright challenged the idea of authority or expertise itself. Inspired by R. D. Laing's controversial theories about schizophrenia, *'dentity Crisis* is an oddly moving comedy in one act and two scenes. The action centers on a young, depressed woman named Jane and her mother, Edith. The play opens as Edith returns from the dry cleaner with Jane's bloodstained dress, which has been ruined after an unsuccessful suicide attempt. Despite the initial impression, it soon appears that Jane is the only character in the play who is "sane." Edith manufactures and discards versions of reality with breathless speed, and Robert, the other occupant of the house, manifests four distinct personalities, alternately Jane's brother, father, and grandfather, as well as the Count de Rochelay, a foreign suitor of the perversely promiscuous Edith. Even Jane's psychoanalyst, Mrs. Summers, is bizarrely inconsistent. In scene 1, the role is played by a man, and in scene 2, after a sex-change operation, by a woman (the actor who plays Mr. Summers in the first scene plays his wife in the second). Jane reveals the motive behind her suicide attempt in a poignant and surrealistic monologue concerning a production of *Peter Pan* she had seen as a girl. Life is not worth continuing, she says, if it only leads to death in the end. The play ends with the daughter's loss of her identity, but the audience's sympathy remains with her because it has entered her version of reality and regards the others as mad.

The authoritative Mr. and Mrs. Summers in *'dentity Crisis* are remarkably similar to Ronald and Elaine May Alcott, the two "agents of God" who borrow various guises in *The Nature and Purpose of the Universe*. Like its glib title, the play pokes fun at those who would offer easy explanations of the mysteries of existence and evil. It is a play in thirteen "chapters," each chronicling a different aspect of the tragicomic downfall of the hapless Eleanor Mann. Presiding over the events of the drama are Ronald and Elaine, who pretend to render meaningful the random catastrophes which they inflict upon the Job-like Eleanor. Every now and then they enter the action of the play, purportedly to offer heavenly guidance and solace but actually to intensify the poor woman's suffering. Durang's comedy springs from the characters' absurdly cool responses to horror. When Eleanor is knocked to the kitchen floor and kicked by her drug-peddling son, her husband chides the boy, saying, "Donald, have a little patience with your mother." The play ends as, in a parody of Old Testament piety, Ronald and Elaine bind and gag Eleanor and sacrifice her to a distant and passively vicious God.

Sister Mary Ignatius, teacher at Our Lady of Perpetual Sorrow and the menacingly maternal protagonist of *Sister Mary Ignatius Explains It All for You*, is the writer's classic realization of the banality and willful ignorance of human evil. The play falls into three sections. In the first, Sister Mary catechizes the audience on basic doctrines and practices of the Roman Catholic Church. As Durang noted in several interviews, the humor of this section stems from the unexaggerated reportage of the irrational but devoutly held beliefs of certain Christians: the existence of Heaven, Hell, and Purgatory within the physical universe; the supernatural births of Jesus Christ and Mary; the efficacy of Christ's suffering and death on a cross; the exclusively procreative function of sex; and God's everlasting vengeance against wrongdoers such as Zsa Zsa Gabor, Brooke Shields, and David Bowie. Repeatedly, however, Sister Mary dodges the more interesting issue of God's responsibility for the existence of evil and suffering in the world. The second section presents a Nativity play performed by four of Sister Mary's former students. More than anything else, the play demonstrates the triumph of dogma over narrative in traditional Christianity and portrays an absurdly abbreviated life of Christ. With only three characters, Mary, Joseph, and Misty the camel (two actors impersonate separate humps), and a doll as the infant Jesus, the play spans the time from the Immaculate Conception (of Mary) to the Ascension (of Jesus, Mary, Joseph, and Misty). The third section of the play involves the Nativity-scene actors' disclosure to Sister Mary of the courses their lives have taken after leaving Our Lady of Perpetual Sorrow. Philomena (Misty's front end) has borne a daughter out of wedlock. Aloysius (Misty's back end) has become a suicidal alcoholic who regularly beats his wife. Gary (Joseph) has had homosexual relationships. Diane (Mary), whom Sister Mary especially detests, has had two abortions. Diane engineers the climactic confrontation in order to embarrass Sister Mary and then reveals her intention to kill her, much to the surprise of her three cohorts. Victorious in the end, Sister Mary whips out a gun and kills Diane; then, after assuring herself that he has made a recent confession of his sexual sins, she kills Gary as well. The play ends with a recitation of the catechism by Thomas, a boy currently enrolled in the parochial school.

In the 1980's, Durang turned his attention to other kinds of oppression in society, specifically the normalization of sexuality and family relationships. In *Beyond Therapy*, he again attacks psychoanalysis from a Laingian perspective, portraying the analysts in the play as more bizarre versions of Mr. Summers and his wife in *'dentity Crisis*. Their clients are a heterosexual woman and a bisexual man who meet through an advertisement in the personals column of a newspaper. The complex relationship they form is played mainly for laughs, but the butt of most of the jokes is pop psychology, as well as the notion of anyone's being an expert about how other people ought to live their lives.

Both *Baby with the Bathwater* and *The Marriage of Bette and Boo* have their origins in plays Durang wrote while in college and pertain to American family life. *Baby with the Bathwater* is a grim but humorous indictment of the science of child-rearing. Born as a boy but reared as a girl, Daisy, the baby of the title, is the victim of two inept parents and a manipulative nanny; in the last act he appears in his analyst's office wearing a dress, clearly suffering from a sexual identity crisis. *The Marriage of Bette and Boo* takes the form of a college student's memories of his parents, both of whom are emotionally unbalanced and (for their son Matt, the narrator) unbalancing. The play is a parody of the family dramas of American dramatists Thornton Wilder and Eugene O'Neill. The mother, Bette, idolizes babies but is able to produce only one living descendant because her blood type is incompatible with her husband's. The several stillborn infants she produces she names after animal characters in Winnie the Pooh storybooks. The father, Boo, is an alcoholic whose life is a cycle of a reformation and backsliding. Though a comedy, the play touches on serious philosophical questions concerning God, suffering, death, the absurdity of life, and the meaning of love. It is also the most autobiographical of Durang's plays.

Christopher Durang belongs to the postmodernist wave of American playwrights who emerged during the 1970's, including A. R. Gurney, Tina Howe, and Sam Shepard. These writers fused the experimental techniques of the structuralist theater experiments of the 1960's with the "traditional" domestic drama of the early twentieth century American realists, creating a new form of theater that is simultaneously naturalistic and self-consciously theatrical.

674 *Critical Survey of Drama*

Evolving as it did from collegiate travesties and comedy sketches, Durang's drama violates many of the established principles of the well-made play. However sloppily constructed and politically unsophisticated his plays may be, Durang's genius is to create comedies out of existential anger and to infuse them with energy, thought, and an unbounded sense of liberty.

Other major work

SCREENPLAY: *Beyond Therapy*, 1987.

Bibliography

Brustein, Robert. "The Crack in the Chimney: Reflections on Contemporary American Playwriting." *Theater* 9 (Spring, 1978): 21-29. A discussion of *The Vietnamization of New Jersey*, set against the more serious examination of the work of David Rabe, in *Sticks and Bones.* "He is demolishing cliches," a trademark of Durang in any venue, and in this play, Brustein says, he "has declared a separate peace" with the guilt of Vietnam.

Durang, Christopher. Introduction to *Christopher Durang Explains It All for You.* New York: Grove Weidenfeld, 1990. The introduction to this collection of six plays is a tongue-in-cheek autobiography, written in 1982, that includes anecdotes about playwriting classes under Howard Stein and Jules Feiffer, and early psychiatric counseling. "I was nostalgic for belief, since it offered comfort," Durang says of his early Catholic upbringing.

Flippo, Chet. "Is Broadway Ready for Christopher Durang?" *New York* 15 (March 15, 1982): 40-43. "I was very depressed about how depressed I got," says Durang in this chatty, readable conversation. Discusses his early revues at Harvard University and cabaret pieces for the Yale School of Drama, his collaboration with Sigourney Weaver, and his development as a "fearless satirist." Demures on describing his vision of the world. Three photographs.

Savran, David. *In Their Own Words: Contemporary American Playwrights.* New York: Theatre Communications Group, 1988. A brief overview is followed by a protracted interview, centering on biographical history, the development of *The Marriage of Bette and Boo*, and Durang's writing habits. Durang sees advantages to filmmaking (if the playwright's script is not desecrated as with *Beyond Therapy*), including reaching a larger audience and enjoying more permanence.

Weales, Gerald. "American Theater Watch, 1981-1982." *The Georgia Review* 36 (Fall, 1982): 517-526. Weales offers insightful comments on Durang's comic style, but he is not impressed by his structure or depth. Drawn from interviews in *The New York Times*, this article summarizes critics' first reactions to this new voice, as a satirist whose real theatrical value is yet to be proved.

Joseph Marohl
(Updated by *Thomas J. Taylor*)

LONNE ELDER III

Born: Americus, Georgia; December 26, 1931

Principal drama

Ceremonies in Dark Old Men, pr. 1965, pb. 1969; *Charades on East Fourth Street*, pr. 1967, pb. 1971 (one act); *Splendid Mummer*, pr. 1988.

Other literary forms

Lonne Elder III also wrote screenplays and television scripts. His screenplays include *Melinda* (1972), *Sounder, Part Two* (1976), and *Bustin' Loose* (1981), with Roger L. Simon and Richard Pryor. Among his teleplays are *Ceremonies in Dark Old Men* (1975), based on his play of the same title, and *A Woman Called Moses* (1978), based on a book by Marcy Heidish.

Achievements

Elder's playwriting reputation rests solidly on the drama *Ceremonies in Dark Old Men*, not because his formidable theatrical talents faltered after he created this early work, but because he turned from the stage to write for film and television. *Ceremonies in Dark Old Men* interweaves psychological and social themes in describing a black family. Elder presents a careful dissection of the love and power relations within that family, while also, looked at more broadly, showing the adverse situation of African Americans living in a racially torn nation. Though his themes are somber, Elder injects his work with humor and affection, carefully balancing his audience's sympathy for the disparate characters. Although the play ends tragically, presenting the family's partial dissolution, it carries a positive undercurrent insofar as it charts the family's heroic resistance against difficult circumstances and portrays how a number of characters mature during the struggle.

Elder has received numerous awards, including the American National Theatre Academy Award (1967), the Outer Circle Award (1970), the Vernon Rice Award (1970), and the Stella Holt Memorial Playwrights Award (1970).

Biography

Lonne Elder III was born in Americus, Georgia, on December 26, 1931, to Lonne Elder II and Quincy Elder. While he was still an infant, his family moved to New York and New Jersey. He was orphaned at the age of ten and ended up living with relatives on a New Jersey farm. Rural life, however, was not for him, and, after he ran away a few times, he was sent to live with his uncle, a numbers runner, in Jersey City.

In 1949, Elder entered New Jersey State Teachers College, where he stayed less than a year. He then moved to New York City and took courses at the Jefferson School and the New School for Social Research, while becoming involved in the movement for social equality for black people. In 1952, he was drafted into the United States Army. While stationed near Fisk University, in Nashville, Tennessee, he met the poet and playwright Robert Hayden, who encouraged Elder with his writing.

Back in New York City in 1953, Elder shared an apartment with the aspiring playwright Douglas Turner Ward and began studying acting. Supporting himself through jobs as a dockworker, waiter, and poker dealer, among other things, he pursued his acting career, appearing on Broadway in 1959 in *A Raisin in the Sun* and with the Negro Ensemble Company (cofounded by Ward) in Ward's play *Day of Absence* (pr. 1965). During this time, he met such prominent black writers as Lorraine Hansberry and John Oliver Killens, married Betty Gross (in 1963), and wrote his first play. This work, "A Hysterical Turtle in a Rabbit Race," written in 1961 but never performed or published, broached Elder's favored topic of how a black family can be pulled apart by prejudice and false standards.

In 1965, his masterpiece, *Ceremonies in Dark Old Men*, was performed, earning for him fame and critical success. Along with his other ventures, such as writing television scripts for such shows as *NYPD* and *McCloud*, it netted for him a number of awards and honors, including a fellowship to the Yale School of Drama in 1966-1967. His next play to be produced was the one-act *Charades on East Fourth Street*, which did not have the impact of his previous drama. It was performed in 1967.

In 1970, sick of New York City, Elder moved with his second wife, Judith Ann Johnson, whom he had married in 1969, to California. He was hoping to improve the depiction of African Americans in Hollywood productions, and he did just that in his screenplay *Sounder* in 1972. After the critical success of this film, he continued working in the industry, producing more serious work about black life and tradition, such as his follow-up television script *Sounder, Part Two* (1976) and his television presentation about Harriet Ross Tubman, *A Woman Called Moses* (1978), as well as writing an occasional comedy, such as the 1981 Richard Pryor film *Bustin' Loose.*

In 1988, Elder returned briefly to the theater with *Splendid Mummer*, a historical play about a black expatriate actor who left the United States in the 1820's to practice his art in Europe. The play was liked by critics but was not a popular success and was not published. Elder continued to be primarily devoted to his goal of working in television and film to provide a positive and realistic view of African-American life.

Analysis

Lonne Elder III's major play, *Ceremonies in Dark Old Men*, deals with the survival of the black family under duress. For Elder, the family is not a collection of autonomous individuals but a dynamic set of relationships. In *Ceremonies in Dark Old Men*, Elder focuses on how each family member's decisions crucially hinge on the words and actions of each other member. The playwright indicates, moreover, that under stressful conditions, the equilibrium of such a black family is a fragile thing, because the family is a working unit in a larger society that is controlled by white people to the disadvantage of black persons. The drama records how, under increasing pressure, the family disintegrates in some ways while it grows in others. Thus, Elder combines social criticism with a subtle look at the inner workings of families. In all of his writings, such as his screenplay *Sounder*, his depictions of family life have been outstanding for their realism, compassion, and penetration, while those works that do not describe family connections, such as his play *Charades on East Fourth Street*, have been notably lacking in inspiration.

In much of post-World War II American theater, including such works as Arthur Miller's *Death of A Salesman* (pr., pb. 1949) and Tennessee Williams' *The Glass Menagerie* (pr. 1944, pb. 1945), the family is portrayed as entrapping and destructive of individualism. The family may stifle a son by forcing him to support it, as in Williams' play, or it may ruin his life by giving him false views, as happens to Biff in Miller's work; in either case, however, the family is inimical to self-reliance. By contrast, in *Ceremonies in Dark Old Men*, each family member has a role that is both constricting and sustaining, while each member either grows or diminishes as a result of the family's overall adaptation to the outside world.

At first sight, the family in Elder's play is organized in stereotypical "culture of poverty" fashion, with a female, the daughter Adele, being the de facto head of the house, since she supports the other, male family members. The two sons with the father, the nominal ruler of the house, are shiftless characters; the father, Russell, presides over a defunct barbershop, while his elder son, Theo, is a hapless loser, and the younger one, Bobby, a sneak thief. As the story develops, however, the audience learns that the three are not as parasitical as they first appeared. The father, for example, had been the mainstay of the family, earning a living as a professional dancer until his legs failed and he was unceremoniously dropped from his place. When viewers see the father returning from a day of job-hunting humiliation, they also learn that, as an over-the-hill black man, he has little hope of finding work.

The thrust of the play, however, is not to exonerate any individual but to show that the current operation of the family is, given the way the odds are stacked against prosperity for minority group members, probably the best possible. This view is shown by the simple, but fundamental, device of ending the first act with the beginning of a basic change in the household arrangements (as Theo sets up a viable, if illegal, business) and then jumping ahead a few months for the second act. In this way, in the second act, the audience can see how Theo's changed status, as he takes on a more manly role in the family and supports the others by working long hours, affects the personalities and actions of each of the others, often adversely. Adele, for example, no longer having to bear tremendous responsibility, lets herself go, running around with a notorious skirt chaser. Bobby, who never felt threatened by his brother, since Theo was as ambitionless as he was, now begins sullenly competing with him, becoming a big-time hoodlum.

This is not to say that, because there is more tension in the family after Theo begins working than previously, the old organization was better. Rather, Elder indicates—especially toward the end of the second act, when the family begins to calm down and Adele gives up her playboy boyfriend—that each set of family relationships is highly interdependent and serves as an essential means to help the members orient themselves to the outside world. Elder also indicates that each transition between different familial "steady states" will involve special periods of stress.

In his plays, it is clear that Elder is critical of the position that black persons are forced to occupy in the American economy, and it also may be evident that his anger is more latent than expressed. Rather than have his characters complain about the system, he makes the audience experience the constant feeling of failure that hovers over a family whose members are not fully employed, especially when, to a large degree, their unemployment is not their fault. In relation to one character, however, Elder's social criticism is less oblique. This character, Blue Haven, is a self-styled black activist, who, curiously, is not interested in fighting injustice and oppression through protests and political action; rather, he prefers to steal the clients of white people's liquor and gambling establishments by setting up bootleg and numbers operations of his own. In this portrayal, Elder reveals a satirical side to his talent and shows that he is as critical of black persons as he is of white ones, insofar as he shows that black residents of Harlem are more interested in supporting Blue Haven's "enterprises" than the businesses run by more bona fide progressives.

Elder's treatment of this character also reveals another point about his methods. Throughout most of the play, Blue Haven obtains little sympathy from the audience, being not only a sharper but also a hypocrite. Yet in a powerful monologue that he delivers in a confrontation with Theo, who accuses Blue Haven of exploiting him, Blue Haven presents his own tortured dreams, showing that he is capable of much deeper feeling than it would have been thought possible. This emotional monologue lifts him in the audience's estimation and establishes Elder's goal of giving every character his or her due.

The generosity in Elder's treatment of his characters, seen not only in the way he allows each to develop a voice but also in his mutualistic conception of the family, does have certain drawbacks. Since none of the characters is larger than the others, none, in this tale of wrecked hopes, gains the type of tragic stature obtained by the leading characters in the Williams and Miller plays mentioned above. That is to say, none has the broken splendor of a Willy Loman, because, as each family member's choices are heavily dependent on others' situations, no character ever has to face the anxiety of bearing total responsibility for his or her actions. Thus, a character can never rise to the grandeur associated with an acceptance of such responsibility. Furthermore, as a number of critics have noted, Elder's evenhandedness sometimes hints at a distance between him and his creations, since his equal treatment of each problem reveals that he was not aroused by any of his characters' tribulations. Such an attitude can lead to the pathos and power of a given dramatic situation not being fully asserted.

One compensation for these drawbacks is compassion. Elder refuses to make any of his characterizations, even of such comic figures as Blue Haven, into caricatures. He extends to each a measure of respect and understanding. Further, Elder's undistorted, accepting view of his characters and their world matches their general realism. His characters are aware of their own and others' limitations and are largely accustomed to, though hurt by, their social inferiority. The family members tend to treat each new vicissitude with relatively good humor. Thus, near the end of the first act, when everyone is momentarily glum about future prospects, the father, having leeringly accepted Theo's proposal that he work with Blue Haven but being none too happy about it, engages in a little tap dancing. Although his steps are clumsy, the boys cheer him on, caught up in their infectious attempt to celebrate a dubious alliance. The frequent joking of the father and sons works to this same end, lightening the burdens they must bear.

Elder's ability to create a multisided situation is found in his other published drama, *Charades on East Fourth Street.* This play belongs to a genre, delved into by black playwrights of the 1960's, that might be called "ritual drama." Ritual dramas were a component of the rebellious black arts movement that emphasized theater as a social ritual, such as the Catholic Mass, that worked to renew symbolically a society's cohesion. These works provided a way of going back to the sources of theater, as is evident in such dramas as the medieval mystery plays. Ritual dramas retold the story of Christ's passion, and, as the centerpiece of a worldview, its reenactment served to rededicate viewers to a common purpose as they reempathized with their binding social myth. Numerous modern authors, such as T. S. Eliot, have turned back to the roots of drama, but black writers often gave this turn a perverse twist. Undoubtedly, one of the most brilliant of the black writers' ritual dramas was *Dutchman* (pr., pb. 1964) by LeRoi Jones (who later changed his name to Amiri Baraka). In this play, a black college student flirts with an initially willing white woman on a subway, but the game turns ugly, and she stabs him. All the other white passengers join her in disposing of the corpse. The ritual, then, is the sacrifice of a young black male, portrayed as the glue holding together white society. Thus, *Dutchman*, pretending to reveal white America's ideological foundations, actually serves up an indictment of how, it claims, the United States can unite only by scapegoating its minorities.

It may be surmised from this plot recapitulation that such plays could easily become shrill. Although this is not the case with *Dutchman*, because of the author's use of three-dimensional characters, with the woman becoming a fury only in the last minutes, the same cannot be said for Elder's *Charades on East Fourth Street*. At points, his characters grow strident when they lecture one another about police brutality. This short play revolves around the actions of a band of black youths who have kidnapped a white policeman who they believe is guilty of raping a teenage girl. Then, in keeping with the title, *Charades on East Fourth Street*, the youths force the officer to act out a series of degrading scenes. For example, they strip him and put him in bed with a teenage girl, saying that they will send photographs to his wife. It can be seen that in this sexual charade, he is acting out the same part that he supposedly plays in his oppression of the black community.

As the play progresses, it grows more complex. It turns out, for example, that the gang has grabbed the wrong police officer. Furthermore, the audience learns that the majority of these black teenagers are not convinced of the utility of this kidnapping and are involved in it only because they have been pressured into acting by their leader. In a short (one-act) play such as this one, however, there is no room for excessive ambiguity. The fact that Elder does not give his black revolutionaries much conviction— the kind of fanaticism that Baraka's characters often display—takes the wind out of the story's sails. Without the time to develop the gang's interplay or the anger to make the play an indictment, Elder heroically fails at a genre for which he has no aptitude.

It could be said that Elder's lack of success at agitational drama indicates that, for him, to write well he must follow his bent, which comes from depicting the complexity of characters and the networks they form. His defense of the black family in his most important play, *Ceremonies in Dark Old Men*, does not rest on any encomiums of individual family members' virtues but on an insistence on the value of the family as a mechanism offering support and solidarity in the face of a hostile society. The worth of Elder's works lies in the evocative power of his affirmation, which itself rests on a sophisticated analysis of how a family functions as one, composed of the relationships of people rather than of people standing alone.

Other major works

SCREENPLAYS: *Sounder*, 1972; *Melinda*, 1972; *Sounder, Part Two*, 1976; *Bustin' Loose*, 1981 (with Roger L. Simon and Richard Pryor).

TELEPLAYS: *The Terrible Veil*, 1964; *Ceremonies in Dark Old Men*, 1975 (based on his play); *A Woman Called Moses*, 1978 (based on a book by Marcy Heidish).

Bibliography

Duberman, Martin. "Theater 69." *Partisan Review* 36 (1969): 488-489. In a review of significant new theatrical work of the season, playwright Duberman singles out black drama as especially noteworthy. He has, however, little good to say about *Ceremonies in Dark Old Men*, which he characterizes as too predictable and cliché-ridden. He explains that many black writers, such as Elder, have introduced new themes to the American stage but have been hampered in doing so by their reliance on tired dramatic forms.

Eckstein, George. "Softened Voices in the Black Theater." *Dissent* 23 (Summer, 1976): 306-308. Eckstein analyzes the changes through which black drama has gone, from the heady, often outspokenly nationalist and/ or revolutionary drama of the mid-1960's to the more reserved drama of the mid-1970's, which puts a greater stress on mere survival and family values. He chooses the works of Elder, as they have evolved in the transition from stage to screen, to signal these changes.

Fenderson, Lewis H. "The New Breed of Black Writers and Their Jaundiced View of Tradition." *CLA Journal* 15 (September, 1971): 18-24. This essay does not discuss Elder at length but does situate his and other black writers' work in terms of the whole development of the black novel and theater in the 1960's. It provides a strong account of the flavor and diversity of that period.

Harrison, Paul Carter. *The Drama of Nommo.* New York: Grove Press, 1972. This highly original look at black drama studies it within categories developed from African aesthetics. One example is Harrison's use of the concept of "nommo," or life force. In discussing *Ceremonies in Dark Old Men*, he argues that "the father, Mr. Parker, performs poorly at checkers, which alerts us to the limited Nommo force he has available." On the whole, Harrison finds the play weak because it does not sufficiently bring to light the characters' own recognition of the moral implications of their actions.

Jeffers, Lance. "Bullins, Baraka, and Elder: The Dawn of Grandeur in

Black Drama." *CLA Journal* 16 (September, 1972): 32-48. Looking at *Ceremonies in Dark Old Men*, Jeffers points to the resilience of the characters as they face oppressive circumstances. He states that one of Elder's themes is "that the genius and energy of young black America are thwarted and trampled upon, but they remain alive." He believes, however, that Elder lacks the identification with his characters shown by fellow playwright Ed Bullins.

James Feast

T. S. ELIOT

Born: St. Louis, Missouri; September 26, 1888
Died: London, England; January 4, 1965

Principal drama

Sweeney Agonistes, pb. 1932, pr. 1933 (fragment); *The Rock*, pb., pr. 1934; *Murder in the Cathedral*, pb., pr. 1935; *The Family Reunion*, pb., pr. 1939; *The Cocktail Party*, pr. 1949, pb. 1950; *The Confidential Clerk*, pr. 1953, pb. 1954; *The Elder Statesman*, pr. 1958, pb. 1959; *Collected Plays*, pb. 1962.

Other literary forms

In addition to being a successful liturgical dramatist, T. S. Eliot was an editor, an essayist, and a poet of great distinction. He became assistant editor of *The Egoist* in 1917 and founded *The Criterion* in 1922, serving as editor of the latter from then until its demise in 1939. As an essayist, Eliot explored the place of modern literature with regard to tradition, discussed the relationship between literature and ethics, and emphasized the need for a modern idiom. Among his extremely influential collections of essays are *The Sacred Wood* (1920) and *After Strange Gods* (1934), both dealing with the individual's debt to tradition, the latter propounding a moral standpoint; *The Use of Poetry and the Use of Criticism* (1933); and *On Poetry and Poets* (1957). In *For Lancelot Andrewes* (1928) and *The Idea of a Christian Society* (1939), the impact of his 1927 confirmation in the Church of England on his life and letters is particularly evident.

Eliot's poetry has had a greater influence, not only in England and America but also in world literature, than that of any of his contemporaries. *Prufrock and Other Observations* (1917), *Poems* (1919; printed by Leonard and Virginia Woolf), and *The Waste Land* (1922) illustrate his growing despair over personal problems as well as modern social trends; *Ash Wednesday* (1930) and *Four Quartets* (1943), produced following his confirmation, are meditations concerning spiritual illumination. In *Old Possum's Book of Practical Cats* (1939), Eliot demonstrated his talent for writing comic verse with equal success. That work has been reprinted widely in many formats and even, in 1983, provided the basis for a Tony Award winning musical, *Cats*.

Achievements

Any assessment of T. S. Eliot's achievements as a dramatist must be made in the light of his own comments about the relationship between past and present, between "tradition and the individual talent." For Eliot, a new work of art causes a rearrangement of the ideal, preexisting order. As

Carol Smith points out, his comments about "historical perspective" are not innovative; what is new is his idea that the "given" order defines the artist, whose chief responsibility is to subsume his individual talent as part of the progress of literary history. Eliot's dramatic works are therefore "classical" in the altered sense of his attempting to employ a modern idiom in the service of the imperatives of history, both literary and religious.

One of Eliot's achievements was the presentation of liturgical drama on the modern stage to a commercial audience. His endeavor in this regard began with his writing both a pageant, *The Rock*, and a ritual drama, *Murder in the Cathedral*, for the limited audiences provided respectively by a benefit to promote church building in London and the Canterbury Festival, audiences preconditioned to dramas of redemption. (*Sweeney Agonistes*, an experimental fragment, was not produced until 1933.) With his later plays, however, Eliot undertook the task of convincing secular audiences that traditional ideas about redemption were viable within a modern framework. *The Family Reunion*, his first full-length experiment in turning drawing-room comedy into religious fable, was not immediately successful; as his close friend and adviser Elliott Martin Browne reports, critics found the work mixed—the most negative reviews said that the play was characterized by "lifeless smoothness" and "difficulty" and was guaranteed to leave the audience "vexed and exhausted." Some modern critics, however, such as Eliot's biographer T. S. Matthews, find the play "extraordinary, ... far superior to his later, 'better made' plays." *The Cocktail Party*, on the other hand, was better received; even those who wrote negative reviews acknowledged that the production bordered on greatness. Browne notes that similar comments were made about *The Confidential Clerk*, although critical reception was influenced by the general belief that Eliot's attempt "to combine the esoteric with the entertaining" was no longer innovative. *The Elder Statesman*, Browne believes, was overinterpreted by gossipmongers intent on reading the play in the light of Eliot's marriage to his secretary, Valerie Fletcher, the previous year.

Quite aside from their mixed commercial appeal, Eliot's plays illustrate his critical theories not only about the connection between drama and poetry but also about the failure of realistic theater. As C. L. Barber notes, Eliot's Aristotelian viewpoint prompted him to criticize modern drama for its lack of rhythm. For Eliot, poetry was more than a distraction, more than an attempt to prettify dramatic diction; never extrinsic to the action, poetry provides an underlying musical pattern that strengthens the audience's response. The presence of such an abstract pattern suggests, as Eliot says in "Four Elizabethan Dramatists" (written in 1924), that the great vice in English drama is realism, for it detracts from the unity of the play. As his large essay *Poetry and Drama* (1951) makes clear, such unity is more than a technical matter of form and content, for the literary is handmaiden to the religious. Eliot's ideal vision of verse drama is one in which "a design of human action and of words" is perpetuated in such a way that the connection between the everyday world and the universal design is illustrated; such a drama, Eliot believed, would provide the proper feeling of "reconciliation" to lead the audience to a spiritual awakening.

Biography

Thomas Stearns Eliot was born on September 26, 1888, in St. Louis, Missouri. His celebrated statement of his allegiances in *For Lancelot Andrewes*—"classicist in literature, royalist in politics, and Anglo-Catholic in religion"—ran counter to the family tradition of Unitarianism; his grandfather, William Greenleaf Eliot, descendant of a pastor of Boston's Old North Church, established the Unitarian Church of the Messiah in St. Louis. Eliot's father himself was a renegade, refusing the ministry for what was eventually the presidency of the Hydraulic-Press Brick Company. His mother, Charlotte Stearns, was a descendant of one of the judges in the Salem witch trials; an intellectual woman, Stearns began a career as a schoolteacher and eventually became active in children's causes.

As Matthews notes, the family saying *"Tace et fac* ('Shut up and get on with it')" suggests a household in which indulgence gave way to duty. As a child, Eliot was considered delicate but precocious; at Smith Academy, he took the Latin prize and excelled in English. Deemed too young at seventeen to enter Harvard, he was sent first to Milton Academy. At Harvard, he was conservative and studious. He became an editor of the *Advocate*, a literary magazine, but his decision to accelerate his undergraduate work in order to pursue a master's degree left him small leisure for such friends as Conrad Aiken. Important influences during his college years included his discovery of Arthur Symons' *The Symbolist Movement in Literature* (1899), a book that led him to imitate the verse of Jules Laforgue; his love for Elizabethan drama; and, finally, his acquaintance with Irving Babbitt, the leader of the New Humanism, an anti-Romantic movement that stressed the ethical nature of experience. Certainly, Babbitt's influence led Eliot to spend one of his graduate years in France, where, resisting the attractive Bohemianism open to a writer of his talents, he decided to pursue a degree in philosophy at Harvard, where he came under the influence of Bertrand Russell.

The fellowship that Harvard awarded Eliot in 1914 proved to alter the course of his life. Enrolled in Merton College, at Oxford, he began his long friendship with Ezra Pound, under whose aegis Eliot published "The Love Song of J. Alfred Prufrock" in *Poetry* magazine in 1915. In England, Eliot met and married his first wife, Vivienne Haigh-Wood. Described as a beautiful and entrancing individual, she nevertheless suffered from a nervous disability that had devastating emotional effects. In increasing financial difficulty, Eliot worked as an usher at a boys' school, an employee at Lloyd's Bank, or free-lance journalist, and an assistant editor of *The Egoist.*

Eliot enjoyed many fruitful friendships, among them those with Bertrand Russell, Virginia Woolf, and I. A. Richards. From 1921 to 1925, when he was publishing reviews in the *Times Literary Supplement,* Eliot's health deteriorated; the unforeseen result of an enforced vacation was *The Waste Land.* In 1922, he founded *The Criterion,* a literary quarterly that was sponsored financially by Lady Rothermere. After a long period of ill health and self-doubt, he joined the Anglican Church. His biographer suggests a number of reasons for the decision, including certain social and "aesthetic" attractions of this particular denomination, the authoritarian cast of the Church, and the long Church "pedigree" that satisfied Eliot's belief in the importance of tradition. His decision to become a British citizen followed soon thereafter, partly, Matthews believes, because Eliot felt that in America "the aristocratic tradition of culture was dead."

Eliot's 1932 return to his native land was, like his first journey away, a new start, for it began his separation from Vivienne, for whom he had become more nurse than husband. To be sure, the attempt to escape from her neurotic persecution made his middle years unhappy ones, years complicated further by the exigencies of World War II. Despite such distractions, however, these were the years in which Eliot began his career as a playwright.

Quite clearly, Eliot's religious conversion provided the themes not only for his poetry but also for his plays. Events in Eliot's personal life, including the death of his estranged wife in 1947, are also reflected in his plays. Conceivably, his sense of alienation and guilt found its way into the portrait of Harry, the putative wife-killer in *The Family Reunion,* as well as into the depiction of the dreary marriage faced by the Chamberlaynes in *The Cocktail Party.* Other elements are identifiable, such as the figure of Agatha in *The Family Reunion;* the only one to understand Harry's spiritual search thoroughly, Agatha is said to be based on Emily Hale, Eliot's longtime friend, who had been a schoolmistress at Scripps College, Smith College, and Abbot Academy. Emily was as shocked by Eliot's second clandestine marriage as she was by his first; at the age of sixty-nine, Eliot married Valerie Fletcher, his secretary.

Before the arrival of that emotional security, however, Eliot had achieved other triumphs. He was awarded the Nobel Prize in 1948, and, in the same year, received the British Empire's Order of Merit. While he was drafting *The Cocktail Party,* he traveled to Princeton, New Jersey, to accept a fellowship at the Institute for Advanced Study. His last two plays—*The Confidential Clerk* and *The Elder Statesman*—were not as popular as *The Cocktail Party;* they do, however, show an increasing understanding of the way in which human relationships may be ameliorated. Indeed, in *The Elder Statesman*, the love experienced by Monica and Charles seems a reflection of the happiness that Eliot himself found with his second wife. For the first time in his dramatic writing, the possibility of redemption through human love is adequately broached; indeed, for the first time, human love seems a model of divine love rather than, as Celia observes in *The Cocktail Party*, a distraction or a second-best choice.

On January 4, 1965, Eliot died in London. At his request, his ashes repose at East Coker, the birthplace of his ancestors and the titular locale of one of the *Four Quartets*; the memorial plaque in the Poets' Corner at Westminster Abbey was placed on January 4, 1967.

Analysis

T. S. Eliot's conservative dramaturgy is clearly expressed in his 1928 essay "Dialogue on Dramatic Poetry" in which, as C. L. Barber notes, he suggests that "genuine drama" displays "a tension between liturgy and realism." To be sure, Eliot differed sharply from the advocates of Ibsenite realism, maintaining throughout his career that untrammeled realism operating outside the limitations of art did not produce classic harmony. In consequence, Eliot relied on a number of traditional forms, including the Mass and Greek drama. On the other hand, he created new verse forms, convinced that traditional forms such as Shakespearean blank verse would be inadequate to express modern experience. In *Sweeney Agonistes*, he made use of the rhythms of vaudeville, believing that such robust entertainment contained the seeds of a popular drama of high artistic quality, comparable to the achievements of the great Elizabethan and Jacobean playwrights.

Modern religious drama, Eliot believed, "should be able to hold the interest, to arouse the excitement, of people who are not religious." Redemption is the theme of all of his plays, a theme explored on different levels. For example, Becket's understanding, in *Murder in the Cathedral*, that salvation is a willing submission to a larger pattern is developed and tempered in the later social comedies.

In almost all of his plays, Eliot presents characters on a continuum of spiritual understanding, including the martyr or saint figure, the "guardians" (the spiritual advisers), the common folk (capable of limited perception or at least of accommodation), and the uncomprehending. In *The Family Reunion* and *The Cocktail Party*, respectively, Harry and Celia experience a sense of having sinned and the desire to atone. Celia's illumination is also characterized by a sense of having failed another person. Her martyrdom is correspondingly more moving, not because it is graphically described, but because it seems inexorable. In *The Confidential Clerk*, Colby, whose search for a human father parallels his desire for a divine one, experiences his *éclaircissement* as a private moment in a garden and works out his salvation as an organist. In the aforementioned plays, guardian figures abound. Agatha councils Harry to follow attendant Eumenides if he wishes to expiate the family curse; Julia, Alex, and Reilly not only show Celia the way to enlightenment but reinstate the Chamberlaynes' marriage; the retired valet Eggerson offers Colby a job as an organist and predicts his eventual entry into holy orders. Eliot's last play, *The Elder Statesman*, is the only one in which human love is an adequate guide to divine love; in that sense, Monica, in her affection for her fiancé and in her unwavering love for her father despite his faults, is a guardian figure.

A development in the characterization of the common people may be seen as well. Because of their foolishness or their attempt to dominate, all of Harry's relatives seem lost to perceptiveness, except, perhaps, for his Uncle Charles, who begins to feel "That there is something I *could* understand, if I were told it." A wider hope is held out in *The Cocktail Party*, for while not all may follow Celia's path, the Chamberlaynes learn to accept the "good life" that is available to them, and even Peter, in love with Celia, may learn to "see" through the same qualities that make him a film producer. Again, while Colby withdraws from the family circle, those who remain—no matter how superficially mismatched—engage in a communion characterized most of all by a desire to understand and to love. Finally, in *The Elder Statesman*, Eliot achieves a balance in his continuum of characters, for he presents the salvation of the Calvertons by love as well as the possibility that, through Monica, Michael might return to find his self-identity, while both Gomez and Mrs. Carghill become lost souls as they pursue their revenge.

Although originally produced for the Canterbury Festival, *Murder in the Cathedral* has achieved the most lasting interest of all Eliot's plays. It is a psychological and historical exploration of martyrdom that, as David R. Clark points out, speaks directly not only to current disputes about the interconnection between Church and State but also to the ever-present contemporary threat of assassination. It is Eliot's most successful attempt to adapt verse forms to drama, particularly in the speeches of the Chorus, whose function, Eliot believed, was to interpret the action to the viewers and to strengthen the impact of the action by reflecting its effects. In the speeches of the Knights and Tempters (characters doubled when the play is staged) as well, attitudes are mirrored by poetic cadence—a fine example of form following content. As Grover Smith notes, the title itself, while commercially attractive, is somewhat misleading, as were other possibilities Eliot considered, among them "The Archbishop Murder Case" and "Fear in the Way," for *Murder in the Cathedral* is less a whodunit than an attempt to startle the unimpassioned believer into percipience and the nonbeliever into understanding.

Like Eliot's first venture into ritualistic drama, *The Rock*, *Murder in the*

Cathedral is based on an actual event, the martyrdom of Thomas à Becket in the year 1170 in the chapel of Saint Benedict in Canterbury Cathedral. Unlike *The Rock*, however, which is a spectacle play delineating the history of the Church, *Murder in the Cathedral* is focused on a dramatic event of great intensity. The play traces the spiritual education of Thomas, whose greatest temptation is self-aggrandizement; the education of the Chorus, who seek to escape both suffering and salvation; and the education of the Knights and the audience, whose worldliness implicates them jointly in the assassination.

Eliot's addition of a Fourth Tempter to Becket's "trial" in part 1 is crucial. The first three tempters are expected and easily rejected. The first, who offers sensual pleasures, resigns Becket to "the pleasures of [his] higher vices." One such vice is offered by the Second Tempter: "Temporal power, to build a good world," power that requires submission to secular law. Becket, who rejects this exercise in intelligent self-interest, also rejects the Third Tempter's offer of a coalition with the barons to overthrow the King; such an action would bestialize Becket, make him "a wolf among wolves." The Fourth Tempter is, however, not so easily answered, for he brings the temptation of spiritual power through martyrdom. Counseling the Archbishop to seek death, he offers as its rewards the joy of wielding power over eternal life and death, the adulation of the masses, the richness of heavenly grandeur, and, finally, the sweetness of revenge, for Becket will then be able to look down and see his "persecutors, in timeless torment."

For Becket, the only way to escape the damning effects of his own spiritual pride is to give up self-will so that he may become part of a larger pattern. As Grover Smith notes, the counsel that Becket gives to the Chorus (ironically quoted to him by the Fourth Tempter) has its roots in Aristotle's image of the still point—on a wheel, for example—as the source of action:

> You know and do not know, that acting is suffering,
> And suffering action. Neither does the actor suffer
> Nor the patient act. But both are fixed
> In an eternal action, an eternal patience
> To which all must consent that it may be willed
> And which all must suffer that they may will it,
> That the pattern may subsist, that the wheel may turn and still
> Be forever still.

In theological terms, Eliot is suggesting that the nature of the relationship between action and suffering depends on the conception of God as the first mover, just as the still point is centered in the wheel. Becket, in willing martyrdom, has substituted his will for God's will. When he understands that he was doing the right deed for the wrong reason, he enters the ideal relationship between man and God—one of submission, of man's consent to be an instrument. In that condition of bringing one's will into conformity with that of God, one paradoxically does not suffer, for he acts as an instrument; neither does he act, for he gives up will. Both Grover Smith and David E. Jones explore the extension of this idea from Aristotle to Dante to clarify the sources of Eliot's vision.

For the women whose barren lives are spent among small deeds, Becket becomes a new center; with their wills in conformity to his, they too become the instruments of God's will, even as the Knights are in the murder of Becket. For Grover Smith, whereas Becket's language is abstract and passionless, his decision hidden in difficult, paradoxical words, that of the women is overtly sensual; for Carol Smith, such language shows that the women have accepted their "Christian responsibility." The women's unwilling participation in the event is a violent disturbance of their willed attitude of noninterference; through Becket, they are touched not only by life but also by death. The key is in the homily delivered by Becket as an interlude in the play, a sermon in which he speaks of an attitude of mourning and rejoicing in martyrdom. Before his death, he warns the women that their joy will come only "when the figure of God's purpose is made complete"—when, in other words, they understand that his martyrdom is the answer to their despair.

The prose in which the Knights speak after the murder has taken place is to some critics jarring, but it is deliberately so on Eliot's part; a far graver criticism is that it is either amusing, or, as Grover Smith suggests, misleading, insofar as the emphasis on the "contest . . . between brute power and resigned holiness" is shifted to an argument about Church and State. Jones disagrees; for him, the prose shakes the audience's sanctimonious complacency. The arguments offered by the Knights are familiar rationalizations. The Second Knight pleads disinterested duty as his reason for the murder, the Third that "violence is the only way in which social justice can be secured," and the Fourth that, since Becket's overweening egotism prompted the murder, the correct "verdict" is "Suicide while of Unsound Mind." The final words of the Chorus, spoken to a Te Deum in the background, serve as a corrective to any distorted view, for they, the "type of common man," not only accept responsibility for "the sin of the world" but also acknowledge that human consciousness is an affirmation of the ultimate design, of which they have willingly become a part.

Produced in March, 1939, *The Family Reunion* was considerably less successful than Eliot's first full-length play, partly because he was attempting to appeal to a secular audience; moreover, his evocation of the Aeschylean Eumenides—the Furies—as a group of well-dressed aunts and uncles and his deliberate blurring of the hero's motives and fate contribute to the weakness of the play. Various critics have traced the antecedents of *The Family Reunion*, including Henry James's "The Jolly Corner," William Shakespeare's *Hamlet*, and Aeschylus' *Oresteia*, sources discussed thoroughly by Grover Smith and David Jones. Eliot attempted to wed the classical and the modern, believing that poetry brought into the audience's world would help to heal social disintegration.

The two levels of the play—the realistic and the spiritual—are not always mutually illuminating. On the surface, the play depicts the homecoming of Harry, Lord Monchensey, to Wishwood, the family mansion that his mother, Amy, has maintained, unchanged, for his benefit. Harry, convinced that he murdered his wife a year ago, is unable to agree with the conventional wishes of his mother or of his featherheaded aunts, Ivy and Violet, or of his blundering uncles, Gerald and Charles. On another level, he arrives convinced that he is pursued by the Furies, only to learn from his Aunt Agatha that to *follow* the "bright angels" is the way to redemption through suffering.

The Family Reunion reflects Eliot's recurring preoccupation with original sin. While Harry's own uncertainty about his responsibility for his wife's death may be unsettling to the audience, the point is surely that for Eliot the *fact* is irrelevant; what is important is that Harry (and Eliot, because of his own marital situation) feels guilty about the wish itself. Indeed, Harry seems to be burdened with a family curse that he must expiate. As Agatha tells him, his father wanted to murder Harry's mother but was prevented from doing so by Agatha, who loved him; Harry has lived to reenact his father's will. Harry's guilt thus is shifted to the larger framework of the *felix culpa*, or fortunate fall.

Again, Harry's character is so unappealing that to call him, as Agatha does, "the consciousness of your unhappy family,/ Its bird sent flying through the purgatorial fire," is not acceptable on the metaphoric level. His rudeness and abrupt repudiation of his mother (which leads to her death) conspire against the suggestion that he is to become a Christian mystic or saint—that, as Agatha says, he is destined for "broken stones/ That lie, fang up" or that, as he says, he is headed for "A stony sanctuary and a primitive altar" or "A care over lives of humble people."

The transformation of the Eumenides from "hounds of hell" to "bright angels" is justified not only by the *Oresteia* of Aeschylus but also by the idea, developed in *Murder in the Cathedral*, that suffering precedes atonement; on a psychological level, however, the idea poses problems. As the evocation of the watchful eyes possessed by both mother and wife, the Eumenides suggest a developing Oedipus complex; interpreted by Agatha as helpful guardians, they suggest a childish transference of affection to Agatha, an affection that is at once incestuous and spiritual. As both Barber and Grover Smith point out, Mary, Harry's childhood sweetheart, simply presents the desired but now impossible fulfillment of human love. For Agatha, however, and eventually for Harry, the Eumenides posit a frontier beyond which all experience is private, save that it is a confrontation between the human spirit and the divine, a purgatorial confrontation under "the judicial sun/ Of the final eye."

In the final analysis, the play is not a triumph of comedy—or of tragedy. With Amy dead, Harry's father has ironically gotten his wish; Wishwood is to be ceded to Harry's brother John, about whom Harry says brutally, "A minor trouble like a concussion/ Cannot make very much difference to John." In the ritualistic chorus performed by Agatha and Mary at the end of the play, Eliot emphasizes the inexorability of the curse around which he has built his plot as well as the possibility of salvation. What is lacking is an explanation of the nature of expiation.

First produced for the 1949 Edinburgh Festival, *The Cocktail Party* is, like *The Family Reunion*, an attempt to express modern concerns in the guise of ritualistic drama. In this case, however, Eliot depends on Euripides' *Alcestis* as his classical antecedent, wisely eliminating the embodiment of the Furies that proved to be so dramatically disruptive. In one view, he effectively reproduced the sophisticated patois of cocktail-party chatter to distract his secular audience from what Grover Smith calls the play's theological "underpattern." Other critics, among them Barber and Carol Smith, suggest that the comic approach was a deliberate attempt at a reversal in which "surfaces" become "depths" and the comic resolution an indication of divine order.

A number of this play's themes are taken from Eliot's earlier plays. There is a reunion, although not in the sense of Harry Monchensey's mythopoeic experience, for the Chamberlaynes literally as well as figuratively re-create their marriage; again, there is the figure of the mystic, this time, however, a more convincing one, in Celia; moreover, there is a guardian, Reilly, who achieves expressed validity in his role as a psychologist. Finally, and perhaps most important, there is a sense that spiritual illumination is not restricted, except in its intensity, to martyr figures.

Superficially, the plot is familiar drawing-room comedy, entailing a series of love affairs. Edward's wife, Lavinia, has inexplicably left him; Peter Quilpe, a filmmaker, is in love with Celia Coplestone, Edward's mistress, while Lavinia is in love with Peter. Comic relief is provided by the scatterbrained Julia Shuttlethwaite, the peripatetic Alexander MacColgie Gibbs, and Sir Henry Harcourt-Reilly, an enigmatic, gin-swilling psychologist. As in the well-made play, the plot revolves around a secret: Julia and Alex have conspired with Reilly to reinvigorate the Chamberlaynes' marriage, in an association called variously "the Christian conspiracy" or, as Jones puts it, "the Community of Christians."

The marital difficulties would be familiar to the audience, but not Eliot's interpretation of them. Having confused desire with affection in his attachment to Celia, Edward must face the fact that he is essentially unloving, whereas Lavinia is by nature unlovable: Thus, Eliot suggests, they are perfectly matched. In addition, Edward, who is indecisive, must learn to face the consequences of making a decision—in this case, the decision that Lavinia should return to him. What he realizes is that her return is tantamount to inviting the angel of destruction into his life.

Possessed by the belief that he is suffering "the death of the spirit," that he can live neither with the role Lavinia imposes on him nor without it, Edward goes to Reilly for help. The language that this counselor uses indicates his role of spiritual guardianship. He speaks of Edward's "long journey" but refuses to send him to his "sanatorium," for to do so would be to abandon him to the "devils" that feast on the "shadow of desires of desires." Instead, he brings him face to face with Lavinia to convince him that the unloving and the unlovable should make the best of a bad job— or, in terms of the blessing he administers, must "work out [their] salvation with diligence." Carol Smith's review of Christian mysticism as a background to the play makes clear that Reilly encourages the Chamberlaynes to follow the "Affirmative Way," in which "all created things are to be accepted in love as images of the Divine," rather than the "Negative Way," which is characterized by detachment from "the love of all things."

Reilly's interview with Celia is substantially different, for while she, like Edward, complains of an awareness of solitude, she focuses less on herself than on a perception that loneliness is the human condition and that communication is therefore illusory. She also complains, unlike Edward, of a sense of sin, of a feeling that she must atone for having failed "someone, or something, outside." She attributes her failure to a self-willed fantasy: In Edward, she loved only a figment of her imagination. Unlike Edward, she has had a vision of the Godhead, an ecstatic exhaltation "of loving in the spirit." It is this vision that she chooses to follow, although Reilly emphasizes that it is an unknown way, a blind journey, a way to being "transhumanized," the "way of illumination." Her way, the "Negative Way" of mysticism, culminates in her crucifixion "very near an ant-hill" in the jungles of Kinkanja.

What Eliot offers in *The Cocktail Party* is a series of gradations of spiritual understanding, gradations that were not presented adequately in *The Family Reunion*. Celia's way of illumination is undoubtedly more believable because her developing perceptions are not expressed in sibylline pronouncements; likewise, the guardians are given authenticity by the comic role their very eccentricity engenders. The common way, represented by the Chamberlaynes, is not appealing but understandable, and, as Reilly says, "In a world of lunacy,/ Violence, stupidity, greed . . . it is a good life." Finally, Peter Quilpe, shocked by the news of Celia's death, comes to understand that he had been loving only the image he had created of her. As Grover Smith comments, "the kind of comedy Eliot devised has been compared generically by some critics to Dante's *Commedia*, for in it the characters either fulfill their greatest potentialities or else are set firmly on the way toward doing so."

In Eliot's fourth play, *The Confidential Clerk*, the theme of redemption is again explored, this time through a dependence on Euripides' *Ion*, a play that deals with hidden paternity. Eliot examines the sense of aloneness expressed so effectively by Celia and the human penchant for re-creating other individuals to conform with one's own desires. In addition, Eliot shows the path that a mystical vocation may take.

Denis Donoghue pertinently remarks that Eliot solved the "false tone" occasioned by Celia's death by shifting his terms: Illumination becomes Art, and the worldly way, Commerce, both terms that avoid doctrinal problems. Metaphorically, an escape into Art (illumination) becomes an escape into a garden, one in which real communication is possible. So it is for the musical Colby Simpkins, about whom Lucasta Angel, Sir Claude Mulhammer's illegitimate daughter, notes that he has his "own world." Taken in by Sir Claude as his presumptive son, Colby is immediately claimed by Lady Elizabeth Mulhammer, a fashionable reincarnation of Julia Shuttlethwaite, as the lost son of her former lover, a poet. Each imagines Colby in terms of personal wish-fulfillment. To Colby, the failed musician, Sir Claude reveals his early yearnings to be a sculptor and his decision to follow in the family business. For Sir Claude, the act of creation is "a world where the form is the reality" and an "escape into living" from an illusory world. Indeed, for Sir Claude, life is a constant compromise, just as it is for the Chamberlaynes, a constant coping with two worlds, neither of which offers perfect fulfillment. It is, as he says, a substitute for religion.

Despite this analogy, Colby is unwilling to accept Sir Claude as a father. Colby expresses his yearning for an ideal father in words that may be read for their religious connotation. He wishes, as he says, to have a father "Whom I had never known and wouldn't know now/ ... whom I could get to know/ Only by report, by documents," a father, he continues, "whose life I could in some way perpetuate/ By being the person he would have liked to be." The analogues to Christ are unmistakable. The revelation that Colby is actually the son of Herbert Guzzard, a "disappointed musician," suggesting a harmony between the mystical and the commonplace that is seldom achieved in *The Family Reunion*, adds to the success of *The Confidential Clerk*.

Like Celia, Colby chooses a life of service, if one more prosaic than joining a nursing order and perishing in Kinkanja. He acknowledges his inheritance by becoming the organist at a small church (rather than continuing to live on Sir Claude's generosity, for Sir Claude is eager to think of Colby as one with whom he shared disillusionment); Eggerson, the retired confidential clerk—who, as Jones notes, was for Eliot "'the only *developed* Christian in the play'"—suggests that Colby will enter the ministry.

As Barber points out, the play presents a succession of individuals who are reaching out after Colby, essentially as a way of gratifying their own expectations. It is only, however, when the audience knows the secret of Colby's birth that many of the early conversations make sense; consequently, Barber suggests, the play is weak in its early acts. Despite this criticism, *The Confidential Clerk* offered Eliot's most convincing and optimistic treatment to that time of the possibility of human communion, pointing the way to his hopeful treatment of human love in his last play, *The Elder Statesman*. It seems less important that Lady Elizabeth's up-to-date spiritualism, her substitute for religion, fails her in her perception that Colby is her son than that she is willing to accept as her real offspring B. Kaghan, a brash, successful businessman, a diamond in the rough. Again, it seems less important that Sir Claude has lost his desired son than that, in the end, he emotionally accepts Lucasta as a daughter. Indeed, the note that Eliot strikes—that, as the Mulhammers say, they are "to try to understand our children" and that both Lucasta and B. Kaghan desire to "mean something" to their newfound parents—is exceptionally conciliatory and suggestive of greater amelioration in the "good life" than is posited in the earlier plays.

Eliot's final play, *The Elder Statesman*, is an extension not only of the idea that one must come to terms with his past, just as Harry Monchensey and the Mulhammers attempt to do, but also that this is, indeed, the only way to redemption. Such atonement on the part of Lord Claverton is presented in words that are less mystical than prosaic; indeed, his past is populated by the blackmailers Federico Gomez, who seeks to capitalize on his knowledge that Lord Calverton had run over a dead man after a drinking party, and Mrs. Carghill, who, as the actress Maisie Montjoy, possesses incriminating love letters. Certainly Calverton's immediate problem—that of being a terminally ill, newly retired man of consequence, suffering from the loneliness of "sitting in an empty waiting room"—is one with which the audience can quickly identify. As Jones points out, *The Elder Statesman* has a "naturalistic surface": The more plays Eliot wrote, the more muted the spiritual enlightenment became, so that eventually the social relationships became primary. Carol Smith, on the other hand, sees the play as a culmination of Eliot's development of the "dramatic fable" that serves as a "transparent mask" for permanent, religious meanings.

The corollary to Calverton's loneliness takes on sinister (and existential) connotations when it is present in Gomez, who has adopted a new name and new country after a prison sentence. As he says, he has returned to face Lord Calverton in order to find the self he left behind. Gomez charges Calverton with "creating him," with engineering his tastes and altering his career. In revenge, he threatens to make others see Calverton for what he really is—a murderer and a hypocrite. Calverton, in fact, has created his own ghosts by dominating the lives of others. The lesson that he must take responsibility for meddling in others' lives is reinforced by his realization that he is no better than those he created. Both Jones and Carol Smith point out that Calverton's and Gomez's careers parallel each other in that their ethical standards merely mirror the society of which they are a part and in that both have changed identities, the "statesman" Dick Ferry having adopted his wife's name for its impressiveness and the Oxford student having changed his name to blend into his new country. Gomez's desire to amalgamate his two personalities and his desire for revenge are satisfied when he meets Calverton's ne'er-do-well son Michael, to whom he offers the lure of easy money and a new identity. Gomez is, in short, reenacting Calverton's earlier role of tempter.

The other ghost that Calverton must face—Maisie Montjoy, known as Mrs. Carghill—has also been "created" by him. As his mistress, who sued him for breach of promise, she was irrevocably affected by his offer of and withdrawal of love. Indeed, their relationship is a parody of the fruitful, redeeming love that comes to Monica Calverton and Charles Hemington. Like Gomez, Mrs. Carghill has gone through a series of name changes reflecting a progressive confusion in identity. Like him, she resorts to blackmail to gain companionship, insisting on what Jones calls the "uncomfortable Christian conception of a man and a woman becoming the inseparable unity of 'one flesh,'" and like him, she seeks revenge by encouraging the weak-willed Michael to emigrate to South America.

The cure that Eliot proposes for Calverton's loneliness, for his series of façades, and for his discomfort with the past also exorcises his ghosts by allowing him to face them: love. Accompanying that love is the relinquishment of power; understanding that Michael is a free agent, Calverton recognizes that he has been trying to dominate his son's choice of friends, lifestyle, and career. If Michael is a free agent, then Gomez and Carghill's revenge has lost its sting, because Calverton is no longer responsible for his son's actions. The model for the cure is the love shared by Monica and Charles, a love that creates a new, viable personage out of the you and the I. Unlike the kind of false images projected by Calverton's desire to dominate, the new individual is created by a submission of wills, a voluntary merging of the selves. It is, in short, a model of divine love. Eliot thus points to an achievable salvation unspoiled by artificial dramatic techniques such as the evocation of the Eumenides or the awkward ritualistic libation in *The Cocktail Party*.

While Jones notes that for one reviewer, at least, the language of the lovers is abstract and lacking in evocative details, Calverton's illumination is clearly expressed: As Calverton says, if an individual is willing to confess everything to even one person—willing, that is, to appear without his mask—"Then he loves that person, and his love will save him." Calverton further realizes that his wish to dominate his children arises not from love but from the desire to foist upon them an image so that he "could believe in [his] own pretences." At peace with himself and with Monica, who has promised to remember Michael as he really is so that he may one day shed his mask and return to his real self, Calverton approaches death with serenity: "It is worth dying," he says, "to find out what life is."

Other major works

POETRY: *Prufrock and Other Observations*, 1917; *Poems*, 1919; *Ara Vos Prec*, 1920; *The Waste Land*, 1922; *Poems, 1909-1925*, 1925; *Ash Wednesday*, 1930; *Triumphal March*, 1931; *Words for Music*, 1934; *Collected Poems, 1909-1935*, 1936; *Old Possum's Book of Practical Cats*, 1939; *Four Quartets*, 1943; *The Cultivation of Christmas Trees*, 1954; *Collected Poems, 1909-1962*, 1963; *Poems Written in Early Youth*, 1967; *The Complete Poems and Plays*, 1969.

NONFICTION: *Ezra Pound: His Metric and Poetry*, 1917; *The Sacred Wood*, 1920; *Homage to John Dryden*, 1924; *Shakespeare and the Stoicism of Seneca*, 1927; *For Lancelot Andrewes*, 1928; *Dante*, 1929; *Charles Whibley: A Memoir*, 1931; *Thoughts After Lambeth*, 1931; *John Dryden: The Poet, the Dramatist, the Critic*, 1932; *Selected Essays*, 1932, 1950; *The Use of Poetry and the Use of Criticism*, 1933; *After Strange Gods*, 1934; *Elizabethan Essays*, 1934; *Essays Ancient and Modern*, 1936; *The Idea of a Christian Society*, 1939; *The Classics and the Man of Letters*, 1942; *The Music of Poetry*, 1942; *Notes Toward the Definition of Culture*, 1948; *Poetry and Drama*, 1951; *Religious Drama: Medieval and Modern*, 1954; *The Three Voices of Poetry*, 1954; *The Literature of Politics*, 1955; *The Frontiers of Criticism*, 1956; *On Poetry and Poets*, 1957; *To Criticize the Critic*, 1965; *The Letters of T. S. Eliot: Volume One, 1898-1922*, 1988.

Bibliography

Bloom, Harold, ed. *Murder in the Cathedral.* New York: Chelsea House, 1988. A collection of the most significant articles, by a variety of critics, on one of Eliot's most famous plays. Some of the articles tend toward obscurity, but most are helpful in placing the play in the larger context of poetic drama. Includes a helpful introduction by Bloom and a bibliography.

Browne, Elliott Martin. *The Making of T. S. Eliot's Plays.* London: Cambridge University Press, 1969. The most exhaustive textual study of Eliot's plays available, this book analyzes the early typescript and manuscript versions of Eliot's dramas, identifying and commenting on all major changes. Browne attempts to reconstruct Eliot's writing process, and so any reader interested in that aspect of Eliot's art might begin here.

Headings, Philip R. *T. S. Eliot.* Rev. ed. Boston: Twayne, 1982. This critical study of all Eliot's works is more devoted to his poetry than to his drama, but the drama chapters are the easiest introduction to Eliot's plays. The revision incorporates criticism published after the first edition, as does the excellent annotated bibliography. Includes a line-drawing portrait of Eliot.

Jones, David E. *The Plays of T. S. Eliot.* Toronto: University of Toronto Press, 1960. The first book-length study to deal exclusively with Eliot's plays, and still one of the best. In addition to separate sections on each of the plays, Jones includes general criticism relating them to Eliot's poetic and critical writings.

Smith, Carol H. *T. S. Eliot's Dramatic Theory and Practice: From "Sweeney Agonistes" to "The Elder Statesman."* Princeton, N.J.: Princeton University Press, 1963. Unlike most other studies of Eliot's drama, this book makes full use of Eliot's own statements on dramatic theory in his critical essays to help illuminate his own plays. Another bonus is Smith's analysis of dramatic elements in Eliot's nondramatic works. The bibliography is helpful, though somewhat dated.

Patricia Marks
(Updated by *John R. Holmes*)

ST. JOHN ERVINE

Born: Belfast, Northern Ireland; December 28, 1883
Died: London, England; January 24, 1971

Principal drama

The Magnanimous Lover, wr. 1907, pr., pb. 1912 (one act); *Mixed Marriage*, pr., pb. 1911; *Jane Clegg*, pr. 1913, pb. 1914; *John Ferguson*, pr., pb. 1915; *The Ship*, pr., pb. 1922; *The Lady of Belmont*, pb. 1923, pr. 1924; *Anthony and Anna*, pb. 1925, pr. 1926; *The First Mrs. Fraser*, pr., pb. 1929; *Boyd's Shop*, pr., pb. 1936; *Robert's Wife*, pr. 1937, pb. 1938; *Private Enterprise*, pb. 1938, pr. 1947; *William John Mawhinney*, pr. 1940 (also as *Ballyfarland's Festival*, pr. 1953); *Friends and Relations*, pr. 1941, pb. 1947; *My Brother Tom*, pr., pb. 1952; *Esperanza*, pr. 1957; *Selected Plays of St. John Ervine*, pb. 1988.

Other literary forms

St. John Ervine was the author of several novels which were highly regarded in their day. His novels, such as *Mrs. Martin's Man* (1914) and *The Foolish Lovers* (1920), display the same strengths as the best of his plays—realism and clarity of design and structure. Ervine also wrote abrasive and controversial drama criticism for several newspapers. Finally, he was the author of several opinionated biographies of literary and public figures, including Oscar Wilde and George Bernard Shaw.

Achievements

Ervine holds an honorable place in the Irish Renaissance; as such, he is aligned with William Butler Yeats, Lady Augusta Gregory, and the Abbey Theatre. His greatest achievements are his early Irish plays, two of which, *Jane Clegg* and *John Ferguson*, have long been recognized as minor classics. After a brief time as manager of the Abbey Theatre followed by wartime military service, Ervine settled in England and was chosen as a member of the Irish Academy. He served as professor of dramatic literature for the Royal Society of Literature from 1933 through 1936. His critical theory supports his practice in his early plays: Dramatic value resides in the author's attempt to present real people dealing with believable human situations. Though he turned from playwriting to novels, criticism, and political and biographical essays, Ervine is best remembered as a spokesman for and practitioner of dramatic realism. His influence on a later generation of Irish playwrights, while indirect, may be seen in the continuation of the realistic tradition. Ervine serves as an exemplar of honest, realistic, economically plotted, straightforward playwriting.

Biography

St. John Greer Ervine was born in Belfast in Northern Ireland on December 28, 1883. He did not take a university degree but was writing plays by his twenty-fourth year. In 1911, he married Leonora Mary Davis and became associated with the Abbey Theatre in Dublin. He served for a brief time as manager of the Abbey Theatre, and, while in that capacity, produced his best play, *John Ferguson*. His British sympathies caused an estrangement between him and the theater players, and on May 29, 1916, the actors declared their unwillingness to work under Ervine's direction. The resultant break with the Abbey Theatre, combined with the escalation of World War I, led Ervine to turn away from Ireland and exclusively Irish subject matter. His service in a regiment of the British Household Battalion and, later, with the Royal Dublin Fusiliers ended in 1918, when he was severely wounded and suffered the loss of a leg.

After the war, Ervine settled in London. His first London success was in 1929, when his play, *The First Mrs. Fraser*, enjoyed an extended run; that success was repeated the next year in New York. His career expanded to include novels, essays on political and ethical subjects, drama criticism, and biographies. He was drama critic for *The Sunday Observer* of London, and in 1929, he was guest drama critic for *The World* in New York. His criticism was controversial, which is usually attributed to Ervine's plainspoken, even harsh criticism of American plays. His reputation for acerbity rests additionally upon his style: Abandoning his polished, sophisticated prose, he wrote in an approximation of a "Broadway" dialect; this caused at least as much outrage as his astringent critical judgments. Indeed, this choice of dialect seems to have been a mistake. As dialect, it is not accurate, and its use seems patronizing, even if that was not Ervine's intent.

After his return to London, Ervine served for three years as professor of dramatic literature for the Royal Society of Literature. His later plays, written after he left Ireland, are less serious than his early work. These later plays, written for a British audience, are sophisticated comedies of manners that rely on wit and topicality for their very considerable effect. Ervine's biographical subjects included men of letters such as Shaw and Wilde; William Booth, founder and General of the Salvation Army; and Lord Craigavon, the first prime minister of Ulster. His biographies reflect his literary, ethical, and political interests; they are partisan rather than objective, polemical rather than scholarly.

With the production of *William John Mawhinney* in 1940, Ervine renewed his association with the Abbey Theatre; one of his next plays, *Friends and Relations*, was produced at the Abbey Theatre in 1941. These were the last of Ervine's works to premiere at the Abbey Theatre, however, and in 1957, Ervine completed his theatrical career with the production of *Esperanza*.

Ervine died in 1971, at the age of eighty-seven, in a nursing home in Sussex.

Analysis

St. John Ervine's early Irish plays are his finest, displaying the strengths characteristic of his best work in all genres. *Mixed Marriage, Jane Clegg, John Ferguson*, and *The Ship* are uniformly serious in plot and theme, realistic in subject matter, and economical in structure. Ervine's virtues as a playwright are traditional ones; each play has a single, unified plot and an unambiguous, uncomplicated theme. Each play displays great economy of construction and a modest level of aspiration, and within this deliberately simple, unassuming framework, it succeeds because of certain very real strengths of structure and characterization.

In his drama criticism, Ervine's touchstone is economy. In every important way, the early plays illustrate that Ervine believed in and followed his own theory: Economy is not a negative value of limiting, cutting, and leaving out; it is, rather, a positive principle. Good theater, to Ervine, is that which exhibits restraint and simplicity in cast size, subject matter, plot line, dialogue, and characterization.

The casts, for example, are uniformly small. *John Ferguson* has the largest cast; there are eleven characters. *Jane Clegg* has seven; *The Ship*, eight; and *Mixed Marriage*, six. There are simply no minor characters whose dramatic function may be described as merely decorative. Every character is important and necessary to the development of the action of the play.

The action of each play is also dictated in part by Ervine's rule of economy. On a superficial level, his plays are devoid of luxuries such as tableau scenes, offstage voices, and unnecessary dramatic business. There is a minimum of exposition; for the most part, each play consists only of those events which are seen by the audience. The exposition in *John Ferguson*, for example, is limited to the information that the Fergusons are going to lose their farm unless they manage to pay the mortgage; the audience learns of the successive trials of John Ferguson's faith in a just God as Ferguson himself experiences them. The exposition in *Jane Clegg* is limited to the information that Henry Clegg has been unfaithful to his wife in the past. This immediacy of action is present in all the early plays. Nothing *has* happened; everything happens onstage during the course of the play.

The plays are all limited to a single plot, which is usually a familiar one and which is uniformly serious. Each of the long plays consists of a single story whose content is that of everyday life. *Jane Clegg* deals with the failure of a marriage, *John Ferguson* with the loss of a farm and the destruction of a family through violence. *The Ship* is a study of the lack of communication between a strong-willed father and his son. *Mixed Marriage* deals with the public forces which destroy the private romance of a Protestant boy and a Catholic girl. The stories are familiar ones, and Ervine does not alter his material so that it appears to be anything other than what it essentially is—newspaper realism, known territory to everyone. At the same time, there is always a single sustained idea which informs and illuminates the play.

The dialogue of Ervine's plays also exhibits his characteristic economy. The language of all the early plays is simple and easily understood and has as its function the furthering of the plot and the revelation of character. Dialogue, Ervine believed, should sound artlessly natural but should actually be an artful construct. None of Ervine's characters chatters aimlessly; no one repeats himself or leaves a sentence or thought unfinished. Ervine eliminates those parts of ordinary talk which would produce conversation rather than dialogue. Even when his characters are supposed to be merely making conversation, there is no excess. Each seemingly meaningless sentence is working to establish character. Again, the principle of economy is used as a positive force to shape an element of Ervine's plays.

The characters in Ervine's plays are, like his plots, familiar and instantly recognizable types, yet they are also extremely believable and vital. The character of Jane Clegg is strong and able to bear suffering; Rainey of *Mixed Marriage* and John Thurlow of *The Ship* are egotists. In each character, there is a single, prevailing element of personality, and each character becomes real and believable within his own "humor." The characters are drawn with little internal complexity; they are not cowardly *and* brave, but rather cowardly *or* brave. Like his dialogue, Ervine's characters appear to be natural but are in fact artful constructs.

One can appreciate Ervine's art most fully by examining the elements of plot and character in his early plays. In general, the plot is the weakest element of each play. All the plays have plots associated with melodrama. *John Ferguson* is the story of a family whose farm is lost to the evil landlord who forecloses, rapes the daughter, and is murdered by the son. *Jane Clegg* is the story of the strong, long-suffering wife who holds her family together while her husband loses her money, embezzles company funds, and finally runs away with a younger woman. *Mixed Marriage* deals with young lovers surrounded by the chaos of a strike which rapidly becomes a religious war; ultimately, the lovers are destroyed by the religious bigotry of the Protestant father. *The Ship* is the story of a strong-willed father who builds a ship that "God couldn't sink" and forces his son to sail on her maiden voyage. The son, who has refused to enter the family business, dies when the ship is sunk after colliding with an iceberg. The plots are both melodramatic and highly conventional; there are no surprising turns, no innovative twists in the action.

An important technique that Ervine used to control the response of the audience is one that is closely related to satire. Within the structure of the plot, there is always an explicit norm with which the audience can identify. The plots of the early plays make, in some way, an attack on stupidity, and there is usually a character who explicitly represents the sane, moral position of playwright and audience. Jane Clegg, John Ferguson, Old Mrs. Thurlow, and Mrs. Rainey are articulate spokespersons for the standards of good sense and morality. One recognizes the standard they offer and judges the other characters and the plot development by this explicit norm.

The plots of the four plays hinge upon dramatic irony of the simplest, most basic sort. John Ferguson's family is destroyed because his brother forgot to mail the money that would have saved the farm; Jack Thurlow dies because his father asks him to sail with the ship just this once. John Rainey loses his children because his religious prejudice is stronger than his desire to unite the Protestant and Catholic strikers.

Although the plots of these plays are simple and melodramatic, this is not a serious weakness in Ervine's art. Perhaps a playwright cannot create great drama from this material, but he can create great theater. Ervine asks his audience to respond in a rather uncomplicated, unsophisticated manner; he manages to get an audience, conditioned to dismiss plots of this nature as slight and hackneyed, to believe implicitly in his stories. The audience understands the familiar, unambiguous plots and themes, applauds the hero and hisses the villain, but not with the self-conscious condescension that one would bring to minstrel-show melodrama. The audience reacts in an unsophisticated way to the plays, but it reacts sincerely.

In large part, this response can be attributed to the vitality of Ervine's characters. His best characters are universal types: The audience recognizes the villainous landlord or the foolish, irritating mother-in-law with a shock of pleasure. Each character is also, within his or her type, absolutely individual.

Ervine is particularly good with certain types of characters. His villains are all lifelike and effective. They are of two types: The first is the unpleasant little vermin, such as Jimmy Caesar in *John Ferguson*; Henry Clegg and the racing tout, Munce, in *Jane Clegg*; and Captain Cornelius in *The Ship*. The second type is the monster of evil, such as Witherow in *John Ferguson*. The villain Witherow has no redeeming qualities; he is unalterably evil. He is a brilliantly drawn one-dimensional character; the audience hates him and is appeased by his death.

Jimmy Caesar and the other little villains are villainous because they are weak and mean-spirited. They are more satisfactory characters than is Witherow because they are more complex, and the audience is able to despise them as well as hate them. They are all incapable of anything as large and important as a foreclosure or a rape. Their villainies are secret and unsavory; they are all cowards. Captain Cornelius is willing to accept money from John Thurlow in return for ruining Jack's farm; Munce is quite willing to ruin lives to get his money from Henry Clegg; Henry himself leaves his wife, children, and mother penniless for another woman and cannot understand why no one is terribly sorry to see him go. Jimmy Caesar, the most vividly drawn of the weak villains, is the unsavory suitor of Hannah Ferguson; he grovels at Witherow's feet, nauseates Hannah when he tries to kiss her, goes home to bed when he is supposedly avenging her honor, eats a hearty breakfast while he confesses his cowardice, and offers to marry Hannah even though her rape has made her "unworthy" of him.

In Mrs. Rainey, Old Mrs. Thurlow, and John Ferguson, Ervine creates strong, sympathetic moral characters. John Ferguson, for example, is uniformly good without being unrealistic. He is devout, gentle, and forgiving, yet, unlike many virtuous characters, absolutely convincing. His moments of doubt are canceled by his monumental Christian goodness and faith. He is a truly decent man who keeps his faith in a just God even as he mourns his ruined son and daughter. Like John Ferguson, Mrs. Rainey in *Mixed Marriage* is consistently good, tender and protective toward her sons, sensible and tolerant toward Michael O'Hara, their Catholic friend, and gentle with Nora, Hugh's girlfriend; most important, she manages to love her husband even though she has no respect for him and disapproves of his tenaciously held prejudices. Mrs. Rainey, Old Mrs. Thurlow, and John Ferguson are all voices of sanity in situations which have suddenly gone insane. Mrs. Rainey pleads for religious tolerance in the middle of a religious war; John Ferguson tries to love and protect the man who has taken his farm and raped his daughter; Old Mrs. Thurlow of *The Ship* tries to reconcile her son and grandson, and when Jack dies in his father's place, she comforts and encourages John Thurlow to continue to live with unchanged goals even though she believes him to be wrong.

St. John Ervine's early plays are good plays, strong and believable in their economy and in characters who force the viewer to accept plots that have become clichés. The deliberate simplicity of construction, the unity of tone and theme, the absolutely vital characters, make Ervine an important playwright. His plays are not complex or difficult to understand; their value lies precisely in their accessibility and believability.

Other major works

NOVELS: *Francis Place, the Tailor of Charing Cross*, 1912; *Mrs. Martin's Man*, 1914; *Alice and a Family*, 1915; *The Foolish Lovers*, 1920; *The First Mrs. Fraser*, 1931 (novelization of his play); *Private Enterprise*, 1948.

NONFICTION: *The Organized Theatre: A Plea in Civics*, 1924; *Parnell*, 1925; *How to Write a Play*, 1928; *God's Soldier: General William Booth*, 1934; *The Christian and the New Morality*, 1940; *Oscar Wilde*, 1951; *Bernard Shaw: His Life, Work and Friends*, 1956.

Bibliography

Bell, Sam Hanna. *The Theatre in Ulster.* Dublin: Gill and Macmillan, 1972. Bell considers Ervine as an Ulster dramatist and compares his work with that of other playwrights of his generation from Northern Ireland. Discusses briefly productions of Ervine's works and mentions their main social and cultural features, though the brevity of this study's overview limits discussion.

Cronin, John. Introduction to *Selected Plays of St. John Ervine.* Washington, D.C.: Catholic University of America Press, 1988. Contains *Mixed Marriage, Jane Clegg, John Ferguson, Boyd's Shop,* and *Friends and Relations.* The introduction provides biographical information and establishes a cultural context for Ervine's work. Includes extracts from Ervine's dramaturgical writings and a bibliography of Ervine's dramatic and numerous other works.

Hogan, Robert, and Richard Burnham. *The Art of the Amateur, 1916-1920.* Atlantic Highlands, N.J.: Humanities Press, 1984. Contains a considerable amount of information regarding the various levels of Ervine's participation in contemporary Irish theatrical affairs. Cites his contributions to public debate and evaluates his theatrical works. The study's documentary approach and elaborate scholarly apparatus provide a detailed context for an assessment of Ervine's plays.

Hunt, Hugh. *The Abbey: Ireland's National Theatre, 1904-1978.* New York: Columbia University Press, 1979. This historical narrative deals in passing with Ervine's plays. Provides a more detailed description of the playwright's sojourn as manager of the Abbey Theatre and assesses its effects. Includes a full list of productions at the Abbey from the theater's foundation, facilitating a preliminary chronology of Ervine's dramatic career there.

Maxwell, D. E. S. *A Critical History of Modern Irish Drama, 1891-1980.* Cambridge, England: Cambridge University Press, 1984. Locates Ervine's drama in the context of developments in realism in the Irish theater and provides a critical analysis of his most noteworthy plays. Draws attention to the Ulster origins of much of Ervine's dramatic material. Contains a bibliography and a chronology of Irish theater.

Elizabeth Buckmaster
(Updated by *George O'Brien*)

SIR GEORGE ETHEREGE

Born: Maidenhead(?), England; c. 1635
Died: Paris(?), France; c. May 10, 1691

Principal drama

The Comical Revenge: Or, Love in a Tub, pr., pb. 1664; *She Would if She Could*, pr., pb. 1668; *The Man of Mode: Or, Sir Fopling Flutter*, pr., pb. 1676.

Other literary forms

In addition to his drama, Sir George Etherege wrote poetry, collected and published posthumously in *Poems* (1963). His correspondence is collected in *The Letterbook of Sir George Etherege* (1928) and *Letters of Sir George Etherege* (1973).

Achievements

In the amazingly vital and varied drama that developed, flourished, and faded in London within a few decades after the restoration of Charles II to the throne in 1660, the most important type was the so-called comedy of manners. The comedy of manners was characterized by strong contemporary realism, by resolution of the main plot in marriage, and by pairs of characters arranged in a hierarchy of wit, from the most witty down to the most foolish. In the Restoration drama, wit is determined in part by the ability of individuals to get their own way and in part by their social grace, best exemplified in the witty (meaning comic, ingenious, and psychologically astute) verbal duels with which the plays abound. It was Etherege's achievement to develop and define this distinctive Restoration form in *The Comical Revenge* and *She Would if She Could* and to bring it to full maturity in *The Man of Mode*.

Biography

Sir George Etherege's life resembled those of the wits, courtiers, and rakes who populated his plays. When he was born, his father had a small place at Court. In 1644, during the Civil War, when the queen escaped to France, Etherege's father followed her into exile, where he died in 1650. Etherege himself was probably reared by his grandfather in England, obtaining along the way a good education and an excellent knowledge of French. In 1654, he was appointed a clerk to George Goswold, an attorney at Beaconsfield. In 1668, *The Comical Revenge*, Etherege's first play, was performed at Lincoln's Inn Fields. It was well received, and Etherege's reputation was at once established. His next play, *She Would if She Could*, was performed at Lincoln's Inn Fields in 1668; although a better play than the first, it was poorly rehearsed and badly performed, and it fared very poorly. By this time, Etherege was a member of the circle of courtiers and wits that included Sir Charles Sedley and the Earl of Rochester. He was made a Gentleman of the Privy Chamber and went, as secretary to the ambassador, to Constantinople. Etherege returned to London in 1671, and for the next few years he, along with the Earl of Rochester, was mixed up in several wild and rather unsavory scrapes, resulting in at least one death.

In 1676, *The Man of Mode* was performed at the Duke's Theatre in Dorset Garden. Remembering his earlier failure, Etherege was careful to have a first-class performance, with the top actors of the period playing the principal parts, particularly with Thomas Betterton, the most famous actor of his time, taking the role of Dorimant. This major play was, as it deserved to be, an enormous success. During this period, Etherege was knighted and then married a rich old widow, daughter of a London merchant. By 1683, he was rapidly squandering his wife's wealth on cards and dice at Locket's, a popular coffeehouse. He was offered a minor diplomatic post, under King James II, at the Diet of the Holy Roman Empire in Regensburg, Bavaria. He gladly accepted the appointment, possibly escaping heavy gambling debts in London and certainly leaving his unloved wife behind. He outraged and antagonized the staid and pompous German ministers there with his informal behavior. During this period, he carried on a large correspondence. Almost four hundred letters have been preserved, which give the best existing portrait of the life and thoughts of a Restoration playwright and wit. When James II was deposed in 1689, Etherege left his post to try to join him in France. Etherege died, possibly first converting to Roman Catholicism, in 1691.

Analysis

Sir George Etherege's first play, *The Comical Revenge*, has no discernible main plot. Rather, it has four more or less unconnected subplots. Three of the plots are derivative of earlier drama; the fourth constitutes Etherege's real contribution to dramatic form. The first of the derivative plots is the "heroic" plot, based no doubt on the romantic plays of Francis Beaumont and John Fletcher (still very popular during this period) and of Sir William Davenant. When the characters of this plot, with their characteristically romantic names, come onstage, the play's usual prose dialogue shifts to rhyming verse. The action in this subplot revolves around highly stylized conflicts between love and honor. Graciana and Lord Beaufort are madly in love; by mischance, however, Graciana's brother has told his best friend, Colonel Bruce, that Graciana will marry him. Colonel Bruce does not care particularly about Graciana, whom he has not met, but would like to be connected to the family of his best friend. Secretly, Graciana's sister Aurelia is madly in love with Bruce, but out of honor cannot tell him. When Colonel Bruce discovers that Beaufort might be his rival for

Graciana, he fights a duel with him, is disarmed, but is magnanimously given his life by Beaufort. Not to be outdone in honor, Bruce falls on his sword. As he lies grievously wounded, Graciana feels honor-bound to pretend to Beaufort that she never loved him but only led him on to test Bruce's love for her. She pledges to Bruce that if he survives she will marry him; if he dies, she will remain forever a virgin. At the last minute, everybody accidentally overhears everybody else confessing his and her true thoughts, all are overcome by how honorable all the rest are, and the right couples get together and live happily ever after.

The second plot is low farcical comedy of a kind to delight those who guffaw at dialect jokes and pratfalls. The humor is meant to come in part from the nearly unintelligible French accent of the servant, Dufoy ("Begar me vil havé de revengé"), and in part from his situation. He looks pale and unhealthy, and when people ask the cause, he claims he is languishing from unrequited love for Betty, a waiting woman. Actually, it soon comes out, he is languishing from a venereal disease. Betty, highly indignant when she discovers that he has been pretending to love her, locks him up in a washtub (the "comical revenge," or "love in a tub" of the title), providing opportunities for various farcical jokes. In the "happy ending," it appears that Dufoy and Betty actually *are* to get married. It is difficult to guess how boisterously audiences may have responded to this kind of comedy.

The third plot seems to derive from the comedy of Ben Jonson, or perhaps of Thomas Middleton. It involves Sir Nicholas Cully, who, as his name suggests, is a gull waiting to be swindled. He falls into the clutches of Wheadle and Palmer, two con artists; thinking all the time that he is the one who is doing the swindling, Cully gets the treatment he deserves. What separates this plot from the first two is its astonishing, almost documentary realism: The language of the street plays against the absurdly elevated "torments" and "despair" of the heroic scenes and the theatrically conventional burlesque French accent of Dufoy. For example, Wheadle and Palmer, having maneuvered Cully into a tavern to play cards, want to shift from the public table where they are seated to a back-room table, where they can cheat their victim in private. Finding a pretext for this move, one of them says, "this table is so wet, there's no playing upon it." That may be the first time in the history of the drama that a character mentions something so homely and realistic as the wetness of a table that has had several glasses and bottles sitting on it.

The fourth plot, which in the play gets no more emphasis than the other three, constitutes Etherege's major contribution to Restoration drama and was to become the central plot of his two comedies to follow. It involves Sir Frederick Frollick, a young rake and gallant and wit about town. Audiences were no doubt accustomed to the nonspecific, timeless settings of William Shakespeare, to the remote and imaginary settings of the romantic plays of Beaumont and Fletcher. Suddenly, Sir Frederick walks in off the very London streets the playgoers themselves have just quitted to see this play. The language he speaks is their language; the class to which he belongs is theirs. His conversation is topical. He is indeed a sad young rake, keeping his wench, intriguing with dozens of women, drinking, carousing, fighting, breaking windows, and otherwise tearing about. He is also, at least to a degree, witty, fashionable, and genteel. As the wealthy widow he is chasing throughout the play admits, he is "the prettiest, wittiest, wildest gentleman about the town." Having gone through his fortune, he must court and wed the widow to mend his estate, as Etherege himself was to do a few years later.

The play as a whole is not memorable. Except for the moments of fine realism in the swindling scenes, the motivation for actions and the conflicts to be overcome are all weakly contrived. The four plots are but faintly connected. At the end, all the players—servants, whores, swindlers, rakes, and romantic lovers—are improbably brought onstage together in a mass marriage ceremony. With the exception of this unlikely event, they could as easily have been in separate plays.

Still, the play contained important innovations, and Etherege, shrewdly observing his audience, must have seen their delight and response to his contemporary rake speaking their language, frequenting the same places of pleasure as they did. He must also have recognized his facility in rendering such a character (so like himself) and his witty language. He made such characters the center of his subsequent plays, wisely phasing out the other subplots or, rather, disguising, shifting, and transforming them until they were no longer recognizable, serving instead as underpinnings to his main plot.

Etherege's second play, *She Would if She Could*, is a considerable refinement upon *The Comical Revenge*. The structure is clearer, simpler, the actions more logically motivated. Three plotlines are discernible, but one of these is clearly the major plot, and the two minor plots are closely integrated with it, supporting its actions and commenting on it thematically. Most important, in the play as a whole, the contrast between the Truewit and the Witwoud, or would-be wit, has become central, setting the pattern for the great comedies of manners of the period.

The Witwouds are at the center of the two minor plots. In one subplot, Sir Oliver Cockwood is a "country knight." In the social geography of the Restoration stage, the courtiers, rakes, and the stylish and witty women all live in the "town," the fashionable West End of London. The "city" is the commercial part of London, where the "cits," the much despised middle class, live. Worst of all, however, is the country. For the wits, the chief pleasures in life were found in association with town and court: the coffeehouses, the playhouses, the pleasure resorts, the fashionable clothing. The severest penance, therefore, would be to live in the country, where every-thing is several years out of date, where the only diversion is going for long walks. Witty young people forced to live in the country by cruel parents who do not trust them among the seductions of London are justified in using any means to escape to the town. Older people from the country are automatically assumed to be foolish and out of fashion.

Sir Oliver Cockwood is typical of the country knights. His name, to begin with, is appropriate (the "wood" having the sense of "would-be"), since his annoyed wife charges that he is impotent. If he stayed in the country, got drunk every night, and hunted foxes during the day, no one would object to him. His fault is that he has come to town to spark it like a young rake and to boast of all of his amorous adventures. He spends most of his time running away from his wife to make ineffectual dates with prostitutes. He becomes a comic butt because of his pretensions to being a man of honor (that is, a duelist and a lover) when he is actually timid and impotent.

In the other subplot, his wife, Lady Cockwood, is equally well named, though with an opposite signification. She tries to make assignations with any young man who will look at her. The problem is that she also wants to maintain her reputation for honor and virtue. She becomes a comic butt because of her pretensions to being modest and chaste, when it is obvious to everyone that she would readily be unchaste if she could. Interestingly, Lady Cockwood's language is a burlesqued echo of the heroic or romantic scenes of *The Comical Revenge*. Her dialogue is filled with such words as "honor," "ruined," "undone," "betrayed," and "false," but with the mean-ings comically reversed. If a young rake fails to keep his assignation with her, he is "wicked." If he finally does show up to commit adultery with her, "truly he is a person of much worth and honor."

The subplots in which these foolish persons partake, by giving examples of Witwouds—failed Truewits—provide a backdrop against which the Truewits of the main plot can be measured. These Truewits are the young men Courtall and Freeman and the young women Gatty and Ariana. The young men are considerable refinements upon Sir Frederick Frollick of *The Comical Revenge*. For example, Frollick's idea of courtship is to get drunk and go to his lady's window in the wee hours of the morning to shout out ribald suggestions to her. He marries at the end a wealthy widow, behavior that Etherege himself was not above. Courtall is above it. He is much more self-assured than Frollick and has his drives, emotions, and true feelings absolutely under control—an important sign of the Truewit. Losing con-trol, however, and thus putting himself at the mercy of others, is the un-mistakable sign of the Witwoud. Courtall needs to marry a rich heiress but will not consider a widow. His wife, in addition to being rich, must also be young, beautiful, as witty as he, and untouched by other men.

Of particular interest in this play are the roles of the female characters. Lady Cockwood is an archetypal character—the lustful woman—who has appeared in both comedy and tragedy from the classical drama onward. Etherege, however, makes specific Restoration uses of her. She is made comic by her pretension to heroic virtue and by the fact that she has so little control of her emotions that she gives herself away at every word. By the lights of the Restoration society, she is not wrong in wishing to have a reputation for chastity, for without such a reputation a woman was lost (with the exception of mistresses of high royalty). At the same time, she was not wrong to possess sexual desire, for women, in this realistic society, were allowed to have at least moderate appetites. She was wrong, and therefore comic, in her extreme pretension of virtue, in her extreme libidinousness, and in her consequent inability to control herself. Control of self was highly valued in Restoration theater because only through self-control, so it was believed, could one's external world be controlled. The world of Restoration theater is one in which a person must control himself or be controlled. Courtall, for example, by pretending to be interested in her, used Lady Cockwood in order to gain access to Gatty and Ariana, who are staying in her house, and then uses her desire to save her reputation to fend her off. He fends her off, interestingly, because her overeagerness has rendered her undesirable.

Gatty and Ariana represent the feminine witty ideal. Envious of the men for their freedom (which the women cannot have, for reputation is important), they decide, while resolving "to be mighty honest" to have as much fun as circumstances will allow. They put on masks (very popular at the time) to disguise their identities, and go strolling in the fashionable Mulberry Garden in hopes of flirting innocently with some handsome and witty men. Though the men whom they encounter (Courtall and Freeman) are tremendously attractive to them, the women easily fend them off with witty conversation and a dissembling of their emotions. This response does not mean that they lack emotions, for in private they admit to each other how much the men tempt them. As Gatty says to Ariana: "I hate to dissemble when I need not. 'Twould look as affected in us to be reserved now we're alone as for a player to maintain the character she acts in the tiring [dressing] room." The scene is in direct contrast with the scene in which Lady Cockwood sends out her maid to pimp for her, and then scolds her (even though they are in private) for doing so.

She Would if She Could, in short, is a didactic play, suggesting which emotions, which pretenses, which modes of behavior are proper—that is, witty—and which are not. The modern theatergoer, losing sight of this and responding to the play as simply a realistic social document, can misinterpret it in certain ways, seeing cruelty, for example, where a Restoration theatergoer would see a didactic point being made.

The finest thing of all in *She Would if She Could* is the witty love dialogue between Courtall and Freeman and the two women. Their first encounter is quite delightful. The girls, in their masks, are strolling through the Mulberry Garden. When Courtall and Freeman see them, they immediately set out after them, planning to engage them in witty repartee, but the women, who have been brought up in the country, are such swift walkers that the men are soon panting and puffing, quite unable to overtake them. Freeman says, "Whatever faults they have, they cannot be broken-winded."

When the men finally do catch up, the women are equally nimble verbally. When the men insist on kissing their hands, Ariana says, "Well, I am not the first unfortunate woman that has been forced to give her hand where she never intends to bestow her heart." They part, agreeing to meet again the next day, each side immensely pleased with the other (though of course the women have not admitted their feelings). The jealous Lady Cockwood, hoping to win the two men for herself, starts a rumor that the men have spoken slightingly of Gatty's and Ariana's honor. The next time Gatty and Ariana meet with the innocent and unsuspecting men, their witty banter suddenly has real bite and sting to it. The men, puzzled by the shift in tone, scarcely know how to reply. The dialogue is wonderfully witty; at the same time, it is subtly and dramatically revelatory of the inner states of the characters.

Etherege's last play, *The Man of Mode*, is in every respect a major work and remains the central document of Restoration comedy. The brilliant opening act is so relaxed and casual as to seem like a slice of life rather than the first act of a tightly constructed play. A minor poet of the time even alluded to Etherege as "one that does presume to say,/ A plot's too gross for any play." Such an impression is deceptive, however, for every word in the first act carefully defines characters and sets up the complex chain of events to follow. On the surface, the first act is a very naturalistic presentation of Dorimant (whose name suggests "the gift of love") in the morning. He is composing a letter to his current mistress, whose suggestive name is Loveit. When his friend Medley drops in on him, it emerges in conversation between them that he is tired of Loveit and wants to break off with her so he can begin with a new girl, Bellinda. He plans to use Bellinda in his plot to break with Loveit, who is passionately jealous; Bellinda will call on her just before Dorimant is expected to arrive, and will insinuate that Dorimant has been seeing someone else. Dorimant will walk in, and Loveit, who has no control of her emotions, will fall on him in a passion; he will then instantly break with her and stalk out. While Dorimant is recounting his plot to Medley, an old woman selling fruit arrives at his door. She is, in addition, a bawd who keeps a watchful eye out for young women in whom young men might be interested. She brings information to Dorimant that an extremely beautiful and wealthy heiress has come to town and has seen Dorimant and is attracted to him. The woman's name is Harriet, and she has been brought to town from the country by her mother, Lady Woodvill. Dorimant immediately begins plotting to get to know her. Young Bellair, another friend, drops in, and Medley and Dorimant begin teasing him about his coming marriage to Emilia. Marriage, to the young rakes, is nearly equivalent to suicide, as it means the end of their bachelor freedom and a limitation on their openly chasing after new mistresses. Young Bellair is in love and takes their teasing lightly. Then they discuss Sir Fopling Flutter, newly arrived in town from a long stay in Paris. Fopling wants desperately to be a true-wit, but he is in every way the opposite of Dorimant. Where Dorimant dresses well, Fopling dresses extravagantly. Where Dorimant has several affairs, Fopling strives only for the reputation of having several affairs. Where Dorimant is casually witty and literate, Fopling works hard to achieve these graces, even affecting a French accent (the last lingering echo of Dufoy in *The Comical Revenge*) to let everyone know he has been abroad. Dorimant decides to use him in his plot to break with Loveit: He will pretend to be jealous himself, and charge her with chasing after Fopling.

At this point, a messenger calls Young Bellair outside the room, and while he is out, Dorimant confesses to Medley that he has encouraged Young Bellair to marry Emilia. Dorimant has tried in the past to seduce her, with no luck. He thinks that once she is married and no longer needs to worry about her maidenhood, she will be more accessible to him. Young Bellair comes back in with the news that his father, Old Bellair, is in town. The father, not knowing anything about Emilia, has conspired with Lady Woodvill to arrange a marriage between Young Bellair and Harriet. If Young Bellair does not agree to the marriage, he will lose his inheritance. Young Bellair leaves in distress. As a last bit of business in the act, before Dorimant and Medley go off to dine, Dorimant receives a note from a former girlfriend fallen on hard times and sends her some money.

No brief summary can hope to render the quality of this act, one of the finest things in Restoration drama. The witty repartee, the different levels of language, the naturalness, all make it a virtuoso performance, but one should not lose sight of the function of the act in terms of the unfolding action of the play. First, it has introduced Dorimant, the main character. He is witty, relaxed, capable of dealing with all social classes on their own terms, shamefully indulgent of his servants, most of whom have not yet got out of bed by the end of the act. At the same time, he is the supreme gallant, with, as Medley says of him, "more mistresses now depending" than the most eminent lawyer in England has cases. The audience sees abundant proof of this. In the course of one morning, he is forming plans to cast off one mistress, Loveit, as he begins to close with a new one, Bellinda, and tries to get Emilia married off in hopes that matrimony will make her more vulnerable to him. At the same time, he is already beginning to think ahead to Harriet, whom he has not even met, and, at last, sends money to a girlfriend from sometime in the past. The audience also gets an insight into Dorimant's modus operandi. He thinks in terms of power plays and manipulation. People, to him, are to be used: He employs the fruiterer to bring him information of new beauties come to town; he uses his mistress-to-be to help him break off with Loveit; he uses Young Bellair to make Emilia more accessible; he plans to use Fopling also in his plot to rid himself of Loveit. He states his attitude more baldly in a later scene: "You mistake the use of fools, they are designed for properties and not for friends." In this respect, almost all are fools to Dorimant.

In addition to Dorimant, the first act introduces the audience to two other major characters, Medley and Young Bellair, and gives capsule profiles to prepare the audience in advance for seeing the other important characters: Loveit, Fopling, Old Bellair, Lady Woodvill, and Harriet. Finally, the groundwork is laid for the main action of the play, Dorimant's pursuit of Harriet, and for the four subplots: Dorimant's breaking off with Loveit; his coming to terms with his new mistress, Bellinda; Young Bellair's attempt to marry the woman he loves without being disinherited; and the fun they will all have with the foolish Sir Fopling Flutter, especially when Dorimant tries to foist him off on Loveit.

The play now unrolls quickly. Old Bellair meets Emilia and, not knowing she is his son's fiancée, begins chasing her himself. She humors him in his infatuation, hoping it will help later when she confesses her love for his son. In the meantime, Young Bellair has met Harriet. Harriet has no intention of marrying him but has only pretended to go along with the match as an excuse to get out of the country and come to London. She and Young Bellair act out a courtship for the sake of their parents, in order to buy time. At the proper moment, Young Bellair and Emilia sneak off and get married. They fall on their knees before Old Bellair, and he is prevailed upon to give them his blessing. He cannot say his son has made a bad choice, since it was the choice he was thinking of making himself. In the meantime, Dorimant's plans go off almost but not quite perfectly. Loveit rages at him jealously, and he storms off, charging her with chasing after Fopling. Bellinda is timid but at last submits to a meeting with him in his room, but Loveit is suspicious and almost catches Bellinda in the act, so that Bellinda would have lost her reputation on her very first fall from grace. She cleverly talks her way out of being discovered but vows never to take such a chance again. Dorimant, though charging Loveit with receiving Fopling's advances (as an excuse for dropping her), still wants her to spurn Fopling publicly, thus showing that he holds complete power even over a cast-off mistress. He even brings Medley along to be a witness of Fopling's discomfiture. Loveit, however, realizing that Dorimant is using her, greets Fopling with open arms and walks off with him. Medley jibes: "Would you had brought some more of your friends, Dorimant, to have been witnesses of Sir Fopling's disgrace and your triumph." Dorimant begs Medley not to tell everyone for a few days, to give him a chance to make amends. He wants his reputation as a perfect manipulator of women to remain intact. In the meantime, Dorimant has met Harriet, and they have a duel of brilliant repartee, almost like the love song of two wary but amorous birds of prey. The final scene shows Dorimant in high gear, running from woman to woman, keeping all bridges unburned. First, he convinces Loveit that he is courting Harriet only for her fortune, as he has gone through his own inheritance, and that he will come back to her as soon as he can. She is sufficiently satisfied to snub Fopling publicly the next time he enters—and Medley declares Dorimant's reputation clear. Dorimant convinces Bellinda that she should take another chance with him, keeps his lines of communication open with Emilia, and gains permission from Lady Woodvill to pay his court to Harriet. A marriage seems in the offing, but it has not happened by the end of the play, and Dorimant is still free to go in any direction he chooses.

It is a play, then, in which a vain, arrogant man, renowned for his deceptions, seductions, cruel manipulations, and constant infidelities, has by the end achieved the admiration of all the men, has all the women at his beck, and has the prospect of a rich, witty, beautiful young girl's hand in marriage. It may seem a considerable leap to maintain that *The Man of Mode* is a didactic play (even liberated modern audiences have difficulty with the morality of the play), but such it is. Although courtship is at the center of Restoration drama, *The Man of Mode* and similar masterpieces of the period are not romantic works; on the contrary, they are cynically realistic. The plays abound with cautionary examples of bad marriages—marriages inappropriately arranged by parents, resulting in spouses who detest each other, are rude to each other in public, and betray each other at every chance—or, at the other extreme, "love" matches in which neither partner has any money, condemned to sink into sordidness. The appropriate marriage is one in which at least one of the partners has enough money to make them both comfortable for life (since a gentleman, by definition, does not work for a living) and the partners are so perfectly matched in wit and attractiveness that they can continue to be interesting and exciting to each other even after the novelty of the chase is over. It is a serious and realistic business, and a misstep has the lifetime repercussion of an unhappy marriage. That is why this drama can be so ruthless and competitive. The stakes are high. The good-natured, trusting person is the one who will be exploited; the shrewd, perceptive person has the best chance of winning.

Since accurate judgment of one's partner is of the utmost importance in this dangerous game, part of the didactic purpose of the play is to serve as a sort of field guide to help the audience tell true wit from would-be wit—and, of course, through poking fun at the fools and fops, to laugh members of the audience out of any foolishness or foppery they may have acquired. With these practical purposes in mind, the Restoration comedy of manners, by its end, will have arranged the characters into a hierarchy from the most witty—in other words, most desirable (if most dangerous)—down to the least witty (or most to be reviled and mocked).

An examination of the hierarchy of wit in *The Man of Mode* will demonstrate how complex and subtle this ranking can be. The characters are divided, first, into young characters and old characters, and the audience is asked to judge each character according to the behavior appropriate to his or her station in life. Dorimant is obviously at the top of the pecking order among the young men. He is the cleverest and wittiest in speech, he dresses in perfect taste, he is the most perceptive in judging the motives and the weaknesses of others yet the most astute in concealing his own. Another essential quality is his "malice." His pleasure in manipulating others and triumphing over them—which can seem so ugly to modern audiences—is the very quality that gives him the competitive edge over others.

Young Bellair is next in the pecking order. He is attractive and clever, and some modern audiences prefer him to Dorimant. That is to miss the point. In Dorimant's accurate summation: "He's handsome, well-bred, and by much the most tolerable of all the young men that do not abound in wit." Young Bellair's crippling defect is that he has not as much malice as Dorimant, so he does not disguise his emotions, being genuinely in love with Emilia. Because of his lack of malice, he is unsuspicious of malice in others, and Dorimant, pretending friendship, is using him. In the play's most cruel—if most realistic and psychologically astute—line, Dorimant says that, since he has been unable to seduce Emilia, he is encouraging the marriage between her and Young Bellair because "I have known many women make a difficulty of losing a maidenhead, who have afterwards made none of making a cuckold."

Sir Fopling Flutter obviously finishes last. With his Frenchified language and excessively fashionable clothing, he is the laughingstock of the town. He attempts to maintain a reputation as a lover, but all the characters easily see through him, and correctly so, for underneath, he appears to be all but sexless. Dorimant has an easy time making Fopling a tool in his plot to cast off Loveit.

Harriet is at the top of the pecking order of the young women. She is the wittiest in dialogue, the most handsomely yet naturally dressed, and, as the characters admiringly point out, she is as full of malice—of pleasure in using and abusing others—as Dorimant. Although she has been described and discussed throughout the play, Etherege, for dramatic effect, does not allow her to appear onstage until the third act. That act is a replay of the first act, as Harriet rises in the morning, the scene almost point for point paralleling the first, to underline what an even and perfect match Dorimant and Harriet are. She is constantly on guard against him, and so she is the only female who can resist him, meaning, at the end, the only one who might possibly get him in marriage.

Emilia, Young Bellair's fiancée, is next in line. Like Young Bellair, her single failing is that she has not enough malice, and for that reason, she is not suspicious enough of it in others. Like Young Bellair, she is sufficiently clever to make use of Old Bellair and Lady Woodvill to get them into a position to agree to the marriage between her and Young Bellair, but again like Young Bellair, she is no match for Dorimant. She is second in the pecking order because, by play's end, she still has not been seduced by Dorimant, but she is clearly in danger. When Bellinda tries to warn her that Dorimant is not to be trusted, she innocently disputes this, saying he is a completely good, trustworthy man—thus indicating that she has her guard down.

Bellinda is third, because she has let Dorimant seduce her. Still, she is shrewd, clever, and witty enough to keep herself from being found out by the others, so she has, for the time being, preserved her reputation. Loveit is last because, unable to control her jealous passions, she has let everyone in town know that she is having an affair with Dorimant. It is her lack of self-control that has allowed Dorimant to work his will on her to begin with, and to continue triumphing over her even after he has cast her off. An outward sign of her lack of wit is in her language. Instead of the repartee of the others, she speaks in the exaggerated tones of the heroic lovers of *The Comical Revenge*: "Traitor!... Ingrateful perjured man!"

What is the proper role for the older characters, who are beyond the courtship stage of their lives? Medley and Lady Townley are good examples. They do not come forward and obtrude their advice where it is not wanted, but help out the young lovers when they are asked and generally provide the gracious and civilized background against which the young people play out their courtship. They also—somewhat like a Greek chorus—keep track of the young people's reputations and make judgments (which young ladies' reputations are unblemished, which are in danger, which young men are the most perfect gallants with women). The negative examples of the older characters are Old Bellair and Lady Woodvill, who both feel that they can choose marriage partners for their children and yet whose language immediately marks them as so far behind the times, so out of touch socially, that they would make disastrous choices. Luckily, however, they are also so socially inept that the young people manipulate them easily.

The Man of Mode suggests that self-interest—Dorimant's "malice"—is necessary to the successful functioning of society. In a reaction against this Restoration worldview in the eighteenth century, later playwrights left out the cruelty and malice in their dramas of courtship. The result was sentimental theater, frankly unrealistic. If Dorimant and Harriet are removed from the play, Young Bellair and Emilia will come to the top of the pecking order. Like them, the sentimental dramas of the eighteenth century are "tolerable" but do not "abound with wit."

Other major works

POETRY: *The New Academy of Complements*, 1669; *A Collection of Poems, Written upon Several Occasions*, 1673; *Restoration Carnival*, 1954 (V. De Sola Pinto, editor); *Poems*, 1963 (James Thorpe, editor).

NONFICTION: *The Letterbook of Sir George Etherege*, 1928 (Sybil Rosenfeld, editor); *Letters of Sir George Etherege*, 1973.

MISCELLANEOUS: *The Works of Sir George Etherege: Containing His Plays and Poems*, 1704; *The Works of Sir George Etherege: Plays and Poems*, 1888 (A. W. Verity, editor).

Bibliography

Dobree, Bonamy. "His Excellency Sir George Etherege." In *Essays in Biography, 1680-1726.* 1925. Reprint. Freeport, N.Y.: Books for Libraries Press, 1967. In 1685, Etherege went to Ratisbon, in Bavaria, as James II's envoy, and three years later he left for Paris after the accession of William and Mary. Dobree does not discuss the plays but provides an amusing account of Etherege's licentious behavior and the eventual diminishment of his powers.

Etherege, George. *The Plays of Sir George Etherege.* Edited by Michael Cordner. Cambridge, England: Cambridge University Press, 1982. This careful edition has a concise introduction that sketches the sparse facts known about Etherege's life, summarizes the status of the texts, and annotates some important works in both the primary and the secondary bibliographies. The introductory and textual notes are all informative.

Holland, Norman N. *The First Modern Comedies: The Significance of Etherege, Wycherly, and Congreve.* Cambridge, Mass.: Harvard University Press, 1959. Reprint. Bloomington: Indiana University Press, 1967. Holland provides "readings" of Etherege's three plays, devoting a chapter to each. His essay entitled "Scenes and Heroes" fills in some essential background to Restoration comedy, and "The Critical Failure" analyzes questions of morality that these plays raise. The copious notes are useful to beginning students of the period.

Hume, Robert D. *The Development of English Drama in the Late Seventeenth Century.* New York: Oxford University Press, 1976. Hume's detailed scholarly survey of five hundred pages combines theorizing with detailed commentaries on specific plays. The essay on "The Man of Mode: Wit Comedy" tackles the following tough question: "Is Dorimant to be admired?" Hume's perceptive analysis concludes that Dorimant is "glamorous but reprehensible."

Huseboe, Arthur R. *Sir George Etherege*. Boston: G. K. Hall, 1987. This volume in the Twayne series is the best introduction to Etherege. It includes a chronology, a biographical chapter incorporating later research, separate chapters on the three plays and the minor works, a valuable annotated bibliography, and notes. The epilogue summarizes the course of Etherege scholarship.

Mann, David D. *Sir George Etherege: A Reference Guide*. Boston: G. K. Hall, 1981. This vade mecum to Etherege scholarship is designed to help scholars find their way in Restoration drama. Although it needs to be supplemented with bibliographies of recent work, this guide is extremely useful for the period it covers.

Underwood, Dale. *Etherege and the Seventeenth-Century Comedy of Manners*. 2d ed. New Haven, Conn.: Yale University Press, 1969. Underwood interprets Etherege's plays in terms of a "configuration of forces in seventeenth-century thought and manners." The chapter entitled "The Fertile Ground" treats the Restoration libertine in a context of the clash between art and nature. Etherege's language gets special attention, and the plays are viewed under two rubrics: "The Comedy of Love" and "The Comedy of Manners."

Norman Lavers
(Updated by *Frank Day*)

GEORGE FARQUHAR

Born: Londonderry, Ireland; 1678(?)
Died: London, England; late May, 1707

Principal drama

Love and a Bottle, pr. 1698, pb. 1699; *The Constant Couple: Or, A Trip to the Jubilee*, pr. 1699, pb. 1700; *Sir Harry Wildair, Being the Sequel of a Trip to the Jubilee*, pr., pb. 1701; *The Inconstant: Or, The Way to Win Him*, pr., pb. 1702 (adaptation of John Fletcher's play *The Wild Goose Chase*); *The Twin Rivals*, pr. 1702, pb. 1703; *The Stage Coach*, pr., pb. 1704 (with Peter Anthony Motteux; adaptation of Jean de La Chapelle's play *Les Carosses d'Orléans*); *The Recruiting Officer*, pr., pb. 1706; *The Beaux' Stratagem*, pr., pb. 1707.

Other literary forms

George Farquhar wrote a few short poems, one long occasional poem entitled *Barcellona* (1710), numerous prologues and epilogues for plays, a short novel called *The Adventures of Covent Garden* (1698), and one miscellany entitled *Love and Business* (1702), besides contributing letters to two other miscellanies.

Achievements

Farquhar was one of the most popular dramatists at the end of the Restoration period. His success is illustrated by the number of prologues and epilogues he was asked to write for other plays, and by his contributions to popular miscellanies such as *Familiar and Courtly Letters* (1700) and *Letters of Wit, Politicks, and Morality* (1701). The popularity of his plays with actors, particularly *The Beaux' Stratagem* and *The Recruiting Officer*, accounted in no small measure for their survival during the eighteenth century and has played a large part in their continued visibility in the twentieth century.

Farquhar's skill in modifying typical Restoration themes and characters accounted for much of the success of his work. He reintroduced a significant degree of realism into drama and used topical issues for comic effect. Although classed among the Restoration playwrights, he stands somewhat apart from them in his craftsmanship and his philosophy of drama, showing greater variety of plot and depth of feeling. In his later work, he sought to reconcile the liberal sexual attitudes of early comedy of manners with the more severe, increasingly moralistic tone of the early eighteenth century. He thus produced a type of comedy that stands between the traditional Restoration comedy of wit and the later sentimental comedy.

The influence of Farquhar's approach to comedy is most apparent not in the work of succeeding dramatists (although Oliver Goldsmith reveals an indebtedness to Farquhar, particularly in *She Stoops to Conquer*, pr., pb. 1773), but in the novels of Henry Fielding, both in terms of sense of humor and breadth of social milieu. Oddly enough, Farquhar was to exert a considerable influence on the development of eighteenth century German drama, mainly as a result of Gotthold Ephraim Lessing's great enthusiasm for him. His continued influence on the history of German theater is displayed in the work of a major twentieth century dramatist, Bertolt Brecht.

Biography

Many traditions and legends have developed around the sparse facts known about the life of George Farquhar. The earliest documented evidence is contained in the records of Trinity College, which list him as entering in July, 1694, at the age of seventeen, establishing his year of birth as either 1677 or 1678. These records also note Londonderry, Ireland, as his place of birth, and Walker as the name of his previous teacher. Farquhar entered Trinity College, presumably to study for the Church, with a sizarship which entitled him to an allowance of bread and ale in return for serving duties. He won a scholarship less than a year after entering. This four pounds a year was suspended for a time, however, because of his riotous behavior at the Donnybrook Fair. Sometime after February, 1696, he left Trinity without taking a degree.

Not long after, Farquhar became an actor at the Smock Alley Theatre, the only theater in Dublin. His not particularly successful career as an actor ended after he wounded a fellow player in a duel scene, having forgotten to use a blunted foil. It was supposedly on the advice of his friend Robert Wilks, who was later to become one of the most popular actors on the London stage, that Farquhar went to London, probably in 1697, to write plays. *Love and a Bottle*, his first play, was produced at the Theatre Royal in Drury Lane in December, 1698. It reportedly ran for nine nights, a successful debut for the young playwright. That same month, a pamphlet entitled *The Adventures of Covent Garden* appeared anonymously. It has been attributed with some certainty to Farquhar on the basis of hints in the preface, the technique of the writer, and the fact that one of the poems appears in a later text, this time signed by Farquhar.

About a year later, again at Drury Lane, *The Constant Couple* was performed, which Farquhar later described as drawing some fifty audiences in a five-month period. Robert Wilks, who had probably joined the company at Farquhar's request, was immensely popular as Sir Harry, and another actor gained the lifelong nickname of "Jubilee Dicky" as a result of the play. Suddenly, Farquhar had become the most popular dramatist in London.

Between 1700 and 1703, three more plays appeared, all relatively unsuccessful: *Sir Harry Wildair*, a sequel to *The Constant Couple*; *The Inconstant*, an adaptation of John Fletcher's *The Wild Goose Chase* (pr. 1621, pb. 1652); and *The Twin Rivals*. Sometime between the fall of 1700 and the spring of 1702, a date earlier than the once-proposed 1704, Farquhar—in collaboration with Peter Anthony Motteux—adapted Jean de La Chapelle's *Les Carosses d'Orléans* into a farce entitled *The Stage Coach*. The authors probably did not make much money from it, since one-act plays could not stand alone on a program. Adding to his increasing financial difficulties, Farquhar was married, probably in 1703, to Margaret Pemell, a widow by whom he was to have two daughters. Knowing that Farquhar needed money, Pemell tricked him into marriage by having rumors spread that she was an heiress.

During the period from 1704 to 1706, Farquhar did not stage any plays. In 1704, he received a lieutenancy from the Earl of Orrery's Regiment of Foot, which was sent for service in Ireland. This commission assured him of a small yearly income of about fifty pounds. He was soon sent into western England on a recruiting campaign. In 1705, he wrote his poem *Barcellona* on the occasion of the taking of that city by the Earl of Peterborough; the poem was not published until after his death. It was also in 1705, supposedly during a stay at the Raven Inn while recruiting at Shrewsbury, that *The Recruiting Officer* was written. In the spring of 1706, this play was an overwhelming success, first at Drury Lane, then at the Queen's Theatre when some of the Drury Lane players moved to the new rival company.

Despite this success, Farquhar still seems to have had financial difficulties. In the fall or winter of 1706, he sold his commission to pay his debts, reportedly after a promise by the Duke of Ormonde that he would obtain for him another commission. This promise apparently came to nothing. In the meantime, Farquhar became ill. Wilks, seeking him out after an absence from the theater, advised him to write a new play and loaned him twenty guineas. The result was *The Beaux' Stratagem*, written in six weeks during his continued illness. The new play, produced in March, 1707, proved to be another success.

The register of St. Martin's in the Fields lists Farquhar's funeral, paid for by Wilks, on May 23, 1707, although his death must have occurred a few days earlier, rather than on the traditionally accepted date, that of the third performance of *The Beaux' Stratagem* in April. He may have died of tuberculosis.

Analysis

In general, past criticism of George Farquhar's plays has centered on two basic areas: finding possible autobiographical references in both characters and settings, and comparing Farquhar's moral attitudes to those of previous Restoration dramatists. In fact, many critics view Farquhar as the harbinger of the eighteenth century sentimental comedy. Both these views fail to deal adequately with Farquhar's artistic development of comedy. Unlike the writers of previous Restoration drama and subsequent sentimental comedy, Farquhar presents a balanced view of humanity and an equal appeal to the intellect and the emotions. His notion of the proper function of comedy, as expressed in a letter entitled "A Discourse upon Comedy" from *Love and Business*, includes the responsibility to portray the times accurately; the playwright's diversions must be realistic if he is also to carry out his task of instruction. Following these ideas, Farquhar produced drama which rests at some point of balance between the earlier cynical, witty comedy of manners and the later melodramatic sentimental comedy. Thematic development, dramatic conflict, and sources of comedy in Farquhar's three most popular plays—*The Constant Couple, The Recruiting Officer*, and *The Beaux' Stratagem*—illustrate his philosophy of comedy.

The Constant Couple is characterized by a light, often farcical atmosphere centered on situational comedy which instructs both by positive and by negative example. The efforts of several of the characters to attend the Jubilee in Rome gave the play a topical flavor.

Farquhar's habit of sustaining dramatic tension by action rather than by dialogue is a primary characteristic of *The Constant Couple*. The main actions center on Lady Lurewell, Colonel Standard, Sir Harry Wildair, and Angelica Darling, whose names alone suggest positive and negative examples. Angelica virtuously rejects a hypocritical suitor in the beginning, quickly establishing her character. In revenge, this suitor, appropriately named Vizard, tells Sir Harry that Angelica is a prostitute. Sir Harry, who has followed Lady Lurewell from Europe in hopes of a conquest, makes several humorous attempts to solicit Angelica's services; the best he can do is to look foolish and to hum when he discovers his mistake. Meanwhile, Lady Lurewell is involved in making all of her would-be lovers pay for the trickery of a man who seduced her at a young age. Her revenge takes the form of getting her suitors into foolish, farcical situations. Sir Harry finally abandons his wooing of Lady Lurewell to marry Angelica, and Standard is revealed as Lady Lurewell's seducer, who has been faithful to his previous engagement with her. All potentially sentimental situations, such as the reconciliation of Lady Lurewell and Standard, are short and factual rather than long and emotional.

Another aspect of *The Constant Couple* that is typical of Farquhar's plays is his modification of the usual Restoration characters. Sir Harry is not the stereotyped rake, cool and polished, living by his wit alone. Above all, he is good-natured and full of contradictions. He has been a good soldier, but he avoids a duel. He loves fashion as well as French phrases.

In *The Recruiting Officer*, typical Restoration characters and themes are similarly modified. The action centers on recruiting antics and the difficulties of the relationships of two couples: Plume and Sylvia, and Worthy and Melinda. At the play's end, both couples plan to be married. This theme of marriage, a typical Restoration theme, is a common motif in the play, but marriage is no longer a loveless relationship with both parties finding pleasure in affairs. Much of the play is devoted to the growing companionship between Plume and Silvia. This marriage, unlike the marriages in earlier Restoration drama, is not for money alone.

Farquhar's characters are also modified from the previous extremes of the Restoration. Farquhar's fop figure, Brazen, who has hopes of marrying Melinda, represents a fragmentation of the usual Restoration fop. Brazen has none of the typical clothes and affectations of the Restoration fop, and much less of the foolish gullibility. Farquhar instead takes the social qualities of a fop, exaggerates them, and fits them into a military atmosphere. Brazen's bragging, traditional for the fop, encompasses the world of battle and the world of the beau. The social memory and name-dropping tendency of a fop are exaggerated; it is precisely these characteristics of Brazen which leave him open to ridicule by other characters within the play.

The rake figure also undergoes modification in *The Recruiting Officer*. Plume asks the country girl, Rose, to his lodging not to debauch her, but to get her to aid in his recruiting, his main area of manipulation. Plume has a definite share of kindness and good nature. He provides for the subsistence of his bastard and provides a husband for the mother. He releases the disguised Silvia from her enlistment because he values an obligation to her father above money. Plume's dialogue has its share of wit, but it also reveals his fundamentally kind nature.

Although wit is used to produce comedy in *The Recruiting Officer*, the dialogue also features puns, farce, and comical treatment of social issues. The greater use of the latter as one of the major sources of comedy distinguishes Farquhar from other Restoration dramatists. The recruiting issue underlies a large part of the comedy in *The Recruiting Officer* and often provides for major dramatic conflict. The light atmosphere is set in the prologue, when the action is foretold and ironically compared to heroic times. The recruiting tricks of Kite play upon possibilities, however improbable, of military advancement and even upon the superstitions of the people when he dons his fortune-telling disguise. Less gentle is the comedy of Plume's entering his bastard as a recruit and wanting no one in his company who can write or who is a gentleman.

In Farquhar's *The Beaux' Stratagem*, social issues and modification of traditional Restoration themes and characters again play a prominent role. *The Beaux' Stratagem* is regarded by most critics as Farquhar's finest achievement; its great sense of naturalness, of fidelity to life, continue to make it a great favorite with actors and audiences alike. The action centers on Aimwell's courtship of Dorinda, first of all for her money, but later for love. Archer, Aimwell's friend disguised as a servant, also courts Cherry, the innkeeper's daughter, and Mrs. Sullen, an unhappily married woman. In the meantime, a series of scenes alternates between the inn, whose owner is a highwayman, and the manor, in which a robbery and a midnight love scene occur.

Farquhar's use of the social issue of the recent war against France and the resulting anti-French sentiment pervades all levels of the play. In the inn, Frenchmen pay double the regular fee. Scrub, Mr. Sullen's servant, parodies the French, while Aimwell quips that he would not like a woman who was fond of a Frenchman. Count Bellair, Mrs. Sullen's suitor, and Foigard, Bellair's chaplain, both come in for a large portion of the anti-French comedy.

The concept of social equality also becomes a major source for comedy, including the financial inequality created by primogeniture. Gibbet, the highwayman, excuses himself because he is a younger brother. Aimwell initiates dramatic conflict because of his status as a younger brother. In *The Beaux' Stratagem*, Farquhar stresses the fact that class differences do not correspond to levels of virtue. He achieves this emphasis by showing the same goodness in Cherry and Lady Bountiful, and the same corruption in Boniface and Sullen. In the robbery scene, Archer himself is cleverly associated with the thieves by Mrs. Sullen's cry of "Thieves, Murder." The same fundamental human qualities are thus shown to exist both in the inn and in the country mansion.

As in *The Recruiting Officer*, the plot of *The Beaux' Stratagem* deals with a modified marriage theme. The subject of marriage is not discussed using the common gaming imagery of the earlier Restoration drama, and the only slave imagery is used to describe Mrs. Sullen's marriage. In this instance, the marriage conflict is a conflict between law and nature. Sullen lies with his wife because of the law, and the natural differences between them do not come within the bounds of divorce law. In the conclusion, however, the maxim of nature as the first lawgiver is upheld.

The roster of traditional figures, as in *The Recruiting Officer*, is again modified. Count Bellair in *The Beaux' Stratagem* is a different variety of fop. He is obviously less foolish than the traditional fop since Mrs. Sullen chooses the Count to be part of her manipulations. Bellair shows extraordinary intelligence, for a fop, in initiating his own manipulation to get into Mrs. Sullen's closet. In creating Count Bellair, Farquhar took one aspect of the traditional fop, the beau, and exaggerated it. Bellair functions exceedingly well in this role, but he is also ridiculed because of his French qualities and becomes emblematic of the deeper conflict of social ideas in Farquhar.

In these three plays, the treatment of theme, dramatic conflict, and sources of comedy contributes to an increased realism. The stiff, artificial characters of early Restoration drama have no place in Farquhar's theater. A Dorinda who admits to Aimwell that she does not know herself would not have been understood by earlier audiences; a Mrs. Sullen who verbalizes her unhappiness would have astonished them. The audience at the turn of the century, however, was different: It was mainly a middle-class audience with an awakening sense of social consciousness.

Farquhar opened the window to a blast of fresh air for English comedy. By placing his characters in the world of innkeepers, military recruits, and highwaymen, Farquhar directed attention to humor rather than wit, and, in so doing, broadened the scope for comedy. His plays may well be less sharp-tongued than those of the dramatists who preceded him, but his work displays a greater naturalness and a deeper sense of life. His is the more human view of the world.

Other major works

SHORT FICTION: *The Adventures of Covent Garden*, 1698.
POETRY: *Barcellona*, 1710.
MISCELLANEOUS: *Love and Business*, 1702; *The Complete Works of George Farquhar*, 1930 (Charles Stonehill, editor); *The Works of George Farquhar*, 1988 (Shirley Strum Kenny, editor).

Bibliography

Berman, Ronald. "The Comedy of Reason." *Texas Studies in Literature and Language: A Journal of the Humanities* 7 (Summer, 1965): 161-168. Berman asserts that "Restoration comedy is one of the great forms of the drama of ideas" and that *The Beaux' Stratagem* is characteristic: "The confrontation of social laws which are inexorable, rational, and transactional by passions which, after all, invalidate them, is a cultural comment."

Farmer, A. J. *George Farquhar*. London: Longmans, Green, 1966. This forty-page British Council pamphlet with a select bibliography is a good introduction to Farquhar. Farmer admits the licentious tone of the early plays but finds a "gradual improvement" in the later ones. Moreover, Farquhar's characters advance beyond the earlier libertines to become more like Henry Fielding's Tom Jones.

James, Eugene Nelson. *The Development of George Farquhar as a Comic Dramatist*. The Hague: Mouton, 1972. After a brief introduction, "The Traditions in Farquhar Criticism," James marches through the plays a chapter at a time. *The Recruiting Officer* is judged "climactic" for its form, and *The Beaux' Stratagem* is the "fulfillment of a promise." Rich source notes.

Milhous, Judith, and Robert D. Hume. *Producible Interpretation: Eight English Plays, 1675-1707*. Carbondale: Southern Illinois University Press,

1985. "By 'producible interpretation' we mean a critical reading that a director could communicate to an audience in performance," the authors note. *The Beaux' Stratagem* is "an effective stage vehicle," and the authors devote twenty-seven pages to discussing possibilities of stage interpretation. An insightful essay.

Palmer, John. *The Comedy of Manners.* London: G. Bell & Sons, 1913. Reprint. New York: Russell & Russell, 1962. Palmer treats Farquhar along with Sir George Etherege, William Wycherley, William Congreve, and Sir John Vanbrugh. Palmer answers the old condemnation of these writers as immoral by defending the artist in general: "Responding to a genuine inspiration he will leave the moral result of his endeavours to look after itself."

Perry, Henry Ten Eyck. *The Comic Spirit in Restoration Drama.* New Haven, Conn.: Yale University Press, 1925. Perry examines the same quintet studied by John Palmer (above), but he is more concerned with theory and practice than with moral consequences. Farquhar is praised for moving away from Sir John Vanbrugh's influence toward "the freer ether of eighteenth-century sentiment." Roebuck in *Love and a Bottle* is "Farquhar himself."

Rothstein, Eric. *George Farquhar.* New York: Twayne, 1967. This volume in the Twayne series is an excellent introduction to and overview of both Farquhar's life and his work, leaving background materials to be read elsewhere. Rothstein's vigorous prose makes his account wonderfully readable, especially in the chapter entitled "Jeremy Collier and *The Twin-Rivals.*" The secondary annotations are frank and tart.

Eril Barnett Hughes
(Updated by *Frank Day*)

EDNA FERBER

Born: Kalamazoo, Michigan; August 15, 1885
Died: New York, New York; April 16, 1968

Principal drama

Our Mrs. McChesney, pr., pb. 1915 (with George V. Hobart); *$1200 a Year*, pr., pb. 1920 (with Newman A. Levy); *Minick*, pr., pb. 1924 (with George S. Kaufman); *The Royal Family*, pr. 1927, pb. 1928 (with Kaufman); *Dinner at Eight*, pr., pb. 1932 (with Kaufman); *Stage Door*, pr., pb. 1936 (with Kaufman); *The Land Is Bright*, pr., pb. 1941 (with Kaufman); *Bravo!*, pr. 1948, pb. 1949 (with Kaufman).

Other literary forms

Edna Ferber hoped she would be remembered as a playwright, but even during her lifetime, she was considered primarily a novelist and writer of short stories; nevertheless, the ease with which several of her major novels, among them *Show Boat* (1926), *Saratoga Trunk* (1941), and *Giant* (1952), have been adapted to musical theater and film proves that memorable characterization is the greatest strength her works possess. Strong characterization appears even in her first novel, *Dawn O'Hara* (1911), and Ferber achieved national success with the Emma McChesney stories, which were published originally in *American* and *Cosmopolitan* magazines, quickly reprinted as collections from 1913 to 1915, and finally distilled as Ferber's first dramatic collaboration, *Our Mrs. McChesney*.

Ferber's works were perfectly attuned to American popular taste. This was especially true of the novels and short stories written in the years between the two world wars, when her career was at its height. Her first venture in autobiography, *A Peculiar Treasure* (1939), written just prior to the outbreak of World War II, appropriately finishes this period. This work especially shows Ferber's identification with European Jewry suffering under Nazi persecution and ominously foreshadows the horrors of the Holocaust.

Giant was Ferber's last successful major novel, and it appears that even as she wrote her somewhat anticlimactic second autobiographical volume, *A Kind of Magic* (1963), she was aware that her popularity had waned. She continued to write until her death, however, managing to sell film rights to her unsuccessful last novel, *Ice Palace* (1958), even before its publication.

Achievements

Ferber's reputation as a novelist and writer of short stories made possible her ventures into drama and autobiography. Paradoxically, the adaptation of several of her major novels to musical theater (*Show Boat*), film (*Saratoga Trunk, So Big, Giant, Ice Palace*), and even television (*Cimarron*, 1929) served to reduce public recognition of the novels from which the adaptations were derived. Correspondingly, two substantial autobiographies, coupled with a biography by Ferber's great-niece Julie Goldsmith Gilbert, discouraged scholarly research.

Ferber's novels are large in scope yet regional in character, and Ferber considered it an accomplishment that she was able to write with apparent ease about so many locations in which she had never lived, describing not only the Midwest, where she was reared, but the South, the West, and even the Arctic. She rightly believed that her strength lay in the ability to isolate the distinctive character of each region and describe it in terms appropriate to the popular imagination.

The Midwest of Emma McChesney, the South of *Show Boat*, even the Texas of *Giant* no longer exist, however, and this has served to make some of Ferber's finest works period pieces. Stronger, more contemporary statements have been made about the plight of minorities; anonymous corporate greed has exceeded that of individual families; and novels of manners are generally out of favor. The works of Willa Cather and William Faulkner, although also regional, can survive on the universal applicability of the situations they describe, but Ferber's work cannot.

Ferber's greatest popularity came in the nostalgic period between the two world wars and during the Depression, when Americans sought escape from overwhelming reality. *So Big* (1924) won the Pulitzer Prize in 1925, and this led to a flurry of publication which slowed only after 1941. Today, most of her works are out of print, even some of her best-known books— books which sold thousands of copies before the advent of the paperback and which won the unsolicited plaudits of Rudyard Kipling and both Theodore and Franklin D. Roosevelt.

The situation is even more dismal in the case of Ferber's plays, this despite her often brilliant collaborations with George S. Kaufman. When *The Royal Family, Dinner at Eight*, or *Stage Door* are mentioned, a glimmer of recognition comes to the eye of a well-read person, but even these works are not generally associated with Ferber's name. Sometimes they are remembered as Kaufman's work, perhaps because his name always preceded Ferber's on the title page and in billing, but they are as likely to be recalled only as films.

Ferber was adept at female characterization, and strong women, who were also usually amiable, fill the pages of her works. This was considered by many an innovation which made Ferber in her own time a popular counterweight to Ernest Hemingway, but it has not continued to save her literary reputation.

Biography

Edna Ferber considered her earliest years turbulent and unhappy, particularly the time before her family's move to Appleton, Wisconsin. This unhappiness had essentially two causes: awareness that as the child of middle-class Jewish merchants, she was often not accepted by rough-edged Midwestern farmers, and her recognition of the isolated and difficult nature of plains life in the last quarter of the nineteenth century. Her parents, Jacob and Julia, made several moves, evidently seeking a more comfortable life for the family, and Edna was born in Kalamazoo, Michigan, on August 15, 1885. (Ferber, perhaps from the vanity to which she confesses in her autobiography, gave the date as 1887, and this was the year published in *The New York Times'* obituary.) By 1888, Jacob, though he seems to have prospered moderately in Kalamazoo, moved his family to Chicago, where his wife, Julia Neumann Ferber, had been reared, and the Ferbers lived for a year in the large Neumann house on Calumet Avenue. Jacob's desire for independence, as well as his idea that his dry goods business would be more successful in an isolated town, prompted him to move the family again, this time to Ottumwa, Iowa, and the Ferbers lived in this farming and coal-mining town from 1890 to 1897. Edna Ferber always considered the place brutal and crude; it was a struggle to maintain even a modicum of comfort in this primitive town, which quite often was openly anti-Semitic. Jacob's progressive blindness was first diagnosed in the Ottumwa years, and this served to place more business and family responsibilities on Julia. A successful lawsuit for slander brought by a fired employee cost the Ferbers several thousand dollars and hastened their move to Wisconsin.

Appleton provided more congenial surroundings. There was a small Jewish community there, good schools, and the pleasant atmosphere of a Midwestern college town. Ferber excelled in declamation and debate for Ryan High School's Forum Debating Society, and her first prize at a statewide declamation contest paved the way at age seventeen for her position as reporter on the Appleton *Daily Crescent*, the town's newspaper. Ferber, like Willa Cather, planned a career in journalism, and in 1905, she accepted an offer to work on the Milwaukee *Journal*.

Milwaukee proved a big change for the nineteen-year-old Ferber. She was suddenly on her own, living in a boarding house whose principal tenants were German-speaking engineers employed in the steelworks and engineering plants in and around the city. She drew on this experience for her first novel, *Dawn O'Hara*, a few years later. Milwaukee also provided more chances than ever to attend the theater, and some of Ferber's earliest writings were drama and music reviews published in both the *Journal* and the *Daily Crescent*. Her health suffered, however, and forced her return to Appleton after three years.

Though Ferber had planned to return to Milwaukee after recovering her strength in Appleton, she never did. On a secondhand typewriter, she wrote an essay entitled "Why I Lost My Job," entered it in a contest sponsored by the Chicago *Tribune*, and won first prize; encouraged by this success, she began to write *Dawn O'Hara*. Upon Jacob's death in 1909, Julia returned to Chicago with Edna and her older sister Fannie (the Fannie Fox who wrote the famous cookbook); this was the beginning of Ferber's Chicago period, and for the next thirteen years, she lived in hotels and furnished apartments. She continued to write free-lance articles for the *Tribune*, but she directed her energies primarily toward fiction.

Short stories in the style of O. Henry poured from her typewriter, and her 1911 success with *Dawn O'Hara* enabled her to publish much of this material. Good reviews for *Buttered Side Down* (1912) continued the momentum, but it was the McChesney stories, which were published in nationally circulated magazines, that brought her popular success. They introduced an admirable and determined traveling saleswoman named Emma McChesney, a character derived from Ferber's mercantile and Midwestern background. These successes led Ferber to divide her time, somewhat awkwardly, between Chicago and New York. She was able to use her training in journalism to cover the 1912 Republican and Democratic National Conventions for the Franklin P. Adams syndicate; it was at this time that she met William Allen White, who would remain a friend and confidant for the rest of her life. The dramatic rights to the McChesney stories were sold to Joseph Brooks at the end of 1913, and in 1915 they appeared as the play *Our Mrs. McChesney*, a difficult collaboration with George V. Hobart. Ethel Barrymore, as Emma McChesney, saved this mediocre play, although Ferber always maintained that Barrymore had been miscast.

Although Ferber could have allowed her reputation to rest on the McChesney character alone, she wisely sought new literary horizons. Returning by ship from a European holiday, she met a young Chicago lawyer, Newman A. Levy, who was a playwright and artist by avocation, and this meeting resulted in the play *$1200 a Year*. Although a dismal failure, the play anticipated the direction her future works in drama would take and led to more successful collaborations with George S. Kaufman. *The Royal Family*, *Dinner at Eight*, and *Stage Door* remain minor classics, although they stand more effectively as literature than as revivals. Her novel *Fanny Herself* (1917), which enjoyed only moderate success, enabled Ferber to see that her greatest abilities lay in the novel, the direction her career would ultimately take.

So Big, *Show Boat*, and *Cimarron* appeared in quick succession during the post-World War I years, and Ferber was firmly established as a New York-based writer and a popular success. She frequented the Algonquin Round Table and met Marc Connelly, Robert E. Sherwood, Deems Taylor,

Alexander Woollcott, George Oppenheimer, and other literary notables in that circle. These were her most productive years.

Ferber's move to Connecticut and Treasure Hill, the country home she built there in the late 1930's, continued to feed her muse. Her autobiography *A Peculiar Treasure* was written while her house was being built, and *Nobody's in Town* (1938), a collection of short stories, also appeared at this time. The onset of World War II, however, reduced her literary output considerably, and it was only at the war's end that her novel *Great Son* (1945) appeared. It was not until 1952 that *Giant*, her novel on life among the oil-rich families of Texas, brought her new acclaim.

In the early 1960's, Doubleday, the publisher with which Ferber had enjoyed such a successful association, encouraged her to write a novel that she had been planning on the American Indian, tentatively entitled "The Squaw." Ferber was doing research for this projected work even as she was suffering from a painful facial nerve disease and finally from the stomach cancer that eventually took her life. She carried on gallantly to the last, dining regally at her favorite restaurants and enjoying the company of her sister's family. She had never married.

Analysis

"Stagestruck" Edna Ferber, as she described herself, could not help writing plays, though she never attempted to do this alone. It appears, from a reading of those she wrote with George S. Kaufman, that she relied on Kaufman's skill for timing and dialogue but that the characterizations are essentially her own. A consistent development in Ferber's dramatic skills can be traced, beginning with her collaboration with Newman A. Levy, *$1200 a Year*.

Ferber wrote *$1200 a Year* with Levy during 1920, which was a transitional year in her life. Still living in Chicago but contemplating a permanent move to New York, she was at once attracted and repelled by city life and the large sums of money that could be earned there. She wrote to William Allen White that she hated the play even as she and Levy were writing it, that everyone but she seemed to be earning $100,000 a year, and that she was eager to work on her novel *The Girls* (1921). She describes the multiple coats of "paint" and "varnish" that she and Levy were applying to the play in an effort to make it stageworthy. This less than enthusiastic approach to the task may well have been one of the reasons for the play's dismal failure. Sam Harris, who had agreed to produce the play, closed it after a week of Baltimore tryouts. Nevertheless, *$1200 a Year* reveals a good deal about Ferber as a developing playwright.

Broadly drawn characterizations and stereotypes developed through hyperbole appear throughout the work. The once-moneyed Massachusetts aristocracy, represented by the appropriately named Winthrop family, contrasts with the prosperous immigrant Cyrus McClure, the Scot who built the Wickley, Pennsylvania, steel mill, which supports most of the town's affluent working class. These personalities, in turn, contrast with those of the mill workers, recent immigrants who have supplied the brawn that the system demands and so have prospered. Paul Stoddard, the protagonist, is a professor of economics at Dinsmore, the university maintained by McClure's money. Stoddard teaches his students, among them McClure's son Steven, the mysteries of political economy, and although he understands theoretically how to make great sums of money, he struggles to survive on his meager professor's salary of $1200 a year.

Stoddard's lectures and research have dealt with the growth of fifteenth century English trade guilds. This has angered Cyrus McClure, who is a member of the Dinsmore Board of Trustees and who fears that the mill workers' children attending the university will convince their parents to agitate for the establishment of unions at the mill.

When Stoddard first appears, McClure and the other trustees have already issued an ultimatum that the young professor delete this potentially inflammatory material from his lectures. Stoddard has met these demands by submitting his resignation. He decides to leave the threadbare aristocracy of college life and apply for a worker's job at McClure's mill. He completes the transformation to worker by living among the workers of the mill district.

Six months later, he has acquired all the material things he and his wife, Jean, have always wanted and has acquired as well a new group of friends, among whom is mill hand Chris Zsupnik. In his free time, Stoddard lectures to receptive audiences, outlining his theories on the potential power of workers, and his words soon have an effect. Significantly, the effect is most pronounced among American academics and other underpaid professionals who flock to join the ranks of unskilled laborers. These new workers create such an imbalance in the labor supply that colleges and universities all over America begin to close. What is more, factory and mill owners such as McClure threaten to cut wages to absorb the new supply of workers and maintain a market for the goods they produce. Another group of casualties includes academics who cannot make the transition to the working class. Jean's older brother, Henry Adams Winthrop, who knows little of any historical event that has occurred since the Peloponnesian War, is now utterly unemployable.

Of necessity, a reversal now occurs. Stoddard's fellow workers become convinced that the academic is merely doing a form of practical research and attempting to see if his theories really work. Jean is never comfortable with her working-class neighbors, even though she does like what Stoddard's higher salary can buy. Jean is a characteristic Ferber heroine: She takes decisive action and bargains with McClure on her own. McClure shrewdly uses his interview with Jean to convince his mill workers that he, and not Stoddard, is their true friend.

The play is now at an impasse, which can be solved only by *deus ex machina*, which arrives in the form of Cleveland Welch, talent scout for the Mastodon Art-Film Company. He offers Stoddard five thousand dollars a week to play the lead in a great new heartthrob film to be entitled *Brains and Brawn*. The film will be the life story of Paul Stoddard, who has put theory to practice in order to conquer the illiterate tyrant Cyrus McClure. When McClure hears Welch's offer, he asks what Stoddard would consider a fair salary for a university professor. The audience never hears Stoddard's reply, for the curtain descends just as he is about to name a figure.

Ferber's first autobiographical memoir, *A Peculiar Treasure*, describes the special affection she had for immigrants to the United States, an affection apparent in the sympathetic portrait of the Zsupnik family in *$1200 a Year*. Her father's background and her life at Appleton and Milwaukee provided inspiration for many of these characters in her comedy.

Although a failure, *$1200 a Year* foreshadows themes that would be developed in subsequent Ferber plays. Topics such as socialism in America following the Russian Revolution, immigration, unfair distribution of wealth, the advancing labor movement, and how America chooses its heroes provide the play's background. Still, *$1200 a Year* never becomes a diatribe on American life. Hyperbole allows the audience to see absurdity where it exists and to draw the obvious conclusion that the common interest is served only by fair dealing; anything else is merely a short-term advantage.

Dinner at Eight was successful in its first production and shows a more mature development of similar themes. In this play, Ferber and Kaufman explore American classes and manners against the background of New York during the Depression. The changed circumstances in which many Americans found themselves in 1932 are obviously at the root of the play's action, but once again, the audience is allowed to discover this on its own. The Jordan family, described in terms Ferber had earlier used for the Winthrops, represents the Yankee aristocracy. Oliver Jordan has come to realize that the family shipping line, which had always seemed a sure source of continuing income, is threatened with bankruptcy. His wife, Millicent, seems blissfully unaware of this; her greatest concern is planning a pretheater dinner for Lord and Lady Ferncliffe, who have just arrived in town.

The guest list is planned to combine business and social requirements. Don Packard, whose manners still betray his Western mining days, and his Passaic-born wife, Kitty, receive Millicent's invitation only through Oliver's urgent petition. Oliver hopes to enlist Dan's aid to rescue the Jordan line. One of Oliver's old flames, Carlotta Vance, an apparently wealthy but faded actress, also receives an invitation; Larry Renault, an equally faded actor, is to be her dinner companion. Oliver's physician, J. Wayne Talbot, and his wife, Lucy, will complete the guest list. (Kaufman worried that the social complications that the play relates would invite comparisons with *The Grand Hotel*, which had been produced the same year; this was indeed the case, for *Dinner at Eight* rivaled *The Grand Hotel* in complexity.)

As the dinner preparations continue, the audience learns that Oliver, struggling to keep the Jordan Line afloat, has an incurable heart disease; that Carlotta has sold her Jordan stock, thereby making Oliver's business problems more acute; that Dan has been maneuvering behind the scenes to acquire control of the Jordan company; that Kitty has been having an affair with Wayne Talbot; and that the Jordans' daughter Paula, though engaged, has been enjoying her own liaison with the alcoholic actor Larry Renault. Ironically, the Ferncliffes, who leave New York for Florida at the last moment, never appear at the party in their honor, and their place is filled, somewhat unwillingly, by Millicent's sister Hattie and her husband, Ed. Larry Renault never appears either, for he commits suicide after learning that he cannot get even a supporting part in an upcoming play.

As usual in Ferber's plays, external events influence the action but are never incorporated into the play. The audience recognizes that the Depression is the fundamental cause of much of what happens, but beyond an occasional reference to difficult times, no one mentions it. Each of the characters has brought on personal disaster by some individual failing: Oliver through lack of diligent management; Dan because of his preoccupation with money-making; Larry by his alcoholism; Talbot through his womanizing. This allows Ferber to maintain her fundamentally optimistic view of American life. The seeds of decadence are present, and a few succumb to them, but others, such as Hattie and Ed, retain the common sense and attachment to simple pleasures that allow them to avoid the disasters that afflict the major characters.

In *Stage Door*, her next play after *Dinner at Eight*, Ferber introduces a large cast of characters to portray manners and emphasize conflict. This 1936 collaboration with Kaufman features thirty-two actors, each of whom plays a character with a remarkably different personality. Even the minor characters become essential to advance the play's action.

The plot is relatively simple. There is only one scene, at the Footlights Club, a boardinghouse for aspiring actresses. Life at the club is one of genteel and somewhat Bohemian poverty. The young women are without jobs more often than with them. They discreetly jockey for position and sometimes grant their favors to assorted "stage-door-Johnnys," writers, producers, and movie moguls.

Terry Randall is the single exception. She refuses a film offer made through David Kingsley, a Broadway producer who has sought greener pastures in Hollywood. She encourages an idealistic writer named Keith Burgess but does not criticize his decision to write screenplays for Hollywood. She resents, though silently, Jean Maitland's exploitation of the Footlights Club to publicize an already successful film career. Rather than rely on the financial support of her father, she works at Macy's department store and seeks auditions during her lunch hour. In short, Terry remains in control of her life throughout the play and never sacrifices her idealism. Inspired by her example, Kingsley decides to return to Broadway as the producer of a play that he rescues from the clutches of movie executive Adolph Gretzl, who had planned to use the play only to publicize Maitland's latest film. *Stage Door* concludes with idealism triumphant. Terry will star in the rescued play and will marry Kingsley, the man whom she has rescued from the dangers of materialism.

It is interesting that Julie Cavendish, in the Ferber-Kaufman collaboration *The Royal Family*, best sums up the way Ferber saw her relationship to the theater. (Indeed, Ferber's single experience as an actress was her portrayal of Julie in a 1940 revival of the play staged in Maplewood, New Jersey.) Julie, a character based on Ethel Barrymore, Ferber's girlhood stage heroine, sees her life as a grand drama. Like Ferber, she is a woman who wants all that life can offer. Ferber, however, had infinitely more common sense and considerably more business acumen than Julie possessed. Her popular appeal made possible the unquestioned success that she enjoyed during her lifetime, even if it has not assured her immortality as a writer.

Other major works

NOVELS: *Dawn O'Hara*, 1911; *Fanny Herself*, 1917; *The Girls*, 1921; *So Big*, 1924; *Show Boat*, 1926; *Cimarron*, 1929; *American Beauty*, 1931; *Come and Get It*, 1935; *Saratoga Trunk*, 1941; *Great Son*, 1945; *Giant*, 1952; *Ice Palace*, 1958.

SHORT FICTION: *Buttered Side Down*, 1912; *Roast Beef Medium*, 1913; *Personality Plus*, 1914; *Emma McChesney & Co.*, 1915; *Cheerful—By Request*, 1918; *Half Portions*, 1919; *Mother Knows Best*, 1927; *They Brought Their Women*, 1933; *Nobody's in Town*, 1938; *One Basket*, 1947.

NONFICTION: *A Peculiar Treasure*, 1939, 1960 (revised with new introduction); *A Kind of Magic*, 1963.

Bibliography

Dickinson, Roger. *Edna Ferber*. Garden City, N.Y.: Doubleday, Doran, 1925. In this brief pamphlet, the author offers a glowing biographical sketch of Ferber, the novelist and dramatist. Although dated, it provides useful information on the author's life and literary influences. Contains a bibliography.

Ferber, Edna. *A Peculiar Treasure.* Garden City, N.Y.: Garden City Publishing, 1940. This autobiography provides a unique perspective on Ferber's own personal and artistic development. Of particular interest is the description of her collaboration with George S. Kaufman. Numerous illustrations.

Gilbert, Julie Goldsmith. *Ferber: A Biography.* Garden City, N.Y.: Doubleday, 1978. Gilbert describes, with style and wit, Ferber's life and work. She calls Ferber a romantic realist, not opposed to working with the system, yet creating her own unique niche within it. Rather than proceeding chronologically, Gilbert begins her narrative with Ferber's death and moves through the major turning points in her life. Illustrated.

Goldstein, Malcolm. *George S. Kaufman: His Life, His Theatre.* New York: Oxford University Press, 1979. In addition to rendering an insightful account of the man, this work is considered a standard source on the theater of the period. Details Kaufman's collaborations with many dramatists, including Ferber.

Mordden, Ethan. *The American Theatre.* New York: Oxford University Press, 1981. In this insightful investigation of what is peculiarly American in American theater, the author writes a straight chronicle, following the evolution of the American stage as art and industry from its beginnings to 1980. His discussion of Ferber focuses on the play *The Royal Family.* Contains a useful guide for further reading.

Morris, Lloyd. *Curtain Time: The Story of the American Theatre.* New York: Random House, 1953. Although dated, this richly illustrated history of the American stage contains a brief discussion of Ferber and Kaufman's *The Royal Family* as a satirical portrait of the Barrymore family. Gives behind-the-stage information on the play's effect on the life of John Barrymore.

Wilson, Garff B. *Three Hundred Years of American Drama and Theatre.* Englewood Cliffs, N.J.: Prentice-Hall, 1973. In this general survey of the history of American drama and theater, Wilson traces the development of plays and playwriting as complementary activities to the development of acting, stagecraft, theater architecture, and management. In his discussion of Ferber's plays, he briefly touches upon George S. Kaufman's collaboration with Ferber on the plays *Minick* and *The Royal Family.* Illustrations, bibliography.

Robert J. Forman
(Updated by *Genevieve Slomski*)

HENRY FIELDING

Born: Sharpham Park, Somersetshire, England; April 22, 1707
Died: Lisbon, Portugal; October 8, 1754

Principal drama

Love in Several Masques, pr., pb. 1728; *The Temple Beau*, pr., pb. 1730; *The Author's Farce, and The Pleasures of the Town*, pr., pb. 1730; *Tom Thumb: A Tragedy*, pr., pb. 1730 (revised as *The Tragedy of Tragedies*, pr., pb. 1731); *Rape upon Rape: Or, Justice Caught in His Own Trap*, pr., pb. 1730 (also known as *The Coffee-House Politician*); *The Letter-Writers: Or, A New Way to Keep a Wife at Home*, pr., pb. 1731; *The Welsh Opera: Or, The Grey Mare the Better Horse*, pr., pb. 1731 (revised as *The Grub-Street Opera*, pb. 1731); *The Lottery*, pr., pb. 1732; *The Modern Husband*, pr., pb. 1732 (five acts); *The Old Debauchees*, pr., pb. 1732; *The Covent Garden Tragedy*, pr., pb. 1732; *The Mock Doctor: Or, The Dumb Lady Cur'd*, pr., pb. 1732 (adaptation of Molière's *Le Medecin malgré lui*); *The Miser*, pr., pb. 1733 (adaptation of Molière's *L'Avare*); *Don Quixote in England*, pr., pb. 1734; *The Intriguing Chambermaid*, pr., pb. 1734 (adaptation of Jean-François Regnard's *Le Retour imprévu*); *An Old Man Taught Wisdom: Or, The Virgin Unmask'd*, pr., pb. 1735; *The Universal Gallant: Or, The Different Husbands*, pr., pb. 1735 (five acts); *Pasquin: Or, A Dramatic Satire on the Times*, pr., pb. 1736; *Tumble-Down Dick: Or, Phaeton in the Suds*, pr., pb. 1736; *Eurydice: Or, The Devil's Henpeck'd*, pr. 1737, pb. 1743 (one act); *Eurydice Hiss'd: Or, A Word to the Wise*, pr., pb. 1737; *The Historical Register for the Year 1736*, pr., pb. 1737 (three acts); *Miss Lucy in Town*, pr., pb. 1742 (one act); *The Wedding-Day*, pr., pb. 1743 (five acts; also known as *The Virgin Unmask'd*); *The Fathers: Or, The Good-Natured Man*, pr., pb. 1778 (revised for posthumous production by David Garrick).

Other literary forms

The focus of Henry Fielding's work progressed from drama to satire to the novel to legal inquiries and proposals, with some overlap and with a nearly constant overlay of critical and political journalism. Among his novels, his masterpiece *Tom Jones* (1749) is a monument of English literature, though *Joseph Andrews* (1742) is highly regarded and *Amelia* (1751) was his own favorite. *Shamela* (1741) burlesques Samuel Richardson's novel *Pamela* (1740-1741), and the strongly satiric *Jonathan Wild* (1743) attacks the contemporary prime minister of England, Sir Robert Walpole. Political satire formed the staple of *The Champion*, a thrice-weekly journal in which Fielding was a leading partner in 1739 and 1740, but social commentary and drama criticism played a large role in *The Covent-Garden Journal*, which came out during 1752. In the early 1750's, Fielding authored several influential tracts aimed at reforming his country's criminal and poor laws, and in 1754 he wrote a moving and contemplative travel book, *The Journal of a Voyage to Lisbon* (1755).

Achievements

Fielding was a central figure in the theatrical world of the 1730's, and he continued to be influential as a literary and social critic almost up to his death in 1754. He wrote in popular and established forms, but his cleverness and vigor raised his work well above the level set by his contemporaries. Fielding exploited the ballad opera, a form originated by John Gay, with particular success. By adding broad farce and often surreal fantasy to Gay's inspiration of setting satiric lyrics to popular tunes sung in operatic style, Fielding produced one of his best plays, *The Author's Farce*. He combined farce, burlesque, and fantasy to create *The Tragedy of Tragedies*, another masterpiece. Both plays, often classified as dramatic satires, were hugely popular by the standards of the time.

Beyond his contribution as a playwright, Fielding's management of the Little Theatre in the Haymarket set a dangerously bold pace in terms of showmanship and satire. He attacked the shortcomings of society in general and of the theater in particular but found his chief target in the Whig government of Robert Walpole. Fielding's popularity, his influence in the theater, and the potency of his satire are usually credited with bringing on the Licensing Act of 1737, an instrument of political censorship which limited the staging of plays to a select list of theaters and required the Lord Chamberlain's approval before a new play could be staged or an old one altered. The Licensing Act ended Fielding's theatrical career on an ironic note; he had made the stage at once so lively and so central to England's political life that its control and suppression had become a political necessity.

Shorn of topical relevance and their original sense of daring, only two or three of his plays are still performed. They have wit and pace, and they certainly repay the discriminating reader, but they no longer exert the tremendous popular appeal that was Fielding's first goal. As a contributor to dramatic tradition, Fielding presents another irony; he was restless within the forms he chose, but his experimentation forced and complicated those forms rather than breaking through and extending them. Had his career as a playwright not ended so early—in part through his own doing—he might well have made a more substantial contribution to the genre. As it was, his interest turned to the novel, and he joined Daniel Defoe and Richardson in establishing a great new English literary tradition.

Biography

Born on April 22, 1707, Henry Fielding grew up quietly in Somerset and

Dorset. When he was eleven, however, his mother died, and after a year of turmoil, during which his father remarried and quarreled violently with his mother's relatives, young Henry was sent to Eton. After making as much as possible of the excellent if strict and structured education offered by this famous school, Fielding chose, about 1724, to enjoy life in London rather than enter a university.

In 1728, his comedy *Love in Several Masques* was staged at the Theatre Royal. Instead of pursuing a stage career at once, however, Fielding enrolled at the University of Leyden, where he remained for a year, probably studying classical literature. In 1729, Fielding returned to England, where his second play, *The Temple Beau*, was accepted by the theater in Goodman's Fields. This coup inaugurated ten years of immersion in the London theater world, a brilliant career in the course of which Fielding became both widely known and respected and widely disparaged and attacked. His third play, a ballad opera called *The Author's Farce*, opened at a more prestigious theater, the Little Theatre in the Haymarket, where it met with great success; it was followed immediately by *Tom Thumb*, a minor masterpiece which Fielding reworked the following year as *The Tragedy of Tragedies*. This satire on Robert Walpole, a parody of heroic tragedy, is today Fielding's most widely known dramatic production.

After his spectacular initial success, Fielding's ability to please the public became less certain. *Rape upon Rape* was found only acceptable, and its afterpiece, *The Letter-Writers*, had to be withdrawn. A new and highly political afterpiece, however, *The Welsh Opera*, played to enthusiastic houses. Already the government was aware of Fielding; the play's even more outspoken revision, *The Grub-Street Opera*, was suppressed before it could open.

In 1732, Fielding continued to increase the pressure he had caused by his inflammatory satire with *The Lottery*, an attack on the combination of financial corruption and public foolishness represented by lottery-ticket jobbers. This play did well, but *The Modern Husband*, a strong satire on public—rather than political or financial—morals, had a mixed reception, as did *The Old Debauchees*, which is a much darker work than Fielding's lighthearted style usually produced. *The Old Debauchees'* afterpiece, *The Covent Garden Tragedy*, was a flat failure and had to be replaced by *The Mock Doctor*. This ballad opera was the first of Fielding's two successful adaptations of Molière. The second, a highly successful farce entitled *The Miser*, was produced the following year, followed by another ballad opera, *The Intriguing Chambermaid*.

Fielding was now well established as a popular London playwright, a figure to be reckoned with among his literary peers, and a man well able to earn a decent, if uneven, income through his art. At the same time, he had already made enemies among both politicians and literary critics and had himself been the butt of sharp satiric comment.

At this juncture, late in 1734, Fielding married. For information about how he lived, passed his days, dealt with his necessities, and satisfied his tastes—whatever these were—one must rely on generalizations about the period. No Fielding diaries have been found and very little of his correspondence exists. He and his new wife, the former Charlotte Cradock, lived in the heart of London while he opened *An Old Man Taught Wisdom*, a successful ballad opera/farce, and *The Universal Gallant*, a comedy which failed emphatically.

The death of Fielding's mother-in-law, which came soon after this failure, left his wife with a small estate. After dealing with financial matters related to the estate, the couple managed to spend a good deal of the year 1735 at Fielding's family home in East Stour, but Fielding apparently did not take well to rural life. By the time he was back in London for the fall season, he had succeeded in gaining control of the Little Theatre, where he organized a group of young actors referred to as the "Great Mogul's Company of Comedians." *Pasquin*, a dramatic satire, which was more specific in its personal reference than any of Fielding's other works, made the new company's name. This was followed with a farce, *Tumble-Down Dick*, which was aimed at his theatrical compatriots.

Fielding continued to provide competition and stimulation to the new theatrical season with a provoking and innovative schedule at the Little Theatre, also offering a short farce of his own, *Eurydice*, to Drury Lane, a rival house. *Eurydice* failed, giving Fielding the opportunity to rework it (twice), ending up with *Eurydice Hiss'd*, a short farce which played for more than a month as a popular afterpiece to *The Historical Register for the Year 1736*. The latter, while it provides the broad social satire suggested by its title and takes aim at the theatrical world as well, is largely a political allegory to which Walpole's government, hard-pressed and near its end, was sensitive. Fielding's next offering, a play called *The Fall of Bob, Alias Gin* (now lost), apparently did much to end his career in the theater, although after his works had lost some of their notoriety, he did produce a few minor pieces.

The Licensing Act of 1737 closed the Little Theatre as well as those in Lincoln's Inn Fields and Goodman's Fields. Moreover, it closed all stages to Fielding, whose development as a dramatist had increasingly led him to the kind of material that would never pass a government censor. Fielding's engagement in anything with which he was involved had been intensely energetic and provocative; he was always searching, pushing, and trying something new. Faced with chains and muzzles, he simply shifted his energies to two, or perhaps three, new careers.

Ostensibly, Fielding became a lawyer instead of a playwright. He resumed his formal education, studying at the Middle Temple, and was admitted to the bar in 1740. He practiced as a barrister, riding the Western Circuit and generally working hard for small financial reward. In 1748, however, he was made a Justice of the Peace for the city of Westminster, and for the next six years he served as a stern but sympathetic judge, concerned with discerning and remedying the causes of crime as well as reforming and improving the city's means of protecting itself, its rudimentary police force. During this period, Fielding continued to interest himself in politics and the drama through three journals, *The Champion* (1739-1741), *The Jacobite Journal* (1747-1748), and *The Covent-Garden Journal* (1752).

Not satisfied by law and journalism, Fielding channeled into prose fiction the creative powers cut off from the stage. In 1741, very soon after he abandoned *The Champion* and less than a year after he began to practice law, Fielding published *Shamela*, a parody of Richardson's *Pamela*. This led the next year to *Joseph Andrews*, the first of his three great novels. *Joseph Andrews*, published anonymously, begins as another attack on Richardson's ethical and moral vision but soon goes off in its own direction, a picaresque work—in the tradition of *Don Quixote de la Mancha*—which is centered on the inscrutable character of Parson Adams. Fielding next published his *Miscellanies* (1743), a collection of both old and new works that was especially notable for the inclusion of *Jonathan Wild*. This intense and bitter satire equates political greatness with criminal notoriety, insisting that greed, ruthlessness, cunning, and singleness of vision propel men to success in crime and government alike. Six years later, *Tom Jones*, Fielding's masterpiece and one of the world's great novels, made original literary contributions, which the plays had not managed to produce. *Amelia*, which Fielding published at the end of 1751, lacks the robust spirit and characters of *Tom Jones* but sold well when it first appeared. Fielding himself favored the book and was disappointed with its critical reception.

By the time *Amelia* was published, Fielding was nearing the end of his life. Making do with the inadequate resources of the legal system, constantly exposed to the diseases of those brought before him in court, and fundamentally weakened, perhaps, by the pace of his own somewhat intemperate life, Fielding required constant medical attention. He did not, however, slow down until the summer of 1754, when he decided to travel to Portugal for his health. During the slow, uncomfortable journey, he wrote *The Journal of a Voyage to Lisbon*, a work of shrewd, humorous observation. It was his last effort. On October 8, 1754, Fielding died, widely mourned by friends who, however much they had valued him, were unlikely to appreciate the scope and variety of his achievements or grasp the extent of the contributions he had made in the forty-seven years of his life.

Analysis

In a period of only nine years, Henry Fielding wrote and staged more than twenty plays. Such a sustained outburst recalls the careers of Elizabethan dramatists Thomas Dekker and John Fletcher, who in the early 1600's turned out three or four scripts a year to feed London's voracious appetite for new plays. The decade of the 1730's was another theatrically hungry period. Five theaters competed for reputation, audience, and income; their managers vied for the best authors, plays, and actors. The pressure of competition added farces, burlesques, operas, pantomime, and even puppet shows to the repertory of drama by standard playwrights. In the struggle to keep up and get ahead, authors and companies freely borrowed material from the French and Italian theaters and readily used singers, dancers, jugglers, and anything else that attracted customers. Innovative theater often brought quick profits, but it challenged many dramatic conventions (especially notions of genre) and often sacrificed dramatic quality to gain immediate impact.

A review of Fielding's plays shows that he attempted to work in one traditional dramatic style, the comedy of manners, but, more important, to cater to the popular taste for new dramatic entertainments. Fielding first tried his hand at five-act comedies in the style of William Congreve and Sir John Vanbrugh. When he met limited success with this form, Fielding turned to farce, one- and two-act plays designed as afterpieces to the main performance. These short plays, at which Fielding proved adept, emphasized broad characterization, limited plots, and busy stage action. If Fielding had worked only in these two styles, however, his modern reputation as a dramatist would be negligible. The theatrical rivalry of his era led Fielding to experiment with dramatic form and stage technique; he experimented both to find innovations that would please audiences and to poke fun at rival playwrights. His experimental dramas (which he once called the "unshaped monsters of a wanton brain") defy categorization because they mix freely and imaginatively elements of manners comedy, farce, burlesque, and ballad opera. Fielding's plays represent different levels of achievement. Skillful as he could be at following convention or manipulating it, Fielding often pursued thematic concerns at the expense of form. His themes are as numerous as the plays themselves: the moral state of London society, the political health of the nation under the administration of Prime Minister Robert Walpole, the condition of modern marriage, and the quality of contemporary theater.

The emphasis on theme made Fielding only a mediocre practitioner of the five-act comedy. His Congrevian comedies were progressively ill-received by audiences, and modern scholarship has devoted attention to them primarily because of Fielding's reputation in other genres. The thematic emphasis was more congenial in farce, where conventions were less firm, but at the same time, the form worked against any substantial thematic exploration or revelation. Fielding's "unshaped monsters," plays in which form is shaped almost organically as a means of expressing theme, are his major achievement. They are amusing, imaginative, and energetic; even though two centuries have dulled some of the pointed satire, they are a delight to read. In the 1730's these experimental plays, mingling dramatic elements in unexpected ways for irreverent purposes, sometimes pleased and sometimes puzzled. Modern readers—accustomed to Gilbert and Sullivan operettas, Marx Brothers films, and Monty Python skits—can easily visualize these works in performance. A term Fielding used for one of this group, "dramatic satire," might serve for all of them.

Tracing the sequence of Fielding's five-act comedies, one sees clearly how the conventions of the genre and Fielding's interests grew steadily. The Congrevian comedy of manners followed patterns that had codified during four decades of Restoration theater. The staple plot presents a witty hero in pursuit of love and fortune through fashionable London society. Love begins as a hunt for pleasure—like a fox hunt, a chase of elaborate ceremony—with the hunter well equipped by a solid inheritance. The hero, a skeptic about the virtues of marriage, enjoys the hunt until he meets a woman whose wit and intelligence match his own. Now the hero's pursuit changes: Love's quality matters more to him than variety, and his wealth enables him to avoid mindless conformity to society's customs. The lovers display their attractive characters and mutual affection in brilliant dialogue, and they overcome whatever obstacles arise: rival lovers, disagreeable guardians, legal complexities. By manipulating other characters, the lovers bring their courtship to a successful conclusion which sees deserving heads, hearts, and fortunes united. Although the dramatist might make, in the course of things, satiric points about contemporary values and attitudes, Congrevian comedy emphasizes the mutual attraction of the young lovers. John Loftis has called this celebration of attraction, as it matures from a physical desire to incorporate intellectual parity, the "gaiety of sex." Congrevian comedy entertains and improves by championing the pursuit of love.

Fielding's first two comedies, *Love in Several Masques* and *The Temple Beau*, remain faithful to the conventions and emphases of the type. In the first play, Merital seeks to win Helena, whose guardians, an aunt and uncle, wish to marry her to the foolish man-about-town, Apish. The aunt, Lady Trap, is an obstacle in another sense: She is trying to seduce Merital. The lovers elope after Merital pretends friendship with Apish to gain access to Helena. In the second play, Veromil, though defrauded of his inheritance by a rascally brother, pursues Bellaria because he loves her. His rival is a high-living rake and supposed law student, Henry Wilding, who courts Bellaria as a means of recouping his wasted fortune. The timely intervention of an old family servant exposes the fraud and secures social recognition for Veromil's marriage to Bellaria. Although the plays attack the contemporary feeling that money and concern for the family name are more important than love, their satire does not obscure the zesty pursuit of love.

This is not the case, however, in Fielding's other five-act comedies. Perhaps because comedy is a traditional vehicle for lashing vice and exposing folly, Fielding increasingly gave precedence to theme over conventions of character and plot. A moralist, like many eighteenth century authors, he could not help paying more attention to political, professional, and social corruption than he did to literary traditions. Though this emphasis weakened the public appeal of his five-act plays, it shows his thinking and underlies his growing sense of dramatic freedom.

Rape upon Rape, which claims to present contemporary life as any observer could remark it, is more a thesis play than a comedy. The title (which offended Fielding's contemporaries and had to be changed) both describes the literal action and also becomes a symbolic indictment of the English judicial system. Hilaret's plans to elope with Captain Constant are upset when she is accosted by the rakish Ramble. Her cry of "rape" causes Ramble to be apprehended, but he then charges her with swearing a false accusation. Both are hauled before Justice Squeezum, who solicits bribes from men and women alike: money from the former and sex from the latter. Managing to escape Squeezum's solicitations, Hilaret learns that Constant has been carried to the same court on a false rape charge. Although Hilaret and Constant are true lovers, who proceed to expose Squeezum's corruption and manage to marry, little attention is paid to celebrating their mutual attraction. The play offers some amusing moments, but there is, not surprisingly, little gaiety in the themes of pandering, attempted rape, and injustice.

Fielding's subsequent five-act comedies move even further from the model. There are courting lovers in *The Modern Husband*, but they are not the central couple; there are no unmarried lovers in *The Universal Gallant*, nor are the married people especially attractive people in either play. The main action of *The Modern Husband* is a strong indictment of aristocratic power and middle-class groveling: Lord Richly awards power and prestige to men who prostitute their wives to him and then uses those couples to seduce others. The play shows Richly attempting to use Mr. and Mrs. Modern to bring Mr. and Mrs. Bellamant within his circle. Fortunately, the Bellamants are faithful to each other and clever enough to thwart Richly's design. *The Universal Gallant* contrasts the overly suspicious Sir Simon Raffler, whose wife is faithful, with the trusting Colonel Raffler, whose wife is regularly unfaithful. Entangled with these couples are Captain Spark, who boasts (without justification) of numerous conquests, and the beau Mondish, who goes quietly about several amours. Sex abounds in both plays, but, again, little of it is lighthearted. The Bellamants and the

Simon Rafflers find only distress in love; the couples endure, but with little sense of celebration.

Fielding found farce a better medium than comedy for exaggerated char- acterization and pointed satire. Eighteenth century farce did not have as many conventions as manners comedy, but its assumptions were well under- stood. In the prologue to *The Lottery*, Fielding comments on two impor- tant differences between the types. First, while "Comedy delights to punish the fool,/ Farce challenges the vulgar as her prize"; that is, the characters satirized in farce are more mean-spirited than self-deluded (and probably of a low social class). Second, farce identifies and attacks its targets by a "magnifying right/ To raise the object still larger to the sight"; that is, it allows exaggeration, hyperbole, and caricature. Formally, farce differs from comedy by dispensing with subplot, speeding up the pace, and emphasizing humor rather than wit in dialogue.

The Lottery is a good example of the latitude that farce gave Fielding's interests. The play exposes the foolishness of those who literally mortgage their futures to a one-in-ten-thousand chance and deplores the corruption of those who capitalize on foolish hopes. Mr. Stocks, who sells lottery tick- ets, knows "what an abundance of rich men will one month reduce to their former poverty." The brief plot follows the rocky love affair of Mr. Stock's younger brother Jack, who has no inheritance and whose beloved puts all their hopes for a happy married life on winning a ten-thousand-pound first prize. Fortunately, the lovers' natural affection survives the inevitable dis- appointment when their ticket does not win.

Eurydice shows a more imaginative use of farce's freewheeling style. The play depicts the visit of Orpheus to the Underworld in pursuit of his wife, Eurydice. Orpheus, singing ballad opera instead of strumming the lyre, charms Pluto, god of the Underworld, into granting permission for Euryd- ice to return to earth. Eurydice, however, is reluctant to return to modern London, where married love is accorded little respect; if Orpheus is like other modern husbands, he will soon lose interest in her. She wonders if she is not better off in a kingdom where she is free to govern herself. After much singing about the advantages and disadvantages of either choice, Eurydice finally decides to stay, and Orpheus departs alone, warning other husbands to appreciate their wives while they have them. *Eurydice* was not well received by its first audience, which took an unexpected dislike to one character, the ghost of an army beau. This reception led Fielding to write a sequel, *Eurydice Hiss'd*, about an author whose play, though imperfect, is unjustly scorned by theatergoers.

The Lottery and *Eurydice* are typical English farces, with a certain zani- ness that results from making the plot fit the satiric theme. There was another tradition of farce, however, that Fielding explored in the 1730's. This other tradition was French; its major practitioner was Molière. Its sat-

ire is general (the incompetence of doctors, the social vanity of the nou-
veau riche), its structure built on the traditional devices of fast-paced
action, intrigue, and disguise rather than on ludicrous situations. One
might call it the "well-made farce": The plot leaves no loose ends. Such
plays demand especially skillful actors; Fielding, who was always aware of
how much a play's success depended upon its cast, twice adapted material
from the French to match the talent of a specific actress—in *The Intriguing
Chambermaid* and *The Mock Doctor*. Taking stock situations such as the
clever servant who outwits a master and the couple for whom marital life
and marital strife are synonymous, these farces move briskly to unfold,
develop, and tie together the action. *The Intriguing Chambermaid* and *The
Mock Doctor*, both successful pieces, show that Fielding could adapt as
well as be original in the art of farce.

Fielding, like many of his contemporaries, spoke slightingly of farce
because it was without classical precedent and therefore less literary: "The
stage . . . was not for low farce designed/ But to divert, instruct, and mend
mankind" through comedy. Fielding moved progressively away from comedy, however, as his own interests and theatrical developments in the 1730's
did more to shape his drama than did the desire to succeed as a regular
dramatist. Fielding found two vehicles, ballad opera and burlesque, ideal
for presenting satire in drama. Ballad opera combined farce, music, and
ingenious paralleling; it originated with John Gay's *The Beggar's Opera* (pr.
1728), a tale of London's underworld in which thieves and prostitutes sing
arias (set to native English tunes) about their lives, which show embarrassing similarities to those of the rich and powerful. Burlesque exaggerated
theatrical conventions in order to poke fun at them and to indict a public
taste for such inferior entertainment. (Sometimes, however, "inferior"
meant only "what was currently successful at a rival theater.")

Fielding never wrote pure burlesque or ballad opera, preferring to draw
on these forms for devices which, when mixed with elements of comedy
and farce, could produce ingenious and distinctive plays. As suggested earlier, Fielding's subtitle to *Pasquin—A Dramatic Satire on the Times*—may
be the most useful way of describing these plays. "Satire" comes from the
Latin *satura*, which means a medley; Fielding's dramatic satires are indeed
medleys for the stage, collections of parts and techniques and themes
which the critical purist may find offensive but which the responsive reader
often finds delightful. Fielding, never able to give up hope of becoming
famous for his five-act comedies, often apologized for the dramatic satires,
calling them products of "his unskilled muse," because they pleased the
fancy more than the judgment. Those who read the dramatic satires today
could hardly disagree more. Written to "combat the follies of the town,"
these plays do suffer somewhat because some contemporary allusions are
lost, but Fielding is one of the great detectors of human folly, and the truth

of his observations is not limited to any time, any place, or any social class.

Four plays—*The Tragedy of Tragedies*, *The Author's Farce*, *Pasquin*, and *The Historical Register for the Year 1736*—are Fielding's masterpieces in dramatic satire. They demonstrate his inventiveness, his versatility, his wit, and his thematic concerns. *The Tragedy of Tragedies* (a three-act version of the two-act afterpiece *Tom Thumb*) is a fantastic burlesque of heroic tragedy. The court of King Arthur and Queen Dollalolla is attacked by a race of warriors led by the giantess Glumdalca. The invaders are defeated by Arthur's champion, Tom Thumb, a knight as big as the digit whose name he bears. In reward, Tom is allowed to marry the Princess Huncamunca, but the proposed union causes much jealousy. Lord Grizzle, who loves Huncamunca, refuses to see her wed to one "fitter for [her] pocket than [her] bed." The queen and Glumdalca despair because they both love Tom. The giantess must forsake Tom because of their physical difference, and the queen's marriage vows intrude, although Dollalolla finds that in Cupid's scale, "Tom Thumb is heavier than my Virtue."

While Tom celebrates his engagement by murdering two bailiffs who arrest his courtier friends for debt, Grizzle attempts to woo Huncamunca. He succeeds quickly, but only because the Princess is ready to marry either man—or any man. Grizzle vows to kill Tom by leading a rebellion. Meanwhile, King Arthur is visited by a ghost who prophesies Tom's death. When the loyal army confronts the rebels, Grizzle kills Glumdalca, but Tom slays Grizzle. The celebration at court is spoiled, however, when news comes that upon meeting the victors in their march home, "a Cow, of larger size than usual/ . . . in a Moment swallowed up Tom Thumb."

As farce, *The Tragedy of Tragedies* is humorous, but as burlesque it is brilliant. As he exaggerates tragic conventions, Fielding also mocks their language by mimicking it. Inflated rhetoric, overblown metaphor, inappropriate diction, and ironic simile provide an aural equivalent of the visual farce. The king inquires thus about Dollalolla's health: "What wrinkled Sorrow,/ Hangs, sits, lies, frowns upon thy knitted brow?" Huncamunca describes pining for Tom: "For him I've sighed, I've wept, I've gnawed my Sheets." The parson prays for the fruitfulness of Tom's marriage: "So when the Cheshire Cheese a Maggot breeds,/ . . . By thousands, and ten thousands they increase,/ Till one continued Maggot fills the rotten Cheese." Glumdalca laments the emotional storm raised in her by the sight of Tom: "I'm all within a Hurricane, as if/ The World's four winds were pent within my Carcass." A giantess filled with one wind to expel is awesome; the notion of four winds pent within her is catastrophic.

The printed text of the play adds another target to the burlesque: It is a mock scholarly edition with critical apparatus. Fielding names his editor H. Scriblerus *Secundus* in the tradition of Martinus Scriblerus, whom Alexander Pope and Jonathan Swift had created to satirize pedantic scholarship. In a preface filled with Latin tags and authoritative references, Scriblerus argues that *The Tragedy of Tragedies*, conforming perfectly to classical precedent, is renowned throughout Europe. The footnotes increase the fun. Fielding had borrowed lines from actual plays (sometimes crucially altered, sometimes not) for his burlesque; the footnotes invert the procedure by demonstrating that *The Tragedy of Tragedies* was actually written in Elizabethan times and has itself been borrowed from and pillaged by all subsequent dramatists.

The Author's Farce also ridicules, in a somewhat freer form than *The Tragedy of Tragedies*, theatrical tastes of the day. It tells of a struggling playwright named Luckless who is having great difficulty getting his piece performed or published. Luckless is sure the work is just the thing to please contemporary audiences: a puppet show, called *The Pleasures of the Town*, which uses live actors. The inversion is typically Fielding; he teases the current rage for puppet actors performing cut-down standard plays by positing live actors performing Punch-and-Joan (as Judy was universally known then) antics.

The play is not pure burlesque but a mixture of comic traditions. Act 1 is traditional manners comedy. It shows Luckless unable to pay his rent because he is unable to sell his play. Witty though impoverished, Luckless fends off the financial and amorous demands of his landlady, Mrs. Moneywood, because he is really in love with her daughter, Harriot. Luckless' friend Witmore aids him in his battles against dunning creditors and stingy booksellers. When Witmore pays off the back rent, the ingenious Luckless dupes Moneywood into turning the cash over to him. When the publisher Bookweight refuses Luckless an advance, Bookweight is abused and thrown out of the apartment. At least Luckless gains some emotional satisfaction, and he possesses the pluck, the hauteur, and the quick-wittedness of the Congrevian hero.

Act 2 is closer to farce. Ten rapid scenes show Luckless trying to get his puppet show staged immediately. Two theater managers (representing Colley Cibber and Robert Wilks of Drury Lane) turn the play down because the author has no "interest"—that is, no standing within the ruling theatrical clique. Taking his case directly to other managers and to the actors, Luckless arranges for a performance that very night. Bookweight, discovered at his shop overseeing instant dedications and rapid translations written by his stable of hacks, now willingly listens to Luckless because he has "interest." A crier advertises the performance, "in which will be shown the whole Court of Dullness with abundance of singing and dancing and several other entertainments . . . to be performed by living figures, some of them six foot high."

The third act, the actual performance of Luckless' play, combines farce and burlesque. *The Pleasures of the Town* opens with a scene of the archetypal feuding couple, Punch and Joan; the arguing, singing, and dancing please popular taste but in no way relate to what follows. The next scene introduces a deceased poet on his way to the Goddess of Nonsense's Underworld court; the poet meets several other travelers fresh from London who are on the same route. There is Don Tragedio, who died after one performance; Sir Farcical Comic, who was hissed to death; Mr. Pantomime, whose neck the audience wrung; and Madam Novel, who went unread. Preeminent among these victims of shifting audience taste is Don Opera, who was so overwhelmed with the audience's approbation and his own dying aria that he swooned to death. Don Opera has been chosen as the fittest spouse for the Goddess of Nonsense. After an irrelevant scene presenting a card game among four shrieking harridans, the stage is set for the wedding. At this moment, *The Pleasures of the Town* turns into a ballad opera and emotional outbursts are rendered in song. There is plenty of passionate carrying-on: Nonsense discovers that Opera is already wed to Novel, and Opera protests that death has freed him from his vows. Unconvinced, Nonsense invites wooing from Farcical, Pantomime, and the others. Spurned, Opera proclaims his undying affection for Novel.

This dramatic moment is interrupted by Parson Murdertext, who has brought Constable to arrest Luckless for staging a sacrilegious play. The characters in the puppet show argue with Murdertext and Constable, thus blurring the line between play and play-within-the-play. That line grows even fainter as Harriot and Witmore enter with the ambassador from the Javanese kingdom of Bantom. The newcomer proclaims Luckless as the long-lost heir to Bantom's throne. A messenger enters to announce that the old Javanese king has just died, and Luckless is immediately proclaimed Henry I of Bantom. He appoints all the characters (not the actors) in the puppet-show to important government posts. Punch returns to identify himself as Harriot's lost brother, and Moneywood proclaims herself the impoverished Queen of Brentford. The play concludes with a dance.

Without a well-annotated text, modern readers will miss many of the injokes, yet none will miss Fielding's general indictment of the foolishness that passes as entertainment. Sudden reversals of fortune, reliance upon spectacle in place of development, and heavy use of coincidence are all marks of amateurishness or incompetence that mar drama, whether their victim is an eighteenth century play, a Hollywood movie, or a television sitcom.

Pasquin, a dramatic satire that shows Fielding's seemingly limitless inventiveness, follows one of the few traditions for a satiric play: a rehearsal of another play. George Villiers' *The Rehearsal* (pr. 1671), which mocked the heroic plays of John Dryden and Robert Howard, originated the form, which became standard in the self-conscious theater of the late seventeenth and early eighteenth centuries. Fielding's twist on the formula is to include two rehearsals—one of a comedy and one of a tragedy—in the same play. For two and a half acts, *Pasquin* shows Trapwit leading the actors through a comedy about how to win an election; for another two and a half acts, *Pasquin* presents Fustian taking the cast through his tragedy on the death of Queen Commonsense.

There is much comment and satire in *Pasquin* on now-familiar theatrical topics: the plight of actors and actresses, the looming specter of debtor's prison for authors and performers, hasty production of plays, scenes written by formula, reliance in dialogue upon bombast and innuendo (Trapwit, for example, protests that "except about a dozen, or a score, or so, there is not an impure joke" in his comedy), and production opportunity allowed only to already-successful authors. Fielding's main target in *Pasquin*, however, is not the theater; his subjects are political and intellectual. *Pasquin* has more in common with Swift's *Gulliver's Travels* (1726) and Pope's *The Dunciad* (1728-1743) than it does with other plays of the period. Trapwit's comedy is a merciless exposure of election campaigning, and Fustian's tragedy is an indictment of three professions: law, medicine, and religion. The play's title suggests the wide-ranging assault: Pasquin was the name of a Roman statue that was annually festooned with satiric epigrams and verses.

Like Swift, Fielding shows that people get the politicians they deserve. Trapwit's comedy observes the conduct of a contemporary election. Lord Place and Colonel Promise, the court's candidates (representing the Whig party of Sir Robert Walpole), vie for seats in Parliament with Sir Henry Foxchase and Squire Tankard, the country candidates (representing the Tory party). As the Mayor and aldermen sit in a tavern discussing the election, Place and Promise arrive and begin campaigning; they simply bribe each voter. In contrast to this method, which Trapwit calls "direct bribing," Foxchase and Tankard engage in indirect bribing: They buy meat and drink freely for the tavern crowd, patronize the merchants with prodigious orders for silks and clothing, and lament the corruption of courtiers who openly buy votes. The Mayor and aldermen rally for a moment to the newcomers and their slogan of "Liberty, property, and no excise."

Meanwhile, Place and Promise have been active among the ladies of the town, filling their ears with stories about the masquerades and fashionable gowns which could be theirs if the Court candidates win. Mrs. Mayoress and Miss Mayoress conclude that the lord and the colonel are "the finest men . . . the prettiest men . . . the sweetest men" and that the Mayor must vote for them. Miss Mayoress also persuades Miss Stitch, by the gift of a fan, to seek her beau's vote for the Court. The ladies carry the day with the Mayor, and when Foxchase and Tankard win the election, the Mayor is much chagrined that he has supported the losing party. Unable to give up her dreams of Court preferment, Mrs. Mayoress convinces her husband to certify that the losers are really the victors. As she announces this startling development to the surprised courtiers, she encourages them, "when we have returned you so [that is, duly elected] it will be your fault if you don't prove yourself so." Mrs. Mayoress refers to the wonderful knack of eighteenth century incumbents, especially Walpole's supporters, for keeping their seats by parliamentary maneuvering—regardless of an election's outcome.

Fustian's play, more allegorical than Trapwit's, is set at the court of Queen Commonsense in the days when she ruled England. Three of her chief ministers—Law, Physic, and Firebrand (who stands for religion)—are unhappy because the reign of logic and reason in the land has diminished their power. For example, when two men suing each other over property lose it to their own lawyers, the queen is ready to reform the legal system, but Law sees only a decline in his authority and income. When news comes that Queen Ignorance, with an army of "singers, fiddlers, tumblers, and rope-dancers," has invaded the island, the disgruntled courtiers threaten to join the rebels unless Commonsense yields them more power. Nevertheless, the queen bravely contends:

> Religion, law, and physic were designed
> By Heaven, the greatest blessings of mankind;
> But priests and lawyers and physicians made
> These general goods to each a private trade;
> With each they rob, with each they fill their purses,
> And turn our benefits into our curses.

Commonsense's refusal to surrender brings on a battle. Gradually, her followers are slain until only a poet remains; his support of Commonsense has been so weak of late that he readily goes over to the enemy. Firebrand stabs Commonsense, and the reign of Ignorance is established. Only the ghost of Commonsense remains to harass Ignorance's minions on occasion. The play ends, like Pope's *The Dunciad*, with universal darkness covering just about all.

In neither *The Author's Farce* nor *Pasquin* is Fielding's satire subtle. No characters are fully realized, plots jump as need be, and the dialogue has more sarcasm than wit. Fielding's ingenuity is in the juxtaposition of diverse and eclectic elements; the plays please through surprise and bluntness.

The Historical Register for the Year 1736 is less imaginative in its theatrical technique but more daring in its political attack. It, too, is cast as a rehearsal, this time of the playwright Medley's work about the previous year's events on the island kingdom of Corsica (which is obviously a symbol of Walpolian England). Medley's play alternates comments on the theater and on the nation because "There is a ministry in the latter as well as the former, and I believe as weak a ministry as any poor kingdom could boast of."

In linking the two worlds of the prime minister and the theater manager, Medley observes that "though the public damn both, yet while they [the ministers] receive their pay, they laugh at the public behind the scenes." Through Medley's play, Fielding takes the audience behind the scenes.

Act 1 begins by assembling some observers of the rehearsal and showing what kind of reception Medley might expect. Medley and the actors, happy merely to have a script to perform and a stage to use, convene. The critic Sourwit joins them, immediately damning whatever he sees. Lord Dapper looks on, so weak-brained that the most obvious satire must be explained to him. As the rehearsal commences, Medley reads a prologue, an ode to the New Year (with immortal lines such as "This is a day in days of yore/ Our fathers never saw before") which burlesques the vapid verse of the poet laureate and theater manager Colley Cibber. The first scene displays a cabal of politicians who respond to financial crisis by voting another tax. Finding everything already taxed, one politico proposes a tax on learning, but another counters, "I think we had better lay it on Ignorance," which "will take in most of the great fortunes in the Kingdom." Lord Dapper is present proof that the speaker is right. Fielding manages to abuse both politicians and, through them, the masters they serve.

Act 2 continues the assault with an opening scene in which fashionable ladies (formula comedies always open the second act with fashionable ladies) adore the latest opera singer, whose performances currently pack the theaters. They display their enthusiasm by carrying his "babies" (little wax dolls in his image), certainly an ironic tribute to a castrato. Since these dolls are more valuable than lapdogs or spouses, one lady protests, "If my husband was to make any objection to my having 'em, I'd run away from him and take the dear babies with me." In the next scene, the women attend an auction (the current faddish pastime), where the satire turns political. Up for sale are items such as a cloth remnant of political honesty, a piece of patriotism big enough to show off but too small to hold attention, a few grains of modesty, and an unopened bottle of courage; the buyers disparage the goods. Fielding's comment is twofold: There is only enough virtue in political society to give the illusion of honesty, and even that little claims no great market. The act ends with the entrance of the madman Pistol, who claims the title of "Prime Minister Theatrical"; when a mob hisses, he takes the sound as a sign of approbation. Pistol is a caricature of Theophilus Cibber, who, like his father, Colley, aspired to this title by hearing applause in a round of catcalls.

The third act dramatizes Medley's thesis that in the contemporary world "a man of parts, learning, and virtue is fit for no employment whatever . . . that honesty is the only sort of folly for which a man ought to be utterly neglected and condemned." The theatrical and political implications of this view are worked out as a modern-day Apollo casts the players for a performance of Shakespeare's *King John* with little regard to their competency. Like the theater managers of *The Author's Farce*, the god makes his decisions on the basis of "interest," the auditioner's relationship to someone in power. The consequences of such thinking are dramatized as Pistol becomes Prime Minister Theatrical by usurping his father and as Quidam, the model of a modern politician, bilks five citizens of the little money with which he had bribed them at election time. Quidam's fraud is accomplished through a pantomime dance which demonstrates that politics is nothing but theater; Pistol's accession shows how political theater is. The dance concludes the play, yet it is not a proper dramatic ending, simply one that caters to the people's taste. If the actors laugh while they dance, the target of their laughter is clear. Though Fielding's plays are diverse in method and form, they are alike in motivation. Fielding used the stage as early eighteenth century writers used every literary genre: as a forum for the discussion of current events. With journalistic promptness and intensity, Fielding (like other dramatists of the 1730's) built plays around current events in London: examples of private morality and immorality, political issues and personalities, and trends in the theater. Like a journalist, Fielding wrote rapidly. If a play succeeded, it was imitated or redone in a bigger and better version; if a play failed, it was pulled from the stage and replaced. Fielding was adept at writing quickly as well as ingeniously, whether reviving old material or concocting new combinations of dramatic staples. These "unshaped monsters of a wanton brain" could never bring Fielding the literary fame that successful five-act comedies would have brought, but several of them are masterpieces of the 1730's, one of the liveliest and most experimental eras of English theater.

Other major works

NOVELS: *An Apology for the Life of Mrs. Shamela Andrews*, 1741 (commonly known as *Shamela*); *The History of the Adventures of Joseph Andrews, and His Friend Mr. Abraham Adams*, 1742 (commonly known as *Joseph Andrews*); *The History of the Life of the Late Mr. Jonathan Wild the Great*, 1743, 1754 (commonly known as *Jonathan Wild*); *The History of Tom Jones, a Foundling*, 1749 (commonly known as *Tom Jones*); *Amelia*, 1751.
NONFICTION: *The Journal of a Voyage to Lisbon*, 1755.
MISCELLANEOUS: *Miscellanies*, 1743 (3 volumes).

Bibliography

Dircks, Richard J. *Henry Fielding*. Boston: Twayne, 1983. This study is designed to provide an introduction to Fielding in such a way as to integrate his central ideas and vision of life as they are experienced in his works as a dramatist, journalist, pamphleteer, and novelist. Emphasis is placed on Fielding's major works. Includes only those biographical de-

tails that are necessary to provide a coherent sketch of the author's career. Provides a reading that is informed by scholarship. Excellent bibliography, chronology.

Hatfield, Glenn W. *Henry Fielding and the Language of Irony.* Chicago:
University of Chicago Press, 1968. The author examines the eighteenth
century as a language-conscious age and stresses the importance of
Fielding's preoccupation with language. He argues that, for Fielding,
irony is a way of speaking the truth in a corrupt medium. Fielding's
sensitivity to those he considered to be the linguistic prostitutes of his
age and his lifetime search for a means of expressing social truths are
the book's major concerns.

Hunter, J. Paul. *Occasional Form: Henry Fielding and the Chain of Circumstance.* Baltimore: The Johns Hopkins University Press, 1975. This
work attempts to place Fielding's career and major works in relation to
historical forces operating on his mind and art, chronicling his anxiety
and adjustment to circumstance. Fielding, according to Hunter, stands
between two eras; he is a reactionary pioneer who commutes between
old and new values. Provides extensive analysis of Fielding's major
works.

Lewis, Peter. *Fielding's Burlesque Drama: Its Place in the Tradition.* Edinburgh, Scotland: University of Edinburgh Press, 1987. Lewis argues that
because of the overwhelming success of Fielding's novels, the author's
drama has been neglected—with the exception of the *Tom Thumb* plays.
Emphasizes the burlesque and satirical dimension of Fielding's plays and
places his work in the history of burlesque theater. Illustrations.

Rivero, Albert J. *The Plays of Henry Fielding: A Critical Study of His
Dramatic Career.* Charlottesville: University Press of Virginia, 1989. Taking a new approach to Fielding's dramatic career, Rivero tells the story
of this career by focusing on the plays themselves and by offering a
detailed critique of ten representative plays. Discusses dramatic technique, construction, themes and provides some historical context to the
plays.

Rogers, Pat. *Henry Fielding: A Life Story.* New York: Charles Scribner's
Sons, 1979. This well-written biography attempts to discuss the major
turning points in the author's life and career. Although mentioned in the
context of his life, Fielding's major works are not discussed at length.
Aimed at a general audience. Contains illustrations, family tree, biographical index, and reading list.

Simpson, K. G., ed. *Henry Fielding: Justice Obscured.* New York: Barnes
& Noble Books, 1985. This collection of essays attests the diversity of
Fielding's experience as a citizen, magistrate, political writer, and
dramatist—varied aspects that influenced the nature of his writing. At
the heart of the collection is a concern with the formation of the writer's

values and their expression in his works. Richness and range of vision in the essays.

Robert M. Otten
Richard N. Ramsey
(Updated by *Genevieve Slomski*)

CLYDE FITCH

Born: Elmira, New York; May 2, 1865
Died: Châlons-sur-Marne, France; September 4, 1909

Principal drama

Beau Brummell, pr. 1890, pb. 1908; *Frederick Lemaître*, pr. 1890, pb. 1933 (one act); *Betty's Finish*, pr. 1890; *Pamela's Prodigy*, pr. 1891, pb. 1893; *A Modern Match*, pr. 1892; *The Masked Ball*, pr. 1892 (adaptation of Alexandre Bisson and Albert Carré's play *Le Veglione*); *The Social Swim*, pr. 1893 (adaptation of Victorien Sardou's play *Maison neuve*); *The Harvest*, pr. 1893; *April Weather*, pr. 1893; *A Shattered Idol*, pr. 1893 (adaptation of Honoré de Balzac's novel *Le Père Goriot*); *An American Duchess*, pr. 1893 (adaptation of Henri Lavedan's play *Le Prince d'Aurec*); *Mrs. Grundy*, pb. 1893; *His Grace de Grammont*, pr. 1894; *Lovers' Lane*, wr. 1894, pr. 1901, pb. 1915; *Gossip*, pr. 1895 (with Leo Ditrichstein; adaptation of Jules Claretie's play); *Mistress Betty*, pr. 1895; *Bohemia*, pr. 1896 (adaptation of Henri Murger's novel *Scènes de la vie de Bohème*); *The Liar*, pr. 1896 (adaptation of Bisson's play); *The Superfluous Husband*, pr. 1897 (with Ditrichstein; adaptation of Ludwig Fulda's play); *Nathan Hale*, pr. 1898, pb. 1899; *The Moth and the Flame*, pr. 1898, pb. 1908 (revision of *The Harvest*); *The Head of the Family*, pr. 1898 (adaptation of Adolf L'Arronge's play *Hasemanns Töchter*); *The Cowboy and the Lady*, pr. 1899, pb. 1908; *Barbara Frietchie*, pr. 1899, pb. 1900; *Sapho*, pr. 1899 (adaptation of scenes by Alphonse Daudet and Adolphe Belot and adaptation of Daudet's novel); *Captain Jinks of the Horse Marines*, pr. 1901, pb. 1902; *The Climbers*, pr. 1901, pb. 1906; *The Last of the Dandies*, pr. 1901; *The Marriage Game*, pr. 1901 (adaptation of Émile Augier's play *Le Mariage d'Olympe*); *The Way of the World*, pr. 1901; *The Girl and the Judge*, pr. 1901; *The Stubbornness of Geraldine*, pr. 1902, pb. 1906; *The Girl with the Green Eyes*, pr. 1902, pb. 1905; *The Bird in the Cage*, pr. 1903 (adaptation of Ernst von Wildenbruch's play *Die Haubenlerche*); *The Frisky Mrs. Johnson*, pr. 1903, pb. 1908 (adaptation of Paul Gavault and Georges Berr's play *Madame Flirt*); *Her Own Way*, pr. 1903, pb. 1907; *Major André*, pr. 1903; *Glad of It*, pr. 1903; *The Coronet of the Duchess*, pr. 1904; *Granny*, pr. 1904 (adaptation of Michel Georges-Michel's novel *L'Aïeule*); *Cousin Billy*, pr. 1905 (adaptation of Eugène Labiche and Édouard Martin's play *Le Voyage de M. Perrichon*); *The Woman in the Case*, pr. 1905, pb. 1915; *Her Great Match*, pr. 1905, pb. 1916; *The Toast of the Town*, pr. 1905 (revision of *Mistress Betty*); *Wolfville*, pr. 1905 (with Willis Steell; adaptation of Alfred Henry Lewis' stories); *The Girl Who Has Everything*, pr. 1906; *Toddles*, pr. 1906 (adaptation of André Godfernaux and Tristan Bernard's play *Triplepatte*); *The House of Mirth*, pr. 1906 (with Edith Wharton; adaptation of Wharton's novel); *The Straight Road*, pr. 1906; *The Truth*, pr. 1906, pb. 1907; *Her Sister*, pr. 1907; *Girls*, pr. 1908 (adaptation of Alexander Engel and Julius Horst's play *Die Welt ohne Männer*); *The Blue Mouse*, pr. 1908; *A Happy Marriage*, pr. 1909; *The Bachelor*, pr. 1909; *The City*, pr. 1909, pb. 1915; *Plays*, pb. 1915 (4 volumes).

Other literary forms

Clyde Fitch's nondramatic works have never been collected. He wrote one novel, *A Wave of Life*, which appeared in *Lippincott's* magazine in February, 1891, and which was later published by Mitchell Kennerley, with a foreword by Montrose J. Moses. Before the novel was published, Fitch had served his literary apprenticeship by writing short stories for a variety of commercial and church-related magazines. In 1889 alone, *The Independent*, *The Christian Union*, *The Churchman*, *Puck*, *Life*, and the children's magazine *Young Hearts* had accepted his stories, and in 1891, Fitch gathered a number of his vignettes of childhood into a volume entitled *The Knighting of the Twins*, which was published by Roberts Brothers in Boston; one of the stories, "An Unchronicled Miracle," was dedicated to Walter Pater. Known for his association with the Pre-Raphaelite movement, the author of *Studies in the History of the Renaissance* (1873) answered Fitch's whimsical verse that suggested that "even a cat may look on a king" with a pleasant, congratulatory note. *Some Correspondence and Six Conversations* (1896) and *The Smart Set* (1897), both collections of letters and discussions, were published by Stone and Kimball in Chicago. Fitch's nondramatic works are out of print and difficult to obtain; some of the short stories in such magazines as *Puck* and *Life* have not been identified.

Achievements

While Fitch was awarded no prizes or honors, he deserves mention as one of the first American playwrights to achieve popular success on his home ground. Indeed, the theatrical climate was ripe for his combination of romance and realism with purely American settings; most Broadway plays were either comedies of manners imported from England or farces translated from the French or German. Fitch wrote, then, when many serious as well as satiric publications were concerned not only with "Anglomania" but also with the development of a national literature. Given such a receptive audience, Fitch frequently produced a number of plays within one season.

To be sure, he was criticized for his "artificial" plotting, for tailoring his plays to available actresses, and for both borrowing from successful foreign plays and taking poetic license with history. Nevertheless, his development from farce to drama was sure and steady, and his careful attention to scenic detail and acting method earmarked him as a major influence on the realistic stage. Fitch's later experimentation, notably in *The City*, would make him memorable.

Fitch's works generally met with wildly enthusiastic responses from audiences but were often less generously received by critics, many of whom felt that his mechanical, "well-made" plots were indicative of a superficial point of view. Others, however, believed that his carefully tailored dramatic structures were foils for a social consciousness that would not be accepted in an undisguised form. In one sense, at least, such negative criticism was justified. The lighthearted *Captain Jinks of the Horse Marines*, starring Ethel Barrymore as the enterprising and charming Bronxite who pretends to be an Italian soprano, was resoundingly successful; the more serious *The Truth*, treating the marital consequences of inveterate lying, was not—at least in the United States. Marie Tempest made the play one of the first American successes throughout Europe, but at home, reception was cool, perhaps because the title betokened a more serious treatment than the public wished. Certainly, *The Climbers* had similar trouble, refused by all the New York producers because of what they believed to be a twin disability: a death and a suicide. The producers were wrong: Fitch's audience, which was both nurtured on the new realism of Theodore Dreiser and Stephen Crane and rooted in the nostalgia of the nineteenth century, appeared in droves, not only to witness the January-May marriage of the widowed Mrs. Hunter and the wealthy, socially inept Johnny Trotter, but also to hear about the self-denying love between Blanche Sterling and Edward Warden.

Critics and audiences agreed that Fitch excelled in the details of his settings. Producers were content to give him free rein, knowing that the playwright who worked almost eighteen hours a day and who was concerned in *Barbara Frietchie*, for example, that a fan failed to blow the curtains realistically enough to simulate a Maryland breeze, would mount a production with the finest attention to detail. Such attention came from his own aesthetic predilections: Once he achieved financial success, he traveled to Europe every spring, collecting the Della Robbias, the Louis IV furniture, the rare books, and the Watteaus that spilled over in his New York salon.

For Fitch, the collection of such paraphernalia, which might be regarded as mere affectation, was much in concert with his immersion in the theater. Without family attachments, he saw his work as defining his life; in words reminiscent of Henry James, Fitch wrote that he spent his time "studying and observing life" and that he had one goal—"to develop always." Praised for his "psychology," ideas, and theatrical savvy abroad, he failed to win serious critical acclaim at home, yet a modern reassessment suggests that his enthusiastic audiences were wiser than the savants. Fitch is important, not simply as one of the first American playwrights to achieve solid popularity but also as a transitional figure between nineteenth century melodrama and twentieth century realism.

Biography

Born in Elmira, New York, on May 2, 1865, William Clyde Fitch was the first of five children and the only son of Alice Maud Clark of Hagerstown, Maryland, and William Goodwin Fitch, a staff member to General Heintzelman during the Civil War. When he was four, the family moved to Schenectady, where he later joined with friends to form the Amateur Club and the Hookey Club and edited *The Rising Sun*, the pages of which express Fitch's early verve and vitality. His childhood frailty and love of beauty, learned from his charming, vivacious mother and sisters, made him an anomaly as he grew older; preferring the company of girls, to whom he wrote precocious love notes, and affecting individualistic aesthetic costumes, he marked himself as an original as early as his attendance at the Hartford Public High School.

Fitch's reputation followed him through preparatory school in Holderness, New Hampshire, and to Amherst College, where his classmates and Chi Psi fraternity brothers found his picturesque appearance no deterrent to his good humor and inventiveness. In fact, his first dramatic effort was a second act to a *Harper's* operetta, *Il Jacobi*, written in haste to complete an evening program for his fraternity. During his college years, he acted, produced, and painted scenery, frequently transposing effects from, for example, Daly's theater in New York, where he was an avid visitor. His college acting career included performances in Oliver Goldsmith's *She Stoops to Conquer* (pr. 1773) and in Richard Brinsley Sheridan's *The Rivals* (pr. 1775).

After graduating from Amherst College in 1886, Fitch went to New York, attempting both journalism and tutoring—which he disliked—to support himself. His novel *A Wave of Life* and short stories for *The Churchman* were written at a boardinghouse on West Fifty-third Street. The beginnings of his successful career can be traced to two experiences: He presented a letter of introduction to E. A. Dithmars, the drama critic for *The Times*, who provided the entrée to opening nights; and he spent some time in Paris with his mother in 1888, where he composed and read the one-act original play *Frederick Lemaître*.

By 1889, Fitch had established himself in New York and increased his circle of acquaintances to include such artists and writers as Oliver Herford of *Life* and William Dean Howells. His old friend Dithmars spurred Fitch's dramatic career by introducing the young playwright to the actor Richard Mansfield, who wanted a tailor-made play about Beau Brummell. After several false starts, including an argument with Mansfield about the ending, the play opened on a shoestring budget on May 17, 1890, at the Madi-

son Square Theatre, where it was a huge success. Five months later, Felix
Morris produced *Frederick Lemaître* in Chicago with the Rosina Vokes
Company.

Soon before Fitch went to London to work on the unsuccessful comedy
Pamela's Prodigy, he countered the critic William Winter's charges that
Mansfield's kindness had made him only the titular author of *Beau Brummell*. His apprenticeship years, from 1890 to 1892, were devoted to adapting and rewriting, commissions appearing at financially opportune times.
Of his works in this period, his adaptation of *The Masked Ball* from Bisson
and Carré's French play *Le Veglione* proved the most important, catapult-
ing John Drew and Maude Adams to stardom and assuring the reputation
of Charles Frohman.

Fitch's output of plays produced between 1891 and 1898 (the two biggest
successes were *Nathan Hale*, which opened at Hooley's Theatre in Chicago, and *The Moth and the Flame*, first produced in Philadelphia) testifies
to his unremitting industry, broken only by his lavish entertainment for his
growing circle of theatrical acquaintances and his frequent trips abroad. He
became, in fact, one of the first commercially successful American dramatists; Frohman, who had looked to the British playwrights Arthur Wing Pi-
nero and Henry Arthur Jones for his productions, tapped the young playwright. *Barbara Frietchie*, which opened at the Philadelphia Broad Street
Theater on October 10, 1899, surpassed even *Nathan Hale* in popularity,
bringing in ten thousand dollars in a single week. Inspired by a photograph
of Fitch's mother as a girl and written for Julia Marlowe, the play, a
romanticized version of the events surrounding the American revolutionary
war hero, evoked an ongoing discussion about poetic license. His next
major success was *The Cowboy and the Lady*, which was well received on
the circuit and in New York in 1899, but it was criticized because of the
swearing which Fitch, who had never been West, employed as local color.
Clearly, Fitch proved himself a master of versatility. As the year 1901
opened, no fewer than three Fitch plays, aside from *Barbara Frietchie*,
were on the boards in New York: *The Climbers*, a comedy of manners;
Lovers' Lane, a rural romance; and *Captain Jinks of the Horse Marines*,
described as a "fantastic comedy."

Indeed, Fitch frequently had more than one play running at the same
time. His Greenwich, Connecticut, homesite, purchased in March, 1902,
and christened Quiet Corner, was to alleviate some of the intense pressure
under which he worked in his studio in New York, a studio crammed with
keepsakes and theatrical books, flowers and memoirs—and guests. In
addition, Fitch traveled some six months of the year, sometimes taking a
"cure" such as the one at Parma, Italy, where he met actress Lily Langtry.
Throughout all, he continued to write; in 1902, suffering from illness and
exhaustion, he produced both *The Stubbornness of Geraldine* in November

and *The Girl with the Green Eyes* in December, both with the same attention to fine detail that fostered his reputation as a realist.

Although many of Fitch's plays were written while he was traveling—as, for example, was *Her Own Way*, written for Maxine Elliott partly in Florence and read aloud to friends in London—Fitch's plays are thoroughly American, a fact recognized by William Dean Howells, who favorably reviewed *Glad of It* in *Harper's Weekley* early in 1904. In a letter of thanks to Howells, Fitch acknowledged the novelist's influence, writing that, although he himself was lost in the midst of "shams," Howells' name was a signpost to the true path.

The composition and rehearsal of the less than successful *The Coronet of the Duchess* in 1904 were typical of Fitch's work habits at Quiet Corner, where he and his menagerie of pets entertained a constant flow of visitors and where he composed his plays under a favorite apple tree, his birdcages hanging above him and his company chattering around him. After the next year, in which *Her Great Match*, *Wolfville*, and *The Toast of the Town* were produced, Fitch gave a series of lectures in Philadelphia and New York and at Yale and Harvard, in an attempt to educate the public, as he put it, about their responsibility: "Hardened theater" was the result, he believed, of a constant and unhealthy cry for novelty and a refusal to take the drama seriously.

In one sense Fitch heeded his own words when, in 1906, in the midst of *Toddles*, *The House of Mirth* (produced with the cooperation of Edith Wharton), and *The Girl Who Has Everything*, he began to write *The Truth* for Clara Bloodgood. This play, which depicts the effect of inveterate lying, seems to be an oblique commentary on the falseness of the theatergoing public itself, which *prefers* to trivialize the truth into melodrama, just as the heroine *prefers* to jeopardize a happy marriage for the sake of fibbing and flirtation. Perhaps not surprisingly, the initial reception was not as enthusiastic as that of *The Straight Road*, opening the same night. Reviewers became more warm in their praise, however, even comparing Fitch to Henrik Ibsen; the French wildly applauded Marie Tempest in the foreign presentation of the play.

Fitch's years of overwork began to take their toll; suffering from perpetual indigestion and a weak heart, he virtually retired to Katonah, New York, in 1907. The last year of his life found him writing *The City*, a play that justifies his self-assessment as a major contributor to the American drama. Indeed, his last reading of the play, five days before he left for his last trip to Europe, left him exhausted. His continued illness on the trip ended in his death in Châlons-sur-Marne on September 4, 1909.

Analysis

Clyde Fitch's generally undeserved reputation as a playwright who wrote exclusively for star performers gained currency with his first success, *Beau Brummell*, written at the request of Richard Mansfield through the influence of the reviewer E. A. Dithmars. Mansfield, unhappy with Blanchard Jerrold's version, was initially pleased with Fitch's script. With the play in rehearsal at Palmer's Theatre in January, 1890, Mansfield suddenly withdrew the play, then decided to go ahead at the Madison Square Theatre in May. Even then, the production was fraught with problems; Mansfield, financially overdrawn, was forced to cut corners. Costumes were at a premium, borrowed or provided out of the actors' own trunks. In addition, actor and playwright argued over the last act, Mansfield insisting on a happy ending. Fitch's compromise—bringing back the king and Brummell's old friends at the very moment of the Beau's death—made the play a success.

Based on the life of the eighteenth century dandy George Bryan Brummell, the friend of the prince regent George IV, the play is a potpourri of romance, wit, and nostalgia that does, nevertheless, depict enough character development in Beau to gain the audience's sympathy when he finally dies impoverished in France. His first-act appearance is characterized by superficial wit, polished manners, and exquisite sensibility as contrasted with the bluff, natural mien of his nephew, Reginald Courtenay. The romantic interest involves Reginald's clandestine love for an unnamed woman whose father refuses consent, and Beau's financially motivated proposal to Mariana Vincent, Reginald's beloved.

While Beau's mistaken identification of Mr. Vincent as a merchant peddler and his difficulty in disentangling himself from his mistress, Mrs. St. Aubyn, provide comic relief, the second act presents Brummell in a more ennobling light as he confesses to Mariana that, although he proposed because of her wealth, he finds that he loves her in her own right. His quarrel with the prince regent is occasioned by his attempt to protect her father; flustered by having his flirtation with Mrs. St. Aubyn exposed to public scrutiny by the clumsiness of Mr. Vincent, the prince is offended by Brummell's familiarity.

Again, in act 3, Brummell becomes more humanized as Mariana, convinced that he has saved her father's honor by snubbing the prince regent, refuses to give up her engagement at the urging of Mrs. St. Aubyn, who, out of jealousy, offers to intercede with the prince if Mariana will not marry. Knowing that her wealth can save Beau from his creditors, Mariana agrees to marry him; then she meets Reginald, whose letters have been stopped by connivance between the servants. Beau, in a self-sacrificing gesture, releases her from her engagement and is led away by the bailiffs.

Beau, with his "glory gone," is depicted in the fourth act in abject poverty, his faithful servant Mortimer having pawned all of his possessions. Fitch's melodramatic genius created the act in which Brummell sees his old friends in a vision, Mortimer assisting as he goes through the empty formalities of greeting his nonexistent guests. That the guests actually return to play their parts at the end of the play satisfied both Mansfield's desire for a happy ending and Fitch's realization that no happy ending was possible.

The Truth began as a casual remark in 1906 to Fitch's business agent about a character who could not avoid telling lies. He elaborated the plot in less than two hours after being asked to write a play for the actress Clara Bloodgood and was convinced that the result was "psychologically and technically" his best work. Initially, the critics were less convinced; reviews after the first night, on which he also opened *The Straight Road*, were unenthusiastic. As the record shows, however, the second tour of the play, in October, 1907, was very successful; in addition, European audiences and reviewers were extraordinarily enthusiastic over the performance of Marie Tempest, whom Fitch met at Versailles. Indeed, her success abroad was the indirect cause of the suicide of Bloodgood, depressed over the lack of American response.

Becky Warder, the play's protagonist, seems to lie for the sheer inventiveness and challenge of juggling varieties of truth. Perhaps if Fitch had been a greater playwright, he would have explored, as the twentieth century playwright Luigi Pirandello did, the existential ramifications of such a condition. Fitch, however, concentrated on the effects of Becky's lying upon her marriage. Like his later play *The City*, *The Truth* ends with a reconciliation based on self-knowledge.

Act 1 is reminiscent of the eighteenth century comedy of manners. Becky carries on a flirtation with Lindon, under the pretext of reconciling him with his wife, Eve; she entertains his wife between his visits; she deceives her husband not only about Lindon but also about the price of a bonnet and about money sent to her sponging father. Through it all, she protests that she loves her husband. The audience can judge that she does indeed try to convince Lindon to return to Eve; nevertheless, she cannot stop lying.

The converse, that a sincere man can awaken a woman to good, is only suggested, not underscored, because it is the character of Becky that is emphasized, not that of Warder. Indeed, the sudden appearance of Becky's father and Mrs. Crespigny—the landlady with whom he has been living, from whom he has been borrowing, and whom he has been refusing to marry—interrupts the theme. Mrs. Crespigny, both comic and sincere in her awe at the Warders' residence, is a variation of the "prostitute with the heart of gold," yet she encourages Roland in his profligate habits rather than helping him. The act seems to fall into two halves: Tom Warder confronts his wife with the detectives' evidence that Eve has gathered against Lindon and Becky, and Roland and Mrs. Crespigny arrive to ask for money. Warder, who discovers that Becky has lied about sending money to her father and that she has indeed seen Lindon, no longer trusts her when she does tell the truth concerning her refusal to give in to Lindon's propositioning.

The function of the Crespigny subplot becomes clear when the third act opens; Becky decides to live with her father once Tom has left her, and the act takes place at the landlady's cheap boardinghouse. In this play as in *The City*, Fitch merely touches on the effect of upbringing and heredity in shaping character. Becky's father himself is a consummate liar—in fact, his scheme to reconcile Becky and her husband is based on a lie. Its double function—to save him from a second marriage and to resume his life-style without Becky's interference—is predicated on her agreeing to play a charade. His telegram to Tom that Becky is seriously ill brings Tom to the boardinghouse; Becky is to play the part of an invalid and so evoke her husband's pity.

At the final moment, Becky cannot play the game. "If I can't win his love back by the truth I'll never be able to keep it, so what's the use of getting it back at all?" she asks. In a scene reminiscent of the one with which Fitch ends *The City*, Tom forgives Becky—not because she is without fault, but because she has finally learned to be herself without shamming. "We don't love people because they are perfect," he says. "We love them because they are themselves."

In the final analysis, the play presents a problem that borders on the tragic; thus, the denouement seems too easy, although Fitch made an effort not to provide a *deus ex machina*, a solution achieved by external means, but rather one brought about by character change. The change in Becky wrought by her father's confession of his own propensity for lying and by the disagreeable surroundings of the boardinghouse seems, however, temporary at best.

Fitch's last play, *The City*, produced posthumously in New York in 1909, was conceived while he was at work on an English adaptation of a German farce, *The Blue Mouse*. *The City* is said to contain the best and the worst of Fitch: While it is a thesis play—arguing that the city is a crucible which reveals a person's essential strengths and weaknesses—it is also a melodrama, and while the dialogue is witty, it calls attention to itself at the expense of the plot. The play displays Fitch's gifts as a distinctively American playwright, dealing with a theme that is one of the staples of modern American literature: urbanization and its consequences.

Fitch was convinced that he had written his best play, and modern assessments agree. As usual, he read the script to a circle of friends in Katonah. The reading, which took place only five days before he sailed on his annual trip to Europe, lasted until two o'clock in the morning, during which time Fitch rewrote and removed scenes as he read. Although the play was not produced until December, 1909, some three months after his death, his production notes were clear, and his company, under the direction of stage manager John Emerson, attempted to reproduce Fitch's directions. Perhaps encouraged by the death of a favorite playwright, the audience's mood of expectation reportedly became hysterical at the end of the play. For once, the critics agreed with the audience, and *The City* finally earned for Fitch the critical acceptance that he had wanted.

In part, the play is an examination of the secret tensions that underlie an average American home and therefore may be seen within the context of Ibsen's realism; like Ibsen, Fitch was not reluctant to confront, onstage, matters such as incest, adultery, and suicide. Fitch was considerably more conventional than Ibsen, however, and so even *The City* presents the audience with a satisfying "happy" ending.

In the opening act, the tension in the Rand family, comfortably established in Middleburg, seems to lie between the security of the small town and the lure of the city. The father, a successful banker, opposes the social aspirations of his wife and daughters, Teresa and Cicely, and the professional ambitions of his son, George, Jr., all of whom want to move to New York. Underlying that tension, however, is the idea that to stay in Middleburg, or in any small town, for that matter, is not to be "safe." George Rand, the pillar of the community, has engineered illegal bank deals; moreover, he is being blackmailed by George Frederick Hannock, his illegitimate son. Before the close of the act, Rand falls dead, a victim of a heart attack apparently precipitated by another demand from Hannock and the necessity of confessing his hypocrisy to his son George.

For the family, the death means release to go to the city, where George establishes himself as a financier and political aspirant. Fitch does more, however, than simply show that Rand was wrong to force his family to stay in Middleburg or that the city offers unlimited opportunity. George, it is revealed, copies his father's suspect business practices by gambling with his partner's investment and selling at a favorable time; Hannock threatens to publicize the deal, which could send George to prison.

With every event, George is put to the test: Honesty will lose for him not only the nomination but also his fiancée, as plain dealing would have lost him money. His political success is threatened by Teresa's pending divorce and by Hannock's drug addiction and dubious associates. The realistic depiction of family problems becomes melodrama, however, when George tries to tell Cicely that in her secret marriage to Hannock, she has committed incest; Hannock shoots Cicely to prevent her knowing the truth. Fitch piles incident upon incident. George's final test in the second act is whether to allow Hannock to kill himself before the police arrive. Hiding his shady financial dealings protected his reputation; likewise, he has made a deal with Teresa: To save his nomination, she will live in apparent harmony with her husband. Hannock's death, which might be passed off as an accident, would hide the worst of the story of incest and crime and salvage George's own engagement to Eleanor, a woman who, as her father says, must "look up to" the man she marries.

The brief third act opens with George's confession to his fiancée's father and his old friend and political supporter. His determination is not to return to Middleburg, a decision that underlines Fitch's refusal to draw the conventional good/bad distinction between country and city. In perhaps the best speech in the play, George defends the city:

> *She* gives the man his opportunity; it is up to *him* what he makes of it! A man can live in a small town all his life, and deceive the whole place and *himself* into thinking he's got all the virtues, when at heart he's a hypocrite! . . . *But the City!* . . . there she strips him naked of all his disguises—and all his hypocrisies . . . and then she says to him, Make good if you can, or to Hell with you! And what is in him comes out to clothe his nakedness, and to the City he can't lie! *I know*, because *I tried*!

His truth-telling has an immediate effect on others: Teresa and her husband drop their twin divorce suits, convinced that unselfish consideration of their children is more rewarding than personal gratification.

George's more difficult confession is to Eleanor, to whom he says that he disguised lying and cheating as "business diplomacy" and as "the commercial code." His excuse—that he simply patterned himself on others around him—is, he says, finally no excuse at all, since, as a grown man, he was in possession of his own judgment. Eleanor's response, that someone who makes a fresh start because "it is the right thing to do" and because "he *had to be honest with himself*" is "twice the man" he was the day before, provides the kind of satisfying ending that Fitch's audiences enjoyed.

Fitch is noteworthy, then, in giving the theme of the city a new twist: As the small town is no guarantor of virtue—not only because it does not provide a test but also because it allows one to deceive oneself with the approval of one's neighbors—so the city is no guarantor of vice. Indeed, for George Rand, it is a place where, in the midst of millions of people, he has learned to live with himself.

Other major works

NOVEL: *A Wave of Life*, 1891.

NONFICTION: *Some Correspondence and Six Conversations*, 1896; *The Smart Set*, 1897; *Clyde Fitch and His Letters*, 1924 (Montrose J. Moses and Virginia Gerson, editors).

CHILDREN'S LITERATURE: *The Knighting of the Twins*, 1891.

Bibliography

Andrews, Peter. "More Sock and Less Buskin: In the Hands of a Rococo

Yankee Named Clyde Fitch the American Stage Came of Age with a Gasp of Scandalized Shock." *American Heritage* 23 (April, 1972): 48-57. Written for the general public, this essay follows a chronological order in describing the playwright's role in the American theater. Photographs of the flamboyant Fitch and some of the stars he directed make the work appealing.

Eaton, Walter Prichard. "The Case of Clyde Fitch." In *The American Theatre As Seen by Its Critics, 1752-1934*, edited by Montrose J. Moses and John Mason Brown. New York: W. W. Norton, 1934. This reprint of a seminal study is as welcome now as it was when it first appeared in 1910. Eaton shows that Fitch placed high value on entertaining his audiences and that the dramatist taught Americans the value of setting and emotional landscape. His plays, therefore, exerted much influence on the theater.

Meserve, Walter J. "Clyde Fitch and the Social World." In *An Outline History of American Drama.* Totowa, N.J.: Littlefield, Adams, 1965. Meserve analyzes the playwright's theory of drama, which he quotes from Archie Bell's 1909 biography, *The Clyde Fitch I Knew.* He suggests that Fitch's plays, presenting contemporary issues before a backdrop of melodrama, may be judged as models for social comedy on the American commercial stage.

Mordden, Ethan. "Clyde Fitch, Mrs. Fiske, Shaw, and Barrie." In *The American Theatre.* New York: Oxford University Press, 1981. This historical survey attempts to identify the American characteristics of Fitch's theater. In the chapter on comedy from 1900-1915, Mordden examines the plays and contrasts them to those of George Bernard Shaw. He also compares Fitch to Eugene O'Neill and provides an informative chapter on satire.

Moses, Montrose J. "Concerning Clyde Fitch and the Local Sense." In *The American Dramatist.* 1925. Reprint. New York: Benjamin Blom, 1964. Moses discusses Fitch's personality, revealed in his correspondence, and his dramaturgy. The playwright wrote good dialogue, but he had the qualities of a novelist: sharp visual sense and powers of observation. The actresses who were to play the roles were his models for the redaction of the female characters.

Phelps, William Lyon. "Clyde Fitch." In *Essays on Modern Dramatists.* 1921. Reprint. Freeport, N.Y.: Books for Libraries Press, 1970. Phelps remembers Fitch as an eccentric, independent child; the adult, too, was aloof, but he eagerly discussed his writing techniques with Phelps's drama students at Yale University. Those conversations are recalled here. Phelps also analyzes five masterpieces and reveals that his friend had deep knowledge of the female psyche and a keen sense of wit.

Quinn, Arthur Hobson. "Clyde Fitch and the Development of Social Comedy." In *A History of the American Drama, from the Civil War to the Present Day.* 2 vols. 1927. Reprint. New York: Appleton-Century-Crofts, 1964. In this excellent work, Quinn discusses Fitch's adaptations, translations, and original works, and he identifies his place in the history of theater. He analyzes the French and German influences on Fitch's dramaturgy as well as on his conception of realism and the topics that he introduced to American audiences.

Patricia Marks
(Updated by *Irene Gnarra*)

JOHN FLETCHER

Born: Rye, England; December 20, 1579 (baptized)
Died: London, England; August, 1625

Principal drama

The Woman's Prize: Or, The Tamer Tamed, pr. c. 1604, pb. 1647; *The Woman Hater*, pr. c. 1606, pb. 1607 (with Francis Beaumont); *The Faithful Shepherdess*, pr. c. 1608-1609, pb. 1629; *The Coxcomb*, pr. c. 1608-1610, pb. 1647 (with Beaumont); *Philaster: Or, Love Lies A-Bleeding*, pr. c. 1609, pb. 1620 (with Beaumont); *The Captain*, pr. c. 1609-1612, pb. 1647 (with Beaumont); *Bonduca*, pr. 1609-1614, pb. 1647; *Valentinian*, pr. 1610-1614, pb. 1647; *Monsieur Thomas*, pr. 1610-1616, pb. 1639; *The Maid's Tragedy*, pr. c. 1611, pb. 1619 (with Beaumont); *A King and No King*, pr. 1611, pb. 1619 (with Beaumont); *The Night Walker: Or, The Little Thief*, pr. c. 1611, pb. 1640; *Cupid's Revenge*, pr. 1612, pb. 1615 (with Beaumont); *Four Plays, or Moral Representations, in One*, pr. c. 1612, pb. 1647 (commonly known as *Four Plays in One*; with Beaumont); *The Two Noble Kinsmen*, pr. c. 1612-1613, pb. 1634 (with William Shakespeare); *The Masque of the Inner Temple and Grayes Inn*, pr., pb. 1613 (masque; with Beaumont); *Henry VIII*, pr. 1613, pb. 1623 (with Shakespeare); *Wit Without Money*, pr. c. 1614, pb. 1639; *The Scornful Lady*, pr. c. 1615-1616, pb. 1616 (with Beaumont); *The Nice Valour: Or, The Passionate Madman*, pr. 1616(?), pb. 1649; *The Mad Lover*, pr. 1616(?), pb. 1647; *Love's Pilgrimage*, pr. 1616(?), pb. 1647; *The Queen of Corinth*, pr. 1616-1617, pb. 1647; *The Knight of Malta*, pr. 1616-1618, pb. 1647; *The Tragedy of Thierry, King of France, and His Brother Theodoret*, pr. 1617(?), pb. 1621 (commonly known as *Thierry and Theodoret*; with Beaumont); *The Chances*, pr. c. 1617, pb. 1647; *The Loyal Subject*, pr. 1618, pb. 1647; *Sir John van Olden Barnavelt*, pr. 1619, pb. 1883 (with Philip Massinger); *The Humorous Lieutenant*, pr. 1619, pb. 1647; *The Custom of the Country*, pr. c. 1619-1620, pb. 1647 (with Massinger); *The Little French Lawyer*, pr. 1619-1623, pb. 1647 (with Massinger); *Women Pleased*, wr. 1619-1623, pb. 1647; *The Island Princess: Or, The Generous Portugal*, pr. 1619-1621, pb. 1647; *The False One*, pr. c. 1620, pb. 1647 (with Massinger); *The Double Marriage*, pr. c. 1621, pb. 1647 (with Massinger); *The Wild Goose Chase*, pr. 1621, pb. 1652; *The Pilgrim*, pr. 1621, pb. 1647; *The Beggar's Bush*, pr. before 1622, pb. 1647 (with Massinger); *The Prophetess*, pr. 1622, pb. 1647 (with Massinger); *The Sea Voyage*, pr. 1622, pb. 1647; *The Spanish Curate*, pr. 1622, pb. 1647; *The Maid in the Mill*, pr. 1623, pb. 1647 (with William Rowley); *The Lover's Progress*, pr. 1623, pb. 1647 (revised by Massinger, 1634); *A Wife for a Month*, pr. 1624, pb. 1647; *Rule a Wife and Have a Wife*, pr. 1624, pb. 1647; *The Elder Brother*, pr. 1625(?), pb. 1637 (with Massinger); *The Fair*

Maid of the Inn, pr. 1626, pb. 1647 (with Massinger?); *Wit at Several Weapons*, pb. 1647 (with Beaumont?); *The Dramatic Works in the Beaumont and Fletcher Canon*, pb. 1966-1985 (6 volumes).

Other literary forms

John Fletcher apparently wrote very little or no poetry. He may have collaborated with other playwrights in the composition of court masques, but no direct evidence has been introduced identifying his hand in entertainments of that kind.

Achievements

Although Fletcher wrote many plays alone, he is best known for those he composed in collaboration with Francis Beaumont. In fact, much of the criticism of these playwrights' work regards them as an inseparable team. This practice has tended to obscure the technical brilliance of Fletcher's own plays, many of which were revived successfully on the Restoration stage. In their collaboration, however, the two dramatists came to be recognized as the inventors and chief practitioners of a style of drama, tragicomedy, that won enthusiastic applause from audiences at the Jacobean public theaters. Fletcher published a definition of the new genre in the preface to one of his earliest plays, *The Faithful Shepherdess:*

> A tragi-comedy is not so called in respect of mirth and killing, but in respect it wants deaths, which is inough to make it no tragedie, yet brings some neere it, which is inough to make it no comedie: which must be a representation of familiar people, with such kinde of trouble as no life be questioned, so that a God is as lawfull in this as in a Tragedie, and meane people as a comedie.

While the play to which this preface was appended proved unpopular with its audience, Fletcher, with the older Beaumont, went on to instant success in *Philaster*, one of his first collaborative efforts in the new form. This event was also notable because it cemented the playwrights' connection with William Shakespeare's company, the King's Men. Beaumont and Fletcher continued to write for that company for the rest of their careers.

What attracted Jacobean playgoers to *Philaster* was its complicated but relatively fresh plot (no sources have been identified), romantic setting, and suspenseful denouement: The heroic prince discovers that the page who has served him faithfully throughout the play is in fact a woman—a woman who is deeply in love with him. The happy ending, however, leaves the audience with a sense of having been manipulated; Beaumont and Fletcher take little care to develop their characters or to motivate action. Even so, *Philaster* won the playwrights a reputation with the gentlemen and ladies who increasingly made up the audience at the Blackfriars playhouse.

Before Beaumont's retirement in 1613, he and Fletcher worked together on several other plays, only a few of which were in fact tragicomedies. Other than *Philaster*, *A King and No King* is probably the best example of the genre. *A King and No King*, like many Jacobean plays, depends on the frisson of an incestuous love: The hero believes that he has engaged in intercourse with his sister. As it turns out, the two are not in fact brother and sister, the hero's parentage having been misrepresented by a deceitful queen. Despite this happy evasion of tragedy, the purpose of titillating the viewers was deftly accomplished. The dramatic rhythm of relaxation and sudden surprise is reinforced by a style of verse that alternates between realistic conversation and high-flown rhetoric. This characteristic of the verse (informal talk that suddenly gives way to elevated poetry) was widely admired by the audiences of Beaumont and Fletcher's era and by Restoration audiences, for whom the plays became regular revival fare. Indeed, their tragicomedies were staged more frequently in the period from 1660 to 1700 than were the works of Shakespeare, who was judged too rough-edged, or Ben Jonson, who was regarded as too satiric.

Beaumont and Fletcher also composed tragedies—*Cupid's Revenge*, *The Maid's Tragedy*—and witty comedies—*The Coxcomb*, *The Scornful Lady*—in the Jonsonian vein. These plays demonstrate the versatility and range of these playwrights, but they helped propel the Jacobean stage into decadence. The dominant scene in *The Maid's Tragedy*, for example, contains a wedding-night confession by the heroine to her warrior-hero husband that she has been and intends to continue to be the king's mistress. This situation brings the style and tone of *The Maid's Tragedy* perilously close to the realm of soap opera.

After Beaumont's death, Fletcher continued to work in collaboration, primarily with Philip Massinger and William Shakespeare. The plays produced during this period were largely tragedies and tragicomedies that responded to the audience's desire for spectacular entertainment. The teaming of Fletcher and Shakespeare likewise suggests that the style of tragicomedy developed by Fletcher strongly influenced Shakespeare's own play production. Romances such as *Pericles, Prince of Tyre* (pr. c. 1607-1608), *The Winter's Tale* (pr. c. 1610-1611), and *The Tempest* (pr. 1611) display the same fascination for plot turns, type characters, exotic settings, and elevated verse found in Beaumont and Fletcher's tragicomedies. When left to his own devices, however, Fletcher also turned his hand to comedy that explored the manners of upper-class Englishmen. Most of these plays are distinguished by complicated plots, humorous characters, and witty dialogue. His ease in writing comedy has led many critics to conclude that Fletcher was the author of the comic scenes in the tragicomedies, while Beaumont was responsible for the tragic scenes and characters. Fletcher's comedies, with their themes of youthful love and sexual combat, caught the fancy of Stuart courtiers and helped to lay the groundwork for the Restoration comedies of manners.

Although he ended his career by composing sophisticated comedies, Fletcher has been recognized by commentators on the Jacobean stage as the innovator of tragicomedy and as the period's foremost dramatic collaborator. His name seems destined to be linked with that of Beaumont or Massinger in future critical analyses as well. The body of work turned out by Fletcher with his fellow playwrights is truly impressive: some fifty plays in the Second Folio (1679). Considerable time and print have been spent in attempts to determine the relative contributions of each playwright to the comedies, tragedies, and tragicomedies printed in the First and Second Folios—a task that is still going on and may never be satisfactorily completed. As a result, much valuable criticism of the style and content of the individual plays still remains to be done.

Biography

John Fletcher was born in Rye, Sussex, where he was baptized on December 20, 1579. His father, Richard, was a clergyman who attended Cambridge and was later made president of Corpus Christi College, Cambridge, Dean of Peterborough, and eventually Bishop of London. Elizabeth I reportedly admired his talent as a scholar and bestowed special favor on him. John Fletcher's uncles, Giles and Phineas Fletcher, were poets with respected reputations, and their successes added honors to the family name. These conditions of birth and social standing were somewhat unusual among playwrights of the age and doubtless helped to reinforce Fletcher's reputation as an entertainer of gentlemen.

Although John Fletcher no doubt attended lectures at his father's alma mater, he may have been forced to leave Cambridge in 1596 when, perhaps in part because of an ill-advised second marriage, Bishop Fletcher was suspended by the queen. Later in that same year, he died, and Fletcher was probably taken under the wing of his uncle Giles, who may have helped to pay off the family's large debts. Just when Fletcher began writing plays is not known, but it is certain that he was hard at work in collaboration with Beaumont early in the first decade of the seventeenth century. After Beaumont left the profession in 1613, Fletcher continued as the chief playwright for the King's Men, working alone or with Philip Massinger, William Shakespeare (on *The Two Noble Kinsmen* and *Henry VIII*), and several others. Fletcher's death in August, 1625, was caused by the plague; he was buried in St. Saviours Church, Southwark, the district in which he had resided throughout his career in London.

Analysis

Una Ellis-Fermor (*The Jacobean Drama: An Interpretation*, 1936) observes that the "names of Beaumont and Fletcher are often associated so closely with tragi-comedy that their work and that form of play are loosely spoken of as if they were coexistensive." Although she goes on to state that only five plays in the tragicomic genre are accepted as bearing the stamp of their mutual authorship, recent critical assessments have not been very successful in altering the prevailing opinion. Certainly, there are good reasons for the tenacity of the popular view, including the fact that Fletcher named and defined the genre in the preface to one of his earliest plays, *The Faithful Shepherdess*. The play may have been inspired by Giambattista Guarini's *Il pastor fido* (1585), but it bears little resemblance to the realistic "sad shepherd" plays, marked by dancing and festivity, with which the English audience of that day was familiar. In fact, with its shepherd and shepherdess lovers poeticizing about passion and lust, *The Faithful Shepherdess* more nearly approximates the prose romances of Edmund Spenser and Sir Philip Sidney.

Set in Thessaly, the play introduces the virgin shepherdess Clorin who, having vowed to purge all passion from her heart in memory of her dead lover, lives beside his grave and dispenses healing herbs to those wounded by love or lust. This devotion sets the standard against which one is to judge the behavior of all the other characters—especially the central couple, Perigot and Amoret, pastoral lovers who vow to exchange only chaste kisses. The comedy of errors that develops tests this resolve, and their love. Amarillis, Amoret's rival, wantonly pursues Perigot, who dutifully rejects her. She vows to gain revenge against Amoret by magically transforming herself into Amoret's double. Despite her altered appearance and her use of every conceivable weapon of seduction, Amarillis finds Perigot unable to love in any but a chaste fashion. As might be expected, when Perigot next encounters the true Amoret, he is so incensed by what he believes is her blatant cynicism that he strikes her with his sword. Later, Amarillis takes pity on the grieving Perigot, who believes he has killed his true love; she admits to disguising herself as Amoret and offers to do so again to prove her case. When the real Amoret reappears, seeking to reassure Perigot of her love, he believes she is intentionally deceiving him and once again wounds her with his sword. Through the good offices of Clorin, however, the two lovers are finally reconciled and Amarillis, along with two other unchaste lovers, is cured of her affliction. In the main plot and in subplots involving other pastoral characters (among them, a satyr, a river god, and the Caliban-like Sullen Shepherd), Fletcher sets up moral and ethical contrasts: He disguises vice as virtue and virtue as vice in an attempt to dramatize conflicts between essentially one-dimensional characters. Although the action is occasionally brought to the brink of tragedy only to be saved by some intervention of fortune, the plot depends on a kind of mechanical alteration of moods. Almost more an exercise in poetic composition—with impressive variations in sound effects and imagery, for example, used to indicate subtle differences between characters—the play's style has been nicely characterized by Eugene Waith as "the product of refined sensationalism." Whether because the contemporary audiences perceived this flaw or were simply unprepared to believe or care about the rather stylized figures delivering, in long poems of closely rhymed verse, explanations for their attitudes and desires, the play proved a failure on the stage.

As in *The Faithful Shepherdess*, *Cupid's Revenge* turns on the contrast between lust and love. Princess Hidaspes, a virtuous woman who recalls Clorin, is given one wish on her birthday, and she wishes for the destruction of Cupid's altars. When this occurs, a vengeful Cupid forces Hidaspes to fall in love with the court dwarf, who is later killed by the king. Hidaspes then expires from a broken heart. In a second story, Prince Leucippus, Hidaspes' brother, falls in love with Bacha, an unchaste woman who has wooed both the prince and the king (Leontius) by means of a mask of chastity. Thus, male and female members of the royal household are made to suffer because of love—degradation (in the case of Leucippus and Leontius) and death (Hidaspes). As in *The Faithful Shepherdess*, *Cupid's Revenge* is filled not with well-motivated dramatic characterizations but rather with representations of the moral dimensions of love.

An incident inserted in *Cupid's Revenge* primarily to play upon the sympathies of the viewers concerns Urania, daughter to Bacha, who loves Leucippus and disguises herself as a page in order to be near him after his banishment. She is murdered when she rushes between her lover and a messenger sent by Bacha to kill him. Leucippus' discovery of Urania's true identity provides the occasion for a melodramatic statement on the fortunes of true love. This situation was repeated by Fletcher and Beaumont in the popular and dramatically fresh *Philaster*. The hero, a disinterested prince who has been compared by many critics to Hamlet, finds himself living in the court of an evil king, usurper of his throne. Philaster falls in love with Arethusa, the king's daughter, but is informed by Megra, a scheming, lascivious lady of the court, that his beloved has deceived him with Bellario, a young page who has served as their messenger. Aroused to a sudden anger, Philaster attacks Bellario and Arethusa but is quickly arrested by the usurping king. After a revolt by the people helps Philaster win back his throne, his marriage to Arethusa is made public. Megra revives the old charge against Arethusa, and Philaster orders Bellario stripped and beaten. Only then is the page revealed to be Euphrasia, a noble's daughter who is hopelessly in love with Philaster; the revelation results in the banishment of Megra. Hero and heroine live happily ever after, although the continued presence of Philaster's "loyal" servant (often compared to Viola in *Twelfth Night*) seems to strike a melancholy note.

Philaster carries on the debates about love and lust, loyalty and deceit, that were a part of Fletcher's earlier work. By setting the action in a distant time not associated with the pastoral, Beaumont and Fletcher manage to avoid much of the confusion that resulted from a pastoral setting. The characters here are types—the lover, the lustful lady, the usurper—whose actions are not carefully motivated; they behave in a manner required by the situation. There can be little doubt that the poetry spoken by these characters, which is often refined and beautiful, helped considerably in holding the contemporary playgoer's attention. More than any other element, however, the scenes depicting Philaster striking his loyal servant and Bellario disclosing her true identity are typical of Beaumont and Fletcher's successful plays. They are suspenseful and surprising; they wrench potentially tragic situations into the realm of romantic happiness, usually at the last possible moment.

A somewhat different, more serious tone prevails in *A King and No King*. As in *Philaster*, King Arbaces faces a romantic dilemma, but unlike Philaster, he falls in love with his sister—when they meet after a long separation. Although promised to Arbaces' rival Tigranes, the captured King of Armenia, Panthea returns her brother's love, thereby setting the stage for what appears to be an incestuous affair. The shock of this situation is created through dubious maneuvering, but one can readily see that it is the type of dilemma requiring the radical, even sensational resolution typical of Beaumont and Fletcher's tragicomic style.

Just as Arbaces concludes that the only course for a sinner like him is suicide, he learns that his real father is the Lord-Protector, who had helped the queen "produce" an heir, allowing her to present his newborn infant as her own son. Panthea emerges as the true heir to the throne, thereby legitimating Arbaces' love for her. The two are married, Tigranes finds Spaconia to be his true love, and the terrible atmosphere of evil that dominates the play in its earlier stages seems banished like a bad dream. The audience has followed the hero and heroine to the brink of tragedy, but once again, through a miraculous discovery, a happy ending has been imposed. What gives this play greater weight than even *Philaster* is the way in which Arbaces' struggle with his emotions has been thoroughly explored. He emerges as more than a type, although his flaws, which have seemed so real throughout the body of the play, seem to disappear with the discovery and resolution. Arbaces emerges in this regard as a "problem" character similar to Shakespeare's Angelo (*Measure for Measure*) and Bertram (*All's Well That Ends Well*).

Although the central dilemma of *The Maid's Tragedy*—what a worthy man should do after learning that his bride is the king's mistress—could have been resolved through the devices of tragicomedy, Beaumont and Fletcher chose instead to make the play into a tragedy. The result is a compelling, artful play. Amintor is persuaded to marry Evadne by the predictably evil king; in order to do so, Amintor breaks off his engagement with Aspatia—and breaks her heart. When Evadne informs Amintor that their marriage is only a cover-up, he swears vengeance, but when he learns he has been cuckolded by the king, he decides against taking revenge because of his strong feeling of loyalty toward the throne. Amintor does divulge his awful secret to his fellow warrior Melantius, who also happens to be Evadne's brother. Melantius confronts his sister with the truth and says that she must repair the damage to her marriage—and to the country—by murdering the king: "All the gods require it." In another of those contrived but riveting scenes so typical of Beaumont and Fletcher plots, Evadne comes to Amintor, her hands covered with the king's blood, to ask his forgiveness, only to find him weeping over the body of Aspatia. Aspatia, despairing of happiness, had disguised herself as a man (a favorite convention in the tragicomedies) and provoked a duel with Amintor, falling on his sword and killing herself. When Amintor realizes what Evadne has done, he rejects her, in blank verse that rivals Shakespeare's in sheer dramatic strength. Evadne cannot withstand his rebuke and soon commits suicide. Finally, Amintor, struck by the horrible sight of these women who died for him, likewise gives up the struggle.

Despite the tragic impact of this final scene, it is difficult to describe either Amintor or Aspatia as characters with the capacity for suffering of a Hamlet or Ophelia. Both are sentimental figures. Whether, as one critic has observed, Aspatia represents the pure heroine of the Elizabethan period brought down by the sophisticated and corrupt Jacobean heroine is a matter for debate. She certainly traces her origins back to the disguised page characters of the earlier tragicomedies. The regular introduction of debates over honor and loyalty, the sudden twists of plot, the prominence of an intriguing and vengeful figure such as Melantius, and the almost operatic verse style are all elements that look ahead to the heroic drama of John Dryden and Sir William Davenant. Other than *A King and No King,* *The Maid's Tragedy* is probably the most carefully constructed and emotionally rich of the plays written by Beaumont and Fletcher.

In addition to tragicomedy and tragedy, the two playwrights also worked together on a number of comedies. Two of the best of these are *The Scornful Lady* and *The Coxcomb.* In *The Scornful Lady*, a play originally written for the Queen's Revels Children, two pairs of male lovers woo different ladies. The brothers Loveless, the older a sober fellow who engages in combats of wit with the Lady and the younger a prodigal who woos and wins a rich widow, are the comic heroes of this comedy of manners. The main action concerns Elder Loveless' attempt to purge the humor of the Lady, who longs for her lover when he is away but abuses and mocks him when he is present; he vies for her favor with the good-looking Walford, who, upon losing the contest, settles for the Lady's sister. In this situation one can clearly see the influence of Jonson on Fletcher; the humor scheme is worked in similar fashion in Jonson's *Epicoene: Or, The Silent Woman* (pr. 1609, pb. 1616). Young Loveless also woos a lady, a beautiful and wealthy widow, but in a style that is considerably more boisterous than that of his brother, and he, too, faces a rival—Morecraft, a moneylender who had previously fleeced him. Young Loveless might be called a "playboy" in modern usage, and he and his companions nearly drive the steward of his beloved's house mad with their drinking and carousing. Although his speech lacks the verbal pyrotechnics to be found in the dialogue of Restoration comedy, Young Loveless does stand for the power of revelry and good fun, and the stratagems and spicy wit which finally bring him and his brother their desired prizes were a model for subsequent playwrights.

Like *The Scornful Lady, The Coxcomb* follows a dual plot structure and depends somewhat heavily on the humor scheme for its effects. Antonio, the coxcomb or cuckold, proves to be so generous that the moment he learns of his friend Mercury's love for his wife (Maria), he literally forces her into Mercury's arms. Antonio even resorts to a disguise to bring the two together for what appears to be a lust-satisfying tryst. To the end, however, Antonio apologizes profusely for his wife's "excessive" virtue. The subplot (really a second story) concerns Viola, a fair maid who is scorned by her lover Ricardo. Forced to wander the countryside alone, Viola is robbed and nearly raped by an oversexed "gentleman." She is finally befriended by two milkmaids, a circumstance that allows her to praise the inherent virtues of country life. Her short verse encomium provides an effective contrast to the rough-and-tumble prose speech of the rustic characters. When Ricardo is finally reunited with Viola, he begs forgiveness for the wanton behavior that led him to scorn her. How this romantic tale relates to the more tragicomic one involving Antonio, Maria, and Mercury, however, remains unclear. Both heroes might be viewed as humor types who are, because of their blindness, susceptible to being cuckolded. Despite its disjointed plot, *The Coxcomb* is a comedy of lively contrast between city and country life, urban and rustic foolery.

A similar farce, *Wit at Several Weapons*, has been variously attributed to Fletcher alone, to Beaumont and Fletcher, and even to such revisers as Middleton. It is the story of Sir Perfidious Oldcraft, who strives to make his son, Wittypate, less of a dunce. After a complicated series of intrigues, the father discovers that Wittypate has been deceiving him from the beginning and, in fact, truly does possess wit. This recognition makes Oldcraft so happy that he immediately gives the boy a large allowance. In the subplot, a character named Sir Gregory Fop also finds himself the victim of trickery, but the result is a happy one: marriage to an attractive heiress. Even though the action, with its emphasis on intrigue and duping, smacks of Jonson, Beaumont and Fletcher do not intrude the element of keen satire here. Indeed, the mood is one of high spirits, involving stock characters speaking humorous but not ingenious verse.

When Beaumont retired from the stage in 1613, Fletcher continued to write plays on his own and in collaboration with others. He had become a valued member of the King's Men, recognized as a skilled and popular creator of tragicomedies, tragedies, and comedies. Indeed, there is convincing evidence that Fletcher was composing successful plays on his own even during the period of his collaboration with Beaumont. *Bonduca* and *Valentinian* are two tragedies written by Fletcher that appealed to the Globe and Blackfriars audiences. *Bonduca* dramatizes events related to the wars between Britons and Romans, and it may have been inspired by Shakespeare's *Cymbeline* (pr. c. 1609-1610). Although the play is named after the English queen Bonduca, she has very little part in it. The tragic hero is a brave lad named Hengo, who is deceitfully killed by the Roman Judas. Caratach, a courageous old soldier who is the other major figure in the play, avenges the murder by slaying Judas. The death scene, with its rhapsodizing about Britain and youthful death, smacks of the kind of pathos that Fletcher achieves in the verse of the tragicomedies. Whether Caratach was intended as a dramatic copy of Sir Walter Raleigh, at that time a prisoner in the Tower and widely regarded as a champion of the good old cause, is difficult to determine. There can be no doubt, however, that *Bonduca* was intended to be a play about English patriotism and loyalty.

Valentinian achieves a greater tragic impact than does *Bonduca*, primarily because its villain is the Roman emperor who rapes Lucina, the honest wife of a brave soldier named Maximus. Fletcher spins out the action by means of contrast between the brave and loyal army captains and the dissolute world of the court, with the emperor Valentinian announcing to the prostrate Lucina: "Justice shall never hear you; I am justice." Here is the mood and style of a work such as *The Maid's Tragedy*, with its helpless victims and seemingly omnipotent villains. When Lucina dies, Maximus, instead of seeking direct revenge against Valentinian, becomes a Machiavellian intriguer who employs servants to taunt and then poison the villain, betraying his own friend Aecius as one step toward this end. After Maximus marries the emperor's widow, he foolishly tells her of his deeds, and she proceeds to poison him in turn, by crowning him with a poisoned wreath. This serpentine plotting corrupts the tragic mood of *Valentinian*, which is also marred by special effects and what one critic has called "Fletcher's flamboyant declamation."

Fletcher's chief collaborator after Beaumont was Philip Massinger. The two men produced at least ten plays together, most of them tragedies and comedies. *The False One* and *Sir John van Olden Barnavelt* are two representative examples of this collaboration. The former tragedy depicts Caesar's affair with Cleopatra in Egypt, although the title does not refer to the queen but to a Roman named Septimius, who is responsible for the murder of his old general, Pompey. In a bold move, Septimius vows to murder Caesar, and much of the action concerns the intrigues against him. In the end, however, Caesar outwits and defeats his enemies, which makes it difficult to regard the ending as tragic. Massinger was probably responsible for the opening and closing scenes of the play, while Fletcher depicted the love scenes involving Caesar and Cleopatra and invented the breathtaking masque of Nilus. Honor and nobility are at stake throughout, but the action and characters do not achieve the heights or complexity found in Shakespeare's play dealing with similar materials.

Sir John van Olden Barnavelt deals with a contemporary rather than an ancient event in history—the downfall and death of the well-known Dutch statesman in May, 1619. There are also allusions in this tragedy to the execution of Sir Walter Raleigh, which had taken place the previous year, making it difficult to understand how the play was allowed on the stage (it was not published until 1883). Massinger's interest in political themes and foreign policy (see his *Believe as You List*, pr. 1631) is evident in this aspect of the play, while Fletcher no doubt wrote the scenes that deal with Barnavelt's emotional side. The play suffers from hasty composition: It was written and put into production within three months of Barnavelt's death. Of particular importance, however, is the fact that Fletcher lent his talent to a play dealing with the topic of absolutism. He is no doubt the author of a sensational scene in which three executioners throw dice to decide who will carry out the beheading.

Besides Massinger, Fletcher was also working with Shakespeare during this period (1613-1620), and *Henry VIII* and *The Two Noble Kinsmen* bear the mark of Fletcher's hand. In *Henry VIII*, the spectacular celebrations and the episodic plot are reminiscent of the style of *A King and No King* and *Thierry and Theodoret*. Little attention is given to Henry himself, the best speeches and scenes going to Wolsey (whose famous farewell may indeed have been written by Fletcher) and Cranmer. The same emphasis on spectacle, especially scenes of pageantry, can be seen in *The Two Noble Kinsmen*.

Although Fletcher collaborated with other playwrights after 1616, the main body of his work in this period was in his own hand and in his favorite genres: comedy and tragicomedy. Tragicomedy was apparently more attractive for him than tragedy because he was either incapable of or uninterested in exploring internal conflict by means of the soliloquy. As William Appleton has put it in *Beaumont and Fletcher: A Critical Study* (1956), "Rarely can Fletcher conceive of the tragedy of the individual caught in an infernal machine of his own making. He concentrates instead on the tragedy of circumstance."

A few tragicomedies from Fletcher's later works should suffice to illustrate his dramatic style at this stage in his career. In some ways, Fletcher's interests reveal a return to the themes and characters of his earliest plays. *The Mad Lover* features a hero named Memnon, who leaves his career as a vainglorious warrior to woo the beautiful Princess Calis. This rejection of war in favor of love was a subject treated in earlier tragicomedies, such as *Philaster* and *A King and No King*. Memnon, however, follows a rigid code of honor in his love that is mocked by other characters in the court of Paphos, where a cynical view of romance prevails. His chief rival for Calis' hand turns out to be his own brother, Polydor, who wins the princess' heart even as he tells her she must love his brother. In a spectacular denouement typical of Fletcher, Polydor has himself sent to Calis in a coffin, bearing a will that directs her to marry Memnon. When Memnon enters, however, he sees his apparently dead brother and declares his intention to follow him to the grave. At this point, Polydor arises, still pleading for his brother as suitor. Memnon, however, perceives the truth—that Calis loves Polydor deeply—and decides to return to war. This heroic gesture places Memnon in the first order of heroic lovers that will come to dominate the Restoration stage. He also qualifies as one of Fletcher's most memorable tragicomic figures, changing from an essentially foolish soldier to a romantic Platonist.

In *The Loyal Subject*, Fletcher likewise gives the action coherence by organizing it around the theme of duty to self and sovereign. Based on an earlier play by Thomas Heywood (*The Royal King and Loyal Subject*, pr. 1602?, pb. 1637), Fletcher's tragicomedy concerns the staunch loyalty of the general Archas to the weak and easily flattered Duke of Moscow. That devotion is contrasted to the Machiavellianism of Boroskie, who seeks to widen a rift that has resulted in Archas' resignation. Archas is then subjected to exile, imprisonment, and torture, but at every instance of national crisis, he acts to aid his country. Only after Archas' daughters are able to convince the duke of their father's loyalty is he allowed to live. Before this happens, Archas is brought to a point at which he threatens to kill his son Theodore for speaking out against the cruel duke and Boroskie. This disaster is deftly avoided by a general resolution in which Archas is forced to relent when his youngest son is threatened with death. The resolution allows Archas to remain true to his personal and political codes of honor. It also has suggested to certain critics that Fletcher meant his audience to be thinking about the fate—and principled character—of Sir Walter Raleigh as it listened to Archas' declamations (particularly when added to numerous contemporary references related to Raleigh). Certainly the extravagant rhetoric, overwrought scenes of conflict, and surprising convolutions of plot serve to place the play squarely in the Fletcher canon.

One final tragicomedy gives some sense of the range of Fletcher's last plays. *The Island Princess* has as its central character a woman, the Princess Quisara, who offers her hand to any suitor brave enough to rescue her brother, the King of Sidore, from captivity. When the Portuguese captain Armusia manages the release, it appears as if a joyous marriage will follow. The king, however, fears the Portuguese will attempt to take over his island and requires that Armusia change his religion before he marries Quisara. Armusia refuses and is thrown in prison, where Quisara, moved by her love's defiance, decides to join him. They are soon rescued by friends of Armusia, who also manage to unmask a priest responsible for poisoning the king's mind against Armusia. (He turns out to be the enemy king who held Quisara's brother captive at the opening of the action.) The king now welcomes his new brother-in-law, declaring that he is "half-persuaded" to become a Christian. As this happy resolution takes place, it becomes clear that the play has not really concerned religion or the conflict of East and West. The exotic setting proves to be only the backdrop for a tragicomic study of honor. It should also be added that *The Island Princess* looks forward to such Restoration plays as John Dryden's *The Indian Emperor* (pr. 1665), where the setting provides the occasion for spectacle and heroic flights of rhetoric. Fletcher's late comedies, in particular *The Chances*, *The Wild Goose Chase*, and *Rule a Wife and Have a Wife*, likewise foreshadowed the comedy of manners, which was to prove so popular during the Restoration.

The rich legacy of Fletcher's work, and that of his collaborators, was warmly received in the Restoration. It appears that the complex and suddenly turning plots, remote but familiar settings, effectively imitated manners, and high-flown rhetoric of the tragicomedies accurately reflected the taste of the age. Fletcher was also skilled at capturing the rhythm and diction of elevated conversation, which clearly contributed to his talents as a writer of comedy. "Sophistication" is a word that recurs in critical commentary on the comedies and tragicomedies, while assessments of the tragedies written alone and in collaboration often employ the words "facile" or "extravagant." That Fletcher was an innovator cannot be denied, but he (along with Beaumont and Massinger) was also an entertainer. He was to some extent lucky in sensing the taste of the age and in devising plays to indulge that taste. Even though one rarely finds a Fletcher play in theatrical repertories today, many of the comedies and some of the seriocomic pieces one sees on the modern stage feature scenes and characters that trace their lineage back to the theatrical genius of John Fletcher.

Bibliography

Appleton, William W. *Beaumont and Fletcher: A Critical Study.* Folcroft, Pa.: Folcroft Press, 1969. Appleton analyzes the early collaborations, then proceeds to a critical investigation, unfortunately too brief, of Fletcher's independent plays and later collaborations. He discusses the influence and critical reputation of Fletcher in the Restoration and in the 1700's.

Finkelpearl, Philip J. *Court and Country Politics in the Plays of Beaumont and Fletcher.* Princeton, N.J.: Princeton University Press, 1990. Considers the plays in connection with the author's three worlds: the country, the playhouse, and the Mermaid Tavern. Analyzes eight plays in depth for their political relevance. Among the themes discussed are the Anti-Prince, corruption of royal power, and tyrannicide.

Leech, Clifford. *The John Fletcher Plays.* Cambridge, Mass.: Harvard University Press, 1962. This good overview of Fletcher's dramatic production contains separate chapters on the comedies, the tragicomedies, and the tragedies. Leech discusses Fletcher in connection with William Shakespeare and provides an appendix on dates of plays by these two writers plus Ben Jonson and Philip Massinger. The index is too slight.

Maxwell, Baldwin. *Studies in Beaumont, Fletcher, and Massinger.* Chapel Hill: University of North Carolina Press, 1939. Reprint. New York: Octagon Books, 1966. Questions various conclusions of E. H. C. Oliphant in *The Plays of Beaumont and Fletcher: An Attempt to Define Their Respective Shares and the Shares of Others* (1927). Maxwell places a major emphasis on the dating of certain plays, with comments on sources, topical allusions, and actors who performed the plays.

Pearse, Nancy Cotton. *John Fletcher's Chastity Plays: Mirrors of Modesty.* Lewisburg, Pa.: Bucknell University Press, 1973. Pearse attempts to defend Fletcher's aesthetics and morality and to oppose the contention that Francis Beaumont deserves the credit for all the moral quality of their collaborations. Investigates seventeenth century ideas about chastity and concludes that Fletcher creates chaste women who are greatly concerned with marriage and constancy. Not fully convincing to every reader.

Squier, Charles L. *John Fletcher.* Boston: Twayne, 1986. A general study which contains individual chapters on the tragicomedies (where his influence and reputation were greatest), the tragedies (where he had little interest or strength), and the comedies (where his real genius appeared). Includes a section on Fletcher's critical reputation in the last two centuries and on stylistic idiosyncrasies. Annotated bibliography.

Waith, Eugene M. *The Pattern of Tragicomedy in Beaumont and Fletcher.* Edited by Benjamin Nangle. New Haven, Conn.: Yale University Press, 1952. Waith believes that patterns began to form in the collaborations by 1608 and were fully developed by 1611 in *A King and No King.* Identifies eight different elements—ranging from characters to atmosphere—that comprise the patterns. This valuable study contains analyses of nine early plays and many later ones. Lengthy index.

Robert F. Willson, Jr.
(Updated by *Howard L. Ford*)

SAMUEL FOOTE

Born: Truro, England; January 27, 1720 (baptized)
Died: Dover, England; October 21, 1777

Principal drama

The Diversions of the Morning, pr. 1747-1754 (series of vaudeville sketches); *The Auction of Pictures*, pr. 1748; *The Knights*, pr. 1749 (revised, pr., pb. 1754); *Taste*, pr., pb. 1752; *The Englishman in Paris*, pr., pb. 1753; *The Englishman Returned from Paris*, pr., pb. 1756; *The Author*, pr., pb. 1757; *The Minor*, pr., pb. 1760; *The Liar*, pr. 1762, pb. 1764; *The Orators*, pr., pb. 1762; *The Mayor of Garratt*, pr., pb. 1763; *The Patron*, pr., pb. 1764; *The Commissary*, pr., pb. 1765; *The Tailors*, pr. 1767, pb. 1778; *The Devil upon Two Sticks*, pr., pb. 1768; *The Lame Lover*, pr., pb. 1770; *The Maid of Bath*, pr., pb. 1771; *The Nabob*, pr. 1772, pb. 1778; *The Handsome Housemaid: Or, Piety in Pattens*, pr. 1773 (as *Piety in Pattens*); *Primitive Puppet Shew*, pr. 1773; *The Bankrupt*, pr. 1773, pb. 1776; *The Cozeners*, pr. 1774, pb. 1778; *The Trip to Calais*, pr. 1775, pb. 1778; *The Capuchin*, pr. 1776, pb. 1778 (revision of *The Trip to Calais* with new last half); *Dramatic Works*, pb. 1929 (M. M. Belden, editor).

Other literary forms

Although Samuel Foote is known chiefly for his dramatic works, he wrote several critical essays and letters and translated a French comedy. His *The Roman and English Comedy Consider'd and Compar'd* (1747) and *A Treatise on the Passions* (1747) are well written and sound, but they are short and reflect traditional, conservative Augustan literary and dramatic criticism. *A Letter from Mr. Foote, to the Reverend Author of the "Remarks, Critical and Christian," on "The Minor"* (1760) and *Apology for "The Minor"* (1771) are significant because in them Foote delineates his critical ideas concerning affectation, hypocrisy, comedy, farce, the humorist, and the man of humor. Foote's thinking as presented in these two essays is strikingly similar to Henry Fielding's ideas on these topics as stated in the famous preface to *Joseph Andrews* (1742). Several of Foote's prologues and prefaces, such as the preface to *Taste* and the preface to *The Minor*, are critically important for their discussions of the aims and purposes of his satires. (The prologue to *Taste* that was written and spoken by actor David Garrick seems also to present some of Foote's views.) Foote's *The Comic Theatre, Being a Free Translation of All the Best French Comedies, by Samuel Foote and Others* (1762) was an ambitious undertaking, and although he wrote the preface for it, he translated only one play, *The Young Hypocrite*, leaving "the others" to translate the remainder of the five volumes.

Achievements

In his time, Foote was known as the English Aristophanes, a sobriquet originally used by the opposition in a libel suit but one which stuck because of Foote's dramatic satires of living persons and of contemporary scandals. G. H. Nettleton has described Foote as Henry Fielding's direct descendant, because he fully developed the latter's personalities, localized mimicry, and contemporary satire. In formulating his comic theory, Foote emphasized the corrective purpose of comedy, whose ridicule he considered to be more effective than law or reason in combating folly and vice. There were indeed times when Foote's satire achieved this purpose. When Foote played Lady Pentweazel in his comedy *Taste*, for example, he wore a huge headdress made with large, loose feathers that fell off his head to litter the stage throughout the play. His ridicule of the absurd hats then in vogue was credited with reforming this extreme fashion.

Perhaps Foote's greatest achievement was breaking the monopoly of Drury Lane and Covent Garden, the only two theaters in London that had official permission to produce plays and that did so primarily during the winter, when the social season was at its height. Foote made significant strides in breaking this monopoly when he evaded the 1737 Stage Licensing Act by advertising his performances not as drama but as entertainments, scheduling them for early in the day, and describing them under various names such as *The Diversions of the Morning*, *The Auction of Pictures*, "a dish of chocolate," or "an invitation to a dish of tea." None of these had a set content but instead contained combinations of successful old material, reworked material, and new material based on the latest social and political gossip—much like television shows such as *Laugh In* and *Saturday Night Live* two hundred years later. The result of Foote's "diversions," according to Simon Trefman (in his 1971 book on Foote), was the first theatrical matinee.

Foote finally broke the monopoly when the king awarded him a summer patent to the Haymarket Theatre that allowed him to operate between May fifteenth and September fifteenth of each year. Foote's resourcefulness and energy were tremendous, and so was his success. He wrote, produced, and directed his plays and, for most of the season, played the leading roles in them. Most of his plays enjoyed long runs, commanding large audiences not only at his establishment but elsewhere. *The Englishman in Paris*, for example, became part of the repertoire at Drury Lane and Covent Garden and was regularly played for more than twenty years. In addition, Foote was able to give steady employment to almost fifty actors during each season and to run his performances for fifty to sixty nights. Trefman claims that no one else in the history of English theater had ever drawn such crowds by the sheer power of satiric invention.

Foote was interested in new and experimental theatrical devices. The framing techniques he used in *Taste* and *The Orators* provided both unity for the segments that made up the pieces and a plausible explanation for poor and inexperienced performers, with whom they might be staged. He also experimented with puppets in his *Primitive Puppet Shew*. Foote's performances were successful not only in England but also in Ireland and Scotland.

Biography

Samuel Foote, although he receives very little attention today, was one of the leading playwrights, actors, and theater managers in mid-eighteenth century England. Foote's father was an attorney and magistrate who served as mayor in Truro, Cornwall, as Member of Parliament for Tiverton, as commissioner of the Prize Office, and receiver of fines. His mother was Eleanor Dinely Goodere, the daughter of baronet Sir Edward Goodere of Hereford.

Samuel was the youngest of three sons. The oldest son, Edward, was trained as a clergyman but was unable to support himself financially and depended on Samuel. There is very little recorded about the second son, John.

Foote attended Truro Grammar School and, in 1737, entered Worcester College, Oxford, whose founder, Sir Thomas Cookes, was related to the Foote family. During his tenure at Oxford, Foote is said to have become a competent Greek and Latin scholar. He was an undisciplined student, however, and his frequent unauthorized absences led the College to disenroll him on January 28, 1740.

After leaving Oxford, Foote entered London's Inner Temple to study law, but he soon left to replenish his depleted fortune. On January 10, 1741, he married Mary Hicks, an old acquaintance from Truro. After spending her dowry, Foote neglected and deserted her. This marriage produced no children, but Foote's will mentions two sons, Francis and George, and Trefman suggests that these children were the result of a short-lived liaison between Foote and one of his servants.

Foote made his first appearance as a professional actor on February 6, 1744, at the Haymarket Theatre in the role of Othello. Foote's forte, however, was not tragedy but comedy and impersonation. Foote mimicked many of the luminaries of his day, including Charles Macklin, Thomas Sheridan (father of playwright Richard Brinsley Sheridan), David Garrick, Arthur Murphy, and Henry Fielding. This comedic flair marked his private life as well, and he was a noted conversationalist. Even Samuel Johnson found Foote's humor attractive, observing " . . . he has wit too, and is not deficient in ideas, or in fertility and variety of imagery . . . he never lets truth stand between him and a jest, and he is sometimes mighty coarse."

Foote had friends at court, including the Duke of York, although these relationships often seemed to be troublesome rather than advantageous. His lifelong connection with wealthy, handsome, socialite Francis Blake Delaval, for example, did lead to many high times at Delaval's family seat. On the other hand, when Delaval commissioned Foote to facilitate the marriage between a supposedly wealthy elderly widow, Lady Isabella Pawlett, and Delaval, the result was strikingly similar to a stage farce: legal battles, social scandal, and very little money for either Foote or Delaval—most of Lady Isabella's wealth proving to be part of an irrevocable trust for her daughter. Another scheme—in which Foote and some demimondaines were to accompany Delaval and Sir Richard Atkins on a yacht trip to Corsica and help Delaval secure the vacant throne of that country—ended in the death of Sir Richard.

The temptations of high-living friends with money to waste led to other problems for Foote. Although he worked hard, was a prolific playwright, and was much in demand as an actor, debts plagued him for most of his life. A low point was reached in 1742, when he was imprisoned for nonpayment of debts, having been charged by creditors ranging from his mother to Lady Viscountess Castlecoma. The passage of a bill for the relief of insolvent debtors led to Foote's release, but although his economic difficulties were never to become that acute again, they never entirely disappeared.

Foote traveled often for both work and recreation. It became habitual for him to travel to Dublin and Edinburgh to act, and he regularly spent his holidays in Paris. His trips to Paris inspired *The Englishman in Paris* and *The Englishman Returned from Paris*.

Foote's strongest competition as a theater manager came from the licensed winter theaters, Drury Lane and Covent Garden. In order to make a living, Foote rented and managed the Little Theatre in the Haymarket during the summer months—an insecure undertaking because he did not have legal permission to operate his theater. There he began what came to be a wildly popular form of entertainment consisting of imitations of various actors and celebrities and satiric sketches loosely grouped in programs that were commonly called *The Diversions of the Morning*.

This situation changed in 1765 as a result of a sad accident. While visiting the aristocratic Lord and Lady Mexborough, Foote's friends teased him into claiming that he was a good horseman. In backing up this false claim, Foote mounted the Duke of York's spirited horse and was thrown immediately. The hard fall shattered Foote's leg in several places and the duke's personal physician had to amputate it. Feeling guilty for his role in this affair, the duke used his influence to obtain for Foote the summer patent rights to the theater, a patent good for the remainder of Foote's life.

In 1767, Foote bought and refurbished the Haymarket Theatre. He successfully managed it and played most of the lead roles or acted in the afterpieces until 1776, when George Colman was finally able to rent the patent from him. Several times before this, Foote had contemplated retiring and leasing his theater rights, but his reluctance to give up his extremely favorable position in the theater world had always made him reconsider. He only gave the lease to Colman because of the mounting pressure of a battle Foote was waging against the Duchess of Kingston, the last and perhaps most disastrous lawsuit resulting from Foote's habit of satirizing persons involved in contemporary scandals. (An earlier lawsuit over Foote's lampoon in *The Orators* of the one-legged Dublin printer George Faulkner had been won by Faulkner.)

The Duchess of Kingston, the one-time Countess of Bristol, had begun life as Elizabeth Chudleigh. While Chudleigh was maid of honor to the Princess of Wales, she met and married the heir to the Earl of Bristol—in secret, so that her standing at Court was not jeopardized. A few years later, she found a man she preferred, the wealthy and elderly Duke of Kingston. Becoming the duchess involved a series of shady legal maneuvers, but the transfer was accomplished; after the duke's death, however, the duchess was indicted for bigamy and her trial became the focus for gossip in the best social circles.

Almost inevitably, Foote made the duchess' greed and hypocrisy the subject of a satire, *The Trip to Calais*, enraging the duchess. She retaliated by using her connections to prohibit the play's continued production. Foote did rewrite the play, with a new second act, as *The Capuchin*, but the duchess and her supporters were not appeased. A newspaper war ensued. One of Chudleigh's hangers-on, William Jackson, editor of *The Public Ledger*, bribed a servant whom Foote had discharged, John Sangster, to sue Foote for homosexual assault, and covered the matter extensively in his scandal sheet.

When the matter finally came to trial, the charge was found to be totally unsubstantiated, and Foote was acquitted. Although Foote appeared in forty-nine mainpieces and twenty-six afterpieces while awaiting trial, the most acting he had done since the loss of his leg, after the verdict was rendered, he began to suffer from recurring seizures.

In order to rebuild his health, Foote started for Paris, but he died en route at the Ship Inn at Dover. On October 27, 1777, his friends buried him in Westminster Abbey.

Analysis

Samuel Foote developed his theory of comedy over a fifteen-year period in several critical works. According to Foote, the main purpose of comedy is to correct vice and folly by ridiculing them while pleasing and delighting the imagination. By representing fashionable foibles and extravagant humors, comedy teaches people to avoid folly. Foote's comic design was to amend the heart, improve the understanding, and please the imagination.

In his *A Letter from Mr. Foote*, Foote outlined the requirements of comedy: Comedy should be true to nature; it must represent exactly the peculiar manners of a people; it must faithfully imitate singular absurdities and particular follies. Comic imitation and representation provide an example to the entire community.

Foote himself likened his comic-satiric method to that employed by Aristophanes, William Shakespeare, Molière, John Dryden, Alexander Pope, Jean de La Bruyère, and Nicolas Boileau. For Foote, character was the greatest comic requisite, and his definitions of two comic character-types—the "humorist" and the "man of humor"—constitute his major contribution to comic theory. According to Foote, the humorist possesses some internal disposition which makes him say or do absurd and ridiculous things while firmly convinced that his actions are correct and acceptable. Foote's man of humor is the pleasant person who enjoys the humorist's eccentricities or affectations and exposes them.

Foote's plays *Taste* and *The Orators* exemplify his comic method, although an analysis of any of Foote's plays must necessarily be incomplete since it depends on the printed version, while almost every performance was different. *Taste* was first produced at Drury Lane on January 11, 1752. Foote's target in this play was the booming art market of the time, the notoriously ignorant and gullible society poseurs who craved antiques and works of old masters only because of the current fad, and the dishonesty of dealers and auctioneers who preyed upon them. The play, staged only five times during the 1752 season, was a failure because, according to the critical judgment of the day, the audience lacked taste and did not understand the method or objectives of Foote's satire. Foote's satiric approach was high burlesque. In order to appreciate high burlesque, an audience must be aware of certain standards of true taste and judgment and therefore be able to recognize the discrepancy between these standards and the pretensions of the characters in the play. Audiences who were devoted to a similar mad pursuit of trends were unlikely to appreciate Foote's humor on the subject.

Foote's theory of taste is similar to the theories of the leading formulators of a standard of taste in the eighteenth century such as David Hume, Edmund Burke, Sir Joshua Reynolds, James Beattie, Oliver Goldsmith, and Joseph Addison. All held the same fundamental requisites to a standard of taste: sensibility, imagination, judgment, education, common sense, morality, and objectivity. In *Taste*, Foote develops these principles by exhibiting the follies of people who lack these requisites. Foote's "connoisseurs," Lord Dupe, Novice, Lady Pentweazel, Squander, and Sir Positive Bubble, are so overcome by the fashionable craze for mutilated objects that are promoted as antiques, for foreign artworks, and for foreign artists that what little intellect they may have suspends operation.

Foote, in the preface to *Taste*, presents his views on education and morality as necessary to a standard of taste. He says that he is determined to satirize the barbarians who have prostituted the study of antiquity to trifling superficiality, who have blasted the progress of the elegant arts by unpardonable frauds and absurd prejudices, and who have vitiated the minds and morals of youth by persuading them that what serves only to illustrate literature is true knowledge and that active idleness is real business.

In the context of the play itself, the virtuosi do not know art. Lady Pentweazel thinks that the *Mary de Medicis* and the *Venus de Medicis* were sisters in the Medici family instead of paintings. Novice and Dupe think that they can evaluate the age and worth of a coin or medal by tasting it. Puff, the auctioneer, is able to convince Dupe, Novice, and Sir Positive that broken statuary and china are more valuable than perfect pieces. Lord Dupe demonstrates a complete lack of common sense when he purchases a canvas that has all the paint scraped off it. Carmine, Puff, and their associates even convince the dupes that a head from Herculaneum dates from before the biblical account of the Creation.

Satire is invariably based on human foibles evident in the time in which it is written, but in good satire, such as that of Aristophanes, the point being made is more widely applicable. *Taste* reflects conditions that existed in Foote's day, but its humor is generalizable not merely to any era in which works of art are bought and sold by fashionable and ignorant collectors; it also has something to say about the way in which people come to be so easily misled, no matter what the issue or era.

The Orators, a three-act comedy which presented different aspects of another currently fashionable preoccupation, was first produced on Wednesday, April 28, 1762, in Foote's Haymarket Theatre. Unlike *Taste*, *The Orators* was highly successful, appearing thirty-nine times in the first year.

The Orators is a framed play. In the printed version (as was the case with many of Foote's plays, the staged version varied from one performance to the next), this play comprises three parts. The first is a long satire on oratory, the second is a mock trial of the Cock-Lane ghost (introduced so that students at Foote's onstage oratory class could practice judicial oratory in the trial of a currently notorious apparition), and the third features amateur debating clubs such as the Robin Hood Society. The parts are united by the four or five principal characters that appear in each, not by plot, because there is none—even within the individual parts.

Originally advertised as "A Course of Comic Lectures on English Oratory," the play is set in a theater. Harry Scamper and Will Tirehack, two Oxford dandies looking for amusement, enter, seat themselves in a side box, and after questioning the candle-snuffer about what the lectures will contain, call for the theater's manager, Mr. Foote, played by the author himself. They want him to assure them that they will be amused. From a box on the other side of the stage, Ephraim Suds, a soap-boiler, wants reassurance that the lectures will be educational—that he will learn to give speeches. Foote declares that both needs will be met; in the course of his explanation, it is revealed that Foote operates a school of oratory guaranteed to train even the most burr-tongued Scotsman to be a golden-throated speaker. This prepares the way for the introduction of the other major character, Donald, a young Scot with a broad accent.

After the opening lecture on the principles of oratory, Foote allows his "students" to practice what they have learned in various professions and situations. This framework provides not only unity but also an excuse for poor performers. In one scene, the actors are merely beginning students, in another they are rehearsing. This device enabled Foote to use a series of less skilled (and less expensive) actors and to vary lines on short notice without in any way diminishing the humor of the play.

Foote wrote *The Orators* primarily to satirize the British Elocutionary Movement and its leader, Thomas Sheridan, whose success as an actor gave weight to his pronouncements on delivery. From the days of the early Greeks, rhetoric had been regarded as possessing five aspects: *inventio, dispositio, elocutio, pronuntiatio,* and *memoria* (or discovery of a thesis, arrangement of argument, style, delivery, and memory). It was the belief of more conservative rhetoricians of Foote's day that Sheridan had devalued rhetoric by extending Cicero's definition of *pronuntiatio* and making it seem that it was the whole of the art of ancient rhetoric rather than merely one of five parts, and a lesser one at that.

Foote gives a good picture, though satirized and therefore exaggerated, of the tenets of Sheridan's elocutionary theory in act 1 of *The Orators*. At the beginning of his lecture he refers to Sheridan's *Lectures on Elocution* (1762), which delineates Sheridan's plan "to revive the long-lost art of oratory, and to correct, ascertain, and fix the English language." To achieve these goals, Sheridan wanted to establish an academy, but the institution had to be structured on his plan alone. Foote ridicules Sheridan's egocentrism by saying that he (Foote) wants to be made perpetual professor of his own academy.

Foote mimics Sheridan's intention to "correct, ascertain, and fix the English language" in the character of Ephraim Suds, who has just finished taking Sheridan's course of oratory. Suds has learned little from Sheridan's teaching, for he mispronounces words, such as "empharis" for "emphasis," and speaks ungrammatical English.

Sheridan not only believed his academy could perfect the English language; he also envisioned his school as an Irish center for the study of correct English speech, and he thought that students would flock to it from

Scotland, Wales, America, and the other British colonies abroad, in order to correct provincialisms in speech. Foote satirizes these ideas by demonstrating the effects of Sheridan's education on Donald, a Scottish orator who has studied for one year under Sheridan and six weeks under Foote. Donald continues to speak with a heavy Scottish accent and uses dialectal diction which Scamper and Tirehack cannot understand.

Foote also uses Donald to satirize Sheridan's emphasis on pronunciation—his belief that a good orator could, by following proper accents, read a work he did not understand. In an exaggerated paraphrase of Sheridan's discussion of pronunciation, Donald contradicts the ancient rhetoricians Demosthenes and Cicero, who called delivery the fourth rather than the first part of oratory. Scamper and Tirehack notice the contradiction and complain. Again, Foote attacks Sheridan and the Elocutionists for their emphasis on voice and gesture to the exclusion of the other four major procedures in rhetoric.

Donald becomes furious at Scamper and Tirehack's correction, and they tell him that he must tell the truth. Donald replies that he can tell the truth "logically," satirizing internal or artistic proofs which are based not upon empirical evidence but upon probability. The Elocutionists wanted to persuade and to win debates through a grandiloquent style, and they did not care about truth; they excluded from rhetoric considerations of subject matter and arrangement of argument and thereby reduced it to style, voice, and gesture alone.

Foote suggests a motto for a treatise that Sheridan planned to write. He adds, however, that Sheridan is probably already well provided with an apt Latin or a Greek one. Here, Foote's comment is most likely a strike at Sheridan's greatest shortcoming, his total inability to understand the Greek and Latin rhetoricians from whom he quoted so often, and the consequential diminishing of ancient oratory.

Although today his work is known only to specialists, Foote's colorful and successful theatrical career offers rich insights concerning the practical exigencies and the underlying values of the eighteenth century English style.

Other major works

NONFICTION: *The Roman and English Comedy Consider'd and Compar'd*, 1747; *A Treatise on the Passions*, 1747; *A Letter from Mr. Foote, to the Reverend Author of the "Remarks, Critical and Christian," on "The Minor,"* 1760; *Apology for "The Minor,"* 1771.

TRANSLATION: *The Comic Theatre, Being a Free Translation of All the Best French Comedies, by Samuel Foote and Others*, 1762 (with others).

Bibliography
Belden, Mary Megie. *The Dramatic Work of Samuel Foote.* Hamden,
Conn.: Archon Books, 1969. Belden acknowledges the biographical work
of Percy Fitzgerald (below) and states that her purpose is to extend
Fitzgerald's 1910 study by providing contemporary sources of information. She briefly touches upon Foote's life and then focuses on a description and evaluation of the plays. She concludes with a critical analysis of
Foote's theory of comedy, proclaiming that his importance lies in revealing the character of his contemporary society. Bibliography and index.
Chatten, Elizabeth N. *Samuel Foote.* Boston: Twayne, 1980. Chatten focuses
on a discussion of Foote's dramatic works and essays on drama, evaluat-
ing them in the light of social history. She describes him as a witty
social satirist who resides firmly within eighteenth century literary tradition. Chronology, annotated bibliography, and index.
Fitzgerald, Percy. *Samuel Foote: A Biography.* London: Chatto & Windus,
1910. This standard biography of Foote chronicles his life in a lively and
popular style. The plays are discussed and the satirical targets explained.
Index and portrait of Foote.
Theatre Survey: The American Journal of Theatre History 14 (Fall, 1973).
This entire issue is devoted to the first publication of Foote's satire, *Piety
in Pattens*, from manuscripts found in the Huntington and Folger libraries. It is valuable for its extensive notes, commentary, and introductory
essay, "Samuel Foote and the Revolt Against Sentimental Drama." Illustrations, playbills, and bibliography.
Trefman, Simon. *Sam. Foote, Comedian: 1720-1777.* New York: New York
University Press, 1971. Foote achieved his enormous popularity through
his audacious and libelous wit, attracting an audience that came to see
his satires of well-known people. Trefman examines how Foote's plays
reflected his controversial battles with the theater monopolies and how
he took advantage of the newspaper's thirst for mudslinging to increase
his audience. Complete listing of Foote's London performances, bibliography, and index.
Wharton, Robert Verner. "The Divided Sensibility of Samuel Foote." *Educational Theatre Journal* 17 (1965): 31-37. Wharton claims that by viewing Foote only as a wit, mimic, and master satirist, a substantial vein of
sentimentalism is overlooked in his comedies. This sentimentalism is
then explored in Foote's major comedies.

Mary C. Murphy
(Updated by *Gerald S. Argetsinger*)

JOHN FORD

Born: Near Ilsington, England; April 17, 1586 (baptized)
Died: Unknown; after 1639

Principal drama

The Witch of Edmonton, pr. 1621, pb. 1658 (with Thomas Dekker and William Rowley); *Perkin Warbeck*, pr. c. 1622-1632, pb. 1634; *The Sun's Darling*, pr. 1624, pb. 1656 (with Dekker); *The Broken Heart*, pr. c. 1627-1631, pb. 1633; *The Lover's Melancholy*, pr. 1628, pb. 1629; *'Tis Pity She's a Whore*, pr. 1629(?)-1633, pb. 1633; *The Fancies Chaste and Noble*, pr. 1631(?) or 1635-1636(?), pb. 1638; *Love's Sacrifice*, pr. 1632(?), pb. 1633; *The Lady's Trial*, pr. 1638, pb. 1639; *The Queen: Or, The Excellency of Her Sex*, pb. 1653.

Other literary forms

In addition to his plays, John Ford published two long poems and three prose pamphlets. *Fame's Memorial: Or, The Earl of Devonshire Deceased* (1606) is an elegy praising Charles Blount, who had married Penelope Devereux (on whom Sir Philip Sidney based his Stella) after her divorce from Lord Rich. *Christ's Bloody Sweat: Or, The Son of God in His Agony* (1613) is a religious poem on the efficacy of repentance. *Honor Triumphant: Or, The Peer's Challenge* (1606) argues four propositions in mock style; *The Golden Mean* (1613) praises Stoicism; and *A Line of Life* (1620) describes the Stoic conduct of a man, a public man and a good man.

Achievements

Many critics have acclaimed John Ford as the outstanding dramatist of the Caroline period (1625-1649), and his plays give ample evidence of the justice of this claim. Today, almost any full-year course on the drama surrounding William Shakespeare will include *The Broken Heart*, *'Tis Pity She's a Whore*, and *Perkin Warbeck*. These plays are being produced and evoke a positive response from modern audiences. Although he is not known for innovation, Ford creatively employed such common forms of the age as tragicomedy, revenge tragedy, and the visual elements of the masque. His plays are rich in resonances from other dramatists of the period (particularly Shakespeare, Ben Jonson, and John Webster), but what he borrows, he transforms for his own use. In no way is Ford a surface dramatist. He was deeply interested in Burtonian psychology, but he was never a slave to its formulas; in his drama, he was continually probing into the depths of personality, and he was particularly interested in exploring the human psyche in relationship to or confrontation with other human beings.

Biography

Very little is known about John Ford's life other than a few isolated facts. He was baptized on April 17, 1586, the second son of a Devonshire country gentleman. He was admitted to Middle Temple in 1602, expelled for not paying a board bill in 1606, readmitted in 1608, and involved in a dispute over the wearing of hats in 1617. His father died in 1610, leaving Ford a paltry ten pounds, and six years later, his income was increased by a bequest of twenty pounds a year from his elder brother's estate. Nothing is known of his style of life—whether he was ever married or engaged in a profession—and no record has yet been found of his death.

Analysis

John Ford's fascination with the psychology of love in its many-faceted applications to social life is evident in his earliest produced play, *The Witch of Edmonton*, which he wrote in collaboration with Thomas Dekker and William Rowley. Here also is evident Ford's propensity to the sensational as well as the association of love with death, which was to reappear in many of his subsequent plays. In the first scene, Frank Thorney has just been married to Sir Arthur Clarington's serving maid, Winnifride, who is with child. The marriage is to be kept in the dark until Frank can secure his inheritance. Sir Arthur abets this deception by writing a letter certifying that no marriage has taken place, even though he is frustrated in his hopes of maintaining a relationship with Winnifride, who takes her marriage and her new status most seriously. The reason for the secrecy becomes gradually yet shockingly apparent as the audience realizes that Frank, who seems to have a strong and genuine love for his bride, nevertheless intends to secure his inheritance through a bigamous marriage with his longtime neighbor Susan Carter. There is irony throughout the scene of his second courtship, but particularly in Susan's outburst of hymeneal joy at having her heart settled with her one true love and winning the right to dismiss her unwanted suitors. Frank, who seems to like Susan well enough, blames his situation on fate—an ever-present force in Ford's dramas.

The violent outcome of this wedding is predicted in the imagery as Susan's father remembers a proverb relating weddings with hangings. One of her former suitors remarks on the unity of the newly married couple, but with an undesirable cutting edge as he compares them to a "new pair of Sheffield knives, fitted both to one sheath." To Susan as to Ford, real love involves unity and the sharing of souls, and she is disturbed to discover that Frank is unable to share with her the source of his obvious discontent. In a pleading not unlike Portia's to Brutus in Shakespeare's *Julius Caesar*, she coaxes him to display his mind: "You shall not shut me from partaking/ The least dislike that grieves you; I'm all yours. . . . I must know/ The ground of your disturbance." Frank assures Susan that the cause has nothing to do with her, blaming his unrest on "the poison'd leeches twist about my heart." He comes close to revealing his bigamy, telling of a palmist who predicted that he should have two wives, but Susan naturally assumes that the second will appear only after her death and, with saintly humility, wishes that "fate" might give him a second wife to outmatch his first—that is, herself.

Frank's two wives are brought together for a brief scene in which Frank is leaving on a journey with his first wife, dressed as a page for the occasion, and stops to say a farewell to Susan. Winnifride, apprised of the situation, is horrified at Frank's lawlessness and callousness in committing bigamy for money, but she has little choice but to follow his lead, and her love for him seems to survive. Susan, in ignorance of the situation, ironically pleads with Frank's "page" to be servant, friend, and wife to him on their journey. Susan contrives to bid farewell to Frank privately; she delays their parting as long as possible, exacerbating Frank's impatience until a white dog enters the scene and Frank suddenly murders Susan, wounds himself, ties himself up (with the dog's help), and cries out "murder." In the supernatural scenes of the play, from which it gets its title and which are generally ascribed to Dekker, the dog is both the witch's familiar and the representative of the Devil himself. In the scenes by Ford, such as this, the dog almost seems to be a bodily representation of the force of fate, tainted as it is in this play with more than a touch of evil.

Later, in Frank's sickroom, where he is recovering from his wound, the dog enters just as Susan's sister discovers the incriminating knife. When she leaves, Frank is visited by the ghost of Susan and by a very live Winnifride before the authorities enter, and both Frank and his remaining wife are carted off to jail. In the final scene of the play, Winnifride is free but faints under the heaviness of her emotion and the weight of her continuing love for her condemned husband. A wave of pity for the bigamist-murderer seems to come over the crowd—a pity which Ford would evidently induce in his audience. This is strengthened by Frank's final speech on his way to execution. In deep penitence, he comments on the rightness of his own death, asks for forgiveness, and seeks to obtain financial security for Winnifride, whom he has never ceased to love, though his ways of demonstrating that love are aberrant in the extreme. Ford's obvious sympathy for the murderer, who planned the bigamy long before any "dog" urged him to go further, is an indication of a moral ambiguity which many critics have found in his plays, but it is also an empathetic examination of a kind of love, pure on the part of both Susan and Winnifride and tainted on Frank's, which can survive in spite of circumstances and a society which would threaten to smother it completely.

Dekker also collaborated with Ford on another early play (it is almost impossible to date Ford's plays precisely), a delightful marriage of morality

play and masque entitled *The Sun's Darling*. Raybright, an Everyman figure who is the offspring of the sun, travels through the domains of the four
seasons, each of which attempts to entice him to stay, while his companion,
Humour, enlists counterforces to lure him on the the next segment of the
year. Each act, representing a season, is a masque in its own right, and
each introduces separate masquelike episodes, with songs, dances, and
poetic combats presenting various virtues and vices. The most insidious vice
of the play is undoubtedly the Spanish confectioner in Spring's entourage,
who brags that he "can teach sugar to slip down your throat a thousand
ways." Perhaps the most outlandish is the personified Detraction, who
claims that scholars are merely "petty penmen [who] covet/ Fame by Folly."
The production ends with a final masque performed by the four elements
and the four humours, after which the Sun itself descends to make its comments on health and harmony in the perfect interaction of these eight
dancers.

There is much about love in the play, as each of the seasons courts
Raybright, but he discerns that much of what is presented as love is merely
an attempt to buy him with the various gifts the seasons offer. In Autumn
and Winter, the season-acts most often ascribed to Ford on the basis of
style, it is interesting to note that the ideas of love grow more complex.
There is mutuality in the love offered by Autumn, who recognizes that
Raybright, in representing the sun, has as much to offer the season as
Autumn has to offer him. "Let us be twins in heart," she suggests, after
which Humour and her companion Folly have a harder time convincing
Raybright to leave. He does leave eventually, and as he approaches Winter,
the love imagery of the play becomes theological if not downright messi-
anic. Raybright, the son of the Sun, is the "excellently good" one for
whom they have been waiting. He comes with justice and impartial law.
The clowns who oppose his coming are waging "war against heaven" and
thereby subject themselves to the "thunder-stroke" which is able to cast
them "From heaven's sublime height to the depth of hell." In terms of the
Book of Revelation, Raybright will appear like a star, and "Night shall be
chang'd into perpetual day."

The Lover's Melancholy, which is probably the first play Ford wrote
without a collaborator, examines love in what is almost a clinical study. The
play opens with a veritable symphony of frustration. When Menaphon returns from a year's trip abroad, he is met by his soul-friend Amethus, who
laments that his loved Cleophila (a kinswoman of Menaphon) has remained
cold to him, because she cares only for her aging and infirm father.
Menaphon, in return, discovers that his love, Thamasta, who also happens
to be Amethus' sister, is still "intermured with ice"—absence having done
nothing to make her heart grow fond. The illness of Cleophila's father,
Meleander, is related to love, since its genesis was the disappearance of his

loved daughter, Eroclea. The classic case of love melancholy, however, is that of Palador, the Prince of Cyprus, whose kingdom has been in a sharp decline since Eroclea's departure. She had been promised to him in marriage by his tyrant father, but only as a trick to lure her to court, where she was to be raped by lecherous courtiers—a fate from which she had been saved by her father, who was promptly dismissed from court as his reward. This was certainly a factor in producing his melancholy state.

The sickness suffered by the prince has descended through him to the state. Ford presents this on the stage via another returned traveler, Rhetias, who determines to play the role of court railer. His soliloquy against court foolery at the beginning of the second scene of the play is aided by the entrance of two court sycophants, Pelias and Cuculus, who provide excellent targets for his barrage of satire. At the end of the scene, Rhetias finds a partner in raillery in Corax, the physician who has been called into court to heal the prince's malady. The description of a sick court is enhanced by Meleander himself, as, in beautifully mad poetry, he pictures the decadence perpetrated by the former tyrant, moans over the futility of court life, and pleads for a funeral without pomp, ceremony, or expense. Even Thamasta shows a side of love melancholy as she conceives of herself in love with the youth, Parthenophill, whom Menaphon has brought back from his travels. "Love is a tyrant/ Resisted," she proclaims—a complaint which might have come from any one of the multifarious treatises on melancholy produced in the sixteenth and seventeenth centuries. This aberrant love, however, is easily treated when she discovers at the end of one particularly well-wrought scene that the object of her misguided affection is indeed a woman. "Cupid," Parthenophill points out, "Comes to make sport between us with no weapon."

The presence of a physician in the court, and hence in the play, gives Ford his chance to examine love melancholy as a form of diseased love. When Prince Palador enters like the melancholy Hamlet, reading a book, Corax caustically reminds him that he had prescribed exercise, not sonnets. Later, two court counselors open the door for a lecture by asking Corax to explain the nature of melancholy, which he does fairly directly out of Robert Burton's *The Anatomy of Melancholy* (1621). Being a master of stagecraft, Ford, through Corax, arranges for a "masque of melancholy" to be presented before the prince, in which Burtonian characters of Lycanthropia, Hydrophobia, Delirium, Phrenitis, Hypochondriacal Melancholy (including a delightful poem against tobacco), and Wanton Melancholy all make their appearance on the stage with appropriate speeches. Prince Palador perhaps assumes that he is getting off lightly, since love melancholy is not among the characters, but thus relaxed (as Claudius perhaps relaxed after the dumb show), he is an easy target for Corax, who, claiming that the condition is too serious and complex to be presented by art

(art versus nature being one of the concerns of the play), describes love melancholy to him and suggests that Parthenophill, pale and wan for a lad, is a *living* example of the disease. As visibly moved as Claudius, Palador abruptly dismisses the gathering, and Corax has his diagnosis confirmed: "Love . . . will be seen." Corax's cure is surely made easier by the fact that Parthenophill is in truth Eroclea, who had been in Athens under the care of Rhetias and opportunely found a way to return with Menaphon after the death of Palador's tyrannical father. Even so, the prince has to be prepared for her return with a closely paralleled parable, and he accepts her actual presence only very slowly, thinking it might be some trick—perhaps Parthenophill disguised as Eroclea. Ford fashions their meeting with another demonstration of the mutuality necessary for real love. When she enters the scene, she finishes his speech as if she were privy to the thoughts of his mind, and she also reveals that she has been carrying his picture next to her breast in exactly the same fashion that, it has been earlier revealed, he has been carrying hers.

In addition, the healing of Meleander is carefully wrought by the scholar-physician Corax. He first prepares Meleander (who enters raging, with a poleax) by staring him down, having donned a frightful mask. He then tries to establish empathy with him by claiming that he, Corax, has a daughter who has been snatched away, leaving him with a crazed head and an acute lack of sleep. It works; Meleander does thereafter claim a special affinity for Corax, admits "I hug my afflictions," and fetches Cleophila to praise her virtues and compare them with those of the lost Eroclea. In the final scene of the play, Meleander is reached with another court device, perhaps even more dramatic than the masque of melancholy. Meleander has been drugged, delivered to a barber to have his four-years' beard removed, and carted to a tailor to fit him with fresh clothes. When he wakes, to the sound of music, he is met with a procession of messengers. First Aretus, the court tutor, announces that all of Meleander's honors have been restored, and Amethus then presents him with a staff of office, indicating a healing to take place in the state as well as in the individual. Sophronos, Meleander's brother and the father of Menaphon, hands him the picture of Eroclea which Palador had worn next to his heart and which he no longer needs, further announcing that the prince is ready to address Meleander as father. When Cleophila enters with her sister, the meeting of father and daughter is natural and joyful as the story of her disappearance is related. When Prince Palador finally enters, he joyfully greets Meleander as father with the "prince's sweetness," which completes his cure. He makes all necessary explanations and arranges for the marriages, bringing the comedy to a healthy close.

In many ways, *The Broken Heart* is a study in courtship and marriage. The play opens with Orgilus discussing his relationship with his betrothed,

Penthea, which has been thwarted by, to use his words, a "poisonous stalk/ Of aconite" in the person of Penthea's brother, Ithocles, who, in spite of the betrothal, has compelled Penthea to marry Bassanes, an older and richer, though hardly wiser, nobleman. At first, Orgilus, who is later referred to as a married bachelor, seems to show some real concern for Penthea as he informs his father, Crotolon, that he is leaving Sparta for Athens not only to escape from the jealousies of Bassanes and to ease the pain he feels in Penthea's presence, but also to free her "from a hell on earth," caught between her present husband and her former lover. All of this, however, turns out to be little more than subterfuge, of which Orgilus is a master. He soon returns in disguise as a scholar, spies on her in an unconscionable way, continually describes his love for her in terms bordering on the lascivious, and even in one painful scene tries by psychological pressure to force her to violate her marriage vows, claiming that their prior betrothal was the more valid contract. His attempts on her honor fall little short of attempted rape, and her resistance serves but to whet his already sharp appetite for revenge.

Orgilus' lack of integrity is also manifest in his extraction of a promise from his own sister, Euphrania, that she will never marry without his consent. In doing this, Orgilus is taking control of his sister's marriage in the same way that Ithocles had manipulated Penthea's. Euphrania's love for Prophilus seems genuine, pure, and controlled throughout. It outlasts the delay imposed upon them by having to wait for permission from the supposedly absent Orgilus, and it survives his close examination of the relationship, disguised as student who by accident becomes the messenger by whom they exchange letters while their love is still secret. Because Prophilus is a close friend of the hated Ithocles, Orgilus' permission is wrenched from him only with the greatest difficulty, although once it is given, his rancor seems to be forgotten if not totally dissipated.

The marriage between Penthea and Bassanes is indeed a hellish affair. Orgilus deems it a "monster-love" because she had been previously betrothed to him, but surely it is monstrous in its own right. The cliché of an older man's fear of cuckoldry when married to a young, attractive woman comes to life on the stage. In the audience's first glimpse into their home, Bassanes is arranging for a mason to have the front window "dammed up" lest it afford passersby a glimpse of Penthea's beauty. She is continually spied upon by Brausis, a delightfully doughty old woman described in the *dramatis personae* as her overseer. Bassanes is even jealous of Penthea's brother, but perhaps this is not untoward in a Ford play. In spite of this oppressive picture of his personality, there is also a note of pathos in it. Although he was the benefactor of Ithocles' pandering, he did not devise it; the court he describes is indeed a dangerous place for an attractive woman; and his appreciation of her beauty has a numinous quality to it. At

her first entrance, he exclaims: "She comes, she comes! So shoots the
morning forth,/ Spangled with pearls of transparent dew." His own intoxi-
cation with her beauty justifies his belief that others might be equally
affected.

The mad jealousy of Bassanes is dramatically revealed to all when he
breaks in on a conference between his wife and her brother and imagines
their incest. Ithocles, long since repentant of this marriage which he forced
on his sister, now takes decisive steps to remove her from the oppression of
this home and put her under his own protection. The shock of public horror at his behavior and the losing of his wife bring Bassanes to a sudden
but believable repentance, and he genuinely laments the loss of a love he
was not fit to enjoy. Ironically, his repentance comes too late to transform
him into a fit husband at the same moment that Ithocles, through painful
repentance, has belatedly become a fit brother.

In this state, Ithocles earnestly attempts to elicit his sister's forgiveness,
but every opening gesture he makes is met with scornful barbs forged in
the deep center of pain which Penthea feels from having been wrenched
from her betrothed love and forced into a relationship which she therefore
considers adulterous. She relents only when, sensitized to the psychological
conditions of impossible love, she senses the nature of her brother's recent
illness and evokes from him a confession of his love for Calantha, the
daughter of his king, who is at the moment being newly courted by
Nearchus, prince of neighboring Argos. Penthea recovers from her bitterness to visit Calantha, in the guise of asking her to be the executrix of
her will. Using a familiar Renaissance form, she prettily bequeaths her
youth to chaste wives who marry "for ties of love,/ Rather than ranging of
their blood"; then her fame is left to memory and truth. Calantha is beginning to enjoy the game, when suddenly Penthea shatters the tradition and
unexpectedly leaves Ithocles her brother to Calantha. The princess is irate
at the presumption of this suggestion but withholds any comment on the
suggestion itself. In the next scene, however, Calantha takes a ring that has
been given to her by Nearchus and rejects it by tossing it to Ithocles,
suggesting that he "give it at next meeting to a mistress." It is Ithocles' turn
for presumption now, as he returns the ring to the princess herself, causing
some resentment among the supporters of Nearchus. The love between
Calantha and Ithocles is evidently genuine and reciprocal, and Nearchus,
making a choruslike comment on the theme of marriage, shows genuine
humility and understanding.

By the next scene, Calantha and Ithocles have courted and grown mature in their love, and she asks her dying father, the king, for permission to
marry, which is readily granted. Ithocles has proved himself worthy on the
battlefield and in the court and through repentance has cleansed himself of
his earlier inclinations to control the lives of others. Calantha is a magnifi-

cent woman, a queen, knowing herself and her own love and managing to keep love, passion, and will in perfect balance. Unfortunately, however, their love is to be consummated only in death. Ithocles dies magnificently under the revenger's dagger as Orgilus first catches him fast in a trick chair and then coolly deprives him of life. Calantha is leading the festivities at the wedding celebration for Euphrania and Prophilus when, on successive changes of the dance, she hears of the deaths of her father, her best friend Penthea, and her betrothed. Giving no evidence of the shock she feels at the news brought by successive messengers, she continues the dance to its conclusion. Then, as the reigning queen, she comments on Penthea's death; provides for the continuing rule of her country in a wedding contract with Nearchus which, as Bassanes comments, is actually her will and testament; and then, placing her mother's wedding ring on Ithocles' lifeless finger as a symbol of the consummation of a timeless love, she dies, indeed of a "broken heart."

In *Love's Sacrifice*, Ford is concerned with human relationships between the sexes in which no fulfillment is possible. The play opens with the banishment of Roseilli, an honest courtier, from the court. The only explanation he can surmise for his banishment is that somewhere behind the action is Fiormonda, the woman he has been unsuccessfully wooing for some time and who wants only to be rid of him.

When the duke enters with his duchess, Bianca, it at first seems as if they are a well-mated pair. Their entrance is announced by courtiers praising the duke for choosing Bianca not because of family or connections but simply because of her beauty, to which Fernando adds virtue. Onstage, the duke affirms that he values only two things: his duchess and his trusted friend Fernando. Intimations of things to come present themselves shortly after their departure, however, when the trusted Fernando laments his all-consuming love for the duchess. He is hardly through with this speech when Fiormonda enters to court him. He deftly puts her off by praising not only her beauty but also her loyalty to her dead husband, but this serves only as a cue for Fiormonda to produce the ring that her husband instructed her to give to the one she could love as much as she had loved him. The scene is interrupted (a blessing to Fernando and a curse to Fiormonda) by the entrance of Bianca, asking Fernando's help in convincing the duke to recall Roseilli, the man Fiormonda had just succeeded in getting out of her way.

The intrigue does not stop here. The beginning of the second act discloses still another courtier enamored of Fiormonda, and the court gets a good laugh as, from the upper stage, it overhears and sees Mauruccio practicing ridiculous speeches, designing outlandish costumes, and devising foolish gifts as he outlines his assault upon his beloved—the only member of the court who is not in stitches at the entire proceeding. Thus, the audience is introduced to a court with its love triangles, quadrangles, and octangles, none of which promises to produce anything but pain.

The unhealthy quality of the love in this play is underscored by a quantity of disease imagery, with love referred to as a leprosy at least three times. The center of this disease in the court is the duke's new counselor, Ferentes, who initiates an intriguing scene in which two young ladies and one older one all discover they are pregnant, having been bribed into bed with a promise of marriage from the same man. This source of the disease is effectively purged, however, in a scene reminiscent of Thomas Kyd, in which Ferentes is stabbed by all three of the women in a court masque presented in honor of a visiting abbot (Bianca's uncle). To justify this action, each woman displays her newborn infant.

The primary love business of the play, between Fernando and Bianca, is strong, poignant, and confusing. At his first opportunity, Fernando speaks most eloquently of his love, evidently for the third time, and is put down with equal force and eloquence by a diatribe on chastity from Bianca, who takes her marriage vows seriously. In spite of being charged never to speak of love again, upon pain of exposure and certain death, Fernando cannot contain himself and once more pleads his plight. The situation is ominous. D'Avolos has noted Fernando's passion and, by means of displaying a pair of pictures, has trapped him into disclosing the object of his desire. With the duke away, Fiormonda has maneuvered the couple into a chess game (fraught with double entendre) and then, pleading sickness, has managed to leave them alone except for D'Avolos, who is sent back to spy upon them. The situation is too much for Fernando; even though warned, he is soon on his knees declaring his love. Again he is chastely humbled by Bianca, who deplores his "bestial dalliance" and warns that if he opens his "leprous mouth"again on the subject, it will mean "the forfeit of thy life." Fernando agrees to silence, but with Donne-like eloquence declares that if his heart is ripped open at his death, there the observer will read "Bianca's name carv'd out in bloody lines." From his observation post, D'Avolos completely misreads this scene and reports to Fiormonda that the couple are on their way to bed, to which she, playing the role of a good revenger, vows "to stir up tragedies as black as brave."

This misreading is the only preparation there is in the play for the next turn in the relationship, which surprises the reader in the very next scene. Bianca suddenly becomes the initiator in the game of love, appears in Fernando's bedroom while he is fast asleep, and wakes him with her declaration of mutual love. Even though she comes with "shame and passion," caught up by the "tyranny" of love, there is also an invitation in her words: "if thou tempt'st/ My bosom to thy pleasures, I will yield." Her invitation, however, has a barb in it; though she is torn by the passion of her love, she is also constant to her "vow to live a constant wife." Her impossible solution to this dilemma is to follow her passion in offering herself to Fernando but also to follow her conscience in declaring that, should he accept, "Ere yet the morning shall new-christen day,/ I'll kill myself." Fernando at first hopes this is some jest, but finally he takes her at her word, vowing to master his passion and sublimate their love into a spiritual relationship, though he is still uneasy enough to ask if she will later laugh at him for refusing the wondrous gift. At the end of the scene, she echoes Fernando's own avowal of constancy.

The reader is never quite sure of her mood after this. In one scene she contrives, in public, to wipe Fernando's lips and adds in an aside, "Speak, shall I steal a kiss? believe me, my lord, I long." There is something too coquettish in these lines coming from the woman vowed to death should her lover go beyond the kiss. Furthermore, in the final scenes of the play, she confesses to the duke, her husband, that she desired Fernando madly, tried her best to seduce him, but was unable to overcome his scruples. Perhaps she wanted both Fernando and death; this would not, certainly, be beyond the scope of Ford's imagination. Perhaps in this scene, she was merely trying to save his life in the face of the revenge-fury that Fiormonda had worked up in the duke. The latter seems most likely, in that she attributes Fernando's technical chastity not to the concern for her life but rather to his constant loyalty to the duke himself—an idea which, as far as the audience can tell, never entered Fernando's head, though perhaps it should have.

Typical of Ford's plays, the love which is impossible in life finds its consummation in death, as has been foreshadowed throughout the play. There is something noble about the way in which Bianca bravely bares her breast to receive death from her husband's dagger. She may be seeking death as the only way out of her dilemma, using her cruel and seemingly needless taunting of the duke (by proclaiming Fernando's superiority) as a device to be sure he is angry enough to complete the deed. She warns him that he will suffer when he comes to accept the validity of her physical chastity, but he cannot believe this, and his one moment of relenting is quickly overcome by the urging of Fiormonda, the real revenger, from the upper stage. The duke's anger is inflamed, the murder committed.

When the duke, again at Fiormonda's urging, approaches Fernando to complete his revenge, he finds him armed and unhesitatingly challenges him to a duel to the death. Fernando, however, upon hearing that Bianca is dead, drops his sword and bares his breast, willing to be sacrificed in the same manner that she had been, thus joining her in a death union symbolically apparent on the stage. He is denied this symmetry, however, for the duke, finally convinced of his wife's chastity if not her constancy, tries to stab himself, though he is stopped before completing his self-immolation. Instead, he arranges for a coffin and a funeral procession for his wife's body, and the abbot returns in time to add his dignity and pomp to the occasion. After an eloquent tribute to his dead wife, the duke opens the burial vault, only to find Fernando there ahead of him, still quite alive but dressed in his winding sheet. He answers the duke's attempt to drag him out by gulping poison to join his Bianca. The bliss of their union in death (assuming that such is possible) is, however, short-lived. The duke, after proclaiming that when the day comes that he should die he would like to be buried in one monument with his wife and friend, makes the waiting time short by stabbing himself to join them. The love triangle presumably moves from the human stage into an eternal tension.

Whether Ford is trying to say that all attempts at a solution by means of death are in vain or is quietly mocking himself, the situation suggests that there is neither glory nor promise nor fulfillment in love's sacrifice, which seeks to find on the other side of the grave what it is denied in life. On this side of the tomb, life goes on. The dukedom is perpetuated when Fiormonda, the sole surviving heir, offers the dukedom along with herself to Roseilli, who seems to be worthy of the post and establishes justice by consigning D'Avolos to the hangman. Fiormonda, however, who is the real source of evil in the play, lives to become the new duchess. Roseilli vows to live a celibate life within marriage. This, given his love for her, punishes him almost as much as it does Fiormonda, but it also reiterates the theme of the play, which is dominated by love, or at least by passion, without any fulfillment.

The play widely regarded as Ford's best, *'Tis Pity She's a Whore*, is a study of a single but hopelessly tainted love—that between Giovanni and his full sister Annabella. The other loves that emerge serve but to cast light upon the central pair of lovers.

In the opening speech of the play, the friar is in the process of urging young Giovanni to abandon love. For several lines, Ford artistically delays revealing the nature of the friar's objection until Giovanni reveals the state of his psyche by genuinely asking a question, the answer to which is totally obvious both to the friar and to the play's audience: "Shall then, for that I am her brother born,/ My joys be ever banish'd from her bed?" What Giovanni wants from the friar is some means of justifying his love and of consummating it, but what he gets is a formula for exorcising the "leprosy of lust/ That rots thy soul," as the friar describes his condition. Giovanni agrees to the regime, even though it seems obvious that it will not succeed, and the scene ends by introducing two powerful forces at work within the play: revenge and fate.

Undoubtedly the greatest critical problem in this play is the simple fact that although Giovanni's passion is by common definition a sick love, it is by far the healthiest love in the play. Giovanni and Annabella join strengths, not weaknesses; they augment each other's personalities through giving, never by preying upon each other. Giovanni is praised for his "government, behaviour, learning, speech,/ Sweetness, and all that could make up a man," and Annabella's virtues are lauded throughout the play as she is courted by at least three others and described by father, brother, and nurse. The quality most conducive to a genuine love in Ford's plays is mutuality, and this brother-sister love abounds with it. Giovanni justifies his love to the friar by describing their unity, and it is the primary mark of their first love scene when it is discovered that Annabella has long had the same feeling for her brother but has not dared to speak it. In this scene, both brother and sister seem to be free from a sense of guilt. Their mutual vows, "love me or kill me," speak of the strength of their love in the face of the opposition of the world, not a mutual guilt. By their next meeting, their love has been consummated, and the poetry of their union marks it as complete. When Giovanni tries to rationalize his love to the friar in terms of school principles, it turns out to be mere sophistry, but the real and convincing argument is her beauty, in which almost every cliché of Renaissance poetry is created anew.

It is also in the presence of the friar that some hint of division comes between Giovanni and Annabella. Although little noted by critics, it is surely her pregnancy that brings Annabella to her knees, weeping in contrition before the friar, who responds by offering her a fine condensation of Dante's *Inferno*. The means to salvation he suggests is for her to marry her suitor, Soranzo, not only to cover her pregnancy but also to live totally loyal to him all her days. The marriage is easily achieved, and that very day Annabella and Soranzo exchange vows. Loyalty and commitment, however, are harder to muster, and when Soranzo discovers the pregnancy and excoriates her as a common whore engaging in "belly sports," she taunts him with high praise of her former lover, a man whom Soranzo could never match. He ought to be proud, she insists, to "have the glory/ To father what so brave a father got." Though she is hardly an obedient wife (evidently continuing her relations with Giovanni), Annabella does grow in penitence, wishing in love, like John Milton's Eve, to take the penalty due Giovanni upon herself. When the friar enters in the middle of her soliloquy, he is delighted and agrees to deliver a letter to Giovanni, both suggesting that he join her in repentance and also warning him against the revenge-fury of Soranzo.

The change in Giovanni is more subtle, but there is a definite shift in his attitude from love of a woman to love of the pleasure itself. Ford has underlined this in the structure of his play, for just as the friar interrupted Annabella's soliloquy of repentance, he enters in the middle of Giovanni's soliloquy glorying that even after her marriage, he finds "no change/ Of pleasure in this formal law of sports." Annabella was once more than a sport, and though he can still speak of "united hearts" and a love to the death, the emphasis is on the pleasure. In their final meeting, "lying on a bed," Giovanni is upset at Annabella's sudden resolve to "be honest," and certainly his anger and resentment at being denied his pleasure contributes to the impetus to murder. Even after he is convinced that their end is near and the talk turns to eschatology and life after death, his mind is on pleasure: "May we kiss one another, prate or laugh,/ Or do as we do here?" Annabella, however, does not know the answer, but Giovanni, convinced that death is on the way and that only after death is there any possibility for their love, frustrates Soranzo's elaborate plans for revenge by sacrificing his love upon his own dagger. Like Shakespeare's Othello, he exacts three kisses from her, finally resolving to "kill thee in a kiss" as she begs Heaven to forgive him and cries for mercy. The final scene of the play, in which Giovanni, quietly and rationally demented, enters the banquet scene carrying her bleeding heart on the tip of his dagger, is one that few can forget.

It is not only the sensationalism of this final scene or the disturbingly sympathetic treatment of an incestuous love that makes this play memorable. The poetry is of a consistently high caliber, forming a mirror of the souls of the characters. Recurring motifs, particularly of music and the full and ebbing sea, bind the play together. The pervasive resounding of love associated with death, accentuated by images of piercing and ripping, artistically creates a unified tone and foreshadows the end. Further, Ford's masterful use of the irony inherent in the situation, in which only the audience and the friar know of the clandestine love, adds enjoyment and understanding to the experience of the play.

This work also receives Ford's most complete examination of the role fate plays in life, a topic which obsessed him. In the very first scene of the play, Giovanni is convinced that he is compelled into his love by a force beyond him, not by what the friar describes as his "wilful flames." When Giovanni resolves to tell his sister of his love, he proclaims (perhaps protesting too much), " 'tis not, I know,/ My lust, but 'tis my fate that leads me on." He uses the idea of fate in pleading his love, insisting, " 'tis my destiny/ That you must either love, or I must die," and fate justifies the incest: "Wise nature first in your creation meant/ To make you mine; else't had been sin and foul." Annabella also uses fate to justify her actions, as she unconvincingly tries to convince Soranzo that he should accept an impregnated bride: "Why, 'tis thy fate." Later, in soliloquy, she echoes an earlier pair of star-crossed lovers as, regarding Giovanni, she laments: "Would thou hadst been less subject to those stars/ That luckless reign'd at my nativity." The friar tries to make a distinction between fate as nature's dictates and the destiny which is the will of Heaven. Both of the minor, bungling revengers, Richardetto and Hippolita, indicate that they are trying to control fate, and against this background it is interesting that Giovanni also, as he begins to assume the role of avenger, changes from a victim of destiny to one who would manufacture his own fate. He does not, however, outlive his revenges, and a sword in the fist of Vasques deals him the final blow, which otherwise he had determined to inflict upon himself. He dies declaring the irrelevance of mercy in the fact of the justice he has met, and wishing to "enjoy this grace,/ Freely to view my Annabella's face."

Perkin Warbeck has been termed a tragedy by some critics and a history play by most. It is about a legitimate king and an infamous claimant to the throne, yet it has no villain, unless it be Margaret of Burgundy, who never appears in the play, although her murky influence is felt behind Warbeck's claim to the throne. Henry himself is presented as an efficient king who rules well, with both foresight and insight, keeping always the good of his kingdom as his first goal and using mercy and goodness whenever they coincide with his major purpose. James of Scotland joins forces with Perkin Warbeck, out of a genuine though misguided sense of right. He is a weak but not a sinister character. He quickly takes the expedient course when he perceives that no English forces are rising to back Warbeck and when the forces of Spain and the empire are discovered to be totally behind the current English king. Warbeck himself is not without dignity in the play. Totally convinced that he is the duke who should rightfully have inherited the throne of England, he behaves in all respects like a king. Ford heightens his sense of nobility in the closing act of the play by contrasting him with Lambert Simnel, a previous pretender to the throne who is presented on the stage as a tempter of Warbeck. Simnel has bought his life by accepting the abject position of the king's falconer, and it is made plain that a similar choice is open to Warbeck. Convinced that he is indeed of royal blood, however, he will have none of it, and in a conventional but moving speech on the nobility of death, he is taken off to his own in royal dignity, a genuine, almost heroic figure who has almost persuaded the audience.

Interested as Ford is in the proper rules of succession and in affirming the legitimacy of the Tudor and Stuart lines, the play is just as much concerned with the quality of love, the dominant theme in his plays. In *Perkin Warbeck*, there are two examples of deep spiritual love of man for man. One instance is King Henry's attachment to his counselor, Lord Stanley. When Clifford reveals Stanley's complicity in the Warbeck plot, the king is shaken; Stanley had saved Henry's life on the battlefield and placed the crown on his head. Since that time, there had been nothing the king would not have done for him. The king's feelings for Stanley are poignantly evident in the scene of Stanley's condemnation. The king confides to his couselors that his heart would pardon Stanley, that there is "a chancery of pity in our bosom," but his better sense (awakened by a few strong words from his advisers) knows that this is impossible. Even so, he absents himself from the trial, fearing his own strong emotions. Stanley himself seems to underline the strength of their relationship as he responds to his sentence: "O the king,/ Next to my soul, shall be the nearest subject/ Of my last prayers!" In the face of this love, the reasons for his complicity in the plot remain a mystery.

Even stronger than this relationship is that between the Scots' Lord Huntley and Daliell, the suitor for his daughter Katherine's hand. Since she is an attractive girl with royal blood flowing in her veins, her father feels that she might well be a fit choice for King James himself, yet he is so fond of Daliell that he finally agrees to give his blessing to the match if Katherine should answer Daliell's plea with proper passion, though he does not agree to recommend the match to her. When Kate shatters the dreams of both men by turning her passion toward Warbeck, whom her father sees as a mere impostor, the relationship between Huntley and Daliell deepens and the older man invites Daliell to "Come with me, for I feel thy griefs as full/ As mine; let's steal away and cry together." This friendship is deepened at the wedding feast, where the music sounds to Huntley "Like to so many choristers of Bedlam/ Trolling a catch." In spite of a good nature which has learned to make light of hardships and a determination to be merry in a court where flattery keeps him secure, there is a touch of bitterness in Huntley's resignation to kings who are "earthly gods" with "anointed bodies" and in the renunciation of his child, who has chosen a "dukeling mushroom" for a husband. Daliell cuts through this mood of the older man, and with a more humble, continuing, and faithful love adds a tincture of consolation to their meeting. When Huntley asks for pardon for slighting Daliell's suit, the younger man offers him "a love, a service,/ A friendship to posterity," and Huntley expresses his gratitude for "some ease,/ A partner in affliction," after which the two men together endure the remainder of the wedding feast. They next appear after Warbeck has been rejected by King James, and although they enter together, they leave separately. Huntley, after a moving farewell to his daughter, returns to Scotland, but Daliell, in an act of faithfulness resembling that of Lear's Kent, asks permission to join Katherine and her husband in their sojourn to Cornwall. When Huntley appears for a brief moment at the end of the play, he does not converse with Daliell, but the two men are obviously united in their attitudes toward Katherine.

The major examination of love in the play involves Katherine. Although when Daliell begins to address her, Huntley suspects that an arrangement has already been made between them, the passion which he supposed to exist is the one thing lacking. Instead of responding to his suit, Katherine pleads duty to her father as an excuse to say no. Highly appreciative of his virtues, she gently and coolly suggests a Platonic courtly-love relationship. In sharp contrast to this is Katherine's first response to Warbeck. She merely watches his arrival in court from the sidelines, when the Countess of Crawford, observing her, remarks, "Madam, y'are passionate." To this passion is added the press of duty to accept Warbeck for a husband, but it is not duty to her father. In spite of Huntley's vociferous objections to the match, King James himself has insisted upon it, claiming an "Instinct of Sovereignty" to authenticate his choice. Katherine is nothing loath to accept this higher authority. She must be hurt deeply, however, when her father refuses his blessing upon the match and goes off to commiserate with Daliell.

From this point on, Katherine's love is a blend of commitment, duty, and faithfulness marked by a desire to share every life experience with her husband. She begs to go off to war with him, and when she is denied this, she extracts from him a promise that he will never again leave without her. Later, when Warbeck is dismissed by King James, his first reaction is not concern for his kingdom but a fear that James will find a way to retract the marriage and separate him from his new wife. Kate affirms her faithfulness to her husband. With bravery and courage, she is ready for what amounts to exile, exhibiting no bitterness toward the king, who commanded her into the marriage. She evinces a majestic sense of pride, vowing that she will not return as long as Warbeck is banished from the king's presence.

At the end of the play, Katherine is not allowed to share Warbeck's death, but she does share the humiliation which he has already turned into triumph by royally refusing to capitulate either to the king's taunts or to Lambert Simnel's demeaning compromise. In a magnificent bit of stagecraft, characteristic of Ford, Katherine climbs up onto the stocks in which he has been fixed. Though the Earl of Oxford is shocked and angered by the indignity, Katherine answers him with an affirmation of her marriage vows and her intention to live or die with her husband. Fate, however, which plays an important part in this play, as it does in Ford's others, decrees otherwise, and Perkin is taken off to his death, while Katherine is escorted to her apartment, her true love thwarted by a tragic misconception of birth and role.

The question of love is again examined in *The Lady's Trial* and this time it is social: Is it possible for love and marriage to succeed across socioeconomic lines? The well-born Auria has married Spinella with no dowry except her youth and beauty. His bosom friend, Aurelio, had warned him against this move, and indeed, shortly after the marriage, Auria is forced to leave Genoa to seek his fortune in the desperate arena of fighting Turkish pirates—not without an "I told you so" from Aurelio. Spinella's real dowry is faithfulness, honor, and an inner nobility. With humility and scorn, she spurns the suit of the ranking lord, Adurni, who, in her husband's absence, has trapped her into a bedroom replete with seductive music and a full banquet spread for the two of them. Aurelio, who discovers them together, threatens to expose her infamy. Although by hiding at Auria's return, she evinces some doubt of his willingness to believe her innocence, a mutual, perfect trust is reestablished at the close of the play, and all is well.

The theme is perhaps even more expressly considered in the subplots of the play. Levidolche has married beneath her station one Benatzi, whom her uncle, Martino, has designated a mere "trencher-waiter." The upper ranks of society beckon, however, and after becoming the mistress of Adurni, she divorces her husband, whose fortunes then degenerate until he becomes a galleyslave to the Turks. When Adurni's affections begin to cool (as he plans his seduction of Spinella), Levidolche writes a passionate letter seeking to enter into a relationship with Malfato, a lowly gentleman of the court, Spinella's uncle and ward. She confides her thoughts on rank to Futelli, whom she has hired to deliver the letter (and who betrays her by bringing it to Adurni first). "The properest men," she states, "should be preferr'd to fortune." Futelli leads her to admit that Adurni is not a man she admires by suggesting that "The title of a lord was not enough/ For absolute perfection," which she answers by describing the real perfections of Malfato. He, however, scorns her letter completely and publicly, mistakenly believing that Adurni was behind the solicitation, seeking to dupe Malfato into a marriage that would serve as both a cover-up for and pregnancy insurance against his own illicit relationship with the woman he would marry off. Infuriated at her betrayal by the two men, Levidolche seeks an avenger and hires Benatzi, who has been freed from the Turks by Auria and is now in disguise as a returned soldier and outlaw. His fee, however, is not money but marriage, and he insists on a wedding before the commission is fulfilled. She confesses her adultery and looseness, but he affirms his faith in her ability to reform. As he leaves, Levidolche smiles, confiding to the audience that "Love is sharp-sighted,/ And can pierce through the cunning of disguises./ False pleasures, I cashier ye; fair truth, welcome!"

This change of heart and life, induced by trust, is evidently genuine and lasting. When Levidolche's uncle, Martino, first sees her with this disheveled, disreputable piece of man-flesh, he accuses her of going public in her whoredom, setting up shop and crying "A market open; to't and welcome," but when he is informed of the marriage and let in on her secret that this creature is in reality her former husband, to whom she now intends absolute fidelity, her uncle is won over and convinced of her ability to achieve faithfulness. In the final scene of the play, Levidolche proclaims her new life-style to the entire court, and they, too, believe, accepting her fully into their society. She blushes to face Malfato but is forgiven by him, and she is supported financially in her new start by Adurni, Spinella, and her sister Castanna. This is indeed what Robert Grams Hunter would call "comedy of forgiveness."

The theme is reiterated on still another level of society, in which it approaches farce. Amoretta has a fixation: Although lacking social status herself, she refuses to marry anyone less than a count and believes that she is really fit for a duke. Futelli and his friend Piero plot to cure her of this disease by having her courted by one Guzman, in the disguise of a Spanish grandee, and by Fulgoso, one of the newly rich who has devised for himself a long and honorable family tree. In four long and delightful pages, Futelli coaches Guzman on the proper method to approach Amoretta, describing correct courtship in terms of military strategy. When Piero enters, counseling Fulgoso, the two would-be lovers challenge each other to a bloody resolution of their rivalry, but when they discover their mutual gluttony, they decide to have a sumptuous dinner together instead. In the wooing scene, in which Amoretta's heavy lisp adds to the foolishness, both Guzman and Fulgoso plead their cases by giving long and hilarious recitations of their family ancestries, and eventually they become so ridiculous that they are literally kicked off the stage with a cruelty reminiscent of Ben Jonson. Amoretta is cured and readily agrees to accept the mate of her father's choice, who later turns out to be Futelli.

Although there may be no such genre, this play can surely be best classified as a revenge comedy. It is almost as if Ford looked at his earlier tragedies and asked what psychological factors might have kept the blood from the stage. Many elements of revenge tragedy are present. There is an age-discrepancy between Auria and Spinella, and when Auria leaves court, he warns his young wife not to give even the slightest appearance of infidelity, charging her to remember "whose wife thou art." Against this charge, Aurelio, who has the innate potential to become an Iago figure, is commissioned to watch her. His love for Auria, which is twice mentioned in the play, is enough to create jealousy. He has warned Auria that his wife's youth and beauty are "baits for dishonour," and would naturally like to prove his forebodings justified. Further motivation is provided in that Auria has made Aurelio his heir, to inherit all of his assets except "Some fit deduction for a worthy widow/ Allow'd, with caution she be like to prove so." In addition to this, Aurelio is provided with "occular proof" which seems totally convincing to him when he finds Spinella locked in the bedroom with Adurni. His threat to inform his newly returned friend of this infidelity is ominous, and it is little wonder, remembering Auria's departing charge, that Spinella chooses to hide rather than to face her husband after he has heard Aurelio's accusations. Hiding, however, could well be interpreted as an admission of guilt, adding one more bit of evidence to the already convincing testimony.

What is the psychological ambience that resolves all of these elements into comedy rather than tragedy? The answer is in the quality of love in the play. Auria answers Aurelio's accusations with common sense and a luminous sense of trust in his wife, a quality that is completely absent in revenge tragedy. The evidence against her is circumstantial, he explains to Aurelio, and other interpretations are equally satisfactory. It is Auria's relationship with his friend that is threatened, not that with his wife. What a refreshing current this is in the murky waters of Renaissance drama: One can trust the person he loves; accusations dissolve into nothing in the clear, binding matrix of love. The one thing that hurts Auria is that Spinella's absence seems to say she did not trust him to have faith in her. His dealing with this seems a bit cruel, for upon their meeting, he pretends not to recognize her. Spinella retains her dignity and is eloquent against both liars and those who believe them. To this, Aurelio confesses that his accusations were engendered more by his suspicions than knowledge, but Auria then suggests the disparity in their ages as a possible cause of her dissatisfaction, to which she answers that there was none. Adurni, who had previously confessed to Auria that his confrontation with Spinella had changed his entire attitude toward women, convincing him that good women exist, enters to ask pardon of Spinella. When Auria seems not to accept even this as evidence of her innocence, Spinella strikes at the heart of their relationship: "You can suspect?/ So reconciliation, then, is needless." To allay Auria's suspicions would be irrelevant; if he has suspicions, the relationship is already beyond salvation. The reader, however, knows that he has none, but is worried about *her* suspicions of him. This worry removed, their relationship of mutual trust is reaffirmed. The real "lady's trial," then, appears not to be the obvious external assault on her virtue, portrayed in the first half of the drama, but the inward trial of the mutual trust, the real basis of love and marriage—the kind that makes tragedy impossible.

The other strain in which the play skirts on tragedy is in Levidolche's cry for revenge, which seems genuine and threatening. Her method of hiring a revenger is also typical of revenge tragedy, as she drops a purse with a note in it from a second-story window in the dark of night, so that it appears mysterious to all those on the lower stage. Benatzi, disguised as Parado, is certainly a fit instrument for revenge. Like Bosola, he has been both a soldier and a galley slave, and he makes a ragged appearance on the stage— an outsider to society. It is only when her renewed love for him proves to be genuine and permanent that the audience knows the revenge will not take place, though some suspense is maintained right up to the moment that he is disarmed in court. The play ends in merriment as Futelli is to wed Amoretta, Adurni is betrothed to Spinella's sister Castanna, and Fulgoso and Guzman enter to make their final foolish speeches before Auria dismisses all to attend the revels celebrating both marriages and his own promotions.

Love is not the only theme of Ford's drama, but it does, perhaps, best illustrate the deep and pervasive interest in psychological motivation which is evident in all of his extant works.

Other major works

POETRY: *Fame's Memorial: Or, The Earl of Devonshire Deceased*, 1606; *Christ's Bloody Sweat: Or, The Son of God in His Agony*, 1613.

NONFICTION: *Honor Triumphant: Or, The Peer's Challenge*, 1606; *The Golden Mean*, 1613; *A Line of Life*, 1620.

MISCELLANEOUS: *The Works of John Ford*, 1869 (Alexander Dyce, editor; includes previously uncollected poetry); *The Nondramatic Works of John Ford*, 1991 (edited by L. E. Stock et al.).

Bibliography

Anderson, Donald K., Jr., ed. *"Concord in Discord": The Plays of John Ford, 1586-1986.* New York: AMS Press, 1986. The first book of essays on Ford, this collection presents the work of thirteen scholars and includes many useful discussions: Robert Heilman on the perverse in Ford's plays, Eugene Waith on the staging and spectacle of Ford's concluding scenes, David Bergeron on brother-sister relationships, Larry Champion on Ford's early works as a foreshadow of his later tragedies, Richard Ide and Mark Stavig both on aspects of *'Tis Pity She's a Whore*, and Anderson on Ford's manipulation of the audience in *The Fancies Chaste and Noble*.

_____. *John Ford.* New York: Twayne, 1972. Rich in insights into Ford's dramaturgy and imagery, this well-written study provides a sensitive, balanced understanding of all Ford's plays and poems. To judge by the numerous references to this work by others, Anderson's book has had a strong influence on Ford studies. The work includes the chapters "Ford and His Age" and "Ford and the Critics" as well as an annotated bibliography. Anderson also wrote the bibliographic chapter on Ford in *The Later Jacobean and Caroline Dramatists* (1978), by Terence P. Logan and Denzell S. Smith.

Champion, Larry. *Tragic Patterns in Jacobean and Caroline Drama.* Knoxville: University of Tennessee Press, 1977. This excellent book on the changing societal values of later Renaissance drama discusses plays by William Shakespeare, Ben Jonson, Cyril Tourneur, John Webster, Thomas Middleton, and Ford. Readers interested in Ford's place among his literary peers and in the ways the dramas of the age "effectively capture the spiritual uncertainties of an increasingly analytical age" should consult Champion's book.

Farr, Dorothy. *John Ford and the Caroline Theatre.* London: Macmillan, 1979. Farr studies Ford's plays and their suitability for the specific theaters where they were first staged, but such a narrow-sounding topic should not deter the general reader. Farr writes effectively about many aspects of Ford's art, and not incidentally, her remarks about the indoor, private theaters of the time of Charles I provide an informative supplement to most readers' greater knowledge of the open-air, public theaters of the Elizabethan age.

Neill, Michael, ed. *John Ford: Critical Re-Visions.* Cambridge, England: Cambridge University Press, 1988. Eleven essays cover topics such as stage history, imagery, use of melodrama, the question of decadence, metatheater in *Love's Sacrifice*, and gender in *Perkin Warbeck.*

Sensabaugh, George F. *The Tragic Muse of John Ford.* Stanford, Calif.: Stanford University Press, 1944. This famous study presents Ford as a modernist in temperament, someone who celebrates "scientific determinism" and "unbridled individualism" and who makes "sin seem . . . pure." For a book-length presentation of the opposite, orthodox view, the reader should consult Mark Stavig's *John Ford and the Traditional Moral Order* (1968). Most studies of Ford adopt a position somewhere between the two poles defined by Sensabaugh and Stavig.

Howard C. Adams
(Updated by *Glenn Hopp*)

RICHARD FOREMAN

Born: New York, New York; June 10, 1937

Principal drama

Angelface, pr. 1968, pb. 1976; *Elephant-Steps*, pr. 1968 (music by Stanley Silverman); *Ida-Eyed*, pr. 1969; *Real Magic in New York*, pr. 1970; *Total Recall: Or, Sophia = (Wisdom) Part II*, pr. 1970, pb. 1976; *Dream Tantras for Western Massachusetts*, pr. 1971 (music by Silverman); *HCohtienla: Or, Hotel China: Parts I and II*, pr., pb. 1972; *Dr. Selavy's Magic Theatre*, pr. 1972 (music by Silverman, lyrics by Thomas Hendry); *Evidence*, pr. 1972; *Sophia = (Wisdom) Part III*, pr. 1972, pb. 1973; *The Cliffs*, pr., pb. 1973; *Honor*, pr. 1973; *Particle Theory*, pr. 1973; *Une Semaine sous l'influence de . . .* , pr. 1973, pb. 1976; *Vertical Mobility*, pb. 1974; *Pain(t), and Vertical Mobility: Sophia = (Wisdom) Part IV*, pr. 1974, pb. 1976; *Pandering to the Masses: A Misrepresentation*, pr. 1975, pb. 1977; *Hotel for Criminals*, pr. 1975 (music by Silverman); *Rhoda in Potatoland (Her Fall-starts)*, pr. 1975, pb. 1976; *Livre de splendeurs (Part I)*, pr., pb. 1976; *Plays and Manifestos of Richard Foreman*, pb. 1976; *Book of Splendors (Part II): Book of Levers: Action at a Distance*, pr. 1977, pb. 1986; *Boulevard de Paris (I've Got the Shakes)*, pr. 1977, pb. 1986; *Madness and Tranquility (My Head Was a Sledgehammer)*, pr. 1979; *Luogo + Bersaglio*, pr. 1979, pb. as *Place + Target*, 1986; *Penguin Touquet*, pr. 1980, pb. 1986; *Madame Adare*, pr. 1980 (music by Silverman); *Café Amerique*, pr. 1981, pb. 1986; *Egyptology (My Head Was a Sledgehammer)*, pr. 1983, pb. 1986; *La Robe de chambre de Georges Bataille*, pr. 1983; *The Golem*, pr. 1984; *Miss Universal Happiness*, pr. 1985; *Birth of the Poet*, pr. 1985 (with Kathy Acker); *Reverberation Machines: Later Plays and Essays*, pb. 1985; *The Cure*, pr. 1986; *Film Is Evil: Radio Is Good*, pr., pb. 1987; *Symphony of Rats*, pr. 1988; *What Did He See?*, pr. 1988; *Lava*, pr. 1989; *Eddie Goes to Poetry City: Part Two*, pr. 1991; *Love and Science: Librettos by Richard Foreman*, pb. 1991; *The Mind King*, pr. 1992; *Unbalancing Acts: Foundations for a Theater*, pb. 1992; *Samuel's Major Problems*, pr. 1993.

Other literary forms

Richard Foreman has been involved in all aspects of theater. In addition to his plays, he has written several manifestos that explain the genesis of his theater work from a philosophical point of view, and he has also directed several plays and produced numerous videos.

Achievements

Foreman is one of the founders of the contemporary American theatrical avant-garde. His Ontological-Hysteric Theatre—for which Foreman is the sole playwright, director, and designer—is influenced by the theories of Bertolt Brecht and Gertrude Stein. Foreman's intent is to distance the audience from their normal expectations of a pleasurable theater experience and to make spectators aware of the process of perception. To force this awareness, he often obscures the stage picture with bright lights, leaves his scripts meaningless, non-narrative, and nonlinear, and uses loud sounds to unsettle the spectator from passive complacency. Foreman has also applied his avant-garde aesthetic to texts by other writers, and even as a director, his signature remains unmistakable. Foreman's style was the harbinger of the postmodern theater work of artists such as the Wooster Group and John Jesurun. Foreman has received three *Village Voice* Obie Awards, two New York State Creative Artists Public Service Awards, a Rockefeller Foundation Playwrights Grant, a Guggenheim Playwriting Fellowship, and a Ford Foundation Playwrights Grant.

Biography

Richard Foreman was born in New York City on June 10, 1937, and was reared in Scarsdale, an affluent New York suburb in Westchester County. He became interested in theater as an adolescent, encouraged by an indulgent high school teacher who allowed him to express his already iconoclastic vision in inappropriately surreal set designs for school plays. During this time, Foreman studied the writings of Brecht, whose theories permeated Foreman's thought and would later profoundly influence his theater work. At Brown University, from which he was graduated magna cum laude in 1959, Foreman became interested first in film and then in playwriting, and was introduced to the writings of José Ortega y Gasset, which also influenced his later, rigorous style. Foreman studied with John Gassner at Yale University, from which he received his M.F.A. in 1962.

Foreman married his high school friend Amy Taubin in 1962. They moved to New York City, where Taubin pursued an acting career and Foreman joined the playwriting unit of the Actors' Studio, writing conventional plays in the style of Clifford Odets and Arthur Miller. From 1962 to 1967, Foreman and Taubin immersed themselves in the New American Cinema movement evolving in Lower Manhattan, and became captivated by the avant-garde work of filmmakers Ken Jacobs, Michael Snow, and Jack Smith. Foreman gradually began applying the avant-garde film aesthetic to his own playwriting, leaving gaps and rough spots where he had once sought closure and polish. He presented *Angelface*, his first Ontological-Hysteric Theatre production, in 1968, at the Cinematheque on Wooster Street in Manhattan's SoHo district, and began collaborating with musician Stanley Silverman on experimental musical productions for the Music Theatre Group/Lenox Art Center.

Foreman dislodged his productions from his Wooster Street loft in 1976 and began working occasionally in Europe through the early 1980's. He spent most of this period either in Paris or touring to different performance spaces in Europe, such as Teatro Nuovo in Turin, Italy, and the Mickery Theatre in Amsterdam, Holland. Some of Foreman's later works were first performed in Europe: *Livre de splendeurs* was first shown in Paris, and *Luogo + Bersaglio* was first performed, in Italian, in Rome.

In 1982, Foreman began directing occasional productions for Joseph Papp's New York Shakespeare Festival, where he mounted Botho Strauss's *Trilogie des Wiedersehens* (1976; *Three Acts of Recognition*, 1982) and Molière's *Don Juan: Ou, Le Festin de Pierre* (1655; *Don Juan*, 1755) in 1982, H. Leivick's *Der Golem* (1921; *The Golem*, 1966) in 1984, and Vaclav Havel's *Largo Desolato* (1985; English translation, 1985) in 1986. He has also directed productions of *Don Juan* for the Guthrie Theatre in Minneapolis, Minnesota (1981), and Arthur Kopit's *End of the World with Symposium to Follow* (1984) for the American Repertory Theatre (1987) in Cambridge, Massachusetts. Foreman has directed operas as well: *The Fall of the House of Usher* (1988), by Arthur Yorinks and Philip Glass; *Where's Dick?* (1989), by Michael Korie and Stewart Wallace; and *Don Giovanni* (1991), by Wolfgang Amadeus Mozart. Although his Ontological-Hysteric Theatre no longer has a home base, Foreman still writes, designs, and directs his own productions, often using space borrowed from other avant-garde performance artists, such as the Wooster Group.

Analysis

Richard Foreman began his theater career as a playwright and progressed toward international recognition as one of the most influential auteurs of the contemporary American avant-garde. Foreman's writing style helped to establish what has come to be called the postmodern aesthetic, in which character no longer exists as a theatrical element, and the "theater of images," in which aural and visual elements of a production become more important than the literary. His scripts for the Ontological-Hysteric Theatre represent only the workings of his mind while he writes them.

As a designer, Foreman constructs a playing space jumbled with objects and sensory input, which he then obscures from the spectator by shining blinding white lights into their eyes. Although he still presents Ontological-Hysteric Theatre productions, over which he maintains absolute control, Foreman has begun to direct other classic and contemporary plays, yet his unique directorial style is always apparent in his work.

Foreman established his Ontological-Hysteric Theatre in 1968, in a long, narrow loft that he converted into a performance space in the SoHo neighborhood of Manhattan. The name Ontological-Hysteric, although chosen rather capriciously, has come to symbolize many of Foreman's preoccupations. In both his playwriting and his subsequent staging of his own texts and those of other playwrights, Foreman's goal is to materialize the workings of consciousness and to make spectators aware of how they perceive their world.

Foreman sees consciousness as a perceptual mechanism that filters the world through the senses, and he believes that habit has taught people to limit their sensory input. To free them to explore their perceptual potential, Foreman constructs a rigorous attack on habitual ways of seeing the world and seeing art. Foreman's early Ontological-Hysteric Theatre works, such as *Sophia = (Wisdom) Part III, Pain(t), and Vertical Mobility, Pandering to the Masses*, and *Rhoda in Potatoland (Her Fall-starts)*, insistently aimed to reshape spectators' perceptions by focusing on form and structure. He created a perceptually challenging environment that forced the audience to participate actively in constructing the theater experience.

In contrast to realistic theater (which strives to provide catharsis and to resolve its ambiguities and questions in a happy conclusion), Foreman's art avoids moral issues and the linear development of traditional plots. He forces spectators to expend their energies on "blasting" themselves into productions in which the entire framework of traditional theater—plot, characterization, and settings—has been discarded. The required perceptual work replaces the usual theater experience, in which the audience passively awaits catharsis through identification with a hero.

Foreman was considerably influenced by the theories of Brecht, whose alienation effect forced spectators into critical contemplation of the actions presented in his epic dramas. Brecht discouraged the identification processes of more realistic theater, which he believed rendered spectators passive and unable to move toward political change. Brecht's stagings were presentational. He used placards to announce his drama's episodes, intentionally interrupting the seductive narrative flow. His performers were taught to present quoted characterizations that maintained the separation between actor and character and gave the spectators room to contemplate the play's meanings.

Where Brecht encouraged critical distance in order to allow political self-determination, however, Foreman was emphatically apolitical: He wanted his spectators to contemplate purely perceptual concerns. His work, however, departs from traditionally Brechtian techniques. Particularly in his early Ontological-Hysteric Theatre pieces, preferring to work with non-actors, he discouraged his performers from acting as anyone other than themselves, and he directed them to deliver their lines in a flat monotone. Sometimes, performers' dialogue was recorded on tape and played back during performance, dissociating them from their voices. The performers moved through a series of complex, carefully choreographed movements and tasks. Actors in Foreman's early productions were merely demonstrators for his perceptual experiments.

Foreman established his unique style while other artists were also disrupting the conventions of traditional theater. In the late 1960's and early 1970's, the Performance Group, the Living Theatre, and the Open Theatre staged their productions environmentally, using the whole theater instead of only the stage behind the proscenium. All three encouraged their performers to interact physically with the audience and created texts that were often didactic, reflecting the radical political sentiment of the era.

Foreman, a staunch formalist, was at that time diametrically opposed to what he called such "expressionistic" theater. He maintained the proscenium/spectator arrangement, carefully orchestrating his stage pictures in static or slow-moving tableaux behind the proscenium frame; he prohibited his actors from interacting with spectators and maintained the "fourth wall" convention, in which spectators expect to feel as though they are looking into a world from which they cannot be seen; and he offered no didactic meanings for his spectators to consider from a political perspective. Within these conventional outlines, however, Foreman's theater was revolutionary in other ways.

Along with Robert Wilson and Lee Breuer, Foreman's work helped coin the term "theater of images." Despite his theoretical concern with language, Foreman's theater is distinctly nonliterary. The theater of images increases the value of its visual and aural elements, displacing the text's primacy as the motivating principle. As a result, plot and character lose their places as the predominant bearers of meaning. Since the theater of images is dominated by sights and sounds that occur in space and time, within the immediate theater experience, sense impressions and the present-tense manipulation of perception become primary.

It is impossible to understand the full impact of a Foreman play by reading it on a page, because the experience of time and space is so important to his work. The atomization of movement and motion allows spectators' minds to roam freely, considering each part of the stage picture. The carefully constructed tableaux allow theatrical time to pause or even slow to a standstill, so that the spectator can choose which elements of the complex picture to relish visually and which objects to connect with others placed around the space.

Foreman takes a phenomenological approach to the stage space and his props. His aesthetic is similar to Gertrude Stein's, whose notion of a "continuous present" informed her landscape plays, which also stripped things to their essences. Wrenched out of context, objects become things without associations that impose meaning. To this end, Foreman constructs his scenography to render the ordinary extraordinary. Potatoes in *Rhoda in Potatoland (Her Fall-starts)* become larger-than-life. Clocks, such as the grandfather clock in *Sophia = (Wisdom) Part III*, become animate objects that enter the playing space. People become objects related to other objects. The potatoes that come crashing through windows in *Rhoda in Potatoland (Her Fall-starts)* are as much performers as the human beings inhabiting Foreman's cerebral landscape.

Spectators are also kept from finding meaning in Foreman's plays by the intentionally disorienting, uncomfortable process of perceiving the work. Lights shine directly in the spectators' eyes, making it difficult to see the stage. Loud noises startle the spectators out of passive contemplation, jolting them back into full awareness. The texts constantly comment on Foreman's process of creating them, calling attention to the arbitrary nature of words themselves. Snatches of familiar music are used to seduce the spectator into a feeling of ease, then are abruptly curtailed.

Foreman's scripts are plotless, self-reflective meditations on the act of writing. Although nothing ever happens in the conventional sense of action and linear narrative in a Foreman play, his scripts are often humorous and ironic, and they invite spectators to share in their witty investigations of how meaning is being created or withheld in the present theatrical moment. Where Brecht's writing was episodic, Foreman's is atomic, a succession of brief, discrete moments intended to replicate the workings of his mind in the process of writing his plays.

Although there are no carefully crafted, fictional characters in Foreman's work, each person onstage represents a part of Foreman's consciousness. In his early work, a group of characters reappeared in different productions over several years. His works from this early period resembled something of a soap opera, in that the plotless productions never gave spectators the pleasure of a satisfactory ending. The character Max, whom some critics saw as Foreman's fictional counterpart, was a kind of artist figure constantly defining himself intellectually in relation to Rhoda. Rhoda, who was always played by Foreman's lover, Kate Mannheim, and who had a direct influence upon his writing and staging, represented the archetypal woman. She symbolized the dark continent of sexuality and repressed psychology that could not be explained by rational male intellect. These strict gender dichotomies, which some feminist critics find misogynous, are very apparent in Foreman's early work and, despite minor alterations, operate throughout his oeuvre.

While Foreman's theater is clearly ontological because of its obsession with questions of consciousness and being, his theater is aptly named "hysteric" in that it also deals with a more surrealist world of dreams, sexual desire, and anxieties. Foreman uses the ubiquitous Max and Rhoda to represent his consciousness and fears. Rhoda, in particular, represents Foreman grappling with the nature of sexuality and a more irrational world not easily explained by his otherwise rampant intellect.

Foreman's scenography further illustrates his theoretical and philosophical preoccupations. Foreman's sets are distinguished by their jumble of outsized objects, the strings stretched in a maze across the performance space that carves it into geometric patterns, the words or phrases of language decorating the space as though they, too, were objects, and the brightly colored streamers and other fanciful or bizarre props and materials that make for something of a carnivalesque atmosphere. Foreman's scenography is intended to force the eye to scan the stage picture. No one object or person is more important than another, and the taut strings are used to move the eye around the playing space. Miscellaneous words often dangle from the strings in Foreman's design, inviting the spectators to read the stage in a careful, perceptive way.

Foreman is preoccupied with the mechanisms of perception, which his scenography continually challenges. The hallmark of Foreman's productions are the bright white lights turned to shine in spectators' eyes, obscuring often tantalizing images within the stage picture; loud, irritating buzzers that interrupt the dialogue; bells that determine the beginning and the end of bits of action; and taped voices that dissociate the performers from their bodies or order them around. During productions at his Wooster Street loft, Foreman would sit at a table directly in front of the playing space, controlling the lights and the sound. Because many of the performers' cues were on an audiotape, he could change a performance's pace by adjusting the speed of the tape.

After spending a period from the late 1970's to the early 1980's in Europe, where his Ontological-Hysteric Theatre preoccupations were translated into French and toured avant-garde performance spaces, Foreman returned to the United States and began to focus on directing. Since he brings his own unique aesthetic to any play he undertakes, Foreman is often accused of "trashing" classical texts. His unusual scenography and presentational directing style might indeed seem out of place in plays such as Vaclav Havel's *Largo Desolato*, which has its own internal meanings that some critics believed were obscured by Foreman's external devices. His treatments of Molière's *Don Juan* and the classic folktale *The Golem*, however, were applauded for rejuvenating these texts from a new, contemporary perspective.

Still, Foreman's most exciting directorial work seems to be accomplished on the fringes of established theater, in conjunction with avant-garde performance groups. Foreman's *Miss Universal Happiness*, for example, was a collaboration with the Wooster Group at the Performing Garage in SoHo. The Wooster Group's performances for this piece were physical and presentational, in the post-Brechtian style that is the Group's hallmark.

Miss Universal Happiness was purportedly a political piece, although Foreman is avowedly apolitical. The *mise en scène* had revolutionary overtones: The men wore combat clothes, the women dressed in rags and ripped stockings, and all the performers wore sombreros, vaguely referring to

Third World revolutions and political strife. Yet more than revolutionary struggle, the performance was a self-reflexive commentary on how meaning is produced in theater. A teenage boy, the youngest member of the Wooster Group, began the piece by displaying his "lead lined" raincoat, which "protects you from ambiguities and obscurities" in the script. The remark was a wry warning to spectators that they should not try hard to look for meaning.

In the mid-1980's, Foreman departed from the slow, static tableaux that had once characterized his style. The stage images in *Miss Universal Happiness*, for example, were created by manic direction. The performers played musical chairs, but every time the music stopped, there was one chair too many, and another player was added to, instead of subtracted from, the game. Miss Universal Happiness, a parody of the Statue of Liberty, ran about the space dressed in black, wearing a black crown, and holding a tennis racket instead of a flame. Foreman did, however, maintain the artifice of his trademark scenography. A man in a rabbit suit appeared with two oversize oblong objects that could have been either missiles or cold capsules. Two big painted eyes were set up on easels in the back of the space, to watch *Miss Universal Happiness* progress.

Foreman's piece *Birth of the Poet*, with a script by Kathy Acker, was presented in Rotterdam, Holland, and then at the Brooklyn Academy of Music's Next Wave Festival in 1985. Acker's text was as disjunctive and fragmented as Foreman's. There were no characters in *Birth of the Poet*, which consisted of many long, rambling speeches about workers, productivity, and nuclear energy, delivered along with aggressively pornographic imagery and language. To emphasize the technological theme, the performers maneuvered golf carts around the space and moved manically among huge set pieces by sculptor David Salle.

Each of the three production elements—script, set, and music by Peter Gordon—were conceived individually, then brought together by Foreman's direction, a method that echoed the chance performances of composer John Cage. Foreman's signature devices were missing from this production. There were no strings pulled taut across the stage, and Foreman's usually witty, ironic text was replaced by Acker's pornographic script, which the performers shouted through microphones worn like headsets. Yet Foreman's concerns were still in evidence. Part of Foreman's theatrical project is to expose the process of creating performance. In *Birth of the Poet*, the battery packs that feed the microphones the performers wore were visibly strapped to their waists, and the dissociation of their voices from their source through amplification was intentional.

Foreman's concern with language was still clear in *Birth of the Poet*. A tubular steel structure hung from the flies with colorful cloth banners stretched from end to end. For the first hour or so of performance, one

word—"talent"—and fragments of other words were on view. These fragments were meaningless until later in the performance. When the structure
was moved offstage—by stagehands whose presence also emphasized the
process of creating performance normally hidden from the audience's
view—complementary word fragments at other angles formed complete
words.

Foreman's trademark bright lights were present, but obscuring the spectators' view was meaningless in *Birth of the Poet*, since little happened
onstage. The space looked empty and disinterested, despite designer David
Salle's unusual images: gigantic, two-dimensional ears of corn, a full-stage
human body made of steel tubing and purple cloth, a giant steel hand that
becomes a cage, a giant steel vagina, and expressionistic painted backdrops
of a man's head, a dog's head, and a woman bent over at the waist peering
through her legs at the audience.

After *Miss Universal Happiness*, Foreman shifted gears, moving away
from the frenzied acting so amenable to the style of the Wooster Group.
His next plays, beginning with *The Cure*, maintained a calmer and meditative pace conducive to greater reflection. Instead of a large number of actors, there were only three in *The Cure*. While all three wore radio microphones, they spoke softly to elicit an intimate glimpse into more interior
states. For Foreman, this was also the beginning of a greater interest in
developing more psychologically based acting while retaining the structural
and perceptual dynamics of his earlier work. *The Cure* is poetic both in
structure and in tone, and more coherent than previous plays.

Film Is Evil, Radio Is Good is striking in its move toward considering the
ethical consequences of the manipulation of perceptual processes. It demonstrates that cinematic images seduce viewers to the point of confusion
about the nature of material reality, deliberately using the second com-
mandment—prohibiting graven images—as a point of departure. Set as an
old-fashioned radio studio and using New York University theater students
as chorus, the play examines the critical freedom that hearing language
involves versus the authoritarian imposition of images of film, combined
with its narcissistic allure, that denies critical distance. Yet there is a deep
ambivalence evident, given Foreman's own relation to the visual, that is
demonstrated by the central use of a film, *Radio Rick in Heaven and Radio
Richard in Hell*, in which Foreman appears as an authoritarian figure, but
who magically disappears after prostrating himself before the camera.

This socially conscious extension of his own theories of perception
reaches a political level in *Symphony of Rats*. Ron Vawter of the Wooster
Group plays the President of the United States, whose judgments are
guided by voices from "outer space," which in theatrical terms mean the
words of Foreman as author. Foreman represents this connection even more
by the appearance of his face on video monitors serving as the heads of

two giant "spacemen" flanking the stage. This meditation on the social source of language that confuses the nature of internally and externally produced thought is derived in part from French poststructuralist theory. Reflection on the social origins of thought and perception resulted in Foreman's reassessing his early work as also being "political," but not in the sense of the exposition of ideological positions. His direction of Vawter's acting as riding the line between external and internal questioning showed, again, his movement toward the use of psychological technique.

What Did He See? and *Lava* entail Foreman's further self-assessment of earlier work. *What Did He See?* involves questioning the nature of hermetic, possibly solipsistic, experimentation as a form of escapism, while *Lava* involves moving through conceptual categories of cognitive processes. Category One is the logical use of language and gesture in defining reality, common to conventional drama. Category Two is the random use of language and gesture, characteristic of Foreman's earlier plays. Category Three represents the space between these two, the gaps in understanding that defy conceptualization and that indicate a more spiritual form of experience.

In his 1993 play *Samuel's Major Problems*, Foreman designed a playing space that further demonstrates his unique style. A clear plastic screen separates the actors from the spectators, thus forbidding any interaction with the viewers. The plastic screen also creates the effect of a display window in which viewers see their reflecting images while also being seen from behind it as outsiders passively looking in on the action.

Continuing Foreman's interest in psychological acting and in bringing to life his characters' consciousness, *Samuel's Major Problems* reveals the principal character's fright in a nightmarish battle in which a devilish couple (a man and a woman) inflict both physical and mental stress upon the character. Samuel, the principal character, a bedeviled hunchback, is stabbed, following a New Year's Eve party, by the woman, who at times represents the Devil and at others Death. The tormented Samuel finds that he is on his own, cannot get medical help, and is trapped in his nightmare and hallucinations, in an eerie play that is masterfully manipulated by Foreman.

While Foreman's early plays were intent upon exemplifying the atomistic processes of perception, Foreman's plays after *The Cure* show a tendency toward more coherent dialogue *about* the nature of perception, while never eliminating exemplification entirely. What remains are scenic, gestural, and aural techniques that prevent simple empathic responses from the audience and that indicate that Foreman's theater remains a theater of the mind.

Other major works

FILM/VIDEO PRODUCTIONS: *Out of the Body Travel*, 1975 (video); *City Archives*, 1977 (video); *Strong Medicine*, 1978 (16mm film); *Radio Rick in*

Heaven and Radio Richard in Hell, 1987 (16mm film); *Total Rain*, 1990 (video).

Bibliography

Bigsby, C. W. E. *Beyond Broadway.* Vol. 3 in *A Critical Introduction to Twentieth-Century American Drama.* New York: Cambridge University Press, 1985. Bigsby's chapter on Foreman is at once explanatory and critical, anlayzing Foreman's manifestos and early plays. He points to the inconsistencies and shortcomings of some of Foreman's theories within actual theater practice and its reception. He also connects the work to that of the absurdists and the novels of Alain Robbe-Grillet.

Davy, Kate. *Richard Foreman and the Ontological-Hysteric Theatre.* Ann Arbor, Mich.: UMI Research Press, 1981. This in-depth book details Foreman's working methods as writer, director, scenographer, and composer. It is also invaluable as an analysis of the dramatic theories of Bertolt Brecht and Gertrude Stein insofar as they have influenced Foreman's own theory and practice.

Foreman, Richard. "A Conversation with Richard Foreman." Interview by Charles Bernstein. *The Drama Review* 36 (Fall, 1992): 103-130. In this interview, Foreman describes developments and shifts in his working methods and philosophy. He also reveals his literary and philosophical influences as well as the types of theater against which he is reacting— Jerzy Grotowski's, in particular.

Halstead, Jack. "Re-Viewing Richard Foreman and Theater of Images." *Journal of Dramatic Theory and Criticism* 4 (Spring, 1992). Halstead elaborates on Foreman's earlier Ontological-Hysteric Theatre practice in terms of mimesis and writing, viewing these issues from the standpoint of poststructuralist theory. He draws clear parallels between Foreman's work and the ideas of Roland Barthes and Jacques Derrida.

Marranca, Bonnie, ed. *The Theatre of Images.* New York: Drama Book Specialists, 1977. Marranca introduces Foreman's *Pandering to the Masses: A Misrepresentation* with an essay clarifying Foreman's goals regarding memory, perception of the present, the framing of perception, and the operations of self-consciousness.

Munk, Erika. "Film Is Ego, Radio Is God: Richard Foreman and the Arts of Control." *The Drama Review* 31 (Winter, 1987): 125-135. This review-essay on *Film Is Evil, Radio Is Good* contemplates how far Foreman has pushed reflection about his own authority by concentrating on a medium—film—that inevitably reinforces his authority. Munk surmises that technological forms throw one back on a self that finds it increasingly difficult to recognize itself.

Jill Dolan
(Updated by *Jon Erickson*)

MICHAEL FRAYN

Born: London, England; September 8, 1933

Principal drama
The Two of Us, pr., pb. 1970; *The Sandboy*, pr. 1971; *Alphabetical Order*, pr. 1975, pb. 1977; *Donkeys' Years*, pr. 1976, pb. 1977; *Clouds*, pr. 1976, pb. 1977; *Liberty Hall*, pr. 1980; *Make and Break*, pr., pb. 1980; *Noises Off*, pr., pb. 1982; *Benefactors*, pr., pb. 1984; *Plays: One*, pb. 1985; *Balmoral*, pb. 1987 (revised version of *Liberty Hall*); *Look Look*, pr., pb. 1990; *Plays: Two*, pb. 1991.

Other literary forms
Michael Frayn began his career as a journalist, contributing reviews, then satirical essays, and later personal observations about his travels to *The Guardian* and *The Observer*. Much of his journalistic writing has been republished in collections of his work. Frayn turned to the novel while still writing for newspapers, eventually abandoning journalism. Frayn has written several novels, most of them published before he moved on to the theater, where he has enjoyed his greatest success. In addition to his original drama, he has translated and adapted plays by Anton Chekhov (of which Frayn's adaptation of *Three Sisters* in 1983 received especially favorable notice), Leo Tolstoy, and Jean Anouilh and has written documentaries as well as original scripts for television; with *Clockwise* in 1986, he became a screenwriter. Interested in moral sciences since his Cambridge University days, when he was especially influenced by the work of philosopher Ludwig Wittgenstein, he has also written a nonfiction work, *Constructions* (1974), which is best described as a philosophical treatise on perception, language, and time.

Achievements
Already established as a respected journalist and novelist, in middle age Frayn won even greater acclaim as a playwright. His first plays, amusing and well-crafted comedies, suggested that yet another clever farceur, someone akin to the early Alan Ayckbourn, had arrived on the scene. More discerning viewers, however, began to note that beyond the laughter, Frayn was a serious writer employing comedy to explore philosophical themes—the relationship of language and perception, of order and misrule, of human beings' illusory control of self and environment. Soon after arriving on the theatrical scene, Frayn was winning awards as author of the best comedy of the year (for *Alphabetical Order*, *Donkeys' Years*, and *Noises Off*). In 1980, *Make and Break*, more reflective than his previous plays, won awards as

both the year's best comedy and the year's best play. In 1984, *Benefactors*, his darkest comedy, not only won awards as the year's best play but also afforded Frayn a place among such contemporary British dramatists of the first rank as Harold Pinter and Tom Stoppard. His subsequent work for the stage, however, has fallen off in quality and quantity, achieving neither the popular success of *Noises Off* nor the critical acclaim of *Benefactors.* In 1990, *Look Look*, a complex comedy about the interrelationship of actor and audience, confused its actual viewers and closed after a handful of performances.

Biography

Michael Frayn's family lived in Mill Hill in northwest London but moved to Holloway soon after his birth and then to Ewell, a southwest suburb, where he was reared. His father was an asbestos salesman who occasionally took Michael and his sister to the nearby Kingston Empire, a music hall, as a special treat. Frayn remembers borrowing some music-hall routines for the home entertainments—puppet shows and conjuring acts—that he devised for an audience of three—father, mother, and sister. At Christmastime, the elder Frayn became the star performer in the comic sketches that he himself wrote. Michael and his sister were relegated to supporting roles, and Mrs. Frayn formed an audience of one. Michael Frayn's mother, who had earlier worked as a shop assistant and occasional model in Harrods, London's grandest department store, died when he was twelve, a disorienting experience for the boy. At that time, his father removed him from the private day school, which the boy hated, and enrolled him in the good state-run Kingston Grammar School, where he was far more comfortable.

Frayn got along with his chums by playing the fool and by cleverly mimicking his teachers while doing a minimum of schoolwork. That changed when an English master, aware of the boy's incipient talent for writing, challenged him to produce even better work. These were the years in which Frayn discovered poetry, music, religion, and politics. He and his friends declared themselves atheists and formed a model communist cell in the school. Although his interest in Communism soon waned, it led him to study the Russian language. He subsequently traveled to the Soviet Union, employing it as the setting of his *The Russian Interpreter* (1966), a spy novel. In addition, he has become Great Britain's foremost translator of Russian drama, specifically the plays of Chekhov, which are peopled with characters as bewildered, as troubled, and as comic as Frayn's own.

Frayn actually perfected his Russian when he was drafted into the army in 1952 and sent to language school at Cambridge University. He returned to Cambridge as an undergraduate after completing his national service in 1954. In addition to studying philosophy, he dabbled in university theatricals, collaborating on a musical revue and playing a servant in a production of Nikolai Gogol's *Revizor* (1836; *The Inspector General*, 1890). Trapped onstage in Gogol's play for what seemed an eternity when a door refused to open and the audience started a slow handclap, he vowed never again to tread the boards, an experience that may have provided an inspiration for *Noises Off*, a play about theatrical mishaps.

After being graduated from Cambridge in 1957, Frayn worked for *The Guardian* (Manchester) and two years later began a satirical humor column, which he has himself likened to the work of American columnists Russell Baker and Art Buchwald. Like Joseph Addison and Richard Steele in *The Spectator* (1711-1712), Frayn invented a cast of characters, among them two couples reappearing with great frequency: Christopher and Lavinia Crumble, who knew everything, and Horace and Doris Morris, who knew nothing at all. The relationship of contrasting couples, the fortunate Kitzingers and the unfortunate Molyneuxs, would become the basis of his most acclaimed work, *Benefactors*.

After further newspaper work on *The Observer*, Frayn decided that the novel would allow him greater latitude for the exploration of character and ideas. Between 1965 and 1973, he published five novels to generally favorable reviews, the most effective among them *Towards the End of the Morning* (1967; U.S. edition, *Against Entropy*, 1967), a comic exploration of Frayn's familiar newspaper world. A television script brought him to the attention of theatrical producer Michael Codron, who urged him to write a play. Frayn's first attempt was *The Two of Us*, a collection of four one-acts, with all the characters played by two actors and ending in a farcical disaster of a dinner party. Although it entertained audiences for half a year, the play did not amuse the critics. Intrigued, nevertheless, by the possibilities of dramatic presentation, Frayn believed that he could do better. His subsequent plays have proved him right.

Frayn married Gillian Palmer in 1969 and has three daughters with whom he enjoys a close relationship, but he and his wife separated in 1981. He settled in London with Claire Tomalin, literary editor of the London *Sunday Times.*

Analysis

Like Chekhov, his inspirational mentor, Michael Frayn is at his best when he allows his audience an intimate glimpse of characters attempting to make order out of the routine chaos of their mundane existence. There are no grand confrontations, no melodramatic plot twists, merely bursts of wasted energy frequently followed by a deepening frustration as his characters— reporters, salesmen, actors, and architects—perceive a world that ought to be changed, but their ineffectual efforts and plans make no impression upon it. Only the characters change, surrendering to the inevitable, as, comically, a disordered world continues its mad spin, signifying nothing.

Frayn's third play and first critical success, *Alphabetical Order*, locates what would become his abiding concerns. In the library of a provincial newspaper office, several middle-aged reporters, who resemble little boys lost, take refuge amid the office debris. Their daily routine dictates that they enlighten the surrounding world, yet they would rather run and hide from the world, mothered by the head librarian, Lucy, who indulges their whims just as she allows a haphazard filing system to take care of itself. Their personal lives are in as much disarray as the room itself, cluttered with baskets and boxes of news items, even a broken chair. Lucy lives with John, is interested in Wally, and offers sympathy to Arnold, whose unloved wife, Megan, is in the hospital.

When Lucy hires a young woman, Leslie, as her assistant, the newcomer immediately takes control. When a reporter cuts his hand and Lucy cannot find the key to the first-aid kit, Leslie's first act is to break open the kit with a smartly delivered blow with a leg from the broken chair. Not only does Leslie rearrange the furniture, but also all the clutter is soon neatly filed away. More significant, Leslie imposes order on chaos by rearranging relationships as well. She enters into an affair with John, freeing Lucy for Wally; Lucy resists the neat arrangement, however, and takes Arnold into her home instead, thus dashing the hopes of Nora, the features editor.

The newly imposed order is short-lived. A seemingly more efficient library has no effect on a newspaper that is failing. When the paper's closing is announced, the library's habitués, with Leslie out of the room, revolt. Throwing caution to the winds, grown men reduced to little boys convert folders and clippings into missiles to pelt one another. Chaos has dictated order, which in turn has dictated chaos. When Leslie, the youngest and most recent employee, enters to announce that she is in the vanguard of those who will take over the paper to run it themselves, she reasserts the notion that order will rule once more, but to what purpose? Her fellow employees' lives are as messy as ever, and Leslie's failing relationship with John further suggests that her compulsion for efficiency does not extend to that area of her life that really matters.

Critics have viewed Leslie as the villain of the piece, seeing her as the symbol of arid organization in confrontation with the confused humanity of Lucy, the heroine. Frayn himself takes a different view. Perhaps, he suggests, *Alphabetical Order* demonstrates that order and disorder are interdependent, that any extreme provokes its opposite. Lucy's inefficiency is only a perception; her library functions. Leslie's order, too, is only a perception. She is hardly responsible for the paper's failure, but as she rules her roost, the paper grinds to a halt. A semblance of change occurs, but the essential remains the same.

In an essay entitled "Business Worries," originally written for *The Observer* and collected in *At Bay in Gear Street* (1967), Frayn offers a reason for not going to the theater: An audience sits in fear—a fear of something going wrong onstage. A carefully rehearsed play represents an ordered world that should comfort an audience that lives in an uncertain world in flux. Actors, however, can trip and fall, cigarette lighters can fail to light, cues can be missed. In *Noises Off*, Frayn takes theatrical accidents to their extreme, but an audience can view it all happily, knowing that the disorder onstage is, in fact, the order of art. Frayn's award-winning farce presents a predetermined world in which accidents are programmed to occur. First produced in 1982, *Noises Off*, a play in which an actual unforeseen mishap occurring to an actor is accepted by the viewer as yet one more comic disaster planned by the author, so delighted audiences that it achieved a four-and-a-half-year run, breaking all records at London's Savoy Theatre, and has afforded Frayn financial independence. In addition to its nearly two-year Broadway run, *Noises Off* has been translated into thirty-six languages including Russian, the language that Frayn has so frequently translated into English. Despite the failure of an Americanized film adaptation in 1992, *Noises Off* is one of the most successful stage farces of the last quarter-century. What has, however, surprised its author is that the laughter has obscured for most audiences, who may consider it mindless entertainment, that the play has a general application even for them. It is about, Frayn insists, what everyone does in life: keep a performance going.

Noises Off, whose title derives from a British stage term for offstage sound effects, parodies the innocuous sex farces, such as Anthony Marriott and Alistair Foot's *No Sex Please, We're British* (1973), which have become a staple of London's commercial theater. In act 1, the audience witnesses the combination technical dress rehearsal of the first act of a farce called "Nothing On," performed by third-rate actors whose careers have been limited to barely professional companies that play middle-class seaside resorts such as Weston-Super-Mare. Whatever can possibly go wrong does, but only mildly in act 1. In act 2, Frayn changes the perspective. The audience witnesses the performance of "Nothing On" again, but this time from a backstage view. The actors are seen directly behind their set preparing to make their entrances. In act 1, an inept company at least attempted to work together to put on a play. Four weeks later, the inevitably developing professional jealousies and personal entanglements have turned the backstage area into a battlefield. As a result, "Nothing On" is falling apart. In act 3, the perspective is reversed again. Four more weeks have gone by, and the audience witnesses that first act yet again from an audience's usual point of view. By then, however, "Nothing On," the play-within-the-play, has totally collapsed as *Noises Off*'s actual audience, perceiving the changes brought to the performance by the realities of human involvements, collapses from laughter.

Perhaps in repeating the first act of "Nothing On" three times with variations within the framework of *Noises Off*, Frayn had in mind the repetition of the two acts of Samuel Beckett's *En attendant Godot* (1952; *Waiting for Godot*, 1954), another play about actors of sorts keeping a performance going. In *Waiting for Godot*, too, the essential does not change, but the characters' despair—and the audience's—deepens. What keeps the audience happy at *Noises Off* is that, as the characters fail to find solace in the rehearsed world of performance, the audience knows that for once everything has gone right. Here, chaos represents order.

Frayn's view of *Noises Off* being about the necessity of keeping life going provides a key to his darkest comedy, *Benefactors*, whose subtleties took playgoers by surprise following, as it did, a knockabout farce. For the author, it is the petty jealousies and pique, the link to *Noises Off*, that is at the root of what he considers to be, within the context of a thought-provoking domestic comedy, society's "progressive collapse." The bleakest aspect of *Benefactors* is that, in wrecking their own lives, the two couples who constitute its cast—friends who are white, middle-class, reasonably comfortable, basically good, and committed to helping others—unwittingly destroy the hopes of a better, more comfortable life for a class of people further down the social and economic scale, the residents, some white, more of them black, of a public housing enclave in southeast London. The real victims, who never come onstage in the play, are the inhabitants of a slum area, euphemistically referred to by the local housing authority as a "twilight area," who pay for the casual bickering and increasingly strained relationships between the two couples in the foreground of the play and provide *Benefactors* with its too-easily ignored "noises off."

Like the self-deluded architect-protagonist of Frayn's failed second play, *The Sandboy*, liberal-minded David Kitzinger believes he is helping others by designing high-rise local housing. When his wife, Jane, brings their hapless neighbor Sheila into their home as general factotum, Sheila's husband, Colin, an unemployed journalist, is upset by the growing relationship between Sheila and David, supposedly his best friend. He takes action by turning public sentiment against David's housing scheme. The relationships among the four persons who had thought of themselves as two friendly couples undergo obvious and subtle shifts that end with the collapse of one marriage and a total change in dependency in the other. No one by the end, as the four characters relate their own perceptions of what took place some years earlier, is quite sure just what did happen, but people, David finally understands, have a way of wrecking any possibility of meaningful change. The Kitzingers had played at being benefactors for the Molyneuxs, but if Sheila's marriage is destroyed, she has at least achieved a measure of independence she had never known before. Colin, too, is a benefactor. Whatever his motive for opposing David's plan, he has, he convinces himself, actually saved the inhabitants of the area undergoing redevelopment from the dehumanizing conditions that David's efficient scheme would impose upon them. Colin even provides Jane a new career working for another housing trust that plans to rehabilitate rather than rebuild.

What adds impact to the play is Frayn's choice of names for the streets bounding the area for which David has been designing the new housing—"Basuto Road, Bechuana Road, Matebele Road, Mashona Road, and Barotse Road." "Basuto Road" becomes an evermore despairing refrain as the architect's plans undergo extensive modifications until they are at last rejected. By evoking, through the dispossessed people of the Basuto Road enclave, an echo of Basutoland, once an outpost of the British Empire, now the independent enclave of Lesotho surrounded by a hostile South Africa, Frayn suggests that Great Britain's privileged class has not only failed itself but also, ultimately, betrayed its responsibilities to those who had come there from the far reaches of the empire in search of a better life. In like manner, South Africa has exploited the Basutos, who must leave their infertile land to search for a livelihood among a people who oppress them. In *Benefactors*, chaos breeds chaos, and the need for order is implied by the discipline of the dramatist's art. Basuto Road, for Frayn, becomes a ruined Eden. Lured by false hopes, desperately in need of help, the dispossessed are betrayed even by their so-called benefactors, who are too involved in their own petty concerns to comprehend the damage that their intentioned good works can do.

Benefactors concludes ambiguously with the audience only certain that David, Jane, Colin, and Sheila—each one pitted against the others in a quest for self-fulfillment—have been involved in "progressive collapse." By the end of the play, the phrase has become not merely an architectural term but a dramatist's diagnosis of an unhealthy society's desperate need for change while it perpetuates, in a frantic flurry of compromise and accommodation, the desperation of stasis. Possessing wider implications than any of his other plays. *Benefactors*, still within a comic framework, reinforces Frayn's pessimistic view of the human search for order, sanity, and compassion.

Other major works

NOVELS: *The Tin Men*, 1965; *The Russian Interpreter*, 1966; *Towards the End of the Morning*, 1967 (U.S. edition, *Against Entropy*, 1967); *A Very Private Life*, 1968; *Sweet Dreams*, 1973; *The Trick of It*, 1989; *A Landing on the Sun*, 1991; *Now You Know*, 1992.

NONFICTION: *The Day of the Dog*, 1962; *The Book of Fub*, 1963 (U.S. edition, *Never Put Off to Gomorrah*, 1964); *On the Outskirts*, 1964; *At Bay in Gear Street*, 1967; *Constructions*, 1974; *The Original Michael Frayn: Columns from the "Guardian" and "Observer,"* 1983.

SCREENPLAY: *Clockwise*, 1986; *First and Last*, 1989.

TRANSLATIONS: *The Cherry Orchard*, 1978 (of Anton Chekhov's play *Vishnyovy sad*); *The Fruits of Enlightenment*, 1979 (of Leo Tolstoy's play *Plody prosveshcheniya*); *Three Sisters*, 1983 (of Chekhov's play *Tri sestry*);

Number One, 1984 (of Jean Anouilh's play *Le Nombril*); *Wild Honey*, 1984 (of an untitled play by Chekhov); *The Seagull*, 1986 (of Chekhov's play *Chayka*); *Uncle Vanya*, 1987 (of Chekhov's play *Dyadya Vanya*); *Plays*, 1988 (a selection of Chekhov's plays); *The Sneeze*, 1989 (an adaptation of several of Chekhov's one-act plays and short stories).

Bibliography
Cushman, Robert. "Michael Frayn and Farce Go Hand in Hand." *The New York Times*, December 11, 1983, pp. B1, 4. Introducing *Noises Off* to the Broadway audience prior to its New York premiere, Cushman points to its genesis in an essay that Frayn wrote as a journalist for *The Guardian.* The key sentence of the essay, entitled "Business Worries," about a theater audience's apprehensions, is: "All the time one is waiting aghast for some embarrassing disaster to occur." Cushman offers evidence that comic events in his plays and novels stem from Frayn's own experience.
Gussow, Mel. "Echoes of Chekhov Haunt Frayn's *Benefactors.*" Review of *Benefactors. The New York Times*, January 5, 1986, pp. B3, 15. Gussow suggests that a quotation from Anton Chekhov's notebooks in Frayn's introduction to his translation of *Three Sisters* could serve as an epigraph to *Benefactors:* "We struggle to change life so that those who come after us might be happy, but those who come after us will say as usual: it was better before, life now is worse than it used to be."
Henry, William A., III. "Tugging at the Old School Ties." *Time*, January 27, 1986, 66. Henry underscores the relationship of Frayn's life to his work—both plays and novels—in what is primarily a review of the Broadway production of *Benefactors*, which Frayn apparently prefers to the original London production. Henry suggests that "one traditional measure of a superior play is that it can sustain widely varying interpretations." *Benefactors*, according to Henry, "meets that test." The article has two photographs, one of Frayn, the other of a scene from the Broadway production of *Benefactors.*
Kaufman, David. "The Frayn Refrain." *Horizon* 29 (January/February, 1986): 33-36. Written soon after the American premiere of *Benefactors*, this article suggests that Broadway is in need of such serious yet entertaining plays. He notes that Frayn finds American critics, especially John Simon (see below), to be more perceptive about the play than were the British critics. Frayn confesses that he himself learned what his play is about from reading sound critical analyses. The article, biographical in part, is illustrated with a photograph of Frayn and scenes from the Broadway production of *Benefactors.*
Simon, John. "Frayn and Refrayn." Review of *Benefactors* and *Wild Honey*. *New York* 17 (September 3, 1984): 62-63. One year before the American premiere of *Benefactors*, Simon, an American critic, reviewing the

London production, was overwhelmed by the play's intelligence and haunting power. Disturbed by the performance, he read the text: "Creepingly, imperceptibly," he writes, "it overpowers you." Simon reveals the play's complexity by suggesting that it is about change as "the ultimate changelessness" and concludes, "*Benefactors*, finally, is a play about everything."

Albert E. Kalson